MW01123205

The Guide to Cooking Schools

The Guide to Cooking Schools

1997

Ninth Edition

ShawGuides

NEW YORK

ShawGuides and The Guide to Cooking Schools are trademarks of ShawGuides, Inc.

Inquiries concerning this book should be addressed to: Editor, ShawGuides, P.O. Box 1295, New York, New York 10023, Phone: (212) 799-6464, Fax: (212) 724-9287, E-mail: info@shawguides.com, URL: www.shawguides.com.

Please note that the information herein has been obtained from the listed cooking schools and organizations and is subject to change. The editor and publisher accept no responsibility for inaccuracies. Schools should be contacted prior to sending money and/or making travel plans.

Library of Congress Catalog Card Number 88-92516
ISSN 1040-2616
ISBN 0-945834-23-3

Printed in the United States of America by
R. R. Donnelley & Sons Company

Introduction

The Guide to Cooking Schools *is the only comprehensive, international resource to information about culinary and wine educational programs. This ninth annual edition, the largest to date, contains detailed descriptions of 322 career and professional and 474 nonvocational and vacation programs (73 new to this edition), 101 culinary apprenticeships, 61 wine appreciation programs, 27 food and wine organizations, and 46 food and wine publications. All schools have stated that they provide instruction in English and all listings are free.*

New to this edition is a list of 104 addresses of schools that have established sites on the World Wide Web. You can read and print out these schoolsí brochures and communicate directly with them via e-mail, using your own computer and modem or one provided by the increasing number of libraries and enterprises that offer Internet access.

The detailed listings for all the schools and programs contained in this and our other guides are now on-line in a searchable database on ShawGuides' Web site. You can search for schools by name, location, month, tuition, and specialty. Listings are continually updated and those schools that have Web sites can be accessed directly through their listing on site. We look forward to adding new services and features in response to your requests. Please let us know what most interests you. Our URL (Uniform Resource Locator or Web address) is http://www.shawguides.com and our e-mail address is info@shawguides.com.

Section I, Career and Professional Programs, contains information about programs in 46 states and 13 countries and U.S. Department of Labor-registered culinary apprenticeships in the U.S., Puerto Rico, and the Bahamas. Most are offered by career schools, colleges, and universities and are geared to the aspiring or professional cook or chef. Some are continuing education programs for the professional who desires specialized expertise. In addition to contact name, address, phone and fax numbers, e-mail address, and URL, the following is requested from each program sponsor: description of institution, months of operation, year culinary program was established, length of program, accreditation, admission dates, total enrollment and number of enrollees each admission period, student to faculty ratio, age demographics, teaching facilities, course emphasis, daily and weekly schedule, post-graduate and continuing education opportunities, faculty, tuition and fees, lodging, refund policy, scholarship and loan availability, and the percentages of applicants that are accepted, graduates who find employment, students who attend part-time, and financial aid recipients.

Section II, Nonvocational and Vacation Programs, contains information about programs in 43 states and 24 countries in venues that include cookware shops, restaurants, hotels, resorts, and private homes. Many are vacation programs that feature daily classes as well as food-related excursions and dining at notable restaurants. In addition to contact information, sponsors provide the following: year established, months of operation, length and focus of programs, maximum class or group size, method of instruction, facilities, special activities, faculty, cost, and refund policy.

Section III, Wine Courses, includes the following information about programs taught by wine connoisseurs who are members of the American Wine Society and/or the Society of Wine Educators: year established, course length and frequency, maximum enrollment, cost, vintage range, and number of wines sampled, specialties, instructor qualifications, cost, location, and contact.

Section IV, Food and Wine Organizations, describes the goals and objectives, publications, activities, dues, and membership services of 21 organizations.

Section V, Appendix, contains contacts for schools accredited by the American Culinary Federation Educational Institute, recommended reading resources, career program tuition rankings, page-referenced indexes to scholarships, children's classes, and advertisers, school Internet addresses (URLs), a list of abbreviations, and currency conversion ratios as of September, 1996.

Although we strive to make each listing as accurate and complete as possible, changes do occur. Please check the listing on our Web site for the most current information or contact the school directly. Request the names of graduates or previous attendees you can contact whose needs are similar to yours. Did the program fulfill their expectations? What were the weak and strong points? What questions should you ask before you enroll?

Please let us know if you feel that any listing is an inaccurate representation of a school's program or if you are acquainted with new schools that should be listed. They can fill out the listing questionnaire on our Web site, e-mail it to us, and have it accessible on the Internet within a few days.

The editor and publisher thank the school and organization directors for their cooperation and assistance. We're especially grateful to Lisa McConnell and Stacey Shane-Nusbaum for their dedication to this project.

We wish you enjoyment and success in all your culinary endeavors.

*Shaw**Guides***

Contents

1

Career and Professional Programs

LAWSON STATE COMMUNITY COLLEGE
Birmingham/September-May

This college offers a 21-month certificate in Culinary Arts. Program started 1949. Accredited by SACS. Admission dates: quarterly. Student to teacher ratio 23:1. 50% obtain employment within 6 months.

FACULTY: 2 full-time.

COSTS: Annual tuition approximately $200. Admission requirements: high school diploma or equivalent and admission test.

LOCATION: The 2,000-student 50-acre suburban campus is 100 miles from Detroit.

CONTACT: Roosevelt Daniels, Lawson State Community College, Commercial Food Preparation, 3060 Wilson Rd., SW, Birmingham, AL 35221; (205) 925-2515.

WALLACE STATE COMMUNITY COLLEGE
Hanceville

This college offers an 18-month diploma and 24-month degree. Program started 1979. Accredited by SACS. Admission dates: October, January, April, July. Total enrollment: 20. Student to teacher ratio 15:1. 98% obtain employment within 6 months.

FACULTY: 2 full-time.

COSTS: Tuition is $1,100-$1,300 in-state. Admission requirements: high school diploma or equivalent.

CONTACT: Culinary Director, Wallace State Community College, Commercial Foods & Nutrition, Box 2000, Hanceville, AL 35077; (205) 352-6403.

UNIVERSITY OF ALASKA – FAIRBANKS
Fairbanks/January-April, August-December

This university offers a 2-year certificate and 2-year AAS degree in Culinary Arts. Program started 1879. Accredited by NASC, ACCSCT. Admission dates: fall, spring. Total enrollment: 30-45. 85% of applicants accepted. Student to teacher ratio 8-10:1. 95% obtain employment within 6 months.

COURSES: Externship provided.

FACULTY: 3 full-time, 7 part-time.

COSTS: Annual tuition in-state $69/credit hour, out-of-state $207/credit hour. Admission requirements: high school diploma or equivalent.

CONTACT: Frank U. Davis, CCE, CEC, University of Alaska-Fairbanks, Tanana Valley Campus, 510 Second Ave., Fairbanks, AK 99701; (907) 474-5196, Fax (907) 474-7335.

ART INSTITUTE OF PHOENIX
(See display ad page 27) **Phoenix/Year-round**

This private school specializing in the creative and applied arts offers an 18-month AAS degree in Culinary Arts. Program started 1995. Accredited by ACCSCT. Calendar: quarter. Curriculum: core. 96 credit hours of culinary courses required. Admission dates: September, January, March, July. Total enrollment: 16. 10-16 enrollees each admission period. 90% of applicants accepted. 100% of students receive financial aid. 40% under age 25, 47.5% age 25-44, 12.5% age 45 or over. Student to teacher ratio 10:1. Facilities: nearly 8,000-sq-ft added in 1996 includes 1 pastry and 2 production kitchens, storage, dining room, gallery/reception areas.

COURSES: Focus on skills that are required in the workplace. Schedule: Monday-Friday between

7:30am and 4:30pm; evening classes. Internships will be available at the Sheraton Crescent in Phoenix and other locations.

FACULTY: 4 full- and 10 part-time faculty, all with or working toward bachelor's degrees. Includes Director Bill Sy, Terry Barkley, Daniel Levinson, Cathrin Yoder, Lauren House.

COSTS: $208/credit hour, $3,328 quarterly. Total tuition and fees are $22,018. Application fee $50, administration fee $100. Admission requirements: high school diploma or equivalent, 150-word essay, interview. 1 full tuition scholarship, $3,000 merit scholarships to all who qualify. 24 loans granted last year averaging $3,500 each. School-sponsored apartments within a short walk range from $330-$390/month.

CONTACT: Stacy Sweeney, Director of Admissions, Art Institute of Phoenix, 2233 W. Dunlap Ave., #300, Phoenix, AZ 85021; (800) 474-2479, Fax (602) 997-0191, URL http://www.aii.edu.

MARICOPA SKILL CENTER
Phoenix/Year-round

This community college division offers 14- to 27-week certificates in Cook's Apprentice, Kitchen Helper, Baker's Helper, and Pantry Goods Maker. Program started 1964. Accredited by NCA. Curriculum: culinary. Admission dates: any Monday. Total enrollment: 25. Facilities: commercial kitchen.

COURSES: Entry level.

FACULTY: 3 full-time: Dan Bochichio, CWC, and 2 assistants.

LOCATION: Center of Valley of Sun, a metropolitan area.

CONTACT: Barbara Lary, Maricopa Skill Center, Public Relations, 1245 E. Buckeye Rd., Phoenix, AZ 85034; (602) 238-4300, Fax (602) 238-4307, E-mail lacybarbara@gwc.maricopa.edu.

PIMA COMMUNITY COLLEGE
Tucson/September-May

This state-supported college offers a 2-year certificate, 2-year AAS degree in Culinary Arts. Program started 1972. Accredited by NCA. 72 credit hours of culinary courses required. Admission dates: January, May, August. Total enrollment: 50. 22 enrollees each admission period. 100% of applicants accepted. 92% enrolled part-time. Student to teacher ratio 18:1. 90% obtain employment within 6 months. Facilities: 1 kitchen, 2 classrooms.

COURSES: Gourmet, cooking, garde manger, baking. Schedule: 35 hours/week 4-year degree continuation at Northern Arizona University.

FACULTY: 11 full-time and part-time.

COSTS: Annual tuition in-state $28/credit hour, out-of-state $141/credit hour. Other fees $20 -$40 per semester Admission requirements: high school diploma and 1 year food service experience. Off-campus housing $200-$600/month.

CONTACT: Camille Stallings, Dept. Chair, Pima Community College, Hospitality, 1255 N. Stone Ave., Tucson, AZ 85703; (800) 860-7462, #6283, (520) 748-4500, Fax (520) 884-6201.

SCOTTSDALE COMMUNITY COLLEGE
Scottsdale/August-May

This state-supported college offers a 9-month certificate, 2-year AAS degree in Culinary Arts. Program started 1985. Accredited by NCA. Calendar: semester. Curriculum: core. 35 credit hours of culinary courses required. Admission dates: August. Total enrollment: 30. 30 enrollees each admission period. 60% of applicants accepted. 30% under age 25, 50% age 25-44, 20% age 45 or over. Student to teacher ratio 7:1. 90% obtain employment within 6 months. Facilities: 1 kitchen, 2 classrooms, 1 student-run dining room.

COURSES: Hospitality management, culinary principles, menu planning, hot foods, bakery/pastry, garde manger; student-operated restaurant. Schedule: 35 hours/week.

FACULTY: 2 full-time, 2 part-time.

COSTS: Annual tuition in-state $1,600, out-of-state $5,400. Course fee is $250/semester

Application deadlines: May for August. Admission requirements: high school diploma and 1 year food service experience. 2 scholarships awarded last year averaging $500 each.

LOCATION: The 10,000-student 160-acre campus is on Salt River-Pima Indian Community land in the greater Phoenix area.

CONTACT: Sarah Labensky, Professor, Scottsdale Community College, Culinary Arts Program, 9000 East Chaparral Rd., Scottsdale, AZ 85250; (602) 423-6241, Fax (602) 423-6200.

(See display ad page 4)

SCOTTSDALE CULINARY INSTITUTE
Scottsdale/Year-round

This private institution offers an accelerated 15-month 78-credit-hour AOS degree in Culinary Arts and Sciences and Restaurant Management. Founded in 1986. Accredited by ACCSCT, ACFEI. Calendar: every 6 weeks. Curriculum: culinary. 2,017 hours of culinary courses required. Admission dates: January, February, April, May, July, August, October, November. Total enrollment: 330. 36 enrollees each admission period. 70% of applicants accepted. 70% of students receive financial aid. 35% under age 25, 50% age 25-44, 15% age 45 or over. Student to teacher ratio 15:1. 97% obtain employment within 6 months. Facilities: include 5 modern, full-service kitchens, bakery, meat fabrication shop, student-run Mobil 3-star L'Ecole restaurant.

COURSES: Emphasis is classic French techniques and principles of Escoffier. Schedule: 7-8 hours/day. Final 12 weeks are a national paid externship program; 80% of positions become permanent. Continuing education for professionals.

FACULTY: 17 full-time, 2 part-time. Founder/Director Elizabeth Leite developed a commercial foods curriculum at Scottsdale Voc-Tech Institute. Her staff of American- and European-trained professionals are selected for their teaching skills. An advisory board of chefs, restaurateurs, and hospitality managers recommend curriculum.

COSTS: Tuition is $15,385. A one-time $785 fee covers uniforms, knives, and textbooks. A $25 fee accompanies application. $100 deposit to enroll, tuition arrangements completed 30 days prior to start. Admission requirements: high school diploma or equivalent, application, essay, 2 letters of recommendation. 150 scholarships awarded last year averaging $1,000 each. Housing adjoins the campus.

LOCATION: Phoenix metropolitan area.

CONTACT: Scottsdale Culinary Institute, Admissions, 8100 E. Camelback Rd., Ste. 1001, Scottsdale, AZ 85251; (602) 990-3773, (800) 848-2433, Fax (602) 990-0351, URL http://www.chefs.com/culinary/.

TUCSON CULINARY ALLIANCE
Tucson/Year-round

This professional job bank, mentoring service, and provider of foodservice training offers a 2-year AOS degree in Hotel/Restaurant Management and Cook Certification with the ACFEI. Established in 1993. Registered with U.S. Dept. of Labor Bureau of Apprenticeship Training. Calendar: semester. Curriculum: culinary, core. 288-576 hours of culinary courses required. Admission dates: open. Total enrollment: 5-10/year. 90% of applicants accepted. 25% of students receive financial aid. 5% under age 25, 95% age 25-44, Student to teacher ratio 1:1. 100% obtain employment within 6 months.

COURSES: Depends on apprentice's needs and goals.

FACULTY: Advisory committee includes Program Director Robert Shell, CCC, CCE, Lorraine Adler, Lonnie Lloyd, Neal McLaren, and Jim Murphy.

COSTS: Total cost is $1,500-$2,000. $275 nonrefundable deposit. Admission requirements: 18 years old, high school diploma or equivalent, pass pre-apprenticeship courses. Full or partial tuition reimbursement provided by employers.

LOCATION: 120 miles south of Phoenix.

CONTACT: Robert B. Shell, CCC, CCE, Program Director, Tucson Culinary Alliance, 3124 E. Pima St., Bldg. B, Tucson, AZ 85716; (520) 327-3594 (AMs).

CALIFORNIA

BERINGER VINEYARD'S SCHOOL FOR AMERICAN CHEFS
St. Helena/January

This nonprofit school offers one 2-week post-graduate course. Established in 1989. Total enrollment: 8. 8 enrollees each admission period. 25-30% of applicants accepted. Student to teacher ratio 8:1. Facilities: Beringer Vineyards' Culinary Arts Center: one kitchen for practicing and one for public dinner preparation.

COURSES: Tailored to student requests. Required courses are wine and food pairing, wine tasting, and elementary viticulture. Schedule: 44 hours/week.

FACULTY: School Director Madeleine Kamman was born in Paris, taught French cuisine in the US for over 30 years, authored 9 cookbooks, and hosts a PBS TV series.

COSTS: None. Tuition, ingredients, and wines are provided by Beringer Vineyard. Application deadlines: one year prior to admission. Admission requirements: American citizen, age 21 with high school diploma or equivalent, 2 years experience as working chef. Off-campus lodging averages $250 per week.

LOCATION: The Napa Valley, 90 minutes from San Francisco.

CONTACT: Administrator, Beringer Vineyards, Culinary, 2000 Main St., St. Helena, CA 94574; (707) 963-7115 #2225, Fax (707) 963-2385.

CABRILLO COLLEGE
Aptos/August-May

This community college offers a 30-unit certificate and 60 unit AS degree in Culinary Arts & Hospitality Management. Program started 1972. Calendar: semester. Curriculum: core. Admission dates: August, January. Total enrollment: 200+. 150-200 enrollees each admission period. 100% of applicants accepted. 70% enrolled part-time. 100% obtain employment within 6 months. Facilities: restaurant kitchen, quantity foods kitchen, bake shop, lecture/demonstration room, student-run restaurant.

COURSES: Include culinary arts, baking and pastry arts, cake decorating, garde manger, culinary specialties, chocolate.

FACULTY: 2 full-time 4 part-time.

COSTS: Annual tuition for full-time students is $498 in-state, $3,768 out-of-state. Admission requirements: high school diploma or equivalent. 7 scholarships awarded last year averaging $500 each. Off-campus housing available.

LOCATION: 100 miles south of San Francisco, on the coast.

CONTACT: Katherine Niven, Director of Culinary Arts, Cabrillo College, Culinary Arts & Hospitality Management, 6500 Soquel Dr., Aptos, CA 95003, USA; (408) 479-5749, (408) 479-6100.

CAKEBREAD CELLARS AMERICAN HARVEST WORKSHOP
(See also page 157)   **Napa Valley/Summer**

Cakebread Cellars winery sponsors an annual four-day event for ten invited chefs and sommeliers who produce 5-course dinners using local products and Cakebread Cellars wines.

COURSES: Features visits to food growers and a farmer's market.

FACULTY: Workshop director Narsai David, a San Francisco television and radio host, and the Cakebread Cellars staff.

CONTACT: Cakebread Cellars, 8300 St. Helena Hwy., Box 216, Rutherford, Napa Valley, CA 94573-0216; (707) 963-5221, Fax (707) 963-1067.

CALIFORNIA CULINARY ACADEMY
San Francisco/Year-round   *(See display ad page 7)*

This proprietary institution offers a full-time 18-month AOS degree in Culinary Arts, 30-week certificate in Baking and Pastry Arts; over 200 courses/year for professionals and novices. Founded in 1977. Accredited by ACFEI, ACCSCT. Calendar: 16-week term. Curriculum: culinary. Admission dates: vary, 2 times/month. Total enrollment: 700 in degree program. 90 degree, 22 certificate enrollees each admission period. 85% of applicants accepted. 75% of students receive financial aid. 35% under age 25, 65% age 25-44. Student to teacher ratio 20-25:1. 93% obtain employment within 6 months. Facilities: 14 production kitchens, auditorium, 2 restaurants, confiseries, butcher & seafood prep kitchens, garde manger, baking/pastry kitchens.

COURSES: Degree program covers food preparation & presentation, baking & pastry, nutrition, wine, menu, facilities planning; certificate program covers baking & pastry, chocolate, candies, decorating, pastillage. Schedule: 7 hours/day, morning and afternoon shifts. 3-month externship for degree students. 200+ courses/year for professionals & novices.

FACULTY: Full-time staff of 30 chefs averaging 15 yrs experience, 3 maitres d'hotel, 6 part-time, guest professionals.

COSTS: Approximately $25,000 ($11,000) for degree (certificate) program, which includes meals, uniforms, textbooks, equipment and student accident insurance. Application fee $35. $500 deposit due within 15 days of acceptance; balance by first class. Admission requirements: high school diploma or equivalent; industry experience recommended. Housing service provides assistance in finding lodging and transportation. Approximate cost of housing is $5,200.

LOCATION: Near San Francisco's Civic Center, two blocks from City Hall.

CONTACT: California Culinary Academy, Admissions, 625 Polk St., San Francisco, CA 94102; (415) 771-3536, (800) BAY-CHEF, Fax (415) 771-2194, URL http://www.baychef.com.

CITY COLLEGE OF SAN FRANCISCO
San Francisco/August-May

This college offers a 4-semester AS degree in Hotel and Restaurant Operations, Award of Achievement and ACFEI certificate. Program started 1935. Accredited by WASC, ACFEI. Calendar: semester. Curriculum: core. Admission dates: August, January. Total enrollment: 240. 86 enrollees each admission period. 90% of applicants accepted. Student to teacher ratio 20:1. 90% obtain employment within 6 months. Facilities: 8 kitchens and classrooms, student-run restaurant.

COURSES: Elementary and advanced foods, bake shop, advanced pastry, meat analysis, garde manger, and general education. Schedule: 6 hours/day, 9 months/year. 240-hour externship.

FACULTY: 12 full-time.

COSTS: Annual tuition in-state $390, out-of-state $3,720. Application deadlines: November for spring, April for fall. Admission requirements: age 18, or high school diploma. 23 scholarships awarded last year averaging $1,000 each.

CONTACT: Lynda Hirose, City College of San Francisco, Hotel & Restaurant, 50 Phelan Ave., San Francisco, CA 94112; (415) 239-3152, Fax (415) 239-3913.

COLUMBIA COLLEGE
Sonora/August-May

This college offers a 2-year AS degree in Culinary Arts/Hospitality Management. Program started 1977. Accredited by WASC. Admission dates: August, January. Total enrollment: 75. 30 enrollees each admission period. 99% of applicants accepted. 40% of students receive financial aid. 20% enrolled part-time. 40% under age 25, 50% age 25-44, 10% age 45 or over. Student to teacher ratio 10:1. 100% obtain employment within 6 months. Facilities: 2 kitchens, 5 classrooms, a Mobil 3-star restaurant.

COURSES: Cooking, baking, wines, bartending, garde manger, sausages and cured meats, service, restaurant management and marketing. 41 credit hours of culinary courses required. Schedule: 30 hours/week, 10 months/year.

Go *Professional*

Recipe for
SUCCESS
Choose the
program that
suits your
taste, mix
well with
your talent
and enter
one of the
world's most
exciting
careers.

A̲t the California Culinary Academy, we offer:

- 16-month Culinary Arts AOS degree program
  30-week Baking & Pastry Arts certificate program
- Financial Aid available to those who qualify
  Lifetime Placement service for graduates
- ACFEI and ACCSCT accreditation
  San Francisco's diverse food culture
- International Chef/Instructors

1-800-BAY-CHEF

CALIFORNIA
**CULINARY
ACADEMY**

625 Polk St San Francisco CA 94102

FACULTY: 2 full-time, 5 part-time. Qualifications: full-time: lifetime teaching credential and industry experience; part-time: full-time employment and 15 years experience.

COSTS: Annual tuition in-state $286, out-of-state $2,800. Health and student fees $20 per semester. 70% refund first month of semester. Application deadlines: July, December. Admission requirements: admission test. On-campus housing: 180 spaces; average cost is $400/month. Average off-campus housing cost $500 per month.

LOCATION: The 3,000-student campus is 120 miles from San Francisco.

CONTACT: Francis T. Lynch, Program Coordinator, Columbia College, Hospitality Management, 11600 Columbia College Dr., Sonora, CA 95370; (209) 533-5135, Fax (209) 533-5104, E-mail francis@mlode.com.

CONTRA COSTA COLLEGE
San Pablo

This college offers a 2-year certificate. Program started 1962. Admission dates: August, January. Total enrollment: 75-100. 90% of applicants accepted. Student to teacher ratio 20-25:1. 90% obtain employment within 6 months.

FACULTY: 3 full-time, 1 part-time.

COSTS: $100. Admission requirements: admission test.

CONTACT: Steve Cohen, Contra Costa College, Culinary Arts, 2600 Mission Bell Dr., San Pablo, CA 94806; (510) 235-7800.

THE CULINARY INSTITUTE OF AMERICA AT GREYSTONE
St. Helena   *(See display ad page 66) (See also page 65)*

The Culinary Institute of America's Greystone Campus offers fundamental to advanced 3- to 5-day and 3-, 6-, 9-, 12- and 21-week intensives for foodservice professionals. Program started 1995. Accredited by Council of Private and Post-Secondary Vocational Education of State of California. Calendar: year-round. Admission dates: on-going. Student to teacher ratio 18:1. Facilities: 15,000-sq-ft open teaching kitchens that include Bonnet Cooking Suites & Bongard Hearth ovens, 125-seat Ecolab Theater, on-campus vineyards and gardens.

COURSES: Professional cooking, professional baking and pastry, garde manger, skill development, baking and pastry arts certificate program, wine, career exploration, special subjects, custom programs. Other than certificate program, Greystone is exclusively devoted to continuing education.

FACULTY: 8 full- and part-time instructors plus visiting instructors, which include chef/owners of fine restaurants. Also drawn from the 125 instructors at the Hyde Park, NY, campus.

COSTS: Tuition ranges from $625 for 30 hours of instruction to $5,520 for a 12-week course. Deposit ranges from $100-$1,200. Application deadlines: on-going. Admission requirements: for cooking production classes, a minimum of 6 months experience in a professional kitchen. 18-room guest house on campus. Rooms available by the week.

LOCATION: One-and-a-half hours north of San Francisco, in the Napa Valley.

CONTACT: Holly Briwa, Education Office Manager, The Culinary Institute of America, Education Dept., 2555 Main St., St. Helena, CA 94574, USA; (800) 333-9242, (707) 967-0600 (Education Dept.), Fax (707) 967-2410, URL http://www.ciachef.edu..

CYPRESS COLLEGE
Cypress/January-May, August-December

This college offers a 1-year certificate, 2-year AS degree in Food Service Management and Hotel Operations. Program started 1975. Accredited by WASC. Calendar: semester. Curriculum: core. Admission dates: August, January. Total enrollment: 90. 35 enrollees each admission period. 90% of applicants accepted. 45% of students receive financial aid. 55% enrolled part-time. 25% under age 25, 50% age 25-44, 25% age 45 or over. Student to teacher ratio 16:1. 85% obtain employment within 6 months. Facilities: 1 kitchen, 4 classrooms, student-run dining room.

COURSES: Basic food production, advanced cooking techniques, quantity food production, international gourmet foods, dining room service, food and beverage costing and kitchen management, menu planning and design, and kitchen planning design. Schedule: full-time, part-time, evenings. 255-hour salaried externship.

FACULTY: 1 full-time, 4 part-time.

COSTS: Tuition in-state $13 per unit, out-of-state $114 per unit. Lab fees: $5 per lab. Full refund before second week. Application deadlines: Wednesday of the first week. Admission requirements: high school diploma or equivalent. Average off-campus housing cost $250-$750/month.

LOCATION: The 16,200-student campus is in an urban setting 35 minutes from downtown Los Angeles.

CONTACT: David Schweiger, Cypress College, Hospitality Management/Culinary Arts, 9200 Valley View St., Cypress, CA 90630; (714) 826-2220 #208, Fax (714) 527-8238.

DIABLO VALLEY COLLEGE
Pleasant Hill/Year-round

This college offers a program in Culinary Arts, Baking & Patisserie, Restaurant Management and Hotel Administration. Program started 1971. Accredited by ACFEI, WASC. Calendar: semester. Curriculum: core. Admission dates: August, January. Total enrollment: 750. 50 enrollees each admission period. 100% enrolled part-time. 25% under age 25, 45% age 25-44, 30% age 45 or over. Student to teacher ratio 24:1. 100% obtain employment within 6 months. Facilities: include a fully-equipped food production kitchen, demonstration laboratory, 130-seat open-to-the-public restaurant.

COURSES: Advanced food preparation, catering, garde manger, menu planning, costing, nutrition, California Cuisine and baking. Schedule: weekdays, 8 hours/day. One semester local externship.

FACULTY: 5 full-time, 14 part-time. Qualifications: BA degrees and 7 years industry experience. Includes Jack Hendrickson, Dept. Chair Linda Sullivan, Nader Sharkes, Robert Eustes.

COSTS: In-state tuition for first semester is $225. Fees and deposits: $13/unit for residents, $127/unit for non-residents, $135/unit for international students. Application deadlines: August, January. Admission requirements: high school diploma or equivalent. Average off-campus housing cost is $500 per month.

LOCATION: The 23,000-student 100-acre suburban campus is off Contra Costa Blvd. & 680 Fwy.

CONTACT: Jack Hendrickson, Diablo Valley College, Culinary Arts Dept., 321 Golf Club Rd., Pleasant Hill, CA 94523; (510) 685-1230 #555, Fax (510) 825-8412.

EPICUREAN SCHOOL OF CULINARY ARTS
(See also page 160) **Los Angeles/Year-round**

This private school offers a 6-month Professional Chef diploma. Established 1985. Admission dates: 3 times yearly. Total enrolment: 15. 45 enrollees each admission period. 100% of applicants accepted. 35% under age 25, 35% age 25-44, 15% age 45 or over. Student to teacher ratio 15:1. Facilities: teaching kitchen with 5 work stations.

COURSES: Classic French and contemporary cuisines, breads and pastries, food costing and accounting. Schedule: Monday-Sunday, part-time, evenings. 20-hour externship at a restaurant or catering kitchen. Assistantships available at the school.

FACULTY: Karen Unland, Carol Cotner. 4 part-time instructors are CIA and CCC graduates.

COSTS: Tuition is $2,600. A 50% deposit is required.

CONTACT: Shelley Janson, Director, Epicurean School of Culinary Arts, 8759 Melrose Ave., Los Angeles, CA 90069; (310) 659-5990, Fax (310) 659-0302.

GLENDALE COMMUNITY COLLEGE
Glendale/January-May, August-December

This college offers 2-year certificates in Culinary Arts, Restaurant Management, Hotel Management, and Dietary Services. Program started 1974. Accredited by state. Calendar: semester. Curriculum: culinary. Admission dates: August. Total enrollment: 338. 95% of applicants accepted.

50% enrolled part-time. 25% under age 25, 60% age 25-44, 15% age 45 or over. Student to teacher ratio 35:1. 80-85% obtain employment within 6 months.

COURSES: Restaurant and cost control management, quantity foods & purchasing. Other required courses: wine & beverages, catering, baking, dining room service, international cooking, and nutrition. Schedule: part-time, days and evenings, 18-week semester. Externship.

FACULTY: 1 full-time, 5 part-time. Qualifications: BS or MS degree, at least 6 years experience.

COSTS: Annual tuition in-state $30/unit, out-of-state $120/unit. Admission requirements: high school diploma or equivalent.

CONTACT: Yeimei Wang, Prof. of Food & Nutrition and Coordinator, Glendale Community College, Culinary Arts Dept./Food & Nutrition Studies, 1500 N. Verdugo Rd., Glendale, CA 91208; (818) 240-1000 #5597, Fax (818) 549-9436.

GROSSMONT COLLEGE
El Cajon/August-May
This college offers a 1-year certificate, 2-year degree. Program started 1969. Accredited by WASC. Calendar: August, January. Curriculum: culinary, core. Admission dates: January, August. Total enrollment: 90. 100% of applicants accepted. 10% of students receive financial aid. 50% enrolled part-time. 10% under age 25, 70% age 25-44, 20% age 45 or over. Student to teacher ratio 25:1. 100% obtain employment within 6 months.

FACULTY: 3 full-time.

COSTS: Annual tuition in-state $150/semester, out-of-state $103/unit.

CONTACT: Cathie Robertson, Grossmont College, 8800 Grossmont College Dr., El Cajon, CA 92020; (619) 465-1700 #327.

JUDY PECK PRINDLE "THE ART OF FOOD STYLING" SEMINARS
Los Angeles/October
This program offers a 3-day weekend seminar that covers the role of the food stylist in TV and stills and the techniques of preparing food for the camera. 22 hours of culinary courses. Total enrollment: 30. 30 enrollees each admission period.

FACULTY: Judy Peck Prindle has worked for Kraft, General Foods, Pillsbury, General Mills, and over 20 other food companies.

COSTS: $900 includes workbook, breakfasts, and lunches. Prepayment required.

LOCATION: Ms. Prindle's photography studio.

CONTACT: Judy Peck Prindle, Judy Peck Prindle "The Art of Food Styling" Seminars, 106 N. Mansfield Ave., Los Angeles, CA 90036; (213) 939-7009, Fax (213) 939-4219.

LANEY COLLEGE
Oakland/Year-round
This community college offers a 2-year AA degree in Culinary Arts, 1-year certificate in Retail Baking. Program started 1948. Accredited by WASC. Admission dates: August, January. Total enrollment: 200. 60 enrollees each admission period. 80% of applicants accepted. 70% of students receive financial aid. 10% enrolled part-time. 25% under age 25, 50% age 25-44, 25% age 45 or over. Student to teacher ratio 12:1. 100% obtain employment within 6 months. Facilities: include 7 kitchens and classrooms, a student-run restaurant, retail bakery.

COURSES: 6 hours/day, 4 days/week.

FACULTY: 5 full-time, 4 part-time.

COSTS: Tuition in-state $15/unit, out-of-state $110/unit.

CONTACT: Wayne Stoker, Laney College, Culinary Arts, 900 Fallon St., Oakland, CA 94607; (510) 464-3407.

LEDERWOLFF CULINARY ACADEMY
Sacramento/Year-round

This private vocational school offers diplomas in Professional Baking and Professional Cooking. Founded in 1990. Accredited by ACCSCT.

COURSES: Schedule: 33 hours/week full-time, 25 hours/week part-time.

FACULTY: 12 full-time.

COSTS: Annual tuition is $15,995 for Professional Cooking, $7,995 for Professional Baking. Application fee is $75; other fees range from $170 to $500. Refund policy pro rata. Admission requirements: high school diploma or equivalent and admission test.

LOCATION: A 22,000-square-foot historic landmark building..

CONTACT: Ron Lederman, Lederwolff Culinary Academy, Admissions, 3300 Stockton Blvd., Sacramento, CA 95820, USA; (916) 456-7002, Fax (916) 456-7603.

LET'S GET COOKIN' AND WESTLAKE CULINARY INSTITUTE
(See also page 162)   ### Westlake Village/Year-round

This private school offers a 24-session professional series, 6-session baking series, 3-session catering series, certificate granted upon completion. Established 1984. Calendar: 24-session. Curriculum: culinary. 100 hours of culinary courses required. Admission dates: variable. Total enrollment: 36. 12 enrollees each admission period. 80% of applicants accepted. 5% of students receive financial aid. 100% enrolled part-time. 10% under age 25, 70% age 25-44, 20% age 45 or over. Student to teacher ratio 12:1 with 2 assistants. 90% obtain employment within 6 months. Facilities: 1,000-sq-ft combination demonstration/participation facilities, cookware store.

COURSES: Include classical food preparation, skills, methods, techniques and presentation, international cuisines, menu costing and planning. Schedule: one session/week, offered Monday, Friday, Sunday.

FACULTY: 25-member guest and regular faculty. Includes owner/director, Phyllis Vaccarelli, CCP and Cecilia DeCastro, CCP who coordinates professional programs for UCLA Extension.

COSTS: $2,250 for the professional series, $495 for the baking series, $225 for the catering series. For 24-session: $100 initial deposit, $750 by 1st class, $750 by the 8th class, $750 by the 16th class. Refunds prorated through the 4th session. Admission requirements: commitment, written application, basic skills, attitude.

LOCATION: North of Malibu, 30 minutes from Los Angeles.

CONTACT: Phyllis Vaccarelli, Owner/Director, Let's Get Cookin', 4643 Lakeview Canyon Rd., Westlake Village, CA 91361; (818) 991-3940, Fax (805) 495-2554.

LOS ANGELES TRADE-TECHNICAL COLLEGE
Los Angeles/January-May, August-December

This college offers a 1-year certificate, 2-year AA degree in Culinary Arts and Professional Baking. Program started 1941. Accredited by WASC. Calendar: semester. Curriculum: culinary, core. Admission dates: August, January. Total enrollment: 200. 60 enrollees each admission period. 75% of applicants accepted. 40% of students receive financial aid. 40% under age 25, 40% age 25-44, 20% age 45 or over. Student to teacher ratio 25:1. 80% obtain employment within 6 months. Facilities: include 2 kitchens, 6 classrooms.

COURSES: 21 hours/4-day week.

FACULTY: 9 full-time. Qualifications: AA degree, ACF certification, industry experience.

COSTS: Annual tuition in-state $150+, out-of-state $250+. $600 for tools, uniforms, books. Deposit $175/semester. Refund before end of 2nd week. Application deadlines: first day of semester. 15 scholarships awarded last year averaging $250 each.

CONTACT: Steven L. Kasmar, Director, Los Angeles Trade-Technical College, Culinary Arts, 400 West Washington Blvd., Los Angeles, CA 90015; (213) 744-9480, Fax (213) 748-7334, E-mail stevel.kasmar@tradetechpo1.

NAPA VALLEY COOKING SCHOOL
St. Helena/Year-round   *(See also page 164) (See display ad above)*

Napa Valley College offers a 13-month certificate (Professional Training for Fine Restaurants) that consists of 8 months of school and 5 months of externship. Established in 1996. Curriculum: culinary. 1,050 training hours, 800 externship hours of culinary courses required. Admission dates: August. Total enrollment: 14-16. 14-16 enrollees each admission period. 75% of applicants accepted. 50% of students receive financial aid. 50% under age 25, 50% age 25-44. Student to teacher ratio 14:1. Facilities: modern, light teaching kitchen with patio overlooking.

COURSES: Basic to intermediate techniques, food and wine education. Special emphasis on skills for entry and advancement in fine restaurants. Schedule: 8am-2:30pm weekdays. Salaried externship in a Napa Valley restaurant the final semester.

FACULTY: Northern California chef-instructors. Guest lecturers include area chefs, growers, specialty food producers, viticulturists, and winemakers. Includes Executive Chef, George Torassa, ACF.

COSTS: Approximately $10,000. Deposit is $150. A nonrefundable $25 application fee is required. Application deadlines: June 30 for August. Admission requirements: high school diploma or equivalent. 6 months industry experience. 7 loans granted last year averaging $10,000 each. Average off-campus housing cost is $400+/month.

LOCATION: Napa Valley, 75 minutes from San Francisco.

CONTACT: Sue Farley, Coordinator, Napa Valley Cooking School, 1088 College Ave., St. Helena, CA 94574; (707) 967-2930, Fax (707) 967-2909.

ORANGE COAST COLLEGE
Costa Mesa

This college offers a 1-year certificate, 2-year AA degree. Program started 1964. Accredited by WASC, ACFEI. 1,120 hours of culinary courses required. Total enrollment: 350. 100% of applicants accepted. Student to teacher ratio 15:1. 100% obtain employment within 6 months.

COURSES: Culinary and cook apprenticeship program.

FACULTY: 15 full-time.

COSTS: Tuition in-state $120/year, out-of-state $102/unit. Admission requirements: high school diploma or equivalent.

LOCATION: 25,000-student suburban campus in southern California.

CONTACT: Dan Beard, Professor, Orange Coast College, Hospitality Department, 2701 Fairview Blvd., Box 5005, Costa Mesa, CA 92628-5005; (714) 432-5835, Fax (714) 432-5609.

OXNARD COLLEGE
Oxnard/January-May, August-December

This college offers a 1-year certificate, 2-year degree. Program started 1985. Accredited by WASC. Admission dates: August, January. Total enrollment: 75-125. 30 enrollees each admission period. 100% of applicants accepted. Student to teacher ratio 20:1. 95% obtain employment within 6 months.

FACULTY: 1 full-time, 5 part-time.

COSTS: Tuition in-state $15/unit, out-of-state $115/unit. Admission requirements: high school diploma or equivalent.

CONTACT: Frank Haywood, Oxnard College, Hotel & Restaurant Management, 4000 S. Rose Ave., Oxnard, CA 93033; (805) 986-5869, Fax (805) 986-5865.

RICHARDSON RESEARCHES, INC.
(See display ad above)   **Hayward/March, June-July, October**

This product development and research company for the confectionery food industry offers 8 to 10 five-day certificate courses per year. Established 1976. 18 enrollees each admission period. Student to teacher ratio 9:1. Facilities: the company's 4,000-square-foot professional facility, which has 3 kitchen areas, a lecture room, and a specially-equipped laboratory.

COURSES: Theoretical and practical aspects of confectionery and chocolate technology: Chocolate Technology, Confectionery Technology, Continental Chocolates, and Lite/Sugar-Free/Reduced Calorie and No Sugar Added. Schedule: 8 hours/day.

FACULTY: Terry Richardson, a graduate of the London Borough Polytechnic in Confectionery and Chocolate Technology, worked for major companies and holds several patents for new products and processes. Margaret Knight has a BS in Food Science.

COSTS: Tuition ranges from $1,280-$1,450. A $150 nonrefundable deposit is required with balance due a month prior. Cancellations 10 working days prior forfeit $500.

LOCATION: 30 minutes from the San Francisco Airport and 20 minutes from the Oakland Airport.

CONTACT: Richardson Researches, Inc., 23449 Foley St., Hayward, CA 94545; (510) 785-1350, Fax (510) 785-6857.

SAN JOAQUIN DELTA COLLEGE
Stockton/August-May

This college offers a 1-semester certificate, 3-4 semester certificate in Basic and Advanced Culinary Arts, and a 2-semester certificate in Dietetic Services Supervisor. Program started 1979. Accredited by WASC. Admission dates: rolling. Total enrollment: 60. 20-30 enrollees each admission period. 100% of applicants accepted. 40% of students receive financial aid. 40% enrolled part-time. 30% under age 25, 60% age 25-44, 10% age 45 or over. Student to teacher ratio 15:1. 90% obtain employment within 6 months. Facilities: 2 kitchens, 2 classrooms and a student-run restaurant.

COURSES: Culinary arts, baking, restaurant operations, nutrition, menu planning, food purchasing, and catering. Schedule: part-time, evenings. 1-semester salaried externship.

FACULTY: 2 full-time, 3 part-time. Qualifications: Master's degree. Includes Char Britto, RD, FADA, and John Britto, CEC.

COSTS: Tuition in-state $13/unit, out-of-state $115/unit. Students supply equipment and supplies. Refunds granted first 2 weeks of class. Application deadlines: ongoing. Admission requirements: high school graduate or age 18. $3,500 in scholarships awarded last year averaging $200-$750 each.

Housing $400/month.

LOCATION: North of San Francisco.

CONTACT: Hazel Hill, Ed. D., Division Chairperson, San Joaquin Delta College, Culinary Arts Department, 5151 Pacific Ave., Stockton, CA 95207; (209) 474-5516, Fax (209) 474-5600.

SANTA BARBARA CITY COLLEGE
Santa Barbara/August-May
This college offers a 1-year certificate, 2-year AS degree in Culinary Arts and Restaurant-Hotel Management. Program started 1970. Accredited by WASC, ACFEI. Calendar: semester. Curriculum: core. Admission dates: fall, spring. Total enrollment: 120. 50 enrollees each admission period. 80% of applicants accepted. 60% of students receive financial aid. 70% under age 25, 20% age 25-44, 10% age 45 or over. Student to teacher ratio 10-15:1. 100% obtain employment within 6 months. Facilities: include 6 kitchens and classrooms, a gourmet dining room, coffee shop, bake shop, lecture/lab room with individual stoves, cafeteria, and snack shop.

COURSES: International cuisine, wines, bar management, production service, nutrition, meat analysis, garde manger, baking, and restaurant ownership. Schedule: 6:30am-2:30pm weekdays.

FACULTY: 3 full-time, 6 part-time, and 10 lab teaching assistants.

COSTS: Annual tuition in-state $500, out-of-state $3,360. Application deadlines: May, December. Admission requirements: high school diploma or equivalent. Average off-campus housing cost $250 per month.

LOCATION: The 12,000-student suburban campus is 90 miles from Los Angeles.

CONTACT: John Dunn, Santa Barbara City College, Hotel/Restaurant & Culinary Department, 721 Cliff Dr., Santa Barbara, CA 93109-2394; (805) 965-0581, Fax (805) 963-7222.

SANTA ROSA JUNIOR COLLEGE
Santa Rosa
This college offers a 1-year certificate. Accredited by WASC. Total enrollment: 25-40. Student to teacher ratio 20-24:1. 100% obtain employment within 6 months.

FACULTY: 3 full-time, 10 part-time.

COSTS: Tuition in-state $60/semester, out-of-state $96/unit.

CONTACT: Harriett Lewis, Santa Rosa Junior College, Consumer & Family Studies Dept, 1501 Mendocino Ave., Santa Rosa, CA 95401; (707) 527-4395.

SHASTA COLLEGE
Redding
This college offers a 1-year certificate, 2-year AA program. Program started 1975. Total enrollment: 125. Student to teacher ratio 25:1. 100% obtain employment within 6 months.

FACULTY: 1 instructor.

COSTS: Annual tuition in-state $130, out-of-state $100/unit. Admission requirements: high school diploma or equivalent and admission test.

CONTACT: Kathleen Kistler, VP, Instruction, Shasta College, Culinary Arts, 1155 N. Old Oregon Tr., P.O. Box 496006, Redding, CA 96049-6006; (916) 225-4600.

SOUTHERN CALIFORNIA SCHOOL OF CULINARY ARTS
South Pasadena/Year-round *(See also page 166) (See display ad page 15)*
This nonprofit school offers a 1-year full-time/2-year part-time Professional Culinary Arts diploma, 3-month Advanced Professional Cooking and Advanced Professional Baking diplomas, 3-month Food Styling certificate program. Established 1994. Calendar: quarter. Curriculum: culinary, food arts. 1,865 hours of culinary courses required. Admission dates: fall, winter, spring, summer. Total enrollment: 140. 36 enrollees each admission period. 90% of applicants accepted. 40% enrolled part-time. 15% under age 25, 70% age 25-44, 15% age 45 or over. Student to teacher ratio 12:1. 100% obtain employment within 6 months. Facilities: 3 kitchens for garde manger, bak-

ing & pastry, hot food production; learning resource center, classrooms, food styling lab; student-run bakery and cafe.

Courses: Include culinary arts, garde manger, baking and pastry, hot food production, food styling, sanitation, nutrition, supervision, purchasing & food service principles. Schedule: 25 hours full-time, 12-½ hours part-time. Externship provided. Continuing education: classes available year-round.

Faculty: 7 full-time, 5 part-time. Includes Director and Executive Chef Christopher F. Becker, Executive Chef Instructor Robert Danhi, Chef John Jensen, Chef Terry Hahn and Pastry Chef Instructor Leslie Bilderback.

Costs: Tuition is $14,014. Registration fee $75. 1-month tuition payment required as deposit. Tuition billed monthly. Pro-rata refund policy. Application deadlines: up to 1st day of class based on availability. Admission requirements: high school diploma or equivalent and entrance test required. 4 scholarships awarded last year averaging $500-$1,000 each. Off-campus lodging averages $625/month.

Location: The 12,000-square-foot school facility is in an historic suburb, 12 minutes from downtown Los Angeles.

Contact: Cristina Williams, Admissions Director, Southern California School of Culinary Arts, 1420 El Centro St., S. Pasadena, CA 91030; (818) 403-8490, Fax (818) 403-8494.

TANTE MARIE'S COOKING SCHOOL
San Francisco/Year-round   *(See also page 166) (See display ad page 17)*
This small private school offers 6-month certificate programs in culinary arts (full-time) and pastry (part-time), nonvocational courses, and culinary travel programs. Established in 1979. Curriculum: culinary. 360 hours of culinary courses required. Admission dates: March, September. Total enrollment: 24. 12-14 enrollees each admission period. 95% of applicants accepted. 10% under age 25, 80% age 25-44, 10% age 45 or over. Student to teacher ratio 12:1. 95% obtain employment within 6 months.

Courses: Culinary courses cover basic French techniques, breads and pastries, desserts, ethnic cuisines, food purchasing and handling, menu planning, and taste refinement. Schedule: 10am-4pm weekdays. 4-week internship in a local quality restaurant.

Faculty: Founder Mary Risley studied at Le Cordon Bleu and La Varenne; Catherine Pantsios, former chef/owner of Zola's; Cathy Burgett; guest instructors.

Costs: Tuition is $13,200 for the 6-month culinary certificate course, $5,280 for the 6-month part-time pastry course. A $300 nonrefundable deposit is required. Admission requirements: high school diploma. 2 scholarships awarded last year averaging $4,000 each. Housing in local apartments.

Location: On San Francisco's Telegraph Hill, near Fisherman's Wharf and public transportation.

Contact: Peggy Lynch, Administrator, Tante Marie's Cooking School, Inc., 271 Francisco St., San Francisco, CA 94133; (415) 788-6699, Fax (415) 788-8924.

UCLA EXTENSION, HOSPITALITY/FOODSERVICE MANAGEMENT
Los Angeles/Year-round   *(See also page 167)*
This self-supported continuing higher education institution offers 6 certificate programs: Professional Cooking, Professional Catering, Professional Baking, Vintage, Hotel Management, and Restaurant Management. Calendar: quarter. Student to teacher ratio 15:1.

Courses: 14 Professional Cooking courses, 13 Professional Catering courses, 10 Professional Baking courses. Each includes 6 core business courses and an internship. Schedule: 3-4 hours once weekly weeknights or Saturday. Nonvocational courses are also offered.

Faculty: Local restaurant chefs, culinary specialists, and graduates of the CIA and CCA.

Costs: Tuition is $7,300 for Professional Cooking, $6,000 for Professional Catering, $4,800 for Professional Baking, $1,900 for Vintage. A nonrefundable $95 application fee is required.

Contact: UCLA Extension, Hospitality/Foodservice Management, 10995 Le Conte Ave., Room 515, Los Angeles, CA 90024-0901; (310) 206-8120, Fax (310) 206-7249.

COLORADO

COLORADO INSTITUTE OF ART – SCHOOL OF CULINARY ARTS
(See display ad page 27)   **Denver/Year-round**
This private school offers an 18-month AAS degree in Culinary Arts. Program started 1994. Accredited by ACCSCT. Calendar: quarter. Curriculum: core. 1,716 hours of culinary courses required. Admission dates: January, April, July, October. Total enrollment: 300. 100 enrollees each admission period. 98% of applicants accepted. 75% of students receive financial aid. 15% enrolled part-time. 30% under age 25. Student to teacher ratio 20:1. 90% obtain employment within 6 months. Facilities: include 5 kitchens, classrooms, full dining facility.

COURSES: Basic skills, baking and pastry, food production, garde manger, a la carte, dining room, sanitation, nutrition, management, cost control, wines and spirits, facilities design, and general education courses. Schedule: day and evening classes, Monday/Saturday. Continuing education provided.

FACULTY: 11 full-time, 11 part-time. Qualifications: professional certification, AAS degree, and 20 years experience.

Costs: Quarterly tuition: $3,090. Application fee $50, tuition deposit $100. Other fees: $250/quarter lab fee, $275 general fee, $600 supply kit. Application deadlines: rolling. Admission requirements: high school diploma or equivalent and essay. 2 scholarships awarded last year averaging $9,750 each.

LOCATION: 3 miles from downtown Denver.

CONTACT: Barbara Browning, V.P., Director of Admissions, Colorado Institute of Art, 200 E. 9th Ave., Denver, CO 80203; (800) 275-2420, Fax (303) 860-8520, E-mail browninb@aii.edu.

COLORADO MOUNTAIN COLLEGE CULINARY INSTITUTE
Dillon/Year-round
This collaboration between Keystone Resort and Colorado Mountain College offers a 3-year AAS and Certificate of Apprenticeship from ACF. Program started 1993. Accredited by NCA. Calendar: trimester. Curriculum: core. Admission dates: June. Total enrollment: 32. 12-15 enrollees each admission period. 25% of applicants accepted. 35% of students receive financial aid. 50% under age 25, 50% age 25-44. Student to teacher ratio 6:1. 100% obtain employment within 6 months. Facilities: include 10 full-service kitchens and classrooms and 25 food and beverage outlets.

COURSES: 6,000 hours of structured work experience combined with 850 hours of classroom lecture required for graduation. Schedule: 40 hours/week paid work experience, 8 hours classroom work. 6,000-hour ACF apprenticeship.

FACULTY: 1 full-time, 12 resort chefs part-time. Includes Doug Schwartz, Chris Wing, Bob Burden, Julie Licktiege, Alisa Mathews.

COSTS: Annual tuition in-district $1,300, out-of-state $4,500. Application deposit is $500 and includes culinary texts and tool set. Application deadlines: April 15, August 15. Admission requirements: personal interview. 8 scholarships awarded last year averaging $800 each. On-campus housing $250 per month, off-campus housing $250-$400 per month.

LOCATION: The AAA 5-Diamond Keystone ski resort, 70 miles west of Denver.

CONTACT: Doug Schwartz, Colorado Mountain Culinary Institute, Admissions, P.O. Box 10,001, Glenwood Springs, CO 81602; (800) 621-8559, (970) 468-4153, Fax (970) 945-7279, URL http://www.coloradomtn.edu/aas_culinary_arts.html.

COOKING SCHOOL OF THE ROCKIES
Boulder/Year-round   *(See also page 168) (See display ad page above)*
This private school offers a 6-month Culinary Arts diploma program that consists of 5 months of training in Boulder, the sixth month in Carpentas in Provence, France. Established in 1996. Accredited by Dept. of Higher Education and the state. Calendar: January, July. 1,050 hours of culinary courses required. Total enrollment: 24. 12 enrollees each admission period. 33% under age 25, 33% age 25-44, 33% age 45 or over. Student to teacher ratio 4:1. Facilities: modern, fully-equipped kitchens.

COURSES: Classical, modern, and regional French and Italian cooking. Schedule: 9:30am-4pm weekdays.

FACULTY: Robert Reynolds, French-trained former chef/owner of San Francisco's Le Trou Restaurant; Michael Comstedt, former chef/owner of Boulder's Greenbriar Restaurant; Mary Copeland, former head pastry chef at Palais du Chocolat in Washington, DC.

COSTS: $17,500 tuition includes airfare and room and board in France. A 10% deposit is required with application, $5,000 is due on acceptance, 50% of balance is due 60 days prior, balance is due 30 days prior. Admission requirements: high school diploma.

LOCATION: 25 miles northwest of Denver; 20 miles west of Avignon in the south of France.

CONTACT: Joan Brett, Director, Cooking School of the Rockies, Professional Culinary Arts Program, 637 S. Broadway, Ste. H, Boulder, CO 80303; (303) 494-7988, Fax (303) 494-7999, E-mail jbrett3768@aol.com.

CULINARY INSTITUTE OF COLORADO SPRINGS
Colorado Springs/Year-round

This division of Pikes Peak Community College offers a Certificate in Culinary Arts, 2-year degree in Culinary Arts/Food Management. Program started 1986. Accredited by NCA. Calendar: semester. Curriculum: core. 54 credit hours of culinary courses required. Admission dates: August, January, June. Total enrollment: 35. 10-15 enrollees each admission period. 100% of applicants accepted. 90% of students receive financial aid. 50% under age 25, 48% age 25-44, 2% age 45 or over. Student to teacher ratio 10:1. 100% obtain employment within 6 months. Facilities: include kitchen, student-run cafeteria and catering service/classroom.

COURSES: Food preparation, restaurant management, wine and spirits, food and beverage management, and sanitation. Other required courses: computer, English, math, accounting. Schedule: 8 hours/day, 5 days/week for 11 months. Continuing education: language classes available.

FACULTY: 3 full-time, 1 part-time. Qualifications: ACFEI certification. Includes George J. Bissonnette, CCE, CEC, Dept. Chair; Gary Hino, CC, Robert Hudson, CSC.

COSTS: Annual tuition in-state $4,125, out-of-state $5,775. Application deadlines: 1 month prior to each semester. Admission requirements: high school diploma or equivalent and admission test. Average off-campus housing cost $250 and up.

LOCATION: The 15,000-student campus is in an urban setting 2 miles from Colorado Springs.

CONTACT: George Bissonnette CCE, CEC, Dept. Chair, Culinary Institute of Colorado Springs, TISO Div., PPCC, 5675 S. Academy Blvd., Colorado Springs, CO 80906; (719) 540-7371, Fax (719) 540-7453, URL http://www.ppcc.cccoes.edu.

JOHNSON & WALES UNIVERSITY AT VAIL
(See also page 94)
Vail/Year-round

This university branch offers a 1-year accelerated AAS degree in Culinary Arts for those with a bachelor's degree or higher. Program started 1993. Accredited by NEASC, ACICS-CCA. Calendar: 12-month. Curriculum: culinary. 99 quarter credit hours of culinary courses required. Admission dates: June. Facilities: 16,000-sq-ft of kitchen and restaurant space, 2 additional restaurants.

COURSES: Laboratory courses, professional development, menu design and analysis, nutrition, sanitation, cost control, garde manger, advanced patisserie/dessert, advanced dining room procedures, international cuisine and classical French cuisine. Schedule: Monday-Friday.

FACULTY: 8 full/part-time. Includes Matthew Broussard, CWC, Karl Guggenmos, BS, GMC, David Hendrickson, AOS, CWC, CCE, Michael Koons, CEC, CCE, Steve Nogle, AS, CEC, CCE, Todd Rymer, MS, David Sanchez, AOS, Paul Ferzacca, AOS.

COSTS: Tuition is $17,867. Other costs: $375 general fee, $565 supplies. Annual, term or monthly payments. Admission requirements: a bachelor's degree from an accredited institution. Request for waiver may be directed to the Director of Culinary Admissions in Providence, RI.

CONTACT: Todd Rymer, Director, Johnson & Wales University at Vail, College of Culinary Arts, 8 Abbott Park Place, Providence, RI 02903; (800) DIAL-JWU #1892, Fax (401) 598-4712, E-mail admissions@jwu.edu, URL http://www.jwu.edu.

SCHOOL OF NATURAL COOKERY
(See also page 169)
Boulder/Year-round

This private trade school specializing in vegetarian cuisine offers Personal Chef Training, 12 weeks; Teacher Training, 8 weeks of Fundamentals and Baking plus individual training; Baking & Pastry, 2 and 5 weeks; Fundamentals, 5 weeks. Established in 1991. Admission dates: January, April, June, September. 8 enrollees each admission period. 95% of applicants accepted. 30% of students receive financial aid. 33% under age 25, 50% age 25-44, 15% age 45 or over. Student to teacher ratio 5:1. 98% obtain employment within 6 months. Facilities: teaching kitchen.

COURSES: Fundamentals covers technique, grains, food energetics, intuitive cooking, meal composition; Teacher Training includes practice teaching; Personal Chef Training covers marketing & management; Baking & Pastry covers sugar, wheat, & dairy alternatives. Schedule: 3-5 hours daily. Continuing education: 1-day and 1-week seminars for professional chefs.

FACULTY: Founder and director Joanne Saltzman, author of *Amazing Grains* and *Romancing the Bean*, Mary Bowman, and Barbara Jacobs, author of *Cooking with Seitan*.

COSTS: Fundamentals $3,500, 2- (5-)week Baking $980 ($2,600), Personal Chef Training $6,530 (includes Fundamentals & 2-week baking), Teacher Training $1,340, Professional Seminars $400/day. Deposit is $500. Cancellations 1 month prior receive full refund. Application deadlines: application suggested 3 months prior to admission. Admission requirements: personal or phone interview; Fundamentals and 2-week Baking required for Teacher Training. Off-campus lodging ranges from $300 to $500 per month.

LOCATION: 35 miles from Denver.

CONTACT: Joanne Saltzman, Director, School of Natural Cookery, P.O. Box 19466, Boulder, CO 80308; (303) 444-8068, Fax available 1/97, E-mail available 1/97.

WARREN OCCUPATIONAL TECHNICAL CENTER
Golden/August-May

This public institution offers a 1-semester (options for 2nd and 3rd semesters) certificate in Restaurant Arts. Program started 1974. Accredited by State, NCA. 540 hours of culinary courses required. Admission dates: August, January. Total enrollment: 60. 45 enrollees each admission period. 98% of applicants accepted. 2% of students receive financial aid. 25% enrolled part-time. 98% under age 25, 2% age 25-44, 1% age 45 or over. Student to teacher ratio 20:1. 95% obtain employment within 6 months. Facilities: kitchen, 60-student classroom, 2 dining rooms and a restaurant.

COURSES: Production, nutrition, baking, safety & sanitation. Schedule: 7:30am to 2:00pm weekdays. Externship provided.

FACULTY: 3 full-time with master's degree in vocational education.

COSTS: Tuition in-state $1,600 per semester, out-of-state $2,464 per semester. Parking fee $50, materials $10. Application deadlines: July. Admission requirements: diploma or GED. Off-campus housing cost is $350/month.

LOCATION: The 1,200-student campus is in a suburban setting.

CONTACT: Sharron K. Pizzuto, C.F.E., Service Instructor, Warren Occupational Technical Center, Restaurant Arts, 13300 W. Ellsworth Ave., Golden, CO 80401; (303) 982-8555, Fax (303) 982-8547.

CONNECTICUT

CONNECTICUT CULINARY INSTITUTE
Farmington/Year-round

This private occupational school offers 360-hour professional training program in Culinary Arts, 250-hour Professional Pastry and Baking program. Founded in 1988. Accredited by CT Dept of Ed., ACCSCT. 360/250 hours (culinary arts/pastry-baking) of culinary courses required. Admission dates: September, January, March, June for day students; September, February for evening students. Total enrollment: 200+. 11 enrollees each admission period. 42% enrolled part-time. 20% under age 25, 37% age 25-44, 27% age 45 or over. Student to teacher ratio 11:1. 92% obtain employment within 6 months. Facilities: include a custom-built 4,500-square-foot area with 2 fully-equipped kitchen-classrooms; another facility is in New Haven county.

COURSES: Emphasis is on the preparation of fine international cuisine and pastry. Topics also include kitchen organization and food identification and purchasing. Home assignments and research are required. Schedule: day classes run 12 weeks, 6 hours daily weekdays; evening classes run 20 weeks, 3 classes per week, 6 hours per class. Continuing education courses include sanitary food handling and low-cholesterol cooking.

FACULTY: Includes V.P. James T. Monroe, Director of Professional Education Leslie Noury, staff instructors, and 25 part-time chef/instructors.

COSTS: Tuition is $5,300. Application fee is $100; materials fee is $345. A $750 deposit is due within 10 days of acceptance, $2,500 is due 30 days prior to class, balance is due 1 week prior. Admission requirements: 18 years or older, high school diploma or equivalent, interview.

LOCATION: Suburban Farmington Valley, 10 miles west of Hartford.

CONTACT: Connecticut Culinary Institute, Loehmann's Plaza, 230 Farmington Ave., Farmington, CT 06032; (860) 677-7869, (800) 76-CHEFS, Fax (860) 676-0679.

GATEWAY COMMUNITY-TECHNICAL COLLEGE
New Haven/Year-round

This college offers a 1-year certificate, 2-year degree in Culinary Arts. Program started 1987. Accredited by state, NEAS. Calendar: semester. Curriculum: culinary. Admission dates: September, January. Total enrollment: 140. 20 enrollees each admission period. 100% of applicants accepted. 40% of students receive financial aid. 60% enrolled part-time. 20% under age 25, 60% age 25-44, 20% age 45 or over. Student to teacher ratio 15:1. 100% obtain employment within 6 months. Facilities: include 1 lab, many classrooms, restaurant.

COURSES: Externship provided.

FACULTY: 2 full-time, 4 part-time.

COSTS: Annual tuition in-state $1,398, out-of-state $4,206. Admission requirements: high school diploma or equivalent and admission test. Average off-campus housing $500/month.

CONTACT: Eugene J. Spaziani, Gateway Community-Technical College, Hospitality Management, 60 Sargent Dr., New Haven, CT 06511; (203) 789-7067, Fax (203) 777-8637.

MANCHESTER COMMUNITY TECHNICAL COLLEGE
Manchester/September-May

This college offers a 1-year certificate. Program started 1977. Accredited by ACFEI. Admission dates: September, January. Total enrollment: 54. 20 enrollees each admission period. 25% of students receive financial aid. 50% enrolled part-time. 50% under age 25, 35% age 25-44, 15% age 45 or over. Student to teacher ratio 18:1. 95% obtain employment within 6 months. Facilities: include classrooms and 2 kitchens.

COURSES: Include 4 culinary, 2 baking, sanitation, nutrition, and co-op ed. Schedule: various options available. Externship provided. Continuing education in decorative work, wines & spirits, hospitality industry, cost control.

FACULTY: 7 full-time with master's degree or equivalent.

COSTS: Tuition per semester in-state $820, out-of-state $2,400. Application fee $10. Admission requirements: high school diploma or equivalent.

LOCATION: 160-acre campus in a suburban setting 10 miles from Hartford.

CONTACT: G. S. Lemaire, Program Coordinator, Manchester Community Technical College, Culinary Arts Dept., 60 Bidwell St., Manchester, CT 06040; (860) 647-6136.

FLORIDA

ART INSTITUTE OF FT. LAUDERDALE
(See display ad page 27)   **Ft. Lauderdale/Year-round**

This proprietary school offers a 9-month diploma in Baking & Pastry and The Art of Cooking and an 18-month AS degree program in Culinary Arts. Program started 1991. Accredited by ACCSCT. Admission dates: January, April, July, October. Total enrollment: 180. 15-40 enrollees each admission period. 90% of applicants accepted. 20% under age 25, 65% age 25-44, 15% age 45 or over.

Student to teacher ratio 18:1. 98% obtain employment within 6 months. Facilities: 8 kitchens and classrooms and a student-run restaurant.

COURSES: General education; 1st yr. includes basic cooking, product identification, baking & pastry, knife skills, & nutrition; 2nd yr. includes garde manger, art history, international cuisine, menu planning, kitchen layout, wine appreciation & restaurant service.

FACULTY: 7 full-time ACF-certified instructors.

COSTS: Annual tuition is $8,940. Application fee $50. Tuition deposit is $100. Application deadlines: open. Admission requirements: high school diploma or equivalent. On-campus housing $290-$1,150 per quarter. Average off-campus housing $600 per month.

CONTACT: Art Institute of Ft. Lauderdale, School of Culinary Arts, 1799 S.E. 17th St., Ft. Lauderdale, FL 33316; (305) 463-3000, Fax (305) 527-1799.

ATLANTIC VOCATIONAL TECHNICAL CENTER
Coconut Creek/Year-round

This public institution offers a 1,080 hour certificate in Culinary Arts. Program started 1976. Accredited by SACS, ACFEI. Calendar: quarter. Curriculum: core. 1,080 hours of culinary courses required. Admission dates: open. Total enrollment: 100. 100 enrollees each admission period. 90% of applicants accepted. 30% of students receive financial aid. 1% enrolled part-time. 25% under age 25, 73% age 25-44, 2% age 45 or over. Student to teacher ratio 15:1. 85% obtain employment within 6 months. Facilities: include student-run restaurant.

COURSES: Hot foods, cold foods, bakery, nutrition, sanitation, supervision, dining room, and management. Schedule: 30 hours/week, evening schedule available.

FACULTY: 8 full-time.

COSTS: Annual tuition $700. Textbook and workbook $35, uniforms $60, and knives. Admission requirements: admission test and basic academic skills. 3 scholarships awarded last year.

LOCATION: The campus is an a suburban setting.

CONTACT: Moses Ball, Atlantic Vocational Technical Center, Culinary Arts, 4700 N.W. Coconut Creek Pkwy., Coconut Creek, FL 33066; (305) 977-2066, Fax (305) 977-2019.

DAYTONA BEACH COMMUNITY COLLEGE
Daytona Beach/Year-round

This college offers a 3-year Certificate of Apprenticeship. Program started 1980. Accredited by ACFEI. Admission dates: open. Total enrollment: 130. 80% of applicants accepted. 100% enrolled part-time. 10% under age 25, 60% age 25-44, 30% age 45 or over. Student to teacher ratio 25:1. Facilities: include kitchen and classroom.

COURSES: Culinary and pastry apprenticeship, sanitation, supervision, nutrition. Schedule: culinary course meets 4 hours on Mondays, pastry course meets for 4 hours on Tuesday.

FACULTY: 5 part-time.

COSTS: State funded vocational program. Fees are $160. Admission requirements: high school diploma or equivalent and admission test.

CONTACT: Denise M. O'Brien, Daytona Beach Community College, Culinary Arts Department, P.O. Box 2811, Daytona Beach, FL 32020-2811; (904) 255-8131, #3735, Fax (904) 254-4492.

FLORIDA CULINARY INSTITUTE
West Palm Beach/Year-round   *(See display ad page 23)*

This proprietary institution, a division of New England Tech offers an 18-month Specialized Associate degree in Culinary Arts, International Baking and Pastry, and Food & Beverage Management. Established in 1987. Accredited by ACFEI, COE. Calendar: quarter. Curriculum: culinary. 90 quarter hours of culinary courses required. Admission dates: January, March, July, September. Total enrollment: 480. 140 enrollees each admission period. 95% of applicants accepted. 80% of students receive financial aid. 50% under age 25, 40% age 25-44, 10% age 45 or over. Student to teacher ratio 18:1. Facilities: include 8 kitchens and 8 classrooms.

FLA. CULINARY INSTITUTE

- Earn a specialized Associate Degree in 18 months in Culinary Arts •
- Earn a specialized Associate Degree in International Baking & Pastry •
- New! Food & Beverage Management •
- American Culinary Federation Educational Institute Accredited •

FLORIDA CULINARY INSTITUTE, 1126 53rd Ct., West Palm Beach, FL 33407
For more information on Culinary Arts or Financial Aid call: (800) 826-9986

COURSES: 6 quarters including food preparation, facilities planning, nutrition, purchasing, baking, classical American and international cuisine, and management. Schedule: six 11-week quarters with 2-week breaks in between. Classes meet 5 hours daily. Internships are served in practicum facility with Cafe Protege, the Institute's gourmet restaurant.

FACULTY: 18 full-time. Includes Department co-chairs Colin Cage and David Pantone, CEPC, Michael Barber, CWC, Dan Birney, CWC, William Boetcher.

COSTS: Cost per academic year is $9,800. Application deadlines: rolling. Admission requirements: high school diploma or equivalent. Advanced credit awarded through a testing program. 90 scholarships awarded last year averaging $900 each. Average off-campus housing cost is $500/month.

LOCATION: 25,000-square-foot facility on Florida's southeast coast, 5 miles from WPB International Airport.

CONTACT: Scott Spitolnick, Admissions Director, Florida Culinary Institute, 1126 53rd Court, West Palm Beach, FL 33407-9985; (800) 826-9986, (407) 842-8324, Fax (407) 842-9503.

GULF COAST COMMUNITY COLLEGE
Panama City/Year-round

This college offers a 2-year AS degree in Culinary Management. Program started 1988. Accredited by SACS, ACFEI. Calendar: semester. Curriculum: core. Admission dates: fall, spring. Total enrollment: 60. 20 enrollees each admission period. 100% of applicants accepted. Student to teacher ratio 16:1. Facilities: include a student-run restaurant.

FACULTY: 2 full-time, 1 part-time. Includes Travis Herr, CEC, CCE, John Holley, Jon Bullard, CCE.

COSTS: Tuition in-state $30/credit, out-of-state $110/credit. Lab fees $8-$9. Refund policy: 100% 4 weeks prior, third day of class 75%. Application deadlines: first day of class. Admission requirements: high school diploma or equivalent. 6 scholarships awarded last year.

LOCATION: The campus is in a suburban setting in Florida's Panhandle.

CONTACT: Travis Herr, Chef/Coordinator, Gulf Coast Community College, Culinary Management, 5230 W. U.S. Hwy 98, Panama City, FL 32401; (904) 872-3850, Fax (904) 872-3836.

INSTITUTE OF THE SOUTH FOR HOSPITALITY & CULINARY ARTS
Jacksonville/Year-round

This 2-year college offers a 1-year diploma and a 2-year AS degree. Program started 1990. Accredited by SACS, ACFEI. Calendar: semester. Curriculum: core. 64 credit hours of culinary courses required. Admission dates: August, January, May. Total enrollment: 150. 50 enrollees each admission period. 100% of applicants accepted. 30% of students receive financial aid. 40% enrolled part-time. 20% under age 25, 79% age 25-44, 1% age 45 or over. Student to teacher ratio 20:1. 95% obtain employment within 6 months. Facilities: 3 kitchens, 4 classrooms, 2 restaurants.

COURSES: Culinary courses. Schedule: weekdays. 2 externships at 150 hours, throughout the community at major properties.

FACULTY: 4 full-time, 6 part-time. Includes Chefs Rick Grigsby, Joe Harrold, and Al Fricke.

Qualifications: ACF certified.

Costs: Annual tuition in-state $832, out-of-state $3,328. Admission requirements: high school diploma or equivalent.

Contact: Dr. Sharon Cooper, Dean, Florida Community College at Jacksonville, Inst. of the South for Hospitality & Culinary Arts, 4501 Capper Rd., Jacksonville, FL 32218; (904) 766-6594, Fax (904) 766-6654, E-mail scooper@fccj.cc.fl.us.

JOHNSON & WALES UNIVERSITY AT NORTH MIAMI
North Miami/Year-round   *(See also page 94)*

This nonprofit university offers a 2-year AAS in Culinary Arts, Baking & Pastry Arts, Food & Beverage Management, Hotel-Restaurant Management, Restaurant/Institutional Management, Travel-Tourism Management and 4-year BS program in Culinary Arts. Program started 1992. Accredited by NEASC, ACICS. Calendar: term. Curriculum: core. 99/189.5 quarter credit hours (AS/BS) of culinary courses required. Admission dates: rolling. Total enrollment: 617. Varied enrollees each admission period. 80% of applicants accepted. 5% enrolled part-time. 38% under age 25, 62% age 25-44. Student to teacher ratio 20:1. 58% obtain employment within 6 months. Facilities: laboratory kitchens, academic classrooms, library, computer laboratory, conference center.

Courses: Culinary fundamentals, advanced culinary technologies, culinary principles. Other required courses: professional studies and academic courses. Schedule: Monday-Thursday, up to 24 hours/week, 9 months/year; weekend programs available. Term-long internships scheduled for all Baking & Pastry, Culinary, Hotel-Restaurant majors. Continuing education: The Culinary Arts Weekend program.

Faculty: 23.

Costs: Tuition is $13,824 for College of Culinary Arts, $11,982 for Hospitality College. Other costs: $375 general fee, $65 new student orientation fee. $100 deposit. Annual, term or monthly payments. Application deadlines: rolling. Admission requirements: high school diploma or equivalent. The number of scholarships awarded and the amount varies. Grant and award programs administered annually. On-campus housing: 250 spaces, average cost: $2,970. Average off-campus housing cost: $350 per month.

Location: The 617-student, 8-acre campus is in South Florida.

Contact: Licia Dwyer, Director of Admissions, Johnson & Wales University at North Miami, Office of Admissions, 1701 N.E. 127th St., North Miami, FL 33181; (800) 232-2433 #7600, (305) 892-7600, Fax (305) 892-7020, E-mail admissions@jwu.edu, URL http://www.jwu.edu.

McFATTER SCHOOL OF CULINARY ARTS
Davie/Year-round

This trade school offers a 1-year certificate. Program started 1996. Accredited by SACS. Calendar: quarter, semester. Curriculum: culinary, core. 1,080 hours of culinary courses required. Admission dates: each 9-week term. Total enrollment: 20. 10-20 enrollees each admission period. 100% of applicants accepted. 50% of students receive financial aid. 10% enrolled part-time. 50% under age 25, 47% age 25-44, 1% age 45 or over. Student to teacher ratio 20:1. 90% obtain employment within 6 months. Facilities: cafeteria, cafe, dining room.

Courses: Baking & pastries, food production, garde manger, service. Other required courses: 30 hours each of sanitation, nutrition, supervisory management. Schedule: 7am-1:45pm, Monday-Friday.

Faculty: 2 full-time, 2 part-time. Includes Program Coordinator/Dept. Head V. Paul Citrullo, Jr., CEC, Chef Kay Bolm, Chef Al Nelfi.

Costs: Tuition is $135 per term. Other costs: books and uniforms. Admission requirements: basic skills testing.

Location: 5 miles from Ft. Lauderdale.

Contact: V. Paul Citrullo, Jr., CEC, Exec. Chef/Director of Culinary Arts, McFatter Vocational Tech Center, 6500 Nova Dr., Davie, FL 33317; (954) 424-4161, Fax (954) 370-1647.

MID-FLORIDA TECHNICAL INSTITUTE
Orlando

This institution offers an 1,800-hour certificate. Program started 1970. Accredited by SACS. Admission dates: open. Total enrollment: 80. 100% of applicants accepted. Student to teacher ratio 15-20:1. 100% obtain employment within 6 months.

FACULTY: 2 full-time, 6 part-time.

CONTACT: Dale Pennington, Mid-Florida Technical Institute, Commercial Cooking-Culinary Arts, 2900 W. Oakridge Rd., Orlando, FL 32809; (407) 855-5880, Fax (407) 855-5880, #700.

NORTH TECHNICAL EDUCATION CENTER
Riviera Beach/Year-round

This public institution offers an 1,800-hour certificate in Commercial Foods and Culinary Arts. Program started 1970. Accredited by SACS. Admission dates: August, October, January, March, June. Total enrollment: 40. 30 day and 30 evening enrollees each admission period. 100% of applicants accepted. 50% of students receive financial aid. 50% enrolled part-time. 70% under age 25, 20% age 25-44, 10% age 45 or over. Student to teacher ratio 15-20:1. 90% obtain employment within 6 months. Facilities: kitchen and classroom.

FACULTY: 2 full-time.

COSTS: Annual tuition in-state $400 to $800. Textbook, uniform and shoes approximately $200. Refund policy: full first week, half second week less $10 fee.

LOCATION: In an urban setting.

CONTACT: R. Robertson, North Technical Education Center, Commercial Foods & Culinary Arts, 7071 Garden Rd., Riviera Beach, FL 33404; (407) 881-4600.

OKALOOSA-WALTON COMMUNITY COLLEGE
Niceville/Year-round

This college offers a 2-year AAS/AS degree in Restaurant Management. Program started 1973. Accredited by SACS. Admission dates: August, January, May. Total enrollment: 25. 40% of students receive financial aid. 5% enrolled part-time. 40% under age 25, 50% age 25-44, 10% age 45 or over. Student to teacher ratio 25:1. 92% obtain employment within 6 months. Facilities: include kitchen and classroom.

COURSES: Culinary courses plus 6 hours elective in commercial baking required.

FACULTY: 1 full-time, 1 part-time.

COSTS: Tuition in-state $26 per semester hour, out-of-state $104 per semester hour. Admission requirements: high school diploma or equivalent and admission test. Average off-campus housing cost $225 per month.

CONTACT: Okaloosa-Walton Community College, Commercial Foods-Industrial Education, 100 College Blvd., Niceville, FL 32578; (904) 678-5111, Fax (904) 729-5215.

PINELLAS TECHNICAL EDUCATIONAL CENTER
N. Clearwater/Year-round

This college offers a 15-month diploma in Culinary Arts. Program started 1965. Accredited by ACFEI, COE. 1,800 hours of culinary courses required. Admission dates: monthly. Total enrollment: 60. 6-10 enrollees each admission period. 100% of applicants accepted. 75% of students receive financial aid. 50% under age 25, 25% age 25-44, 25% age 45 or over. Student to teacher ratio 15:1. 100% obtain employment within 6 months. Facilities: include 2 kitchens, 2 classrooms and a student-run restaurant.

COURSES: Include employability skills and computer literacy. Transformation class also required. Schedule: 6 hours/day, 11 months/year.

FACULTY: 4 full-time.

COSTS: Tuition in-state $247/trimester. Admission requirements: admission test. Average off-campus housing cost $350 per month.

CONTACT: Vincent Calandra, Dept. Chair, Pinellas Technical Educational Center, Culinary Arts Dept., 6100 154th Ave., N. Clearwater, FL 34620; (813) 538-7167, Fax (813) 538-7203.

PINELLAS TECHNICAL EDUCATIONAL CENTER
St. Petersburg/Year-round
This trade school offers an 1,800-hour diploma in Culinary Arts. Accredited by SACS, ACFEI. Admission dates: open. Total enrollment: 52. 10 enrollees each admission period. 100% of applicants accepted. 60% of students receive financial aid. 18% under age 25, 70% age 25-44, 12% age 45 or over. Student to teacher ratio 17:1. 95% obtain employment within 6 months. Facilities: include kitchen, baking lab and classroom.

COURSES: Schedule: days 7:30am-2:10pm, evenings 5:30pm-9:00pm.

FACULTY: 2 full-time, 1 part-time. Includes Dr. Warren Laux, Dr. Tom Maas, Alvin Miller, Fred Lemiesz.

COSTS: Annual tuition $440. Books $42. Admission requirements: admission test.

LOCATION: The 1,950-student campus is in a suburban setting 21 miles from Tampa.

CONTACT: Alvin Miller, Pinellas Technical Educational Center, Culinary Arts Dept., 901 34th St. South, St. Petersburg, FL 33711; (813) 893-2500 #1104.

SARASOTA COUNTY TECHNICAL INSTITUTE
Sarasota
This institution offers a 1,485-hour certificate. Program started 1967. Accredited by SACS. Admission dates: open. 90% of applicants accepted. 100% obtain employment within 6 months.

FACULTY: 1 full-time.

CONTACT: Timothy Carroll, Sarasota County Technical Institute, Culinary Arts, 4748 Beneva Rd., Sarasota, FL 34233; (941) 924-1365 #250.

THE SOUTHEAST INSTITUTE OF CULINARY ARTS
St. Augustine/Year-round
This school offers 1-year (1,080-hour) certificate and 2-year (2,160-hour) diploma programs in Commercial Foods and Culinary Arts. Established in 1970. Accredited by ACFEI, Council on Occupational Education. Calendar: quinmester. Curriculum: culinary. 1,080/2,160 hours (certificate/diploma) of culinary courses required. Admission dates: every 9 weeks. Total enrollment: 600+. Student to teacher ratio 15-20:1. 99% obtain employment within 6 months.

COURSES: Rotation through basic stations, participation in intensives that include epicurean service, advanced bake shop, buffet catering, purchasing & receiving, and a la carte. Specialized certificates awarded for portions of course. 270-hour internship for diploma. Hospitality management programs at area colleges offer credit toward AS degree.

FACULTY: 18 instructors, all ACF-certified or pending, 5 support staff.

COSTS: Total cost is $2,100 in-state; out-of-state residents should call for fees. $15 registration fee, $149/quinmester fee, $50 refundable book deposit, $500 for supplies. Admission requirements: 16 years or older, high school diploma or equivalent on completion. Scholarships are available. Off-campus lodging is $400 per month.

LOCATION: St. Augustine, the nation's oldest city and home of the American Culinary Federation, on Florida's northeast coast.

CONTACT: Chef David S. Bearl, CCC, CCE, The Southeast Institute of Culinary Arts, Commercial Foods/Culinary Arts, 2980 Collins Ave., St. Augustine, FL 32094-9970; (904) 829-1060, (904) 829-1061, Fax (904) 824-6750.

SOUTHEASTERN ACADEMY'S CULINARY TRAINING CENTER
Kissimmee/Year-round
This proprietary institution offers a 30-week diploma in Culinary Arts. Program started 1990. Accredited by ACCSCT, approved for veterans' training. 750 hours of culinary courses required.

Admission dates: every 5 weeks. Total enrollment: 120. 30 enrollees each admission period. 95% of applicants accepted. 90% of students receive financial aid. 20% under age 25, 75% age 25-44, 5% age 45 or over. Student to teacher ratio 10:1. 85% obtain employment within 6 months. Facilities: include 6 kitchens and classrooms, student-run restaurant, bakery.

COURSES: Culinary arts, baking/pastry arts, sanitation, nutrition, professional development. Schedule: 5 hours/day, 5 days/week, 12 months/year, 1 of 3 classes/day. Externship provided.

FACULTY: 10 full-time, 2 part-time. Includes Reimund D. Pitz, CEC, CCE, AAC, Glen Rhoades, Richard Woodring, CWC, Kimberly Pearson, David Weir, David Solomon.

COSTS: Annual tuition in-state and out-of-state $8,030, fees and equipment $665. Tuition deposit $150. Refund policy: prorated except for application fee, uniforms, text and tools. Application deadlines: every 5 weeks. Admission requirements: high school diploma or equivalent. 75 loans granted; $2,625 Direct Student Loans. On-campus dorm (30 weeks) $3,600; off-campus $450-$600/month.

LOCATION: Suburban Orlando.

CONTACT: Reimund D. Pitz, CEC, CCE, AAC, VP/Director, Southeastern Academy, 233 Academy Dr., Box 421768, Kissimmee, FL 34742-1768; (407) 847-4444, Fax (407) 847-8793, URL peoples@gdi.net.

GEORGIA

ART INSTITUTE OF ATLANTA – SCHOOL OF CULINARY ARTS
(See display ad above)   **Atlanta/Year-round**

This proprietary institution offers an 18-month AA degree in Culinary Arts. Program started 1991. Accredited by ACFEI, SACS. 72 credit hours of culinary courses required. Admission dates: January, April, July, October. Total enrollment: 400. 50-75 enrollees each admission period. 75% of students receive financial aid. 10% enrolled part-time. 25% under age 25, 70% age 25-44, 5% age 45 or over. Student to teacher ratio 20-25:1. 96% obtain employment within 6 months. Facilities: include 4 kitchens and 3 classrooms.

COURSES: Culinary skills, food production, baking and pastry, garde manger. Schedule: about 20 hours/week, mornings, afternoons, or evenings.

FACULTY: 17 full- and part-time.

COSTS: Quarterly tuition $3,328. Application fee $50, quarterly lab fee $250. Tuition deposit $100. Application deadlines: rolling. Admission requirements: high school diploma or equivalent and writing sample required. 110 scholarships awarded last year averaging $600 each. On-campus housing $450 per month.

LOCATION: The 1,300-student campus is in Atlanta's uptown Buckhead area.

CONTACT: Robin J. Rickenbach, Director of Admissions, Art Institute of Atlanta, 3376 Peachtree Rd. NE, Atlanta, GA 30326; (800) 275-4242, (404) 266-2662, Fax (404) 266-1383, URL http://www.aii.edu.

ATLANTA AREA TECHNICAL SCHOOL
Atlanta

This institution offers an 18-month diploma. Program started 1967. Accredited by SACS. Admission dates: quarterly. Student to teacher ratio 12:1. 92% obtain employment within 6 months.

FACULTY: 6+ full-time.

COSTS: Tuition $296/quarter full-time, $21/credit part-time. Admission requirements: high school diploma or equivalent and admission test.

CONTACT: Barbara Boyd, Culinary Chair, Atlanta Area Technical School Culinary Arts Program, Health & Human Services, 1560 Stewart Ave. S.W., Atlanta, GA 30310; (404) 756-3700 #3727, Fax (404) 756-0932.

AUGUSTA TECHNICAL INSTITUTE
Augusta/Year-round

This state trade school offers a 4-quarter certificate program in Food Service and a 6-quarter diploma in Advanced Culinary Arts. Program started 1985. Accredited by SACS. 108/37 credit hours (6/4 quarters) of culinary courses required. Admission dates: September, March. Total enrollment: 24. 15 enrollees each admission period. 90% of applicants accepted. 100% of students receive financial aid. 10% under age 25. Student to teacher ratio 12:1. 100% obtain employment within 6 months. Facilities: include 1 kitchen, 2 classrooms, and local restaurants.

COURSES: Basic food preparation, introduction to baking, garde manger, nutrition and menu management, safety and sanitation, and consumer education. Other required courses: office accounting, computer literacy. Schedule: approximately 30 hours/week, 12 months/year. Internship: 150 hours (concludes diploma program), salaried, at various food service institutions. Continuing education: catering, cake decoration, sanitation.

FACULTY: 2 full-time. Includes Willie Mae Crittenden, CCE and Kathleen Fervan, CCE, CEC.

COSTS: Quarterly tuition: $274 in-state, $548 out-of-state. Application fee $15. Cancellations prior to July 5 receive full refund and prior to July 19 receive 75% refund. Admission requirements: high school diploma or GED. Average off-campus housing cost $500 per month.

LOCATION: The 50-acre, 5,000-student suburban campus is 7 miles from Augusta.

CONTACT: Willie Mae Crittenden, Department Head, Augusta Technical Institute, Culinary Arts, 3116 Deans Bridge Rd., Augusta, GA 30906; (706) 771-4000, Fax (706) 771-4016, E-mail NCritten@augusta.tec.ga.us.

SAVANNAH TECHNICAL INSTITUTE
Savannah/Year-round

This public institution offers a 6-quarter and a 4-quarter diploma in Culinary Arts. Program started 1981. Accredited by SACS, ACF. Calendar: quarter. Curriculum: core. 106/69 credit hours (6/4 quarters) of culinary courses required. Admission dates: quarterly. Total enrollment: 24. 4 enrollees each admission period. 100% of applicants accepted. 54% of students receive financial aid. 10% enrolled part-time. 10% under age 25, 85% age 25-44, 5% age 45 or over. Student to teacher ratio 12:1. 100% obtain employment within 6 months. Facilities: include kitchen, classroom, student-run restaurant.

COURSES: Culinary arts, sanitation and equipment, food preparation, baking, garde manger, nutrition, and management. Other required courses: English, math, psychology. Schedule: 30 hours/week. Externship: 150 hours, restaurant. Continuing education: sanitation, cake decorating, restaurant management.

FACULTY: 1 full-time, 1 part-time. Includes Marvis T. Hinson, CFBE, M.Ed and John F. Kelley, Executive Sous Chef.

COSTS: Tuition in-state $216/quarter, out-of-state $348/quarter. Application fee $15. 2 uniforms $50, shoes $40, knives $60, books $100. 100% refund prior to first day of class, 75% first to four-teenth day of class. Application deadlines: 30 days before entry. Admission requirements: high school diploma or equivalent and admission test. 95 loans granted last year.

CONTACT: Marvis Hinson, Department Head, Savannah Technical Institute, Culinary Arts, 5717 White Bluff Rd., Savannah, GA 31499; (914) 351-4553, Fax (912) 352-4362.

HAWAII

KAPIOLANI COMMUNITY COLLEGE
Honolulu/August-May

This college offers a 2-year AS degree in Culinary Arts, Patisserie, School Food Service, and Food Service-Health care; 18-month and 1-semester certificate program in Culinary Arts and Patisserie. Program started 1947. Accredited by ACFEI, WASC. Calendar: semester. Curriculum: core. Admission dates: fall, spring. Total enrollment: 450. 100% of applicants accepted. 25% of students receive financial aid. 50% enrolled part-time. 25% under age 25, 65% age 25-44, 10% age 45 or over. Student to teacher ratio 20:1. 98% obtain employment within 6 months. Facilities: 9 kitchens, 8 classrooms, 5 restaurants.

COURSES: Asian/Pacific and international cuisine, garde manger, confisserie. Schedule: day classes 8am-2pm, evening lab classes 2:30pm-9pm weekdays. Externship: available at local and neighbor island hotels.

FACULTY: 14 full-time, 6 part-time. Qualifications: Industry experience.

COSTS: Annual tuition in-state $504, out-of-state $3,096. $10 fee per semester. 100% refund up to 5 days prior to class. Application deadlines: July 1 and December 1. Admission requirements: age 18, or age 17 with high school diploma or GED. Average off-campus housing cost $500 per month.

LOCATION: The 7,500-student, 47-acre suburban campus is 2 miles from Waikiki.

CONTACT: Frank Leake, Chairman, Kapiolani Community College, Food Service & Hospitality Education Dept., 4303 Diamond Head Rd., Honolulu, HI 96816; (808) 734-9485, Fax (808) 734-9212, E-mail yonemori@kccada.kcc.hawaii.edu.

LEEWARD COMMUNITY COLLEGE
Pearl City/Year-round

This 2-year college offers a 2-year AS degree in Food Service, 1.5-year certificate in Food Service, 1-semester certificate in Food Preparation, 2-semester certificates in Baking and Dining Room. Program started 1974. Accredited by WASC, ACFEI. Calendar: semester. Curriculum: core. 1,612 hours of culinary courses required. Admission dates: August, January. Total enrollment: 80-100. 25-30 enrollees each admission period. 100% of applicants accepted. 40% of students receive financial aid. 20% enrolled part-time. 65% under age 25, 25% age 25-44, 10% age 45 or over. Student to teacher ratio 15-20:1. 90% obtain employment within 6 months. Facilities: 3 kitchens, 5 classrooms, 1 restaurant, 2 cafe/dining rooms.

Courses: Provide students with technical knowledge and basic skills training for a professional food service career.

Faculty: 5 full-time with 15-20 years industry experience, 3 part-time. Includes Tommylynn Benavente, Stanley Ikei, Issac Tamada, Fern Tomisato.

Costs: Semester tuition in-state $391, out-of-state $2,588. 100% refund on or before last day of registration, 80% within first two weeks of class. Application deadlines: July and December. Admission requirements: age 18 or 17 with high school diploma.

Location: The 6,000-student, 49-acre campus is on the Pearl City peninsula between Pearl City and Waipahu.

Contact: Tommylynn Benavente, Program Coordinator, Leeward Community College, Food Service Program, 96-045 Ala Ike, Pearl City, HI 96782; (808) 455-0298, (808) 455-0300, Fax (808) 455-0471, E-mail tlbenave@hawaii.edu.

MAUI COMMUNITY COLLEGE/FOOD SERVICE PROGRAM
Kahului/Year-round
This 2-year college offers a 1-year certificate, a 2-year AS degree-Culinary, and a 2-year AS degree-Baking. Program started 1969. Accredited by ACFEI. 42-43 credit hours of culinary courses required. Admission dates: August, January. Total enrollment: 125. 30 enrollees each admission period. 100% of applicants accepted. 25% of students receive financial aid. 20% enrolled part-time. 80% under age 25, 20% age 25-44. Student to teacher ratio 10:1. 98% obtain employment within 6 months. Facilities: include 2 kitchens, 2 classrooms, 1 restaurant, 1 cafe/dining room.

Courses: Culinary Arts or Baking Specialties. Schedule: 24-30 hours/week, 2 years. Apprenticeship available. Continuing Education: Specialty courses available.

Faculty: 4 full-time, 5 part-time.

Costs: Annual tuition in-state $393, out-of-state $2,565/semester. Application deadlines: January and August. 8-10 scholarships awarded last year averaging $300-$350 each. 2 bedroom cost is $997/semester, 3 bedroom cost is $857/semester.

Contact: Karen Tanaka, Coordinator, Maui Community College, Culinary Arts Dept., 310 Kaahumanu Avenue, Kahului, HI 96732; (808) 984-3225, E-mail mccada::tanaka.

IDAHO

BOISE STATE UNIVERSITY
Boise/Year-round
This university offers a 1-year certificate and a 2-year AAS degree. Program started 1969. Accredited by ACFEI. Admission dates: August, January. Total enrollment: 35-45. Student to teacher ratio 10:1. 98% obtain employment within 6 months.

Faculty: 3 full-time, 1 part-time.

Costs: Tuition is $940 per semester. Admission requirements: high school diploma or equivalent and admission test.

Contact: Vern Hickman, CWC, CCE, Boise State University, Culinary Arts Program, 1910 University Dr., Boise, ID 83725; (208) 385-4199.

COLLEGE OF SOUTHERN IDAHO
Twin Falls/September-May
This community college offers a 2-year AAS, 1-year technical certificate. Program started 1986. Calendar: semester. Curriculum: core. 40 credit hours of culinary courses required. Admission dates: open. Total enrollment: 20. 12 enrollees each admission period. 32% of applicants accepted. 90% of students receive financial aid. 50% under age 25, 40% age 25-44, 10% age 45 or over. Student to teacher ratio 10:1. 90% obtain employment within 6 months.

Courses: Culinary arts, Food production. Internships provided in summer. Cooperative education during school year.

FACULTY: 2 full-time, 6 part-time.

COSTS: Tuition in-state $550/semester, out-of-state $1,200/semester. Application deadlines: 30 days prior to beginning of semester. Admission requirements: high school diploma or equivalent. 12 scholarships awarded last year averaging $300 each. On-campus room & board is $1,625; average off-campus housing cost is $350/month.

LOCATION: South Central Idaho, 120 miles east of Boise.

CONTACT: Chris Mottern, Program Coordinator, College of Southern Idaho, Hotel-Restaurant Management, P.O. Box 1238, Twin Falls, ID 83303-1238; (208) 733-9554 #2407, Fax (208) 736-2136, E-mail cmottern@evergreen2.csi.cc.id.us.

BLACK HAWK COLLEGE – QUAD CITIES CAMPUS
Moline/Year-round

(See also page 179)

This college offers a 1-year certificate and a 2-year AAS degree in Hospitality, Culinary Arts, and Professional Baking. Program started 1988. Accredited by NCA. Calendar: semester. Curriculum: core. 34/62 credit hours (certificate/degree) of culinary courses required. Admission dates: September, January. Total enrollment: 85. 30 enrollees each admission period. 30% of applicants accepted. 30% of students receive financial aid. 70% enrolled part-time. 55% under age 25, 40% age 25-44, 5% age 45 or over. Student to teacher ratio 15:1. 100% obtain employment within 6 months. Facilities: include advanced equipment in several areas of curriculum, and students prepare food for gourmet luncheon and community functions at the college.

COURSES: Sanitation, culinary arts, quantity food, cost/portion control, baking, garde manger, internship, nutrition, general education courses. Schedule: days. Externship: 16 weeks, open, individualized. Continuing education: classes for home economic teachers.

FACULTY: 8 full-time.

COSTS: Tuition in-district $49 per credit hour, out-of-district $105 per credit hour, out-of-state $189 per credit hour. 100% refund through 6th calendar day of term. Application deadlines: ongoing. Admission requirements: high school diploma or equivalent and admission test. 2 scholarships awarded last year averaging $500-$1,000 each. Average off-campus housing cost is $250-$300 per month.

LOCATION: The 161-acre site is in a suburban setting.

CONTACT: Kim Davenport, Black Hawk College-Quad Cities Campus, Culinary Arts, 6600 - 34th Ave., Moline, IL 61265; (309) 796-1311 ext. 4125, Fax (309) 792-3418.

CLEA'S CASTLE COOKING SCHOOL
Oak Park/Year-round

This school offers 12-session cuisine courses, 2-session ice carving courses, 5-session courses in cake decorating, baking, and catering, a 30-hour supervisory development and nutrition course, and a 5-session sanitation and safety course for state certification. Founded in 1974.

COSTS: Tuition ranges from $125-$200.

CONTACT: Clea's Castle Cooking School, 1201 Fair Oaks Ave., Oak Park, IL 60302; (708) 383-8245, (708) 383-1849, Fax (708) 848-8580.

COLLEGE OF DUPAGE
Glen Ellyn/Year-round

This college offers a 1-year certificate and a 2-year AAS degree in Food Service Administration and Culinary Arts. Program started 1966. Accredited by NCA, RBA, NRA Educational Foundation Calendar: quarter. Curriculum: core. 63 quarter credit hours of culinary courses required. Admission dates: September, January, March, June. Total enrollment: 200. 50-125 enrollees each admission period. 100% of applicants accepted. 25% of students receive financial aid. 30%

enrolled part-time. 40% under age 25, 40% age 25-44, 20% age 45 or over. Student to teacher ratio 15:1. 100% obtain employment within 6 months. Facilities: include kitchen, many classrooms, restaurant, dining room.

COURSES: Food preparation, classical cuisine, merchandising, cake decorating, garde manger, wines and international cuisine. Schedule: part-time or evenings. Externship provided.

FACULTY: 4 full-time, 12 part-time. Includes George C. Macht, CHA, CFE, FMP, Chris Thieman, CWC, Rolf Sick, Jim Zielinski, FMP.

COSTS: In-district $29/credit hour. Admission fee $10. Texts, uniforms, tools and fees $500. 100% refund before the first day of quarter, 80% refund through the first week of the quarter. Application deadlines: depend on the quarter. Admission requirements: high school diploma or equivalent. 8 scholarships awarded last year averaging $300 each. 20 loans granted last year averaging $1,500 each. Average off-campus cost is $500 per month.

LOCATION: The 33,000-student campus is in a suburban setting 25 miles from Chicago.

CONTACT: Catherine Leveille, Program Assistant, College of DuPage, Culinary Arts/Pastry Arts, 22nd St. & Lambert Rd., Glen Ellyn, IL 60137; (630) 942-3663, Fax (630) 858-9399, E-mail machtg@cdnet.cod.edu.

COLLEGE OF LAKE COUNTY
Grayslake/August-May

This college offers a 1-year certificate in Culinary Arts or Food Service Management and an AAS in Food Service Management. Program started 1987. Accredited by NCA. Calendar: semester. Curriculum: core. 14 hours of culinary courses required. Admission dates: August, January, June. Total enrollment: 40. 10 enrollees each admission period. 95% of applicants accepted. 10% of students receive financial aid. 50% enrolled part-time. 50% under age 25, 40% age 25-44, 10% age 45 or over. Student to teacher ratio 10:1. 98% obtain employment within 6 months. Facilities: include 2 kitchens and 3 classrooms.

COURSES: Cooking, baking, nutrition and menu planning. Schedule: 4 days/week, part-time/full-time and evening options available. Externship: 16-week part-time.

FACULTY: 5 full-time. Includes C. Wener, M. Eskenazy, J. Lempke, J. Bress. Qualifications: minimum 2-year culinary school or formal internship.

COSTS: Tuition $44 per credit hour. Other fees: lab, equipment, uniforms.

LOCATION: Lake County, IL.

CONTACT: Mr. Cliff Wener, Coordinator, College of Lake County, Food Service Program, Business Division, 19351 W. Washington St., Grayslake, IL 60030-1198; (847) 223-6601 #2823, Fax (847) 223-7248.

COOKING ACADEMY OF CHICAGO
Chicago/January-December

This institution offers a 6-month Culinary Career certificate, and a 6-month Baking & Pastry certificate. Founded in 1992. Accredited by Illinois State Board of Education. Curriculum: culinary. 595 hours of culinary courses required. Admission dates: January, May, September. Total enrollment: 30. 10 enrollees each admission period. 100% of applicants accepted. 50% enrolled part-time. 10% under age 25, 80% age 25-44, 10% age 45 or over. Student to teacher ratio 10:1. 100% obtain employment within 6 months. Facilities: 2 full kitchens, 2 classrooms.

COURSES: Knife skills, soups and stocks, vegetables and starches, meats, fish, poultry, sauces, baking and pastry.

FACULTY: 2 full-time. Qualifications: minimum AAS and 5 years experience.

COSTS: Tuition culinary $3,400, baking & pastry $3,400. Fees: $100. Application deadlines: January 1, May 1, September 1. Admission requirements: high school diploma or equivalent.

LOCATION: 20 blocks west of Wrigley Field.

CONTACT: Nora Christensen, Director, Cooking Academy of Chicago, 2500 W. Bradley Pl., Chicago, IL 60618; (312) 478-9840, Fax (312) 478-3146.

THE COOKING AND HOSPITALITY
INSTITUTE OF CHICAGO

Chicago's premier culinary school. For information, call 312.944.2725

THE COOKING AND HOSPITALITY INSTITUTE OF CHICAGO
(See also page 180) (See display ad above)
Chicago/Year-round
This institution offers a 2-year (70-credit-hour) associate degree in Culinary Arts, 30-week (28-credit-hour) certificate programs in Professional Cooking and Baking and Pastry, a 300-hour certificate program in Restaurant Management. Founded in 1983. Accredited by ACCSCT. Calendar: every 7 weeks. Curriculum: core. Admission dates: 6 times yearly. Total enrollment: 550. 100 enrollees each admission period. 80% of applicants accepted. 60% of students receive financial aid. 35% enrolled part-time. 20% under age 25, 60% age 25-44, 20% age 45 or over. Student to teacher ratio 25:1. 95% obtain employment within 6 months. Facilities: 3 fully-equipped instructional kitchens, on-site restaurant.

COURSES: Professional cooking covers qualitative and quantitative cooking, menu planning, recipe development, sanitation, and job search techniques. Baking and pastry covers production techniques, food as an art form, yeast breads, and decoration. Schedule: flexible schedules available. Variety of continuing education and nonvocational classes.

FACULTY: School founder Linda Calafiore is a past state coordinator of local vocational training programs. Instructors include Mark Facklam, formerly executive chef at Cricket's.

COSTS: Tuition is $16,500 for the degree program and $6,600 for each certificate program. Registration fee is $100. Application deadlines: 2 months before start date. Admission requirements: high school diploma or equivalent. Off-campus housing varies.

CONTACT: Jim Simpson, Director, The Cooking and Hospitality Institute of Chicago, 361 W. Chestnut, Chicago, IL 60610; (312) 944-2725, Fax (312) 944-8557, URL http://www.chicnet.org.

THE CULINARY SCHOOL OF KENDALL COLLEGE
Evanston/Year-round
This nonprofit school, a division of Kendall College offers a 21-month AAS degree in Culinary Arts, 2- and 4-year programs in Hospitality Management. Program started 1985. Accredited by ACFEI, NCA, UMCUS. Calendar: 11-week term. Admission dates: continuous admissions. Total enrollment: 270. 40 enrollees each admission period. 80% of applicants accepted. 82% of students receive financial aid. 30% enrolled part-time. 42% under age 25, 58% age 25-44,. Student to teacher ratio 13:1. 90% obtain employment within 6 months. Facilities: include demonstration, production, and display kitchens, 3 professional kitchens, dining room, banquet area, cafeteria.
COURSES: Culinary skills, business management, nutrition, menu planning, classic cuisine, American and nutritional. Beginning students work in the school's cafeteria, bakery, and catering service; advanced students work in the school's restaurant. A 13-week salaried internship is required. Continuing education: culinary fundamental series in cooking, baking & pastry.
FACULTY: 25 chef/instructors and hospitality specialists as well as visiting lecturers and guest chefs. Include Michael Carmel, CEC, BA in CW, AOS, John Draz, CEC, CCE, AOS, Hubert Martini, AAC, CEC, CCE, Lawrence Smith, Kader Temkkit.
COSTS: Tuition is $13,566 per year, including equipment and activities fee and 2 meals daily. A $30 nonrefundable application fee is required. $150 nonrefundable deposit is due within 30 days of acceptance. Withdrawals the first week of class forfeit $100. Admission requirements: high school diploma or equivalent and ACT/SAT scores or college experience. 36 endowed and restricted scholarships. 240 loans granted/$10,100. Room and board is $764 double, $993 single/term.
LOCATION: 35 minutes from Chicago's Loop by express train.
CONTACT: Kathleen A. Shannon, Coordinator of External Affairs, The Culinary School of Kendall College, 2408 Orrington Avenue, Evanston, IL 60201; (847) 866-1304, Fax (847) 866-6842.

ELGIN COMMUNITY COLLEGE
Elgin/September-July
This college offers a 2-year associate degree in Culinary Arts. Program started 1972. Accredited by Illinois Community College Board, ACFEI. Admission dates: August, January. Total enrollment: 140. 30-40 enrollees each admission period. 80% of applicants accepted. 30% enrolled part-time. 25% under age 25, 65% age 25-44, 10% age 45 or over. Student to teacher ratio 12-30:1. 100% obtain employment within 6 months. Facilities: 4 kitchens, 3 classrooms and a culinary training center.
FACULTY: 3 full-time, 8 part-time. Qualifications: ACF-certification.
COSTS: $35 per credit hour. Books and uniforms $200. Admission requirements: high school diploma or equivalent. Average off-campus housing cost $400-$600 per month.
CONTACT: Michael Zema, Director, Elgin Community College, Hospitality Department, 1700 Spartan Dr., Elgin, IL 60123; (708) 697-1000 #7461, Fax (708) 888-7995.

FOOD ARTS STUDIO
Elmwood Park/Spring, Fall
Food stylist Donna Lafferty offers 2- and 4-day certificate courses (limit 10 students) in styling food for the still and motion camera. Student to teacher ratio 1:1. Facilities: a 250-square-foot professional kitchen with work stations and overhead mirror.
COURSES: Weekend (4-day) course offers 16 (32) hours of instruction and a shopping trip to specialty shops. Other activities: shopping at specialty stores. A yearly food-oriented tour to a country where food styling, cooking, & food photography are taught.
FACULTY: Donna Lafferty has 17 years of experience styling for still and motion advertising. Her clients include Edy's Grand Ice Cream, Kraft Foods, and The Oprah Winfrey Show.
COSTS: $400 for 2 days, $800 for 4 days. Nonrefundable deposit. Admission requirements: students should know how to cook. Motels/hotels recommended.

LOCATION: U.S. classes: a Chicago suburb.

CONTACT: Donna Lafferty, Food Arts Studio, 2733 N. 75th Ct., Elmwood Park, IL 60707-1433; (708) 456-8415.

JOLIET JUNIOR COLLEGE
Joliet/Year-round

This college offers a 2-year certificate/AAS degree in Culinary Arts. Program started 1970. Accredited by NCA, ACFEI. Admission dates: August, January, May, June. Total enrollment: 200. 100 enrollees each admission period. 98% of applicants accepted. 40% of students receive financial aid. 85% under age 25, 15% age 25-44. Student to teacher ratio 20:1. 95% obtain employment within 6 months. Facilities: include 3 kitchens, demonstration kitchen, 3 classrooms and a pastry shop.

FACULTY: 9 full-time.

COSTS: Annual tuition in-state $982, out-of-state $4,118. Admission requirements: high school diploma or equivalent and admission test.

LOCATION: The 11,000-student campus is in a small town setting.

CONTACT: Patrick F. Hegarty, CEC, CCE, Joliet Junior College, Culinary Arts/Hotel-Restaurant Management, 1216 Houbolt Ave., Joliet, IL 60436-9352; (815) 729-9020 #2448, Fax (815) 744-5507.

LEXINGTON COLLEGE
Chicago/September-May

This independent institution offers a 2-year AAS degree in Hotel, Restaurant & Institutional Management. Program started 1977. Accredited by NCA. Calendar: semester. Curriculum: core. 8 hours of culinary courses required. Admission dates: September, January. Total enrollment: 20. 20 enrollees each admission period. 50% of applicants accepted. 85% of students receive financial aid. 10% enrolled part-time. 75% under age 25, 25% age 25-44. Student to teacher ratio 5:1. 95% obtain employment within 6 months. Facilities: include a culinary lab, 3 classrooms, library, computer lab, bookstore, off-campus site for quantity foods.

COURSES: Professional baking, pastries, food & beverage sales & service, garde manger, purchasing, quantity foods, basic food production, professional cooking, food service sanitation, & general education liberal arts & management courses. Other courses required. Schedule: 15 to 17 credit hours/semester, 17-20 hours/week; part-time options available. Externship provided. Continuing education: evenings and weekends.

FACULTY: 4 part-time.

COSTS: Tuition $2,900/semester. Application fee $25, books and equipment $300-350/semester, lab culinary fees $50-100/semester. No refund after fourth week of class. Application deadlines: rolling. Admission requirements: high school diploma or equivalent, with 2.0 average or above. Average off-campus housing cost is $1,600/semester.

LOCATION: An urban setting, 20 miles from downtown Chicago.

CONTACT: Mary Jane Markel, Director of Admissions, Lexington College, Admissions, 10840 S. Western Ave., Chicago, IL 60643-3294; (312) 779-3800, Fax (312) 779-7450.

TRITON COLLEGE
River Grove/August-May

This college offers a 2-year AAS degree in Culinary Management. Program started 1970. Accredited by NCA, ACFEI. Admission dates: September. Total enrollment: 150. 30 enrollees each admission period. 50% of students receive financial aid. 30% enrolled part-time. 30% under age 25, 60% age 25-44, 10% age 45 or over. Student to teacher ratio 12:1. 97% obtain employment within 6 months. Facilities: 5 kitchens and classrooms, demonstration kitchen, ice carving facility, and student-run restaurant.

COURSES: Garde manger, international cooking, ice carving, food production, food theory, menu planning, purchasing, cost control, nutrition, service, and baking. Schedule: Monday-Friday 10 months per year; part-time, evening and weekend options available. Externship provided. Continuing education: international cooking, sanitation, and nutrition.

FACULTY: 3 full-time, 10 part-time.

COSTS: $36.50 per credit hour. Application fee $25. Other fees: approximately $100 per semester. Refund policy: before classes begin. Application deadlines: fall: August 25; spring: January 15. Admission requirements: high school diploma or equivalent. Average off-campus housing cost $300 per month.

CONTACT: Triton College, Hospitality Industry Administration, 2000 Fifth Avenue, River Grove, IL 60171; (708) 456-0300.

WASHBURNE TRADE SCHOOL
Chicago

This independent institution offers an 80-week certificate in Chef Training. Program started 1937. Accredited by City Colleges of Chicago. Calendar: 3 16-week phases. Admission dates: September, January, May. Total enrollment: 150. 25 enrollees each admission period. 75% of students receive financial aid. 25% under age 25. Student to teacher ratio 25:1. 98% obtain employment within 6 months. Facilities: 6 kitchens, 6 classrooms.

COURSES: Schedule: 8:00am-1:35pm Monday-Thursday, 8:00am-12:20pm Friday. Continuing education: ice carving.

FACULTY: 7 full-time.

COSTS: Annual tuition of $3,664 includes books and uniforms. Application fee: $200 if cash-paying student; none if financial aid. Cutlery set: $272. Admission requirements: high school diploma or equivalent and admission test. 2 scholarships awarded last year averaging $4,000 each.

LOCATION: The 4-story campus occupies one-block in Chicago.

CONTACT: Dean Jaramillo, Washburne Trade Program, Chefs Training Program, 3233 W. 31st St., Chicago, IL 60623; (312) 579-6108/6109, Fax (312) 376-5940.

WILLIAM RAINEY HARPER COLLEGE
Palatine/Year-round

This college offers a 1-year certificate in Culinary Arts and Baking. Program started 1975. 420 hours of culinary courses required. Admission dates: year-round. Total enrollment: 150. 25 enrollees each admission period. 95% of applicants accepted. 50% of students receive financial aid. 75% enrolled part-time. 50% under age 25, 40% age 25-44, 10% age 45 or over. Student to teacher ratio 15:1. 100% obtain employment within 6 months. Facilities: include 3 kitchens including production bakery, production kitchen, demo lab, and several classrooms.

COURSES: Garde manger, classical cuisine, cake decorating, basic and advanced culinary, and basic and advanced baking. Other required courses: 200 management contact hours. Schedule: daily August-May; part-time and evening options.

FACULTY: 3 full-time, 4 part-time.

COSTS: Annual tuition is $1,000. Other costs: application fee $20, lab fee $200, books $400. Refund policy: 90% 1st week, 80% 2nd week. Average off-campus housing cost $400-$600 per month.

LOCATION: The 27,000-student, 20-building campus is in a suburban setting, 35 miles from Chicago's loop.

CONTACT: Bruce Borher, Director of Admissions, William Rainey Harper College, 1200 W. Algonquin Rd., Palatine, IL 60067-7398; (708) 925-6700, (708) 925-6000, Fax (708) 925-6031, E-mail bborher@harper.cc.il.us, pbeach@harper.cc.il.us.

WILTON SCHOOL OF CAKE DECORATING
Woodridge/February-November

This private school offers career-oriented 4- to 10-day cake decoration and candy making diploma courses. Founded in 1929. Admission dates: open. 20 enrollees each class period. Student to teacher ratio 15:1. Facilities: the 2,200-square-foot school includes a classroom, teaching kitchen, student lounge, and retail store.

COURSES: The 10-day (70-hour) Master Course covers basic cake decorating and design techniques; 5-day courses cover chocolate, the Lambeth method, Australian techniques, and catering; 3- and 4-day courses cover gum paste and pulled sugar. Schedule: hours vary and some courses can be taken concurrently. Most are conducted on consecutive days with weekends free.

FACULTY: Includes Sandra Folsom, Susan Matusiak, Nicholas Lodge, Wesley Wilton, and Elaine Gonzalez.

COSTS: Range from $75 for 1 day to $650 for a 10-day course. A registration fee of $25-$75 must accompany application. Refund with 14 days written notice.

LOCATION: A southwestern Chicago suburb, 25 miles from downtown.

CONTACT: School Secretary, Wilton School of Cake Decorating and Confectionery Art, 2240 W. 75th St., Woodridge, IL 60517; (708) 963-7100 #211, Fax (708) 963-7299.

INDIANA

IVY TECH STATE COLLEGE
Fort Wayne/Year-round

This college offers a 2-year AAS degree in Hospitality Administration with Culinary Arts or Pastry Arts Specialty. Program started 1981. Accredited by NCA, ACFEI. Calendar: semester. Curriculum: culinary. 60 credit hours of culinary courses required. Admission dates: year-round. Total enrollment: 108. 64 enrollees each admission period. 100% of applicants accepted. 33% of students receive financial aid. 42% enrolled part-time. 15% under age 25, 75% age 25-44, 10% age 45 or over. Student to teacher ratio 10-12:1. 100% obtain employment within 6 months. Facilities: include 5 kitchens and classrooms, pastry arts lab, large full service kitchen with top-of-the-line equipment.

COURSES: Basic foods, soups, stocks and sauces, nutrition, meat cutting, special cuisines, classical cuisines, fish and seafood, pantry and breakfast, garde manger, catering, breads and pastries, cake decoration, chocolates and baking. Schedule: 8am-10pm; part-time evening options are available. Externship: 144-hour, salaried, in an ACF approved site.

FACULTY: 2 full-time, 8 part-time. Includes Program Chair Alan Eyler, CCE, CFBE, and Chef Instructor Jerry Wilson with 35 years industry experience.

COSTS: Annual tuition $1,835 in-state, $3,335 out-of-state. Other fees: books, uniforms, knife kits, and specialty tools. Refund: full during 1st week of class; partial thereafter. Application deadlines: rolling. Admission requirements: high school diploma or equivalent and admission test.

LOCATION: The small campus is in an urban community about 200 miles from Chicago or Indianapolis.

CONTACT: Alan Eyler, CCE, CFBE, Program Chair, Ivy Tech State College, Hospitality Administration, 3800 North Anthony Blvd., Fort Wayne, IN 46805; (219) 482-9171, Fax (219) 480-4177.

IVY TECH STATE COLLEGE
East Chicago, Gary, Valparaiso/Year-round

This college offers a 2-year AAS degree and a 1-year technical certificate in Hospitality Administration. Program started 1981. Accredited by NCA. Calendar: semester. Curriculum: core. Admission dates: January, May, August. Total enrollment: 80. 15 enrollees each admission period. 90% of applicants accepted. 30% of students receive financial aid. 30% enrolled part-time. Student to teacher ratio 12:1. 100% obtain employment within 6 months. Facilities: include 4 kitchens at 3 campuses, catering facilities, restaurant, bake shop.

COURSES: Include portfolio program: wine, culinary/hotel specialty, catering, baking. Schedule: 8am-5pm Monday-Friday or 2 evenings/week; year-round. Externship: 16 weeks. Continuing ed: French studies with Premier Sommelier and Chef of France, special interest courses.

FACULTY: 2 full-time, 7 part-time. Program director Deborah Ward is the only American to have received France's Cross of Gold award.

COSTS: Annual tuition $1,810 in-state, $3,621 out-of-state. Admission requirements: high school diploma or equivalent.

CONTACT: Sharon Purdy, Ivy Tech State College, Hotel & Restaurant Management/Culinary Arts, 410 E. Columbus Dr., East Chicago, IN 46312; (219) 392-3600 #18, (219) 981-1111, Fax (219) 981-4415.

IVY TECH STATE COLLEGE
Indianapolis/Year-round

This college offers a 2-year AAS degree in Culinary Arts, Baking & Pastry Arts, and Hotel Restaurant Management. Program started 1986. Accredited by NCA, ACFEI. 66 credit hours of culinary courses required. Admission dates: August, January. Total enrollment: 200. 40 enrollees each admission period. 100% of applicants accepted. 75% of students receive financial aid. 40% enrolled part-time. 20% under age 25, 70% age 25-44, 10% age 45 or over. Student to teacher ratio 10:1. 98% obtain employment within 6 months. Facilities: 3 kitchens, classrooms, 1 restaurant.

COURSES: Include basic food theory & skills, sanitation, classical French techniques. Externship: 5 months.

FACULTY: 3 full-time, 12 part-time. Qualifications: Associate degree, 5 years experience, certifiable.

COSTS: Annual tuition $3,000 in-state, $4,650 out-of-state. Admission requirements: high school diploma or equivalent and admission test. Average off-campus housing cost $300 per month.

CONTACT: Chef Vincent Kinkade, Chair, Ivy Tech State College, Hospitality Administration, One W. 26th St., Indianapolis, IN 46208; (317) 921-4619.

VINCENNES UNIVERSITY
Vincennes/August-May

This public institution offers a 2-year AS degree in Culinary Arts. Accredited by NCA. 44 credit hours of culinary courses required. Admission dates: open. Total enrollment: 60. 30 enrollees each admission period. 100% of applicants accepted. 90% of students receive financial aid. 5% enrolled part-time. 65% under age 25, 35% age 25-44. Student to teacher ratio 12:1. 100% obtain employment within 6 months. Facilities: include kitchen, 3 classrooms, hands-on lab and restaurant.

COURSES: Quantity foods, pastry and bake shop, haute cuisine, food facility design, hospitality, sanitation, purchasing, supervision, and general education. Other required courses: core curriculum 22 to 23 hours. Schedule: 16-17 hours per 5-day week. Externship provided. Continuing education: ACF regional chefs conduct hands-on classes.

FACULTY: 2 full-time, 1 part-time. Qualifications: combined 58 years in industry with AS and BA degrees.

COSTS: Annual tuition $1,800 in-state, $5,000 out-of-state. Application fee $20. Student activities fee $18. Housing deposit $150. 100% credit adjustment of tuition and fees during the first week of classes. Admission requirements: high school diploma or equivalent. On-campus housing: 3,000 spaces.

CONTACT: Robert H. Bird C.C.E., Assistant Professor, Vincennes University, Culinary Arts Department, Hoosier Hospitality Center., Gov. Hall, Vincennes, IN 47591; (812) 888-5742, Fax (812) 888-5868.

IOWA

DES MOINES AREA COMMUNITY COLLEGE
Ankeny/Year-round

This college offers a 2-year AAS degree in Culinary Arts. Program started 1975. Accredited by NCA, ACFEI. Admission dates: fall, spring. Total enrollment: 50. 20 enrollees each admission period. 100% of applicants accepted. 60% of students receive financial aid. 25% enrolled part-time. 50% under age 25, 45% age 25-44, 5% age 45 or over. Student to teacher ratio 15:1. 90% obtain employment within 6 months. Facilities: include 2 kitchens, demonstration lab, several classrooms and restaurant.

COURSES: Externship provided.

FACULTY: 2 full-time, ACF-certified.

COSTS: Annual tuition in-state, $1,500, out-of-state, $3,000. Application fee $10. Admission requirements: high school diploma or equivalent and admission test. Average off-campus housing cost $300 per month.

LOCATION: The 12,000-student suburban campus is 10 miles from Des Moines.

CONTACT: Robert Anderson, Des Moines Area Community College, Culinary Arts Department, 2006 South Ankeny Blvd., Ankeny, IA 50021; (515) 964-6532, Fax (515) 964-6486.

INDIAN HILLS COMMUNITY COLLEGE
Ottumwa/Year-round

This college offers an 18-month AAS degree in Culinary Arts and 9-month diploma in Culinary Assistant. Program started 1969. Accredited by NCA. Calendar: semester. Curriculum: culinary. 30-64 credit hours of culinary courses required. Admission dates: fall, spring. Total enrollment: 35. 15-20 enrollees each admission period. 100% of applicants accepted. 85% of students receive financial aid. 50% under age 25, 45% age 25-44, 5% age 45 or over. Student to teacher ratio 12:1. 97% obtain employment within 6 months. Facilities: include 3 kitchens, 3 classrooms, student-run dining room.

COURSES: Schedule: 8 hours/day.

FACULTY: 4 full-time. Includes Mary Kivlahan, Tom Shepard, Lisa Larson.

COSTS: $2,379 in-state, $4,192 out-of-state. Admission requirements: high school diploma or equivalent and admission test. On-campus housing: 472 spaces. Average off-campus housing cost is $350/month.

CONTACT: Tom Shepard, Program Director, Indian Hills Community College, Culinary Arts, 525 Grandview, Ottumwa, IA 52501; (515) 683-5195, Fax (515) 683-5184.

IOWA LAKES COMMUNITY COLLEGE
Emmetsburg/Year-round

This college offers a 2-year AAS degree in Culinary Arts. Program started 1974. Accredited by NCA. Admission dates: September, January. Total enrollment: 30-40. 95% of applicants accepted. Student to teacher ratio 10-12:1. 95% obtain employment within 6 months. Facilities: 2 kitchens, 2 classrooms, 1 restaurant, banquet hall.

COURSES: Externship provided.

COSTS: Annual tuition $2,500 in-state, $3,000 out-of-state. Admission requirements: high school diploma or equivalent and admission test. Dormitory spaces available on campus.

CONTACT: Mr. R. Halverson, Professor/Coordinator, Iowa Lakes Community College, South Attendance Center, Culinary Arts Department, 3200 College Dr., Emmetsburg, IA 50536; (712) 852-3554 #256, Fax (712) 852-2152.

IOWA WESTERN COMMUNITY COLLEGE
Council Bluffs/August-May

This college offers a 2-year AAS degree in Culinary Arts. Program started 1974. Accredited by NCA. Admission dates: fall, spring. Total enrollment: 30-40. 10-20 enrollees each admission period. 95% of applicants accepted. 80% of students receive financial aid. 1% enrolled part-time. 75% under age 25, 25% age 25-44. Student to teacher ratio 10-12:1. 95% obtain employment within 6 months. Facilities: include kitchen and 2 classrooms.

COURSES: Externship: 8 to 12 weeks.

FACULTY: 2 full-time, 3 part-time. Includes P. Swope, B. Gauke, B. Leeder, CCE, N. Johnson, L. Harrill.

COSTS: Tuition in-state $54 per credit hour, out-of-state $81 per credit hour. Application deadlines: August. Admission requirements: high school diploma or equivalent and admission test. 2 scholarships awarded last year at $500 each. Room and board $1,300-$1,500/semester.

LOCATION: The 4,000-student school is in a suburban area across the river from Omaha.

CONTACT: Paula Swope, Iowa Western Community College, Food Service Mgmt./Culinary Arts/Retail Baking, 2700 College Rd., Box 4-C, Council Bluffs, IA 51503; (712) 325-3378, (712) 325-3236, Fax (712) 325-3424.

KIRKWOOD COMMUNITY COLLEGE
Cedar Rapids/September-July
This state institution offers a Bakery certificate and 2-year AAS degree in Culinary Arts and Restaurant Management. Program started 1972. Accredited by NCA, ACFEI. 55 credit hours of culinary courses required. Admission dates: fall, spring. Total enrollment: 85. 36 enrollees each admission period. 100% of applicants accepted. 33% of students receive financial aid. 1-2% enrolled part-time. 30% under age 25, 30% age 25-44, 30% age 45 or over. Student to teacher ratio 23:1. 97% obtain employment within 6 months. Facilities: include 2 kitchens, 2 classrooms, restaurant and bakery.

COURSES: Food production, culinary arts, garde manger, artistic display, bakery, wines, purchasing, menu planning, nutrition, restaurant law, sanitation, and general education courses. Other required courses: 14 credit hours. Schedule: part-time or evening options available.

FACULTY: 3 full-time, 2 part-time. Qualifications: college degrees and industry experience. Includes Mary Rhiner, RD, David Dettman, Janelle Kamerlin, Lisa Pisney.

COSTS: Tuition in-state $55/credit hour, out-of-state $110/credit hour. Refund policy: 1st week 80% of tuition; 2nd week 60%. Admission requirements: high school diploma or equivalent and admission test. Average off-campus housing cost $375 per month.

LOCATION: The 10,000-student campus has 9 off-campus sites and 13 other buildings in an urban setting.

CONTACT: Mary Rhiner, Associate Professor, Kirkwood Community College, Business Dept., 6301 Kirkwood Blvd. S.W., Cedar Rapids, IA 52406; (319) 398-5468, Fax (319) 398-5667, E-mail MRhiner@kirkwood.cc.ia.us.

SCOTT COMMUNITY COLLEGE
Bettendorf/Year-round
This college offers a 3-year AAS degree and a 6,000-hour apprenticeship in sanitation and cook certification from ACF. Program started 1991. Accredited by ACFEI. Admission dates: fall. Total enrollment: 30. 10-15 enrollees each admission period. 60% of applicants accepted. 75% of students receive financial aid. 5% enrolled part-time. 30% under age 25, 50% age 25-44, 20% age 45 or over. Student to teacher ratio 10:1. 100% obtain employment within 6 months.

COURSES: Nutrition, sanitation, menu planning, management, beverages, garde manger, hot food, baking, purchasing, and general education courses. Schedule: 8:30am-9:00pm, Monday only. Externship: 6,000-hour, salaried, in restaurant or hotel setting.

FACULTY: 1 full-time, 8 part-time. Qualifications: chef instructors certified by ACF, lecture instructors 4-year degrees, all have industry experience and ACF membership.

COSTS: Annual tuition in-state $1,432.50. Other costs: application fee $25, books, uniform, knives, ACFEI registration $650 (one-time). Refund: tuition only. Application deadlines: May. Admission requirements: admission test. Off-campus housing cost approximately $300-$400 per month.

CONTACT: Jennifer Cook-DeRosa, Scott Community College, Culinary Arts, 500 Belmont Rd., Bettendorf, IA 52722-6804; (319) 359-7531 #279, Fax (319) 359-8139.

AMERICAN INSTITUTE OF BAKING
Manhattan/September-May

This nonprofit educational & research institution offers a 16-week Baking Science and Technology course and a 10-week Bakery Maintenance Engineering program. Established in 1919. Accredited by NCA. Calendar: semester. Curriculum: culinary. Admission dates: August/September, February. 90% of applicants accepted. 25% of students receive financial aid. 40% under age 25, 60% age 25-44,. Student to teacher ratio 15:1. 95% obtain employment within 6 months. Facilities: include a bread shop with 1,500 loaves/hour capacity oven, cake shop with carbon dioxide freezer, in-store bakery, cookie and cracker plant.

COURSES: The Baking Science courses include cake and sweet goods production, bread and roll production, and food product safety. The Maintenance Engineering courses include refrigeration, basic electricity, and motor controls. Schedule: 8am to 5pm weekdays. Continuing education and correspondence courses include the 50-lesson Science of Baking course.

FACULTY: 7 full-time.

COSTS: The 16-week program is $3,000. Registration fee is $45. Nonrefundable $100 deposit is required. Application deadlines: January 15, August 15. Admission requirements: high school diploma or equivalent and at least 2 years of bakery experience (or completion of Bakery Science correspondence course).

LOCATION: The 87,000-sq-ft facility is on 13 acres overlooking the Kansas State University campus, 120 miles west of Kansas City.

CONTACT: American Institute of Baking, 1213 Bakers Way, Manhattan, KS 66502; (800) 633-5137, (917) 537-4750, Fax (913) 537-1493.

JOHNSON COUNTY COMMUNITY COLLEGE
Overland Park/Year-round

This college offers a 2- to 3-year AOS degree. Program started 1975. Accredited by NCA, ACFEI. Admission dates: July, November. Total enrollment: 500. 140 enrollees each admission period. 80% of applicants accepted. 100% enrolled part-time. 50% under age 25, 50% age 25-44. Student to teacher ratio 20:1. 100% obtain employment within 6 months.

COURSES: Externship provided.

FACULTY: 10 full-time.

COSTS: Annual tuition $1,700 in-state, $5,100 out-of-state. Admission requirements: high school diploma or equivalent and admission test. Average off-campus housing cost $500 per month.

CONTACT: Jerry Vincent, Johnson County Community College, Business & Technology Division, 12345 College at Quivira, Overland Park, KS 66210-1299; (913) 469-8500, Fax (913) 469-2560.

KANSAS CITY KANSAS AREA VOCATIONAL TECHNICAL SCHOOL
Kansas City/August-May

This public institution offers a 720-hour certificate in Professional Cooking, certificate in Cooking and Baking. Program started 1975. Accredited by State. Calendar: quarter. Curriculum: culinary. Admission dates: open. Total enrollment: 20. 99% of applicants accepted. 60% of students receive financial aid. 50% enrolled part-time. 90% under age 25, 5% age 25-44, 5% age 45 or over. Student to teacher ratio 5:1. 88% obtain employment within 6 months. Facilities: include working kitchen, classroom, cafeteria, child care center, banquet facilities.

COURSES: Food preparation, cooking and presentation; safety and sanitation, baking, serving. Schedule: 4, 5, or 6 hours/day. Externship provided.

FACULTY: 4 full-time. Includes Sharyn Gassmann, BS, MS, M. Mollentine, L. Benson, S. Cole.

COSTS: Annual tuition $780. Application fee $25. Other fees: $50. Application deadlines: open. Admission requirements: admission test.

LOCATION: 5 miles west of downtown Kansas City.

CONTACT: Sharyn Gassmann, Program Director, Kansas City Kansas Area Vocational Technical School, Professional Cooking, 2220 W. 59th St., Kansas City, KS 66104; (913) 596-5500, Fax (913) 596-5509.

NORTHEAST KANSAS AREA VOCATIONAL TECHNICAL SCHOOL
Atchison/August-May

CONTACT: Northeast Kansas Area Vocational Technical School, 1501 West Riley, Atchison, KS 66002; (913) 367-6204, Fax (913) 367-3107.

WICHITA AREA TECHNICAL COLLEGE
Wichita/August-May

This technical college offers a 9-month certificate. Program started 1975. Accredited by state. Calendar: semester. Curriculum: core. Admission dates: August. Total enrollment: 20. 95% of applicants accepted. Student to teacher ratio 6:1. 95% obtain employment within 6 months.

COURSES: Culinary knowledge and skills.

FACULTY: 6 full-time. 2-certified culinary educators on staff.

COSTS: Annual tuition is approximately $1,600. Admission requirements: high school diploma or equivalent and admission test.

CONTACT: Wichita Area Technical College, Central Campus, Food Service, 324 N. Emporia, Wichita, KS 67202; (316) 833-4360.

KENTUCKY

JEFFERSON COMMUNITY COLLEGE
Louisville/August-May

This college offers a 2-year AAS degree. Program started 1974. Accredited by ACFEI, SACS. 42 credit hours of culinary courses required. Admission dates: August. Total enrollment: 22. 90% of applicants accepted. Student to teacher ratio 11:1. 96% obtain employment within 6 months. Facilities: 2 kitchens and 2 classrooms.

COURSES: Food preparation, American and European pastries, garde manger, menu planning, and catering. Other required courses: nutrition, sanitation, management, food cost and portion control. Schedule: 14 hours/week. Externship provided.

FACULTY: 2 full-time, 1 part-time.

COSTS: Annual tuition $880 in-state, $2,520 out-of-state. Admission requirements: high school diploma or equivalent and admission test.

CONTACT: Dr. Pam Besser, Chair, Business Division, Jefferson Community College, Downtown Campus, 109 E. Broadway, Louisville, KY 40202; (502) 584-0181, #2188, Fax (502) 584-0181 #2414.

KENTUCKY TECH ELIZABETHTOWN
Elizabethtown/Year-round

This public institution offers a 17-month diploma in Food Service Technology. Program started 1966. Accredited by COE. Calendar: semester. Curriculum: core. 1,850 hours of culinary courses required. Admission dates: July, January. Total enrollment: 18. 18 enrollees each admission period. 100% of applicants accepted. 80% of students receive financial aid. 20% under age 25, 70% age 25-44, 10% age 45 or over. Student to teacher ratio 18:1. 95% obtain employment within 6 months. Facilities: kitchen, classroom and restaurant.

COURSES: Food service, quantity food production, short order cooking, bakery, and cake decorating. Schedule: 24 hours/week full-time, Monday-Friday. Externship: 3 months. Continuing ed.

FACULTY: 2 full-time, Brenda Harrington and Maxine Terrill.

COSTS: Annual tuition: $600 in-state, $1,200 out-of-state. Admissions fee $20 and books. Refund policy: 1st 10 school days 100% of tuition. Application deadlines: 1 month before start of semester. Admission requirements: high school diploma or equivalent and admission test. 6 scholarships awarded last year averaging $700 each. Off-campus housing cost is $2,464.

LOCATION: The 20-acre campus is in a small town 40 miles from Louisville.

CONTACT: Rene J. Emond, Registrar, Kentucky TECH Elizabethtown, Food Service Technology, 505 University Dr., Elizabethtown, KY 42701; (502) 766-5133, Fax (502) 737-0505.

KENTUCKY TECH-DAVIESS COUNTY CAMPUS
Owensboro/August-June

This independent institution offers a 5- to 6-quarter certificate/diploma in Culinary Arts. Program started 1971. Accredited by SACS. Calendar: quarter. 1,550-1,600 hours of culinary courses required. Admission dates: August. Total enrollment: 24. 2-6 enrollees each admission period. 100% of applicants accepted. 90% of students receive financial aid. 50% enrolled part-time. 60% under age 25, 35% age 25-44, 5% age 45 or over. Student to teacher ratio 18:1. 85% obtain employment within 6 months. Facilities: include kitchen and classroom.

COURSES: Include culinary and general education courses. Schedule: 30 hours/week full-time, 15 hours/week part-time. 150 hours of cooperative and occupational training. Continuing education: cake decorating.

FACULTY: One full-time, M. VanVactor. Qualifications: BS in Home Economics, MS in Secondary Education, meets state requirements.

COSTS: $175 per quarter. Application fee $25. Application deadlines: August. Admission requirements: TABE test, high school diploma or equivalent. 1-3 scholarships were awarded last year averaging $500 each. 50 loans were granted last year averaging $1,000-$1,500 each.

LOCATION: Western Kentucky, 125 miles from Louisville.

CONTACT: Kaye Evans, Counselor, Kentucky Tech-Daviess County Campus, Student Services, 15th and Frederica St., Owensboro, KY 42301; (502) 686-3255.

SULLIVAN COLLEGE'S NATL. CTR. FOR HOSPITALITY STUDIES
Louisville/Year-round

This division of Sullivan College offers an 18-month AS degree programs in Culinary Arts, Baking & Pastry Arts, Hotel/Restaurant Management, Professional Catering, and Travel & Tourism. Program started 1987. Accredited by SACS, ACFEI. Calendar: quarter. Curriculum: core. 72 credit hours of culinary courses required. Admission dates: January, March, June, September. Total enrollment: 236. 95% of applicants accepted. Student to teacher ratio 17:1. 100% obtain employment within 6 months. Facilities: a la carte kitchen, 3 bakery labs, international, garde manger, basic skills & computer labs, retail bakery, fine dining restaurant (Winston's).

COURSES: Include theory and skills, regional and international cuisine and pastry, business management, nutrition and meal planning, and menu design and layout. Students also participate in a 400-hour off-premise practicum. Schedule: Monday through Thursday. Students work in on-campus restaurant. Externship provided.

FACULTY: 45-member resident faculty and a 38-member adjunct faculty. Includes Culinary Chairman Tom Hickey CEC, and Baking and Pastry Chairman Walter Rhea CMPC, CEC, CCE.

COSTS: Tuition is $17,550 ($8,775 per 9 months). Comprehensive supplies fee is $800 per lab; nonrefundable application fee is $100. Graduates can re-take any course at no charge. Payments arranged, pro-rata refund. Application deadlines: rolling. Admission requirements: high school diploma or equivalent. 128 loans granted last year averaging $2,625 sub, $4,000 unsub. Nearby apartments are $290/month.

LOCATION: Watterson Expressway and Bardstown Road in suburban Jefferson County.

CONTACT: Greg Cawthon, Director of Admissions, Sullivan College's National Center for Hospitality Studies, Watterson Expwy at Bardstown Rd., Box 33-308, Louisville, KY 40232; (800) 844-1354, (502) 456-6504, Fax (502) 454-4880, E-mail jvernon@vernon.sullivan.edu.

WEST KENTUCKY STATE VOCATIONAL TECHNICAL SCHOOL
Paducah

This institution offers an 18-month diploma/degree. Program started 1979. Accredited by SACS. Total enrollment: 36. Student to teacher ratio 18:1. 80% obtain employment within 6 months.

Costs: Annual tuition in-state $150, out-of-state $250. Admission requirements: high school diploma or equivalent and admission test.

Contact: Mary Sanderson, West Kentucky State Vocational Technical School, Culinary Arts, Blandville Rd., Box 7408, Paducah, KY 42002-7408; (502) 554-4991.

LOUISIANA

BOSSIER PARISH COMMUNITY COLLEGE
Bossier City

This institution offers a 9-month certificate. Program started 1986. Accredited by ACFEI. Admission dates: August. Total enrollment: 25. 98% of applicants accepted. Student to teacher ratio 13:1. 100% obtain employment within 6 months.

Faculty: 2 full-time, 4 part-time.

Costs: Annual tuition is $3,100. Admission requirements: high school diploma or equivalent and admission test.

Contact: Tommy Sibley, Bossier Parish Community College, Culinary Arts Department, 2719 Airline Drive North, Bossier City, LA 71111; (318) 746-9851, Fax (318) 742-8664.

CHEF JOHN FOLSE CULINARY INSTITUTE
Thibodaux/Year-round   *(See also page 185) (See display ad above)*

This university offers a 2-year AS degree in Culinary Arts. Program started 1994. Accredited by SACS. Calendar: semester. Curriculum: culinary, core. 66 credit hours of culinary courses. Admission dates: rolling. Total enrollment: 50. 76% of applicants accepted. 60% of students receive financial aid. 25% enrolled part-time. 35% under age 25, 50% age 25-44, 15% age 45 or over. Student to teacher ratio 15:1. Facilities: 2 newly-equipped teaching kitchens, 2 demonstration classrooms.

Courses: Classic culinary knowledge and regional American cuisine. Schedule: 15 hours/week culinary courses, 9 hours/week general education courses. Freshman externship of 360 hours paid work experience. Externships throughout U.S. Continuing education courses year-round.

Faculty: The 3 full- and 2 part-time instructors are Jerald W. Chesser, Ed.D., CEC, CCE, Chef John Folse, CEC, AAC, Robert Harrington, MBA, CEC, Damian Thomas, CSC, MS, Louis Jesowshek, CEC, AAC.

Costs: Semester tuition (full-time) is $1,008 in-state, $2,304 out-of-state. Additional fees and equipment are $725-$750 plus $50 per lab course. Payment at registration. Full refund prior to classes, proportional refund during first 3 weeks. Admission requirements: minimum GPA, ACT score, or top 25% of high school class. 2 scholarships awarded last year averaging $1,000 each. 32

loans granted last year averaging $2,700 each. Off campus housing rates vary.

LOCATION: South Louisiana, 45 minutes from New Orleans, 75 minutes from Baton Rouge.

CONTACT: Dr. Jerald Chesser, Director, Nicholls State University, Chef John Folse Culinary Institute, P.O. 2099, Thibidaux, LA 70310, United States; (504) 449-7100, Fax (504) 449-7089, E-mail jfci-jwc@nich-nsunet.nich.edu, URL http://server.nich.edu/~jfolse.

CULINARY ARTS INSTITUTE OF LOUISIANA
(See display ad above)　　　**Baton Rouge/Year-round**

This proprietary institution offers a 15-month (1,800-clock-hour) certificate in Nutrition, Sanitation, and Restaurant Management. Established in 1988. Accredited by ACCSCT. Calendar: quarter. Curriculum: core. 1,800 hours of culinary courses required. Admission dates: monthly. Total enrollment: 60. 10-20 enrollees each admission period. 99% of applicants accepted. 75% of students receive financial aid. 5% under age 25, 90% age 25-44, 5% age 45 or over. Student to teacher ratio 12:1. 100% obtain employment within 6 months. Facilities: include 8 kitchens and classrooms.

COURSES: Include culinary theory and technique, restaurant management, ice carving, nutrition, and general subjects. Schedule: 8am-2:30pm and 3pm-9:30pm weekdays. Externship provided. Continuing education courses: advanced classical French, Cajun/Creole, tableside service.

FACULTY: Certified Executive Chefs teach culinary courses, academic faculty includes Ph.D.s.

COSTS: Tuition is $17,314, which includes meals, uniforms, cutlery, insurance, and textbooks. A $25 refundable fee must accompany application 30 days in advance. Application deadlines: monthly. Admission requirements: high school graduate with some cooking experience. 3 scholarships awarded last year averaging $2,500-$5,000 each. Loans granted last year averaged $13,000. On-campus housing for 150 students at the LSU apartment complexes, a 5-minute drive from the Institute, is $250-$350 per month. Off-campus lodging is $200-$400 per month.

LOCATION: A leased hotel building overlooking the Mississippi River.

CONTACT: Vi Harrington, Director, Culinary Arts Institute of Louisiana, 427 Lafayette St., Baton Rouge, LA 70802; (800) 927-0839, (504) 343-6233, Fax (504) 336-4880, URL http://www.explore-br.com-caila.

LAFAYETTE REGIONAL TECHNICAL INSTITUTE
Lafayette

CONTACT: Rafael Galindo, Lafayette Regional Technical Institute, 1101 Bertrand Dr., Lafayette, LA 70502; (318) 262-5342, (318) 262-5962.

LOUISIANA TECHNICAL COLLEGE
New Orleans

This school offers a program in culinary arts and occupations.

CONTACT: Tim Gourley, FMP, Louisiana Technical College, Culinary Arts, 9800 Navarre Ave., New Orleans, LA 70124; (504) 483-4626, Fax (504) 483-4643.

LOUISIANA TECHNICAL COLLEGE – BATON ROUGE CAMPUS
Baton Rouge/Year-round

This public institution offers a 1-year diploma/certificate in Culinary Arts. Program started 1974. Calendar: quarter. Curriculum: culinary. 1,248 hours of culinary courses required. Admission dates: year-round. Total enrollment: 10-15. 6 enrollees each admission period. 95% of applicants accepted. 45% of students receive financial aid. 20% enrolled part-time. 30% under age 25, 60% age 25-44, 10% age 45 or over. Student to teacher ratio 12:1. 95% obtain employment within 6 months. Facilities: include 2 kitchens.

COURSES: Sanitation, nutrition, food and beverage management, professional cooking. Schedule: 8:00am-2:40pm weekdays.

FACULTY: 1 full-time. Michael Travasos. Qualifications: bachelor's degree, industry experience.

COSTS: Annual tuition $420. Application fee $9.50. Books, uniforms, equipment $215. No refunds. Average off-campus housing cost is $300 per month.

CONTACT: Rose Fair, Louisiana Technical College-Baton Rouge Campus, Admissions, 3250 N. Acadian Throughway, Baton Rouge, LA 70805; (504) 359-9226, Fax (504) 359-9296.

SCLAFANI'S COOKING SCHOOL, INC.
(See display ad page 46) **Metairie/Year-round**

This proprietary school offers a 4-week (120-hour) certificate of completion program in commercial cooking/baking. Established in 1987. Accredited by State of Louisiana. Calendar: monthly. Curriculum: culinary. 120 hours of culinary courses required. Admission dates: monthly. Total enrollment: 95. 8 enrollees each admission period. 85% of applicants accepted. 60% of students receive financial aid. 25% under age 25, 50% age 25-44, 25% age 45 or over. Student to teacher ratio 8:1. 98% obtain employment within 6 months. Facilities: classroom/dining room, commercial kitchen preparation room, storage area.

COURSES: Culinary arts, baking, food cost math, sanitation & safety, supervisory skills. Schedule: 8:30am-3:30pm, Monday-Friday. Continuing education: 5 points towards ACFEI certification, 120 points towards re-certification.

FACULTY: 2 full-time. Includes Administrative Instructor Frank P. Sclafani, Sr., CEC, and chef/instructor Deborah Raines.

COSTS: Tuition is $1,995 plus $150 registration fee. $150 deposit with application, balance due 14 days before class. Full refund for written cancellation within 3 business days. Admission requirements: age 18 or older; must pass 7th grade level reading and math. Average off-campus housing cost: $15 per day and up.

LOCATION: 3 miles from New Orleans.

CONTACT: Frank P. Sclafani, Sr., CEC, President, Sclafani's Cooking School, Inc., Culinary Arts, 107 Gennaro Pl., Metairie, LA 70001; (504) 833-7861, Fax (504) 833-7872, E-mail sclafani@gnofn.org, URL http://www.neworleans.com/sclafani-cooking-school.

SIDNEY N. COLLIER VOCATIONAL TECHNICAL INSTITUTE
New Orleans

This institution offers a 12-month certificate. Program started 1957. Accredited by SACS. Admission dates: open. Total enrollment: 20. 100% of applicants accepted. Student to teacher ratio 20:1. 80% obtain employment within 6 months.

CONTACT: Edward James, Sidney N. Collier Vocational Technical Institute, Culinary Arts, 3727 Louisa St., New Orleans, LA 70126; (504) 942-8333, Fax (504) 942-8337.

MAINE

SOUTHERN MAINE TECHNICAL COLLEGE
South Portland/September-May

This state-owned institution offers a 2-year associate degree in Culinary Arts. Program started

1956. Accredited by NEASC. Admission dates: rolling. Total enrollment: 70. 75% of applicants accepted. 50% of students receive financial aid. 10% enrolled part-time. 20% under age 25, 40% age 25-44, 40% age 45 or over. Student to teacher ratio 16:1. 90% obtain employment within 6 months. Facilities: include 8 kitchens and classrooms, restaurant.

COURSES: Baking, food development, buffet, classical cuisine, dining room management, and general education courses. Schedule: 6 hours/day, 9 months/year, part-time and evening options available. Continuing education: bartending and cake decorating.

FACULTY: 6 full-time with college degrees and/or ACF certification.

COSTS: Annual tuition in-state $2,088, out-of-state $4,572. Application deadlines: August 1. Admission requirements: high school diploma or equivalent and admission test. On-campus housing: 100 spaces; off-campus housing cost: $50 per week.

CONTACT: Robert Latham, Southern Maine Technical College, Culinary Arts/Hotel, Motel & Rest. Management, 2 Fort Rd., South Portland, ME 04106; (207) 767-9520, Fax (207) 767-9671.

MARYLAND

BALTIMORE INTERNATIONAL CULINARY COLLEGE
Baltimore and Ireland/Year-round   *(See also page 259)*

This private nonprofit college specializing in hospitality education offers associate degrees in Professional Cooking, Professional Baking and Pastry, Professional Cooking and Baking, Food and Beverage Management, and certificates in Professional Cooking, Professional Baking and Pastry and Culinary Arts. Established in 1972. Accredited by ACCSCT. Admission dates: January, April, July, October. Total enrollment: 807. 95% of applicants accepted. 90% of students receive financial aid. 61% under age 25, 36% age 25-44, 3% age 45 or over. Student to teacher ratio 13:1. 85%-90% obtain employment within 6 months. Facilities: Include 30 kitchens & classrooms, hotels, restaurants, bakeshops, lecture theater, & 100-acre Park Hotel-Deer Park Lodge estate in Ireland.

COURSES: Each program builds from a foundation of theories and techniques to advanced techniques and special projects. Core courses include math, science, English, economics, history, and psychology. Degree programs include 3-12 weeks study in Ireland plus a 3-month externship.

FACULTY: 45-member faculty. Academic faculty members hold degrees through the doctorate level. European-trained chefs at the European Educational Centre hold credentials from the City and Guilds of London.

COSTS: Per semester costs are $3,197 for tuition, $564-$1,323 for fees. Nonrefundable $25 application and $100 deposit fees. Admission requirements: high school diploma or equivalent and satisfactory placement test score required. On-campus lodging for 200 students begins at $1,600/semester.

LOCATION: Baltimore's Inner Harbor area and County Cavan, Ireland, 50 miles from Dublin.

CONTACT: Raymond L. Joll, Vice President of Enrollment Management, Baltimore International Culinary College, 17 Commerce St., Baltimore, MD 21202; (800) 624-9926, (410) 752-4710, Fax (410) 752-3730.

INTERNATIONAL SCHOOL OF CONFECTIONERY ARTS, INC.
Gaithersburg/Year-round   *(See display ad on page 49)*

This proprietary school offers 1- to 3-week certificate courses in confectionery arts. Founded in Zurich in 1982. Accredited by ACF. Admission dates: weekly. Total enrollment: 400/year. 12-16 enrollees each admission period. 100% of applicants accepted. 3% of students receive financial aid. 20% under age 25, 70% age 25-44, 10% age 45 or over. Student to teacher ratio 4:1. 100% obtain employment within 6 months. Facilities: 2,400-square-foot area has 16 individual work stations, overhead mirrors, marble tables, and decorating and candy-making equipment.

COURSES: Sugar pulling, blowing, and casting, chocolate decoration, Swiss candy making, cake decoration, gum paste. Schedule: 8am-4:30pm, Monday-Thursday, 8am-noon Friday.

FACULTY: Ewald Notter and wife, Susan, have won gold medals in international competitions and have taught in Japan, Hong Kong, Denmark, Germany, England, Spain, and Finland. They are authors of *The Text Book of Sugar Pulling and Blowing* and *That's Sugar.*

COSTS: Tuition ranges from $220-$680, which includes breakfast, lunch and materials. A 50% deposit is required. Cancellations 14 days prior receive full refund. Application deadlines: 1 month prior. Nearby lodging averages $54/night.

LOCATION: 2 miles from Gaithersburg, 10 miles from Washington, D.C.

CONTACT: Susan Notter, International School of Confectionery Arts, Inc., Admissions, 9209 Gaither Rd., Gaithersburg, MD 20877; (301) 963-9077, Fax (301) 869-7669, E-mail esnotter@aol.com.

L'ACADEMIE DE CUISINE
(See also pages 187, 252) (See display ad above) **Gaithersburg/Year-round**

This proprietary vocational school offers a 1-year full-time Culinary Career Training diploma program, 6- and 9-month part-time certificate courses, continuing education and nonprofessional courses, culinary & cultural program in Gascony, France. Established in 1976. Accredited by ACCET and certified by the Maryland Higher Education Commission. Calendar: semester. Curriculum: culinary. 1,944/108/216 hours (full-time/part-time/pastry) of culinary courses required. Admission dates: January, July, September. Total enrollment: 35 twice a year. 35 enrollees each admission period. 85% of applicants accepted. 50% of students receive financial aid. 90% enrolled part-time. 9% under age 25, 90% age 25-44, 1% age 45 or over. Student to teacher ratio 17:1. 95% obtain employment within 6 months. Facilities: at the 2 campuses, include a 35-station practice and pastry kitchen and 25-seat demonstration classroom.

COURSES: Curriculum is based on classic French technique. Diploma program covers food preparation & presentation, pastries & desserts, wine selection, catering, menu planning, kitchen management. Schedule: first 6 months consists of daily classes, second 6 months is a paid restaurant externship. Placement in fine dining restaurants in metropolitan D.C. Advanced/continuing ed courses: marzipan, wedding cakes, sugar, chocolate, catering, sanitation.

FACULTY: 4 full- and 4 part-time. School President Francois Dionot, graduate of L'Ecole Hoteliere de la Societe Suisse des Hoteliers and founder of the IACP, Pascal Dionot, Bonnie Moore, L'Academie de Cuisine graduates Somchet Chumpapo, Mark Ramsdell, Mike Langan.

COSTS: Tuition for the diploma program is $13,500. A $75 application fee required. Supplies are $450. Certificate course tuition ranges from $2,300 to $4,450; payment plans available. $2,500 tuition deposit required; full deposit refund with 7 days notice. Application deadlines: rolling admissions. Admission requirements: high school diploma or equivalent. 3 scholarships were awarded last year averaging $12,300 each. Nearby lodging is approximately $600 per month.

LOCATION: The Gaithersburg branch is 20 minutes north of Washington, DC; the Bethesda branch is 3 miles northwest of D.C.

CONTACT: Carol McClure, Assistant Director, L'Academie de Cuisine, 16006 Industrial Dr., Gaithersburg, MD 20877; (301) 670-8670, (800) 664-CHEF, Fax (301) 670-0450, URL http://www.L'Academie.com.

MASSACHUSETTS

BERKSHIRE COMMUNITY COLLEGE
Pittsfield
This college offers a 1-year certificate and a 2-year AAS degree. Program started 1977. Accredited by NEASC. Admission dates: fall. Total enrollment: 15.

FACULTY: 2 full-time, 3 part-time.

COSTS: Tuition in-state $2,000, out-of-state $6,300. Admission requirements: high school diploma or equivalent and admission test.

CONTACT: Janet R. Kroboth, Business Division Chair, Berkshire Community College, Culinary Arts Dept., 1350 West St., Pittsfield, MA 01201-5786; (413) 499-4660, Fax (413) 447-7840.

BOSTON UNIVERSITY CULINARY ARTS
Boston/September-May   *(See also page 187)*
This university offers a 4-month certificate in the Culinary Arts (started 1988) and a Master of Liberal Arts with concentration in Gastronomy (started 1994). Program started 1986. Calendar: semester. Curriculum: core. Admission dates: January, September. Total enrollment: 24. 12 enrollees each admission period. 60% of applicants accepted. 50% of students receive financial aid. 20% under age 25, 60% age 25-44, 20% age 45 or over. Student to teacher ratio 6:1. 100% obtain employment within 6 months. Facilities: demonstration room with overhead mirror, classroom, 8 restaurant stations in the laboratory kitchen.

COURSES: Cover basic, classic and modern techniques and theory, ethnic and regional cuisine, food history, dining room theory and practice, purchasing. Master program includes 4 core courses in history and anthropology of food, nutrition and diet, 4 electives. Schedule: 30 hours/week. Continuing education courses are available.

FACULTY: 2 full-time, 30 part-time. Guest chefs have included Julia Child, Albert Kumin, Jacques Pépin, Roger Fessaguet, and Jasper White.

COSTS: Certificate course tuition is $6,200. Application fee is $35. Full refund less $100 after the first week of class. Application deadlines: August 1 and December 1. Admission requirements: applicants must have some foodservice experience. 10 loans granted last year.

LOCATION: The 28,000-student campus is in Kenmore Square.

CONTACT: Rebecca Alssid, Director of Special Programs, Boston University Culinary Arts, 808 Commonwealth Ave., #109, Boston, MA 02215; (617) 353-9852, Fax (617) 353-4130.

BRISTOL COMMUNITY COLLEGE
Fall River
This institution offers a 1-year certificate. Program started 1985. Accredited by NEASC. Admission dates: September, January. Total enrollment: 22-24. 80% of applicants accepted. Student to teacher ratio 6:1. 75% obtain employment within 6 months.

FACULTY: 4 full-time.

COSTS: Tuition in-state $2,000, out-of-state $5,800.

CONTACT: Culinary Director, Bristol Community College, Culinary Arts Department, Fall River, MA 02720; (508) 678-2811, Fax (508) 678-2811.

Some people like to broaden their horizons.

Cambridge School of Culinary Arts

We like to broaden your tastes.
Call now for a catalog, before it's too late.
(617) 354-3836

THE CAMBRIDGE SCHOOL OF CULINARY ARTS
(See display ad above)   **Cambridge/Year-round**

This proprietary school offers a 10-month (756-792-clock-hour) Professional Chef's diploma program, a summer program for cooking enthusiasts, and culinary trips to Europe. Established in 1973. Accredited by ACCSCT and Licensed by the Commonwealth of Massachusetts Dept. of Education. Calendar: quarter. Curriculum: culinary. Admission dates: September, January. Total enrollment: 110-200. 75-100 enrollees each admission period. 80% of applicants accepted. 5% under age 25, 90% age 25-44, 5% age 45 or over. Student to teacher ratio 32:1 lectures; 15:1 hands-on. 90% obtain employment within 6 months. Facilities: 3 large newly renovated kitchens, 3 large demonstration classrooms; gas and electric commercial appliances.

COURSES: Emphasis is on chemistry and principles of fine cooking. Curriculum covers basics, pastry, American and international cuisines, food and business management, butchering, herbs and spices, cheese and wine. Schedule: 21-22 hours/week (attendance 3 times/week) day or evening classes. Continuing ed: wedding & specialty cakes, baking, catering, event planning, advanced baking/catering.

FACULTY: Instructors are master chefs and federally accredited and state-certified teachers. President-Founder Roberta Avallone Dowling earned diplomas from Julie Dannenbaum, Marcella Hazan, Madeleine Kamman, Richard Olney, and owns DeGustibus, Inc., caterers.

COSTS: Tuition is $9,800, payable in 4 installments; application fee $50. Upon acceptance a $100 deposit is required, refundable within 5 days. Application deadlines: rolling. Admission requirements: applicants must be at least age 18 and have a high school diploma or equivalent. Nearby lodging ranges from $500-$1,600/month.

LOCATION: 5 miles from downtown Boston, 1 mile from Harvard Square.

CONTACT: Director of Admissions, The Cambridge School of Culinary Arts, 2020 Massachusetts Ave., Cambridge, MA 02140; (617) 354-3836, Fax (617) 576-1963.

ESSEX AGRICULTURAL AND TECHNICAL INSTITUTE
Hathorne/September-May

This public institution offers a 2-year AAS degree in Culinary Arts and Food Service. Program started 1968. Accredited by NEASC. Admission dates: revolving. Total enrollment: 60. 40 enrollees each admission period. 90% of applicants accepted. 33% of students receive financial aid. 5% enrolled part-time. 60% under age 25, 30% age 25-44, 10% age 45 or over. Student to teacher ratio 15:1. 90% obtain employment within 6 months. Facilities: include 6 kitchens and classrooms, bakery and restaurant.

COURSES: Restaurant operation, baking, garde manger, international cuisine, buffet, specialty food production, cakes and pastries, American regional cuisine, and nutrition. Schedule: 25 hours/week, 15 weeks/semester. Externship provided.

FACULTY: 4 full-time. Includes Division Chair C. Naffah, P. Kelly, L. Bassett, J. Costello.

COSTS: Annual tuition $1,650. Application fee $30. Other fees approximately $1,830. Application deadlines: revolving. Admission requirements: high school diploma or equivalent.

LOCATION: The 180-acre campus is in a suburban setting 20 miles from Boston.

CONTACT: Dr. Donald Glazier, Essex Agricultural and Technical Institute, Admissions, 562 Maple St., Hathorne, MA 01937; (508) 774-0050, Fax (508) 774-6530.

HOLYOKE COMMUNITY COLLEGE
Holyoke/Year-round

This college offers a 1-year certificate in Culinary Arts. Program started 1991. Accredited by NEASC. Calendar: semester. Curriculum: culinary. 29 semester hours of culinary courses required. Admission dates: September, January. Total enrollment: 75. 50 enrollees each admission period. 100% of applicants accepted. 20% enrolled part-time. Student to teacher ratio 12:1 lab, 20:1 lecture. 90% obtain employment within 6 months. Facilities: include 2 kitchens, bakeshop, student-run cafeteria.

COURSES: Food production management, advanced food production, and nutrition. Schedule: 7am-4pm weekdays; classes September-May, with field experience in summer; part-time options available. Externship: 14-week, paid. Continuing education: evening courses in advanced baking, food service supervision, nutrition.

FACULTY: 4 full-time. Includes H. Robert, D. Walsh, W. Grinnan.

COSTS: Annual tuition in-state $2,605, out-of-state $6,275. Application fee $10. Advance payment fee $30. Refund: 100% prior to 1st day of classes, 90% during add/drop period. Application deadlines: day before classes begin. Admission requirements: high school diploma or equivalent.

LOCATION: Western Massachusetts.

CONTACT: Hugh Robert, Department Chair, Holyoke Community College, Hospitality Management, 303 Homestead Ave., Holyoke, MA 01040; (413) 538-7000, Fax (413) 534-8975, E-mail hrobert@hcc.mass.edu.

MASSASOIT COMMUNITY COLLEGE
Brockton

This college offers a 2-year degree. Program started 1982. Accredited by state. Admission dates: September. Total enrollment: 60. Student to teacher ratio 20-35:1. 93.5% obtain employment within 6 months.

COURSES: Externship provided.

FACULTY: 3 full-time, 2 part-time.

COSTS: Annual tuition in-state $950, out-of-state $1,900. Admission requirements: high school diploma or equivalent.

CONTACT: Culinary Director, Massasoit Community College, Culinary Arts Department, 1 Massasoit Blvd., Brockton, MA 02402; (508) 588-9100.

MINUTEMAN REGIONAL VOCATIONAL TECHNICAL SCHOOL
Lexington

This independent institution offers a 3-year diploma, 2-year post-graduate course, and 90-day retraining courses in Culinary, Baking, Hotel and Restaurant Management. Program started 1973. Total enrollment: 150. 25 enrollees each admission period. 95% of applicants accepted. 90% under age 25, 5% age 25-44, 5% age 45 or over. Student to teacher ratio 10:1. 99% obtain employment within 6 months. Facilities: include 6 kitchens and classrooms.

COURSES: Sanitation, nutrition, management, purchasing, computer skills, applied math, and applied science. Schedule: 6-1/2 hours/day, 10 months/year. Externship: 20 weeks, hotel/restaurant.

COSTS: Annual tuition in-state $6,200. Uniform fee: $100. Application deadlines: open. Admission requirements: admission test.

CONTACT: John Fitzpatrick, Director, Minuteman Tech, Foodservice/Hospitality Management, 758 Marrett Road, Lexington, MA 02173; (617) 861-6500, Fax (617) 863-1254.

NEWBURY COLLEGE
Brookline/September-May

This nonprofit institution offers a 2-year AAS degree in Culinary Arts and Food Service Management. Program started 1962. Accredited by NEASC. 42 credit hours of culinary courses required. Admission dates: September, January. Total enrollment: 240. 140 enrollees each admission period. 60% of applicants accepted. 80% of students receive financial aid. 10% enrolled part-time. 75% under age 25, 20% age 25-44, 5% age 45 or over. Student to teacher ratio 17:1. 99% obtain employment within 6 months. Facilities: include 7 production kitchens and the college dining room.

COURSES: Include preparation and presentation of international and regional cuisines, equipment, sanitation, and nutrition, menu planning, and general education subjects. A 12- to 18-week salaried externship is provided.

FACULTY: The 10 full- and 6 part-time faculty members are active industry professionals.

COSTS: Annual tuition is $11,110 and culinary program fee is $1,170. Tuition deposit is $100. Refund with written request prior to April 15 or November 15. Application deadlines: rolling. Admission requirements: high school diploma or GED and a 2.0 GPA. On-campus room and board are provided for 400 students at $6,600 (double occupancy).

LOCATION: A suburban setting, 4 miles from downtown Boston.

CONTACT: Dan Pinch, Asst. Dean of Admission, Newbury College, Admission Center, 129 Fisher Ave., Brookline, MA 02146; (617) 730-7007/7001, (800) NEWBURY, Fax (617) 731-9618, E-mail info@newbury.edu, URL http://www.newbury.edu.

MICHIGAN

GRAND RAPIDS COMMUNITY COLLEGE
Grand Rapids/August-May

This college offers a 2-year AAAS degree in Culinary Arts, Culinary Management, and Baking and Pastry Arts. Program started 1980. Accredited by ACFEI, NCA. Admission dates: January, August. Total enrollment: 360. 95% of applicants accepted. 60% of students receive financial aid. 20% enrolled part-time. 40% under age 25, 50% age 25-44, 10% age 45 or over. Student to teacher ratio 15-22:1. 99% obtain employment within 6 months. Facilities: include kitchens and classrooms, bar, bakery, bistro, banquet rooms, auditorium, 2 formal storerooms, and 2 student-run restaurants.

COURSES: Schedule: 30 hours/week, 34 weeks/year; part-time options available. Externship: 240-hour, summer semester. Continuing education: about 40 non-credit seminars per year on a variety of subjects.

FACULTY: 12 full-time, 7 part-time. Qualifications: equivalent of a bachelor's degree and minimum 6 years industry experience in management.

COSTS: Annual tuition $4,896 in-state, $6,048 out-of-state. Application fee $20. Books, uniforms, cutlery kit: $1,200. Full refund before start of classes. Admission requirements: high school diploma or equivalent and admission test. Average off-campus housing cost: $250 per month.

LOCATION: The 14,000-student, 11-building campus is in an urban setting.

CONTACT: Robert B. Garlough, Grand Rapids Community College, Hospitality Education Division, 151 Fountain, N.E., Grand Rapids, MI 49503-3295; (616) 771-3690, Fax (616) 771-3698.

HENRY FORD COMMUNITY COLLEGE
Dearborn/January, May, August
Program started 1972.
LOCATION: A half mile from Detroit.
CONTACT: Dennis Konarski, CFE, CCE, Culinary Director, Henry Ford Community College, Culinary Arts/Hotel Restaurant Management, 5101 Evergreen Rd., Dearborn, MI 48128; (313) 845-6390, Fax (313) 845-9784, E-mail dennis@mail.henryford.cc.mi.us.

MACOMB COMMUNITY COLLEGE
Mt. Clemens
This college offers a 2-year AAS degree in Culinary Arts. Program started 1972. Accredited by State. Admission dates: fall, spring, summer. Total enrollment: 112. Student to teacher ratio 16-35:1. 99% obtain employment within 6 months.
FACULTY: 3 full-time, 2 part-time.
COSTS: Tuition in-county $42 per credit hour, out-of-county $165 per credit hour. Admission requirements: high school diploma or equivalent.
CONTACT: David Schneider, Macomb Community College, Culinary Arts Department, 44575 Garfield, Mt. Clemens, MI 48044; (810) 286-2000, Fax (810) 286-2038.

MONROE COUNTY COMMUNITY COLLEGE
Monroe/September-May
This independent institution offers a 2-year AOC degree/certificate in Culinary Skills and Management. Program started 1981. Accredited by NCA, ACFEI. Calendar: semester. Curriculum: core. Admission dates: September. Total enrollment: 36. 20 enrollees each admission period. 80% of applicants accepted. 25% of students receive financial aid. 25% enrolled part-time. 35% under age 25, 50% age 25-44, 15% age 45 or over. Student to teacher ratio 18:1. 87% obtain employment within 6 months. Facilities: include 2 kitchens, classroom, restaurant.
COURSES: Restaurant production, baking, buffet, institutional food, management, sanitation, nutrition, garde manger, ice carving, menu planning, purchasing and receiving, a la carte, dining room procedure and general education. Schedule: Monday-Friday, 3 hours/day. Externship provided.
FACULTY: 2 full-time. Includes K. Thomas, CCE, CEC and one technician.
COSTS: Annual tuition in-state $1,290, out-of-state $2,010. Application fee $15. Lab fee additional. Refund policy: prorated until 3 weeks after start of semester. Application deadlines: May 21. Admission requirements: high school diploma or equivalent and admission test. Average off-campus housing cost is $400/month.
LOCATION: The 4,000-student campus is in a rural setting.
CONTACT: Kevin Thomas, Instructor of Culinary Skills, Monroe County Community College, Culinary Arts Department, 1555 Raisinville Rd., Monroe, MI 48161; (313) 242-7300, Fax (313) 242-9711.

NORTHERN MICHIGAN UNIVERSITY
Marquette/August-April
This public institution offers a 1-year certificate, 2-year AAS degree, and 4-year BS degree, program in Culinary Arts, Restaurant and Institutional Management. Program started 1970. Accredited by NCA. Admission dates: September, January. Total enrollment: 47. 18 enrollees each admission period. 100% of applicants accepted. 80% of students receive financial aid. 25% enrolled part-time. 70% under age 25, 30% age 25-44. Student to teacher ratio 18:1. 100% obtain employment within 6 months. Facilities: include 5 kitchens and classrooms, computer lab, restaurant and meat-cutting room.
COURSES: Cooking, baking, garde manger, sanitation, purchasing, and general education. Schedule: Monday-Thursday, 8am-2pm.
FACULTY: 3 full-time. Qualifications: bachelor's or master's degrees.

COSTS: Tuition in state $81 per credit hour, out-of-state $152 per credit hour. Application fee $50. Application deadlines: July 1. Admission requirements: high school diploma or equivalent. On-campus housing: 2,000 spaces at $2,300 per year. Average off-campus housing cost: $2,000 per year.

LOCATION: The 9,000-student campus is in a small town setting.

CONTACT: Walt Anderson, Department Head, Northern Michigan University, Department of Consumer & Family Studies, College of Technology & Applied Sciences, Marquette, MI 49855; (906) 227-2364, Fax (906) 227-1549.

NORTHWESTERN MICHIGAN COLLEGE
Traverse City/Year-round

This college offers a 2-year AAS degree in Culinary Arts. Program started 1978. Accredited by ACFEI. Admission dates: open. Total enrollment: 75. 100% of applicants accepted. 65% of students receive financial aid. 45% enrolled part-time. 50% under age 25, 50% age 25-44. Student to teacher ratio 20:1. 90% obtain employment within 6 months. Facilities: include 3 kitchens, many classrooms, restaurant and bake shop.

COURSES: Externship: 400-hour, salaried.

FACULTY: 2 full-time, 10 part-time.

COSTS: Tuition in-state $52 per credit hour, out-of-state $83 per credit hour. Application fee $15. Admission requirements: high school diploma or equivalent. 5 scholarships were awarded last year averaging $1,000 each. On-campus housing: 120 spaces; average cost $1,950 with meal plan.

LOCATION: A small town campus, 150 miles from Grand Rapids.

CONTACT: Fred Laughlin, Northwestern Michigan College, Culinary Arts Department, 1701 East Front St., Traverse City, MI 49686; (616) 946-4700, Fax (616) 946-2772, E-mail fredlaugh@aol.com.

OAKLAND COMMUNITY COLLEGE
Farmington Hills/September-June

This college offers a 2-year AAS program in Culinary Arts, Food Service Management, Hotel Management, and Chef Apprentice. Program started 1978. Accredited by ACFEI. Calendar: semester. Curriculum: core. Admission dates: September, January, May. Total enrollment: 210. 125 enrollees each admission period. 98% of applicants accepted. 35% of students receive financial aid. 50% enrolled part-time. 20% under age 25, 60% age 25-44, 20% age 45 or over. Student to teacher ratio 15:1. 90% obtain employment within 6 months. Facilities: include 10 kitchens and classrooms and restaurant.

COURSES: Cooking, baking, pastries, garde manger, front-of-house service, sanitation, purchasing, menu planning, cost control. Schedule: 6 hours/day 4 days/week. Continuing education: garde manger, culinary competition, meat cutting, baking.

FACULTY: 9 full-time, 6 part-time. Includes Chairperson Susan Baier, FMP; Kevin Enright, CEC, CCE; Roger Holder, CPC, CCE; Dan Rowlson, CCE; Robert Zemke, RD, MBA; Darlene Levinson, FMP.

COSTS: Annual tuition in-county $46 per credit-hour. Lab fee $330 for production classes.

CONTACT: Susan Baier, Dept. Chair, Oakland Community College, Hospitality/Culinary Arts, 27055 Orchard Lake Rd., Farmington Hills, MI 48334; (810) 471-7786, Fax (810) 471-7739.

SCHOOLCRAFT COLLEGE
Livonia/August-April

This college offers a 2-year certificate/AAS degree in Culinary Arts and Culinary Management. Program started 1966. Accredited by NCA. 40 credit hours of culinary courses required. Admission dates: January, August. Total enrollment: 156. 12-78 enrollees each admission period. 100% of applicants accepted. 40% enrolled part-time. 50% under age 25, 40% age 25-44, 10% age 45 or over. Student to teacher ratio 14:1. 100% obtain employment within 6 months. Facilities:

include 8 kitchens and classrooms, pastry kitchen, butcher shop, bakery, and restaurant.

COURSES: Baking, pastries, a la carte, international cuisine, butchery. Other required courses: sanitation, nutrition. Schedule: 18 hours/week, 8 months/year. Externship: 16-week, salaried, restaurants. Continuing education: sanitation, supervision, olympic cooking trends and concepts, and nutrition.

FACULTY: 5 full-time, 6 part-time. Qualifications: ACF certification.

COSTS: Tuition $73/credit hour. Application fee $10. Lab fees $35-$105. Refund policy: 100% up to 1 week following start. Admission requirements: high school diploma or equivalent and admission test, completion of CAP 090.

LOCATION: This 13,900-student suburban campus is 20 miles from Detroit.

CONTACT: Kevin Gawronski, Culinary Manager, Schoolcraft College, Culinary Arts, 18600 Haggerty Rd., Livonia, MI 48152-2696; (313) 462-4423, Fax (313) 462-4519, E-mail kgawrons@schoolcraft.cc.mi.us.

WASHTENAW COMMUNITY COLLEGE
Ann Arbor/September-June

This college offers a 1-year certificate in Food Service Production Specialist and a 2-year AAS degree in Culinary Arts and Hotel and Restaurant Management. Program started 1975. Accredited by NCA. 40 credit hours of culinary courses required. Total enrollment: 80-120. 50 enrollees each admission period. 90% of applicants accepted. 10% of students receive financial aid. 60% enrolled part-time. 30% under age 25, 40% age 25-44, 25% age 45 or over. Student to teacher ratio 16-25:1. 95% obtain employment within 6 months. Facilities: include kitchen, bake shop, and student-run dining room.

COURSES: 50% culinary courses, 25% business courses, 25% general studies. Schedule: 15-20 hours/week full-time; 3-9 hours/week part-time. Externship: 300-hour, salaried. Continuing education: in summer.

FACULTY: 4 full-time. Qualifications: bachelor's or master's degree and ACF certification.

COSTS: $51 in-district, $73 out-of-district, $92 out-of-state. $23 registration fee/semester. Application deadlines: year-round. Admission requirements: high school diploma or equivalent and admission test. Off-campus housing cost: $400-$600 per month.

LOCATION: The suburban 11,000-student campus is 40 miles from Detroit.

CONTACT: David Placey, Director, Washtenaw Community College, Admissions, 4800 E. Huron River Drive, Ann Arbor, MI 48106-0978; (313) 973-3300, Fax (313) 677-5414.

MINNESOTA

HENNEPIN TECHNICAL COLLEGE
Brooklyn Park, Eden Prairie/September-June

This college offers an 80-credit diploma/certificate in Culinary Arts. Program started 1972. Accredited by NCA, ACFEI. Admission dates: fall, winter, spring. Total enrollment: 60. 10-20 enrollees each admission period. 100% of applicants accepted. 40% of students receive financial aid. 10% enrolled part-time. 25% under age 25, 60% age 25-44, 15% age 45 or over. Student to teacher ratio 15:1. 98% obtain employment within 6 months. Facilities: include 3 kitchens, 3 classrooms and restaurant.

COURSES: Externship: 6- to 8-week and post-graduate assistantships.

FACULTY: Qualifications: ACF certified or certifiable.

COSTS: Annual tuition $2,228 in-state, $4,456 out-of-state. Approximately $550 for supplies. Refund policy: up to 1st 10 days of quarter. Application deadlines: up to start of classes.

LOCATION: The campus is in a suburban setting, 10 miles from Minneapolis.

CONTACT: Mike Jung, CEC, AAC, Hennepin Technical College-Brooklyn Park Campus, Culinary Arts Dept., 9000 Brooklyn Blvd., Brooklyn Park, MN 55445; (612) 425-3800, Fax (612) 550-2119.

NATIONAL BAKING CENTER
Minneapolis/Year-round

This independent institution offers short courses and seminars geared to the professional baker, including foodservice baking. Program started 1914. Curriculum: baking. Admission dates: year-round.

Facilities: one theater-style demonstration bakery, one hands-on bake shop, one classroom, test baking and research areas.

COURSES: Breads and rolls, bagels, ingredient science, cake and pastry, cake decorating, financial and business management, merchandising.

FACULTY: 3 full-time, frequent national and international guest lecturers.

COSTS: Vary with courses and seminars.

CONTACT: Tom McMahon, Project Director, National Baking Center, 818 Dunwoody Blvd., Minneapolis, MN 55403-1192; (612) 374-3303, Fax (612) 374-3332, E-mail mardon@dunwoody.tec.mn.us.

NORTHWEST TECHNICAL COLLEGE
Moorhead/September-May

This college offers a 2-year diploma in Chef Training. Program started 1966. Accredited by State, NCA. Calendar: quarter. Curriculum: core. Admission dates: quarterly. Total enrollment: 40-50. 25 enrollees each admission period. 80% of students receive financial aid. 10% enrolled part-time. 80% under age 25, 15% age 25-44, 5% age 45 or over. Student to teacher ratio 20-25:1. 89% obtain employment within 6 months. Facilities: 2 kitchens, 1 classroom, 2 restaurants.

COURSES: Quantity food preparation, food purchasing and cost controls, menu planning. Schedule: 7am-3pm, 9 months/year; part-time options available.

FACULTY: 2 full-time. Includes Kim E. Brewster, CEC, CCE, Colleen Kraft.

COSTS: Annual tuition in-state $1,996, out-of-state $3,840. Other fees: $60/quarter meal fee, $40/quarter uniform fee, $20 admission application fee. Refund policy: 100% during first 5 days of quarter, 80% 6-10 days, 50% 11-15 days. Admission requirements: high school diploma or equivalent. Off-campus housing cost is $250/month.

LOCATION: The single building campus is in an urban setting.

CONTACT: Kim Brewster, Dept. Chairperson, Northwest Technical College, Chef Training, 1900 28th Ave. S., Moorhead, MN 56560; (800) 426-5603, Fax (218) 236-0342.

ST. PAUL TECHNICAL COLLEGE
St. Paul/Year-round

This college offers a 12-month diploma. Program started 1967. Accredited by NCA. Calendar: quarter. Curriculum: culinary. 66 credit hours of culinary courses required. Admission dates: March, September, December. Total enrollment: 40-50. 25 enrollees each admission period. Student to teacher ratio 16:1. 95% obtain employment within 6 months.

FACULTY: 3 full-time.

COSTS: Tuition in-state $40/credit hour, out-of-state $80/credit hour. Admission requirements: high school diploma or equivalent and admission test.

CONTACT: Culinary Director, St. Paul Technical College, Culinary Arts, 235 Marshall Ave., St. Paul, MN 55102; (612) 221-1300, Fax (612) 221-1416, E-mail ewerthma@spt.edu.mn.us, URL http://www.sptc.tec.mn.us.

SOUTH CENTRAL TECHNICAL COLLEGE
North Mankato/September-July

This college offers a 15-month diploma and 2-year associate degree in Hotel, Restaurant and Institutional Cooking. Program started 1968. Accredited by NCA. Admission dates: September, January, March, June. Total enrollment: 25. 5-7 enrollees each admission period. 100% of applicants accepted. 70% of students receive financial aid. 10% enrolled part-time. 50% under age 25, 40% age 25-44, 10% age 45 or over. Student to teacher ratio 17:1. 95% obtain employment within 6 months. Facilities: include 2 kitchens, bakery and classroom.

COURSES: Food preparation, inventory control, cost control, management, menu design, job preparation, and problem solving. Other Required courses: CPR, first aid, microcomputers, problem solving, employment search skills. Schedule: 6-1/2 hours/day, 5 days/week.

FACULTY: 2 full-time.

COSTS: Annual tuition: in-state $42 per credit, out-of-state $83 per credit. Books and uniforms $520. Refund policy: within 5 days of beginning of quarter. Application deadlines: beginning of each quarter. Admission requirements: high school diploma or equivalent. Off-campus housing cost: $300 per month.

LOCATION: The 1,200-student campus is in an urban setting.

CONTACT: Jim Hanson, Instructor, South Central Technical College, Culinary Arts, 1920 Lee Blvd., P.O. Box 1920, North Mankato, MN 56003; (507) 389-7229, Fax (507) 388-9951, E-mail JimH@tc-mankato.scm.tec.mn.us.

MISSISSIPPI

OFFSHORE COOKING SCHOOL
Ocean Springs/Year-round

This private vocational school offers 1- to 5-week diploma courses in shipboard cuisine. Established in 1990. Accredited by State of Mississippi. Admission dates: weekly. 4 enrollees each admission period. 75% of applicants accepted. 50% of students receive financial aid. 10% under age 25, 50% age 25-44, 40% age 45 or over. 95% obtain employment within 6 months. Facilities: large lab/kitchen and 1 classroom in a restored 1911 manor house.

COURSES: Emphasize southern traditional and cajun cuisine. Steward: includes basic scratch cooking and baking, inventory control, cost control analysis, and menu planning. Specialized House husband/wife weekend and evening courses are offered.

COSTS: $400 weekly, specialized courses begin at $100. Payment is due in advance. Lodging ranges from $100-$200 per week.

LOCATION: A coastal town 60 miles from Mobile, Ala., and 98 miles east of New Orleans.

CONTACT: L.J. Couch, Offshore Cooking School, 703 Cox Ave., Ocean Springs, MS 39564; (601) 875-1333, Fax (601) 872-2537.

MISSOURI

MISSOURI CULINARY INSTITUTE
Lexington/January-November   *(See also page 192)*

This private school offers a 10-week certificate of completion. Established in 1995. Calendar: quarter. Curriculum: culinary. 300 hours of culinary courses required. Admission dates: every 10 weeks starting in January. Total enrollment: 12. Student to teacher ratio 12:1. Facilities: 1 lab kitchen with work stations, demo kitchen and classroom.

COURSES: Basic culinary and baking skills, safety, sanitation, nutrition, menu planning. Schedule: 9am-11:30am, 1:30pm-4pm, Monday-Friday.

FACULTY: 2 full-time, 1 part-time. Includes Dorothy Kopp, who has over 50 years restaurant experience, and Terry Kopp, who owns The Missouri Gourmet restaurant and studied at Le Cordon Bleu.

COSTS: Tuition $2,500. Application and registration fees are $150; other fees and supplies are $850. Full refund for cancellations within 3 days of enrollment; withdrawals during first week forfeit 15% of tuition plus $150. Admission requirements: high school graduation, GED, or school examination. Average off-campus housing cost $150-$500.

LOCATION: The school is in a rural setting, 35 miles from Kansas City.

CONTACT: Terry Kopp, Missouri Culinary Institute, Rte. 1, Box 224F, Lexington, MO 64067; (816) 259-6464.

PENN VALLEY COMMUNITY COLLEGE
Kansas City

CONTACT: Bob Abrams, Penn Valley Community College, Lodging & Food Service Dept., 3201 S.W. Traffic Way, Kansas City, MO 64111; (816) 759-4000.

ST. LOUIS COMMUNITY COLLEGE – FOREST PARK
St. Louis/August-May

This college offers a 2-year AAS degree, apprenticeship leading to ACF certification. Program started 1976. Accredited by NCA. 40 credit hours of culinary courses required. Admission dates: August, January. Total enrollment: 150. 50 enrollees each admission period. 100% of applicants accepted. 40% enrolled part-time. 20% under age 25, 60% age 25-44, 20% age 45 or over. Student to teacher ratio 20:1. 98% obtain employment within 6 months. Facilities: include 2 kitchens and classrooms.

COURSES: Meat analysis, garde manger, pastry, baking, nutrition, food specialties, catering, general education, involvement with Junior Chef Organization. Other required courses: 20 hours. Schedule: 15 hours/week; part-time and weekend options available. Externship: 150-hour, salaried, each semester.

FACULTY: 4 full-time, 25 part-time. Qualifications: masters degree and industry experience. Includes Dept. Chair Kathy Schiffman, Scott Vratarich, Reed Miller, Mike Downey, CCE, CCC.

COSTS: Annual tuition: $1,200 in-state, $1,700 out-of-state. Parking $16. Refund policy: 100% before classes begin, 50% before 2nd week. Application deadlines: 1 week before classes begin. Admission requirements: high school diploma or equivalent and admission test. 15 scholarships were awarded last year averaging $500 each. Off-campus housing cost: $450 per month.

LOCATION: The 7,000-student campus is in an urban setting.

CONTACT: Kathy Schiffman, Dept. Chair, St. Louis Community College-Forest Park, Hotel, Restaurant, Culinary Management Dept., 5600 Oakland Ave., St. Louis, MO 63110; (314) 644-9751, Fax (314) 644-9992.

MONTANA

COLLEGE OF TECHNOLOGY – UNIVERSITY OF MONTANA
Missoula/Year-round

This public institution offers a 1-year certificate and 2-year AAS degree in Food Service Management. Program started 1973. Accredited by ACFEI, NASC. Admission dates: August, January. Total enrollment: 50. 25 enrollees each admission period. 90% of applicants accepted. 3% of students receive financial aid. 5% enrolled part-time. 10% under age 25, 70% age 25-44, 20% age 45 or over. Student to teacher ratio 15:1. 90% obtain employment within 6 months. Facilities: include 4 kitchens and classrooms, and 3 restaurants.

COURSES: Cooking, baking, management, and general education. Schedule: 6 hours/day, 12 months/year.

FACULTY: Qualifications: CEC, CPC, CC. Includes F. Sonnenberg, CEC, R. Lodahl, M.M. Barton, CPC, S. Bartos, CC.

COSTS: Annual tuition $2,500 in-state, $5,500 out-of-state. Application fee $20. Other fees: $400. Refund policy: 80% - 2 weeks. Application deadlines: July. Admission requirements: high school or equivalent and admission test. Off-campus housing cost: $300 per month.

CONTACT: Frank Sonnenberg, College of Technology-University of Montana/Missoula, Culinary Arts Dept., 909 S. Avenue West, Missoula, MT 59801-7910; (406) 542-6811, Fax (406) 243-7899.

NEBRASKA

CENTRAL COMMUNITY COLLEGE
Hastings/September-June

This college offers a 2-year certificate/AAS degree in Culinary Arts. Program started 1971. Accredited by NCA. Calendar: semester. Curriculum: core. Admission dates: open. Total enrollment: 40. 6 enrollees each admission period. 100% of applicants accepted. 80% of students receive financial aid. 80% under age 25, 20% age 25-44. Student to teacher ratio 20:1. 95% obtain employment within 6 months. Facilities: 1 kitchen, 4 classrooms, restaurant.

COURSES: Bake shop, pantry, entrees, international cuisine, advanced sauces, pastries, and garde manger. Schedule: 8am-4pm weekdays.

FACULTY: 2 full-time.

COSTS: Annual tuition in-state $1,230, out-of-state $1,809. Uniform and supplies $40. Admission requirements: high school diploma or equivalent. 4 scholarships awarded last year averaging $200 each. On-campus dormitories available.

LOCATION: The 600-acre campus is 100 miles from Lincoln.

CONTACT: Deborah Brennan, Program Supervisor, Central Community College, Hotel, Motel, Restaurant Management, P.O. Box 1024, Hastings, NE 68902; (402) 461-2458, Fax (402) 461-2454.

METROPOLITAN COMMUNITY COLLEGE
Omaha/Year-round

This college offers a 1- to 2-year AAS degree in Food Arts, Foodservice Management, and Chef Apprentice. Program started 1976. Accredited by NCA, ACFEI. Admission dates: September, December, March, June. Total enrollment: 100. 15 enrollees each admission period. 100% of applicants accepted. 68% of students receive financial aid. 53% enrolled part-time. 40% under age 25, 40% age 25-44, 10% age 45 or over. Student to teacher ratio 12:1. 96% obtain employment within 6 months. Facilities: include kitchens and classrooms, and restaurant.

COURSES: Schedule: 8am-10pm weekdays; part-time options available. Externship: 150-hour, restaurant setting.

FACULTY: 2 full-time, 10 part-time.

COSTS: Tuition in-state $23 per credit hour, out-of-state $42 per credit hour. Other fees: uniforms, tools. Admission requirements: high school diploma or equivalent.

CONTACT: Jim Trebbien, Metropolitan Community College, Food Arts & Management, P.O. Box 3777, Omaha, NE 68103-0777; (402) 449-8400, Fax (402) 449-8333.

SOUTHEAST COMMUNITY COLLEGE
Lincoln/Year-round

This college offers an 18-month AS degree in Culinary Arts. Program started 1988. Accredited by NCA. Calendar: quarter. Curriculum: core. Admission dates: September, March. Total enrollment: 20. 10 enrollees each admission period. 100% of applicants accepted. 30% enrolled part-time. 50% under age 25, 50% age 25-44. Student to teacher ratio 15:1. 95-100% obtain employment within 6 months. Facilities: include kitchen and 2 classrooms.

COURSES: Advanced food, buffet, decorating and catering, professional baking. Schedule: 20 hours/week. Externship: 220-hour, salaried.

FACULTY: 1 full-time, 3 part-time. Qualifications: associate degree. Includes Gerrine Schreck Kirby, CCE, CWC; Jo Taylor, MA, RD; Lois Cockerham, BS; Erin Coudill, MS, RD; Keenan Cain, CWC.

COSTS: Annual tuition in-state $26.50 per credit hour, out-of-state $31.50 per credit hour. Program reservation fee $25. Student activities fee $12. Refund policy: pro-rated on percentage of total course length. Admission requirements: high school diploma or equivalent.

CONTACT: Jo Taylor, Program Chair, Southeast Community College, Food Service Program, 8800 "O" St., Lincoln, NE 68520; (402) 437-2465, Fax (402) 437-2404.

NEVADA

CLARK COUNTY COMMUNITY COLLEGE
North Las Vegas

This college offers a 1-year certificate and a 2-year degree. Program started 1990. Accredited by NASC, ACFEI. Admission dates: open. Total enrollment: 400. 100% of applicants accepted. Student to teacher ratio 15:1. 100% obtain employment within 6 months.

FACULTY: 4 full-time, 18 part-time.

COSTS: Annual tuition in-state $33.50/credit hour with 15 credits/semester, out-of-state $1,550, lab fee is additional.

CONTACT: Giovanni DelRosario, Culinary Director, Clark County Community College, Culinary Arts Department, 3200 East Cheyenne Ave., Z1A, North Las Vegas, NV 89030; (702) 651-4192, Fax (702) 651-4558.

TRUCKEE MEADOWS COMMUNITY COLLEGE
Reno/August-May

This college offers a 2-year AAS degree in Food Service Technology. Program started 1980. Accredited by state. Calendar: semester. Curriculum: core. Admission dates: January, September. Total enrollment: 72. 30-40 enrollees each admission period. 100% of applicants accepted. 30% of students receive financial aid. 70% enrolled part-time. 60% under age 25, 25% age 25-44, 15% age 45 or over. Student to teacher ratio 16:1. 75% obtain employment within 6 months. Facilities: include 8 kitchens and classrooms, and student-run restaurant.

COURSES: Cooking, baking, pastry, garde manger, sauces, business chef, nutrition, sanitation, general education.

FACULTY: 1 full-time, 5 part-time. Includes George Skivofilakas, CEC, CCE, AAC.

COSTS: Tuition in-state $34/credit hour, out-of-state $1,100 + $31/credit hour. Application fee $5. Refund policy: no refund after third class. Application deadlines: prior to first class of each semester. Admission requirements: high school diploma or equivalent. Off-campus housing cost is $400-$500/month.

CONTACT: George Skivofilakas, Professor, Truckee Meadows Community College, Culinary Arts Department, 7000 Dandini Blvd., Reno, NV 89512; (702) 673-7015, Fax (702) 673-7108.

NEW HAMPSHIRE

NEW HAMPSHIRE COLLEGE CULINARY INSTITUTE
Manchester/September-May

This college offers a 2-year AAS degree in Culinary Arts; this can be transferred into a 4-year Hotel/Restaurant degree. Accredited by ACFEI. Admission dates: June. Total enrollment: 120. 65 enrollees each admission period. 80% of applicants accepted. 75% of students receive financial aid. 10% enrolled part-time. 80% under age 25, 15% age 25-44, 5% age 45 or over. Student to teacher ratio 15:1. 100% obtain employment within 6 months. Facilities: include 3 kitchens, bakeshop lab, 2 production labs, and a dining room/classroom.

COURSES: Include culinary skills, bakeshop, food production, garde manger, nutritional cooking, and general education courses. Other required courses: dining room management and classical, regional, and international cuisine. Schedule: 20-30 hours/week; part-time options available. Externship: 600-hour, salaried, with travel opportunities.

FACULTY: 5 full-time, 6 part-time.

COSTS: Annual tuition $9,596. Knife set fee $147, books $200, uniforms $100. Admission requirements: high school diploma or equivalent. On-campus housing cost $4,884 annually.

LOCATION: The 1,200-student campus is situated on 200-wooded acres in a rural setting.

CONTACT: Cindie Farley, Admissions Counselor/Culinary Coordinator, New Hampshire College Culinary Institute, Admissions, 2500 N. River Rd., Manchester, NH 03106; (603) 644-3128, Fax (603) 644-3166.

NEW HAMPSHIRE TECHNICAL COLLEGE
Berlin/Year-round

This college offers a 2-year diploma/certificate/AAS in Culinary Arts. Program started 1966. Accredited by NEASC. Calendar: semester. Curriculum: core. Admission dates: open. Total enrollment: 30. 20 enrollees each admission period. 76% of applicants accepted. 89% of students receive financial aid. 10% enrolled part-time. 60% under age 25, 30% age 25-44, 10% age 45 or over. Student to teacher ratio 15:1. 100% obtain employment within 6 months. Facilities: 2 kitchens plus classrooms.

COURSES: Soups & sauces, food production, meat fabrication, sanitation, baking, patisserie, classical desserts, garde manger, patisserie internationale, charcuterie, buffet, food sculpture & design, menu analysis and restaurant design, marketing. Schedule: Monday-Thursday. Externship provided.

FACULTY: 2 full-time. Includes R. Turgeon, CWC, CCE and K. Hohmeister, working Executive Chef.

COSTS: Annual tuition $2,410 in-state, $5,678 out-of-state. Other fees: $90. Application deadlines: open. Admission requirements: high school diploma or equivalent. Off-campus housing cost is $1,440/semester.

CONTACT: Roger Turgeon, Department Chair, New Hampshire Technical College, Culinary Arts Department, 2020 Riverside Dr., Berlin, NH 03570; (603) 752-1113, Fax (603) 752-6335.

NEW JERSEY

ATLANTIC COMMUNITY COLLEGE
Mays Landing/August-May

This college offers a 2-year AAS degree in Culinary Arts. Established in 1981. Accredited by MSA. Calendar: semester. Curriculum: core. 43 credit hours of culinary courses required. Admission dates: September, January. Total enrollment: 360. 110 enrollees each admission period. 100% of applicants accepted. 54% of students receive financial aid. 95% under age 25, 4% age 25-44, 1% age 45 or over. Student to teacher ratio 20:1. 100% obtain employment within 6 months. Facilities: include 8 kitchens, 4 classrooms, computer lab, a bake shop, retail store, and gourmet restaurant.

COURSES: Include food purchasing, pastry, garde manger, hot food preparation, and nutrition. Schedule: 5 hours daily, mornings or afternoons and limited evening program. An internship is required. Also offers non-credit classes and ACF Apprenticeship program in entry level skills.

FACULTY: 15 full-time international faculty with professional designations.

COSTS: Approximately $3,000 per semester. Nonrefundable application deposit of $300. 100% refund before first class, 50% after 2 weeks. Application deadlines: rolling admission. Admission requirements: high school diploma or equivalent. 17 scholarships awarded last year averaging $1,000 each. Housing is available.

LOCATION: Atlantic Community College, a 536-acre campus in New Jersey's Pinelands, is 17 miles west of Atlantic City's boardwalk and 45 miles from Philadelphia.

CONTACT: Bobby Royal, Director of Admissions, Academy of Culinary Arts - Atlantic Comm. College, Admissions Office, 5100 Black Horse Pike, Mays Landing, NJ 08330-2699; (609) 343-5000, (800) 645-CHEF, Fax (609) 343-4914, E-mail accadmit@nsvm.atlantic.edu, URL http://www.atlantic.edu.

BURLINGTON COUNTY COLLEGE
Pemberton/Year-round

This college offers a 2-year certificate and a 3-year AAS degree in Hospitality Management/Culinary Arts. Program started 1989. Accredited by MSA. Admission dates: open. Total enrollment: 127. 5 enrollees each admission period. 100% of applicants accepted. 50% enrolled part-time. 25% under age 25, 65% age 25-44, 10% age 45 or over. Student to teacher ratio 14:1. 100% obtain employment within 6 months. Facilities: include 14 kitchens and classrooms, pastry kitchen and restaurant.

COURSES: Cooking, baking, nutrition, and sanitation.

FACULTY: 5 full-time. Qualifications: master's degree or state certification.

COSTS: Annual tuition in-state $605 plus fee, out-of-state $51 per credit hour. Tuition deposit $100. Refund policy: 10 days after first day of class. Admission requirements: high school diploma or equivalent and admission test.

CONTACT: William White, Program Director, Burlington County College, Business Studies, Route 530, Pemberton, NJ 08068; (609) 894-9311.

HUDSON COUNTY COMMUNITY COLLEGE
Jersey City/September-May

This college offers a 1-year certificate program and 2-year AAS degree. Program started 1983. Accredited by MSA. Calendar: semester. Curriculum: core. Admission dates: September, January. Total enrollment: 240. Student to teacher ratio 15:1. 100% obtain employment within 6 months. Facilities: 4 kitchens, 3 classrooms, bar.

COURSES: Include bakeshop, garde manger, buffet catering. Schedule: 4 days or 5 evenings. Externship provided.

FACULTY: 10 full-time.

COSTS: Annual tuition $1,080 in-state, $2,160 out-of-state. Admission requirements: high school diploma or equivalent and admission test. 4 scholarships awarded last year averaging $300 each.

CONTACT: Siroun Meguerditchian, Executive Director, Hudson County Community College, Culinary Arts Institute, 161 Newkirk St., Jersey City, NJ 07306; (201) 714-2193, Fax (201) 656-1522.

MIDDLESEX COUNTY COLLEGE
Edison/Year-round

This college offers a 1-year certificate in Culinary Arts. Program started 1987. Accredited by MSA. Admission dates: January, May, September. Total enrollment: 32. 10 enrollees each admission period. 25% of students receive financial aid. 50% enrolled part-time. Student to teacher ratio 18:1. 100% obtain employment within 6 months. Facilities: include 2 kitchens, 3 classrooms.

COURSES: Food selection and preparation, baking, food production, garde manger, food and beverage cost controls and purchasing, sanitation, and general education. Schedule: 12 hours/week; part-time and evening options available. Externship: 180 hours.

FACULTY: 6 full-time, 3 part-time.

COSTS: Annual tuition in-state $2,300, out-of-state $4,600. Application fee $25. Application deadlines: 1 month prior to semester. Admission requirements: high school diploma or equivalent.

LOCATION: The 200-acre suburban campus is 30 miles from New York City.

CONTACT: Marilyn Laskowski-Sachnoff, Department Chair, Middlesex County College, Hotel Restaurant & Institution Management, 155 Mill Rd., P.O. Box 3050, Edison, NJ 08818-3050; (908) 906-2538, Fax (908) 561-1885, E-mail mlsachnoff@aol.com.

SALEM COUNTY VOCATIONAL TECHNICAL SCHOOLS
Woodstown

This college offers a 2-year certificate in Culinary Arts. Program started 1976. Accredited by MSA. Admission dates: September, January. Total enrollment: 30. 75% of applicants accepted. Student to teacher ratio 15:1. 85% obtain employment within 6 months.

FACULTY: 20 full-time.

COSTS: Annual tuition $3,000.

CONTACT: E. Hoffman, Culinary Arts Instructor, Salem County Vocational Technical Schools, Culinary Arts, Box 350, Woodstown, NJ 08098; (609) 769-0101, Fax (609) 769-4214.

NEW MEXICO

ALBUQUERQUE TECHNICAL VOCATIONAL INSTITUTE
Albuquerque/Year-round

This community college offers a Baking certificate, Quantity Foods certificate, Food Service Management certificate, AAS degree. Program started 1965. Accredited by ACFEI. Calendar: trimester. Curriculum: culinary, core. 1,720 hours of culinary courses required. Admission dates: December-January, April-May, August-September. Total enrollment: 200. 150 enrollees each admission period. 100% of applicants accepted. 65% of students receive financial aid. 33% enrolled part-time. 25% under age 25, 65% age 25-44, 10% age 45 or over. Student to teacher ratio 12:1. 100% obtain employment within 6 months. Facilities: baking lab, quantity foods lab, computer lab.

COURSES: Baking, quantity foods, food service management. Schedule: varies.

FACULTY: 11 full- and part-time. Includes Joyce Jones, CWC, Tania Lovato, CWPC, Carmine Russo, CCE, Martin Samudio, CCC, Rudy Garcia, Masters Management.

COSTS: $21/credit hour plus equipment. Application deadlines: 5 days after start of each trimester. 4 scholarships awarded last year averaging $300 each. Off-campus housing available.

CONTACT: Darcy D. Buland, Academic Advisor, Albuquerque Technical Vocational Institute, Culinary Arts, 525 Buena Vista SE, Albuquerque, NM 87106; (505) 224-3755, Fax (505) 224-3781, E-mail d.buland@tv1mail.tv1.cc.nm.us.

SANTA FE COMMUNITY COLLEGE
Santa Fe/Year-round

This college offers a 2-year certificate/AAS degree in Culinary Arts. Program started 1985. Accredited by NCA. 30 credit hours of culinary courses required. Admission dates: August 20, January 10, June 1. Total enrollment: 190. 30 enrollees each admission period. 100% of applicants accepted. 20% of students receive financial aid. 70% enrolled part-time. 50% under age 25, 40% age 25-44, 10% age 45 or over. Student to teacher ratio 14:1. 100% obtain employment within 6 months. Facilities: include 2 kitchens and classrooms, culinary lab and restaurant.

COURSES: Culinary courses, specialty topics, Southwestern cuisine, general studies. Other required courses: nutrition, sanitation, food and beverage management, math, English. Schedule: 24 hours/week, 10 months/year, full, part-time/evening schedules. Externship provided. Continuing education: 12 courses per semester.

FACULTY: 1 full-time, 8 part-time. Qualifications: working executive chef.

COSTS: Annual tuition in-county $17 per credit hour, out-of-county $24 per credit hour, out-of-state $45 per credit hour. Other fees: lab fees. Refund policy: pro-rated. Admission requirements: high school diploma or equivalent.

LOCATION: The new 9,000-student campus is in a country setting.

CONTACT: Bill Weiland, CEC, Santa Fe Community College, Culinary Arts/Hospitality Dept., P.O. Box 4187, Santa Fe, NM 87502-4187; (505) 438-1600, Fax (505) 471-1237.

NEW YORK

ADIRONDACK COMMUNITY COLLEGE
Queensbury/September-May

This proprietary college offers a 1-year certificate and a 2-year AAS degree in Food Service. Program started 1969. Accredited by MSA. Admission dates: fall, spring. Total enrollment: 25. 70-80% of students receive financial aid. 75% enrolled part-time. Student to teacher ratio 10:1. 90% obtain employment within 6 months. Facilities: include 3 kitchens, classroom and restaurant.

COURSES: 1 year of food preparation, 1/2 year of spa cuisine, 1/2 year of American regional cuisine. Externship: 1,000-1,200 hours. Continuing education: baking, wines and other topics.

FACULTY: 1 full-time, 3 part-time.

COSTS: $1,600 annually. Admission requirements: high school diploma or equivalent.

CONTACT: William Steele, Adirondack Community College, Commercial Cooking/Occupational Education, Bay Rd., Queensbury, NY 12803; (518) 793-6208, Fax (518) 745-1433.

THE CHOCOLATE GALLERY
New York/Year-round

This private school specializing in cake decoration and baking offers 2-hour workshops to 2-day hands-on certificate courses. Students may attend one class weekly for 4 weeks or enroll in daily intensives. Established in 1978.

COURSES: Beginning to advanced cake decoration, baking, chocolate, confectionery, desserts.

COSTS: Range from $35 for 2 hours to $250 for 2 days. Full payment must be received 7 days prior.

CONTACT: Joan Mansour, The Chocolate Gallery, 56 W. 22nd St., New York, NY 10010; (212) 675-2253.

THE CULINARY INSTITUTE OF AMERICA
(See also pages 8, 98) (See display ad page 66)   **Hyde Park/Year-round**

This independent, not-for-profit educational institution offers 21-month associate degree programs in Culinary Arts and Baking and Pastry Arts, bachelor's degree programs in Culinary Arts Management and Baking and Pastry Arts Management, and continuing education and nonvocational courses. Established in 1946. Accredited by ACCSCT; curricula registered with NY State Educational Dept. Admission dates: Associate degree 16 (8) times per year for culinary (baking & pastry) arts; bachelor's degree 3 times per year. Total enrollment: 2,000. 72 (associate), 50 (bachelor's) degree enrollees each admission period. 97% of applicants accepted. 88% of students receive financial aid. Student to teacher ratio 18:1. Facilities: 36 professionally-equipped production kitchens and bakeshops, 48,000-volume library, learning resources center, over 2,300 instructional videotapes, nutrition center, student center, bookstore, four student-staffed public restaurants.

COURSES: Associate degree: skill development, American & international cuisines, pastry, nutrition, table service, customer relations, wine & spirits management, menu & facilities planning, baking & pastry arts: breads, desserts, ice carving, showpieces. Bachelor's degrees: marketing communications, finance, foreign languarges, history, culture, gastronomy, computer skills, leadership & management skills. Schedule: 5days/week. Associate degree programs include 18-week externships off campus. Continuing Education Dept. offers 1- to 30-week courses, customized programs, recipe testing, product development, independent learning courses in cooking, baking, & management for foodservice professionals. Fellowships are awarded to a limited number of graduates.

FACULTY: Over 125 chefs and instructors from more than 20 countries, including the highest concentration of ACF-Certified Master Chefs.

COSTS: Estimated cost, including fees and two meals daily, is $26,445 for associate degree programs, $49,780 for bachelor's degree programs, $625-$11,690 for continuing education courses. $150 deposit due 90 days prior. Cancellations 90 days prior to registration or within 3 days of signing enrollment agreement receive refund. Admission requirements: high school diploma or equiv-

alent and at least 3 to 5 months foodservice experience, including work in a professional kitchen. Four on-campus residence halls house 1,150 students; fees range from $1,265-$1,880 per semester.

LOCATION: The 150-acre campus overlooks the Hudson River on U.S. Route 9 in Hyde Park, about 90 minutes north of New York City.

CONTACT: Cathy P. Grande, Dir. of National Recruitment, The Culinary Institute of America, 433 Albany Post Rd., Hyde Park, NY 12538-1499; (800) CULINARY, (Admissions) (800) 888-7850 (Cont. Ed.), Fax (914) 452-8629, URL http://www.ciachef.edu.

ERIE COMMUNITY COLLEGE, CITY CAMPUS
Buffalo/September-May

This college offers a 2-year AOS degree in Hotel Technology/Culinary Arts. Program started 1985. Accredited by MSA. Admission dates: fall. Total enrollment: 80. 80 enrollees each admission period. 60% of applicants accepted. 70% of students receive financial aid. 10% enrolled part-time. 65% under age 25, 20% age 25-44, 15% age 45 or over. Student to teacher ratio 28:1. 75% obtain employment within 6 months. Facilities: include 5 kitchens and classrooms, computer lab and restaurant.

FACULTY: 5 full-time.

COSTS: Annual tuition: in-state $1,980, out-of-state $3,960. Other fees $100. Tuition deposit $50. Refund policy: 100% by 1st week of school. Admission requirements: high school diploma or equivalent and admission test.

LOCATION: The 2,000-student campus is in an urban setting.

CONTACT: Paul J. Cannamela, CCE, AAC, Assistant Professor, Erie Community College, City Campus, Hotel Management/Culinary Arts, 121 Ellicott St., Buffalo, NY 14203; (716) 851-1034, (716) 851-1035, Fax (716) 851-1129.

THE FRENCH CULINARY INSTITUTE
New York/Year-round

(See display ads pages 68 & 69)

This proprietary institution offers 600-hour 6- or 9-month career programs in classic French technique or classic pastry arts culminating in the Grande Diplome. Established in 1984. Accredited by ACCSCT. Calendar: quarter. Curriculum: culinary. 600/600/315 hours (culinary/pastry/bread) of culinary courses required. Admission dates: new classes begin every 6 weeks. Total enrollment: 320. 18 enrollees each admission period. Student to teacher ratio 8-18:1. Facilities: 30,000-sq.-ft. of kitchens, newly-equipped pastry and bread kitchens.

COURSES: Culinary: Basic French classical technique with emphasis on fine dining, a la carte preparation, and service. Pastry Arts: classic French pastry technique and understanding of the tenets of traditional dessert composition. Schedule: full time for 6 months (8:30am-2:30pm weekdays) or part-time for 9 months (5:30 to 10:30pm, 3 evenings/week).

FACULTY: 20 full-time, 9 part-time. Includes Dean of Special Programs Jacques Pépin, Dean of Culinary Studies Alain Sailhac, Dean of Pastry Arts Jacques Torres, and Master Chef/Senior Lecturer Andre Soltner.

COSTS: Tuition for 1997 is $19,660 for the culinary program and $19,435 for the pastry arts program, which includes uniforms, equipment, and registration fee. $500 application fee and $1,000 deposit required. Refund policy complies with ACCSCT guidelines. Admission requirements: high school diploma or equivalent.

LOCATION: New York's SoHo district, adjacent to Chinatown and Little Italy.

CONTACT: Sarah Cirrincione, Director, The French Culinary Institute, Admissions Dept., 462 Broadway, New York, NY 10013-2618; (212) 219-8890, Fax (212) 431-3054.

JEFFERSON COMMUNITY COLLEGE
Watertown

This college offers a 2-year certificate/AAS degree. Program started 1975. Accredited by MSA. Admission dates: August, January. Total enrollment: 120. 100% of applicants accepted. Student to teacher ratio 25:1. 95% obtain employment within 6 months.

COURSES: Externship provided.

FACULTY: 4 full-time.

COSTS: Annual tuition in-state $1,470, out-of-state $2,940. Admission requirements: high school diploma or equivalent.

CONTACT: Edward W. Bushaw, Jefferson Community College, Hospitality & Tourism Dept., Outer Coffeen St., Watertown, NY 13601; (315) 786-2200, Fax (315) 788-0716.

JULIE SAHNI'S SCHOOL OF INDIAN COOKING
Brooklyn Heights/Year-round

(See also page 258)

Cookbook author Julie Sahni offers intensive participation courses, limited to 3 students, that meet over a weekend in her specially designed teaching kitchen. Each course can be taught in any private kitchen in the U.S. as a 1-day introduction for 6 students.

COURSES: Classic and regional Indian cuisine. Sessions emphasize techniques, spices and seasonings, healthful meal planning, historical background, and religious ideology and include shopping at an Indian grocery.

FACULTY: Julie Sahni was executive chef of 2 New York City restaurants, served on the faculty of NYU and Boston University's culinary arts programs, and is author of *Classic Indian Cooking* and *Classic Indian Vegetarian and Grain Cooking*.

COSTS: Each session is $900, which includes materials. A $100 nonrefundable deposit is required 90 days prior. Refund for cancellations 90 days prior or within 3 days of signing enrollment agreement.

LOCATION: Near the Brooklyn entrance to the Brooklyn Bridge.

CONTACT: Julie Sahni, Julie Sahni's School of Indian Cooking, 101 Clark Street, Brooklyn Heights, NY 11201; (718) 625-3958, Fax (718) 625-3456.

MOHAWK VALLEY COMMUNITY COLLEGE
Rome/August-May
(See display ad above)

This college offers a 1-year Chef Training certificate, a 2-year AOS degree in Food Service, 2-year AAS degrees in Restaurant Management and Hotel Technology: Meeting Services Management, and a 2-year AS degree in Nutrition and Dietetics. Program started 1978. Accredited by MSA. Calendar: semester. Curriculum: culinary. Admission dates: August, January. Total enrollment: 120. 30 enrollees each admission period. 90% of applicants accepted. 80% of students receive financial aid. 40% enrolled part-time. 29% under age 25, 65% age 25-44, 6% age 45 or over. Student to teacher ratio 15-25:1. 98% obtain employment within 6 months. Facilities: include 6 kitchens and classrooms, student-run restaurant, cafe.

COURSES: Include sanitation, food preparation, food merchandising, and baking. Schedule: varies. A 225-hour externship is provided.

FACULTY: 3 full-time, 6 part-time. Includes Dennis R. Baumeyer, BS, MS, Linda Irwin, AAS, BS, MS, Marc Lubetkin, AAS, BS.

COSTS: Annual tuition is $2,350 in-state, $4,450 out-of-state. Application fee is $25. Other fees: student activity and insurance fee is $65. Admission requirements: high school diploma or equivalent and admission test.

LOCATION: The 2,500-student college campus is 12 miles from Utica.

CONTACT: Dennis R. Baumeyer, Director, Mohawk Valley Community College, Hospitality Programs, 1101 Floyd Ave., Rome, NY 13440; (315) 339-3470, Fax (315) 339-6934, E-mail baumeyer@mvcc.edu.

MONROE COMMUNITY COLLEGE
Rochester/September-May

This college offers a 2-year certificate/AAS degree. Program started 1967. Accredited by MSA. Calendar: semester. Curriculum: core. Admission dates: fall, spring. Total enrollment: 175. 60 enrollees each admission period. 80% of applicants accepted. 60% of students receive financial aid. 20% enrolled part-time. 50% under age 25, 40% age 25-44, 10% age 45 or over. Student to teacher ratio 18:1. 96% obtain employment within 6 months. Facilities: 4 kitchens, computer lab, dining room.

COURSES: Co-op training. Continuing education available.

FACULTY: 8-10 full- and part-time. Includes Chair E.F. Callens, CEC, CCE, CFE.

COSTS: Annual tuition in-state $2,000. Admission requirements: high school diploma or equivalent.

CONTACT: Eddy Callens, Chairperson, Monroe Community College, Dept. of Food, Hotel, and Tourism Management, 1000 East Henrietta Rd., Rochester, NY 14623; (716) 292-2000, Fax (716) 427-2749.

THE NATURAL GOURMET COOKERY SCHOOL
(See also page 200) (See display ad above)   **New York/Year-round**

This private trade school devoted to healthy cooking offers 600-hour Chef's Training and 110-hour Holistic Culinary Arts Assistants certificate programs and courses for professionals and non-professionals. Established in 1977. Accreditation in process. Curriculum: core. 445 hours of culinary courses required. Admission dates: Chef's Training 4-month full-time/8-month part-time courses begin 9 times a year. Total enrollment: 16. 14-16 enrollees each admission period. 20% of students receive financial aid. 33% enrolled part-time. 10% under age 25, 75% age 25-44, 15% age 45 or over. Student to teacher ratio 16:1. 70% obtain employment within 6 months. Facilities: include 2 kitchens, classroom, and bookstore.

Courses: Preparation of fresh vegetables, nuts, fruits, whole grains, legumes, and healthful condiments; Eastern & Western nutritional theories. Emphasis on vegetarian; instruction in fish, poultry, butter & eggs. Students prepare meals for Friday Night Dinner Club. Schedule: full-time (part-time) Chef's Training program meets weekdays from 9am-4pm (2 evenings and 3 Saturdays or Sundays/month). A 95-hour externship is provided. Assistants take 1 or 2 classes/week assisting the instructor in the public classes. Continuing education: 30 classes, open to the public.

Faculty: Co-presidents Annemarie Colbin, MA, CCP, CHES, founder, syndicated columnist, author of *Food and Healing* and 2 natural food cookbooks; Diane Carlson, director, graduate of the school & owned a cooking school; Jenny Matthau, CCP, director, graduate of the school.

Costs: Tuition is $9,400 for Chef's Training, $3,400 for Assistants. Admission requirements: high school diploma or equivalent; Assistants applicants must have taken a course at the school and have natural food experience. Last year C-CAP scholarship awarded at $1,000, IACP at $1,000. 20 loans granted last year. Nearby lodging begins at $500 per month.

Location: Between 5th and 6th Avenues in Manhattan.

Contact: Director of Admissions, The Natural Gourmet Cookery School, 48 W. 21st St., 2nd Floor, New York, NY 10010; (212) 645-5170, (212) 627-COOK.

NEW SCHOOL CULINARY ARTS
(See also page 200)   **New York/Year-round**

The New School for Social Research offers master class certificate courses in Cooking (25 sessions), Baking (15), Professional Catering (10), Italian Cooking (10), and Restaurant Management (12) and other programs for professionals and nonprofessionals. Established in 1919. Calendar: trimester. Total enrollment: 12 maximum in each Master class. 100% enrolled part-time. 20% under age 25, 60% age 25-44, 20% age 45 or over. Student to teacher ratio 12:1. Facilities: a restored landmark townhouse with indoor and outdoor dining areas and a fully-equipped instructional kitchen.

Courses: Master Class: basic skills, cuisine & pastry preparation, presentation, recipe development; Baking: pastries, breads & doughs, cake decoration, chocolate; Catering: food preparation and instruction in the business of catering. Schedule: Monday-Friday mornings and evenings. Graduates are eligible for apprenticeships. Include restaurant management, cake decorating, opening a coffee bar, creating and selling a new food.

FACULTY: 50+ faculty headed by Gary Goldberg, co-founder Martin Johner, includes Miriam Brickman, Richard Glavin, Arlyn Hackett, Micheal Krondl, Harriet Lembeck, Lisa Montenegro, Robert Posch, Dan Rosati, Stephen Schmidt, Marie Simmons, Karen Snyder, Carole Walter.

COSTS: Master Class $2,215 (+$450 materials fee) for Cooking, $1,350 (+$200) for Baking, $880 (+$195) for Catering. Most other professional courses $45/session (+$5-$14). Tuition-free kitchen assistant & work/study program is open to selected applicants. Full payment upon registration. Full refund less $15 for written cancellation prior to class.

LOCATION: Manhattan's Greenwich Village.

CONTACT: Gary A. Goldberg, Executive Director, New School Culinary Arts, 100 Greenwich Ave., New York, NY 10011; (212) 255-4141, (800) 544-1978, #20, Fax (212) 229-5648, E-mail admissions@newschool.edu, URL http://www.newschool.edu.

NEW YORK CITY TECHNICAL COLLEGE
Brooklyn/September-May

This college offers a 2-year AAS degree and 4-year BS degree in Hospitality Management. Established 1947. Accredited by MSA, state, ALPHA. Calendar: semester. Curriculum: core. Admission dates: September, February. Total enrollment: 800. 125 enrollees each admission period. 50% of students receive financial aid. 50% enrolled part-time. 38% under age 25, 59% age 25-44, 3% age 45 or over. Student to teacher ratio 15:1. 90% obtain employment within 6 months. Facilities: include 5 kitchens, dining room, 3 classrooms, restaurant.

COURSES: Food and beverage cost control, culinary arts, baking and pastry arts, wines, beverage management. Externship: 8 weeks, in Italy, France, Germany, if qualified. Continuing Education: garde manger, cake decorating, other subjects.

FACULTY: 13 full-time, 20-40 part-time. Includes Patricia S. Bartholomew, Chair.

COSTS: Annual tuition in-state $3,200, out-of-state $6,400. CUNY fee is $35. Textbooks $1,000, materials fee $10, uniforms $120. 100% refund prior to first class. Admission requirements: high school diploma or equivalent and admission test. Average off-campus housing cost is $600/month.

LOCATION: Downtown Brooklyn.

CONTACT: Dr. Patricia Bartholomew, Chair, New York City Technical College, Hospitality Management, 300 Jay St., #N220, Brooklyn, NY 11201; (718) 260-5630, Fax (718) 260-5997.

NEW YORK FOOD AND HOTEL MANAGEMENT SCHOOL
New York/Year-round

This proprietary institution offers a 9-month certificate in Commercial Cooking and Catering. Established in 1935. Accredited by ACCST. Admission dates: every 4 to 6 weeks. Total enrollment: 20-25. 80% of applicants accepted. 50% of students receive financial aid. 50% under age 25, 40% age 25-44, 10% age 45 or over. Student to teacher ratio 16:1. Facilities: include 4 kitchens, 5 classrooms and restaurant.

COURSES: Skills development, quantity food production, food preparation, catering, restaurant operation, food purchasing, sanitation, baking and pastry production. Schedule: 5 hours/day, 5 days/week. Externship: 3 months.

FACULTY: 10 full-time.

COSTS: Annual tuition $7,115. Registration fee $100. Other costs: books $168, food lab fee $1,080, kits and uniforms $132. Admission requirements: high school diploma or equivalent and admission test.

CONTACT: Harold Kaplan, New York Food and Hotel Management School, Admissions, 154 West 14th Street, New York, NY 10011; (212) 675-6655.

NEW YORK INSTITUTE OF TECHNOLOGY
Central Islip/Year-round

This independent institution offers a 19-month AOS degree in Culinary Arts. Program started 1987. Accredited by MSA. Calendar: semester. Curriculum: core. Admission dates: fall, spring. Total enrollment: 170. 80/40 enrollees each admission period. 90% of applicants accepted. 95% of students receive financial aid. 75% under age 25, 25% age 25-44, 2% age 45 or over. Student to teacher ratio 16:1. 100% obtain employment within 6 months. Facilities: include 3 kitchens, bakery, 10 classrooms, computer software, 2 restaurants.

COURSES: Schedule: mirrors the industry. Externship: 3-month, in public restaurants and food service establishments.

FACULTY: 9 full-time, 3 part-time.

COSTS: Annual tuition $25,085. Admission requirements: high school diploma or equivalent. 10 scholarships awarded last year averaging $1,000 each. On-campus housing: 150 spaces; average cost: $2,500 per semester.

CONTACT: Prof. Susan Hendee, Dept. Chair, New York Institute of Technology, Culinary Arts Center, 300 Carleton Ave., #66-101, PO Box 9029, Central Islip, NY 11722-9029; (516) 348-3290, Fax (516) 348-3247, E-mail shendee@acl.nyit.edu.

NEW YORK RESTAURANT SCHOOL
(See display ad page 72)   ### New York/Year-round

This private college offers a 16-month AOS degree program in Culinary Arts-Restaurant Management and a 6- to 9-month credit-bearing certificate program in Pastry Arts and Culinary Skills. Established in 1980. Accredited by ACCSCT, NYS Bd. of Regents. 44 credit hours of culinary courses required. Admission dates: rolling admission. Total enrollment: 500. 50 enrollees each admission period. 50% of applicants accepted. 60% of students receive financial aid. 10% enrolled part-time. 30% under age 25, 66% age 25-44, 4% age 45 or over. Student to teacher ratio 17:1 (labs); 25:1 (lectures). 93% obtain employment within 6 months. Facilities: the 30,000-square-foot recently renovated facility includes 5 newly-equipped kitchens, 3 classrooms, and resource center.

COURSES: Include basic food preparation and knife skills, food handling, meat, vegetable, fish, and seafood preparation, international cuisine, and garde manger. Schedule: 35 hours/week full-time or 17-1/2 hours/week part-time. Late night and weekend classes are available. Programs conclude with a 2- to 3-month local externship.

FACULTY: The 28 faculty members all have a minimum of 8 year's experience and many have 4-year degrees and prior teaching background.

COSTS: Tuition is $14,382 for Culinary Arts, $10,830 for Restaurant Management, $8,664 for Pastry Arts, $10,760 for Culinary Skills, $24,000 for AOS degree program. $40 application fee required. Additional fees range from $750-$1,050. $300 deposit required. New York State refund policy and Federal Pro Rata policy. Admission requirements: vary. 10 scholarships were awarded last year. 250 loans were granted last year averaging $3,000 each. The Admissions Office provides assistance in obtaining nearby housing.

LOCATION: Just off Broadway, in SoHo.

CONTACT: Stephen Tave, New York Restaurant School, Admission Dept., 75 Varick St., New York, NY 10013; (212) 226-5500, Fax (212) 226-5644, E-mail NYRScoll@chelsea.ios.com.

NEW YORK UNIVERSITY
New York/Fall, Spring, Summer   *(See also page 201)*

The Dept. of Nutrition and Food Studies, School of Education, offers bachelor's, master's, and doctoral degree programs in Food Studies, Food and Restaurant Management, and Nutrition that grant BS, MA, MS, and Ph.D. degrees. Established in 1986. Accredited by MSA. Total enrollment: 350, many part-time. Facilities: new teaching kitchen and library, computer, academic resources.

COURSES: More than 50 in food science, food management, food culture and history, food writing, nutrition. Schedule: late afternoon or evenings. Internship required for all students.

FACULTY: 9 full-time academic, 45 part-time academic and professional.

COSTS: Approximately $600/credit. Financial aid available. Some housing available.

LOCATION: Washington Square, Greenwich Village.

CONTACT: Dr. Marion Nestle, Department Chair, New York University, Dept. of Nutrition and Food Studies, 35 W. 4th St., 10th Flr., New York, NY 10012-1172; (212) 998-5580, (212) 998-5592, Fax (212) 995-4194, E-mail nestlem@is2.nyu.edu., URL http://www.nyu.edu/education/nutrition/.

ONONDAGA COMMUNITY COLLEGE
Syracuse

This college offers a 1-year certificate and a 2-year AAS degree. Program started 1979. Accredited by state. Admission dates: fall, spring. Total enrollment: 90-100. Student to teacher ratio 16:1.

COURSES: Externship provided.

COSTS: Annual tuition in-state $1,350, out-of-state $2,700.

CONTACT: Culinary Director, Onondaga Community College, Culinary Arts Department, Onondaga Hill, Syracuse, NY 13215; (315) 469-7741.

PAUL SMITH'S COLLEGE
Paul Smiths/Year-round

This college offers a 2-year AAS degree in Culinary Arts and a 1-year Baking certificate. Established 1980. Accredited by MSA. Admission dates: September, January. Total enrollment: 150. 85% of applicants accepted. 80% of students receive financial aid. 80% under age 25, 15% age 25-44, 5% age 45 or over. Student to teacher ratio 14:1. 99% obtain employment within 6 months. Facilities: include 4 campus Foods Laboratories, an a la carte kitchen, and a 60-seat dining room.

COURSES: Baking certificate curriculum covers journeyman skills, including advertising, merchandising, and management. Students produce goods for an on-campus bakery. During year two, 1 semester is spent in the College's Hotel Saranac, the other is an externship.

FACULTY: 66 full-time, 12 part-time. Includes Robert Brown, CM, and Paul Sorgule, CCE, 1988 Culinary Olympics gold medalist.

COSTS: Annual tuition is $11,000. The Culinary Arts program comprehensive fee is $545 per semester. $25 application fee. $100 deposit due May 1. Application deadlines: rolling. Admission requirements: high school transcript or GED. The Baking Certificate program is open to those who have industry experience or have completed a culinary arts program. Housing averages $2,300/year; board is $2,480/year.

LOCATION: On the shore of the Lower St. Regis Lake, surrounded by 13,100 acres of college-owned forests and lakes in the Adirondack Mountains.

CONTACT: Enrico A. Miller, VP for Enrollment Management, Paul Smith's College, Admissions Office, P.O. Box 265, Paul Smiths, NY 12970; (800) 421-2605, (518) 327-6227, Fax (518) 327-6161, URL http://www.paulsmiths.edu.

PETER KUMP'S NEW YORK COOKING SCHOOL
(See also page 201) (See display ad page 74)   **New York/Year-round**

This private school offers 20- to 26-week diploma programs in the Culinary Arts and Pastry and Baking Arts, 10- to 24-week certificate programs in cooking and baking, continuing education and business courses, and programs for nonprofessionals. Founded in 1974. Career program curricula licensed by New York State Dept. of Education. Admission dates: 13 times/year. Student to teacher ratio 12:1.

COURSES: In addition to theory and hands-on training in the preparation & presentation of classic cuisines, culinary arts courses cover menu planning, kitchen management, butchering, regional cuisines, and wine. Schedule: diploma courses meet 5 days/week for 14 weeks or 3 mornings or evenings/week for 20 weeks; certificate courses meet once weekly for 10-24 weeks. 6-week apprenticeship at a restaurant/pastry shop in New York City or France follows diploma courses.

FACULTY: Over 30 instructors. Founder Peter Kump studied with James Beard & Simone Beck, was IACP president & James Beard Foundation founding president. Director of Pastry & Baking Nick Malgieri won the 1996 James Beard Award for best Baking and Dessert Cookbook.

COSTS: Day (evening) Culinary Arts tuition is $9,300 ($6,900). Pastry and Baking Arts tuition is $8,900 ($6,500). 10% deposit with application; 10% due 30 days prior to course. Admission requirements: proof of 2 years college or 4 years professional work experience (any profession). Loans available to eligible students starting in 1997.

LOCATION: East 92nd Street and West 23rd Street in New York City.

CONTACT: Bill Grant, Director, Peter Kump's New York Cooking School, 307 East 92nd St., New York, NY 10128; (800) 522-4610, (212) 348-6360, Fax (212) 348-6360.

SUNY COLLEGE OF AGRICULTURE & TECHNOLOGY
Cobleskill/August-May

This college offers a 2-year AOS degree in Culinary Arts. Program started 1971. Accredited by MSA, ACFEI. Admission dates: fall, spring. Total enrollment: 100. 60 enrollees each admission period. 85% of applicants accepted. 95% of students receive financial aid. 90% under age 25, 8% age 25-44, 2% age 45 or over. Student to teacher ratio 15:1. 98% obtain employment within 6 months. Facilities: include 5 kitchens.

COURSES: Externship provided. Fellowship available.

FACULTY: 10 full-time.

COSTS: Annual tuition $2,650 in-state, $3,900 out-of-state. Admission requirements: high school diploma or equivalent.

LOCATION: The 750-acre campus is 30 miles from Albany, Schenectady, and Troy.

CONTACT: Dean, SUNY College of Agriculture & Technology, Food Service & Hospitality Administration, Cobleskill, NY 12043; (518) 234-5011, Fax (518) 234-5333.

SCHENECTADY COUNTY COMMUNITY COLLEGE
Schenectady/Year-round

This college offers a 2-year degree and a 1-year certificate. Program started 1980. Accredited by MSA, ACFEI. Calendar: semester. Curriculum: culinary. 795 hours of culinary courses required. Admission dates: September, January, June. Total enrollment: 284. 72 enrollees each admission period. 86% of applicants accepted. 22% enrolled part-time. 54% under age 25, 42% age 25-44, 3% age 45 or over. Student to teacher ratio 20:1. 88% obtain employment within 6 months. Facilities: 7 kitchens, restaurant, 2 dining rooms, banquet room.

COURSES: Other required courses: 600 hours work experience. Externship provided.

FACULTY: 11 full-time, 22 part-time. Includes David Brough, CEC, Paul Cerone, CEC, Wayne Maibe, CCE, Jim Rhodes, CEC, American Academy of Chefs, Toby Strianese, ACFEI Accrediting Team.

COSTS: Annual tuition $2,240 in-state, $4,480 out-of-state. Admission requirements: high school diploma or equivalent and placement testing.

CONTACT: Toby Strianese, Chair and Professor, Schenectady County Community College, Hotel, Culinary Arts & Tourism, 78 Washington Ave., Schenectady, NY 12305; (518) 381-1391, Fax (518) 346-0379, E-mail strianaj@gw.sunysccc.edu.

SULLIVAN COUNTY COMMUNITY COLLEGE
Loch Sheldrake/September-May

This college offers a 2-year AAS degree in Professional and Hotel Technology. Program started 1965. Accredited by MSA. Admission dates: September, January. Total enrollment: 126. 75 enrollees each admission period. 90% of students receive financial aid. 22% enrolled part-time. 78% under age 25, 20% age 25-44, 10% age 45 or over. Student to teacher ratio 14:1. 90% obtain employment within 6 months. Facilities: include 7 kitchens and classrooms, restaurant.

FACULTY: 8 full-time. Qualifications: bachelor's or master's degree.

Costs: Annual tuition for 1996-97 is estimated to be $2,300 in-state, $4,400 out-of-state. Application fee $25. Refund policy: according to Federal regs. Application deadlines: rolling. Admission requirements: high school diploma or equivalent and admission test. On-campus housing: 300 spaces. Average off-campus housing cost: $4,400.

Location: The 405-acre campus is 35 miles from Middletown.

Contact: Edmund Nadeau, Sullivan County Community College, Hospitality Division, LeRoy Rd., Box 4002, Loch Sheldrake, NY 12759-4002; (914) 434-5750, Fax (914) 434-5806.

WESTCHESTER COMMUNITY COLLEGE
Valhalla/September-May

This college offers a 2-year AAS degree in Food Service Administration. Program started 1971. Accredited by MSA. Calendar: semester. Curriculum: culinary, business. Admission dates: all year. Total enrollment: 100. 50 enrollees each admission period. 20% of students receive financial aid. 25% enrolled part-time. 50% under age 25, 30% age 25-44, 20% age 45 or over. Student to teacher ratio 15:1. 100% obtain employment within 6 months. Facilities: include lab/demo kitchen, baking kitchen, production kitchen, bar/beverage management lab, instructional dining room.

Courses: Food preparation, quantity food production, buffet catering, advanced foods, garde manger, bar/beverage management, and menu planning. Schedule: flexible. Continuing education provided.

Faculty: 4 full-time. Qualifications: MS required. Includes Curriculum Chair D. Nosek, D. Salvestrini, J. Snyder, T. Cousins.

Costs: Annual tuition in-state $1,075/semester. Lab fees $15. Application deadlines: 2 weeks before each semester. Admission requirements: high school diploma or equivalent. 5 scholarships awarded last year averaging $850 each.

Location: 30 miles north of New York City.

Contact: Daryl Nosek, Curriculum Chair, Westchester Community College, Restaurant Management, 75 Grasslands Rd., Valhalla, NY 10595-1698; (914) 785-6551, Fax (914) 785-6765.

NORTH CAROLINA

ASHEVILLE BUNCOMBE TECHNICAL COMMUNITY COLLEGE
Asheville/Year-round

This college offers a 2-year AAS degree in Culinary Technology. Program started 1968. Accredited by SACS. 61 credit hours of culinary courses required. Admission dates: begins September of year previous to official enrollment. Total enrollment: 70. 35 enrollees each admission period. 100% of applicants accepted. 16% enrolled part-time. 54% under age 25, 37% age 25-44, 8% age 45 or over. Student to teacher ratio 11:1. 100% obtain employment within 6 months. Facilities: include 2 kitchens, 4 classrooms, restaurant 1 day per week.

Courses: Food preparation, baking, garde manger, classical lab, palate development, butchering, dining room personnel, sanitation, and international cuisine. Externship provided.

Faculty: 2 full-time, 3 part-time. Includes Sheila Tillman, BS, MA, Brian McDonald, Lance Etheridge, John Hofland, Steven Howard.

Costs: Annual tuition $763 in-state, $4,966 out-of-state. Activity fee $7 quarterly. Refund policy: 75% on or before the 20% point. Application deadlines: May 31. Admission requirements: high school diploma or equivalent and admission test. Off-campus housing cost: $300 per month.

Location: The 4,000-student, 127-acre campus is in a suburban setting.

Contact: Sheila Tillman, Chairperson, Asheville Buncombe Technical Community College, Culinary Technology, 340 Victoria Rd., Asheville, NC 28801; (704) 254-1921, Fax (704) 251-6355.

CENTRAL PIEDMONT COMMUNITY COLLEGE
Charlotte/Year-round

This college offers a 2-year AAS degree in Food Service Management and Culinary Arts. Program started 1974. Accredited by SACS, ACFEI. Calendar: semester. Curriculum: culinary, core. Admission dates: fall, winter, spring. Total enrollment: 500. 100-150 enrollees each admission period. 75% of applicants accepted. 10% of students receive financial aid. 25% enrolled part-time. 30% under age 25, 40% age 25-44, 30% age 45 or over. Student to teacher ratio 15:1. 98% obtain employment within 6 months. Facilities: include 5 kitchens, 3 classrooms, baking lab, small quantities lab, restaurant.

FACULTY: 3 full-time C.I.A. graduates, 5 part-time.

COSTS: Annual tuition in-state $800, out-of-state $4,800. Admission requirements: high school diploma or equivalent and admission test. Off-campus housing cost: $400-$500 per month.

LOCATION: near downtown Charlotte.

CONTACT: Robert G. Boll, FMP, CFE, Central Piedmont Community College, Culinary Arts Department, P.O. Box 35009, Charlotte, NC 28235; (704) 330-6721, Fax (704) 330-6581.

GUILFORD TECHNICAL COMMUNITY COLLEGE
Jamestown/Year-round

This community college offers a 1-year and 2-year program in Culinary Technology, Hotel/Restaurant Management, Travel & Tourism. Program started 1989. Applicant for ACFEI accreditation. Calendar: semester. Curriculum: core. 106 credit hours of culinary courses required. Admission dates: year round. Total enrollment: 102. 35 enrollees each admission period. 90% of applicants accepted. 50% of students receive financial aid. 50% enrolled part-time. 50% under age 25, 45% age 25-44, 5% age 45 or over. Student to teacher ratio 7:1. 98% obtain employment within 6 months.

COURSES: Garde manger, baking & pastry, dining room management, nutritional cuisine, customer service. Schedule: day and evening courses. Co-op training.

FACULTY: 2 full-time, 4 part-time. Qualifications: ACFEI certified and minimum 5 years experience. Includes Ronald Wolf, CCC, CCE and Keith Gardiner, CEC.

COSTS: Tuition in-state $13/quarter-hour, out-of-state $108/quarter-hour. Application deadlines: on-going. Admission requirements: placement exam. 7 scholarships awarded last year averaging $250 each.

CONTACT: Ronald S. Wolf, CCC, CCE, Department Chair, Guilford Technical Community College, Culinary Technology, Box 309, Jamestown, NC 27282; (910) 334-4822 #2302, Fax (910) 841-4350, E-mail wolfr@gtcc.cc.us.nc.

WAKE TECHNICAL COMMUNITY COLLEGE
Raleigh/Year-round

This college offers a 2-year associate degree in Culinary Arts. Program started 1985. Accredited by SACS. Calendar: quarter. Curriculum: core. Admission dates: year-round. Total enrollment: 45. 30 enrollees each admission period. 75% of applicants accepted. 10% enrolled part-time. 20% under age 25, 60% age 25-44, 20% age 45 or over. Student to teacher ratio 10:1. 98% obtain employment within 6 months. Facilities: include kitchen and restaurant.

COURSES: Foods, nutrition, sanitation, cost control, wine, inventory control, general education. Schedule: 30 hours/week. Externship provided.

FACULTY: 5 full-time, 1 part-time. Qualifications: BS, HRM, certified chefs. Includes Richard Roberts, Fredi Morf, Carolyn House, Jane Broden.

COSTS: Annual tuition in-state $2,300. Admission requirements: high school diploma or equivalent. Off-campus housing cost is $400+/month.

LOCATION: suburban.

CONTACT: Richard Roberts, Dept. Head, Wake Technical Community College, Culinary Technology, 9101 Fayetteville Rd., Raleigh, NC 27603; (919) 662-3417, Fax (919) 779-3360.

NORTH DAKOTA

NORTH DAKOTA STATE COLLEGE OF SCIENCE
Wahpeton/August-May

This college offers an 18-month diploma/AAS degree in Culinary Arts. Established in 1903. Accredited by NCA. 49 credit hours of culinary courses required. Admission dates: August, January. Total enrollment: 30-35. 18 enrollees each admission period. 100% of applicants accepted. 80% of students receive financial aid. 80% under age 25, 15% age 25-44, 5% age 45 or over. Student to teacher ratio 18:1. 100% obtain employment within 6 months. Facilities: include 2 kitchens and classrooms.

COURSES: Food preparation, baking, catering, gourmet, short order. Other required courses: 23 semester hours. Co-op training between 1st and 2nd year.

FACULTY: 2 full-time.

COSTS: Annual tuition $1,701 in-state, $4,293 out-of-state. Application deadlines: rolling. Admission requirements: high school diploma or equivalent. On-campus housing: 1,700 spaces, average cost: $860.

LOCATION: The 2,492-student campus is located on 125 acres in a small town, 45 miles from Fargo.

CONTACT: Neil Rittenour, Program Director, North Dakota State College of Science, Culinary Arts, 800 North 6th St., Wahpeton, ND 58076; (800) 342-4325, Fax (701) 671-2201.

OHIO

CINCINNATI STATE TECHNICAL & COMMUNITY COLLEGE
Cincinnati/Year-round

This college offers a 2-year ASOB degree in Chef Technology and 30-hour certificate program. Program started 1980. Accredited by ACFEI, NCA. Admission dates: open. Total enrollment: 130. 30 enrollees each admission period. 100% of applicants accepted. 40% of students receive financial aid. 20% enrolled part-time. 40% under age 25, 50% age 25-44, 10% age 45 or over. Student to teacher ratio 15:1. 100% obtain employment within 6 months. Facilities: include commercial kitchen.

COURSES: 7 culinary courses. Other required courses: 23 other courses. Schedule: day and evening options. Co-op externship provided.

FACULTY: 4 full-time.

COSTS: Annual tuition $3,025 in-state, $5,000 out-of-state. Application deadlines: open enrollment. Admission requirements: high school diploma or equivalent and admission test. 10 scholarships awarded last year averaging $1,000 each. Off-campus housing cost: $350 per month.

CONTACT: Richard Hendrix, Dept. Chair, Cincinnati State Technical & Community College, Business Division, 3520 Central Pkwy., Cincinnati, OH 45223; (513) 569-1500, Fax (513) 569-1467.

THE CLEVELAND RESTAURANT COOKING SCHOOL
(See also page XX)   **Cleveland/Year-round**

This private school offers a 4-month professional program and classes for hobbyists, 1-week seminars in May and September. Established in 1986. Curriculum: culinary. Admission dates: January, June, September. Total enrollment: 18. 6 enrollees each admission period. 95% of applicants accepted. 40% under age 25, 40% age 25-44, 20% age 45 or over. Student to teacher ratio 6:1. 100% obtain employment within 6 months. Facilities: include a teaching kitchen, demonstration area, a restaurant kitchen.

COURSES: Cover restaurant planning, food costing and importing, catering management, food journalism, and organic farming. Schedule: 25 hours/week of hands-on cooking. Two months of daily classes are followed by a 2-month externship at Parker's Restaurant.

FACULTY: Chef Parker Bosley, owner of Parker's Restaurant and Catering, and the restaurant staff.

COSTS: $3,200 for the program. Admission requirements: personal interview.

LOCATION: Downtown Cleveland.

CONTACT: The Cleveland Restaurant Cooking School, 2801 Bridge Ave., Cleveland, OH 44113; (216) 771-7130, Fax (216) 771-8130.

COLUMBUS STATE COMMUNITY COLLEGE
Columbus/Year-round   *(See also page 204)*

This college offers a 3-year AAS degree in Culinary Apprenticeship. Program started 1978. Accredited by ACFEI, NCA. 107 credit hours of culinary courses required. Admission dates: September, January. Total enrollment: 60. 35 enrollees each admission period. 100% of applicants accepted. 95% enrolled part-time. 60% under age 25, 40% age 25-44,. Student to teacher ratio 15:1. 100% obtain employment within 6 months.

COURSES: General education, business, foodservice management, culinary courses. Schedule: one full day of class per week. 40 hours per week on apprenticeship.

FACULTY: 7 full-time. Includes Chair C. Kizer, M. Steiskal, D. Cobler, T. Atkinson, J. Taylor.

COSTS: Annual tuition $1,836 in-state. Application deadlines: May 15. Admission requirements: high school graduate, letters of reference, interview.

CONTACT: Carol Kizer, Chairperson, Columbus State Community College, Hospitality Management Department, 550 East Spring St., Columbus, OH 43215; (614) 227-2579, Fax (614) 227-5146.

CUYAHOGA COMMUNITY COLLEGE
Cleveland/Year-round

This college offers a 2-year AAB degree in Culinary Arts, Restaurant Food Service Management, and Hotel/Motel Management. Program started 1969. Accredited by NCA. Calendar: quarter. Curriculum: core. 35 credit hours of culinary courses required. Admission dates: quarterly. Total enrollment: 175. 30 enrollees each admission period. 95% of applicants accepted. 60% of students receive financial aid. 60% enrolled part-time. 20% under age 25, 75% age 25-44, 5% age 45 or over. Student to teacher ratio 15:1. 95% obtain employment within 6 months. Facilities: include 3 kitchens, 2 classrooms, computer lab, restaurant.

COURSES: Management/food preparation, haute cuisine, garde manger. Other required courses: purchasing, accounting, menu planning. Schedule: daily 8am-5pm. Continuing education: safety & sanitation, nutrition.

FACULTY: 5 full-time, 9 part-time. Qualifications: degree and industry experience.

COSTS: Annual tuition in-state $36.50/credit hour, out-of-state $97/credit hour. Application fee $10, lab fees $300. Application deadlines: 3 weeks before quarter. Admission requirements: testing in English/math. 20 scholarships awarded last year averaging $300-$500 each. Off-campus housing cost is $500/month.

LOCATION: Metro area.

CONTACT: Jan DeLucia, Program Manager, Cuyahoga Community College, Hospitality Management, 2900 Community College Ave., Cleveland, OH 44115; (216) 987-4081, Fax (216) 987-4086, E-mail jan.delucia@tri-c.cc.oh.us, URL http://www.tri-c.cc.oh.us.

HOCKING TECHNICAL COLLEGE
Nelsonville

This college offers a 2-year certificate/AAS degree. Program started 1979. Accredited by NCA. Admission dates: September, January, March, June. Total enrollment: 150. Student to teacher ratio 15:1. 95% obtain employment within 6 months.

FACULTY: 5 full-time.

COSTS: Annual tuition in-state $1,500, out-of-state $3,000.

CONTACT: Director, Hocking Technical College, Culinary Arts Department, Nelsonville, OH 45764; (614) 753-3591, Fax (614) 753-9018.

THE LORETTA PAGANINI SCHOOL OF COOKING
(See also page 205)   **Chesterland/Year-round**

This private school in conjunction with Lakeland Community College offers a Professional Chef Training program and a Baking & Pastry Arts certificate program. Program started 1989. Accredited by ACF. Calendar: semester. Curriculum: culinary. 200 hours of culinary courses required. Total enrollment: 36. 12 enrollees each admission period. 80% of applicants accepted. 10% under age 25, 60% age 25-44, 30% age 45 or over. Student to teacher ratio 12:1. 80% obtain employment within 6 months. Facilities: fully-equipped 600-sq-ft professional kitchen and overhead mirror.

COURSES: Classical European with emphasis on technique and hands-on training. Opportunities to apprentice at local restaurant or assist in classes. Continuing Chef's Training available. Schedule: 10 sessions that meet from 8am-3pm or 10am-4pm once weekly or as a 2-week intensive.

FACULTY: 25 full- and part-time.

COSTS: Tuition is $895 for each program. Nonrefundable $150 deposit at registration, balance due 2 weeks prior to class. Admission requirements: successful completion of Basic Techniques of Cooking or Baking.

LOCATION: 25 miles east of Cleveland.

CONTACT: Loretta Paganini, Director, Lakeland Community College, Gingerbread, 8613 Mayfield Rd., Chesterland, OH 44026; (216) 729-COOK, (888) 434-5987, Fax (216) 729-6459, E-mail LPSCInc@msn.com.

OWENS COMMUNITY COLLEGE
Toledo

This 2-year college offers a 2-year AAB degree in Food Service Management. Program started 1968. Accredited by NCA. Calendar: semester. Curriculum: core. 35 semester credit hours of culinary courses required. Admission dates: August, January, June. Total enrollment: 38. 100% of applicants accepted. 55% enrolled part-time. Student to teacher ratio 18:1. 95% obtain employment within 6 months. Facilities: production kitchen and dining room.

COURSES: Food service management. 300 hours of cooperative work experience in summer.

FACULTY: 1 full-time, 4 part-time.

COSTS: Application deadlines: August, January, June. Admission requirements: assessment of reading, writing, and math skills. 3 $1,000 scholarships awarded last year. No on-campus housing.

CONTACT: Marty Johnson, Dept. Chair, Owens Community College, HRI, P.O. Box 10,000 - Oregon Rd., Toledo, OH 43699-1947; (419) 661-7214, Fax (419) 661-7665, E-mail mjohnson@owens.cc.oh.us.

SINCLAIR COMMUNITY COLLEGE
Dayton/Year-round

This college offers a 2-year Associate Degree in Hospitality Management. Program started 1993. Calendar: quarter. Curriculum: core. 97 credit hours of culinary courses required. Total enrollment: 150. 100% of applicants accepted. 30% of students receive financial aid. 20% under age 25, 60% age 25-44, 20% age 45 or over. Student to teacher ratio 20:1. 100% obtain employment within 6 months. Facilities: 3 kitchens, 150-seat dining room, classrooms.

COURSES: Food preparation, garde manger, butchery & fish management, pastry & confectionery, classical foods, baking.

FACULTY: 2 full-time, 5 part-time. Qualifications: certified by ACF and NRA.

COSTS: Tuition in-county $31, in-state $49. Admission requirements: high school diploma or GED.

LOCATION: Downtown Dayton.

CONTACT: Steven Cornelius, Dept. Chair, Sinclair Community College, Hospitality Management, 444 W. Third St., Dayton, OH 45402-1460; (513) 449-5197, Fax (513) 449-4530, E-mail scorneli@sinclair.edu

UNIVERSITY OF AKRON
Akron
This university offers a 2-year certificate/AAS degree. Program started 1968. Accredited by State. Admission dates: fall, spring, summer. Total enrollment: 245. Student to teacher ratio 18:1. 95% obtain employment within 6 months.
COURSES: Externship provided.
FACULTY: 11 full-time.
COSTS: Annual tuition in-state $2,430, out-of-state $5,970.
CONTACT: Jan Eley, Coordinator, University of Akron, Hospitality Management, Gallucci Hall #104, Akron, OH 44325; (330) 972-7026, Fax (330) 972-5101.

UNIVERSITY OF TOLEDO
Toledo
This university offers a 2-year AAS degree. Program started 1980. Accredited by NCA. Admission dates: quarterly. Total enrollment: 30. Student to teacher ratio 5:1.
COURSES: Externship provided.
FACULTY: 1 full-time, 1 part-time.
COSTS: Annual tuition approximately in-state $2,610, out-of-state $3,400.
CONTACT: Benita Wong, University of Toledo, Food Svc. Mgmt./Culinary Arts, Scott Park Campus, Toledo, OH 43606; (419) 530-3335, Fax (419) 537-3194.

OKLAHOMA

GREAT PLAINS AREA VOCATIONAL TECHNICAL CENTER
Lawton/August-May
This institution offers an 18-month certificate. Program started 1971. Accredited by NCA. Calendar: semester. Curriculum: core. 1,080 hours of culinary courses required. Admission dates: open. Total enrollment: 50. 50 enrollees each admission period. 10% of students receive financial aid. 90% under age 25, 10% age 25-44,. Student to teacher ratio 18:1. 90% obtain employment within 6 months.
COURSES: Schedule: 8am-4pm weekdays.
FACULTY: 2 full-time.
COSTS: Annual tuition $300. Admission requirements: high school diploma or equivalent.
CONTACT: Sue Maree, Great Plains Area Vocational Technical Center, Commercial Food Svcs./Fast Foods Mgmt., 4500 W. Lee Blvd., Lawton, OK 73505; (405) 355-6371, Fax (405) 357-6658.

MERIDIAN TECHNOLOGY CENTER
Stillwater/August-May
This institution offers a 1,050-hour certificate. Program started 1975. Accredited by state. Calendar: semester. Curriculum: core. 1,050 hours of culinary courses required. Admission dates: August. Total enrollment: 36. Student to teacher ratio 18:1. Facilities: 1 kitchen, 1 classroom, 2 restaurants.
COURSES: Schedule: 30 hours/week, 10 months.
FACULTY: 3 full-time.
COSTS: Annual tuition in-district $1,250, out-of-district $2,500. Admission requirements: assessment, interview.
CONTACT: Karim Farajollahi, Asst. Supt., Meridian Technology Center, Commercial Food Production, 1312 S. Sangre Rd., Stillwater, OK 74074; (405) 377-3333, Fax (405) 377-9604.

OKLAHOMA STATE UNIVERSITY
Okmulgee

This college offers a 24-month AAS and 20-month diploma in Food Service Management. Program started 1946. Accredited by NCA. 50 credit hours of culinary courses required. Admission dates: August, January, April. Total enrollment: 120. 35 enrollees each admission period. 90% of applicants accepted. 65% of students receive financial aid. 10% enrolled part-time. 70% under age 25, 20% age 25-44, 10% age 45 or over. Student to teacher ratio 16:1. 90% obtain employment within 6 months. Facilities: include 4 kitchens and 4 classrooms.

COURSES: Pastry production, food preparation, garde manger, hot food production, meat identification, dining room management, nutrition, and general education courses. Schedule: Monday-Friday, 6 hours/day, 12 months/year. Externship provided. Continuing education: advanced cooking and sauces, beginning cake decoration, meat identification.

FACULTY: 4 full-time. Qualifications: 5 years experience, college level culinary arts, ACF certified.

COSTS: Annual tuition in-state $44 per credit hour, out-of-state $110. Admission requirements: admission test. On-campus housing: 1,000 spaces, average cost $200-$250 per month.

LOCATION: The 2,000-student campus is in a small town, 45 miles from Tulsa.

CONTACT: Dean Daniel, Department Head, Oklahoma State University, Hospitality Services Technology, 1801 E. 4th St., Okmulgee, OK 74447; (918) 756-6211, Fax (918) 756-1315.

PIONEER AREA VOCATIONAL TECHNICAL SCHOOL
Ponca City

This institution offers a 1-year certificate. Program started 1972. Accredited by NCA. Total enrollment: 36. Student to teacher ratio 6:1. 100% obtain employment within 6 months.

COURSES: Externship provided.

FACULTY: 3 full-time.

COSTS: Annual tuition $400. Admission requirements: high school diploma or equivalent.

CONTACT: Steve Ellenwood, Pioneer Area Vocational Technical School, Commercial Foods, 2101 N. Ash, Ponca City, OK 74601; (405) 762-8336, Fax (405) 765-5101.

SOUTHERN OKLAHOMA AREA VOC. TECHNICAL SCHOOL
Ardmore

This institution offers a 2-year certificate. Program started 1966. Accredited by State. Total enrollment: 40. Student to teacher ratio 20:1.

FACULTY: 1 full-time, 2 part-time.

COSTS: Annual tuition in-district $0, out-of-district $1,600.

CONTACT: J.W. Reese, Southern Oklahoma Area Vocational Technical School, Culinary Arts, 2610 San Noble Pkwy., Ardmore, OK 73401; (405) 223-2070, Fax (405) 226-9389.

OREGON

INTERNATIONAL SCHOOL OF BAKING
Bend/Year-round

This school offers 1- to 2-day customized courses that focus on European bread and pastries. Established in 1986. Total enrollment: 1 or 2/course. Facilities: modern baking facility.

COURSES: Cover ingredient function, troubleshooting, all types of European breads and pastries. Students can select their own curriculum. Schedule: 8-hour daily hands-on sessions.

FACULTY: Director Marda Stoliar has taught European bread making since 1965, owned a French bakery, and is a baking consultant in China, Hong Kong, and Macau for U.S. Wheat Associates.

COSTS: From $300-$400/day/student. Half is due 30 days prior; balance is due at class. A list of nearby lodging is provided on request.

LOCATION: In Oregon's Cascade Mountains, a 3-minute drive from downtown Bend, 15 minutes from the Redmond Oregon Airport.

CONTACT: Marda Stoliar, International School of Baking, 1971 NW Juniper Ave., Bend, OR 97701; (503) 389-8553, Fax (503) 389-3736; E-mail domocorp@empnet.com, URL http://www.empnet.com/domocorp/

LANE COMMUNITY COLLEGE
Eugene/September-June

This independent college offers a 1-year certificate and a 2-year AAS degree in Culinary Arts and Culinary option. Program started 1976. Calendar: quarter. Curriculum: core. 107 credit hours of culinary courses required. Admission dates: open. Total enrollment: 85-105. 25-50 enrollees each admission period. 100% of applicants accepted. 60-70% of students receive financial aid. 3% enrolled part-time. 15% under age 25, 60% age 25-44, 25% age 45 or over. Student to teacher ratio 18:1. 95% obtain employment within 6 months. Facilities: include 2 kitchens, 1 dining room, deli/bake shop, and 4 to 6 classrooms.

COURSES: Introduction to foods, restaurant lab, buffet, baking, sanitation, safety, menu planning, and general education courses. Schedule: 25-32 hours/week. Externship: 325-450 hour, in commercial, institutional, or single proprietor settings. Post-graduate.

FACULTY: 3 full-time, 3 part-time. Qualifications: ACF certifications with BS, AAS degrees, and training from European cooking schools. Includes Willie Kealoha, Guy Plaa, Don Savoie, Wendy McDaniel, Peter Lohr, Duane Partain.

COSTS: Annual tuition $600-$900 per term. Other fees: lab fees, student fees. Admission requirements: limited enrollment. Average off-campus housing cost: $350-$800 per month.

CONTACT: Willie Kealoha, Lane Community College, Culinary Food Service and Hospitality Program, 4000 E. 30th Ave., Eugene, OR 97405-0640; (503) 747-4501, Fax (503) 744-4159.

LINN-BENTON COMMUNITY COLLEGE
Albany/September-June

This college offers a 2-year AAS degree in Culinary Arts/Hospitality Services with Chef Training Option. Program started 1973. Accredited by NASC. Calendar: quarter. Curriculum: core. 82-86 credit hours of culinary courses required. Admission dates: September, January, March. Total enrollment: 30. 15 enrollees each admission period. 100% of applicants accepted. 50% of students receive financial aid. 5% enrolled part-time. 50% under age 25, 50% age 25-44,. Student to teacher ratio 5:1. 100% obtain employment within 6 months. Facilities: include bakery production facility, restaurant.

COURSES: Chef training. Schedule: 7 hours/day, Monday-Thursday. Fellowships awarded.

FACULTY: 6 full-time. Includes S. Anselm, M. Whitehead, M. Young.

COSTS: Annual tuition in-state $1,500, out-of-state $5,355. Application fee $20. Approximately $300 for tools and uniforms. Application deadlines: September. Admission requirements: high school diploma or equivalent. Off-campus housing cost is $250/month.

LOCATION: The 16,000-student campus is in a small town setting 24 miles from Salem and 42 miles from Eugene.

CONTACT: Scott Anselm, Linn-Benton Community College, Culinary Arts/Restaurant Mgmt. c/o Aux. Serv., 6500 SW Pacific Blvd., Albany, OR 97321; (503) 917-4385, Fax (503) 917-4395, E-mail anselm@gw.lbcc.cc.or.us.

WESTERN CULINARY INSTITUTE
Portland/Year-round *(See display ad page 85)*

This private school offers a 12-month accelerated diploma program in Culinary Arts. Established in 1983. Accredited by ACFEI, ACCSCT. Calendar: non standard. Curriculum: culinary. 92 credit hours of culinary courses required. Admission dates: every 6 weeks. Total enrollment: 410. 40 enrollees each admission period. 85% of applicants accepted. 80% of students receive financial aid. 48% under age 25, 49% age 25-44, 3% age 45 or over. Student to teacher ratio 15-30:1 (labs). 97% obtain employment within 6 months. Facilities: include up-to-date, well-equipped kitchens and an open-to-the-public restaurant.

COURSES: Curriculum is 80% participation, based on the principles of Escoffier with emphasis on modern techniques & trends. The 18 courses include culinary fundamentals, purchasing and cost control, intl. cuisines, nutrition, baking and pastry, and wines. Schedule: the 1,491-hour program consists of 44 weeks of instruction and 6-week internship. Monday-Friday. 6-week internship in an approved foodservice operation.

FACULTY: The 18-member faculty is made up of individuals with international experience and training, many of whom have won culinary awards.

COSTS: Tuition $13,265, which includes cutlery, uniforms, and lab fees. A $25 nonrefundable application fee and $100 enrollment fee are required. Financial aid and payment arrangements must be made prior to first class. Admission requirements: high school diploma or equivalent. Admissions representatives assist in finding suitable lodging.

LOCATION: Near Portland State University in downtown Portland.

CONTACT: Mary Harris, Director of Admissions, Western Culinary Institute, Admissions Dept., 1316 S.W. 13th Ave., Portland, OR 97201; (800) 666-0312, (503) 223-2245, Fax (503) 223-0126.

PENNSYLVANIA

BUCKS COUNTY COMMUNITY COLLEGE
Newtown/Year-round

This college offers a 2-year AA degree and a 3-year degree/apprenticeship program. Program started 1968. Accredited by MSA. 60-63 credit hours for degree of culinary courses required. Total enrollment: 180. 40 enrollees each admission period. 80% enrolled part-time. Student to teacher ratio 15-18:1. 90% obtain employment within 6 months. Facilities: include kitchen, dining room, lab, computer labs.

COURSES: Intensive field-related work structure. 200 hour co-op, 400-hour summer internship for HRIM students.

FACULTY: 2 full-time, 4 part-time. Qualifications: ACF-certification and degree preferred.

COSTS: Tuition $66 per credit-hour in-county, $132 per credit-hour out-of-county. Application deadlines: May. Admission requirements: high school diploma or GED, college placement tests. 4 scholarships awarded last year averaging $250-$500 each.

LOCATION: 20 miles north of Philadelphia.

CONTACT: Earl R. Arrowood, Jr., Bucks County Community College, Business Dept., Swamp Rd., Newtown, PA 18940; (215) 968-8241, Fax (215) 968-8005, E-mail arrowoode@bucks.edu.

COMMUNITY COLLEGE OF ALLEGHENY COUNTY
Pittsburgh

This college offers a 2-year AAS degree in Culinary Arts. Program started 1974. Accredited by MSA. 63 credit hours of culinary courses required. Admission dates: fall, spring. Total enrollment: 60. 20-15 enrollees each admission period. 25% of applicants accepted. 50% of students receive financial aid. 50% enrolled part-time. 60% under age 25, 38% age 25-44, 2% age 45 or over. Student to teacher ratio 2:1. 90% obtain employment within 6 months.

COURSES: Include basic foods, culinary artistry, nutrition, baking, costing. Externship: 240 hours.

FACULTY: 12 faculty members with bachelor's degree or CEC.

COSTS: Tuition is $1,020/semester in-county, $2,040 out-of-county, $3,060 out-of-state. Payment at registration. Cancellations prior to class receive full refund. Application deadlines: open.

CONTACT: Willie Stinson, CEC, AAC, Community College of Allegheny County, Culinary Arts/Allied & Health Science, 808 Ridge Ave., Jones Hall, Rm. 012, Pittsburgh, PA 15212; (412) 237-2698, Fax (412) 237-4678.

COMMUNITY COLLEGE OF ALLEGHENY COUNTY
Monroeville

This college offers a 2-year certificate/AAS degree. Program started 1967. Accredited by MSA. Admission dates: open. Total enrollment: 175. Student to teacher ratio 15:1. 100% obtain employment within 6 months.

COURSES: Externship provided.

FACULTY: 2 full-time, 5 part-time.

COSTS: Annual tuition approximately in-state $1,272, out-of-state $2,545. Admission requirements: high school diploma or equivalent.

CONTACT: Linda Sullivan, Community College of Allegheny County, Hospitality Mgmt./Culinary Arts, 595 Beatty Rd., Monroeville, PA 15146; (412) 327-1327.

HARRISBURG AREA COMMUNITY COLLEGE
Harrisburg/Year-round

This college offers a 2-year certificate/AA program in Culinary Arts. Program started 1965. Accredited by MSA, ACBSP. Calendar: semester. Curriculum: core. Admission dates: August, January. Total enrollment: 250. 48 enrollees each admission period. 76% of applicants accepted. 50% of students receive financial aid. 46% enrolled part-time. 32% under age 25, 58% age 25-44, 10% age 45 or over. Student to teacher ratio 15-20:1. 100% obtain employment within 6 months. Facilities: include production kitchen, demonstration kitchen, culinary classroom, weekly luncheons.

COURSES: Culinary arts, quantity foods, and 20 other courses. Schedule: 12-15 credit hours/semester. Externship: 3-month, salaried.

FACULTY: 3 full-time, 3 part-time. Qualifications: bachelor's degree, master's preferred, certifiable by ACF.

COSTS: Annual tuition in-state $116.50 per credit hour, out-of-state $177.75 per credit hour. $25 to enroll. Equipment and uniforms about $265. Tuition deposit $100 after acceptance. Refund policy: full refund before start of classes. Application deadlines: May 1 for fall. Admission requirements: admission test and portfolio.

LOCATION: The 3 campuses (Harrisburg, Lebanon, and Lancaster) with 11,000 students are 100 miles from Philadelphia.

CONTACT: Marcia W. Shore, M.S.Ed., CCE, Harrisburg Area Community College, Hotel, Restaurant, Institutional Management Dept., One HACC Dr., Harrisburg, PA 17110; (717) 780-2674, Fax (717) 231-7670.

HIRAM G. ANDREWS CENTER
Johnstown/Year-round

This proprietary school offers a 4-month diploma and 18-month AST in Kitchen Helper, Cook's/Baker's Helper, and AST Culinary. Program started 1975. Accredited by ACCSCT. Calendar: trimester. Curriculum: core. Admission dates: every 4 months. Total enrollment: 30. 12-15 enrollees each admission period. 40% of students receive financial aid. 25% under age 25, 50% age 25-44, 25% age 45 or over. Student to teacher ratio 15:1. 100% obtain employment within 6 months. Facilities: include 3 kitchens and classrooms and a part-time restaurant.

COURSES: Baking, sanitation, nutrition, food preparation, cooking methods and techniques, menu writing, and table service. Schedule: 6.25 hours/day. Externship: 2 months.

FACULTY: 3 full-time.

COSTS: Annual tuition $35 per day. Admission requirements: high school diploma or equivalent and admission test. On-campus housing: 400 spaces.

LOCATION: The 66-acre campus is in a suburban setting 80 miles from Pittsburgh.

CONTACT: Jack B. Demuth, Voc. Supv., Hiram G. Andrews Center, Culinary Arts Program, 727 Goucher St., Johnstown, PA 15905; (814) 255-8288.

INDIANA UNIVERSITY OF PENNSYLVANIA
Academy of Culinary Arts

1-800-727-0997

E-mail: culinary-arts@grove.iup.edu   www.iup.edu/cularts/index.html

- Accelerated 16-month program
- Affordable, state univ. instructional cost
- 100% job placement
- 36 credits towards B.S. degree
- Accredited by ACFEI Accrediting Commission

INDIANA UNIVERSITY OF PENNSYLVANIA
Indiana/Year-round   *(See display ad above)*

This university offers a 16-month certificate in Culinary Arts. Established in 1989. Accredited by MSA, ACFEI. Calendar: semester. Curriculum: culinary. Admission dates: September. 100 enrollees each admission period. 75% of applicants accepted. 90% of students receive financial aid. 90% under age 25, 8% age 25-44, 2% age 45 or over. Student to teacher ratio 13:1. 99% obtain employment within 6 months. Facilities: include 5 production and 2 demonstration kitchens, computer lab, classroom.

COURSES: Include cuisine and pastry preparation, purchasing, nutrition, wine appreciation, international cuisine, and menu and facility design. Schedule: 37.5 hours/week. A 450-hour salaried externship is required.

FACULTY: 6 full-time, 2 part-time. Includes Albert Wutsch, director, Timothy Brown, Hilary DeMane, Thomas Vieli, Clifford Klinger, Gary Fitting, and Mindy Wygonik.

COSTS: Tuition $4,500/semester. Application fee is $30. A $104 activity fee is required each semester. Instructional deposit (upon acceptance) is $75. All deposits are nonrefundable. Admission requirements: high school diploma or equivalent. 15 scholarships awarded last year averaging $1,500 each. On campus lodging is $2,528 for a double room, $900 single supplement.

LOCATION: 25 miles north of Indiana in rural Punxsutawney.

CONTACT: Kelly Barry, Admissions Coordinator, IUP Academy of Culinary Arts, Reschini Building, IUP, Indiana, PA 15705; (800) 727-0997, Fax (412) 357-6200, E-mail culinary-arts@grove.iup.edu, URL http://www.iup.edu/cularts/index.html.

INTERNATIONAL CULINARY ACADEMY
Pittsburgh/Year-round   *(See display ad page 89)*

This division of Computer Tech offers 2-year (1,800-clock-hour) AST degrees in Culinary and Pastry Arts. Established in 1989. Accredited by ACICS, ACFEI. Calendar: year-round. 1,800 hours of culinary courses required. Admission dates: March, August, October. Total enrollment: 350. 75 enrollees each admission period. 80% of applicants accepted. 80% of students receive financial aid. 20% under age 25, 60% age 25-44, 20% age 45 or over. Student to teacher ratio 25:1. 92% obtain employment within 6 months. Facilities: include 5 professional-size commercial kitchens (includes pastry kitchen), classrooms, resource center, executive dining room, student lounge.

COURSES: Culinary arts covers kitchen & storeroom operations, hands-on preparation & presentation of classic international cuisines. Pastry arts covers baking principles, international & specialty breads, pies & cakes. French pastry, & advanced decoration & design. Schedule: daily, Monday-Thursday. Salaried externship.

FACULTY: 8 ACF-Certified Culinary Educators.

COSTS: Tuition for each program is $16,550, which includes uniforms, books, equipment and all food costs. The $50 registration fee is refundable prior to start of class. Admission requirements: high school diploma or equivalent and aptitude test. Student housing is offered.

LOCATION: In Pittsburgh's Golden Triangle, overlooking the Allegheny River.

CONTACT: Debbie Love, Director of Admissions, International Culinary Academy-A Division of Computer Tech, 107 Sixth St., Fulton Bldg., Pittsburgh, PA 15222; (412) 471-9330, Fax (412) 391-4224, E-mail info@intlculinary.com, URL http://www.intlculinary.com.

MERCYHURST COLLEGE - THE CULINARY AND WINE INSTITUTE
North East/Year-round

This 4-year college offers a 2-year AA degree in Culinary Arts. Program started 1995. Accredited by MSA. Calendar: trimester. Curriculum: core. 36 credit hours of culinary courses required. Admission dates: September, November, March. Total enrollment: 50. 30-35 enrollees each admission period. 57% of applicants accepted. 100% of students receive financial aid. 18% enrolled part-time. 30% under age 25, 60% age 25-44, 10% age 45 or over. Student to teacher ratio 15:1. 100% obtain employment within 6 months. Facilities: 3 professional kitchens, including bake shop, 30-seat dining room, receiving and storage area.

COURSES: Specialized courses in wines and wine-making; emphasis on management and thinking skills along with traditional culinary courses. Schedule: 8am-5pm weekdays. 420-hour paid externship after 3 terms in quality dining facility.

FACULTY: 5 full-time, 5 part-time, with industry experience and educational background. Includes Stephen C. Fernald, CCC, David Wells, Deborah Hilbert, MS, RD, William Kunz, Douglas Moorhead.

COSTS: Tuition is $6,934/year. Fees are $1,500, books $450. Admission requirements: high school graduate or equivalent, math and English placement test. 45 scholarships awarded last year averaging $1,250 each. 41 loans granted last year averaging $3,850 each. On-campus dormitories available at $4,000 room and board/year.

LOCATION: 15 miles from Erie.

CONTACT: James Theeuwes, Director of Admissions, McAuley Division, Mercyhurst College, The Culinary and Wine Institute, 501 E. 38th St., Erie, PA 16546; (800) 825-1926 #2238, Fax (814) 824-2179.

NORTHAMPTON COMMUNITY COLLEGE
Bethlehem/Year-round

This college offers a 45-week specialized diploma in Culinary Arts. Program started 1993. Accredited by MSA. Calendar: trimester. Curriculum: culinary. 45 credit hours of culinary courses required. Admission dates: March, September. Total enrollment: 46. 23 enrollees each admission period. 100% of applicants accepted. 30% of students receive financial aid. 30% under age 25, 60% age 25-44, 10% age 45 or over. Student to teacher ratio 20:1. 98% obtain employment within 6 months.

COURSES: Baking, pastry, nutrition, pantry, skill development, garde manger, and restaurant operations. Schedule: full-time, 30 hours/week.

FACULTY: 4 full-time. Qualifications: culinary degree and 10 years professional experience. Includes Duncan Howden and Scott Kalamar.

COSTS: Annual tuition in-state $1,770, out-of-state $5,500. Other fees: uniforms $150, meals $115, books $200, tools $100. Tuition deposit $50. Refund policy: 100% prior to start date. Admission requirements: high school diploma or equivalent. 1 scholarship awarded last year at $1,000. On-campus housing: 145 spaces; average cost: $2,400 per year. Average off-campus housing cost: $350 per month.

LOCATION: 65 miles southeast of Philadelphia.

CONTACT: Duncan Howden, Assoc. Professor, Northampton Community College, Culinary Arts, 3835 Green Pond Rd., Bethlehem, PA 18017; (610) 861-5593, Fax (610) 861-5093.

ORLEANS TECHNICAL INSTITUTE
Philadelphia

This institution offers a 30-week specialized diploma. Program started 1978. Admission dates: open. 85% obtain employment within 6 months.

FACULTY: 1 to 2 full-time.

COSTS: Annual tuition $3,950. Admission requirements: admission test.

CONTACT: Chandra Davis, Orleans Technical Institute, Culinary Arts Dept., 1330 Rhawn St., Philadelphia, PA 19111; (215) 728-4488.

PENNSYLVANIA COLLEGE OF TECHNOLOGY
Williamsport/Year-round

This college offers a 2-year AAS degree in Food/Hospitality Management, Baking/Pastry Arts, and Culinary Arts. Program started 1981. Accredited by MSA, ACFEI. Calendar: semester. Curriculum: core. 72-73 credit hours of culinary courses required. Admission dates: fall, spring. Total enrollment: 80. 72 enrollees each admission period. 95% of applicants accepted. 86% of students receive financial aid. 15% enrolled part-time. Student to teacher ratio 12:1. 100% obtain employment within 6 months. Facilities: include 10 kitchens & classrooms, retail restaurant, catering & meeting facilities, theatre lounge, bed & breakfast, conference center, retreat center.

COURSES: Cooking, baking, service, sanitation, supervision, management skills, and nutrition. Schedule: Monday-Saturday; part-time and evening options available. Semester-long internships provided.

FACULTY: 10 full-time, 4 part-time. Qualifications: college degree and ACF certification. 70% ACFEI certified, 100% certifiable.

COSTS: Annual tuition in-state $181 per credit hour, out-of-state $215 per credit hour. Application fee $20. Lab fee $13. Tuition deposit $100. Refund policy: 100% first week, 30% second and third. Application deadlines: open admission. Admission requirements: high school diploma or equivalent and admission test. Off-campus housing cost: $250-$450 per month.

LOCATION: The 53-acre, 4,300-student campus is in a small town 200 miles from Pittsburgh and Philadelphia.

CONTACT: Chet Schuman, Director of Admissions, Pennsylvania College of Technology, Hospitality Division, One College Avenue, Williamsport, PA 17701-5799; (717) 326-3761 #4761, Fax (717) 327-4503, URL http://www.pct.edu.

PENNSYLVANIA CULINARY
(See display ad page 92)   **Pittsburgh/Year-round**

This private institution offers a 16-month associate degree in Specialized Technology in the School of Culinary Arts (73 credits) and in Specialized Business in the School of Restaurant Management (78 credits). Established in 1986. Accredited by ACCSCT, ACFEI. Admission dates: January, March, May, June, September, October. Total enrollment: 1,100+. 135 enrollees each admission period. 85% of applicants accepted. 93% of students receive financial aid. 70% under age 25, 27% age 25-44, 3% age 45 or over. Student to teacher ratio 40:1 (lectures); 20:1 (labs). 100% obtain employment within 6 months. Facilities: include 8 kitchens, 6 lecture classrooms, computer classroom, library, and full-service restaurant.

COURSES: Include food preparation and skill development, advanced classical and international cuisine, nutrition, wines and spirits, menu planning and dining room management. Schedule: 25-30 hours/week on one of 5 schedules, including an evening schedule. Both programs include a 16-week paid externship, nationwide.

FACULTY: 23 certified chefs, maitres d'hotel, and educators. Supervised by International Culinary Olympics gold medalist Dieter Kiessling, CMC, AAC.

COSTS: Tuition $4,030 per semester. Application fee $50. Application deadlines: rolling. Admission requirements: high school diploma or equivalent; foodservice experience desirable. On-campus housing for 250 students. Off-campus lodging ranges from $200-$400 per month.

LOCATION: Pittsburgh's cultural district.

CONTACT: Charles Day, Director of Admissions, Pennsylvania Institute of Culinary Arts, 717 Liberty Ave., Pittsburgh, PA 15222; (800) 432-2433, Fax (412) 566-2434, URL http://www.pacul.com.

THE RESTAURANT SCHOOL
(See also page 210) (See display ad page 93)   **Philadelphia/Year-round**

This proprietary institution offers 15-month programs leading to a specialized associate degree in Chef Training (1,806 clock-hours), Pastry Chef Training (2,200 clock-hours), Restaurant Management, and Hotel Management. Established in 1974. Accredited by ACCSCT. Calendar: quarter. Curriculum: core. Admission dates: March, October. 216 enrollees each admission period. 90% of applicants accepted. 95% of students receive financial aid. 10% enrolled part-time. 25% under age 25, 50% age 25-44, 25% age 45 or over. Student to teacher ratio 24:1. 98% obtain employment within 6 months. Facilities: include 4 classroom kitchens, two 100-seat demonstration kitchens, pastry shop, and restaurant.

COURSES: Chef Training combines classroom instruction with apprenticeship; includes business management, dining room service, wines, nutrition. Pastry Chef Training covers culinary & baking skills, baking science, business management, career development. Students produce inventory for school pastry shop. 1,080-hour apprenticeship in an area restaurant. Both programs include a 7-day tour of France.

FACULTY: The 12-member professional faculty have a minimum of 12 years' experience in the restaurant, foodservice, and hotel industry.

COSTS: The $15,800 cost of each program includes trip to France. Other fees $1,000. Application and deposit are $200. Admission requirements: high school diploma or equivalent, reference letters, basic achievement test. On-campus dorm is provided for 17 students.

LOCATION: Restored mansion in University City.

CONTACT: Lynne R. Byck, Director of Admissions, The Restaurant School, 4207 Walnut St., Philadelphia, PA 19104; (215) 222-4200 #6, Fax (215) 222-4219.

The Restaurant School

One of the Nation's First
to specialize in fine restaurants, hotels and resorts

Four Nationally Renowned Majors:
Hotel Management ◆ Chef Training
Pastry Chef Training ◆ Restaurant Management

❑ Specialized Associate Degree in just 15 months
❑ Tuition includes a tour of France or a Cruise and Resort tour
❑ Housing available in historic victorian townhouse

Call now for a school catalogue
4207 Walnut Street Philadelphia, PA 19104   215-222-4200 ext. 6

WESTMORELAND COUNTY COMMUNITY COLLEGE
Youngwood/Year-round

This college offers a 2- and 3-year AAS degree in Culinary Arts with apprenticeship option, 2-year Baking and Pastry degree, 1-semester Baking/Pastry/Deli certificate. Program started 1981. Accredited by ACFEI. Calendar: semester. Curriculum: core. 65-67 credit hours of culinary courses required. Admission dates: August, January. Total enrollment: 147. 121 enrollees each admission period. 100% of applicants accepted. 30% of students receive financial aid. 48.4% enrolled part-time. 62.3% under age 25, 32% age 25-44, 5.7% age 45 or over. Student to teacher ratio 15-20:1. 100% obtain employment within 6 months. Facilities: include 4 specially equipped kitchens and classroom projects simulate student-run restaurant.

COURSES: Garde manger, quantity foods, purchasing and storage, baking, food specialties, and hospitality marketing, as well as ACF Laurel Highlands Chapter Membership. Schedule: day and evening, 15-week fall and spring semesters and 6- and 12-week summer sessions. 1 semester externships and 3-year apprenticeships provided.

FACULTY: 4 full-time, 18 part-time. Qualifications: ACF certification, experience in field, academic requirements. Includes Mary B. Zappone, CCE, Marlene Scatena, RD, Cheryl Shipley, RD, and Carl Dunkel, CWC, CCE.

COSTS: Annual tuition in-county $1,419, out-of-county $2,838. Application fee is $10, lab fee $20. Refund policy: 100% during first week of term. Admission requirements: high school diploma or equivalent and admission test.

LOCATION: Southwestern Pennsylvania; 30 miles from Pittsburgh.

CONTACT: Mary Zappone, Westmoreland County Community College, Hospitality Dept., Armbrust Rd., Youngwood, PA 15697; (412) 925-4000, Fax (412) 925-4293, E-mail zapponm@astro.westmoreland.cc.pa.us.

PUERTO RICO

INSTITUTO DE EDUCACION UNIV.
Hato Rey/Year-round

This independent college-nonprofit organization offers a 12-15 month certificate program in Culinary Arts, Baking, and Food Service Specialist. Program started 1991. Accredited by ACCSCT. Calendar: trimester. Curriculum: culinary. 1,440 hours of culinary courses required. Admission dates: February, September. Total enrollment: 164 (culinary), 60 (baking). 50-60 enrollees each admission period. 95% of applicants accepted. 98% of students receive financial aid. 95% under age 25, 5% age 25-44,. Student to teacher ratio 20:1. 80% obtain employment within 6 months. Facilities: include 2 kitchens and classrooms.

COURSES: Include safety & hygiene, cooking methods, basic sauces, menu planning, bread formulas, cost production. Schedule: 3 blocks of 440 hours. Externship: 120 hours, nearby hotels, restaurants, and bakeries.

FACULTY: 6 full-time culinary, 2 full-time baking. Includes Chef Phillipe Chapuis.

COSTS: Admission requirements: high school diploma or equivalent.

CONTACT: Willie Lucca, Coordinator of Culinary Arts, Instituto de Educacion Univ., Culinary Arts Dept., Barbosa Ave. #404, Hato Rey, PR 00930; (787) 766-2443, (787) 767-2000, Fax (787) 767-4755.

INSTITUTO DEL ARTE MODERNO, INC.
Hato Rey

This institution offers a 1,000-hour certificate. Program started 1987. Accredited by ACCSCT. Admission dates: January, August. Total enrollment: 150. Student to teacher ratio 25:1.

FACULTY: 5 full-time.

COSTS: Annual tuition about $2,900. Admission requirements: high school diploma or equivalent.

CONTACT: Miriam Aponte, Instituto del Arte Moderno, Inc., Culinary Arts Dept., Ave. Monserrate FR-5, Villa Fontana, Carolina, PR 00630; (809) 769-7636.

RHODE ISLAND

JOHNSON & WALES UNIVERSITY
Providence/Year-round

This private nonprofit institution offers a 2-yr AAS degree in Culinary Arts and Baking & Pastry Arts, 2-yr AS degree program in Food & Beverage Mgmt, BS degree programs in Culinary Arts, Food Service Mgmt, Food Mktg., Food Service Entrepreneurship. Other degrees offered at different campus locations. Program started 1914. Accredited by NEASC, ACICS. Calendar: trimester. Curriculum: culinary, core. Admission dates: March, September, November. Total enrollment: 3,500+. 84%-100% of applicants accepted. 98% obtain employment within 6 months. Facilities: modern teaching facilities, including 5 student-run restaurants.

COURSES: Culinary Arts includes basic cooking & baking, classic & intl. cuisines, food preparation, nutrition, communication, menu design; Baking & Pastry includes basic ingredients, production techniques, French pastries, desserts, chocolate & sugar artistry. Schedule: 6 hours daily, Monday-Thursday; morning, afternoon, and evening options. Paid externship at a recognized facility. Student exchange program with École Superieure de Cuisine. Continuing education programs available.

FACULTY: 74 instructors.

Costs: Annual College of Culinary Arts tuition is $13,824. General fee is $375, orientation fee is $65. Annual, term, and monthly payment options. Application deadlines: rolling. Admission requirements: high school diploma or equivalent. Room and board are $4,983/year plus $609 for optional weekend meal plan.

Location: Near Providence's cultural and recreational facilities. Other campuses are located in South Carolina, Virginia, Florida and Colorado.

Contact: William Priante, Director, Culinary Admissions, Johnson & Wales University, College of Culinary Arts, 8 Abbott Park Place, Providence, RI 02903; (800) 342-5598 #4650, (401) 598-4650, Fax (401) 598-2948, E-mail admissions@jwu.edu, URL http://www.jwu.edu.

SOUTH CAROLINA

GREENVILLE TECHNICAL COLLEGE
Greenville/Year-round

This college offers a 1-year certificate and a 2-year degree in Food Service Management. Program started 1977. Accredited by ACFEI, SACS, ABSCP. Admission dates: quarterly. Total enrollment: 85. 5-10 enrollees each admission period. 7% of students receive financial aid. 5.5% enrolled part-time. Student to teacher ratio 15:1. Facilities: include kitchen and 3 classrooms.

Courses: A la carte, bake shop, buffet, nutrition, food production.

Faculty: 5 full-time, 2 part-time.

Costs: Tuition $500 per semester. Application fee $20. Refund policy: 100% during first week. Admission requirements: high school diploma or equivalent and admission test.

Location: The 8,700-student, 57-acre campus is in a suburban setting 150 miles from Atlanta and 170 miles from Charlotte.

Contact: Marge Condrasky, Food Science Dept. Head, Greenville Technical College, Food Science Dept., P.O. Box 5616, Station B, Greenville, SC 29606-5616; (864) 250-8404, Fax (864) 250-8506.

HORRY-GEORGETOWN TECHNICAL COLLEGE
Conway/Year-round

This college offers a 2-year degree in Culinary Arts Technology. Program started 1985. Accredited by SACS, ACFEI. 21 semester credit hours of culinary courses required. Admission dates: August, December, April. Total enrollment: 85. 35 enrollees each admission period. 100% of applicants accepted. 60% of students receive financial aid. 5% enrolled part-time. 20% under age 25, 70% age 25-44, 10% age 45 or over. Student to teacher ratio 10:1. 100% obtain employment within 6 months. Facilities: include 3 kitchens, 2 dining rooms and 2 restaurants.

Courses: Food production, sanitation, nutrition, a la carte, buffet, menu planning. Schedule: 8:00am-3:00pm weekdays. Externship provided. Continuing education courses available.

Faculty: 12 full- and part-time. Includes Dept. Head C. Catino, K. Gerba, G. Busch.

Costs: Tuition in-state $500 per semester, out-of-state $1,000 per semester. Application fee $10. Application deadlines: 2 weeks prior to registration. Admission requirements: high school diploma or equivalent and admission test. Average off-campus housing cost: $250-$350 per month.

Location: The 3,200-student campus is in a small town setting.

Contact: Carmen Catino, Dept. Head, Horry-Georgetown Technical College, Culinary Arts Dept., P.O. Box 1966, 2050 Hwy. 501 East, Conway, SC 29526; (803) 347-3186, Fax (803) 347-4207.

JOHNSON & WALES UNIVERSITY AT CHARLESTON
(See also page 94)   **Charleston/Year-round**

This nonprofit university offers an AAS degree in Culinary Arts, Food & Beverage Management, Hotel-Restaurant Management, Restaurant/Institutional Management; BS degrees in Food Service Management, Hospitality Management. Program started 1984. Accredited by ACICS, NEASC. Calendar: term. Curriculum: core. 99/193.5 quarter credit hours (AAS/BS) of culinary courses required. Admission dates: rolling. Total enrollment: 642. 85% of applicants accepted. 75% of students receive financial aid. 75% under age 25, 16.3% age 25-44, 7.7% age 45 or over. Student to teacher ratio 20:1. 98% obtain employment within 6 months. Facilities: 10 kitchens, 15 classrooms.

COURSES: Culinary Arts. Other required courses: cooperative education practicum. Schedule: Monday-Thursday, 25 hours/week, 9 months/year. Externship: 12 weeks, $5 per hour, resorts/hotels/restaurants.

FACULTY: 18 full-time, 2 part-time.

COSTS: Tuition is $11,760 for College of Culinary Arts, $9,960 for Hospitality College. Other costs: $375 general fee, $65 new student orientation fee. $100 tuition and $100 housing deposits. Annual, term or monthly payments. Application deadlines: rolling. Admission requirements: high school diploma or equivalent. Number and amount of scholarships awarded vary. Grant and award programs administered annually. On-campus housing: 124 apartment units; cost: $3,189. Off-campus housing cost: $375 per month and up.

CONTACT: Mary Hovis, Director of Admissions, Johnson & Wales University at Charleston, Office of Admissions, 701 E. Bay St., PCC Box 1409, Charleston, SC 29403; (800) 868-1522, (803) 727-3000, Fax (803) 763-3018, E-mail admissions@jwu.edu, URL http://www.jwu.edu.

TRIDENT TECHNICAL COLLEGE
Charleston/Year-round
This college offers a 4-semester diploma and associate degree in Culinary Arts. Program started 1986. Accredited by SACS, ACFEI. Admission dates: open. Total enrollment: 57. 30-35 enrollees each admission period. 40% of students receive financial aid. 5% enrolled part-time. 10% under age 25, 75% age 25-44, 15% age 45 or over. Student to teacher ratio 15:1. 100% obtain employment within 6 months. Facilities: include 10 kitchens and classrooms and student-run restaurant.

COURSES: Schedule: 8am-5pm. Continuing education: 6-10 courses per semester.

FACULTY: 3 full-time.

COSTS: Annual tuition $1,536 in-county, $1,776 out-of-county, $2,598 out-of-state. Application fee $20. Admission requirements: high school diploma or equivalent and admission test. Off-campus housing cost: $400 per month.

LOCATION: The 9,700-student campus is in downtown Charleston.

CONTACT: Betty Howe, Dean, Trident Technical College, Division of Hospitality & Tourism, P.O. Box 118067, HT-P, Charleston, SC 29423-8067; (803) 722-5541, Fax (803) 720-5614.

SOUTH DAKOTA

MITCHELL TECHNICAL INSTITUTE
Mitchell/September-May
This school offers an 18-month diploma, certificate, or AAS degree in Culinary Arts. Program started 1968. Accredited by NCA. Calendar: semester. Curriculum: culinary. Admission dates: February. Total enrollment: 40. 18-20 enrollees each admission period. 100% obtain employment within 6 months. Facilities: include 3 kitchens, 3 classrooms, a 54-seat restaurant.

COURSES: Program is being re-structured. New curriculum starts September, 1997. Schedule: 7:30am-3:30pm, 5 days/week.

FACULTY: 2 full-time.

COSTS: Annual tuition $1,260. Application fee $75. Other fees $80. Refund policy: 90% within 2 weeks. Admission requirements: high school diploma or equivalent and admission test. Off-campus housing cost $4,200.

CONTACT: John Weber, Mitchell Technical Institute, Cook/Chef, 821 N. Capitol, Mitchell, SD 57301; (605) 995-3030.

TENNESSEE

MEMPHIS CULINARY ACADEMY
Memphis/Year-round

This private school offers a 40-week diploma program that consists of 10-week basic, 5-week intermediate, and 15-week advanced courses based on classic French and European cuisines. Established in 1984. Student to teacher ratio 12-student classes.

COURSES: Include culinary skills, baking, nutrition, and kitchen rotation. Seminars in pastry, garde manger, kitchen management.

COSTS: Tuition is approximately $3,000 for the basic course, $300 for the intermediate and advanced courses, $3,600 for all three.

CONTACT: Joseph Carey, Memphis Culinary Academy, 1252 Peabody Avenue, Memphis, TN 38104; (901) 722-8892, Fax (901) 722-8893.

OPRYLAND HOTEL CULINARY INSTITUTE
Nashville/Year-round

This 3-year apprenticeship and associate degree program offers a 3-year certificate of Apprenticeship plus AAS degree through Volunteer State Community College. Established in 1987. Accredited by ACFEI. Curriculum: culinary, core. 70 semester credit hours of culinary courses required. Admission dates: August. Total enrollment: 50. 50 enrollees each admission period. 20-25% of applicants accepted. 100% of students receive financial aid. 50% under age 25, 50% age 25-44,. Student to teacher ratio varies. 100% obtain employment within 6 months. Facilities: Opryland Hotel.

COURSES: Schedule: varies.

FACULTY: Richard Gerst, CEC, Executive Chef; Dina Starks, M.S., R.D., Apprenticeship Coordinator.

COSTS: Tuition, fees, books, uniforms provided by Opryland. $500 admission fee payable 2 weeks prior to start, no refund thereafter. Application deadlines: March 1st. Admission requirements: high school diploma or GED; some college preferred. All students are on full scholarships awarded by Opryland Hotel. $400-$500/month; temporary housing available through Opryland Hotel.

LOCATION: Central Nashville.

CONTACT: Dina Starks, M.S., R.D., Culinary Apprenticeship Coordinator, Opryland Hotel Culinary Institute, 2800 Opryland Dr., Nashville, TN 37214; (615) 871-7765, Fax (615) 871-6942.

TEXAS

ART INSTITUTE OF HOUSTON
Houston/Year-round

(See display ad page 23)

This proprietary school offers an 18-month AAS degree in Culinary Arts. Program started 1992. Accredited by ACCSCT, ACFEI. Calendar: quarter. Curriculum: core. 63 quarter credit hours of culinary courses required. Admission dates: January, April, July, September. Total enrollment: 200. 40 enrollees each admission period. 65% of applicants accepted. 75% of students receive financial aid. 10% enrolled part-time. 33% under age 25, 50% age 25-44, 17% age 45 or over. Student to teacher ratio 20:1. 90% obtain employment within 6 months. Facilities: include 3 teaching kitchens, bakery, deli, open-to-the-public restaurant.

COURSES: Basic cooking, food production, garde manger, a la carte, baking, nutrition, sanitation, purchasing and cost controls, dining room management, management by menu. Other required courses: 24 hours of general education. Schedule: 30 hours/week for 18 months, full-time. 2 internships/externships are required, in fifth and sixth quarters.

FACULTY: 12 full- and part-time. Includes Michael F. Nenes, CEC, CCE, Larry Matson, CWC,

Peter Lehr, CEC, Charles Prince, CEC, Cheryl Gordon Lewis.

Costs: Tuition is $3,285/quarter. Application fee $50, general fee $125, lab fee $250/quarter, supply kit $625. Tuition deposit $100. Application deadlines: rolling. Admission requirements: high school diploma or equivalent and interview. Off-campus housing, currently 30 units, cost is $1,130/quarter.

Location: The 1,100-student, 70,000-square-foot facility is in the primary business area of Houston, the Galleria.

Contact: Rick Simmons, Director of Admissions, Art Institute of Houston, 1900 Yorktown, Houston, TX 77056; (800) 275-4244, (713) 623-2040, Fax (713) 966-2700, URL http://www.aii.edu.

DEL MAR COLLEGE
Corpus Christi/Year-round

This state-supported institution offers a 1-year certificate, 2-year AAS degree, and 4-year BS degree in Restaurant Management and Culinary Arts. Program started 1963. Accredited by SACS. Admission dates: June, September, January. Total enrollment: 175. 15 enrollees each admission period. 100% of applicants accepted. 40% of students receive financial aid. 30% enrolled part-time. 30% under age 25, 60% age 25-44, 10% age 45 or over. Student to teacher ratio 15:1. 100% obtain employment within 6 months. Facilities: include 3 restaurants, 4 classrooms and laboratory.

Courses: Saucier, garde manger, elementary baking, advanced pastry, and restaurant management. Schedule: varied, day and night.

Faculty: 4 full-time, 11 part-time.

Costs: Annual tuition in state $1,000, out-of-state $1,800. Admission requirements: high school diploma or equivalent and admission test. Average off-campus housing cost: $250-$350.

Contact: D.W. Haven, Professor & Chair, Del Mar College, Dept. of Hospitality Management, Baldwin at Ayers, Corpus Christi, TX 78404; (512) 886-1734, Fax (512) 886-1795.

EL CENTRO COLLEGE
Dallas/Year-round

This college offers a 2-year AAS degree in Food and Hospitality Services. Program started 1971. Accredited by SACS. Calendar: semester. Curriculum: core. Admission dates: January, August, May-June. Total enrollment: 400. 350-400 enrollees each admission period. 100% of applicants accepted. 40% of students receive financial aid. 65% enrolled part-time. 30% under age 25, 50% age 25-44, 20% age 45 or over. Student to teacher ratio 20-35:1. 90% obtain employment within 6 months. Facilities: include 3 kitchens, 4 classrooms, pastry/bakery labs.

Courses: Schedule: 20-25 hours/week, part-time options available. Apprenticeship-ACF available.

Faculty: 4 full-time, 8 part-time.

Costs: Annual tuition in-county $500, out-of-county $900. Admission requirements: high school diploma or equivalent and admission test. 25 scholarships awarded last year averaging $600-$1,000 each.

Location: Downtown/Center City.

Contact: C. Gus Katsigris, El Centro College, Food & Hospitality Services Institute, Main at Lamar Streets, Dallas, TX 75202; (214) 860-2202, Fax (214) 860-2335.

GALVESTON COLLEGE
Galveston/Year-round

This college offers a 2-year certificate and a 2-year AAS degree in Food Preparation, Management Development, Culinary Hospitality Management. Program started 1987. Accredited by SACS. Calendar: semester. Curriculum: core. Admission dates: January, September. Total enrollment: 15-45. 10-12 enrollees each admission period. 75% of applicants accepted. 100% of students receive financial aid. 10% enrolled part-time. 25% under age 25, 60% age 25-44, 15% age 45 or over. Student to teacher ratio 15:1. 70% obtain employment within 6 months. Facilities: include kitchen, bake shop and classroom.

COURSES: Schedule: 8am-6pm weekdays, 12 months/year; part-time and evening options available. Externship provided.

FACULTY: 2 full-time. Includes Bruce Ozga, Director. Qualifications: Texas Chefs Assn., Galveston Chapter Director; bachelor's degree in Foodservice Management, Johnson & Wales University.

COSTS: Annual tuition $279 in-state, $459 out-of-state. Admission requirements: high school diploma or equivalent and admission test.

CONTACT: Phil Harris, Galveston College, Culinary Arts Dept., 4015 Avenue Q, Galveston, TX 77550; (409) 763-6551 #304, Fax (409) 762-9367.

LE CHEF COLLEGE OF HOSPITALITY CAREERS
Austin/Year-round

This independent nonprofit institution offers a 17-month (59 credit-hour) Culinary Arts program and 2-year (72 credit-hour) AAS degree in Culinary Arts and Food and Beverage Management. Established in 1985. Accredited by ACFEI, SACS. Curriculum: culinary, core. Admission dates: continuous. Total enrollment: 100. 60% of applicants accepted. Student to teacher ratio 25:1 or more. 94% obtain employment within 6 months. Facilities: a culinary lab, 2 classrooms, audio/visual library, storage room, student lounge.

COURSES: The 1-year program covers cuisine and pastry preparation, pantry production and garde manger, production and control, and planning and presentation. The degree program includes culinary and food and beverage courses as well as general education courses. Schedule: 5 hours daily, 4 days/week; morning, noon, and evening options. The degree program includes a 720-hour paid externship. Short courses and seminars are also offered.

FACULTY: Founder/President Ronald Boston, CDM, CFBE, was Texas Chef of the Year; V.P. Joseph Schroeder; Chefs Andre Touboulle, Chris Wilson, Matt Collins CWC; 5-member general ed faculty with advanced degrees.

COSTS: Tuition is $12,882 for Culinary Arts, $20,229 for the degree program. A $50 nonrefundable registration fee is required. 30-day satisfaction guarantee. Thereafter, refunds are pro-rated according to state and federal regulations. Admission requirements: high school diploma, GED, or (Culinary Arts Program only) pass test to show proof of Ability to Benefit.

LOCATION: North central Austin, convenient to transportation, less than 30 minutes from Texas Hill Country.

CONTACT: Le Chef College of Hospitality Careers, 6020 Dillard Circle, Austin, TX 78752; (888) LeChef, (512) 323-2511, Fax (512) 323-2126, E-mail LeChef@onr.com, URL http://www.onr.com/chef/lechef.html.

ODESSA COLLEGE
Odessa

This college offers a 2-year certificate/AAS degree. Program started 1990. Admission dates: open. Total enrollment: 35-50. 75% of applicants accepted. Student to teacher ratio 10-15:1. 100% obtain employment within 6 months.

COURSES: Externships provided.

FACULTY: 5 full-time.

COSTS: Annual tuition in-state $550, out-of-state $800-$1,000. Admission requirements: high school diploma or equivalent and admission test.

CONTACT: Jennifer Cochran, Director, Odessa College, Culinary Arts, 201 W. University, Odessa, TX 79764; (915) 335-6583, Fax (915) 335-6860.

SAN JACINTO COLLEGE NORTH
Houston

This college offers a 2-year and 3-year AAS degree. Program started 1986. Accredited by SACS. Admission dates: September, January. Total enrollment: 20-30. 90% of applicants accepted.

Student to teacher ratio 12:1. 50% obtain employment within 6 months.
FACULTY: 3 full-time.
CONTACT: George J. Messinger, San Jacinto College North, Chef's Apprenticeship Training, 5800 Uvalde, Houston, TX 77049; (713) 459-7150, Fax (713) 459-7100.

ST. PHILIP'S COLLEGE
San Antonio/Year-round
This college offers a 2-year AAS degree and 3-year apprenticeship in Hospitality Management. Program started 1979. Accredited by SACS. Admission dates: August, January, June. Total enrollment: 250. 250 enrollees each admission period. 80% of students receive financial aid. 50% enrolled part-time. Student to teacher ratio 50:1. 85% obtain employment within 6 months. Facilities: include 7 kitchens and classrooms and a restaurant.
FACULTY: 5 full-time.
COSTS: Annual tuition in-state $500, out-of-state $900.
CONTACT: William Thornton, St. Philip's College, Hospitality Operations, 2111 Nevada, San Antonio, TX 78203; (210) 531-3315.

UTAH

SALT LAKE COMMUNITY COLLEGE
Salt Lake/Year-round
This college offers a 2-year full-time and 3-year part-time Apprentice Chef program. Program started 1984. Accredited by NASC, ACFEI. Calendar: quarter, semester. Curriculum: culinary, core. Admission dates: rolling. Total enrollment: 110. 40-50 enrollees each admission period. 90% of applicants accepted. 40-50% enrolled part-time. Student to teacher ratio 14:1. 100% obtain employment within 6 months. Facilities: include kitchen, 8 classrooms, video/reference library.
COURSES: Food preparation, sanitation, baking, menu design, and nutrition. Other required courses: AAS degree requires 24 credits in general education. Schedule: full-time Monday-Friday, 5 hours daily; part-time Mondays only 2pm-8pm; Aug.-Nov. and Jan.-Apr. Continuing education: specialized classes and workshops available for culinary professionals.
FACULTY: 8 full-time and part-time.
COSTS: In-state full-time tuition: $482 per quarter, $1,446 per year; part-time program rates: $77 per class, $154 per semester, and $308 per year. A $20 application fee ($5 for part-time program) is required. Admission requirements: high school diploma or equivalent and admission test. Average off-campus housing cost $300 per month.
CONTACT: Joe Mulvey, Apprenticeship Director, Salt Lake Community College, P.O. Box 30808, Salt Lake City, UT 84130-0808; (801) 957-4066, Fax (801) 957-4612.

UTAH VALLEY STATE COLLEGE
Orem/August-April
This college offers a 2-year AAS degree in Culinary Arts. Program started 1992. Accredited by NASC. Admission dates: open. Total enrollment: 35. 15 enrollees each admission period. 90% of applicants accepted. 80% of students receive financial aid. 10% enrolled part-time. 50% under age 25, 50% age 25-44, 10% age 45 or over. Student to teacher ratio 12:1. 100% obtain employment within 6 months. Facilities: include 3 kitchens, 3 classrooms, restaurant & food service operation.
COURSES: Food production, nutrition, sanitation, garde manger, and buffet. Schedule: 8am-1pm daily. Externship: 5-week, salaried, in hotels or restaurants.
FACULTY: 3 full-time. Qualifications: certified chef, work experience.
COSTS: Annual tuition in state $579, out-of-state $2,080. Other fees: $130. Refund policy: 100% first week, 75% second week, 50% third week. Admission requirements: high school diploma. Average off-campus housing cost $200 per month.

CONTACT: Greg Forte, Utah Valley State College, Business, 800 W. 1200 South, Orem, UT 84058; (801) 222-8000, Fax (801) 226-5207.

VERMONT

NEW ENGLAND CULINARY INSTITUTE
(See also page 216) (See display ad page 102)   **Montpelier and Essex/Year-round**

This private institution offers a 2-year AOS degree program in Culinary Arts and an upper level 1-1/2-year Bachelors degree in Service & Management. Established in 1979. Accredited by State of Vermont, ACCSCT. Curriculum: culinary. Admission dates: August, November, March, May. Total enrollment: 448. 84 enrollees each admission period. 90% of applicants accepted. 70% of students receive financial aid. 70% under age 25, 28% age 25-44, 2% age 45 or over. Student to teacher ratio 7:1. 100% obtain employment within 6 months. Facilities: 11 kitchens, 14 classrooms. Montpelier: 2 restaurants, bake shop, catering, banquet dept, 2 cafeterias. Essex: 2 restaurants, catering, banquet, bakery.

COURSES: 75% of class time is spent preparing food for the public. Remaining class time covers cooking theory, food & wine history, wine & beverage management, tableservice, service management & purchasing. At least 45 hours of a structured physical fitness plan. Schedule: 8-10 hours/day, 5 to 6 days/week. Each year consists of a 24-week on-campus residency, followed by an 18- to 20-week internship.

FACULTY: The 40-member faculty are chosen on the basis of experience and teaching ability. The Institute has a 19-member administrative staff and 3 advisory boards. Includes Jim Dodge, Michel LeBorgne, David Miles, and Jozef Herrewyn.

COSTS: The annual $19,365 fee includes room, board, and uniforms. Other costs include a nonrefundable $25 application fee, $550 for books and equipment. $200 dormitory deposit. A $100 enrollment deposit is due within 30 days of acceptance, first tuition payment of $5,570 is due 75 days before registration. Admission requirements: high school diploma or equivalent and 3 reference letters; advanced placement second year students must pass an exam. Dormitory lodging is available for 160 students; other nearby lodging is $300-$500 per month.

LOCATION: The rural Montpelier campus is 3 hours from Boston. The Essex Junction campus is at The Inn at Essex country hotel, in a Burlington suburb.

CONTACT: New England Culinary Institute, Admissions Department, 250 Main St., Dept. S, Montpelier, VT 05602; (802) 223-6324, Fax (802) 223-0634.

VIRGINIA

ATI CAREER INSTITUTE – SCHOOL OF CULINARY ARTS
Falls Church/Year-round

This private school offers a 12-month diploma in Culinary Arts. Program started 1990. Accredited by COE. Calendar: 6-week terms. Curriculum: core. Admission dates: every 6 weeks. Total enrollment: 250. 48 enrollees each admission period. 80% of applicants accepted. 80% of students receive financial aid. 25% under age 25, 65% age 25-44, 10% age 45 or over. Student to teacher ratio 18:1. 95% obtain employment within 6 months. Facilities: include 3 kitchens, 5 classrooms.

COURSES: Culinary theory, nutrition, sanitation, sauces and entrees, baking, garde manger, hospitality management, and electronic accounting. Schedule: 5 hours/day, Monday-Friday. Externship: 12-weeks required.

FACULTY: 10 full-time. Guest chefs are frequent lecturers.

COSTS: Tuition is $13,783, including books and equipment. Nonrefundable application fee: $65. Admission requirements: high school diploma or equivalent. Off-campus housing is $600/month.

LOCATION: The 20,000 square-foot campus, on the Beltway, is 15 miles from Washington, D.C.

CONTACT: John W. Martin, Director of Culinary Arts, ATI Career Institute, School of Culinary Arts, 7777 Leesburg Pike, Ste. 100 South, Falls Church, VA 22043; (703) 821-8570, Fax (703) 556-9892, URL jmarti7031@aol.com.

JOHNSON & WALES UNIVERSITY AT NORFOLK
(See also page 94)   **Norfolk/Year-round**

This university offers a 12- and 18-month AAS degree in Culinary Arts. Program started 1986. Accredited by NEASC, ACICS. Calendar: 12 week terms. Curriculum: core. 99 quarter credit hours of culinary courses required. Admission dates: rolling. 81% of applicants accepted. 1% enrolled part-time. Student to teacher ratio 14.5:1. Facilities: newly-equipped kitchens, mixology and dining room labs, classrooms, computer lab.

FACULTY: 30 instructors.

COSTS: Annual tuition is $11,562. General fee is $375, orientation fee is $65. Annual, term, and monthly payment options. Application deadlines: rolling. Admission requirements: high school diploma or equivalent.

CONTACT: Tammy Jaxtheimer, Director of Admissions, Johnson & Wales University, 2428 Almeda Ave., Norfolk, VA 23513; (757) 853-3508 #251, Fax (757) 857-4869, E-mail admissions@jwu.edu, URL http://www.jwu.edu.

WASHINGTON

ART INSTITUTE OF SEATTLE – SCHOOL OF CULINARY ARTS
(See display ad page 23)   **Seattle/Year-round**

This 2-year college offers a 6-quarter AOS degree in Culinary Arts. Founded 1996. Accredited by ACCSCT. Calendar: quarter. Curriculum: core. 1,300 hours of culinary courses required. Admission dates: rolling. Total enrollment: 250. 60 enrollees each admission period. 65% of applicants accepted. 70% of students receive financial aid. 35% under age 25, 55% age 25-44, 10% age 45 or over. Student to teacher ratio 17:1. Facilities: newly constructed kitchens/classroom space.

COURSES: First 3 quarters cover culinary arts, last 3 allow student to specialize in either baking & pastry, Northwest foods & wines, or edible visual arts. Schedule: Monday-Friday, am and pm classes. Internship program with restaurants & resorts in the Western U.S.

FACULTY: 176 instructors with industry experience.

COSTS: Total tuition is $19,530. $50 nonrefundable application fee. Application deadlines: rolling. Admission requirements: high school diploma and admissions interview. Scholarships and loans available. Student housing available.

LOCATION: On the waterfront overlooking Puget Sound.

CONTACT: Doug Worsley, VP, Dir. of Admissions, Art Institute of Seattle, Admissions Dept., 2323 Elliott Ave., Seattle, WA 98121, USA; (800) 275-2471, (206) 448-6600, Fax (206) 448-2501, E-mail adm@ais.edu.

BELLINGHAM TECHNICAL COLLEGE
Bellingham/September-July

This 2-year technical college offers certificates of completion in Culinary Arts and Baking, Pastry, & Confections. Program started 1957. Accredited by ACFEI, NACS. Calendar: quarter. Curriculum: core. 1,488/1,290 hours (culinary/baking) of culinary courses required. Admission dates: quarterly and other times with instructor's permission. Total enrollment: 52. 40 enrollees each admission period. 30% of students receive financial aid. 20% enrolled part-time. 10% under age 25, 80% age 25-44, 10% age 45 or over. Student to teacher ratio 20:1. 94% obtain employment within 6 months. Facilities: instructional space, industrial kitchen/bake shop, fine dining restaurant, deli/baking.

FACULTY: Michael Baldwin, CEC, and William Pifer, Master Baker, AIB.

COSTS: Quarterly tuition and fees are $647 for Culinary Arts, $525 for Baking, Pastry &

Confections. $30 application fee. Full refund prior to class, refunds pro-rated during first 3 weeks, no refund after 20th day. Application deadlines: anytime during school year. Admission requirements: 18 years or older, high school graduate, placement test. 3 scholarships awarded last year averaging $3,500 each. 9 loans granted last year averaging $1,462-$3,216 each.

LOCATION: Northwestern Washington, 86 miles from Seattle, 80 miles from Vancouver, BC.

CONTACT: Michael Baldwin, Culinary Arts instructor, Bellingham Technical College, Culinary Arts, 3028 Lindberg Ave., Bellingham, WA 98225; (360) 715-8350, Fax (360) 676-2798, E-mail jBlume@CTC.edu.

CLARK COLLEGE CULINARY ARTS PROGRAM
Vancouver/Year-round

This community college offers 1-year certificate and 2-year AAS degree programs in Cooking, Baking, and Bakery and Restaurant Management. Program started 1958. Calendar: quarter. Curriculum: culinary, core. Admission dates: January, March, June, September. Total enrollment: 80. 30 (cooking), 20 (baking) enrollees each admission period. 80% of applicants accepted. 50% of students receive financial aid. 25% under age 25, 65% age 25-44, 10% age 45 or over. Student to teacher ratio 5:1. 95% obtain employment within 6 months. Facilities: the modernized facility operates like a large hotel kitchen. Students make all food products sold on-campus and prepare meals for evening functions.

COURSES: Cooking includes food preparation, advanced meat cutting, ice carving, wine appreciation, cake decoration & pastillage. Baking includes fundamentals the 1st year & specialized courses the 2nd year; includes theory, merchandising, bake shop management. Schedule: 8am to 1:30pm, Monday-Thursday. 5-week internships available.

FACULTY: 12-member faculty. Includes cooking instructors Larry Mains, CEC, George Akau, CCE, and Glenn Lakin and baking instructors Per Zeeverg and Jean Williams.

COSTS: Cost for each 2-year program is $2,700 in-state, $10,092 out-of-state. Program can be 9 or 18 months. Pay by quarter. No refund after third week of a 10-week quarter. Application deadlines: first-come, first-served basis during any quarter. Admission requirements: high school diploma or equivalent. 35 scholarships awarded last year averaging $200-$500 each. 30 loans granted last year for full-tuition. Off-campus housing provided close to campus.

LOCATION: Minutes from Portland, Oregon.

CONTACT: Larry Mains, Clark College, Culinary Arts, 1800 E. McLoughlin Blvd., Vancouver, WA 98663-3598; (360) 992-2143, Fax (360) 992-2861.

EDMONDS COMMUNITY COLLEGE
Lynwood/October-July

This college offers a 6-quarter ATA or certificate. Program started 1988. Accredited by state. Calendar: quarter. Curriculum: core. 850 hours of culinary courses required. Admission dates: fall, winter, spring. Total enrollment: 45. 15 enrollees each admission period. 90% of applicants accepted. 25% of students receive financial aid. 15% under age 25, 80% age 25-44, 5% age 45 or over. Student to teacher ratio 20:1. 100% obtain employment within 6 months. Facilities: kitchen, classroom, restaurant.

COURSES: Contemporary Northwest cuisine, fine dining service, restaurant/food service management. Other required courses: service and management. Schedule: 7:30am-2pm weekdays, 10 months. Externship provided.

FACULTY: 2 full-time, 2 part-time. Includes Walter Bronowitz, CWC, CCE; John Casey.

COSTS: Annual tuition in-state $435/quarter, out-of-state $1,313/quarter. Application deadlines: 1 month prior to start of quarter. Admission requirements: high school diploma or equivalent.

LOCATION: The 12,000-student suburban campus is 20 minutes from Seattle.

CONTACT: Walter N. Bronowitz, Chef/Instructor, Edmonds Community College, Culinary Arts, 20000 - 68th Ave. West, Lynnwood, WA 98036; (206) 640-1329, Fax (206) 771-3366.

NORTH SEATTLE COMMUNITY COLLEGE
Seattle/September-June

This college offers a 1-year certificate and a 2-year AAS degree in Culinary Arts, Hospitality and Restaurant Cooking. Program started 1970. Accredited by NASC. Calendar: quarter. Curriculum: core. Admission dates: quarterly. Total enrollment: 80. 25 enrollees each admission period. 90% of applicants accepted. 25% of students receive financial aid. 10% under age 25, 80% age 25-44, 10% age 45 or over. Student to teacher ratio 18:1. 90% obtain employment within 6 months. Facilities: include 2 kitchens and classrooms, restaurant, bakery.

COURSES: Restaurant cooking and commercial cooking. Schedule: 7:30am-2pm.

FACULTY: 4 full-time.

COSTS: Annual tuition $1,750 in-state, $6,000 out-of-state. Uniform, supplies $750. Application deadlines: rolling. Admission requirements: high school diploma or equivalent and admission test. Average off-campus housing cost: $750/month.

CONTACT: Darrell Mihara, North Seattle Community College, Culinary Arts Dept., 9600 College Way North, Seattle, WA 98103-3599; (206) 527-3779, Fax (206) 527-3635.

OLYMPIC COLLEGE
Bremerton/September-May

This college offers a 3-quarter certificate and 2-year AAS degree. Program started 1978. Accredited by State. 1,170 hours of culinary courses required. Admission dates: continuous enrollment. Total enrollment: 38. 20 enrollees each admission period. 85% of applicants accepted. 60% of students receive financial aid. 15% enrolled part-time. 30% under age 25, 70% age 25-44, 15% age 45 or over. Student to teacher ratio 16:1. 90% obtain employment within 6 months. Facilities: central kitchen, one classroom, two restaurants.

COURSES: Classical cooking, restaurant baking, dining room service, restaurant management. Other required courses: math, English, computers, business. Schedule: 33 hours/week, 9 months/year. Continuing education: English composition, computers, business management.

FACULTY: 2 full-time.

COSTS: Annual tuition: in-state $1,296, out-of-state $5,094. $50 lunch fee quarterly. Admission requirements: high school diploma or equivalent. Average off-campus housing cost: $275/month.

LOCATION: Puget Sound (west), 60 miles from Seattle or 1-hour ferry ride.

CONTACT: Steve Lammers, Chef Instructor, Olympic College, Commercial Cooking/Food Service, 16th & Chester, Bremerton, WA 98310-1688; (360) 478-4576, Fax (360) 478-4650.

RENTON TECHNICAL COLLEGE
Renton/Year-round

This college offers a 1,620-hour certificate/AAS degree in Culinary Arts/Chef and Culinary Arts/Baker. Program started 1968. Accredited by ACFEI, NASC. Admission dates: open. Total enrollment: 30. 10-30 enrollees each admission period. 100% of applicants accepted. 30% of students receive financial aid. 20% under age 25, 75% age 25-44, 5% age 45 or over. Student to teacher ratio 12:1. 100% obtain employment within 6 months. Facilities: include kitchen, bakery, demonstration classroom and 3 restaurants.

FACULTY: 2 instructors and 5 assistants full-time. Includes Chef Instructor David Pisegna, CEC, CCE, and Baking Instructor Erhard Volcke, CMB.

COSTS: Tuition $530 per quarter. Registration fee: $25. Other costs: books, uniforms. Tuition deposit: $500-$530 per quarter. Refund policy: 80% within first 5 days, 40% sixth to fifteenth day. Admission requirements: high school diploma or equivalent and admission test.

LOCATION: 20 minutes south of Seattle.

CONTACT: Kristi Frambach, Associate Dean, Renton Technical College, Culinary Arts Dept., 3000 N.E. Fourth St., Renton, WA 98056; (206) 235-2352, Fax (206) 235-7832.

SEATTLE CENTRAL COMMUNITY COLLEGE
Seattle/Year-round

This college offers a 6-quarter Culinary Arts certificate, a 3-quarter Pastry certificate, and a 7-quarter Hospitality Management AA degree. Program started 1942. Accredited by ACFEI. Calendar: quarter. Curriculum: culinary. 1,750 hours of culinary courses required. Admission dates: quarterly. Total enrollment: 100-125. 30 enrollees each admission period. 85% of applicants accepted. 30% of students receive financial aid. 2% enrolled part-time. 29.8% under age 25, 41.1% age 25-44, 29.1% age 45 or over. Student to teacher ratio 20:1. 97% obtain employment within 6 months. Facilities: include 3 kitchens, 8 classrooms, cafeteria, cafe, gourmet restaurant.

COURSES: Professional cooking, baking, specialty desserts and breads, nutrition, buffet catering, costing,, computerized menu planning, management, ice carving, business law. Schedule: 8am-2:30pm, Tuesday-Friday. Last quarter internship in local restaurants or hotels.

FACULTY: 7 full-time, 2 part-time. Includes Keijiro Miyata, CEC, Linda Hierholzer, CCE, Diana Dillard, CIA graduate, David Madayag, CEC, John Balmores, and Melissa Dallas, JD.

COSTS: In-state tuition $460/quarter, out-of-state $1,830/quarter. Full refund first week of class. Application deadlines: 2 weeks before quarter. Admission requirements: admissions test or college transcripts. 20-25 scholarships awarded for each program. Off-campus housing cost: $300-$500/month.

LOCATION: Campus is located in Capitol Hill district of Seattle, a short walk to downtown.

CONTACT: Joy Gulmon-Huri, Program Manager, Seattle Central Community College, Hospitality & Culinary Arts, 1701 Broadway, Mailstop 2BE2120, Seattle, WA 98122; (206) 587-5424, Fax (206) 344-4323, E-mail jgulmon@seaccc.sccd.ctc.edu, URL http://www.edison.sccd.ctc.edu/instruct/programs.html.

SKAGIT VALLEY COLLEGE
Mt. Vernon/September-May

This college offers a 1-year certificate and a 2-year ATA degree in Culinary Arts/Hospitality Management. Program started 1979. Accredited by state, ACF. Calendar: quarter. Curriculum: core. Admission dates: open. Total enrollment: 60. 6 enrollees each admission period. 100% of applicants accepted. 60% of students receive financial aid. 20% under age 25, 70% age 25-44, 10% age 45 or over. Student to teacher ratio 15:1. 100% obtain employment within 6 months. Facilities: include kitchen, classrooms, restaurant.

COURSES: Schedule: 5 days/per week, 9 months/year. Externship provided.

FACULTY: 3 full-time.

COSTS: Annual tuition in-state $1,125, out-of-state $5,500. Admission requirements: high school diploma or equivalent.

LOCATION: 60 miles north of Seattle.

CONTACT: Lyle Hildahl, Director, Skagit Valley College, Culinary Arts-Hospitality Management, 2405 College Way, Mt. Vernon, WA 98273; (360) 428-1109, Fax (360) 428-1612.

SOUTH PUGET SOUND COMMUNITY COLLEGE
Olympia

This college offers a 2-year ATA degree, Food Service Tech. and Food Service Management. Accredited by state. Calendar: quarter. 119 credit hours of culinary courses required. Admission dates: September, January, April, June. Total enrollment: 40. 12 enrollees each admission period. 85% of applicants accepted. 60% of students receive financial aid. 10% enrolled part-time. 80% under age 25, 15% age 25-44, 5% age 45 or over. Student to teacher ratio 20-25:1.

FACULTY: 2 full-time, 4 part-time.

COSTS: Annual tuition in-state $32 per credit hour, out-of-state $124 per credit hour. Admission requirements: high school diploma or equivalent and admission test.

CONTACT: Fred Durinski, Food Service Director, South Puget Sound Community College, 2011 Mottman Rd., SW, Olympia, WA 98502; (360) 754-7711, #347, Fax (360) 664-0780.

SOUTH SEATTLE COMMUNITY COLLEGE
Seattle/Year-round

This college offers an 18-month certificate/AAS degree in Food Service Production and Pastry and Specialty Baking. Program started 1975. Accredited by ACFEI, NASC. Curriculum: core. Admission dates: September, January, March, June. Total enrollment: 130-160. 100% of applicants accepted. 25% of students receive financial aid. 25% under age 25, 65% age 25-44, 10% age 45 or over. Student to teacher ratio 15:1. 98% obtain employment within 6 months. Facilities: include 4 kitchens, 6 classrooms and 2 waited service dining rooms.

COURSES: Food preparation and theory, restaurant baking, purchasing, meat cutting, and general education. Schedule: 7am-1:40pm, Monday-Friday.

FACULTY: 7 full-time, 8 part-time. Qualifications: extensive industry experience.

COSTS: Annual tuition in-state $1,304, out-of-state $5,224. Off-campus housing cost: $400-$500 monthly.

LOCATION: The 35-acre campus is in a suburban setting.

CONTACT: Daniel Cassidy, Associate Dean, South Seattle Community College, Hospitality & Food Science Division, 6000 16th Ave. S.W., Seattle, WA 98106-1499; (206) 764-5344, Fax (206) 764-5393.

SPOKANE COMMUNITY COLLEGE
Spokane/September-June

This college offers a 2-year AAS degree in Culinary Arts, Pastry, and Baking. Program started 1962. Accredited by NASC, ACFEI. Calendar: quarter. Curriculum: culinary, core. Admission dates: March. Total enrollment: 75-100. 30 enrollees each admission period. 95% of applicants accepted. 40% of students receive financial aid. 70% under age 25, 25% age 25-44, 5% age 45 or over. Student to teacher ratio 20:1. 90% obtain employment within 6 months. Facilities: include 2 kitchens, bake shop, pastry shop, 6 classrooms, restaurant.

COURSES: Schedule: 7:30am-2:30pm weekdays, 9 months/year. Externship: 3-6 months, in area hotels and restaurants.

FACULTY: 4 full-time.

COSTS: Annual tuition approximately $1,400. Admission requirements: high school diploma or equivalent and admission test.

CONTACT: Doug Fisher, Spokane Community College, Culinary Arts Dept., 1810 N. Greene St., Spokane, WA 99207; (509) 533-7283, (509) 533-7372, Fax (509) 533-8059.

WEST VIRGINIA

SYMPOSIUM FOR PROF. FOOD WRITERS AT THE GREENBRIER
White Sulphur Springs/March

This resort sponsors a 2-day conference for professional food writers that consists of lectures, seminars, informal discussions, and receptions. 90 enrollees each admission period. Facilities: the Mobil 5-star, AAA 5-diamond Greenbrier resort.

COURSES: Topics include food writing for newspapers and magazines, recipe development and writing for cookbooks, culinary history, and food writing for film.

FACULTY: About 15 noted professionals. 1997 speakers include Nancy Barr, Heidi Haughy Cusick, Don Fry, Harold McGee, Andres Schloss, Marie Simmons, and guests Julia Child and Anne Willan.

LOCATION: The Allegheny Mountains, 15 minutes from the airport in Lewisburg, 75 miles from Roanoke, Va. Amtrak service available.

CONTACT: Lynne Bostic, Symposium Coordinator, Symposium for Professional Food Writers, The Greenbrier, White Sulphur Springs, WV 24986; (800) 624-6070, (304) 536-7892, Fax (304) 536-7893.

WEST VIRGINIA NORTHERN COMMUNITY COLLEGE
Wheeling

This college offers a 2-year certificate/AAS degree. Program started 1975. Accredited by NCA. Admission dates: open. Total enrollment: 26. 100% of applicants accepted. Student to teacher ratio 9:1. 85% obtain employment within 6 months.

FACULTY: 3 full-time.

COSTS: Annual tuition in-state $42 per credit hour, out-of-state $120 per credit hour. Admission requirements: high school diploma or equivalent and admission test.

CONTACT: James Panacci, West Virginia Northern Community College, Culinary Arts Dept., College Square, Wheeling, WV 26003; (304) 233-5900, Fax (304) 233-5900 # 4402.

WISCONSIN

CHIPPEWA VALLEY TECHNICAL COLLEGE
Eau Claire

This college offers a 2-year degree. Program started 1978. Accredited by NCA. Admission dates: February. Total enrollment: 36. 100% of applicants accepted. Student to teacher ratio 18:1. 90%-95% obtain employment within 6 months.

FACULTY: 3 full-time.

COSTS: In-state $45 per credit hour, out-of-state $295 per credit hour. Admission requirements: high school diploma or equivalent.

CONTACT: Culinary Director, Chippewa Valley Technical College, Restaurant & Hotel Cookery; Hospitality Mgmt., 620 W. Clairemont Ave., Eau Claire, WI 54701-1098; (715) 833-6200.

FOX VALLEY TECHNICAL INSTITUTE
Appleton/September-May

This independent institution offers a 2-year diploma/degree in Culinary Arts and Food Service Production. Program started 1972. Accredited by NCA. Calendar: semester. Curriculum: core. 68 credit hours of culinary courses required. Admission dates: fall, winter. Total enrollment: 100. 15-25 enrollees each admission period. 90% of applicants accepted. 60%-80% of students receive financial aid. 50% enrolled part-time. 80% under age 25, 15% age 25-44, 5% age 45 or over. Student to teacher ratio 6-12:1. 100% obtain employment within 6 months. Facilities: include 5 kitchens and classrooms including full quantity production kitchen, full bakery, full restaurant kitchen, and student-run restaurant.

COURSES: Quantity production, catering, restaurant cooking, baking, deli operations, and general education courses. Schedule: 7 hours/day, 4-5 days/week. Externship provided.

FACULTY: 9 full-time. Includes R. Kimball, H. Dean, A. Exenberger, M. Davis, M. Lang.

COSTS: Annual tuition in-state $2,100, out-of-state $10,000. Application fee $20. Refund policy: 100% before classes and pro-rated after classes begin. Application deadlines: August, November. Admission requirements: high school diploma or equivalent and admission test. 15 scholarships awarded last year. On-campus housing: limited spaces; average cost: $250 per month. Average off-campus housing (shared apartments) cost: $150 per month.

CONTACT: Donna Elliott, Dean, Service Occupations, Fox Valley Technical Institute, Culinary Arts Dept., 1825 N. Bluemound Dr., Appleton, WI 54913; (414) 735-5638, Fax (414) 735-2582, URL http://www.foxvalley.tec.wi.us.

MADISON AREA TECHNICAL COLLEGE
Madison/August-May

This college offers a 2-year AAS degree in Culinary Arts. Program started 1950. Accredited by ACFEI. Calendar: semester. Curriculum: core. 71 credit hours of culinary courses required. Admission dates: August, January. Total enrollment: 60. 36 enrollees each admission period. 75% of applicants accepted. 50% of students receive financial aid. 20% enrolled part-time. 60% under age 25, 35% age 25-44, 5% age 45 or over. Student to teacher ratio 15:1. 100% obtain employment within 6 months. Facilities: include 3 large labs and classrooms.

COURSES: Baking, sanitation, nutrition, gourmet foods, decorative foods, food costs and purchasing analysis, and general education. Schedule: 7:30am-2:30pm weekdays.

FACULTY: Qualifications: certified by state and ACFEI. Includes D. McNicol, M. Egan, P. Short.

COSTS: Tuition in-state $51.20/credit hour. Advanced registration fee is $50. Refund policy: 80% first 14 days, 60% next 15 to 28 days. Application deadlines: July 1 for fall, November 15 for spring. Admission requirements: high school diploma or equivalent and admission test. Average off-campus housing cost is $400-$870.

CONTACT: Mary G. Hill, Chairperson, Madison Area Technical College, Culinary Trades Dept., 3550 Anderson St., Madison, WI 53704; (608) 246-6368, Fax (608) 246-6316.

MILWAUKEE AREA TECHNICAL COLLEGE
Milwaukee

This college offers a 2-year AAS degree. Program started 1955. Accredited by NCA, ACFEI. Admission dates: August, January. Total enrollment: 150. 80 enrollees each admission period. Student to teacher ratio 20:1. 98% obtain employment within 6 months.

FACULTY: 11 full-time.

COSTS: Annual tuition in-state $2,260, out-of-state $8,244. Admission requirements: high school diploma or equivalent and admission test.

CONTACT: Culinary Director, Milwaukee Area Technical College, Culinary Arts, 700 West State St., Milwaukee, WI 53233; (414) 297-6255.

MORAINE PARK TECHNICAL COLLEGE
Fond du Lac/August-May

This college offers a 2-year AA degree in Culinary Arts, a 1-year technical diploma in Food Service Production, Culinary Basics certificate, and Deli/Bakery certificate. Program started 1980. Accredited by NCA. Calendar: semester. Curriculum: core. 1,140 hours of culinary courses required. Admission dates: July-August, November-December, flexible. Total enrollment: 36. 16 enrollees each admission period. 90% of applicants accepted. 40% of students receive financial aid. 30% enrolled part-time. 20% under age 25, 65% age 25-44, 15% age 45 or over. Student to teacher ratio 6:1. 95% obtain employment within 6 months. Facilities: include 3 kitchens, 2 classrooms.

COURSES: Food production, sanitation, meat analysis, restaurant management, catering. Other Required courses: various general education (270 hours). Schedule: varied, mornings. Continuing education: school food service, deli-bakery, IDDA certification.

FACULTY: 3 full-time, 2 part-time. Includes Ron Speich, David Weber, Mary Martin.

COSTS: Tuition for the Culinary Arts degree is $2,700 per year, $1,260 for the certificate program, and $2,470 for the 1-year diploma. Tuition deposit $100. Application deadlines: May. Admission requirements: high school diploma, placement test, and interview. 3 scholarships awarded last year averaging $2,000 each. 6 loans granted last year averaging $500-$1,000 each. Off-campus housing cost: $300 per month.

LOCATION: East central Wisconsin.

CONTACT: Donna Dixon, Moraine Park Technical College, Service Occupations Division, 235 North National Ave., P.O. Box 1940, Fond du Lac, WI 54936-1940; (414) 924-3289, Fax (414) 929-2478, URL http://www.job.careernet.org.

NICOLET AREA TECHNICAL COLLEGE
Rhinelander/August-May

This college offers a 1-year diploma in Food Service Production, 2-year associate degree in Culinary Arts, certificate in Baking, Catering, Kitchen Assistant, Food Service Management, School Food Service Assistant. Accredited by North Central. Calendar: semester. Curriculum: core. Admission dates: fall. Total enrollment: 15/program. 15 enrollees each admission period. 85% of students receive financial aid. 10% enrolled part-time. 50% under age 25, 40% age 25-44, 10% age 45 or over. Student to teacher ratio 10:1. 90% obtain employment within 6 months.

COURSES: Culinary fundamentals for restaurant and institutional cooking. Schedule: 8am-4pm weekdays, varies. Internships encouraged in summer between 1st and 2nd year.

FACULTY: Includes Linda Arndt, BS in Culinary Arts and trained at La Varenne, Kyle M. Gruening, BS, MS in Culinary Arts.

COSTS: Full payment due 10 days prior to beginning of semester. Admission requirements: high school diploma or equivalent, basic competency scores on ASSET. Off-campus housing is available, cost varies.

CONTACT: Linda Arndt, Culinary Instructor, Nicolet Area Technical College, Culinary Arts, P.O. Box 518, Rhinelander, WI 54501; (715) 369-4410, Fax (715) 365-4445, E-mail larndt@nicolet.tec.wi.us.

THE POSTILION SCHOOL OF CULINARY ART
Fond du Lac/Year-round

This private school offers a diploma course consisting of four 100-hour participation sessions that emphasize classic French technique, economy, and building a chef's larder. Established in 1951. Accredited by State of Wisconsin. Student to teacher ratio 8 students per class. Facilities: the professionally constructed teaching kitchen of a Victorian home.

COURSES: 2 weeks (100 hours minimum) each of basic, advanced, menu planning, and cost accounting. A catering course is optional. Other Courses: professional pastry, butchering, sausage making, ice cream.

FACULTY: Owner/instructor Mme. Kuony was educated in Belgium, France, and Switzerland.

COSTS: Each 2-week segment is $1,600, which includes meals. Nonrefundable $200 registration fee required. $300 deposit is required with enrollment, with the $1,100 balance due on the date of entry. Application deadlines: class dates announced at the beginning of the year. Admission requirements: students must begin with the basic class, regardless of experience. Inexpensive lodging is available at nearby motels.

LOCATION: On the south side of Fond du Lac at the southern tip of Lake Winnebago, about an hour from Milwaukee and 120 miles from Chicago.

CONTACT: Mme. Liane Kuony, Owner, The Postilion School of Culinary Art, 220 Old Pioneer Rd., Fond du Lac, WI 54935; (414) 922-4170.

WAUKESHA COUNTY TECHNICAL COLLEGE
Pewaukee/August-May

This college offers a 1-year diploma and 2-year associate degree in Culinary Arts, and a 3-year ACF apprenticeship in Culinary Management. Program started 1971. Accredited by NCA, ACFEI. Calendar: quarter, semester. 68 credit hours of culinary courses required. Admission dates: August, January. Total enrollment: 65. 30 enrollees each admission period. 100% of applicants accepted. 40% of students receive financial aid. 35% enrolled part-time. 60% under age 25, 35% age 25-44, 5% age 45 or over. Student to teacher ratio 14:1. 95% obtain employment within 6 months. Facilities: include 3 kitchens, 4 classrooms, bar lab, restaurant, computer lab.

COURSES: Technical culinary arts training and principles of business management. Internship: semester long, working under certified ACF chef.

FACULTY: 3 full-time, 3 part-time. Qualifications: All have college degrees and industry experience. Includes James Holden, CEC, CCE, Timothy Graham, CFBE, FMP, Phil Lowry, CHA, Keith Owsiany, Michael Leitzke, CEC, Jack Kastner, CEC.

COSTS: Annual tuition: in-state $52.50/credit hour, out-of-state $80/credit hour. Cutlery $150, uniforms $100. Refund policy: 80% within 60 days. Application deadlines: August.

CONTACT: William R. Griesemer, Associate Dean, Waukesha County Technical College, Ctr. for Hospitality Mgmt. & Culinary Arts Studies, 800 Main St., Pewaukee, WI 53072; (414) 691-5254, Fax (414) 691-5155.

AUSTRALIA

CANBERRA INSTITUTE OF TECHNOLOGY
Canberra City

This institution offers a 3-year diploma and a 3-year part-time trade certificate. Program started 1992. Admission dates: February, July. Total enrollment: 450. 25% of applicants accepted. 75% under age 25, 20% age 25-44, 5% age 45 or over. Student to teacher ratio 15:1. 100% obtain employment within 6 months. Facilities: 6 kitchens, 4 restaurants, computer lab, butchery, bakery, bars.

FACULTY: 30 full-time, 50 part-time. Qualifications: industry and educational.

CONTACT: Pam Robertson, Head, Canberra Institute of Technology, School of Tourism and Hospitality, P.O. Box 826, Canberra City, 2601, Australia; (61) 6-273125, Fax (61) 6-2073209.

CROW'S NEST COLLEGE OF TAFE
Sydney/February-November

This college offers a 1-year certificate and diploma hospitality courses. Program started 1989. Admission dates: January. Total enrollment: 135. 8% of students receive financial aid. 40% enrolled part-time. 80% under age 25, 20% age 25-44. 80% obtain employment within 6 months. Facilities: include 3 kitchens, 4 classrooms and commercial bar.

FACULTY: 10 full-time, 12 part-time.

COSTS: A$150 per year. Refund 3 weeks prior to admission.

CONTACT: Joan Davis, Crow's Nest College of Tafe, Tourism & Hospitality, West St., Crows Nest, Sydney, NSW , Australia; (61) 2-99654434, Fax (61) 2-99654408.

DANDENONG COLLEGE
Dandenong

This institution offers a 3-year diploma. Program started 1986. Accredited by state. Admission dates: February. Total enrollment: 200. 20% of applicants accepted. Student to teacher ratio 15-20:1. 100% obtain employment within 6 months.

FACULTY: 20 full-time, 10 part-time.

COSTS: In-state A$0, out-of-state A$7,000. Admission requirements: high school diploma or equivalent.

CONTACT: George Hill, Head of Department, Dandenong College, Hospitality Studies, 121 Stud Rd., Dandenong, VIC 3175, Australia; (61) 3-7975610, Fax (61) 3-7975458.

WILLIAM ANGLISS INSTITUTE
Melbourne/Year-round

This career institute specializing in the hospitality, travel and food industries offers certificate programs in Commercial Cookery and Advanced Culinary Skills, and diploma and advanced diploma in Hospitality. Students can link to degree courses at Victorian universities. Program started 1940. Accredited by national, state, and local. Calendar: semester. Curriculum: core. Admission dates: every 1 or 2 months (commercial cookery), 3 times a year (cookery), February & July (advanced course). Total enrollment: 4,000. varies enrollees each admission period. 50% under age 25, 40% age 25-44, 10% age 45 or over. Student to teacher ratio 15:1. 91% obtain employment within 6 months. Facilities: a $25 million teaching facility with 4 well-equipped bakeries, 6 kitchens, 3 restaurants , bars, computer rooms, butchery and confectionery centers.

COURSES: Apprenticeship: 3 1/2-4-years in breadmaking and baking, pastry, cookery and butchering. Continuing education: short evening courses in cooking and wine.

FACULTY: More than 100 full-time. Includes Director Dr. Christine French.

COSTS: Courses vary in cost depending on length. Admission requirements: cookery open to all applicants over 18. Advanced course open to those who have completed an apprenticeship.

CONTACT: Chris Coates, Associate Director, William Angliss Institute, 555 La Trobe St., P.O. Box 4052, Melbourne, VIC 3000, Australia; (61) 3-96062111, Fax (61) 3-96701330, URL http://www.angliss.vic.edu.au.

CANADA

ALGONQUIN COLLEGE
Nepean/Year-round

This college offers a 2-year diploma in Culinary Management, a 1-year certificate in Cook Training, and a 40-week certificate in Baking Techniques. Program started 1960. Calendar: semester. Curriculum: core. 1,280 hours of culinary courses required. Admission dates: September, January. Total enrollment: 140. 90 & 50 enrollees each admission period. 50% of applicants accepted. 71% under age 25, 25% age 25-44, 4% age 45 or over. Student to teacher ratio 15-20:1. 90% obtain employment within 6 months. Facilities: include 2 production kitchens, 3 demonstration labs.

COURSES: Baking, menu planning, food demonstration & applications, institutional cooking, food and beverage control, management and computer applications. Schedule: 20 hours/week, 8am-10pm. Continuing education: cake decorating, bread baking, Italian regional cooking.

FACULTY: 5 full-time, 5 part-time. Includes Philippe Dubout, Mike Durrer, Serge Desforges, Alain Peyrun-Berron, Roger Souffez, Alan Fleming, Mario Ramsay.

COSTS: Annual tuition in-state C$637.50/semester, out-of-state C$4,607.50/semester. Books, supplies, uniforms: C$850. Application deadlines: March 1. Admission requirements: secondary school diploma or 19 years of age.

CONTACT: Mike Durrer, Coordinator, Cook/Culinary Programs, Algonquin College, Admissions Office, 1385 Woodroffe Ave., Nepean, ON K2G 1V8, Canada; (800) 565-4723, (613) 727-0002, Fax (613) 727-7632.

CANADORE COLLEGE OF APPLIED ARTS & TECHNOLOGY
North Bay/September-April

This college offers a 2-year diploma in Culinary Management. Program started 1984. Accredited by Canadian Federation of Chefs de Cuisine. Admission dates: September. Total enrollment: 50. 35 enrollees each admission period. 10% of applicants accepted. 75% of students receive financial aid. 10% enrolled part-time. 84% under age 25, 15% age 25-44, 1% age 45 or over. Student to teacher ratio 20:1. 90%-100% obtain employment within 6 months. Facilities: include kitchen with specialized equipment, restaurant.

COURSES: Food preparation, baking, sanitation, food and beverage management, nutrition, wines, contemporary cuisine, cost control, menu planning, quantity cooking, garde manger, international cuisine. Schedule: 28 hours/week, 8 months/year; part-time options available. Externship provided.

FACULTY: 8 full-time.

COSTS: Annual tuition in state C$1,550, foreign C$8,375. Admission requirements: high school diploma or equivalent.

CONTACT: Michael Lamb, Coordinator, Canadore College of Applied Arts & Technology, School of Hospitality & Tourism, 100 College Dr., P.O. Box 5001, North Bay, ON P1B 8K9, Canada; (705) 474-7600, Fax (705) 494-7462.

CULINARY INSTITUTE OF CANADA
Charlottetown/September-May

This 2-year career school, a division of Atlantic Tourism & Hospitality Institute (an affiliate of Holland College), offers an 80-week diploma program. Established in 1984. Calendar: semester. Curriculum: core. 2,000 hours of culinary courses required. Admission dates: September. Total enrollment: 130. 65 enrollees each admission period. 60% of applicants accepted. 90% of students receive financial aid. 5% enrolled part-time. 70% under age 25, 28% age 25-44, 2% age 45 or over.

Student to teacher ratio 16:1. 95% obtain employment within 6 months. Facilities: include training kitchens, classrooms, labs, restaurants.

COURSES: Schedule: 30 hours training. A 16-week externship is included in the program. Continuing education: short courses available.

FACULTY: 40.

COSTS: Annual tuition C$8,570. Tuition deposit $100. $4,300 due each semester. Application deadlines: February 15. Admission requirements: high school diploma. 20 scholarships awarded last year averaging $500 each. Average off-campus housing cost is $500/month.

CONTACT: Richard MacDonald, Executive Director, Culinary Institute of Canada, Atlantic Tourism & Hospitality Institute, 305 Kent St., Charlottetown, PEI C1A 1P5, Canada; (902) 566-9550, Fax (902) 566-9568.

DUBRULLE FRENCH CULINARY SCHOOL
(See also page 231) **Vancouver/Year-round**

This private school offers two 17-week diploma programs: Professional Culinary Training and Professional Pastry & Desserts. 12-week diploma program: Professional Breadmaking. Established in 1982. Certified by the Ministry of Labour under the Private Trade Schools Act. Curriculum: culinary. Admission dates: January, April/May, July (Breadmaking), September/October. Facilities: the 6,000-square-foot facility has classrooms, 3 teaching kitchens with fully-equipped working stations, student dining areas.

COURSES: Emphasis is on classic French methods and techniques; 80% practical, 20% theory. Schedule: 30 hours/week weekdays, day and evening. Accreditation may be given towards the B.C. Apprenticeship program.

FACULTY: Classically-trained chefs.

COSTS: Culinary and Pastry programs C$6,650 each, Breadmaking C$4,700. Canadian Student loans are available. Non-residents can obtain a student visa. Accommodation assistance is provided.

LOCATION: A block from Broadway and Granville, 3 hours from Seattle.

CONTACT: Robert Sung, Director of Admissions, Dubrulle French Culinary School, 1522 W. 8th Ave., Vancouver, BC V6J 4R8, Canada; (604) 738-3155, (800) 667-7288, Fax (604) 738-3205.

GEORGE BROWN COLLEGE OF APPLIED ARTS & TECHNOLOGY
Toronto/Year-round

This college offers sixteen 1- & 2-year full-time certificate & diploma programs & 30 part-time programs. Full-time courses include 2-yr Culinary Management, 1-yr Chef Training, 1-yr Baking Techniques, General Food Preparation, Prof. Sommelier & Chinese Cooking. Program started 1965. Accreditation tentative with CHRIE. Calendar: annual. Curriculum: core. Admission dates: September, January annually. Some classes may begin at other times as announced. Total enrollment: 2,500 full-time, 3,500 part-time. Student to teacher ratio 24:1. 85% obtain employment within 6 months. Facilities: include 4 culinary and 3 bake laboratories, each with 24 individual work stations; demonstration kitchens with overhead mirrors.

COURSES: Culinary Management: basic, classical food preparation & presentation with theory, demonstrations, preparations for the student-run restaurant. Baking Techniques: breads, pastries, cakes, decorating. Schedule: full-time programs meet 5 days/week; most part-time programs meet 1 evening/week for 15 weeks. 3 weeks of scheduled industry experience in hotels and restaurants.

FACULTY: More than 20 internationally-trained chef professors as well as former hotel general managers and food and beverage professionals. Includes Canadian wine expert Jacques Marie.

COSTS: Resident (nonresident) tuition for most diploma programs is approximately C$2,000 (C$10,000) for 32 weeks; for certificate programs it's C$544 to C$1,694/program. Cancellation penalty is C$100 for full-time programs with appropriate notice. Financial assistance available to Canadians. Application deadlines: March 1 full-time; ongoing for certificate program. Admission requirements: minimum requirement for admission to a diploma program is an Ontario Secondary School Diploma or an equivalent from within North America. 100 scholarships awarded last year averaging $500 each. Furnished room averages C$100-C$150 per week.

LOCATION: The 4-story facility, completed in 1987, is in downtown Toronto at 300 Adelaide St. E. at the college's St. James campus.

CONTACT: Brian Cooper, Dean, George Brown College, Information Services, 300 Adelaide St. E., Toronto, ON M5A 1N1, Canada; (800) 263-8995, (416) 415-2230, Fax (416) 415-2501, URL http://www.gbrownc.on.ca.

GEORGIAN COLLEGE OF APPLIED ARTS AND TECHNOLOGY
Barrie/September-April

This college offers a 2-year diploma in Culinary Management. Program started 1988. Admission dates: August. Total enrollment: 85. 50 enrollees each admission period. 50% of applicants accepted. Student to teacher ratio 24:1. 100% obtain employment within 6 months. Facilities: include large-quantity kitchen, 2 small-quantity kitchens, bake lab, classrooms, student-run restaurant.

COURSES: Bake theory/lab, menu planning, food/beverage control, creative cuisine. Externship provided. Post-graduate study available through Rochester Institute of Technology and Rye.

FACULTY: 7 full-time, 1 to 2 part-time.

COSTS: Annual tuition in-country C$1,109, out-of-country C$9,215. Application fee C$25. Application deadlines: March until program full. Admission requirements: high school diploma or equivalent. On-campus housing: 252 spaces; average cost: C$400 per month. Average off-campus housing cost: C$400-C$800.

LOCATION: The E-building, 3,500-student campus is in an urban/rural area.

CONTACT: Bill Gordon, Academic Director, Georgian College of Applied Arts and Technology, School of Hospitality & Tourism, One Georgian Dr., Barrie, ON L4M 3X9, Canada; (705) 722-1592, Fax (705) 722-5123, URL http://www.georcoll.on.ca.

HUMBER COLLEGE OF APPLIED ARTS & TECHNOLOGY
Etobicoke

This institution offers a 1-year certificate, 2-year diploma, and a 3-year AS degree. Program started 1975. Admission dates: September, January. Total enrollment: 150. Student to teacher ratio 20:1. 95% obtain employment within 6 months.

COURSES: Externship provided.

FACULTY: 14 full-time, 5 part-time.

COSTS: Annual tuition in-state C$900, foreign C$5,000. Admission requirements: high school diploma or equivalent and admission test.

CONTACT: John Walker, Chairman, Humber College of Applied Arts & Technology, School of Hospitality, Tourism, & Leisure, 205 Humber College Blvd., Etobicoke, ON M9W 5L7, Canada; (416) 675-3111, Fax (416) 675-9730.

LE CORDON BLEU PARIS COOKING SCHOOL
Ottawa/Year-round

This private school offers 12-week certificate courses in French cuisine and pastry (4 of the 6 Classic Cycle courses), 1-day to 1-month intensives, and specialized evening programs. Established in 1988. Calendar: trimester. Curriculum: culinary. 216 hours of culinary courses required. Admission dates: January, April, July, September. Total enrollment: 150. 35 enrollees each admission period. 90% of applicants accepted. 30% under age 25, 50% age 25-44, 20% age 45 or over. Student to teacher ratio 12:1. 75% obtain employment within 6 months. Facilities: include demonstration room, fully-equipped kitchen with individual work spaces, specialized equipment.

COURSES: Basic and Intermediate Cuisine, Basic and Advanced Pastry. Students who wish to receive the Cuisine/Pastry Diplomas or Le Grand Diplome can complete the Superior Cuisine and/or Patisserie courses at Le Cordon Bleu in Paris or London. Schedule: 20 hours/week for full-time classes; customized intensives are available.

FACULTY: All French chefs trained in France. Director is Gerard L. Breissan. Instructors are professional master chefs Philippe Guiet, Jean-Claude Petibon, and pastry chef Michel Denis.

COSTS: Tuition is C$4,700 for Basic Cuisine, C$4,950 for Intermediate Cuisine, C$4,200 for Basic Pastry, and C$4,700 for Advanced Pastry. A C$450 deposit is required; balance due 4 weeks prior. Cancellations 6 weeks prior forfeit C$200. C$50 non-refundable admission fee. Application deadlines: one month prior to session. Admission requirements: high school diploma, minimum age 18 years old. Lodging ranges from C$600-C$1,200.

LOCATION: Chateau Royale Professional Building, about 20 minutes from downtown Ottawa.

CONTACT: Gerard L. Breissan, Le Cordon Bleu Paris Cooking School, 1390 Prince of Wales Dr., #400, Ottawa, ON K2C 3N6, Canada; (613) 224-8603, Fax (613) 224-9966, URL http://www.lebottawa.com.

McCALL'S SCHOOL OF CAKE DECORATION, INC.
(See also page 233)   **Etobicoke/September-May**

This school offers full-time certificate courses in baking, commercial cake decorating (10 days each), and Swiss chocolate techniques (5 days), as well as programs for all levels. Established in 1976. Student to teacher ratio 10 per class. Facilities: the 1,000 square feet of teaching space includes overhead mirrors and two 20-seat classrooms.

FACULTY: Includes school director Nick McCall, and Kay Wong.

COSTS: Professional courses range from C$480-C$750. A 50% deposit is required. Cancellations 1 week prior forfeit deposit.

LOCATION: A western subdivision of Toronto.

CONTACT: Nick McCall, President, McCall's School of Cake Decoration, Inc., 3810 Bloor St. West, Etobicoke, ON M9B 6C2, Canada; (416) 231-8040, Fax (416) 231-9956, E-mail decorate@mccalls-cakes, URL http://www.mccalls-cakes.com.

NIAGARA COLLEGE HOSPITALITY AND TOURISM CENTRE
Niagara Falls/September-June

The College of Applied Arts and Technology offers 3-year cook and baker apprenticeship training and a 2-year diploma in Culinary Skills. Program started 1989. Admission dates: September, January. Total enrollment: 120. 72 & 20 enrollees each admission period. 50% of applicants accepted. 60% of students receive financial aid. 75% under age 25, 20% age 25-44, 5% age 45 or over. Student to teacher ratio 24:1. 100% obtain employment within 6 months. Facilities: production kitchen, baking lab, mixology lab, computer lab, 3 food labs, lecture theatre, learning resource center, 90-seat student-run restaurant.

COURSES: The Culinary Skills program covers food theory and preparation, kitchen management, nutrition, sanitation, and general education courses. Schedule: 21 hours/week. Students must complete an approved summer work experience. The 6,000-hour apprenticeships, administered by the Ministry of Education and Training. A variety of continuing education courses are available.

FACULTY: 6 full-time, 4 part-time. Chef professors are all Certified Chefs de Cuisine.

COSTS: Annual tuition is C$1,312 for Canadian residents, C$7,750 for non-residents. A C$50 application fee and C$735 equipment fee are required. Withdrawals within 10 class days of start of term receive refund less C$50. Application deadlines: April 15, November 15. Admission requirements: secondary school diploma or equivalent. Off-campus lodging ranges from C$90-C$100 per week.

LOCATION: Niagara Falls City.

CONTACT: David A. Davies, Niagara College of Applied Arts and Technology, Hospitality and Tourism Centre, 5881 Dunn St., Niagara Falls, ON L2G 2N8, Canada; (416) 374-7454, Fax (416) 374-1116.

PACIFIC INSTITUTE OF CULINARY ARTS
Vancouver/Year-round   *(See display ad above)*

This small private school offers 2 six-month full-time programs in Culinary Arts and Baking &
Pastry Arts. Established in 1996. Calendar: trimester. Curriculum: culinary. 840 hours of culinary
courses required. Admission dates: January, April, July September. Total enrollment: 136 maximum. 34 maximum enrollees each admission period. Student to teacher ratio 10-12:1. Facilities: 3
commercial training kitchens, demonstration lecture room with overhead mirrors, on-site white
linen teaching restaurant and bake shop.

Courses: French and international cuisines. First 3 months cover the basics, the last 3 months
consists of training in the Institute's restaurant. Schedule: Monday-Friday. One-week practicum.

Faculty: 4 full- and 1 part-time chef instructors, all with international experience.

Costs: C$8,950 per program. A C$895 deposit is required plus C$25 nonrefundable application fee.
Tuition payable in 5 installments. Application deadlines: year-round. Admission requirements: high
school diploma or equivalent. Lodging assistance provided. Ranges from C$350-C$1,000 per month.

Location: City of Vancouver, at entrance to Granville Island Market.

Contact: Sue Singer, Director of Admissions, Pacific Institute of Culinary Arts, 1505 W. 2nd Ave.,
Vancouver, BC V6H 3Y4, Canada; (604) 734-4488, (800) 416-4040, Fax (604) 734-4408, E-mail
admissions@pacinst.ca.

ST. CLAIR COLLEGE
Windsor/September-April

This college offers a 4-semester diploma in Culinary Arts. Program started 1993. Accredited by
Province of Ontario. Calendar: semester. Curriculum: culinary, core. Admission dates: September.
Total enrollment: 80. 40 enrollees each admission period. 75% of applicants accepted. 50% of students receive financial aid. 10% enrolled part-time. 75% under age 25. Student to teacher ratio 22-
25:1. 98% obtain employment within 6 months. Facilities: include 4 kitchens and classrooms, 140
seat restaurant.

Courses: Culinary arts, food preparation, culinary practice, hospitality marketing, nutrition &
menu writing, garde manger, management techniques. Schedule: 20 hours/week, 10 months/year.
Externship: 16-week, 7 hours per week, in hotels and restaurants. Continuing education: bartending.

Faculty: 3 full-time.

Costs: Annual tuition in-state C$1,200, out-of-state C$8,000. 6 scholarships awarded last year
averaging $500 each.

Location: An urban setting, 2 hours from London, Ontario.

Contact: Marg Jeffrey, Chairperson, St. Clair College, Business Hospitality Dept., 2000 Talbot
Rd. W., Windsor, ON N9A 6S4, Canada; (519) 972-2727, Fax (519) 972-0801.

SOUTHERN ALBERTA INSTITUTE OF TECHNOLOGY
Calgary/Year-round

This nonprofit institution offers a 1-year diploma in Professional Cooking and 3-8 week Apprentice Cooking sessions. Program started 1949. 1,328 hours of culinary courses required. Admission dates: September, January, May (November & March for Apprentice). Total enrollment: 195 professional, 216 apprentice. 65 (professional), 48 (apprentice) enrollees each admission period. 30% of applicants accepted. 50% of students receive financial aid. 57% enrolled part-time. 59% under age 25, 34% age 25-44, 7% age 45 or over. Student to teacher ratio 15:1. 97% obtain employment within 6 months. Facilities: 4 large commercial kitchens, 2 commercial bakeries, 2 lab and 7 demonstration classrooms, dining room, computer lab, 2 lecture classrooms, ice plant.

COURSES: Include garde manger, patisserie, kitchen management, fat and ice sculpting. Other required courses include breakfast and short order cooking, technical writing, meat portioning. Schedule: 30 hours/week. Continuing education: includes bar mixology, bed & breakfast, fusion cooking.

FACULTY: 31 full-time, 4 part-time. Qualifications: Journeymans and Red Seal in Cooking. Helmut Schoderbock, Ian Neilson, Otto Daniels, Gerd Steinmeyer, Wolfgang Stampe.

COSTS: Semester tuition is C$1,783; other fees are C$1,073. Application deadlines: year-round. Admission requirements: transcript, resume, statement of career goals. On-campus housing: 204 spaces; average cost: C$7-C$12 per day. Average off-campus housing cost: C$400-C$500.

CONTACT: Reg Hendrickson, Dean, Southern Alberta Institute of Technology, Hospitality Careers Dept., 1301 16th Ave. N.W., Calgary, AB T2M 0L4, Canada; (403) 284-8612, Fax (403) 284-7034.

STRATFORD CHEFS SCHOOL
Stratford/November-March

This nonprofit school offers a 2-semester full-time apprenticeship diploma. Established in 1983. Province of Ontario accreditation as Journeyman available upon passing exam. Calendar: semester. Curriculum: culinary. Admission dates: November. Total enrollment: 70. 35-40 enrollees each admission period. 25% of applicants accepted. 100% obtain employment within 6 months.

COURSES: Gastronomy, nutrition, food styling, wine appreciation, kitchen management, menu preparation, food costing. Other required courses: 2nd-year students research, prepare and serve theme menus in a restaurant setting. Schedule: 45 hours/week. Externship provided.

FACULTY: 14 full-time. Founders/Directors are restaurateurs Eleanor Kane and James Morris.

COSTS: Annual tuition C$2,750 for Ontario residents, C$6,500 for others. C$750 deposit due 30 days after acceptance. Average off-campus housing cost is C$300-C$400/month.

LOCATION: A small town, 90 minutes from Toronto.

CONTACT: Elisabeth Lorimer, Programme Administrator, Stratford Chefs School, 150 Huron St., Stratford, ON N0K 1N0, Canada; (519) 271-1414, Fax (519) 271-5679.

UNIVERSITY COLLEGE OF THE CARIBOO
Kamloops/September-May

This college offers a 12-month certificate in Culinary Arts. Program started 1972. Admission dates: September, November, March. Total enrollment: 50. 16 enrollees each admission period. 80% of applicants accepted. 40% of students receive financial aid. 50% under age 25, 50% age 25-44. Student to teacher ratio 12:1. 75% obtain employment within 6 months. Facilities: include 4 kitchens and classrooms and dining room.

COURSES: Schedule: 30 hours/week.

FACULTY: 6 full-time.

COSTS: Annual tuition C$1,460. Application fee C$15, student fees C$428. Admission requirements: high school diploma or equivalent. Average on-campus housing cost: C$195 per month. Average off-campus housing cost: C$250 per month.

CONTACT: Kurt Zwingli, Department Chair, University College of the Cariboo, Food Training/Tourism, Box 3010, Kamloops, BC V2C 5N3, Canada; (604) 828-5353, Fax (604) 371-5677.

ENGLAND

ASPIC – THE CAMBRIDGE COOKERY SCHOOL
Cambridge/Year-round

This private school offers 3-month certificates and 1-, 2- and 4-week Foundation Courses, programs for caterers and cooks, 5-day intensives for advanced cooks, programs for nonprofessionals. Established in 1994. Curriculum: culinary. Admission dates: September, January, April for 3-month course. 16 enrollees each admission period. Student to teacher ratio 8:1.

COURSES: Geared to those planning a catering career or employment with chalet and boat holiday companies. Include menu planning, costing, ingredient selection, hands-on practice, table setting, wine. Schedule: 10am-3:30pm weekdays.

FACULTY: Founder Alice Percival was born in Kenya, studied in Paris, modeled in London, managed an Essex restaurant, and was a professional caterer. Charlotte Lyon, senior consultant, was Leith's Student of the Year and is owner of Charlotte Lyon Creative Cookery in London.

COSTS: £2,750 (£1,095) for the 3-month (4-week) course. Lodging can be arranged.

LOCATION: Five minutes from the mainline station, walking distance of central Cambridge.

CONTACT: Alice Percival, Principal, ASPIC – The Cambridge Cookery School, 3 Glisson Rd., Cambridge, CB1 2HA, England; (44) 1223-568303, Fax (44) 1223-568304.

BONNE BOUCHE
Devon/Year-round *(See also page 235, 284)*

This private school offers Bonne Bouche professional certificate programs in Catering and Hospitality, extended diploma course, and state recognized National Vocational Qualifications in Food Preparation & Cooking. Established in 1987. Accredited by NVQ, Hospitality Training Found. Curriculum: culinary. 200 hours of culinary courses required. Admission dates: 5 times/year. Total enrollment: 30/year. 6 enrollees/admission period. 85% of applicants accepted. 66% of students receive financial aid. 30% under age 25, 70% age 25-44, 10% age 45 or over. Student to teacher ratio 6:1. 100% obtain employment within 6 months. Facilities: working kitchen, demonstration kitchen, lecture room, wine and food book & video library.

COURSES: Hands-on instruction in the 200+-hour certificate program covers key preparation and cooking techniques, wines, table decoration, business management, and classic, contemporary, vegetarian, and ethnic cuisines. Schedule: 7:30am-2pm weekdays, some weekends. Special training in food hygiene (independently managed) and business management. Continuing education: courses range from 8-40 hours and include food hygiene and advanced techniques.

FACULTY: 2 full-time, 2 part-time. Anne Nicholls, senior tutor, coordinator, and NVQ assessor; Gerald Nicholls, business management and internal NVQ verifier; Moira Clarke, food hygiene; Sri Owen, southeast Asian.

COSTS: Range from approximately £1,600-£2,100, including double occupancy lodging and meals (single supplement available). A 25% deposit is required; participants must insure against cancellation. Application deadlines: as much in advance as possible. Admission requirements: strong motivation and commitment, ability to cope with pressure. State aid available to candidates fulfilling residential requirements. Housing not required except on weekends at £15/person/night.

LOCATION: 16th-century Devon longhouse on 3-acre grounds with gardens, fitness center, croquet lawn; other sports nearby. Rural setting, close to historic sites.

CONTACT: Anne Nicholls, Program Coordinator, Bonne Bouche, Lower Beers House, Brithem Bottom, Cullompton, Devon, EX15 1NB, England; (44) 1884-32257, Fax (44) 1884-32257.

BUTLERS WHARF CHEF SCHOOL
London/Year-round *(See also page 236)*

This private vocational school offers a 6-month full- or part-time Advanced Chefs Diploma course, 6-week full-time Foundation Chefs and Food Service courses, 8-12 month Catering certificate, and courses in Food Preparation & Cooking, Front of House/Food Service, Wine, and Food Hygiene. Established in 1995. Accredited by National Vocational Qualifications. Curriculum: culinary. 240 hours minimum of culinary courses required. Admission dates: flexible. Total enrollment: 250. 60% of applicants accepted. 60% of students receive financial aid. 40% enrolled part-time. 60% under age 25, 35% age 25-44, 5% age 45 or over. Student to teacher ratio 8:1. 100% obtain employment within 6 months. Facilities: training/production kitchen, specialized demonstration theatre, restaurant, study areas.

COURSES: Realistic training in culinary and front-of-house skills. Schedule: 60% practical training, 30% academic, 10% other.

FACULTY: Includes 11 instructors, Director John Roberts, and chefs Gary Witchalls, Nikki Hopkins, Denzil Newton, Mena Dunstane. Guest faculty includes chefs, food and wine experts, restaurateurs.

COSTS: Foundation courses £850 each, certificate course £2,250, basic diploma £1,000, advanced £5,000. Minimum 50% deposit. Admission requirements: enthusiasm and commitment. 30 scholarships awarded (UK residents only) last year averaging £2,500 each.

LOCATION: Central London.

CONTACT: Mr. John Roberts, Director, Butlers Wharf Chef School, Cardamom Bldg., 31 Shad Thames, London, SE1 2YR, England; (44) 171-357-8842, Fax (44) 171-403-2638.

COOKERY AT THE GRANGE
(See also page 236)
Frome/Year-round

This private school offers a 4-week Basics to Béarnaise certificate course and 2-week Beyond Béarnaise advanced programme (February only). Established in 1981. Curriculum: culinary. Admission dates: rolling. Total enrollment: 140/year. 14-20 enrollees each admission period. 65% under age 25, 25% age 25-44, 10% age 45 or over. Student to teacher ratio 8:1. 90% obtain employment within 6 months. Facilities: main kitchen, cold kitchen, herb garden.

COURSES: The 4-week course covers methods and principles of cookery with emphasis on classic techniques using fresh, natural ingredients and styles from around the world. Schedule: 7 hours daily, Monday-Friday.

FACULTY: Jane and William Averill (Grange trained) and teaching staff.

COSTS: Cost for Basics to Béarnaise, including meals and double occupancy housing, is £1,590 to £1,750; Beyond Béarnaise is £780 for two weeks. Fees are inclusive of VAT. A nonrefundable £175 deposit is required, balance is due 6 weeks prior. The Grange has double and single bedrooms. Single room supplement £40/week. Nonresident students (£40/week less) stay for dinner.

LOCATION: The Grange, situated in converted farm buildings surrounded by gardens in rural England, is 90 minutes from London by train.

CONTACT: Jane and William Averill, Cookery at The Grange, Whatley, Frome, Somerset, BA11 3JU, England; (44) 1373-836579, (44) 1373-836579, Fax (44) 1373-836579, URL http://www.hi-media.co.uk/grange-cookery.

THE CORDON VERT COOKERY SCHOOL
(See also page 236)
Altrincham/Year-round

The Vegetarian Society UK, a registered charity and membership organization, offers four 1-week (or 2 weekend) Foundation courses leading to the Cordon Vert diploma, the 4-day Cordon Vert Vegetarian Catering certificate course, and a variety of weekend and day courses. Established in 1984. Curriculum: culinary.

COURSES: Basic and advanced techniques of vegetarian cookery, international cuisines, catering.

FACULTY: Sarah Brown began the courses in 1982, based on her BBC-TV series, *Vegetarian Kitchen*. Tutors include Ursula Ferrigno, Rachel Tyldsley, Lyn Weller, and Deborah Clarke.

COSTS: Resident (non-resident) tuition is £315-£340 (£255-£280) for the 1-week Foundation courses and £420 (£360) for the Catering course. Resident tuition includes full board and lodging. A nonrefundable deposit is required. Lodging in twin-bedded rooms in the school's Lodge.

LOCATION: Ten miles south of Manchester.

CONTACT: Heather Mairs, Cordon Vert Cookery School, The Vegetarian Society, Parkdale, Dunham Road, Altrincham, Cheshire, WA14 4QG, England; (44) 161-928-0793, Fax (44) 161-926-9182, E-mail vegsoc@vegsoc.demon.co.uk, URL http://www.veg.org/veg/orgs/vegsocuk/.

ELISABETH RUSSELL SCHOOL OF COOKERY
London/September-June
This private school offers a 5-week certificate course, a 10-week diploma course, and 4-week courses for those with basic cookery knowledge. Established in 1963. Curriculum: culinary. Student to teacher ratio 6-8 per class.
COURSES: French cookery suitable for home, entertaining, and chalets. Schedule: 10am-4pm, Monday-Thursday.
COSTS: Tuition is £850 for 5 weeks, £1,640 for 10 weeks. Nonrefundable enrollment fee is £50. Tuition is due 3 weeks prior; full refund 5 weeks prior. Lodging is available with nearby families.
LOCATION: 6 miles from London.
CONTACT: Elisabeth Russell, Elisabeth Russell School of Cooking, Flat 5, 18 The Grange, Wimbledon, London, SW19 4PS, England; (44) 181-947-2144.

HARROW HOUSE
East Sussex/Year-round   *(See also page 238)*
This private school (formerly Eastbourne College of Food and Fashion) offers a 1-year diploma course, a 10-week intensive Cookery Certificate Course, a 10-week intensive Sugarcraft Course, a 10-week advanced Cordon Bleu Certificate Course, and short courses. Established in 1907. Recognized as efficient by the British Accreditation Council. Admission dates: all year. Total enrollment: 100. 80% of applicants accepted. 10% of students receive financial aid. 10% enrolled part-time. 75% under age 25, 25% age 25-44. Student to teacher ratio 12:1 per class. Facilities: include 7 specially-equipped teaching kitchens, student-run restaurant, demonstration theatre.
COURSES: Include basic & international cuisines, wines, catering, dress & fashion, typing, home & consumer studies, flower arranging. Advanced course covers famous chef methods, advanced pastry, cake decoration, restaurant presentation. Schedule: 9am-4pm weekdays. During an optional Paris trip, students work in a fine restaurant and visit markets, food companies.
COSTS: Costs are £2,750 (£2,000 nonresident) per term for the 1-year course, £2,990 (£2,200) for the intensive, £3,000 (£2,500) for the advanced course. A £50 nonrefundable fee must accompany application. Residential lodging is £75/week.
LOCATION: The seaside town of Eastbourne, an 80-minute drive from London.
CONTACT: Harrow House College of Food and Fashion, 1 Silverdale Road, Eastbourne, BN20 7AA, England; (44) 1323-730851, Fax (44) 1323-416924, E-mail harrowhouse@mailhost.lds.co.uk.

LE CORDON BLEU
London/Year-round   *(See also page 239) (See display ad page 127)*
This private school acquired by Le Cordon Bleu-Paris in 1990 offers 5- and 10-week Classic Cycle certificate courses in French Cuisine and Patisserie leading to the 30-week Grand Diplome, 10-week summer hospitality management program, 5-week catering program, 3- to 5-week workshops, evening classes, daily demonstrations. Established in 1933. Accredited by California Polytech and University of Denver hospitality management schools. Calendar: quarter. Curriculum: culinary. 1,200 hours (Classic Cycle) of culinary courses required. Admission dates: September, October, January, March, June. Total enrollment: 120/quarter. 100-120 enrollees each admission period. 100% of applicants accepted. 15% of students receive financial aid. 30% enrolled part-time. 40% under age 25, 55% age 25-44, 5% age 45 or over. Student to teacher ratio 9:1. 90% obtain employment within 6 months. Facilities: specialized equipment; classrooms resemble professional kitchens; individual workspaces with refrigerated marble tops; demonstration rooms with video.
COURSES: Classic Cycle consists of 3 cuisine and 3 pastry courses, taken consecutively. Covers

basic to complex techniques: classic, regional, ethnic and contemporary cuisines: marriage of food and wine, catering, planning, presentation, decoration and execution. Schedule: day sessions begin at 9am, 1:30pm, and 4:30pm; twelve 3-hour courses/week. Students assist Master Chefs and are assisted in finding a 3-month internship. Continuing education: Master Chef Catering Course with necessary prerequisites.

FACULTY: All staff full time. Chefs all professionally qualified with experience in Michelin-starred and fine quality culinary establishments. Includes President Andre Cointreau and School Directors Leslie Grey and Susan Eckstein.

COSTS: Tuition ranges from approximately £250 for a week long or evening course to £2,300-£4,000 for a 10-week Classic Cycle course. A 10% deposit is required. Fees payable in Sterling in the form of a bank transfer, Visa, or Mastercard. Application deadlines: first day of course, early enrollment is advised. Admission requirements: enthusiasm for the Culinary Arts. 3 scholarships awarded last year. Students are assisted in finding housing. Monthly rent ranges from £300-£1,000.

LOCATION: London's West End, close to Oxford and Bond Streets.

CONTACT: Le Cordon Bleu, Enrollment Office, 114 Marylebone Lane, London, W1M 6HH, England; (44) 171-935-3503, (800) 457-CHEF, Fax (44) 171-935-7621, URL http://www.cordon-bleu.edu.

LEITH'S SCHOOL OF FOOD AND WINE
(See also page 239) **London/September-August**

This private school offers a 1-year or 2-term diploma consisting of two or three 10- to 11-week certificate courses, a 10-session restaurant management course, and certificate course in wine. Nonprofessional courses. Established in 1975. Calendar: semester. Admission dates: October. Total enrollment: 96. 96 enrollees each admission period. 99% of applicants accepted. 40% under age 25, 55% age 25-44, 5% age 45 or over. Student to teacher ratio 8:1. 90% obtain employment within 6 months. Facilities: include 3 kitchens and a demonstration theatre.

COURSES: Beginner's, Intermediate, & Advanced Certificate in Food & Wine courses run consecutively. Beginner's: basic cookery methods; Intermediate: butchery, exotic fish, commercial catering. Advanced: boned poultry, aspics, advanced patisserie, exotic canapes. Schedule: 10am-4:30pm, Monday-Friday.

FACULTY: 13 full-time, 2 part-time. School founder and cookbook author Prue Leith is former Veuve Cliquot Business Woman of the Year. Principal is Caroline Waldegrave, vice-principals are C.J. Jackson and A. Cavaliero.

COSTS: Tuition ranges from £2,800-£3,150 per course, the cost for all 3 is £8,250. Equipment fee is £200. All prices include VAT. A £100-£200 deposit is required. The school assists in obtaining lodging, which ranges from £80 to £120 per week.

LOCATION: A refurbished Victorian building in Kensington, the center of London.

CONTACT: Judy Van DerSande, Registrar, Leith's School of Food and Wine, 21 St. Alban's Grove, London, W85 BPX, England; (44) 171-229-0177, Fax (44) 171-937-0257.

THE MANOR SCHOOL OF FINE CUISINE
(See also page 239) **Widmerpool/Year-round**

This proprietary institution offers a 4-week certificate in Cordon Bleu cookery. Established in 1988. Calendar: 4 weeks. Curriculum: culinary. Admission dates: rolling. 8 enrollees each admission period. 90% of applicants accepted. 5% of students receive financial aid. 60% enrolled part-time. 40% under age 25, 30% age 25-44, 30% age 45 or over. Student to teacher ratio 8:1. Facilities: include 7 kitchens, lecture room, large dining room, cooking library.

COURSES: Include cuisine preparation, baking, basic nutrition, and menu planning. Schedule: Monday-Friday.

FACULTY: Principal Claire Gentinetta earned the Cordon Bleu Diploma, served as head chef of noted restaurants, and is a member of the Cookery and Food Association, Craft Guild of Chefs, and Chefs and Cooks Circle.

Costs: Resident (nonresident) tuition is £1,162.07 (£1,044.57). A nonrefundable deposit of £100 is required, balance is due 6 weeks prior; refund with 6 weeks written notice. Residents are housed in The Manor (except weekends). Recommendations are provided for local lodging.

Location: The Manor, refurbished 17th century inn, is 9 miles from Nottingham City center and 80 minutes from London's Kings Cross train station.

Contact: The Manor School of Fine Cuisine, Old Melton Road, Widmerpool, Nottinghamshire, NG12 5QL, England; (44) 1949-81371.

OXFORD SYMPOSIUM ON FOOD & COOKERY
University of Oxford/Fall

This annual 2-day weekend program focuses on a theme. Recent themes include Cooks and Others (1995) and Food and Travel (1996). Attendees are invited to submit papers, which are presented and discussed by participants.

Costs: Tuition, which covers lunches and distribution of papers, is £45 for one, £72 for two, £25 for students. Deposit is £25/£40/£10.

Location: St. Antony's College, University of Oxford.

Contact: Harlan Walker, Oxford Symposium on Food & Cookery, 294 Hagley Rd., Birmingham, B17 8DJ, England; (44) 121-429-1779, Fax (44) 121-429-1779.

SONIA STEVENSON
Cornwall/Year-round

This cooking instructor offers 2½- to 4-day participation courses (limit 6-8 students).

Courses: Focus on sauces and fish cookery.

Faculty: Founder of The Horn of Plenty Restaurant near Tavistock, Devon, Sonia Stevenson is a Master Chef of Great Britain and Chef Laureate of the British Academy of Gastronomes.

Costs: Begin at £195.

Location: Venues include Glasgow, Edinburgh, Warwick, London, Cornwall, Northern Ireland.

Contact: Sonia Stevenson, The Old Chapel, Bethany, Trerulefoot, Cornwall, PL12 5DA, England; (44) 1752-851-813.

SQUIRES KITCHEN SUGARCRAFT SCHOOL
Farnham, Surrey/Year-round   *(See also page 240)*

This private school offers a part-time 1-week school certificate in sugarcraft and cake decorating plus diploma courses. Established in 1987. Admission dates: rolling. 100% of applicants accepted. 100% enrolled part-time. 10% under age 25, 40% age 25-44, 50% age 45 or over. Student to teacher ratio 12:1. Facilities: a kitchen with specialized equipment and materials.

Courses: Include royal icing, sugarpaste, flowers, pastillage, chocolate.

Faculty: 17 full- and part-time. Members of the British Sugarcraft Guild, including Peggy Green. Guest tutors include Eddie Spence.

Costs: Range from £45/day. 25% application deposit required.

Location: A period building in a suburban area, a 2-minute walk to train station, 45 minutes from London.

Contact: Beverley Dutton, Course Coordinator, Squires Kitchen Sugarcraft School of Cake Decoration, 3 Waverly Lane, Farnham, Surrey, GU9 8BB, England; (44) 1252-734309, Fax (44) 1252-714714.

TANTE MARIE SCHOOL OF COOKERY
Surrey/Year-round   *(See also page 240)*

This private school offers a 36-week or 24-week Intensive Tante Marie Cordon Bleu diploma. Established in 1954. Accredited by BACIFHE (British Accreditation Council). Calendar: trimester. Curriculum: culinary. Admission dates: January, April, September. Total enrollment: 84. 24-72 enrollees each admission period. 100% of applicants accepted. 20% of students receive financial aid. 50% under age 25, 45% age 25-44, 5% age 45 or over. Student to teacher ratio 12:1. 100% obtain employment within 6 months. Facilities: include 5 modern teaching kitchens, a mirrored demonstration theatre, and a lecture room.

COURSES: 36-wk course for beginners: three 12-wk terms of basic skills, labor-saving appliances, British cookery, French cuisine. Intensive 24-wk course for experienced cooks: practical & theoretical elements. 4-day wine seminar prepares for Wine Certificate exam. Schedule: 9:30am-4:30pm, Monday-Friday.

FACULTY: 12 full- and part-time. Qualified to work in state schools and many have held catering positions. All undergo teacher training. Well-known TV cookery demonstrators, a noted wine expert, and local tradesmen also present.

COSTS: Tuition is £8,100 (£6,300) for the 36-week (24-week) course, £3,000 for one-term certificate course. Uniform and equipment £100 additional. Overseas students qualify for 24% vocational training tax relief on course tuition. Nonrefundable 10% deposit. First term fee due 4 weeks prior for UK residents, 6 weeks prior for others. Deposit is transferable to another course. Application deadlines: 3 months prior to term. Admission requirements: English language fluency. Overseas students qualify for 24% vocational training tax relief on tuition. The school assists students in finding local lodging, which is £90 per week.

LOCATION: A turn-of-the-century country mansion near the center of Woking, a small country town approximately 25 minutes by train from London.

CONTACT: Margaret A. Stubbington, Registrar, Tante Marie School of Cookery, Woodham House, Carlton Rd., Woking, Surrey, GU21 4HF, England; (44) 1483-726957, Fax (44) 1483-724173.

THAMES VALLEY UNIVERSITY
Berkshire/Year-round

This university offers a 3-year NVQ Level 2 international diploma in Culinary Arts. Year-round Program started 1992. Accredited by City and Guilds. Calendar: semester. Admission dates: September. Total enrollment: 40. 40 enrollees each admission period. 70% of applicants accepted. 10% of students receive financial aid. 60% under age 25, 40% age 25-44. Student to teacher ratio 15:1. 100% obtain employment within 6 months. Facilities: include 4 kitchens, demonstration kitchen, 2 science labs, 3 restaurants, computer lab.

COURSES: Schedule: 20 hours/week; part-time 7 hours/week.

FACULTY: 60 full-time.

COSTS: Annual tuition £4,000.

CONTACT: David Foskett, Thames Valley University, Hospitality Studies, Wellington St., Berkshire, Berkshire, England; (44) 7553-697601, Fax (44) 7553-677682.

FRANCE

ECOLE GASTRONOMIQUE BELLOUET-CONSEIL
Paris/Year-round

This school offers 2- and 3-day intensive seminars. Customized classes also available. Established in 1989. Calendar: semester. Student to teacher ratio 8-10:1 per class.

COURSES: More than thirty individual courses including cakes, individual cakes, petits fours, chocolate, artistic sugar, catering, viennoiserie. Schedule: 8:30am-6pm with lunch offered.

FACULTY: G.J. Bellouet and J.M. Perruchon, Meilleurs Ouvriers de France.

COSTS: Two-day seminar is 3,200 FF, 3-day seminar 4,800 FF, cooking classes and catering 3,400 FF.

LOCATION: Downtown Paris, accessible by Metro: Duroc or Vanneau.

CONTACT: Ecole Gastronomique Bellouet-Conseil, 48, rue de Sevres, Paris, 75007, France; (33) 1-40-56-91-20, Fax (33) 1-45-66-48-61.

ÉCOLE LENÔTRE
Plaisir Cedex/Year-round *(See also page 249)*
This French gastronomy school offers more than sixty 1- to 4-day certificate courses. Established in 1970. Student to teacher ratio 12:1.

COURSES: Classes are 90% participation. Several courses in each of the 9 subject categories: cuisine, catering, oenology & coffee, breads & pastry doughs, patisserie, ice cream & frozen desserts, chocolate & confiserie, sugar & decoration, gastronomy for amateurs. Schedule: 1 day (8 hours) to 4-1/2 days (36 hours). Each course is offered at least twice a year; some are offered once a month. Special a la carte courses for groups of 8 to 12 can also be arranged.

FACULTY: 4 instructors are recipients of the Meilleur Ouvrier de France in pastry-confectionery, pork butchery, ice cream, and bakery-viennoiserie. Founded by Gaston Lenotre and managed by Marcel Derrien, Meilleur Ouvrier de France in pastry-confectionery.

COSTS: Tuition (non-French students), including breakfasts and lunches, ranges from 997 FF (626 FF) to 8,650 FF (5,293 FF). Advance payment is required. The school can reserve rooms in one of Plaisir's hotels, which range from 130 FF-260 FF per night.

LOCATION: About 30 miles from Paris, 6 miles from Versailles.

CONTACT: Marcel Derrien, École Lenôtre, 40, rue Pierre Curie-BP 6, Plaisir Cedex, 787373, France; (33) 1-30-81-46-34, (33) 1-30-81-46-35, Fax (33) 1-30-54-73-70.

ECOLE SUPERIEURE DE CUISINE FRANCAISE GROUPE FERRANDI
Paris/September-June
This professional hotel/restaurant school offers a bilingual 9-month program, awarding a diploma issued by Paris' Chamber of Commerce and preparing students for the C.A.P. certificate. Established 1986. Accredited by French Ministry of Education. Calendar: trimester. Curriculum: culinary. 1,225 hours of culinary courses required. Admission dates: April-August. Total enrollment: 200. 10-12 enrollees/admission period. 90% of applicants accepted. 50% of students receive financial aid. 10% under age 25, 80% age 25-44, 10% age 45 or over. Student to teacher ratio 8:1. 100% obtain employment within 6 months. Facilities: 12 kitchens, tasting lab, auditorium, classrooms, 2 restaurants.

COURSES: General theoretical & practical courses, cooking, baking, pastry, butchery, delicatessen products, fish cookery. Other activities include a 3-day wine country excursion. The 9-month program includes visits to museums, markets, bistros, fine restaurants. Schedule: 8am-4:30pm daily. 6-week restaurant apprenticeships in Paris and provinces arranged for top students.

FACULTY: The curriculum is supervised by a Board of Advisors including well-known French chefs Joel Robuchon and Antoine Westermann.

COSTS: 9-month program costs 86,000 FF. 25% deposit due on acceptance, 50% at first class. Written cancellations 1 month prior forfeit 3,000 FF. Application deadlines: July 30. Admission requirements: proof of medical/accident coverage, long-term student visa, certified birth certificate, undergraduate transcript. 5 loans granted last year. Off-campus lodging $500-$800 per month.

LOCATION: Rue Ferrandi in Paris's Latin Quarter, between St. Germain de Pres and Montparnasse. Convenient to 4 major metro stations.

CONTACT: Stephanie Curtis, Coordinator, ESCF Groupe Ferrandi, Bilingual Program, 10 rue de Richelieu, Paris, 75001, France; (33) 1-40-15-04-57, Fax (33) 1-40-15-04-58.

ÉCOLE DES ARTS CULINAIRES ET DE L'HÔTELLERIE
Lyon/Ecully/Year-round *(See also page 249) (See display ad page 125)*
This school offers programs in cooking and hotel and restaurant management, including the 16-week Cuisine and Culture program, the 2-year Cuisine et Gestion program (taught in French), and short courses for professionals and cooking enthusiasts. Established in 1990. Calendar: semester. Admission dates: October for 16-week program, September and April for 2-year program. Facilities: 13 seminar rooms, 2 computer labs, 8 teaching kitchens, pastry/pantry facilities, video-equipped amphitheatre, sensory analysis lab, restaurants.

ÉCOLE DES ARTS CULINAIRES ET DE L'HÔTELLERIE

Hands-on classes in classical and regional French cuisine, pastry and wine coupled with introduction to and appreciation of France's gastronomic heritage. France's school of culinary arts presided by Paul Bocuse. One-week vacation classes and 16-week, two-year and three-year professional training. French cuisine in France in the Chateau du Vivier. ❧

ÉCOLE DES
ARTS CULINAIRES
ET DE L'HÔTELLERIE

COURSES: Include food preparation and processing, pantry, pastry and bakery workshop, basic cooking and catering, and restaurant cuisine. Seminars cover cheese, wine, cost control, French ingredients, and French culinary culture. Excursions and conversational French classes are provided.

FACULTY: In addition to the Board of Trustees, headed by Paul Bocuse, the permanent teaching staff includes 2 Meilleurs Ouvriers de France, Pastry Chef Alain Berne, and Restaurant Chef Alain Le Cossec.

COSTS: Tuition for the 16-week program is 56,000 FF, which includes lunch and dinner as well as accommodation in the student residence. Tuition for the 2-year program is 48,000 FF/year (lunch and dinner included). Admission requirements: students who complete the 16-week program and pass an exam may take the longer programs. The student residence facility has 114 rooms with private shower; lodging is 2,255 FF/month.

LOCATION: The restored 19th century Chateau du Vivier, in a 17-acre wooded park in the Lyon-Ecully University-Research Zone, 10 minutes from downtown Lyon.

CONTACT: Eleonore Vial, Dean, Anne-Catherine Laurencin, International Programs, Ecole des Arts Culinaires et de l'Hotellerie, Office of International Programs, Chateau du Vivier, B.P. 25, Ecully, Cedex, 69131, France; (33) 4-78-43-36-10, Fax (33) 4-78-43-33-51, URL http://www.mairie-lyon.fr.

L'ECOLE DE PATISSERIE FRANCAISE
Uzes/Year-round

French pastry chef Didier Richeux offers 40 intensive 5-day participation master workshops per year. A school certificate is awarded on completion. Established in 1994. Total enrollment: 2 maximum. Student to teacher ratio 2:1. Facilities: commercial patisserie kitchen with separate ice cream preparation kitchen.

COURSES: Traditional and modern patisserie, including ice creams, sorbets, petits fours, chocolates, celebration cakes, plated desserts, croissants, brioches, croqu'embouches, individual pastries, catering. Individual needs are accommodated. Schedule: Schedule and program are according to student's choice of curriculum, minimum 8 hours/day. Nonparticipant can visit olive oil mill, truffle farms, local markets, feudal castles, and participate in sports activities.

FACULTY: Didier Richeux, co-founder, 18 years experience in pastry cooking & recipient of 17 international awards, including Gold Medal, Cordon Bleu de France; Executive Pastry Chef at Le Cordon Bleu & The Savoy in London, worked at Maxim's in Paris, speaks fluent English.

COSTS: 5,000 FF (Tuesday to Saturday), 9,000 FF (2 weeks). A 25% deposit is required; balance is due 4 weeks before course. Written cancellations at least 4 weeks prior forfeit 1,000 FF. .

LOCATION: 30 minutes north of Nimes Airport, 40 minutes southwest of Avignon, and an hour from Montpellier Airport.

CONTACT: Didier Richeux, L'Ecole de Patisserie Francaise, 12 Rue de la Republique, Uzes, 30700, France; (33) 4-66-22-12-09, Fax (33) 4-66-22-26-36.

LA VARENNE
Burgundy/Summer   *(See also page 252) (See display ad above)*

This private school offers two 3-week residential programs (limit 15 students) that focus on French cuisine: the Intensive Orientation Program for beginners and French Cooking Today for professionals. Established in 1975. Facilities: the school is in the 17th-century Château du Feÿ, a registered historic monument owned by founder Anne Willan.

COURSES: Orientation: fundamentals, pastry, contemporary cuisine, vineyard tours & fine dining. Professionals' course: topics such as classical cooking trends, pastry & chocolate, bistro & regional dishes. Students who pass a written and practical exam earn La Varenne's Diplome d'Etudes Culinaire. Other activities include seminars & escorted excursions to northern Burgundy, Beaune, Paris.

FACULTY: 2/3 of curriculum is taught by La Varenne's cuisine and pastry chefs, the rest by noted French restaurant chefs. Programs are directed by Anne Willan, author of the Look and Cook how-to series featured on PBS, Château Cuisine, and La Varenne Pratique.

COSTS: Fee is $7,695 ($9,075) for the beginner (professional) program, which includes full board & lodging. Nonrefundable $1,000 deposit due within 15 days of acceptance; balance 60 days prior to course. Shared twin lodging at the Château, planned excursions, transportation to/from Paris.

LOCATION: The Château du Feÿ is 90 minutes south of Paris. Amenities include a tennis court and an outdoor swimming pool in season.

CONTACT: La Varenne, P.O. Box 25574, Washington, DC 20007; (800) 537-6486, (202) 337-0073, Fax (703) 823-5438, E-mail 102635.2040@compuserve.com.

LE CORDON BLEU
Paris/Year-round   *(See also page 252) (See display ad page 127)*

This private school acquired by Andre J. Cointreau in 1984, re-opened in 1988, with five locations world-wide in Paris, London, Tokyo, Ottawa, and Sydney, offers 9-months of basic, intermediate and superior level diploma programs in Pastry and Cuisine leading to Le Grande Diplome, 10-week International Culinary Hospitality Program, Master Chef Catering Program, 1- to 5-week programs. Established in 1895. Accredited by international hospitality management schools. Calendar: quarter. Curriculum: culinary. Admission dates: quarterly. Total enrollment: 150. 150 enrollees each admission period. 65% under age 25, 30% age 25-44, 5% age 45 or over. Student to teacher ratio 10:1. Facilities: specialized equipment; classrooms resemble professional kitchens; individual workspaces with refrigerated marble tops; demonstration rooms with video.

COURSES: The Classic Cycle: 3 levels of Cuisine & 3 levels of Pastry taken consecutively or together, Courses cover basic to complex techniques; classic, regional, ethnic, contemporary cuisines; food & wine; catering; planning; presentation; decoration & execution. Schedule: Classic Cycle courses Monday-Saturday at 9am, 1:30pm, 4:30pm and some evenings. Basic Cuisine and Intermediate Pastry three 5-week intensive courses in the fall. Students assist chef at least once and are assisted in finding a 3-month internship. Continuing education: Professional Chef and Master Chef Catering Courses, 1-2 week intensives.

FACULTY: 10 full-time master chefs, international staff. School Director is Catherine Baschet. Culinary staff consists of French Master Chefs from Michelin-starred restaurants and fine hotels, including two holding the title of Meilleur Ouvrier de France.

COSTS: Tuition ranges from 220 FF for a ½ day demonstration to 4,590 FF for a 4-day hands-on course. 10-week Classic Cycle courses range from 22,950 FF in pastry to 36,550 FF in cuisine. 10% deposit required and refundable, less 10%, for written cancellations 4 weeks prior. 6 scholarships awarded last year. Students are assisted in finding lodging. Monthly rent 1,800 FF-6,500 FF.

LOCATION: Paris' 15th arrondissement, centrally located in the southwestern part of the city.

CONTACT: Sabine Bailly, Director of Registration, Le Cordon Bleu, 8, rue Léon Delhomme, Paris, 75015, France; (800) 457-CHEF, (33) 1-53-68-22-50, Fax (33) 1-48-56-03-96, URL http://www.cordonbleu.edu.

RITZ-ESCOFFIER ECOLE DE GASTRONOMIE FRANCAISE
(See also page 257) (See display ad page 128)   **Paris/Year-round**

This culinary school in the Hotel Ritz, named for the hotel's first chef, Auguste Escoffier, offers 1- to 6-week Cesar Ritz diploma and Pastry diploma courses (year-round), an advanced level 12-week Ritz-Escoffier diploma course (January, April, September), and short courses for professionals and enthusiasts. Established in 1988. Calendar: semester. Curriculum: core. Admission dates: courses begin each week. Student to teacher ratio 8-10 per class. Facilities: 2,000-sq-ft custom-designed facility includes a main kitchen, pastry kitchen, conference room/library, changing rooms.

COURSES: The Cesar Ritz and Pastry diploma courses consist of demonstrations, hands-on practice, and theory. Those who complete 1-5 weeks receive a certificate; those who complete the 6-week course & pass a practical exam receive a diploma. Schedule: 25-28 hours/week. Diploma recipients may apply for internship in the Hotel Ritz's restaurant kitchens.

Stag Ogilvy

Ritz Escoffier
École de Gastronomie Française
PARIS

The ultimate gourmet French cooking school
located in the legendary Ritz Hôtel
where renowned Chef Auguste Escoffier reigned
in the kitchens a century ago.

*Food lovers and professionals discover
the art of fine cuisine
in a most exceptional environment.*

- Diploma courses for professionals.
- Week-long courses and day work shops
for passionate amateurs.
- Daily demonstration Classes for Paris visitors.

All courses taught in French
with English translations.

"Good cooking is the source of true happiness"
Auguste Escoffier

HÔTEL RITZ
15, PLACE VENDÔME - 75041 PARIS CEDEX 01
TÉL. 33 (1) 43 16 30 50 - FAX. 33 (1) 43 16 31 50*
TOLL-FREE IN U.S. : (800) 966.5758
*As of October 18, 1996, replace the 1 with 01

FACULTY: 7 full-time, 3 part-time. School director Marie-Anne Dufeu has 10 years experience. Instructors are Chefs de Cuisine Jean-Louis Taillebaud and Aime Barroyer and Chef Patissier Gilles Maisonneuve.

COSTS: In 1996, Cesar Ritz Diploma Course 5,850 FF/week, Pastry Diploma Course 5,550 FF/week, Ritz-Escoffier Diploma Course 71,000 FF for 12 weeks. A 25% deposit must accompany enrollment with balance due 4 weeks before course. Written cancellations 4 weeks prior forfeit 500 FF; no refunds thereafter. Admission requirements: Ritz-Escoffier diploma course students must have Cesar Ritz diploma or equivalent experience; no previous experience for Cesar Ritz & Pastry courses. A list of nearby lodging is provided; special rates at the Hotel Ritz are available.

LOCATION: Central Paris, near 3 main subway entrances and most major department stores.

CONTACT: Marie-Anne Dufeu, Ritz-Escoffier Ecole de Gastronomie Francaise, 15, Place Vendome, Paris Cedex 01, 75041, France; (33) 1-43-16-30-50, (800) 966-5758, Fax (33) 1-43-16-31-50.

HONG KONG

CHOPSTICKS COOKING CENTRE
Kowloon/September-December, March-June

(See also page 258)

This private trade school offers a 1-week Intensive Course for individuals and groups, a 4-week Intensive Course for individuals, ½-and 1-day courses, and classes. Established in 1971. Calendar: quarter. Curriculum: culinary. Admission dates: February-May, August-November. Total enrollment: 20. 10 enrollees/admission period. 90% of applicants accepted. 95% enrolled part-time. 10% under age 25, 70% age 25-44, 20% age 45 or over. Student to teacher ratio 12:1. 90% obtain employment within 6 months. Facilities: professional restaurant kitchen with facilities for practical sessions.

COURSES: Include Chinese regional dishes, dim sums, Chinese roasts, cakes and pastries, breads. Schedule: 8-12 hours/week. Part-time and evening options available.

FACULTY: Professional chefs from various hotels and restaurants. School principal Cecilia J. Au-Yang, domestic science graduate and author of a series of 35 cookbooks, Executive Director Caroline Au Yeung, a graduate of HCIMA.

COSTS: 1-week course is $700 group, $1,400 individual; 4-week course is $2,850 basic, $3,350 advanced. Short courses and classes range from $60-$600. Registration fee is $50. Nonrefundable course deposit is $500. All fees are nonrefundable. Application deadlines: 3-6 months in advance. Local lodging averages $2,200/month.

CONTACT: Cecilia Au-Yang, Principal, Chopsticks Cooking Centre, 108 Boundary St., G/Fl., Kowloon, Hong Kong; (852) 2336-8433, (852) 2336-8037, Fax (852) 2338-1462.

IRELAND

BALLYMALOE COOKERY SCHOOL
Midleton/September-July

(See also page 258)

This proprietary school offers a 12-week certificate course in Food & Wine and a variety of short courses. Established in 1983. Calendar: quarter. Curriculum: culinary. Admission dates: September, January. Total enrollment: 44. 44 enrollees each admission period. 90% of applicants accepted. 50% under age 25, 40% age 25-44, 10% age 45 or over. Student to teacher ratio 6:1. 100% obtain employment within 6 months. Facilities: include a specially-designed kitchen with gas and electric cookers, a mirrored demonstration area, and gardens that supply fresh produce.

COURSES: Most courses are hands-on and emphasize traditional Irish and French classic cookery, international cuisine, vegetarian, and seafood cooking. Schedule: 40 hours/week.

FACULTY: 4 full- and 4 part-time. Includes Principal Darina Allen, IACP-certified Teacher & Food Professional, her brother, Rory O'Connell, both trained in the Ballymaloe House restaurant kitchen, and her husband Tim Allen. Guest chefs are featured.

Costs: The 12-week course is IR £3,575. Deposit with booking: 10% of fee for 3-month course, 25% for short course. Application deadlines: subject to availability. Students live in cottages during the 3-month course and may assist in the restaurant. Self-catering cottage lodging is IR £35/week double, £48 single.

Location: Airport & train station pick-up can be arranged. A mile from the sea, outside the village of Shanagarry in southern Ireland, a 4-hour drive from Dublin.

Contact: Tim Allen, Ballymaloe Cookery School, Kinoith, Shanagarry, County Cork, Midleton, Ireland; (353) 21-646785, Fax (353) 21-646909.

ITALY

AVIGNONESI WINE AND FOOD WORKSHOPS
Florence/May and October *(See also page 261)*
This wine-producing estate offers five 10-day programs each year that are designed for wine and food professionals.
Contact: Pamela Sheldon Johns, 1324 State St., #J-157, Santa Barbara, CA 93101, United States; (805) 963-7289, E-mail CulinArt@aol.com.

SCUOLA DI ARTE CULINARIA "CORDON BLEU"
Florence/Year-round *(See also page 274)*
This private school offers professional programs in spring and fall and nonvocational/vacation programs year-round. Professional curriculum consists of 13-17 one- to nine-session hands-on courses, a total of 260-360 hours of instruction. Established in 1985. Calendar: quarter, semester. 183 hours of culinary courses required. Admission dates: July, November for professional programs; year-round for other courses. Total enrollment: 150. 50-70 enrollees each admission period. 90% of applicants accepted. 90% enrolled part-time. 15% under age 25, 45% age 25-44, 40% age 45 or over. Student to teacher ratio 6:1. 90% obtain employment within 6 months. Facilities: the school's 40-square-meter teaching kitchen.
Courses: Include basic to advanced cooking, pastry, breads, holiday menus, regional specialties, specific subjects, wine history. Schedule: morning, afternoon, evening, and customized schedules are available.
Faculty: 2 full-time instructors. Cristina Blasi & Gabriella Mari, 11 years experience, sommeliers and olive oil experts, authored a book on ancient Roman cooking, members Commanderie des Cordons Bleus de France, IACP, Italian Assn. of Cooking Teachers.
Costs: Tuition is 6,000,000 Lira (6,400,000 Lira) for the fall (spring) program, 7,300,000 Lira for both. 30% deposit due 1-month prior; balance at start of course. Deposit not refundable. Application deadlines: August, December. Off-campus housing available in apartments and hotels.
Location: Central Florence.
Contact: Gabriella Mari, Co-Director, Scuola di Arte Culinaria "Cordon Bleu", Via di Mezzo, 55/R, 50121 Firenze-Florence, Italy; (39) 55-2345468, Fax (39) 55-2345468, URL http://www.ats.it/kiosco/cordonbl.

MASTER CLASSES IN VENICE WITH MARCELLA & VICTOR HAZAN
Venice/March-October
Cookbook author Marcella Hazan and her husband, Victor offer 5-day participation master classes at their residence, a 16th century palazzo. Admission dates: classes offered once a month. Student to teacher ratio 6 per class.
Courses: Format is loosely structured, focusing on the techniques and improvisation of classic Italian cuisine. Other activities include a visit to the Rialto market and dinner at a fine local restaurant. Schedule: 10am-3pm for 5 consecutive days.
Costs: Tuition is $2,500. $200 deposit is required, which becomes nonrefundable when class date is confirmed and accepted. Balance is due 120 days prior. Cancellations 45 days. A list of recom-

mended hotels and travel information is provided.

LOCATION: Central Venice.

CONTACT: Susan Cox, Hazan Classics, P.O. Box 285, Circleville, NY 10919; (914) 692-7104, Fax (914) 692-2659.

JAPAN

LE CORDON BLEU TOKYO
(See also page 277) (See display ad page 127)   **Tokyo/Year-round**

This private school acquired by Le Cordon Bleu Paris. Cuisine and Pastry diplomas: 9-month programs of basic, intermediate, superior levels. Le Grand Diplome: 9-month program of cuisine and pastry. Introductory courses to cuisine, pastry, catering, bread baking. Daily demonstrations, evening sessions. Established in 1991. Accredited through international hospitality management schools. Calendar: quarter. Curriculum: culinary. Admission dates: quarterly. Facilities: classrooms resemble professional working kitchens; individual work spaces with refrigerated marble tables, convection ovens; specialty appliances.

COURSES: Classic Cycle core curriculum consists of 3 levels of cuisine and pastry, taken consecutively or together. Covers basic to complex techniques, wine and food pairing, catering, presentation. Schedule: Monday-Saturday, some evenings. Assistance in finding a 3-month internship is provided. Offered at the Paris and London schools.

FACULTY: 7 full-time French and English Master Chefs from Michelin-star restaurants and fine hotels.

COSTS: 10% deposit is required and refundable, less 10%, 4 weeks prior. Assistance is provided in finding lodging.

LOCATION: Tokyo's Daikanyama district.

CONTACT: Yann Brochet, School Director, Le Cordon Bleu, Roob-1, 28-13 Sarugaku-cho, Daikanyama, Shibuya-ku, Tokyo, 150, Japan; (81) 3 5489 01 41, (800) 457-CHEF, Fax (81) 3 5489 01 45, URL www.cordonbleu.edu.

MEXICO

SEASONS OF MY HEART COOKING SCHOOL
(See also page 279)   **Oaxaca/Year-round**

This private school offers a 1-week course twice a year and long weekend courses year-round for culinary professionals; 1-day to 1-week courses for nonprofessionals. Established in 1993. Curriculum: culinary. Total enrollment: 2-20. 100% of applicants accepted. 3% of students receive financial aid. 50% enrolled part-time. 10% under age 25, 50% age 25-44, 40% age 45 or over. Student to teacher ratio 2-10:1. Facilities: Rancho Aurora, a working farm, has a handmade kitchen with 5 stations, outdoor kitchen with parilla, wood-fire and pre-hispanic cooking utensils.

COURSES: "Seven Days for Seven Moles", traditional foods, herbs, pre-hispanic foods, culinary and anthropological studies. Schedule: 6 days, mornings and afternoons. Students come on a non-paid work study basis to be determined individually. Continuing education: archeological tours, herbal studies, farming, extended work-study.

FACULTY: 1 full-time. Susana Trilling, teacher, writer, lecturer, chef, caterer, IACP member. Part-time teachers, cheese makers, bread bakers, chocolate makers, chefs, farmers, herbal healers.

COSTS: $1,295 for 1-week course, which includes meals, lodging, and planned activities. A $200 deposit is required; $150 is nonrefundable. Cancellations 2 weeks prior forfeit $200, no refund thereafter unless space is sold. Application deadlines: 2-weeks to 1-month prior. Admission requirements: student is working in or has studied culinary arts full-time. 1 scholarship awarded last year at $650. Lodging options are private bungalow with view of ranch, bed & breakfast, or other posada in Oaxaca City.

LOCATION: Ranch surrounded by archeological sites in the mountains outside Oaxaca.

CONTACT: Susana Trilling, Director, Seasons of My Heart Cooking School, Rancho Aurora, P.O. Box AP 42, Admon 3, Oaxaca, 68101, Mexico; (951) 6-52-80, (800) 758-1697 (US), Fax (951) 6-52-80.

NEW ZEALAND

CENTRAL INSTITUTE OF TECHNOLOGY
Upper Hutt/Year-round

This trade school offers a 3-year diploma and a 1-year certificate in Hospitality Operations-Management. Year-round 1978. Accredited by State. Calendar: semester. Curriculum: core. 1,480 hours (diploma), 500 hours (certificate) of culinary courses required. Admission dates: August. Total enrollment: 300. 90 enrollees each admission period. 50% of applicants accepted. 40% of students receive financial aid. 65% under age 25. Student to teacher ratio 14:1. 50% obtain employment within 6 months. Facilities: 3 kitchens, 20 classrooms, 2 restaurants.

COURSES: Schedule: 20 hours/week, 30 weeks.

FACULTY: 24 full-time.

COSTS: Tuition: in-country NZ$1,600, out-of-country NZ$10,500. Application deadlines: August 15. Admission requirements: high school diploma or equivalent and admission test. On-campus housing cost: NZ$130 per week.

CONTACT: Tim Lockyer, Head of Department, Central Institute of Technology, Faculty of Commerce, P.O. Box 40-740, Upper Hutt, New Zealand; (64) 4-527-6398 #6758, Fax (64) 4-527-6364, E-mail tim@staff.cit.ac.nz.

THE NEW ZEALAND SCHOOL OF FOOD AND WINE
Christchurch/Year-round

This proprietary institution offers a 15-week full-time certificate in Foundation Cookery Skills, which includes New Zealand certificate in wine. Established in 1994. Accredited by New Zealand Qualifications Authority. Calendar: trimester. Curriculum: culinary. Admission dates: January, May, August. Facilities: include demonstration kitchen with overhead mirrors and practical kitchen with commercial equipment.

COURSES: Foundation Skills: Based on Leith's Bible; concepts of French cuisine, food presentation, menu planning, costing, catering, cuisines of Australasia; wine & vineyard tours. Food & The Family: integrates skills of early childhood education with cookery.

FACULTY: 10 full-time and part-time tutors.

COSTS: Tuition is approximately NZ$3,750 (plus tax). A NZ$250 deposit is required; balance due 20 days prior. Full refund until day 7 of course. Registered with the New Zealand Qualifications Authority (NZQA); students eligible for student visas.

LOCATION: Christchurch, a city of 300,000 in South Island.

CONTACT: Celia Hay, The New Zealand School of Food and Wine, 63 Victoria St., Box 25217, Christchurch, So. Island, New Zealand; (61) 3-3797-501, Fax (61) 3-3797-501.

SCOTLAND

EDINBURGH COOKERY SCHOOL
Edinburgh/September-July

This school offers full-time 10-week foundation, intermediate, and advanced certificate courses, a 22-week Intensive Certificate course, and a 1-year Combined Cookery, Secretarial and French certificate course in conjunction with Basil Paterson College. Established in 1988. Admission dates: September, October, January, April, summer months. 20 enrollees each admission period. Student to teacher ratio 12 per hands-on class. Facilities: include domestic and commercial gas cookers, electric ovens, and Aga cookers.

Costs: Tuition, exclusive of VAT, is £3,500 for the Intensive Certificate course, £1,685 for the other certificate courses, £875 for 4-week course. Housing is £65/week (space limited).

Contact: Edinburgh Cookery School, The Coach House, Newliston, Kirkliston, Edinburgh, EH29 9EB, Scotland; (44) 131-667-3960, Fax (44) 131-662-9320.

TOP TIER SUGARCRAFT
Inverness/Year-round

This school and mail order business offers 1-, 2-, and 3- week demonstration and participation courses for beginners and experts. Established in 1985. Student to teacher ratio 8 per class. Facilities: 600-square-foot classroom with specialized equipment.

Courses: Sugarpaste, royal, floral, chocolate, marzipan, pastillage, and personalized wedding cake instruction. New courses in cold porcelain work, which is suitable for window display and table centerpieces. Other activities include sightseeing in the Highlands. Schedule: 10am-3pm daily. Also available: day and weekend courses.

Faculty: Principal teacher Diana Turner, British Sugarcraft Guild member and judge, has more than 10 years of experience in sugarcraft work.

Costs: Day classes begin at £30; weekend courses begin at £60; week-long programs cost ú750 per week, including meals and accommodations. A £100 deposit is required; full refund with 1 month notice. Meals and accommodations with a Scottish family.

Location: A mile from Culloden Battlefield, 5 miles from Inverness.

Contact: Diana Turner, Top Tier Sugarcraft, 10 Meadow Rd., Balloch, Inverness, IV1 2JR, Scotland; (44) 1463-790456, Fax (44) 1463-790456.

SOUTH AFRICA

SILWOOD KITCHEN CORDONS BLEUS COOKERY SCHOOL
Rondebosch Cape/Year-round

This school offers three 1-year culinary career courses that begin each January: the Certificate Course, the Diploma Course, and the Grande Diploma. Established in 1964. Accredited by HITB-Hospitality Industries Training Board. Calendar: 4 terms. Curriculum: core. Approximately 1,400 hours of culinary courses required. Admission dates: last Thursday in January. Total enrollment: 44. 44, divided into groups of 11 enrollees each admission period. 60% of applicants accepted. 96% under age 25, 4% age 25-44. Student to teacher ratio 11:1. 100% obtain employment within 6 months. Facilities: a 200-year-old coach-house converted into a demonstration and experimental kitchen, 3 additional kitchens, demonstration hall, and a library.

Courses: Cooking and baking, icing, wine, table art, mise en place, floral art. Schedule: cooking and baking practicing, wine, table art, mise en place, floral art.

Faculty: 11-member faculty. Includes school principal Alicia Wilkinson, nutrition instructors Jeanette Rietmann, menu reading instructor Alisa Smith, and practical supervisors Louise Faull, Peggy Loebenberg, Carianne Wilkinson, Pauline Copus and Shirley Henderson.

Costs: Tuition is R20,680 for the Certificate course, R8,470 for the Diploma course, and R825 for the Grande Diploma. A R1,000 deposit must accompany application. Application deadlines: September. Housing is R500 to R1,000/month.

Location: Cape Town.

Contact: Mrs. Alicia Wilkinson, Silwood Kitchen, Silwood Rd., Rondebosch Cape, South Africa; (27) 21-686-4894, (27) 21-685-4378, Fax (27) 21-685-4378.

National Apprenticeship Training Program for Cooks

**American Culinary Federation
Educational Institute (ACFEI)**

Culinary Apprenticeship is a three-year on-the-job training program complemented by related instruction from an educational institution. The program began under the Carter Administration in 1976 with a grant from the U.S. government and is now the 7th largest apprenticeship program in the United States, with over 17,000 cooks being trained since its inception.

The apprenticeship program offers career-oriented cooks an alternative to private culinary institutions and vocational-technical schools. Apprentices, who generally range in age from 18 to 40 (average age 24), receive three years (6,000 hours) of on-the-job training while earning an income. The first 500 hours are a probationary period, after which the apprentice is eligible to join the ACFEI and become registered with the Department of Labor. In addition to a 40-hour work week, the apprentice attends school part-time (a minimum of 192 hours per year) and may also have the opportunity to earn an associate degree. The average cost for school is between $500 and $3,000 during a three-year period.

To qualify for the program, applicant must be at least 17 years of age, have a high school diploma or equivalent, and have passed all entry-level academic and aptitude examinations as prescribed by the Apprenticeship Committee of the ACFEI. Consideration is given to those who have had high school foodservice training or on-the-job experience. A five-step screening process includes an orientation seminar, documentation of prior experience, and personal interviews.

The program is planned in six semi-annual stages, which can be shortened or lengthened according to the individual's ability. The apprentice keeps a weekly Log Book in which recipes and food preparation techniques are recorded. Those who complete the apprenticeship can: prepare, season, and cook soups, sauces, salads, meats, fish, poultry, game, vegetables, and desserts; produce baked goods and pastries; fabricate meat portions from primal cuts; prepare a buffet dinner; select and develop recipes; plan, write, and design complete menus; plan food consumption, purchasing, and requisitioning; operate a working budget in food and labor costing; recognize quality standards in fresh vegetables, meats, fish, and poultry; demonstrate supervisory abilities and inter-relate with other departments in a food operation; and demonstrate basic artistic culinary skills, including ice carving, tallow sculpturing, cake decorating, and garniture display work.

In addition to work skills, the apprentice completes 30 hours minimum class time at an accredited post-secondary institution in each of 12 areas of related instruction: 1) Introduction to Food Service (Industry Survey); 2) Sanitation and Safety; 3) Basic Food Preparation (Introduction to Cooking); 4) Business Math (Food Cost Accounting); 5) Food and Beverage Service; 6) Nutrition; 7) Garde Manger; 8) Menu Planning and Design; 9) Baking; 10) Purchasing; 11) Supervisory Management; 12) Advanced Food preparation.

On completion of the program, the apprentice is identified as a Certified Cook and may be offered employment at the training establishment or recommended for job placement.

CONTACT: ACFEI Programs Coordinator, American Culinary Federation, P.O. Box 3466, 10 San Bartola Rd., St. Augustine, FL 32085; (800) 624-9458 or (904) 824-4468, Fax (904) 825-4758.

The following information about 101 ACFEI apprenticeships in effect June, 1996, was provided by the American Culinary Federation. and the program coordinators.

ALABAMA

ACF BIRMINGHAM CHAPTER

This chapter has 25 apprentices, 15 under age 25, 10 age 25 or over. Costs are $3,500 in-state, $5,000 out-of-state. Beginning salary is $5/hr with 40 cent increases every 6 mos. The 15 locations are country club, restaurant, hotel, corporate dining room, private club. Most desirable settings are local fine-dining restaurants and country clubs. Housing cost is $350-$500/mo. Degree program through Jefferson State Community College.

CONTACT: George White, Acting Coordinator, Jefferson State Junior College, 2601 Carson Rd., Birmingham, AL 35215; 205-856-7898 (work phone), Fax 205-853-0701.

ACF GREATER MONTGOMERY CHAPTER

CONTACT: Mary Ann Ward, CEC, CCE, Trenholm State Technical College, 1225 Air Base Blvd., Montgomery, AL 36108; 205-262-4728 (work phone), 205-272-7245 (home phone).

ACF METRO MOBILE CHEFS ASSN.

CONTACT: Levi Ezell, CEC, CCE, AAC, Chef/Instructor, Carver Technical College, 414 Station Street, Mobile, AL 36603; 334-473-8692 (work phone).

ARIZONA

CHEFS ASSOCIATION OF GREATER PHOENIX

This chapter has 8 apprentices, 4 under age 25, 4 age 25 or over. The 9 locations are resorts. Degree program through Scottsdale & Phoenix Community Colleges. Baking apprenticeship available.

CONTACT: Camron Clarkson, CWC, 2210 E. Sunnyside Dr., Phoenix, AZ 85028; 602-404-9566.

CHEFS ASSOCIATION OF SOUTHERN ARIZONA, TUCSON

CONTACT: Ed Doran, 4123 E. Glenn Street, Tucson, AZ 85712; 520-469-8175.

RESORT & COUNTRY CLUB CHEFS OF THE SW ACF

CONTACT: Robert Chantos, CEC, Desert Samaritan Care Center, 2145 West Southern Ave., Mesa, AZ 85202; 602-890-4816 (work phone), 602-991-2411 (home phone), Fax 602-890-4829.

ARKANSAS

ACF CENTRAL AR CULINARY SCHOOL OF APPRENTICESHIP

This chapter has 35 apprentices, 5 under age 25, 30 age 25 or older. There are 10 on the waiting list. Cost is $1,100/year plus books, uniform, knife kit. Beginning salary is minimum wage or determined by employer. The 12 locations include hotels, hospitals, owner-operated small restaurants, foodservice management companies.

CONTACT: Sharon B. McCone, RD, LD, Executive Director, ACF Central Arkansas Culinary School of Apprenticeship, Box 13226, Maumelle, AR 72113; (501) 590-2722, Fax (501) 851-6684, E-mail acfcark@juno.com.

ACF LITTLE ROCK, AR CHAPTER

This chapter has 11 apprentices, 4 under age 25, 7 age 25 or over. Costs are $650/yr. Beginning salary is $4.75/hr with 5% increases every 6 mos. 8 locations. Most desirable settings are hotel, restaurant, country club.

CONTACT: Edward Hornyak, CEC, 6 Silver Birch Court, Little Rock, AR 72212; 501-225-5622 (work phone), 501-843-3416.

CALIFORNIA

ACF CHEFS ASSOCIATION SAN JOAQUIN VALLEY

CONTACT: Bill McComas, 1175 E. Alluvial, Fresno, CA 93720; 209-322-7280 (work phone), 209-297-0125 (home phone), Fax 209-298-8837.

ACF SAN FRANCISCO CHAPTER

CONTACT: Kay Stickney, Restaurant & Hotel Apprentice & Training Program, 1650 S. Amphlett Blvd., Ste. 312, San Mateo, CA 94402; 415-574-6700 (work phone), Fax 415-341-9725.

ACF SANTA BARBARA

CONTACT: Tim Fox, 208 Natoma, #2, Santa Barbara, CA 93101; 805-564-4333.

CALIFORNIA CAPITOL CHEFS ASSOCIATION

This chapter has 43 apprentices, 33 under age 25. Waiting list is 1 yr. Costs are $15 for books & materials. Beginning salary is $5.40/hr with increases every 6 mos. The 26 locations are restaurants and convalescent homes. Most desirable settings are Red Lion Hotel & El Paso Country Club. Housing cost is $425/mo. Degree program through Sierra College. Baking apprenticeship available.

CONTACT: Jon Greenwalt, CEC, AAC, 5475 Asby Lane, Granite Bay, CA 95746; 916-791-2554.

CHEF DE CUISINE OF BAKERSFIELD

This chapter has 3 apprentices, under age 25, 3 age 25 or over. Waiting list is 1 yr. Costs are $500. Beginning salary is $5/hr with increases every 6 mos. The 2 locations are country club & hotel. Most desirable settings are Red Lion Corporation. Housing cost is $1000/mo. Degree program through Bakersfield Community College. Baking apprenticeship available.

Contact: William P. Coyle, CCE, Bakersfield College-Food Service, 1801 Panorama Dr., Bakersfield, CA 93305; 805-395-4345 (work phone), 805-397-7271 (home phone), Fax 805-395-4241.

CHEFS DE CUISINE ASSOCIATION OF CALIFORNIA

This chapter has 15 apprentices, 14 under age 25, 1 age 25 or over. Costs are $150. Beginning salary is variable with increases every 6 mos. The locations are hotel, private club, restaurant. Housing cost is variable. Degree program through California Polytechnic is completed by 100%. Baking apprenticeship available.

CONTACT: Leroy Blanchard, CEC, Culinary Arts Dept., 400 W. Washington Blvd., Los Angeles, CA 90015; 213-744-9480 (work phone), 310-514-0427 (home phone), Fax 213-748-7334.

NORTHERN CALIFORNIA CHEFS ASSOCIATION

CONTACT: Michael Piccinino, CEC, CCE, 6945 Pine Dr., Anderson, CA 96007; 916-225-4829 (work phone), 916-241-6162 (home phone), Fax 916-225-4881.

ORANGE EMPIRE CHEFS ASSOCIATION

This chapter has 25 apprentices. Costs are $100 one time ACF fee, $55 annually & $13/unit. Beginning salary is negotiable with negotiable increases negotiable. The 30 locations are hotel, country club and restaurant. Most desirable settings are Ritz Carlton, Laguna Niguel, Sutton Place Hotel, and Westin. Housing cost is $400-$600/mo. Degree program through Orange Coast College is completed by 25%. Baking apprenticeship available.

CONTACT: Bill Barber, CWC, Orange Coast C.C., 2701 Fairview Rd., P.O. Box 5005, Costa Mesa, CA 92628-5005; 714-432-5835 (work phone).

SAN FRANCISCO CULINARY/PASTRY PROGRAM

This chapter has 15 apprentices. Waiting list is 12-18 mos. Beginning salary is 55% of journeyman wage with 5% increases every 6 mos. The 5-7 locations are full-service hotels and restaurants. Degree program through City College. Baking apprenticeship available.

CONTACT: Joan Ortegea, Director, 760 Market St., Suite 1066, San Francisco, CA 94102; 415-989-8726 (work phone), Fax 415-989-2920.

SANTA CLARA COUNTY CHEFS ASSOCIATION

CONTACT: Eric Carter, 1572 Monteval Lane, San Jose, CA 95120; 408-254-5627 #258 (work phone), Fax 408-254-5665.

SOUTHERN CALIFORNIA INLAND EMPIRE CHEFS ASSOCIATION

CONTACT: Jesse Moreno, 1723 Rhone Avenue, Highland, CA 92346; 909-864-2737 (work phone), Fax 909-864-7404.

COLORADO

ACF COLORADO CHEFS DE CUISINE ASSOCIATION

CONTACT: Dudley Cable-Larche, CCC, 1250 Welton Street, Denver, CO 80204; 303-575-4808 (work phone), Fax 303-575-4840.

ACF CULINARIANS OF COLORADO

This chapter has 33 apprentices, 3 under age 25, 30 age 25 or over. Costs are $1,150. Beginning salary is 70% of journeyman wage with 5% increases every 6 mos. The 30 locations are restaurant, hotel, club, hospital, and caterer. Most desirable settings are located in Denver. Housing cost is $300+/mo. Degree program through Community College of Denver is completed by 5%.

CONTACT: Dudley Cable-Larche, CEC, Chairman Apprentice Committee, 820 - 16th St., Ste. 421, Denver, CO 80202; 303-571-5653 (work phone), Fax 303-571-4050.

KEYSTONE RESORT APPRENTICESHIP PROGRAM

This chapter has 35 apprentices, 17 under age 25, 17 age 25 or over. Costs are $1,200/year. Beginning salary is $6.50/hr with increases based on performance. The 10 locations are resort, 9 restaurants, conference center. Most desirable settings are Keystone Ranch, Aspenglow Stube, Ski Tip Lodge. Housing cost is $260/mo. Degree program through Colorado Mountain College is completed by 100%.

CONTACT: CME Admissions, PO Box10,001, Glenwood Springs, CO 81602; 800-621-8559 (work phone), Fax 970-945-7279.

CONNECTICUT

CHEFS OF WESTCHESTER & LOWER CONNECTICUT

CONTACT: Brian Martin, Black Goose Grill, 972 Post Rd., Darien, CT 06820; 203-655-7107 (work phone), 914-667-0984 (home phone).

FLORIDA

ACF CENTRAL FLORIDA CHAPTER

This chapter has 300 apprentices, 80 under age 25, 20 age 25 or over. Costs are $615. Beginning salary is $6.50/hr with 25 cent increases annually. The 50 locations are restaurant, corporate and resorts. Most desirable settings are Swan (Westin) Hotel, Peabody Hotel, Sheraton Plaza. Baking apprenticeship available.

CONTACT: Valerie Shelton, Mid Florida Tech, Culinary Arts O/TEC, 2900 W. Oak Ridge Road, Orlando, FL 32809; 407-855-5880 #286 (work phone).

ACF FIRST COAST CHAPTER

This chapter has 25 apprentices, 15 under age 25, 10 age 25 or over. Waiting list is 3 mos. Costs are $300/yr. Beginning salary is $5.50/hr with 25 cent increases every 6 mos. The 20 locations are restaurant, hotel, resort, private club, country club. Most desirable settings are River Club, Ritz Carlton Amelia Island, Omni Hotel. Housing cost is $400/mo. Degree program through Florida Community College at Jacksonville is completed by 100%. Baking apprenticeship available.

CONTACT: Don Pleau, CWC, Ponte Vedra Inn & Club, 200 Ponte Vedra Blvd., Ponte Vedra, FL 32082; 904-285-1111 (work phone).

ACF GREATER FT. LAUDERDALE CHAPTER

This chapter has 22 apprentices, 6 under age 25, 16 age 25 or over. Costs are $200. Beginning salary is $6-$8 with 25-50 cent increases every 3-6 mos. The 12 locations are restaurant, resort, hospital. Most desirable settings are Marriott Harbor Beach Resort, Bonaventure Hotel Resort, Lauderdale Yacht Club. Degree program through Atlantic Vocational Technical Center. Baking apprenticeship available.

CONTACT: Ken Carver, CEC, AAC, 8200 S.W. 3rd St., N. Lauderdale, FL 33068; 305-722-8487 (home phone), Fax 305-977-2091.

ACF GULF TO LAKES CHEFS CHAPTER

This chapter has 16 apprentices, 5 under age 25, 11 age 25 or over. Costs are paid by school. Beginning salary is subject to local wage scales with 25 cent increases every 6 mos. The 12 locations are restaurant, corporate, resort, hotel, inn, nursing care home. Most desirable settings are full service resorts, hotels and restaurants. Degree program through Lake County Vocational Tech Center.

CONTACT: James Aro, CEC, Chef Instructor, 2001 Kurt St., Eustis, FL 32726; 904-742-6486 #152 (work phone), 904-483-2546.

ACF PALM BEACH COUNTY CHEFS

This chapter has 28 apprentices. Costs are $300/yr. Beginning salary is $6/hr with 50 cent increases every 6 mos. The 10 locations are restaurant, hotel, resort, private club, country club, corporate dining room. Housing cost is $400/mo. Degree program through Palm Beach Community College is completed by 80%.

CONTACT: Ken Wade, CEC, AAC, 3926 Bluebell St., Palm Beach Gardens, FL 33410; 407-744-1300 (work phone), Fax 407-744-9948.

ACF TAMPA BAY CULINARIANS

Costs are $37.50/credit, total credits 64. Most desirable settings are hotels, supermarkets, restaurants. Housing cost is $350-$400. Degree program through Willsborough Community College. Baking apprenticeship available.

CONTACT: George J. Pastor, Ed. D., AAC Program Mgr., Hillsborough Community College, PO Box 30030, Dale Mabry Campus, Tampa, FL 33630; 813-253-7316 (work phone), Fax 813-253-7400.

ACF TREASURE COAST CHAPTER

This chapter has 30 apprentices, 10 under age 25, 20 age 25 or over. Costs are $160 plus texts and materials. Beginning salary is $5-$6/hr with increases every 3 mos. The 15 locations are country club, resort, corporate, institutional and restaurant. Most desirable settings are Indian River Plantation, Harbor Ridge CC, Indian River Estates.

CONTACT: Alain Piraux, Indian River Plantation, 555 NE Ocean Blvd, Stuart, FL 34996; 407-225-3700 (work phone), 407-225-2454 (home phone), Fax 407-225-2130.

DISNEY WORLD CULINARY APPRENTICESHIP

This chapter has 137 apprentices. Costs are $2,175 for 3 yrs. Beginning salary is $6.20/hr.

CONTACT: Kevin Keating, CEC, CCE, Walt Disney World Co.-Culinary Development, P.O. Box 10,000, Lake Buena Vista, FL 32830-1000; 407-824-5233 (work phone).

GULF COAST CULINARY ASSOCIATION

CONTACT: Jim O'Brien, CWC, P.O. Box 208, Pensacola, FL 32597; 904-432-3707 (work phone).

SARASOTA BAY CHEFS ASSOCIATION

CONTACT: Stephen Hodge, 8437 Gardens Circle 4, Sarasota, FL 34243; 941-355-9733 (work phone), Fax 941-351-4537.

TAMPA BAY CHEFS & COOKS ASSOCIATION

This chapter has variable apprentices. Costs are $1,200 approx., $34 per credit. Beginning salary is open. Degree program through Hillsborough Community College is completed by 70%. Baking apprenticeship available.

CONTACT: Patrica Sparano. CWC, Hillsborough Community College, 4001 Tampa Bay Blvd., Tampa Bay, FL 33614; 813-932-8612 (work phone).

VOLUSIA COUNTY CHEFS & COOKS

This chapter has 28 apprentices, 12 under age 25, 16 age 25 or over. Costs are $700 in-state, $900 out-of-state. Beginning salary is $5-$6/hr with increases annually. The 30 locations are restaurant, hotel, country clubs. Most desirable settings are country clubs, hotels, & gourmet restaurants.

CONTACT: Jeff Conklin. CEC, Daytona Beach Community College, Daytona Beach, FL 32120-2811; 904-255-8131 #3735 (work phone), 904-423-7994 (home phone), Fax 904-254-4465.

WEST CENTRAL FLORIDA PROFESSIONAL CHEFS

CONTACT: Ray Mickiewicz, 4115 Henderson Blvd., Suite A, Tampa, FL 33629; 813-499-5484 (work phone).

GEORGIA

ACF INC., GREATER ATLANTA CHAPTER

CONTACT: John Brantley, CEC, 3571 Forrest Glen Trail, Lawrenceville, GA 30244; 770-381-8618 (work phone).

GOLDEN ISLES OF GEORGIA, CULINARY ASSOCIATION

CONTACT: Joe Santangini, Cloister Hotel Sea Island, Sea Island, GA 31522; 912-638-3611 #5725 (work phone), 912-638-7370 (home phone), Fax 912-638-5159.

HAWAII

CHEFS DE CUISINE ASSOCIATION OF HAWAII

CONTACT: William Trask, CEC, Ilikai Hotel, 1777 Ala Moana Blvd., Honolulu, HI 96816; 808-949-3811 (work phone), 808-735-5641 (home phone), Fax 808-947-4523.

MAUI CHEFS ASSOCIATION

This chapter has 6 apprentices, 4 under age 25, 2 age 25 or over. Waiting list is 1 yr. Costs are $261 in-state, $1,557 out-of-state/semester. Beginning salary is $10.50-$11/hr with increases every 6 mos. The 3 locations are resort and restaurant. Most desirable settings are Westin Maui and Kea Lani Resort. Housing cost is $600-$800/mo. Degree program through Maui Community College is completed by 50%.

CONTACT: Christopher Speere, Culinary Educator, Maui CC, 310 Kaahumanu Ave., PO Box 1284, Kaahului, HI 96732; 808-242-1210 (work phone), 808-575-2353 (home phone), Fax 808-242-1251.

ILLINOIS

ACF CHICAGO CHEFS OF CUISINE

CONTACT: Jeff M. Lemke, CWC, 23808 Sunset Drive, Lake Zurich, IL 60047; 708-382-4240 (work phone).

INDIANA

ACF GREATER INDIANAPOLIS CHAPTER

CONTACT: Frank Lee, CWC, Hillview Country Club, 1800 E. King St., Franklin, IN 46131; 317-736-5555 (work phone), Fax 317-736-5555.

ACF SOUTH BEND CHAPTER

This chapter has 20 apprentices, 7 under age 25, 13 age 25 or over. Costs are $3,825 for 3 years(6,000 hrs). Beginning salary is $7.50/hr with 8% increases every 1,000 hrs. The 14 locations are restaurant, hotel, private club, country club, college, hospital. Most desirable settings are restaurant, hotel, country club. Degree program through Lake Michigan College is completed by 65%.

CONTACT: Denis F. Ellis, CEC, AAC, University of Notre Dame, Dining Hall, Notre Dame, IN 46556; 219-239-5416 (work phone), 219-486-2922 (home phone).

ACF CHEF DE CUISINE/QUAD CITIES

This chapter has 25 apprentices, 13 under age 25, 12 age 25 or over. Waiting list is 1 yr. Costs are $4,500 for 3 years. Beginning salary is $5/hr with 25 cent increases every 6 mos. The 22 locations are country club, hotel and restaurant. Housing cost is $300-$350/mo. Degree program through Scott Community College.

CONTACT: Jennifer Cook-DeRosa, Culinary Arts/Apprent. Facilitator, Scott Community College, 500 Belmont Rd., Bettendorf, IA 52722; 319-359-7531 #278 (work phone).

ACF GREATER DES MOINES CULINARY ASSOCIATION

CONTACT: Robert Anderson, Des Moines Area CC, 2006 S. Ankeny Blvd., Andeny, IA 50021; 515-964-6200 #6566 (work phone).

KANSAS

ACF GREATER KANSAS CITY CHEFS ASSOCIATION

CONTACT: Patrick Sweeney, CEC,AAC, Johnson County Comm. College, 12345 College @ Quivira, Overland Park, KS 66210; 913-469-8500 #3611 (work phone).

LOUISIANA

ACF NEW ORLEANS CHAPTER

This chapter has 190 apprentices, 123 under age 25, 67 age 25 or over. Costs are $3,600. Beginning salary is with 25 cent increases every 6 mos. The 75 locations are restaurant, hotel, country club, private club. Housing cost is $350-$550. Degree program through Delgado Community College is completed by 90%.

CONTACT: Iva Bergeron, CCE, Delgado Community College, 615 City Park Ave., Bldg. 11, New Orleans, LA 70119-4399; 504-483-4208 (work phone), Fax 504-483-4893.

MARYLAND

CENTRAL MARYLAND CHEFS ASSOCIATION

This chapter has 26 apprentices, 24 under age 25, 1 age 25 or over. Beginning salary is $5/hr with increases every 6 mos. Most desirable settings are hotel, country club, restaurant. Degree program through Anne Arundel Community College. Baking apprenticeship available.

CONTACT: Terry Green, CCE, Western School, 100 Kenwood Ave., Baltimore, MD 21228; 410-887-0852 (work phone), 301-855-4018 (home phone), Fax 410-887-1024.

MASSACHUSETTS

EPICUREAN CLUB OF BOSTON

This chapter has 5 apprentices, 1 under age 25, 5 age 25 or over. Beginning salary is variable with variable increases annually. 7 locations. Housing cost is $700 and up. Degree program through Bunker Hill Community College is completed by 60%.

CONTACT: Christoph Leu, Executive Chef, 10 Huntington Ave., Boston, MA 02116-5798; 617-424-7524 (work phone), Fax 617-424-7586.

MICHIGAN

ACF MICHIGAN CHEFS DE CUISINE ASSOCIATION

This chapter has 65 apprentices. Costs are $1,500. Beginning salary is $6/hr with increases every 6 mos. The 60 locations are hotel, restaurant, country and city club, hospital. Most desirable settings are In Oakland County. Degree program through Oakland Community College.

CONTACT: Kevin Enright, CEC, CCE, Chef/Coordinator, Oakland Community College, 27055 Orchard Lake Rd., Farmington Hills, MI 48018; 810-471-7785 (work phone), Fax 810-471-7553.

ACF OF NORTHWESTERN MICHIGAN

This chapter has 36 apprentices. Costs are $2,800 for 3 yrs. Beginning salary is $6/hr with increases every 6 mos. The 22-25 locations are institutional, hotel, country club, restaurant. Housing cost is $280/mo. Degree program through Lake Michigan College.

CONTACT: Andrew Colvin, CC, Shanty Creek-Schuss Mountain, Bellair, MI 49615; 616-533-8621 (work phone), 616-946-3198 (home phone).

MISSOURI

ACF CHEFS & COOKS OF SPRINGFIELD/OZARK

This chapter has 19 apprentices, 19 under age 25, age 25 or over. Beginning salary is minimum wage with increases every 6 mos. The 6-8 locations are hotel, country club, restaurant.

CONTACT: Steve Zeppenfeld, CEC, 5661 S. Franklin Ave., Springfield, MO 65810; 417-881-4744 (work phone).

CHEFS DE CUISINE OF ST. LOUIS

CONTACT: Sven-Erik Engdorf, 9442-A Mary Glen Drive, St. Louis, MO 63126; 314-644-9276 (work phone).

NEBRASKA

ACF PROFESSIONAL CHEFS OF OMAHA

This chapter has 20 apprentices, 10 under age 25, 10 age 25 or over. Costs are $3,300. Beginning salary is $7/hr with variable increases annually. The 15 locations are hotels, casinos. country clubs, upscale restaurants. Degree program through Metro Community College is completed by 80%.

CONTACT: Jim Trebbien, CCE, Metropolitan Community College, Bldg. 10, P.O. Box 3777, 30th & Fort Sts., Omaha, NE 68103-0777; 402-449-8394 (work phone), 402-238-2199 (home phone), Fax 402-449-8333.

NEVADA

HIGH SIERRA CHEFS ASSOCIATION

This chapter has 12 apprentices, 2 under age 25, 10 age 25 or over. Costs are $185 dues, $500-$1,000 over 3 years. Beginning salary is $6.87/hr (varies with hotel) with increases annually. The 6 locations are hotel and casino. Most desirable settings are Harrah's, Horizon, Caesar's. Housing cost is $300-$500/mo. Degree program through Lake Tahoe & Truckee Meadows Community Colleges. Baking apprenticeship available.

CONTACT: Paul J. Lee, CWC, Harrah's Lake Tahoe, PO Box 8, Lake Tahoe, NV 89449; 702-588-6611 #2205 (work phone), Fax 702-586-6609.

THE FRATERNITY OF EXECUTIVE CHEFS OF LAS VEGAS

This chapter has 11 apprentices, 11 under age 25, age 25 or over. Waiting list is variable. Costs are $165. Beginning salary is 80% of cook's helper's wages with increases annually. The 4 locations are resort. Most desirable settings are Mirage, Caesar's, Hilton. Housing cost is $350-$500. Degree program through University of Las Vegas. Baking apprenticeship available.

CONTACT: Joe DelRosario, CWC, CCE, Community College of Southern Nevada, 3200 E. Cheyenne, N. Las Vegas, NV 89030; 702-651-4192 (work phone), 702-438-1330 (home phone), Fax 702-699-0339.

NEW HAMPSHIRE

GREATER NORTH NEW HAMPSHIRE CHAPTER

This chapter has 16 apprentices, 15 under age 25, 1 age 25 or over. Beginning salary is minimum wage with increases every 2,000 hrs. The 7 locations are Balsams Grand Resort Hotel, Gasparilla Inn, The Cloister. Housing cost is free. Degree program through New Hampshire Technical College.

CONTACT: Phil Learned, CEC, AAC, The Balsams Resort Hotel, Dixville Notch, NH 03576; 603-255-3861 (work phone), 207-392-2162 (home phone), Fax 603-255-4670.

NEW JERSEY

ACF NORTHERN NEW JERSEY CHAPTER

CONTACT: Joe Amabile, CEC, Bergen County Tech High School, 200 Hackensack Avenue, Hackensack, NJ 07601; 201-343-6000 #2255 (work phone), 201-343-1104 (home phone).

PROFESSIONAL CHEFS OF SOUTH JERSEY

CONTACT: John Carbone, CCE,CEC,AAC, P.O. Box 157, Port Republic, NJ 08241; 609-646-4950 (work phone), 609-652-1726 (home phone).

NEW MEXICO

ACF CHEFS OF SANTA FE

CONTACT: Maurice Zeck, CEC, AAC, 100 E. San Francisco St., Santa Fe, NM 87501; 505-982-5511 (work phone).

ACF PASO DEL NORTE CHAPTER

CONTACT: Richard Cannarsa, PO Box 371, Santa Teresa, NM 88008-5858; 915-577-6059 (work phone).

ACF RIO GRANDE VALLEY CHAPTER

CONTACT: Darryl Wilson, 3507 Lomas, NE, Albuquerque, NM 87192; 505-268-2443 (work phone), Fax 505-268-0725.

ACF S.W. NEW MEXICO & TEXAS

CONTACT: Tatsuya Miyazaki, 930 El Paseo Road, Las Cruces, NM 88001; 505-526-7144 (work phone).

NEW YORK

ACF CAPITOL DISTRICT CENTRAL NY

CONTACT: Scott A. Vadney, 43 Berwyn Street, Schenectady, NY 12304; 518-346-1202 (work phone).

ACF OF GREATER BUFFALO

This chapter has 3 apprentices, 3 under age 25, age 25 or over. Beginning salary is negotiable. The locations are private clubs. Most desirable settings are full service with extensive catering. Degree program through Niagara Cnty Comm. College or Erie Comm. College is completed by 100%. Baking apprenticeship available.

CONTACT: Samuel J. Sheusi, CEC, CCE, 5084 Dana Dr., Lewiston, NY 14092; 716-731-4101 (work phone), 716-297-4551 (home phone).

ACF PROFESSIONAL CHEFS/COOKS ASSOCIATION ROCHESTER

This chapter has 4 apprentices, 3 under age 25, 1 age 25 or over. Costs are $150 plus $3,000/yr. Beginning salary is $4.25-$5/hr with increases every 6 mos. The 10 locations are country club and hotel. Most desirable settings are Locust Hill Country Club, Lodge of Woodcliffe Hotel and Country Club, Mario's Restaurant. Degree program through Monroe Community College.

CONTACT: Jeffrey S. Clark, CEC, Apprenticeship Chairman, 3 Broezel St., Rochester, NY 14613; 800-851-3951 (work phone), 716-458-7277 (home phone).

NORTH CAROLINA

ACF INC. CHARLOTTE CHAPTER

CONTACT: John McAllister, CEC, 5709 Cornflower Circle, Charlotte, NC 28212; 704-786-3104 (work phone), 704-568-1071.

ACF SANDHILLS/CROSS CREEK CHEFS ASSOCIATION

CONTACT: Gary Kowal, CEC, P.O. Box 4000, Carolina Vista, Pinehurst, NC 28374; 919-295-6565 (work phone), 919-692-5872 (home phone).

ACF TRIANGLE CHEFS

Costs are $13.25/credit hour. Beginning salary is variable with increases every 6 mos. The locations are restaurant, hotel, country club. Degree program through Wake Technical Community College.

CONTACT: Fredi Morf, CCE, Culinary Instructor, 1316 Hickory Hollow Ln., Raleigh, NC 27610; 919-839-0691 (work phone).

TRIAD PROFESSIONAL CHEFS ASSOCIATION

CONTACT: S. Mitchell Mack, HIFS, 3121 Highpoint Rd., Greensboro, NC 27407; 919-242-9161 #4112 (work phone).

WESTERN NORTH CAROLINA CULINARY ASSOCIATION

CONTACT: Dennis R. Trantham, CC, Route 4, Box 256A, Canton, NC 28716; 704-648-7195 (work phone).

OHIO

ACF CLEVELAND CHAPTER

CONTACT: Richard Fulchiron, CEC, Cuyahoga Community College, 2900 Community College Ave., Cleveland, OH 44115; 216-987-4087 (work phone), 216-243-0714 (home phone), Fax 216-987-4096.

ACF COLUMBUS CHAPTER

This chapter has 70 apprentices, 50 under age 25, 20 age 25 or over. Costs are $6,000 for 3 yrs. Beginning salary is $5/hr & up with variable increases variable. The 40 locations are hotel, country club, private club, restaurant. Most desirable settings are restaurant, hotel, club. Degree program through Columbus State Community College is completed by 60%.

CONTACT: Carol Kizer, CCE, Columbus State Community College, 550 E. Spring St., Columbus, OH 43215; 614-227-2579 (work phone), 614-488-8907 (home phone), Fax 614-227-5146.

OKLAHOMA

ACF CULINARY ARTS OF OKLAHOMA

This chapter has 12 apprentices. Beginning salary is minimum wage. The 6 locations are restaurant, hotel, resort, country club. Most desirable settings are country clubs. Degree program through OSU-Oklahoma City. Baking apprenticeship available.

CONTACT: Geni Thomas, CEPC, CEC, 4337 Dahoon Dr., Oklahoma City, OK 73120; 405-755-0550 #155 (work phone), 405-752-1279 (home phone), Fax 405-751-8971.

ACF TULSA CHAPTER

CONTACT: Robert M. Boyce, CWC, OSU, 5531 S. Toledo Pl., Tulsa, OK 74135-4325; 918-486-6575 (work phone), 918-496-3221 (home phone), Fax 918-486-6576.

PENNSYLVANIA

ACF BERKSHIRE LEHIGH CHEFS

CONTACT: Dennis Moyer, Berks Career & Technology, Box 1370 RD1, Lees Port, PA 19533; 610-374-4073 (work phone), Fax 610-378-5191.

ACF LAUREL HIGHLANDS CHAPTER

This chapter has 61 apprentices, 39 under age 25, 22 age 25 or over. Costs are $3,120 for 3 yrs. Beginning salary is minimum wage with increases every 1,000 hrs. The 35 locations are restaurant, hotel, club, resort, institution. Most desirable settings are club, hotel, restaurant. Degree program through Westmoreland County Community College.

CONTACT: Mary Zappone, CCE, Westmoreland Cty. Community College-Cul. Arts, Armbrust Rd., Youngwood, PA 15697-1895; 412-925-4016 (work phone), 412-836-0103 (home phone), Fax 412-925-4293.

ACF PITTSBURGH CHAPTER

This chapter has 60 apprentices, 40 under age 25, 20 age 25 or over. Costs are $4,000. Beginning salary is negotiable with 25 cent increases every 6 mos. Most desirable settings are hotels, clubs, restaurants. Degree program through Community College of Allegheny Cty is completed by 80%.

Baking apprenticeship available.

CONTACT: Paul Passafume, 274 Washington Street, Whitacre, PA 15120; 412-578-5513 (work phone), 412-462-3572 (home phone).

CENTRAL PENNSYLVANIA CHEFS ASSOCIATION

CONTACT: Charles Gipes, 43 N. Ninth St., Lemoyne, PA 17043; 800-692-7315 (work phone), Fax 717-243-6648.

DELAWARE VALLEY CHEFS ASSOCIATION

CONTACT: William Tillinghast, 3191 Janney Street, Philadelphia, PA 19134; 215-895-1143 (work phone), 215-426-4254 (home phone)

SOUTH CAROLINA

SOUTH CAROLINA UPSTATE PROFESSIONAL CHEFS

This chapter has 7 apprentices, 4 under age 25, 3 age 25 or over. Costs are $500/semester. Beginning salary is $5.50/hr with increases every 6 mos. The 10 locations are hotel, city club, corporate, hospital, college. Most desirable settings are Hyatt Regency, Milliken Corporation, Pointsett Club, Hilton. Housing cost is $250/mo. Degree program through Greenville Technical College.

CONTACT: Ben Black, CSC, Greenville Technical College, ACFEI, P.O. Box 5616, Greenville, SC 29606-5616; 864-250-8474 (work phone), 864-292-8213 (home phone), Fax 864-250-8455.

TENNESSEE

OPRYLAND HOTEL CULINARY INSTITUTE

This chapter has 50 apprentices, 25 under age 25, 25 age 25 or over. Waiting list is 1 yr. Beginning salary is $5.25/hr with 25 cent increases every 6 mos. The locations are restaurant, hotel, club kitchens, in-house butcher shop, bakery, pastry shop of the Opryland complex. Degree program through Volunteer State Community College.

CONTACT: Dina D. Starks, RD, Apprenticeship Coordinator, 2800 Opryland Dr., Nashville, TN 37214; 615-871-7765 (work phone), Fax 615-871-6942.

TEXAS

ACF CAPITOL OF TEXAS CHEFS

This chapter has 8 apprentices, 8 under age 25, age 25 or over. Costs are $500/yr. Beginning salary is $6-$7/hr with 25-40 cent increases every 6 mos. The 12 locations are hotel, resort, country club, conference centers. Most desirable settings are Hill country, downtown, university area. Degree program through Austin Community College is completed by 50%-60%.

CONTACT: Tom Ciapi, CEC, CCE, 11605 Fruitwood Place, Austin, TX 78758; 512-261-7339 (work phone), 817-836-6534 (home phone)

ACF PROFESSIONAL CHEFS ASSOCIATION OF HOUSTON

CONTACT: Bill Wagner, Marriott Mgmt Services, 14950 Heathrow Forrest Pkwy, Houston, TX 77032; 713-449-7911 (work phone), 713-362-0332 (home phone), Fax 713-449-5889.

TCA-BRAZOS VALLEY CHAPTER

This chapter has 13 apprentices. Waiting list is 30 applicants long. Costs are none. Beginning salary is $6/hr with state mandated increases annually. The 5 locations are educational and institutional. Most desirable settings are Texas A&M University. Housing cost is $450/mo. Baking apprenticeship available.

CONTACT: Victoria Beck, Administrative Dietitian, Texas A&M University-Dept. of Food Services, College Station, TX 77843-1374; 409-845-9312 (work phone), 409-696-8721 (home phone).

TCA-DALLAS

CONTACT: James Goering, CCE, CEC, El Centro College, Main @ Lamar, Dallas, TX 75202-3604; 214-746-2217 (work phone), 214-241-4487 (home phone), Fax 214-746-2335.

TCA-HEART OF TEXAS CHAPTER

This chapter has 4 apprentices. Costs are $1,500 over 3 yrs plus fees. Beginning salary is minimum wage with increases every 6 mos. The 1 locations are university. Most desirable settings are Baylor University. Housing cost is $250/mo.

CONTACT: Allen Meyers, CEC, P.O. Box 1401, Mexia, TX 76667; 817-755-3432 (work phone), 817-765-3813 (home phone).

TCA-HOUSTON

CONTACT: George Messinger, 4906 Fairdale, Pasadena, TX 77505; 713-459-7150 (work phone), 713-487-1098 (home phone), Fax 713-459-7132.

TEXAS CHEFS ASSOCIATION

This chapter has 100 apprentices. Costs are less than $1,000/yr. Baking apprenticeship available.

CONTACT: Texas Chefs Assn., 2161 N.W. Military Hwy., Ste. 206, San Antonio, TX 78213; 210-377-1092 (work phone).

UTAH

ACF BEEHIVE STATE CHEFS CHAPTER

This chapter has 80-100 apprentices. Costs are 1,550. Beginning salary is $6.50/hr. The locations are restaurant, hotel, retirement home, club. Housing cost is $650/mo. Degree program through Salt Lake Community College is completed by 34%. Baking apprenticeship available.

CONTACT: Joe Mulvey, Salt Lake Community College-Apprenticeship Office, 4600 S. Redwood Rd., Salt Lake City, UT 84130-0808; 801-942-1954 (work phone), 801-571-4766 (home phone), Fax 801-944-9064.

VERMONT

NORTH VERMONT CHEFS & COOKS ASSOCIATION

Costs are $835/yr. Most desirable settings are Marriott, Perry Restaurant Group, restaurants in Stowe locations. Baking apprenticeship available.

CONTACT: Patrick R. Miller, 2575, Stowe, VT 05672; 802-253-4236 (work phone), 802-253-9901 (home phone), Fax 802-253-4236.

VIRGINIA

ACF NATIONS CAPITOL CHEFS

This chapter has 12 apprentices, 7 under age 25, 5 age 25 or over. Waiting list is 1 yr. Costs are $2,500/yr. Beginning salary is $6.75/hr with increases every 6 mos. The 12 locations are restaurant, hotel, country club. Most desirable settings are ANA Hotel, Congressional Country Club, Vista International Hotel. Degree program through North Virginia Community College.

CONTACT: Forest Bell, 6289 Dunaway Ct., McLean, VA 22101; 301-469-2018 (work phone), 703-893-3823 (home phone), Fax 301-469-2035.

BLUE RIDGE CHEFS ASSOCIATION

CONTACT: Bill King, CEC, 3425 Pippin Ln., Charlottesville, VA 22903; 703-894-5436 (work phone), 804-295-0614 (home phone), Fax 703-894-0534.

VIRGINIA CHEFS ASSOCIATION

This chapter has 25 apprentices, 22 under age 25, 3 age 25 or over. Costs are $3,000 in-state plus $1,250 for books & materials. Beginning salary is $6.50/hr with 25 cent increases annually. The 20 locations are restaurant, country club, hotel, grocery store, central commissary and hospital. Most desirable settings are Colonial Williamsburg, Tobacco Company Restaurant. Housing cost is $300-$500/mo. Degree program through J. Sargeant Reynolds Community College is completed by 100%. Baking apprenticeship available.

CONTACT: Bruce Clarke, 3204 Old Gun Rd. East, Midlothian, VA 23113; 804-367-8880 (work phone), 804-272-0522 (home phone).

WASHINGTON

WASHINGTON STATE CHEFS ASSOCIATION

CONTACT: John V. Melchior, 322 S. 276th Street, Auburn, WA 98011; 206-464-3084 (work phone), Fax 206-464-3058.

WEST VIRGINIA

ACF WEST VIRGINIA CHAPTER

CONTACT: Dan Ferguson, CWC, 216 Rockledge Drive, Nitro, WV 25143;, 304-776-3559 (home phone).

WISCONSIN

ACF CHEFS OF MILWAUKEE, INC.

This chapter has 26 apprentices, 10 under age 25, 16 age 25 or over. Costs are $2,200. Beginning salary is $5-$6/hr with 5%-10% increases every 6 mos. The 48 locations are restaurant, hotel, private club, country club, catering. Most desirable settings are restaurant, hotel, country club. Degree program through Milwaukee Area Technical College is completed by 60%.

CONTACT: John Reiss, CCC, CCE, Milwaukee Area Technical College, 700 W. State St., Milwaukee, WI 53233; 414-297-6861 (work phone), Fax 414-297-7990.

ACF FOX VALLEY CHAPTER

This chapter has 27 apprentices. Costs are $1,400 for 3 yrs. Beginning salary is $5/hr with increases each semester. The 19 locations are restaurant, hotel, resort, convention center, country club. Most desirable settings are American Club Resort, Paper Valley Hotel, Oneida Golf and Riding Club. Housing cost is $300/mo. Degree program through Fox Valley Technical College.

CONTACT: Albert Exenberger, CEC, Apprentice Instructor, Fox Valley Technical Institute, 1825 N. Bluemound Dr., PO Box 2277, Appleton, WI 54913-2277; 414-735-5600 #735 (work phone), 414-722-7960 (home phone).

ACF MIDDLE WISCONSIN CHEFS

CONTACT: Gregory Krzyminski, Mid-State Technical College, 500 32nd Street N., Wisconsin Rapids, WI 54494; 715-423-5650 (work phone), 715-422-5345 (home phone), Fax 715-422-5345.

BAHAMAS

BAHAMAS CULINARY ASSOCIATION

This chapter has 53 apprentices. Costs are $150. Beginning salary is $120/wk with increases annually. The 208 locations are. Most desirable settings are Princess Towers Hotel, Sun International, & Carnival's Crystal Palace Hotel. Degree program through Bahamas Hotel Training College.

CONTACT: Christopher Smith, CCE, Sr. Tutor-Coord. Apprenticeships, Bahamas Hotel Training College, P.O. Box N 4896, Nassau, Bahamas; 809-326-5860 (work phone), 809-393-4463 (home phone), Fax 809-325-2459.

BAHAMAS HOTEL TRAINING COLLEGE

This chapter has 25 apprentices. Waiting list is 1 yr. Costs are $1000/yr. Beginning salary is $120/wk with increases annually. The 8 locations are resort, hotel, restaurant. Most desirable settings are Bahamas Princess Country Club, Lucaya Beach Hotel, Princess Casino. Baking apprenticeship available.

CONTACT: Bernard Dawkins, Chef Instructor, PO Box F-41679, Freeport, Grand Bahamas; 809-352-2896 (work phone), 809-352-4912 (home phone), Fax 809-352-9002.

2

Non-Vocational and Vacation Programs

ALABAMA

SOUTHERN LIVING COOKING SCHOOL
Birmingham/Spring and Fall

Southern Living magazine conducts cooking shows, co-sponsored by nationally-known food brands and local newspapers, that feature the demonstration of more than a dozen recipes containing sponsors' products. Started in 1975.

EMPHASIS: Southern cuisine.

FACULTY: Professional home economists from *Southern Living*.

COSTS: $1-$10/session.

LOCATION: Auditoriums and community centers in Birmingham and other southern cities.

CONTACT: *Southern Living* Cooking School, P.O. Box 2581, Birmingham, AL 35202; (205) 877-6000, Fax (205) 877-6200.

ARIZONA

CULINARY CONCEPTS
Tucson/Year-round

This retail kitchenware store/school offers 40 mostly participation classes/month including a certificate course, series for youngsters, and dinner workshops. Established in 1994. Maximum class/group size: 28. Facilities: 900-sq-ft teaching kitchen with 8 workspaces. Also featured: wine appreciation, beer-making, private classes.

EMPHASIS: A variety of topics, guest chef specialties.

FACULTY: Proprietor Judith Berger.

COSTS: $35-$45/session. Refund 72 hours prior.

LOCATION: Shopping plaza in north-central Tucson.

CONTACT: Judith B. Berger, Culinary Concepts, Plaza Palomino, 2930 N. Swan, #126, Tucson, AZ 85712; (520) 321-0968, Fax (520) 321-0375.

THE HOUSE OF RICE STORE
Scottsdale/Year-round

This retail store/school offers single-session participation classes. Founded in 1977. Maximum class/group size: 12. Also featured: private group classes.

EMPHASIS: Chinese, Japanese, Vietnamese, Thai, and Hawaiian cuisines.

FACULTY: Owner Kiyoko Goldhardt, Chau Liaw, Lan Nguyen Altman, and Kenneth Ikeda.

COSTS: $16-$25/class. Pre-payment required. Refund 1 week prior.

LOCATION: A mile east of downtown Scottsdale.

CONTACT: Kiyoko Goldhardt, The House of Rice Store, 3221 N. Hayden Rd., Scottsdale, AZ 85251; (602) 949-9681, (602) 947-6698, Fax (602) 947-0889.

KITCHEN CLASSICS
Phoenix/Year-round

This kitchen store offers demonstration and hands-on classes four times a week. Established in 1987. Maximum class/group size: 12-32. Facilities: retail store with full kitchen and dining areas. Also featured: classes for youngsters.

FACULTY: Local restaurant chefs and in-store chefs.

COSTS: $25/class. Refund 48 hours prior.

CONTACT: Shauna Pyland, Manager, Kitchen Classics, 4041 E. Thomas Rd., Phoenix, AZ 85018; (602) 954-8141.

LES GOURMETTES ON THE CAMEL'S BACK
Scottsdale/January, April, October, November

This resort program conducted by Les Gourmettes Cooking School offers one-day cooking vacations each month. Two hours of demonstration instruction/day. Program started 1994. Maximum class/group size: 20.

EMPHASIS: Southwestern cuisine, guest chef specialties.

FACULTY: Les Gourmettes owner Barbara Fenzl, the Food and Beverage staff of Gardiner's Resort, guest chefs.

COSTS: Approximately $350-$450/day, which includes double occupancy lodging, meals, use of tennis courts and fitness corral. Commuter, single, and casita lodging rates available.

LOCATION: 9 miles from the Phoenix/Sky Harbor Airport.

CONTACT: Georganne Cavouras, Gardiner's Resort on Camelback, 5700 E. McDonald Dr., Scottsdale, AZ 85253; (602) 948-2100, (800) 245-2051, Fax (602) 483-3386.

LES GOURMETTES COOKING SCHOOL
Phoenix/September-May

This school offers 10-15 demonstration classes and series quarterly. Established in 1982. Maximum class/group size: 15. Also featured: summer classes for children, culinary travel, vacation program at John Gardiner's Tennis Ranch.

EMPHASIS: French, Southwest, and other cuisines.

FACULTY: School proprietor Barbara Fenzl, CCP, studied at Le Cordon Bleu and Ecole Lenotre. Guest instructors have included Giuliano Bugialli, Hugh Carpenter, Lydie Marshall, Jacques Pépin, Anne Willan.

COSTS: $35-$85/class. Pre-payment required.

LOCATION: Central Phoenix.

CONTACT: Barbara Fenzl, Les Gourmettes Cooking School, 6610 N. Central Ave., Phoenix, AZ 85012; (602) 240-6767, Fax (602) 266-2706.

SWEET BASIL GOURMETWARE & COOKING SCHOOL
Scottsdale/Year-round

This cookware store conducts occasional demonstrations and 15-20 one- to three-session participation courses/month. Founded in 1993. Maximum class/group size: 10 hands-on/25 demo. Facilities: 400-sq-ft kitchen with 6 workspaces, gas and electric appliances.

EMPHASIS: Low fat, ethnic, regional cuisines, specific subjects.

FACULTY: 8 instructors include school director Stacey Schulz, IACP award winner Barbara Colleary, nutritionist TJ Majeras.

COSTS: $30-$85/course.

LOCATION: 12 miles from Phoenix.

CONTACT: Martha Sullivan, Owner, Sweet Basil Gourmetware & Cooking School, 10701 N. Scottsdale Rd., #101, Scottsdale, AZ 85260; (602) 596-5628, Fax (602) 596-5629.

THE TASTING SPOON
Tucson/September-May

This school in a private residence offers 3-4 classes/week, 2-3 Lunch and Learn sessions/month, diploma courses in spring and fall, 10-session international series, regional series, basics & advanced series. Founded in 1978. Maximum class/group size: 10-12. Also featured: wine tastings.

EMPHASIS: Techniques, beginning to advanced recipes, international cuisines.

FACULTY: Chefs Jeff Azersky, Doug Levy, James Murphy, Donna Nordin.

COSTS: $35-$40/class, $12 for Lunch and Learn, $375 for series. Payment with registration, refund 72 hours prior. Credit cards accepted.

LOCATION: Northwest Tucson.

CONTACT: Virginia Selby, Director, The Tasting Spoon, P.O. Box 44013, Tucson, AZ 85733-4013; (520) 327-8174.

ARKANSAS

HARRIET NEIMAN
Fayetteville

This catering facility offers 3-4 demonstration and participation classes/month. Started in 1992. Maximum class/group size: 8-13. Facilities: 36-sq-ft demonstration station. Also featured: children's classes, private instruction.

EMPHASIS: Ethnic, especially Mediterranean, easy techniques.

FACULTY: Harriet Neiman studied at La Varenne, Linda Gaddy studied at Le Cordon Bleu.

LOCATION: 2 hours from Tulsa, 4 hours from Little Rock.

CONTACT: Harriet Neiman, 40 N. Crossover Rd., Fayetteville, AR 72701; (501) 521-3739.

CALIFORNIA

ACADEMY OF COOKING – BEVERLY HILLS
Beverly Hills/Year-round except January and August

Meredith's Marvelous Morsels catering firm offers 12 participation classes/month. Established in 1990. Maximum class/group size: 10. Facilities: restaurant kitchen with 10 work stations. Also featured: children's and private classes, culinary tours in southern California.

EMPHASIS: Afternoon tea, buffet, brunch menus; California, international, vegetarian cuisines.

FACULTY: Meredith Jo Mischen studied with chefs at New York's Plaza and Waldorf-Astoria Hotels.

COSTS: $50/class. Class credit 72 hours prior.

CONTACT: Meredith Jo Mischen, Director, Academy of Cooking - Beverly Hills, 400 S. Beverly Dr., #214, Beverly Hills, CA 90212; (310) 284-4940, Fax (310) 271-9464.

ALL SEASONS COOKING SCHOOL
Beverly Hills/September-June

Caterer Dahlia Haas conducts 3 sessions/year that utilize seasonal produce and include holiday menus. Established in 1994. Maximum class/group size: 15. Facilities: newly-equipped kitchen in a country setting. Also featured: classes for youngsters, private instruction.

EMPHASIS: Cooking for family and everyday, healthy menus.

FACULTY: Dahlia Haas has been a caterer in Los Angeles for 12 years.

COSTS: $50-$75, depending upon the menu; holiday meals are $75. 48 hour cancellation notice required.

LOCATION: Central Beverly Hills.

CONTACT: Dahlia Haas, Owner, All Seasons Cooking School, 1109 Tower Rd., Beverly Hills, CA 90210; (310) 276-3110, Fax (310) 201-7701.

AMY MALONE SCHOOL OF CAKE DECORATING
La Mesa/Year-round

This private school offers 40 morning and evening participation and demonstration classes/quarter. Established in 1977. Maximum class/group size: 14 hands-on/30 demo.

EMPHASIS: Cake decorating, candy-making, creative garnishes, desserts, and food presentation.

FACULTY: Amy Malone is a graduate of the Wilton, Betty Newman May, John McNamara, and Frances Kuyper Schools of Cake Decorating and was guest instructor at L'Academie de Cuisine.

COSTS: $15-$75/class. $10 deposit. Refund 5 days prior.

LOCATION: 10 miles east of San Diego.

CONTACT: Amy Malone, Amy Malone School of Cake Decorating, 4212 Camino Alegre, La Mesa, CA 91941; (619) 660-1900, E-mail amymalone@aol.com.

THE APPLE FARM
Philo/Year-round

This 30-acre apple farm offers twice monthly hands-on farm weekend cooking courses and single session demonstration classes. Established in 1995. Maximum class/group size: 8 hands-on/12 demo. Facilities: new kitchen.

EMPHASIS: Meals prepared using the farm's produce and other seasonal foods.

FACULTY: Sally Schmitt, former chef-owner of the French Laundry in Yountville.

COSTS: Farm weekends are $170, which includes most meals (lodging not included). Lodging recommendations are provided. 50% deposit on booking, refund 2 weeks prior.

LOCATION: Anderson Valley in Mendocino County, on Hwy. 128.

CONTACT: Sally Schmitt, Owner, The Apple Farm, 18501 Greenwood Rd., Philo, CA 95466; (707) 895-2461, Fax (707) 895-2461.

THE ART OF THAI COOKING
Oakland/February-October

Cookbook author Kasma Loha-unchit conducts hands-on programs that include 4-week beginner and intermediate courses and on-going advanced classes. Established in 1985. Maximum class/group size: 12. Facilities: fully-equipped private kitchen. Also featured: private instruction, market visits, classes in private homes, food and cultural tours to Thailand.

EMPHASIS: Thai, Chinese, Southeast Asian.

FACULTY: Kasma Loha-unchit is a Thai chef and author of *It Rains Fishes: Legends, Traditions and the Joys of Thai Cooking*, Julia Child Award winner.

COSTS: $30-$35/session for classes. 18- to 27-days tours of Thailand are $2,850-$3,250, including airfare, meals, and lodging. Nonrefundable series deposit is $50.

LOCATION: 20 minutes from San Francisco.

CONTACT: Kasma Loha-unchit, The Art of Thai Cooking, P.O. Box 21165, Oakland, CA 94620; (510) 655-8900, Fax (510) 655-8900, E-mail kasma@lanminds.com, URL http://users.lanminds.com/~kasma. Also: 105 Echo Ave., Oakland, CA 94611-4309.

BORDER GRILL
Los Angeles/Year-round

This restaurant conducts quarterly demonstration classes. Program started 1992. Maximum class/group size: 65.

EMPHASIS: Latin cuisines.

FACULTY: Susan Feniger and Mary Sue Milliken, chef-owners of the Border Grill and authors of *City Cuisine, Mesa Mexicana*, and *Cooking With Too Hot Tamales*.

COSTS: $50/session. Credit cards accepted.

CONTACT: Border Grill, 1445 Fourth St., Los Angeles, CA 90401; (310) 451-1655, Fax (310) 394-2049, E-mail mail@bordergrill.com, URL http://www.bordergrill.com.

BRISTOL FARMS COOKING SCHOOL
Pasadena/Year-round

This gourmet specialty foods and cookware store offers 20 one- to six-session demonstration and participation courses/month. Program started 1985. Maximum class/group size: 20 hands-on/40 demo. Facilities: kitchen with 18-burner stove, grill, 3 convection ovens, video. Also featured: children's and private classes, field trips, tours.

EMPHASIS: International and regional cuisine, baking, low fat cooking, basic cooking techniques.

FACULTY: Director Grace-Marie Johnston and assistant manager Michelle Moore. Guest instructors have included Graham Kerr, Paul Prudhomme, Stephen Pyles, Patricia Wells, Jacques Pépin.

COSTS: $40-$55/session. Payment prior to class. Class credit 48 hours prior.

LOCATION: Next to South Pasadena Bristol Farms Market, 15 minutes from Los Angeles.

CONTACT: Grace-Marie Johnston, Cooking School Director, Bristol Farms Cooking School, 606 Fair Oaks Ave., S. Pasadena, CA 91030; (818) 441-5588, Fax (818) 441-8994.

CAKEBREAD CELLARS
Napa Valley/January, April, July, November

This winery offers 4 demonstration classes/year.

EMPHASIS: Seasonal specialties.

FACULTY: Resident chef Brian Streeter, a New England Culinary Institute graduate, and guest chefs.

COSTS: $75/class.

CONTACT: Cakebread Cellars, 8300 St. Helena Hwy., Box 216, Rutherford, CA 94573-0216; (707) 963-5221, Fax (707) 963-1067.

CAROLE BLOOM, PATISSIERE
Carlsbad/Year-round

This private school offers 2-3 demonstration, participation sessions/week. Established in 1978. Maximum class/group size: 8 hands-on/12 demo. Facilities: specially-equipped professional kitchen. Also featured: private instruction.

EMPHASIS: European pastries and desserts, chocolate, pralines, special occasion cakes, ice creams.

FACULTY: Carole Bloom contributes to *Fine Cooking* and *Bon Appétit*, produces a cooking show, and is author of four cookbooks, including *The International Dictionary of Desserts, Pastries, and Confections*, and *Sugar & Spice*.

COSTS: $85/class. Pre-payment required. Refund 48 hours prior.

LOCATION: 15 miles north of San Diego.

CONTACT: Carole Bloom, 7067 Rockrose Terr., Carlsbad, CA 92009; (619) 931-5920, Fax (619) 931-0423, E-mail cbloom@adnc.com.

CASTROVILLE ARTICHOKE FESTIVAL
Castroville/September

The Castroville Artichoke Festival is an annual 2-day festival in the artichoke capitol that features specialty dishes and activities. Established in 1959. Also featured: arts & crafts, games, music.

EMPHASIS: Artichoke preparations.

COSTS: $4 general admission.

LOCATION: The Monterey peninsula, 50 miles south of San Jose.

CONTACT: Carmen Kloncz, Chairperson, Castroville Festivals, Inc., P.O. Box 1041, Castroville, CA 95012; (408) 633-2465, Fax (408) 633-0485.

CHEF CHARLES
San Diego

FACULTY: Charles Hiigel studied at La Varenne and Le Cordon Bleu. He was owner of Conklin-Chase in Fresno.

CONTACT: Charles Hiigel, 1010 University Ave., Box 281, San Diego, CA 92103; (619) 296-4477, Fax (619) 296-4448.

CHEZ LINDA COOKING
Los Gatos/Year-round

This retail store front offers 10 four-session demonstration and participation courses/month, 2 one-week vacations to France/year that feature demonstrations and visits to wineries, food producers, and markets. Established in 1995. Maximum class/group size: 10 vacation/12-15 demo & hands-on. Facilities: 500-sq-ft home kitchen. Also featured: food & wine pairing classes.

FACULTY: Linda Vandermarliere, who graduated from La Varenne and studied with Madeleine Kamman.

COSTS: $39/class. Trip to France is $3,000, which includes meals, lodging, planned activities. 50% deposit required for trips, balance due 60 days prior.

LOCATION: 5 miles from the San Jose Airport.

CONTACT: Linda Vandermarliere, Chez Linda Cooking, 469 N. Santa Cruz Ave., Los Gatos, CA 95030; (408) 395-5979.

THE COOKING SCHOOL AT JORDANO'S MARKETPLACE
Santa Barbara/Year-round

This cookware store and school offers 16 to 20 one- to four-session demonstration and participation courses/month. Started in 1990. Maximum class/group size: 18 hands-on/30 demo. Facilities: the 14,000-sq-ft space has a large counter, overhead mirror, and professional appliances. Also featured: farms and winery tours, wine tastings, private group and children's classes, culinary tours of Europe.

EMPHASIS: Basic techniques, ethnic and regional cuisines, holiday and entertaining menus, breads and pastries, guest chef specialties.

FACULTY: Director Pamela Sheldon, CCP, author of *The Healthy Gourmet Cookbook,* and more than 30 instructors, cookbook authors, and guest chefs, including Giuliano Bugialli, Hugh Carpenter, Ken Hom, Deborah Madison, and Nick Malgieri.

COSTS: Range from $25-$95. Advance payment required; cancellations 1 week prior receive class credit. Positions available for volunteer kitchen assistants.

LOCATION: 90 minutes north of Los Angeles. There is an airport in Santa Barbara.

CONTACT: Pamela Sheldon Johns, Director, The Cooking School at Jordano's Marketplace, 614 Chapala St., Santa Barbara, CA 93101; (805) 963-7289, Fax (805) 963-0230, E-mail CulinarArt@aol.com. Also: Culinary Arts, 1324 State Street, J-157, Santa Barbara, CA, 93101.

COOKING WITH HEART & SOUL
Calistoga/Year-round

Cooking instructor Jennifer Raymond offers at least six 1- to 4-session demonstration and participation programs/year. Established in 1996. Maximum class/group size: 12-20. Also featured: day trips, market visits, winery tours, sightseeing, private instruction.

EMPHASIS: Low-fat and fat-free vegetarian cooking.

FACULTY: Jennifer Raymond has a master's degree in nutrition and 15 years teaching experience.

COSTS: $20-$40/class. Tours are additional. Inns and motels range from $70-$150/night.

LOCATION: A small resort town in Napa Valley.

CONTACT: Jennifer Raymond, Cooking with Heart & Soul, 1418 Cedar St., Calistoga, CA 94515; (707) 942-2180, E-mail VegiCook@aol.com, VegiCook@napanet.net.

COOKS AND BOOKS COOKING SCHOOL
Danville/Year-round

This cookbook and cookware store, wine shop, and school offers more than 100 demonstration and participation courses/year, 4-part and 6-part series that are hands-on, run continuously; individual single topic classes. Established in 1991. Maximum class/group size: 10-20 demo and hands-on. Facilities: 1,600-sq-ft teaching area. Also featured: local shopping excursions, culinary tours.

EMPHASIS: International cuisines, seasonal and holiday menus, nutritious foods, wine and food pairing, guest chef specialties, and basic services.

FACULTY: In-house instructor D.J. Rae is a CCA graduate. Other instructors are guest chef/instructors, teachers, and cookbook authors.

COSTS: $40-$50/class. Refund 7 days prior; store credit 72 hours to 7 days prior.

LOCATION: 30 miles east of San Francisco.

CONTACT: D.J. Rae, Owner, Cooks and Books, 472 Hartz Ave., Danville, CA 94526; (510) 831-0708, Fax (510) 831-0741.

CUISINE SUR LA MER
Manhattan Beach/Spring and Fall

This gourmet shop and school offers evening demonstrations. Established in 1980.

FACULTY: Includes Disneyland pastry chef George Geary and chefs from local restaurants.

COSTS: $35/class.

LOCATION: Los Angeles area, on the Pacific coast.

CONTACT: Pat Kinnan, Cuisine Sur La Mer, 919 Manhattan Ave., Manhattan Beach, CA 90266; (310) 374-3103.

CULINARY ADVENTURES, INC.
Malibu, N. California/Year-round

Food consultant Doris Felts conducts day-long tours that include lectures, demonstrations, and visits to specialty markets, growers, and manufacturers. Established in 1987. Maximum class/group size: 25. Also featured: consultations, private tours, trips to Napa/Sonoma, New Orleans, Santa Fe, and New Mexico.

EMPHASIS: Food product information for serious cooks.

FACULTY: Doris Felts has taught cooking since 1976, conducts tours for organizations, and consults on southern California food products and sources.

COSTS: Day tours range $65-$95, including lunch and transportation.

LOCATION: Los Angeles area.

CONTACT: Doris Felts, Culinary Adventures, Inc., 23908 De Ville Way, Malibu, CA 90265; (310) 456-2484, Fax (310) 456-3429.

DEPOT
Torrance/Year-round

This restaurant conducts 1-2 Saturday afternoon demonstrations/month. Established in 1992. Maximum class/group size: 60. Facilities: a private dining room of the restaurant. Also featured: wine tastings.

EMPHASIS: Italian, grilling, holiday meals, soups, chef specialties, wine pairing.

FACULTY: Michael S. Shafer, CEC, chef and general manager of Depot, an Urban Grill Room and Bar, also oversees operations in Fino, Misto, and Chez Melange. He received the Gold Medal in the 1988 Culinary Olympics.

COSTS: $35/session. Book in advance, pay in advance.

LOCATION: Los Angeles suburb.

CONTACT: Michael S. Shafer, Depot, 1250 Cabrillo, Torrance, CA 90501; (310) 787-7501, Fax (310) 787-9647.

DRAEGER'S CULINARY CENTER
Menlo Park/Year-round

This school in Draeger's Supermarket offers 350 demonstrations/year at this location. A second school opens in San Mateo in June, 1997. Established in 1991. Maximum class/group size: 35. Facilities: 36-seat classroom with kitchen and overhead mirror. Also featured: wine classes and dinners, market tours, private classes.

EMPHASIS: Ethnic and regional cuisines, fundamentals, baking, vegetarian and healthful foods, entertaining menus, food history.

FACULTY: Guest instructors include well-known chefs, cookbook authors, and culinary professionals.

COSTS: Range from $20-$65 per session. Credit cards accepted. Full payment with reservation. Refund up to 2 weeks prior.

LOCATION: Menlo Park, about 35 miles south of San Francisco.

CONTACT: William K. Wallace, Culinary Director, Draeger's Culinary Center, Draeger's Supermarket, 1010 University Dr., Menlo Park, CA 94025; (415) 688-0688, Fax (415) 326-3718.

ELDERBERRY HOUSE COOKING SCHOOL
Oakhurst/March and November

The Château du Sureau (Estate by the Elderberries) offers two 3-day participation programs. Eight hours of daily cooking instruction are devoted to preparing a 6-course menu. Established in 1985. Maximum class/group size: 12. Facilities: Erna's Elderberry Restaurant's full commercial kitchen, herb garden, local organic vegetable farm. Also featured: bass fishing, golf, hiking, tennis, and visits to Yosemite National Park.

EMPHASIS: Sauces, soups, seafood and meat cookery, desserts.

FACULTY: Chef-Proprietor Erna Kubin-Clanin has 30 years of culinary and restaurant experience.

COSTS: Meals and class only $500 ($175 per day). Nine 2-person guest rooms range from $310-$410 including breakfast. 10% student discount. 50% deposit required; refund 7 days prior minus 10% cancellation fee.

LOCATION: The chateau, a member of Relais & Chateaux, is in a mountain village near Yosemite, 45 minutes from Fresno, 4 hours north of Los Angeles, and less than 4 hours from San Francisco.

CONTACT: Erna Kubin-Clanin, Proprietor, Elderberry House Cooking School, 48688 Victoria Ln., Box 577, Oakhurst, CA 93644; (209) 683-6800, Fax (209) 683-0800.

THE ELIZABETH THOMAS COOKING SCHOOL
Berkeley/Year-round

This school in a private residence offers 6 four-session demonstration courses/year. Established in 1977. Maximum class/group size: 8. Facilities: a remodeled teaching kitchen. Also featured: classes for youngsters, theme classes, private lessons, 1-week intensives, and culinary tours of Berkeley and Napa Valley.

EMPHASIS: French, Italian, American, California, British, and other ethnic cuisines; techniques.

FACULTY: Elizabeth Thomas, a graduate of the London Cordon Bleu, studied with Jacques Pépin and Lorenza de Medici and taught in San Francisco, Washington state, China, Crete, and the West Indies.

COSTS: $40/session, $150 per 4-session course. Payment with reservation.

LOCATION: Overlooking the Golden Gate Bridge, 35 minutes from San Francisco.

CONTACT: Elizabeth Thomas, The Elizabeth Thomas Cooking School, 1372 Summit Rd., Berkeley, CA 94708; (510) 843-3422.

EPICUREAN SCHOOL OF CULINARY ARTS
Los Angeles/Year-round   *(See also page 9)*

This school offers participation classes and private instruction. Maximum class/group size: 30.

EMPHASIS: Baking workshops.

CONTACT: Shelley Janson, Director, Epicurean School of Culinary Arts, 8759 Melrose Ave., Los Angeles, CA 90069; (310) 659-5990, Fax (310) 659-0302.

GARLIC & SAPPHIRES
Del Mar/Year-round

This school offers 2 demonstrations/week, 3 weeks/month. Established in 1988. Also featured: theme changes 3 times per year. Limited hands-on classes also available.

EMPHASIS: Natural gourmet.

FACULTY: Lesa Heebner is author of *Cooking with the Seasons* and TV chef on a San Diego CBS-affiliate.

COSTS: $55/class. Full refund 10 days prior.

LOCATION: 25 minutes from San Diego Airport.

CONTACT: Lesa Heebner, Garlic & Sapphires, P.O. Box 2974, Del Mar, CA 92014; (619) 755-7773, Fax (619) 755-7909, E-mail garnsapph@aol.com.

THE GREAT CHEFS AT THE ROBERT MONDAVI WINERY
Oakville/Spring and Fall

The Robert Mondavi Winery offers two to four 2- to 3-day weekend and 1-day Monday programs per season that feature cooking demonstrations and seminars by noted chefs, private winery tours, and theme lunches and dinners. Established in 1976. Maximum class/group size: 28 for weekend programs, 35 for 1-day programs.

EMPHASIS: International cuisines, table setting, flower arranging, food and wine pairing.

FACULTY: Has included Julia Child, Joachim Splichal, Marc Meneau, and Pierre Gagnaire.

COSTS: One-day sessions range from $150-$180; two-day program is $750; three-day program is

$1,550, including transportation and lodging. Payment must accompany application and credit cards are accepted. Cancellations 6 weeks prior forfeit 10%, 50% within 6 weeks.

LOCATION: Napa Valley; 1.5 hours from San Francisco.

CONTACT: Valerie Varachi, Secretary, The Great Chefs at the Robert Mondavi Winery, P.O. Box 106, Oakville, CA 94562; (707) 226-1395 #3216, Fax (707) 224-3995, E-mail valerie.varachi@mondavi.com, URL http://www.mondavi.com.

HOMECHEF COOKING SCHOOL
Northern California/Year-round

This kitchen store offers a 12-week Basic Cooking Course adapted from professional curriculum, plus over 30 demonstration and participation courses/month. Established in 1976. Maximum class/group size: 20 hands-on/45 demo. Facilities: approximately 1,000-sq-ft classrooms with kitchens. Also featured: private events, free sampler classes, and family workshops.

EMPHASIS: Fine cuisine in home kitchens by home chefs.

FACULTY: Founder Judith Ets-Hokin, CCP, author of the *The Dinner Party Cookbook, The Homechef, Fine Cooking Made Simple, Great Cooking in Minutes*, holds certificates from cooking schools in England, France, and Italy.

COSTS: The Basic Cooking Series is $392 (assistants $260); single classes are $39 for demonstration, $49 for workshops. Flexible scheduling for making-up missed classes.

LOCATION: Four locations in the San Francisco Bay area: San Francisco, Corte Madera (headquarters), Palo Alto, and Saratoga.

CONTACT: Julie R. Khademi, Director, Homechef Cooking School, 5725 Paradise Drive, Suite 360, Corte Madera, CA 94925; (415) 927-3293, (415) 927-3290, Fax (415) 927-4164, E-mail info@homechef.com, URL http://www.homechef.com.

HUGH CARPENTER'S CAMP NAPA CULINARY
Oakville, Napa Valley/May-October

Chef and cookbook author Hugh Carpenter conducts 6-day food and wine tours that feature participation classes. Started in 1992. Maximum class/group size: 16. Facilities: Cakebread Cellars Winery kitchen. Also featured: dining in fine restaurants, private winery tours, seminars on food and wine pairing, a croquet tournament. Hot-air ballooning, Calistoga spa, golf, and tennis also available.

EMPHASIS: California-Asian and cross-cultural cuisine; winery chef specialties.

FACULTY: Hugh Carpenter, founding chef of 6 Chopstix restaurants in Los Angeles, is author of the IACP-award-winning *Pacific Flavors, Chopstix*, and *Hot Wok*; Cakebreads Cellars Executive Chef Brian Streeter.

COSTS: Cost is $975, which includes some meals and planned itinerary. A list of recommended lodging is available. A $150 deposit is required; balance due/refund granted 30 days prior.

LOCATION: Napa Valley, 50 miles northeast of San Francisco.

CONTACT: Hugh Carpenter, P.O. Box 114, Oakville, CA 94562; (707) 944-9112, Fax (707) 944-2221.

JC'S KITCHEN CONNECTION
San Diego/Year-round

This culinary school offers 16 demonstration and participation courses/month. Established in 1991. Maximum class/group size: 12 hands-on/30 demo. Facilities: a specially-designed teaching kitchen. Also featured: children's classes, wine instruction, private classes, catering.

EMPHASIS: International and regional cuisines, guest chef specialties, cutting edge of world cuisine.

FACULTY: Local and celebrity guest chefs, including Giuliano Hazan, Hugh Carpenter, Perla Meyers, Jacques Pépin, and Jim Dodge.

COSTS: Range from $25-$85/class. Credit cards accepted.

CONTACT: Jana Cason, JC's Kitchen Connection, 4885 Ronson Court #G, San Diego, CA 92101; (619) 541-1990, Fax (619) 541-2237.

THE JEAN BRADY COOKING SCHOOL
Santa Monica/September-July
This school in a private residence offers 8 to 12 seven-session demonstration and participation classes/month. Established in 1973. Maximum class/group size: 6-8 hands-on/15 demo. Facilities: a commercially-equipped home kitchen featured in *Bon Appétit*; Campanile restaurant kitchen. Also featured: children's classes, market visits, 1-week seminars for private groups, culinary tours to Europe.
EMPHASIS: A variety of topics; low-fat savories; menus for easy entertaining; guest chef specialties.
FACULTY: Proprietor Jean Brady studied with Lydie Marshall, Jacques Pépin, and Paula Wolfert and attended the Cordon Bleu and La Varenne. Guest chefs include Lydie Marshall, Jacques Pépin, Paula Wolfert, and top local chefs in their restaurant kitchens.
COSTS: Guest chef classes range from $60-$90; 7-session classes are $250.
LOCATION: 20 minutes from Beverly Hills.
CONTACT: Jean Brady, The Jean Brady Cooking School, 680 Brooktree Rd., Santa Monica, CA 90402; (310) 454-4220, Fax (310) 454-4220.

KITCHEN WITCH GOURMET SHOP
Encinitas/September-July
This gourmet shop and school offers 45 demonstration sessions/month. Established in 1981. Maximum class/group size: 14. Also featured: after-school classes for children, private group lessons.
EMPHASIS: Ethnic and regional cuisines, nutrition, vegetarian, macrobiotic, breads, holiday menus, pastries, chocolate, microwave and food processor techniques.
FACULTY: Includes Carole Bloom, Phillis Carey, Suzy Eisenman, Kay Pastorius, Dee Biller, Nadia Frigeri, Nancy Brown, Stella Fong, and George Geary.
COSTS: Range from $16-$27. Credit cards accepted. Deposit 30 days in advance. Refunds granted 3 days prior.
LOCATION: North of San Diego, on the Pacific Coast.
CONTACT: Marie Santucci, Kitchen Witch Gourmet Shop, 127 N. El Camino Real, Suite D, Encinitas, CA 92024; (619) 942-3228.

LET'S GET COOKIN' AND WESTLAKE CULINARY INSTITUTE
Westlake Village/Year-round   *(See also page 11)*
This private school offers 50 one- to six-session demonstration and participation classes/quarter. Maximum class/group size: 10-30. Also featured: classes for young people, day trips, travel abroad.
EMPHASIS: Basic and advanced techniques for the home cook.
FACULTY: Includes cookbook authors and guest chefs.
COSTS: $45-$75/session ($25 for children's classes). Class credit for cancellation 48 hours prior.
CONTACT: Phyllis Vaccarelli, Owner/Director, Let's Get Cookin', 4643 Lakeview Canyon Rd., Westlake Village, CA 91361; (818) 991-3940, Fax (805) 495-2554.

LILY LOH'S CHINESE COOKING CLASSES
Solana Beach/Fall, Winter, spring
This school in a private home offers five 4- to 5-session demonstration and participation courses each season. Started in 1976. Maximum class/group size: 9. Facilities: professionally-designed home kitchen. Also featured: summer 4-session Teenager's Course, culinary tours in southern California.
EMPHASIS: Chinese cuisine.
FACULTY: Shanghai-born Lily Loh has a home economics degree from Purdue University and a masters degree from Cornell, is author of *Lily Loh's Chinese Seafood and Vegetables* and host of two videos.
COSTS: $195/course, $165/teen course. A $50 nonrefundable deposit is required.
LOCATION: Solana Beach, 20 minutes from San Diego airport.

CONTACT: Lily Loh, P.O. Box 1232, Solana Beach, CA 92075; (619) 755-5345, Fax (619) 350-1266, E-mail 74534,1353@compuserve, URL http://www.sandiego-online.com/forums/chinese/chinese.htm.

LUCY'S KITCHEN
Albany/Year-round

Lucy Seligman offers monthly cooking classes that are either demonstration or hands-on. Established in 1994. Maximum class/group size: 6-12. Facilities: Lucy's kitchen or students' home kitchens. Also featured: children's classes, event planning, kitchen organization, private meal preparation.

EMPHASIS: A variety of topics, including Japanese, Italian, Russian, Turkish, and American regional cuisines.

FACULTY: Lucy Seligman graduated from Boston University's Culinary Arts program, owned a cooking school in Japan and Ann Arbor, & studied cooking in Paris, Bangkok, Tokyo, Florence, Orvieto, and Los Angeles. She publishes a Japanese cuisine newsletter.

COSTS: $32-$36/class.

LOCATION: Near Berkeley.

CONTACT: Lucy Seligman, Lucy's Kitchen, 1049 Key Route Blvd., Albany, CA 94706; (510) 527-9385, Fax (510) 527-7190.

MANDOLINE COOKING SCHOOL
Sunnyvale/Year-round

This school in a private residence offers 50 afternoon and evening participation classes per year. Established in 1992. Maximum class/group size: 6. Facilities: a large kitchen with 5 work stations. Also featured: private classes for groups/organizations.

EMPHASIS: Regional Italian, Mediterranean, regional American, vegetarian, and French bistro cuisine, pastry and desserts, bread making, wine pairing, techniques, seasonal ingredients, equipment selection.

FACULTY: Paula Barbarito-Levitt, an IACP-member, studied at Le Cordon Bleu, the New York Restaurant School, and California Culinary Academy and with Giuliano Bugialli and Lydie Marshall.

COSTS: Range from $35-$150. 50% deposit required; 2-week cancellation policy.

LOCATION: A 50-minute drive south of San Francisco and 10 minutes north of San Jose.

CONTACT: Paula Barbarito-Levitt, Mandoline Cooking School, 1083 Robbia Dr., Sunnyvale, CA 94087; (408) 733-4224, Fax (408) 773-1863, E-mail mondoline@aol.com.

MON CHERI COOKING SCHOOL/UCSC EXTENSION
Santa Cruz/Year-round

This university extension-private school cooperative program offers a half dozen 1- to 4-session participation workshops and courses per quarter. Established in 1983. Maximum class/group size: 18-20. Facilities: historic house with modern commercial kitchen.

EMPHASIS: Stress relief cooking and a variety of other topics.

FACULTY: Director Sharon Shipley, an IACP member who received certificates from La Varenne and Le Cordon Bleu; noted guest chefs.

COSTS: Range from $85 for a single session to $165 for four. Credit cards accepted.

LOCATION: Silicon Valley, 40 miles south of San Francisco.

CONTACT: Culinary Arts, UCSC Extension, Humanities Dept., 740 Front St., #155, Santa Cruz, CA 95060; (408) 427-6600 #6695, Fax (408) 427-6608.

MONTANA MERCANTILE
Los Angeles/Year-round

This school offers private and small group instruction, demonstration and participation classes, including a series for beginning cooks. Established in 1976. Maximum class/group size: varies. Also featured: wine instruction, classes taught in Spanish for household staff cooks, home kitchen design.

EMPHASIS: International cuisines and preparation in keeping with busy lifestyles and health concerns.
CONTACT: Rachel Dourec, Director, P.O. Box 17178, Beverly Hills, CA 90209; (310) 472-3220, Fax (310) 472-8846.

NAPA VALLEY COLLEGE – CENTER FOR CULINARY ARTS
St. Helena/Year-round   *(See also page 12)*
This school offers 1- to 6-session demonstration and participation courses. Established in 1990. Maximum class/group size: 12-30. Facilities: new kitchen with 18 burners, 4 ovens, demonstration counter, outdoor dining area. Also featured: wine and food classes, farmer's market visits, catering seminars, culinary trips abroad.
EMPHASIS: Various topics, including basic cooking, bread baking, Indian, Italian, and Mediterranean cuisines.
FACULTY: Includes Bruce Aidells, Catherine Brandel, Michael Chiarello, Gary Danko, Carlo Middione, John Ash.
COSTS: $55-$65/session. Full refund less $5 fee for cancellation 5 days prior.
CONTACT: Sue Farley, Program Coordinator, Napa Valley College, Center for Culinary Arts, 1088 College Ave., St. Helena, CA 94574; 707-967-2930, Fax 707-967-2909.

NATURAL FOODS COOKING SCHOOL
Woodland Hills/Year-round
This school offers a 12-month basic natural foods curriculum that includes two group classes per month and weekend retreats year-round. Established in 1985. Maximum class/group size: 6-15.
EMPHASIS: Grains, pasta, vegetables, breads, fermented foods, catering, food and healing.
FACULTY: Donna Wilson, who also owns the Ginkgo Leaf Bookstore, has operated natural foods stores and restaurants in southern California since 1978.
COSTS: Individual evaluation is $25, nonrefundable; group classes are $25 each, $75 for a series of 5; private classes are $50 per hour.
LOCATION: Woodland Hills.
CONTACT: Donna Wilson, The Ginkgo Leaf, 21109 Costanso St., Woodland Hills, CA 91364; (818) 716-6332, Fax (818) 716-6332, E-mail ginkgo@earthlink.net.

NUTRITIOUSLY GOURMET
Orinda/September-June
This private facility offers 2 demonstration menus/month. Established in 1991. Maximum class/group size: 12. Facilities: large modern kitchen.
EMPHASIS: Creative low-fat cuisine using seasonal ingredients; menus balanced to include 20% of calories as fat, 10% protein, 70% carbohydrate.
FACULTY: Jane A. Rubey, M.P.H., R.D. has taught nutrition courses at the California Culinary Academy and is a regular on KGO radio. She is the author of *Lowfat International Cuisine* and *Fabulous Fiber Cookery*.
COSTS: $30/class. Class credit for cancellations.
LOCATION: Across the bay from San Francisco, 40 minutes from the San Francisco airport, 30 minutes from Oakland airport.
CONTACT: Jane A. Rubey, Nutritiously Gourmet, P.O. Box 1356, Orinda, CA 94563; (510) 254-7582, Fax (510) 254-8693, E-mail gourmet@aimnet.com, URL www.aimnet.com/~gourmet.

PATINA AND PINOT RESTAURANTS
Los Angeles/March-May
These restaurants sponsor Saturday morning demonstration and participation classes and a full day in the kitchen. Established in 1989. Maximum class/group size: 12. Facilities: Patina Restaurant, Pinot Bistro, Cafe Pinot, Pinot Hollywood, Pinot at the Chronicle. Also featured: the full-day class includes working in the pastry kitchen in the morning and in the afternoon prepar-

ing a 5-course dinner for the student's seven dinner guests.
EMPHASIS: Pastries, bistro cooking, spa, vegetarian, potatoes.
FACULTY: Joachim Splichal, chef/owner of Patina & Pinot Restaurants; Octavio Becerra, Executive Chef of Pinot Bistro; Jon Ferow, Executive Chef Pinot Hollywood; Rainer Schwarz, Executive Chef Cafe Pinot.
COSTS: Saturday classes are $55-$100. Day in the Kitchen is $950-$1,250.
LOCATION: Downtown Los Angeles, Valley, Hollywood, and Pasadena locations.
CONTACT: Nina Crowe, Patina and Pinot restaurants, Special Events, 5955 Melrose Ave., Los Angeles, CA 90038; (213) 960-1762, Fax (213) 467-1924.

PEGGY RAHN COOKS
Pasadena/Year-round

This school in a 1918-vintage home offers 50 one- to two-session demonstration and participation workshops per year. Established in 1974. Maximum class/group size: 10 hands-on/20 demo. Facilities: well-equipped, home kitchen with overhead mirror. Also featured: private classes, small group excursions to markets, party classes, and culinary trips.
EMPHASIS: Ethnic cuisines, technique classes, healthful eating.
FACULTY: Peggy Rahn, CCP, food & travel columnist, cookbook/restaurant reviewer, co-host of CBS's "Meet the Cook", teacher at UCLA, studied at La Varenne, Le Cordon Bleu, & the Ritz Escoffier. Guest faculty has included Giuliano Bugialli, and Madeleine Kamman.
COSTS: Range from $50-$75/course. Pre-pay to reserve space. Refund with 24 hour notice.
LOCATION: Ten minutes from downtown Los Angeles, 20 minutes from Burbank.
CONTACT: Peggy Rahn Cooks, 484 Bellefontaine St., Pasadena, CA 91105; (818) 441-2075, Fax (818) 441-5286.

THE RITZ-CARLTON, SAN FRANCISCO
San Francisco/Year-round

This hotel offers weekend and half-day participation classes. Established in 1993.
EMPHASIS: A variety of topics.
FACULTY: Master Sommelier Emmanuel Kemiji and Executive Chef Jean-Pierre Dubray.
LOCATION: Nob Hill.
CONTACT: The Ritz-Carlton, San Francisco, 600 Stockton St., San Francisco, CA 94115; (415) 296-7465.

SEASONAL TABLE, THE COOKING SCHOOL
Santa Monica/Year-round

This school offers two-three 1- to 4-session demonstration courses per week. Established in 1994. Maximum class/group size: 10-25. Facilities: commercially-equipped restaurant kitchen, as well as off-site locations. Also featured: wine instruction, market visits, private classes for individuals, companies, and special events.
EMPHASIS: A variety of topics, including techniques in low fat & vegetarian cooking and baking, seasonal and entertaining menus, wine, restaurant specialties, ethnic cuisines.
FACULTY: Co-owners Karen Berk, founder of Incredible Edibles Cooking School & co-editor of *Southern California Zagat Restaurant & Marketplace Surveys*, & Jean Brady of The Jean Brady Cooking School; guest chefs, cookbook authors, and culinary professionals.
COSTS: Average $50 per session. Full payment in advance; credit with one-week notice.
LOCATION: 20 minutes from Beverly Hills, 15 minutes from Los Angeles International Airport, 1 block from the beach.
CONTACT: Karen Berk, The Seasonable Table Cooking School, 12618 Homewood Way, Los Angeles, CA 90049; (310) 472-4475, Fax (310) 471-3904.

SIAMESE PRINCESS RESTAURANT
Los Angeles/October-May
This restaurant offers Sunday classes. Established in 1987. Maximum class/group size: 20-30. Facilities: the dining room and kitchen.
EMPHASIS: Royal Thai cuisine.
FACULTY: Executive Chef Victor Sodsook, author of *I Love Thai Food* and *True Thai*.
COSTS: Classes are $30. Credit cards accepted.
CONTACT: Chris Chapman, Owner/General Manager, The Siamese Princess, 8048 W. Third St., Los Angeles, CA 90048; (213) 653-2643, Fax (213) 653-1291.

SOUTHERN CALIFORNIA SCHOOL OF CULINARY ARTS
South Pasadena/Year-round   *(See also page 14) (See display ad page 15)*
This nonprofit school offers 12 hands-on courses/month. Maximum class/group size: 12-24. Also featured: workshops and cooking camp for children age 8-15.
EMPHASIS: A variety of topics, including international and vegetarian cuisines, entertaining menus, low-fat cooking, wine and food pairing.
COSTS: $45-$55/class. Payment with booking. Refunds available.
CONTACT: Cristina Williams, Admissions Director, Southern California School of Culinary Arts, 1420 El Centro St., S. Pasadena, CA 91030; (818) 403-8490, Fax (818) 403-8494.

A STORE FOR COOKS
Laguna Niguel/Year-round
This cookware store and school offers 12-14 morning and evening demonstration classes per month and Lunch and Learn classes once a week. Established in 1981. Maximum class/group size: 25 demo. Also featured: classes for private groups.
EMPHASIS: Ethnic and regional cuisines, holiday and seasonal foods, guest chef specialties.
FACULTY: Proprietor and cookbook author Susan Vollmer, Hugh Carpenter, Phillis Carey, Tarla Fallgatter, cookbook authors, and local chefs.
COSTS: Lunch and Learn classes are $15; demonstrations range from $40-$75. Credit cards accepted. Refunds 72 hours prior.
LOCATION: On the Pacific coast, 55 miles south of Los Angeles.
CONTACT: Susan Vollmer, A Store for Cooks, 30100 Town Center Dr., Suite R, Laguna Niguel, CA 92677; (714) 495-0445, Fax (714) 495-2139, E-mail 73571.3511@compuserve.com.

SUGAR 'N SPICE CAKE DECORATING SCHOOL
San Francisco/Year-round
This gourmet bakeware and cake decorating supply store and school offers more than 50 one- to five-session participation courses/year. Established in 1973. Maximum class/group size: 10-15. Facilities: classroom and retail store.
EMPHASIS: Cake decorating and candy making.
FACULTY: Jeanne Lutz is a graduate of Edith Gate's Cake Decorating School and has studied with other professionals. Guest instructors from around the world are featured.
COSTS: Range from $30-$150/course. Supplies vary with each course. Full payment in advance, first come first served. Refund for cancellation 48 hours prior.
LOCATION: The school is moving to a larger facility in 1997.
CONTACT: Jeanne Lutz, Owner, Sugar 'n Spice Cake Decorating School, 2007 41st Ave., San Francisco, CA 94116-1103; (415) 387-1722, Fax (415) 387-7133.

TANTE MARIE'S COOKING SCHOOL
San Francisco/Year-round   *(See also page 16) (See display ad page 17)*
This small private school offers 1-week, weekend, 6-session evening, and single-session morning participation courses, afternoon and weekend demonstrations, and party classes. Maximum class/group size: 16-38. Also featured: 1-week courses that include shopping at the Farmer's

Market, visits to bread bakeries and cheese makers, winery tours, and dining in fine restaurants.
EMPHASIS: General and specific topics, including pastries and regional cuisines.
COSTS: 1-week course $550, weekend courses $40-$125, 6-session courses $450, morning classes $75, demonstrations $40 (5 for $150). Hotel lodging available. $100 deposit for multi-session courses. Full refund 4 weeks prior.
CONTACT: Peggy Lynch, Administrator, Tante Marie's Cooking School, Inc., 271 Francisco St., San Francisco, CA 94133; (415) 788-6699, Fax (415) 788-8924.

UCLA EXTENSION, HOSPITALITY/FOODSERVICE MANAGEMENT
(See also page 16)   **Los Angeles/Year-round**
This school offers a variety of 1- to 10-session demonstration and participation courses, 1-day seminars, and culinary tours.
EMPHASIS: Ethnic and regional cuisines, guest chef specialties, wine and beer appreciation.
COSTS: $45-$60/session. Payment with registration. Refund, less $25, for cancellations 5 days prior.
CONTACT: UCLA Extension, Hospitality/Foodservice Management, 10995 Le Conte Ave., Room 515, Los Angeles, CA 90024-0901; (310) 206-8120, Fax (310) 206-7249.

WEIR COOKING
San Francisco/Year-round
This school in a private home offers weekend and 5-day participation courses, hands-on and demonstration. Established in 1989. Maximum class/group size: 8-9. Facilities: a newly-designed professional commercial kitchen with wood-fired Tuscan oven and 4 work stations. Also featured: courses include Napa and Sonoma Valley tours and dining at fine restaurants. Private classes and visits to restaurants, wineries, and markets.
EMPHASIS: French, Italian, Mediterranean, and American regional cuisines.
FACULTY: Joanne Weir cooked at Berkeley's Chez Panisse, studied with Madeleine Kamman, received the IACP Cooking Teacher Award of Excellence, teaches internationally, & is author of *From Tapas to Meze* & the Williams Sonoma *Seasonal Celebrations* series.
COSTS: $80-$100/class. A 50% deposit, half of which is refundable for cancellations 2 weeks prior, must accompany registration.
LOCATION: Pacific Heights, San Francisco.
CONTACT: Joanne Weir, Weir Cooking, 2107 Pine Street, San Francisco, CA 94115; (415) 776-4200, Fax (415) 776-0318, E-mail weircook@aol.com.

YANKEE HILL WINERY – WHAT'S COOKING AT THE WINERY
Columbia/Year-round
This winery offers weekly demonstration and participation cooking and wine classes since 1995. Established in 1970. Maximum class/group size: 12 hands-on/30 demo. Facilities: 2,500-sq-ft area with 12 workspaces, Swiss baking ovens, pizza oven, candy stove, sausage and salami-making equipment, smoker, wine-making equipment. Also featured: classes for youngsters, private classes, facility rental.
EMPHASIS: Baking, international cuisines taught by native instructors, instruction in a relaxed environment.
FACULTY: The 10 instructors include Yankee Hill Winery owner Ron Erickson, Denise Ganino, Jerry Phillips, Gretchen Erickson, and Ken Churches; guest chefs.
COSTS: $25-$100/class.
LOCATION: Two hours south of Sacramento, in the grape-growing regions of Tuolumne and Calaveras Counties.
CONTACT: Ron Erickson, Owner, Yankee Hill Winery, P.O. Box 330, Columbia, CA 95310; (209) 533-2417, (800) 497-WINE, Fax (209) 533-2417.

YOSEMITE CHEFS' & VINTNERS' HOLIDAYS
Yosemite National Park/November-February
Yosemite Concession Services Corporation conducts a series of seven 2-day/3-night Chefs' and Vintners' Holidays that feature 3 cooking demonstrations or 4 wine seminars and a concluding banquet. Established in 1982. Maximum class/group size: 180. Facilities: Great Lounge of The Ahwahnee hotel.

EMPHASIS: Cuisines of Western chefs, California wines.

FACULTY: Each program features three noted cooking instructors or four wineries. Executive Chef Robert Anderson and his staff prepare the vintner's banquet, visiting chefs prepare the chefs' banquet.

COSTS: Lodging is $215/night. Chefs'/vintners' banquets are $75/$80. Lodging is at the Ahwahnee hotel. Reservations more than 21 days prior require a deposit.

LOCATION: Yosemite National Park, 90 miles from Fresno and 175 miles from San Francisco.

CONTACT: Yosemite Chefs' Holidays & Vintners' Holidays, Yosemite Concession Services Corp., Box 578, Yosemite, CA 95389; (209) 252-4848, Fax (209) 372-1362.

COLORADO

ASIAN COOKERY
Colorado Springs/Year-round
This school in a private residence offers 36 classes/year. Started in 1989. Maximum class/group size: 8-12. Facilities: specially-designed teaching kitchen. Also featured: private classes, specialty classes, dinner parties.

EMPHASIS: Chinese, Malaysian, Thai, Vietnamese, Indian, low-fat, and vegetarian cuisines.

FACULTY: Peng Jones, CCP, studied at the International School of Home Cookery in Malaysia and trained in Oriental food and vegetable carving.

COSTS: $25-$35/session. Payable with registration. Full refund 1 week prior.

LOCATION: A 20-minute drive from the Colorado Springs airport; about 60 miles south of Denver.

CONTACT: Peng Jones, Owner, Asian Cookery, P.O. Box 62674, Colorado Springs, CO 80962; (719) 590-7768.

COOKING SCHOOL OF THE ROCKIES
Boulder/Year-round   *(See also page 18)*
This private school offers a diploma program, short courses, individual classes, and 5-day summer basic techniques intensives that emphasize creativity, organization, presentation.

EMPHASIS: Basic French techniques, Italian cuisine, pastry, baking, nutrition, ethnic cuisines, wine appreciation.

COSTS: Classes range from $35-$75 each; intensives are $395. A list of bed and breakfasts and lodgings is available. $100 nonrefundable deposit required.

CONTACT: Joan Brett, Director, Cooking School of the Rockies, Professional Culinary Arts Program, 637 S. Broadway, Ste. H, Boulder, CO 80303; (303) 494-7988, Fax (303) 494-7999, E-mail jbrett3768@aol.com.

FOOD & WINE MAGAZINE CLASSIC
Aspen/June
Food & Wine Magazine sponsors an annual 3-day weekend festival featuring a variety of events for food and wine enthusiasts and professionals. The 20-hour program offers over 80 lectures, demonstrations, panels, and tastings; a benefit auction; and fine dining. Started in 1983. Maximum class/group size: 70-800. Facilities: hotel and tented park area. Also featured: winemaker dinners.

EMPHASIS: Trade seminars for chefs & restaurateurs cover employee relations, marketing, direct mail, customer relations, insurance; consumer events include chef demonstrations & tastings from over 250 vintners.

FACULTY: Has included Bartholomew Broadbent, Julia Child, Marcella Hazan, Jacques Pépin, Frank Prial.

COSTS: Three-day tickets are about $495. Reserve tastings are $75 to $200 extra. Deluxe hotel and condominiums available. Registration non-refundable less than 30 days prior.

LOCATION: 3 hours from Denver by car, 45 minutes by plane.

CONTACT: Laura Powers, Event Marketing Coordinator, *Food & Wine Magazine* Classic, Events, 425 Rio Grande Plaza, Aspen, CO 81611-9938; (888) 7-WINE-97, Fax (970) 925-9008, E-mail arone@rof.net. Also: Laura Powers, *Food & Wine Magazine*, 1120 Ave. of the Americas, New York, NY 10036, (212) 382-5627.

MIJBANI INDIAN RESTAURANT
Boulder/Year-round

This school & catering service in a private residence offers six 1- to 3-session demonstration and participation courses per quarter. Established in 1993. Maximum class/group size: 6-16 hands-on/20 demo. Also featured: a newsletter, private classes.

EMPHASIS: Western Indian cuisine (without curry powder), techniques, spices, flat breads, chutneys, appetizers, fast foods.

FACULTY: Jessica Shah, a native of Bombay, has 14 years cooking experience, owns a catering service, and writes for local and national publications.

COSTS: $35-$100. Advance payment required.

LOCATION: Boulder, 45 minutes from Denver.

CONTACT: Jessica Shah, 2005 18th St., Boulder, CO 80302; (303) 442-7000, Fax (303) 442-5380.

NATURALLY GRAND JUNCTION COOKING SCHOOL
Grand Junction/Year-round

Cooking instructor Rebecca Wood offers a 16-hour demonstration course and weekend and one-week programs for out-of-towners. Established in 1994. Maximum class/group size: 13 demo. Facilities: private home. Also featured: advanced courses.

EMPHASIS: Grain-based diet, medicinal & energetic properties of foods.

FACULTY: Rebecca Wood authored 5 books on food and health and has taught cooking in London, Rome, and Dublin.

COSTS: $250 for the 16-hour course. A $100 deposit is required 4 weeks prior.

LOCATION: Western Colorado, midway between Salt Lake City and Denver.

CONTACT: Rebecca Wood, NATURALLY GRAND Junction Cooking School, P.O. Box 40408, Grand Junction, CO 81504; (970) 256-9697, (800) 833-1336, Fax (970) 242-7796.

SCHOOL OF NATURAL COOKERY
(See also page 19) ### Boulder/Year-round

This vegetarian cooking school offers a 3-part, 15-session, flexible schedule series 4 times/year. Founded in 1985. Maximum class/group size: 12.

EMPHASIS: Theory and techniques for preparing whole grains, beans, vegetables.

COSTS: Tuition is $250 for Parts I and II, $125 for Part III; materials $55. A 50% tuition deposit plus fee is due 3 weeks prior, refund 3 weeks prior.

CONTACT: Joanne Saltzman, Director, School of Natural Cookery, P.O. Box 19466, Boulder, CO 80308; (303) 444-8068, Fax available 1/97, E-mail available 1/97.

THE SEASONED CHEF
Denver/Year-round

This school offers 12 demonstration and participation classes/month. Established in 1993. Maximum class/group size: 12-15 hands-on/35 demo. Facilities: well-equipped home kitchen. Also featured: classes for youngsters, wine appreciation, market visits, private instruction.

EMPHASIS: Includes basic techniques, healthful cooking, ethnic cuisines, menu planning.

FACULTY: Area cooking school instructors and restaurant chefs, guest chefs and cookbook authors.

Costs: $35-$45/class. Payment with registration, refund for cancellation 1 week prior.
Contact: Sarah Leffen, The Seasoned Chef, 999 Jasmine St., #100, Denver, CO 80220; (303) 377-3222.

SUE'S KITCHEN
Boulder/Year-round
Caterer Susan Cardia-Quint offers more than 15 demonstration and participation day, evening, and weekend classes/term as well as 1- and 2-day sessions. Established in 1995. Maximum class/group size: 6. Facilities: kitchen in a private residence. Also featured: classes for youngsters.
Emphasis: Healthful cuisine, Italian, fish, and grain cookery, allergy-free cooking.
Faculty: Susan Cardia-Quint, trained by her native Italian grandparents, has over 15 years experience, owns a gourmet food take-out service, catering service, and writes food articles for local publications.
Costs: $30-$45/class. Advance payment required.
Location: 45 minutes from Denver.
Contact: Susan Cardia-Quint, Sue's Kitchen, 7433 Singing Hills Dr., Boulder, CO 80301; (303) 530-9683, Fax (303) 530-9683.

TELLURIDE WINE FESTIVAL
Telluride/June
This annual weekend festival features luncheon programs with guest chefs, seminars, tastings of over 200 wines, and a cooking class. Established in 1981.
Emphasis: Wine and food pairing.
Contact: Keith Hampton, Program Director, Telluride Wine Festival, 747 W. Pacific, #324, Box 1677, Telluride, CO 81435; (970) 728-3178, Fax (970) 728-4865.

CONNECTICUT

THE COMPLETE KITCHEN COOKING SCHOOL
Darien/Spring, Fall
This school in a kitchenware store offers more than 30 morning and evening demonstrations per term. Established in 1980. Maximum class/group size: 20.
Faculty: School Director Sigrid Laughlin and guest instructors, including Julia della Croce, Nicole Routhier, Stephen Schmidt, Patricia Wells.
Costs: $45-$75/session. Refunds 48 hours prior.
Location: 40 miles from New York City and New Haven.
Contact: Sigrid Laughlin, Director, The Complete Kitchen Cooking School, 863 Post Rd., Darien, CT 06820; (203) 655-4055, Fax (203) 655-0121.

THE COOK STORE
Storrs/Year-round
This cookware and specialty food shop offers 6-8 demonstration classes/month. Established in 1991. Maximum class/group size: 14. Facilities: fully-equipped teaching kitchen. Also featured: children's after-school and summer classes.
Emphasis: Ethnic cuisines, breads, topics per request. For children: knife skills, kitchen safety, cooking for the family.
Faculty: Proprietor Charles R. Caro, is a former caterer and restaurateur. Other faculty includes Robert Tavarnesi, Barbara Tashman, children's instructor Phyllis J. Caron-Taylor, and sign interpreter Suzanne Silva.
Costs: Usually $10-$15 for adult classes, $5 for children's classes. Food cost is additional. Registration is nonrefundable and payable in advance.
Location: Mansfield, a half-mile from the University of Connecticut's main campus and 45 minutes from Hartford.

CONTACT: The Cook Store, 1132 Storrs Rd., Storrs, CT 06268-2304; (860) 429-5911.

CUCINA CASALINGA
Wilton/Spring, Fall

(See also page 171)
This cooking school offers demonstration and participation classes and culinary tours to Italy. Established in 1981. Maximum class/group size: 12 hands-on/20 demo. Facilities: an open-plan home kitchen. Also featured: private group classes, evening classes, children's summer camp, wine tastings, excursions in the Northeast, tours of Italian neighborhoods in the Bronx.
EMPHASIS: Italian regional cuisine.
FACULTY: Owner/instructor Sally Ann Maraventano graduated Georgetown Univ., studied at the Univ. of Florence, & learned to cook from her mother & Sicilian grandfather, who owned an Italian bakery. Guest instructors include European chefs & American culinarians.
COSTS: Adult (children's) classes are $70 ($40)/session, $195 ($110) for a series of 3. Reservations are required and payment must be received 7 days before class.
LOCATION: Lower Fairfield County, 1 hour north of Manhattan by car or train.
CONTACT: Sally Ann Maraventano, Owner, Cucina Casalinga, 171 Drum Hill Rd., Wilton, CT 06897; (203) 762-0767, Fax (203) 762-0768, E-mail cucina@juno.com.

HAY DAY COOKING SCHOOL
Greenwich, Westport, Scarsdale/Year-round

This school offers 12-18 three-hour demonstration classes/session, 3 sessions/year, in each of its 3 locations. Established in 1982. Maximum class/group size: 45 maximum. Facilities: professional demonstration kitchen-classroom with seating for 45 students, overhead mirror, stovetop, convection oven, P.A. system.
EMPHASIS: Regional and ethnic cuisines, classic techniques, methods and food history.
FACULTY: Guest chefs include Bobby Flay, Bradley Ogden, Marcella Hazan, Jacques Pépin, Michael Romano.
COSTS: $65-$75/class. Payment prior to class; full refund granted one week prior to class.
LOCATION: The Riverside section of Greenwich, a 45-minute drive from New York City; Governor St. in Ridgefield, a 70-minute drive; Post Rd. East in Westport, a 1-hour drive; and Scarsdale, NY, a 30-minute drive.
CONTACT: Nicole J. Courtemanche, Director, Sutton Hay Day, Inc., Information/Reservations, 1071 Post Rd. East, Westport, CT 06880; (203) 221-0100, (203) 454-6649, Fax (203) 454-4923.

PRUDENCE SLOANE'S COOKING SCHOOL
Hampton/Year-round

This school in a private residence offers 4-8 participation workshops, demonstrations, and dinner demonstrations per month. Established in 1993. Maximum class/group size: 8 hands-on/14 demo/14 dinner demo. Facilities: well-equipped teaching kitchen. Also featured: private party classes, culinary weekends, food styling, kitchen design.
EMPHASIS: Ethnic and regional cuisines, techniques, theory, food history and flavoring principles, seasonal and holiday menus.
FACULTY: Prudence Sloane, an IACP member, was awarded the Blue Ribbon Professional diploma from Peter Kump's New York Cooking School, is a food stylist and has studied kitchen design; guest chefs and instructors.
COSTS: $30-$65/session. Full payment to reserve space.
LOCATION: Northeastern Connecticut, 90 minutes from Boston and 3 hours from New York City.
CONTACT: Prudence Sloane, Owner, Prudence Sloane's Cooking School, 245 Main St., Hampton, CT 06247; (203) 455-0596, E-mail eatart@snet.net.

RONNIE FEIN SCHOOL OF CREATIVE COOKING
Stamford/Spring, Fall

This private school offers demonstration and participation classes that emphasize ingredients, techniques, and menus. Established in 1971. Maximum class/group size: 8 hands-on/16 demo.

Facilities: fully-equipped home teaching kitchen. Also featured: children's classes, private instruction, year-round.

EMPHASIS: Regional cuisines, seasonal and holiday menus, food gifts, low-fat cuisine, ethnic foods, use of fresh herbs, and menu structure.

FACULTY: Ronnie Fein writes for food publications (newspapers and magazines) and attended the China Institute and Four Seasons Cooking School. She is author of *The Complete Idiot's Guide to Cooking Basics*.

COSTS: $45-$55. Refund for cancellations 24 hours prior.

LOCATION: North Stamford, 45 minutes from New York City.

CONTACT: Ronnie Fein, Owner, Ronnie Fein School of Creative Cooking, 438 Hunting Ridge Rd., Stamford, CT 06903; (203) 322-7114, Fax (203) 329-3366, E-mail ronskie@aol.com.

THE SILO COOKING SCHOOL
New Milford/March-December

This gourmet foods store and art gallery offers more than 70 demonstration and participation courses/year. Established in 1972. Maximum class/group size: 14 hands-on/30-35 demo. Facilities: well-equipped teaching kitchen. Also featured: custom group and children's classes.

EMPHASIS: Ethnic and regional cuisines, holiday menus, baking, guest chef specialties, wine selection.

FACULTY: Has included Giuliano Bugialli, Michael Romano, Daniel Leader, Jacques Pépin, Madeleine Kamman. School is owned by New York Pops founder Skitch Henderson & wife Ruth.

COSTS: About $75-$85 for master chef classes, $45-$100 for others. Payment with application.

LOCATION: About 80 miles from New York City on the Henderson's Hunt Hill Farm in the Litchfield Hills.

CONTACT: Sandra Daniels, Director, Silo Cooking School, Upland Rd., New Milford, CT 06776; (860) 355-0300, Fax (860) 350-5495.

DELAWARE

WHAT'S COOKING AT THE KITCHEN SINK
Hockessin/September-June

This school in a kitchenware store offers 12-16 demonstration classes/month. Established in 1991. Maximum class/group size: 16. Facilities: 300-sq-ft, 16-seat teaching area with overhead mirror. Also featured: children's workshops, private and party classes.

EMPHASIS: Special occasion menus, guest chef specialties, specific subjects.

FACULTY: Director Lee Wooding, an IACP member, and traveling guest chefs/authors.

COSTS: $26-$45/class. For lodging, the school recommends The Inn at Montchanin Village. Refund for cancellation 1 week prior, 2 weeks prior for outside guests.

LOCATION: Hockessin, a Wilmington suburb, is 40 miles from Philadelphia and 75 miles from Baltimore.

CONTACT: Lee Wooding, Director, What's Cooking at the Kitchen Sink, 425 Hockessin Corner, Hockessin, DE 19707; (302) 239-7066, Fax (302) 239-7665.

DISTRICT OF COLUMBIA

PARIS COOKS
Washington, D.C./October-April

Cooking instructor Elizabeth Esterling conducts 5-session demonstration and participation courses that stress easy, elegant, do-ahead menus. Established in 1977. Maximum class/group size: 5. Facilities: home kitchen.

EMPHASIS: Intermediate and advanced low fat French cuisine.

FACULTY: Elizabeth Esterling holds a degree from La Varenne and is Chevalier du Tastevin, Clos Vougeot. She has written the *Le Cookbook* and contributed to *Small Feasts* and *Simple Feasts*.

COSTS: $200 for 5 sessions.

CONTACT: Elizabeth Esterling, Paris Cooks, 1619 34th St. N.W., Washington, DC 20007; (202) 333-4451, Fax (202) 333-4451.

SMITHSONIAN INSTITUTION
Washington, D.C./Year-round

The Smithsonian Institution Associates Program offers 2 or 3 special interest vacation programs/year that focus on food and cooking. Also featured: lectures and visits to cultural attractions.

COSTS: Includes double occupancy lodging, some meals, all planned activities.

LOCATION: Recent programs in Seattle, New Orleans, and Paris have included cooking classes.

CONTACT: Mary Beth Mullen, Smithsonian Associates, Study Tours and Seminars, 1100 Jefferson Dr. S.W., Room 3045, Washington, DC 20008; (202) 357-4700, Fax (202) 633-9250.

FLORIDA

ARIANA'S COOKING SCHOOL
Miami/Year-round

This cookware store and school offers more than 50 demonstration and participation classes/quarter. Established in 1976. Maximum class/group size: 28. Facilities: a 400-sq-ft kitchen with overhead mirror. Also featured: private bridal showers, birthday parties for children and adults.

FACULTY: The 15+-member faculty includes Wendy Kallergis, Paul Galadga, Ariana Kumpis, Allen Susser, Mark Militello, Sarah Benson.

COSTS: $25-$100/session.

CONTACT: Ariana M. Kumpis, Ariana's Cooking School, 7251 S.W. 57th Ct., Miami, FL 33143; (305) 667-5957, Fax (305) 665-7763.

CARIBBEAN CULINARY ADVENTURES
Key West/November-April

This culinary-focused travel package features 5-night vacations with 3 cooking demonstrations of Caribbean cuisine. Established in 1994. Maximum class/group size: 10-20. Facilities: various Key West restaurants. Also featured: low impact sea kayaking trip, sightseeing bike tour, snorkeling, restaurants, local food markets, locally crafted products. Custom programs for groups of 10 or more.

EMPHASIS: Cuban and Caribbean cuisines.

FACULTY: Donna Shields, MS, RD, IACP member, former instructor at the CIA, food writer and author of the forthcoming *Caribbean Light*.

COSTS: From $600-$975, based on double occupancy for rooms and double/quad occupancy for cottages, includes all planned activities. Lodging is available at historic inns in Old Town. 30% deposit required, balance due 30 days prior. Credit cards accepted.

LOCATION: In Old Town, 10 minutes from Key West airport, a 3-hour drive from Miami.

CONTACT: Donna Shields, Owner, Key West Cooking School, P.O. Box 1636, Key West, FL 33041; (800) 32-FOODS, Fax (305) 295-9305.

CHEF ALLEN'S
Miami/Spring, Summer, Fall

Chef Allen Susser offers demonstration and participation classes and one-on-one sessions in which the student works along with the restaurant staff. Established in 1986. Maximum class/group size: 1-25. Facilities: Chef Allen's restaurant in North Miami Beach.

EMPHASIS: New World cuisine, local fish, tropical fruits, Latin root vegetables.

FACULTY: Chef Susser, graduate and on the faculty of Florida International University School of Hospitality & Restaurant Management. Author of *Allen Susser's New World Cuisine and Cookery*, he studied at Le Cordon Bleu & was chef at Paris' Bristol Hotel.

COSTS: Group classes range from $35-$50. Individual session is $195. Reserve 3 weeks prior.

CONTACT: Chef Allen Susser, Chef Allen's, 19088 N.E. 29th Ave., N. Miami Beach, FL 33180; (305) 935-2900, Fax (305) 935-9062.

CULINARY ARTS CENTER AT OCEAN REEF CLUB
Key Largo/January-April, July, November-December
This private club offers 1- to 4-session demonstration courses, including Miami and Keys food tours and specialty dinners. Program started 1990. Maximum class/group size: 15-35. Facilities: 500-sq-ft kitchen with overhead mirror and seating for 35. Also featured: kid's classes, day trips, visits to food producers, fine dining, sightseeing, market visits, hands-on classes by special request.
EMPHASIS: Contemporary American, regional Florida, Mediterranean, and international cuisines, entertaining menus.
FACULTY: School Manager Carole Kotkin, former owner of Bobbi & Carole's Cooking School; Sarah Benson, contributing editor to *Gourmet*; cookbook authors Steven Raichlen, Joanne Weir, Hugh Carpenter.
LOCATION: 50 miles south of Miami in private club community. Resort amenities include two 18-hole golf courses, lawn and tennis club, marina, nature preserve, fine restaurants, water sports.
CONTACT: Carole Kotkin, Manager, Ocean Reef Club, Culinary Arts Center, 31 Ocean Reef Dr., C-300, Key Largo, FL 33037; (305) 367-2611, Fax (305) 367-2224, E-mail orcsales@oceanreef.com, URL http://www.reefnet.com.

DAMIANO'S AT THE TARRIMORE HOUSE
Delray Beach/October-August
This restaurant offers Wednesday day and evening theme classes. Program started 1992. Maximum class/group size: 25. Facilities: a demonstration kitchen in the restaurant dining room.
EMPHASIS: Low-fat, or fat-free cooking; Italian, Southwest, and Asian cuisines.
FACULTY: Chef Anthony Basil Damiano.
COSTS: $100 ($65) for 3 evening (day) classes. Lodging available at the Seagate Beach Club.
CONTACT: Lisa Damiano, Damiano's at the Tarrimore House, Tarrimore Cooking School, 52 N. Swinton Ave., Delray Beach, FL 33444; (407) 272-4706, Fax (407) 272-0858.

DISNEY INSTITUTE CULINARY ARTS PROGRAMS
Lake Buena Vista/Year-round
This self-contained resort sponsor of more than 60 hands-on programs in eight special interest areas offers culinary programs that range from the basics to entertaining menus. Established in 1996. Maximum class/group size: approximately 15. Facilities: 2 participatory kitchens, each with 14 newly-equipped work stations. Also featured: programs in Disney's animation and story-telling techniques, sports and fitness, design and performing arts, gardening; golf & tennis, spa, special programs for youngsters.
EMPHASIS: Topics include celebrations, techniques, healthy cooking, romantic dinners, baking, international cuisines, wine.
FACULTY: Programs managed by Chef Frank Brough, former executive chef at Ariel's restaurant at Disney's Yacht Club Resort and chef de cuisine at Victoria & Albert's at Disney's Grand Floridian Beach Resort.
COSTS: In 1997, vacation packages begin at $499/person for 3 nights, which includes double occupancy bungalow lodging and 1-day pass to a Walt Disney World theme park. Lodging is in 1-bedroom bungalows that sleep 5 and 1- and 2-bedroom townhouses that sleep up to 6. $200 deposit is due within 2 weeks of booking. Full refund for cancellation 46 days prior. Trip cancellation insurance available.
LOCATION: Walt Disney World Resort.
CONTACT: Frank Brough, Disney Institute, Culinary Dept., P.O. Box 10,000, Lake Buena Vista, FL 32830-1000; (407) 827-1100, Fax (407) 827-4586.

GOING SOLO IN THE KITCHEN
Apalachicola/Year-round

Food and travel writer Jan Doerfer conducts bimonthly 5-day participation courses that are geared to the needs of the solo cook. Instruction is scheduled mornings and evenings, afternoons are free. Maximum class/group size: 12. Facilities: the instructor's 19th-century Key West-style home, overlooking the Apalachicola River.

FACULTY: *Going Solo* newsletter publisher Jane Doerfer's cookbook credits include *The Victory Garden Cookbook* (collaborator), *The Legal Sea Foods Cookbook*, and *Going Solo in the Kitchen.*
COSTS: $975 includes lodging and meals.
LOCATION: Apalachicola, a Natural Estuarine Sanctuary in the Florida Panhandle, is 75 miles from Tallahassee.
CONTACT: Jane Doerfer, Going Solo in the Kitchen, P.O. Box 123, Apalachicola, FL 32329; (904) 653-8848, (800) 445-7685.

HARRIET'S KITCHEN WHOLE FOODS COOKING SCHOOL
Winter Park/September-June

This school offers 12 to 15 demonstration and participation classes/month. Established in 1987. Maximum class/group size: 16 hands-on/35 demo. Facilities: a 500-sq-ft teaching kitchen. Also featured: classes for youngsters, a 9-session Healing Macrobiotic series, sourdough whole grain bread classes, and a 5-day macrobiotic weekend intensive at St. George Island every fall.

EMPHASIS: Macrobiotic and gourmet vegetarian cuisines.
FACULTY: Director Harriet McNear, a Kushi certified teacher and licensed nutrition counselor, studied at the Kushi Institute and the Natural Gourmet Cookery School. Local chefs include Tim Rosendahl, Clair Epting, Richard Blanke, Marc van Couwenberghe, M.D.
COSTS: Classes range from $20-$40, 5-day intensive $650-$850, the 9-session course $220. Spouses receive a 30% discount. Work-study and assistantship positions are available. A 50% deposit is required and refund is granted cancellations 5 days prior.
LOCATION: Near Walt Disney World, 15 miles from Orlando International Airport.
CONTACT: Harriet McNear, Director, Harriet's Kitchen, 1136 Oaks Blvd., Winter Park, FL 32789; (407) 644-2167, Fax (407) 644-2187, E-mail harkit@magicnet.net.

KITCHEN HEARTH
Miami Beach/January-July, September-November

This cookware store offers 4 demonstration and participation classes/month. Established in 1994. Maximum class/group size: 10 hands-on/18 demo. Facilities: kitchen with 10 workspaces. Also featured: classes for youngsters, market visits.

EMPHASIS: A variety of topics, including Italian, Thai, Chinese, and Indian cuisines; baking and cake decorating; low-fat cooking.
FACULTY: Guest chefs from noted local restaurants.
COSTS: $30 for adult classes, $18 for children's classes. Payment with registration; refund with 3 days notice.
LOCATION: Two miles from the historic South Beach district and 15 minutes from Miami International Airport.
CONTACT: Gail Fix, The Kitchen Hearth, 456 Arthur Godfrey Rd., Miami Beach, FL 33140; (305) 538-3358, Fax (305) 538-3431.

THE RITZ-CARLTON, AMELIA ISLAND, COOKING SCHOOL
Amelia Island/Year-round

This resort hotel offers monthly 2-day participation courses that focus on a theme. Established in 1994. Maximum class/group size: 15. Facilities: The Grill kitchen. Also featured: a tour of the food preparation facilities.

EMPHASIS: Seasonal and entertaining menus, regional and ethnic cuisines, macrobiotic recipes.
FACULTY: Matthew Medure, AAA 5-Diamond chef of The Grill; the hotel's food and beverage staff.

Costs: $650/person, $964/couple, which includes lodging, most meals, and resort amenities. Oceanfront resort, 449 rooms, 18-hole championship golf course on property, pools, tennis, AAA 5-Diamond, Mobil Four Star, 8th best resort in 1995 Zagat Survey.
Location: On the Atlantic Ocean, 25 minutes north of Jacksonville.
Contact: Robin Anderson, Restaurant Reservations Coordinator, The Ritz-Carlton, Amelia Island, 4750 Amelia Island Pkwy, Amelia Island, FL 32034; (800) 241-3333, (904) 277-1100, Fax (904) 277-1145.

SARASOTA FOOD AND WINE ACADEMY
Sarasota/Year-round
This wine and gourmet food store offers 20 demonstration and participation courses/year. Established in 1995. Maximum class/group size: 15 hands-on/40 demo. Facilities: 350-sq-ft central teaching station and kitchen. Also featured: wine courses.
Faculty: Special events coordinator Anthony Blue; guest chefs.
Costs: $25-$100.
Location: Adjacent to Michael's On East restaurant, 60 miles south of Tampa.
Contact: Michael Klauber, Director, Sarasota Food and Wine Academy, 1212 East Ave. S., Sarasota, FL 34239; (941) 362-9463, Fax (941) 955-9965, E-mail klauber@gate.net, URL http://www.bestfood.com.

GEORGIA

DIANE WILKINSON'S COOKING SCHOOL
Atlanta/Year-round
Diane Wilkinson offers five 5-day intensive techniques courses and several short courses per year. Established in 1974. Maximum class/group size: 8 for hands-on classes. Facilities: remodeled Mediterranean-style kitchen with 2 fireplaces, one built for open-hearth cooking. Also featured: private classes for individuals and groups.
Emphasis: French and Italian techniques, seasonal foods, reduced fat recipes.
Faculty: Diane Wilkinson, certified by the IACP as a CCP, studied at Le Cordon Bleu, La Varenne, with Marcella Hazan, and has worked in kitchens in France and Italy, including those of Michael Guerard, Claude Deligne, Guenther Seeger, and L'Oustau de Baumaniere.
Costs: Classes are $50, five sessions are $225, the intensive is $650. A $200 deposit is required for the intensive, refundable 3 weeks prior.
Location: Northwest Atlanta, between Buckhead & Cumberland Mall.
Contact: Diane Wilkinson, 4365 Harris Trail, Atlanta, GA 30327; (404) 233-0366, Fax (404) 233-0051.

KITCHEN FARE COOKING SCHOOL
Atlanta/Year-round
This school in a cookware store offers over 125 evening demonstrations/year. Established in 1982. Maximum class/group size: 25. Facilities: a large, home-style kitchen.
Emphasis: Ethnic and regional cuisines, healthy cooking, fish, poultry, holiday menus.
Faculty: A revolving staff of local chefs and professionals.
Costs: $24.50/class. Class credit for cancellations within deadline. MasterCard & Visa accepted.
Location: Buckhead.
Contact: Laura Shapiro, Kitchen Fare Cooking School, 2385 Peachtree Rd., NE, Atlanta, GA 30305; (404) 233-8849.

MR. C'S COOKING CASTLE
Chamblee/March-July, September-November
This school offers up to four 1- to 4-session participation courses/month. Established in 1975. Maximum class/group size: 15. Facilities: 1,200-sq-ft kitchen with 4 workspaces.

EMPHASIS: Cooking techniques, cake decorating, private classes.
FACULTY: Caterers and party planners Cass Chapman, CEC, and Pauline Chapman, Sous Chef.
COSTS: $25/class. 10% nonrefundable deposit.
LOCATION: 10 miles from Atlanta.
CONTACT: Cassius L. Chapman, Mr. C's Cooking Castle, 4330 Chamblee Dunwoody Rd., Chamblee, GA 30341; (770) 455-3636.

RAY OVERTON'S LE CREUSET COOKING SCHOOL
Atlanta/Year-round

Le Creuset Cookshop at Park Place (formerly The Cooking Scene) offers approximately 25 different 1- to 3-session demonstration and Saturday participation classes/month. Established in 1993. Maximum class/group size: 12 hands-on/30 demo-lecture. Facilities: 30-seat demo kitchen with overhead mirror and audio/video system, 8 separate work stations. Also featured: cooking camp for youngsters, private classes, lectures, book signings, and culinary trips.
EMPHASIS: Ethnic and regional cuisines, special occasion dishes, baking, pastry, low fat, healthy and vegetarian, wine tasting, specific subjects.
FACULTY: Cookbook author & cooking show host Ray Overton apprenticed with Nathalie Dupree and is a member of the IACP and AIWF. Guest instructors have included Lydie Marshall, Shirley Fong-Torres, Fabrizio Bottero, and Virginia Willis.
COSTS: Demonstrations are $25/class; participation classes begin at $50. Lodging is available at hotels located across Perimeter Mall. Payment with registration. Refund for cancellations 72 hours prior.
LOCATION: Park Place Shops across from Perimeter Mall.
CONTACT: Ray L. Overton, III, Culinary Director/Owner, Culinary Concepts, Le Creuset Cookshop, 4505 Ashford Dunwoody Rd., Atlanta, GA 30346; (770) 396-5925, Fax (404) 733-6002, E-mail rloiii@aol.com. Also: Culinary Concepts, 89 26th St., NW, Suite #2, Atlanta, GA, 30309-2004; (404) 875-7532.

URSULA'S COOKING SCHOOL, INC.
Atlanta/September-May

This school founded by Ursula Knaeusel offers three 4-session demonstration courses/year. Established in 1966. Maximum class/group size: 40. Facilities: 3-level classroom with 18-foot mirror over a 22-foot granite counter. Also featured: gingerbread house, cutting and decorating classes, bridal shower classes, couples classes.
EMPHASIS: Nouvelle cuisine, time-saving methods and advance preparation.
FACULTY: Ursula Knaeusel's 40+ years of experience include supervising kitchens and operating restaurants in Europe & the U.S., teaching in Central America, the Caribbean, and the U.S. She hosts PBS' *Cooking With Ursula*.
COSTS: $85 for the 4-session course. Payment with registration. Refunds granted cancellations prior to course.
LOCATION: One mile from Interstate 75 and 85 and 4 miles from downtown Atlanta.
CONTACT: Ursula Knaeusel, President, Ursula's Cooking School, Inc., 1764 Cheshire Bridge Rd., N.E., Atlanta, GA 30324; (404) 876-7463, Fax (404) 876-7467.

HAWAII

BIG ISLAND BOUNTY
Hawaii/May

This hotel sponsors an annual 3-day festival which showcases Hawaii's regional cuisine & features gastronomic field trips, seminars on traditional Hawaiian foods, roundtable discussions, receptions and dinners. Established in 1992. Maximum class/group size: varies. Also featured: farmers market, golf, tennis, scuba, fishing, bicycling.
EMPHASIS: Foods of Hawaii.

FACULTY: Noted chefs and culinarians; has included Sam Choy, Peter Merriman, and Alan Wong.
COSTS: A variety of package plans, which include lodging are available. Meals and events can also be purchased separately. The Orchid at Mauna Lani.
LOCATION: The Orchid at Mauna Lani on the Kohala Coast of the Big Island of Hawaii, 20 miles north of the Keahole-Kona airport.
CONTACT: Donna Kimura, Communications Manager, Big Island Bounty, The Orchid at Mauna Lani, One North Kaniku Dr., Kohala Coast, HI 96743; (808) 885-2000, (800) 845-9905, Fax (808) 885-1064.

A CELEBRATION OF HAWAII REGIONAL CUISINE
Hawaiian Islands/Year-round
This full-service travel company sponsors culinary vacation programs that incorporate hands-on classes, wine tastings, seminars, off-site tours, and evening dining events. Established in 1994. Also featured: spa treatments, golf, tennis, cultural and art tours, and enrichment seminars that include floral design, herb gardening, decorative displays, cooking with condiments, and star gazing.
EMPHASIS: Hawaiian regional cuisine, Pacific Rim, vegetarian. Guest chefs.
FACULTY: The founding chefs of Hawaii Regional Cuisine: Peter Merriman (Hula Grill), Mark Ellman (Avalon), Jean-Marie Josselin (A Pacific Cafe), Roy Yamaguchi (Roy's Kahana Bar & Grill), Beverly Gannon (Haliimaile General Store).
COSTS: Land packages begin at $1,000, which includes most meals, ground transport, and first class lodging. A $500 deposit is required; balance due 45 days prior; cancellations over 45 days prior forfeit $250.
CONTACT: Noelle Edwards, Interactive Events, 155 Wailea #14, Wailea, HI 96753; (800) 961-9196, Fax (808) 875-1565, E-mail events@maui.net, URL http://www.maui.net/~events.

CUISINES OF THE SUN
Kohala Coast/July
The Mauna Lani Bay Hotel sponsors an annual 5-day culinary vacation that features daily demonstrations of tropical recipes. Established in 1990. Maximum class/group size: 200. Facilities: on-stage demonstration kitchen. Also featured: resort amenities, including golf, tennis, spa.
EMPHASIS: Tropical cuisines. Theme and region changes each year.
FACULTY: Noted chefs and beverage makers from the regions featured.
COSTS: Approximately $1,500 single, $2,200 double occupancy, which includes some meals, planned activities, and lodging. Daily and individual event options available. Prepayment required for events only; full refund 4 days prior.
LOCATION: The AAA 5-Diamond Mauna Lani Bay Hotel and Bungalows is on the Kohala Coast of Hawaii's Big Island, 20 miles from the airport.
CONTACT: Sharon Bianco, Director of Catering, The Mauna Lani Bay Hotel and Bungalows, One Mauna Lani Dr., Kohala Coast, HI 96743; (800) 367-2323, Fax (808) 885-4556.

GRAND CHEFS ON TOUR
Wailea, Maui/Year-round
The Kea Lani Hotel offers week-long food and wine education programs every 5 or 6 weeks that feature cooking classes, wine seminars, and field trips to wineries, specialty markets, and produce farms. Established in 1996. Maximum class/group size: 25-30. Facilities: Kea Lani Hotel kitchens and open-air classrooms. Also featured: hotel facilities.
EMPHASIS: Cuisines of the Pacific Rim and international guest chefs; wine and food pairing.
FACULTY: Each program features a Pacific Rim chef, a noted guest chef, and a wine expert.
COSTS: A variety of packages, including all-suite and villa lodging, are available. Lodging in luxury suites and villas. Credit cards accepted.
LOCATION: West Maui.
CONTACT: Armida Chamberlain, Public Relations Manager, American Express, co-sponsor, The Kea Lani Hotel, 4100 Wailea Alanui, Wailea, Wailea, Maui, HI 96753; (808) 875-4100, Fax (808)

875-1200, URL http://www.kealani.com/. Also: Cindi Dietrich, Alive Culinary Resources, (707) 433-2499, Fax (707) 433-2498.

JMD EDUCATIONAL CENTER FOR WINE AND FOOD
Aiea/Year-round

This culinary center acquired by U. of Hawaii College of Continuing Ed. in 1992 offers 15 culinary classes/semester and a fine wine series. Established in 1990. Facilities: professional kitchen, exhibition hall, banquet room, wine cellar, garden lanai. Also featured: California wine tours, cultural programs, catering and event planning and facilities.

EMPHASIS: A variety of topics, wine appreciation.

FACULTY: Director David J. Hill managed a restaurant for more than 25 years. The 11-member faculty includes chefs, cookbook authors, and Richard Dean, Master Sommelier, who coordinates the wine series.

COSTS: $35/class. Payment with registration, refund with one working day notice.

LOCATION: The Halawa Valley, near Honolulu.

CONTACT: David J. Hill, Director, JMD Educational Center for Wine and Food, 99-1269 Iwaena St., Aiea, HI 96701; (808) 486-5638, Fax (808) 487-2043.

ILLINOIS

ARG COOKING SCHOOL AND SUPPLY CO.
LaGrange/Fall, Winter, spring

This gourmet equipment catalog supply company and cooking school offers demonstration and participation classes. Established in 1993. Maximum class/group size: 4-12. Facilities: a well-equipped private home kitchen and professional restaurant-style kitchen. Also featured: guided tours of specialty markets and kitchen equipment emporiums.

EMPHASIS: Basic and intermediate Mexican, Caribbean, Latin, and Mediterranean cuisines.

FACULTY: Owner Anthony Garcia has taught Latin and Mediterranean cooking in the Chicago area for 10 years. He trained in Italian restaurants and is primarily self-taught.

COSTS: $40-$60/class. Payable 10 days in advance.

LOCATION: Two locations in the near western suburbs of Chicago.

CONTACT: Anthony Garcia, ARG Cooking School and Supply Co., 106 W. Calendar Court., Suite 223, LaGrange, IL 60625; (708) 485-4876, Fax (708) 354-8773.

BEAUTIFUL FOOD
Glenview/Spring, Fall

Cooking instructor Charie MacDonald offers approximately 20 participation classes/year. Established in 1973. Maximum class/group size: 20. Facilities: the 2,800-sq-ft commercial kitchen of Beautiful Food, her catering and wholesale specialty food business. Also featured: culinary tours.

EMPHASIS: Fresh foods, techniques, breads, pastas, pastries, soups, low-cholesterol foods.

FACULTY: Charie MacDonald studied at Le Cordon Bleu, the Ecole des Trois Gourmands (Provence), and with Simone Beck. A charter member of the IACP, she founded Beautiful Food in 1982.

COSTS: Class fee is $45, payable in advance. The trip cost of $5,000 includes airfare to/from Nice, meals, lodging, and ground transport. A deposit of $2,000 is required by December 1.

LOCATION: Glenview, northwest of Chicago near O'Hare International Airport.

CONTACT: Beautiful Food, 1872 John's Dr., Glenview, IL 60025; (708) 657-8403, Fax (708) 657-8685.

BLACK HAWK COLLEGE – QUAD CITIES CAMPUS
(See also page 31)   **Moline/Year-round**

This college offers two 4- to 6-week demonstration and participation courses. Maximum class/group size: 15-25. Also featured: wine instruction, kids' classes, market visits, dining in fine restaurants, sightseeing, visits to food producers.

EMPHASIS: Baking.

COSTS: $35-$50/sessiom.

CONTACT: Kim Davenport, Black Hawk College-Quad Cities Campus, Culinary Arts, 6600 - 34th Ave., Moline, IL 61265; (309) 796-1311 #4125, Fax (309) 792-3418.

CARLOS' RESTAURANT
Highland Park/Year-round

This restaurant offers luncheon demonstrations and A Day in the Kitchen individual participation classes. Established in 1993. Maximum class/group size: 25 demo.

EMPHASIS: Contemporary French cooking.

FACULTY: Executive Chef Jacky Pluton.

COSTS: Luncheon classes are $40; the full-day class is $140 per person, which includes the class for one and dinner for two.

LOCATION: Highland Park, 25 miles north of Chicago.

CONTACT: Carlos Nieto, Owner, Carlos' Restaurant, 429 Temple Ave., Highland Park, IL 60035; (847) 432-0770, Fax (847) 432-2047.

CHEZ MADELAINE
Hinsdale/Fall, Winter, spring

This school in a private home offers 35-40 one- to three-session demonstration and participation classes/year. Established in 1977. Maximum class/group size: 6-10. Also featured: evening menu classes.

EMPHASIS: Basics, techniques, ethnic cuisines, seasonal and holiday menus, preserving, soups, stocks, baking.

FACULTY: Madelaine Bullwinkel received the Diplome from L'Academie de Cuisine, is author of *Gourmet Preserves, Chez Madelaine*, and is a member of Les Dames d'Escoffier. Occasional guest instructors and cookbook authors.

COSTS: $60-$75. Payment must accompany application.

LOCATION: Hinsdale, 20 miles west of Chicago, 20 minutes from O'Hare airport.

CONTACT: Madelaine Bullwinkel, Owner, Chez Madelaine Cooking School, 425 Woodside Ave., Hinsdale, IL 60521; (630) 325-4177, Fax (630) 655-0355.

THE COOKING AND HOSPITALITY INSTITUTE OF CHICAGO
Chicago/Year-round   *(See also page 33)*

This school offers more than a dozen demonstration classes and series for nonprofessionals. Maximum class/group size: 30.

EMPHASIS: Topics include seafood, herbs, pasta, charcuterie, catering, techniques.

COSTS: $50/session, $200-$275/series.

CONTACT: Jim Simpson, Director, The Cooking and Hospitality Institute of Chicago, 361 W. Chestnut, Chicago, IL 60610; (312) 944-2725, Fax (312) 944-8557, URL http://www.chic.edu.

COOKING CRAFT, INC.
St. Charles/September-May

This gourmet shop and deli offers 2 to 3 evening demonstrations per week and some participation courses. Established in 1982. Maximum class/group size: 24 demo. Also featured: classes for children, private sessions.

EMPHASIS: Basics.

FACULTY: The main instructor has over 10 years of teaching experience. Other instructors specialize in ethnic topics.

COSTS: $18-$22/class. Payment upon registration; full refund with 72 hours notice.

LOCATION: Mid-size commuter town on the Fox River, 40 miles west of Chicago.

CONTACT: Anne Lorenz, Owner/Director, Cooking Craft, Inc., 1415 W. Main St., St. Charles, IL 60174; (603) 377-1730, Fax (603) 377-3665.

CUISINE COOKING SCHOOL
Moline/September-June

This school in a private residence offers approximately 50 participation classes/year. Established in 1979. Maximum class/group size: 10. Facilities: a remodeled large kitchen with 5 work stations and AGA range. Also featured: food and wine pairing, classes for youngsters, private instruction, culinary tours.

EMPHASIS: French and Italian cuisines.

FACULTY: Owner/teacher Marysue Salmon studied at La Varenne and with Simone Beck and earned a BS degree in Food Science from Iowa State University.

COSTS: $37.50/class. Hotels are located nearby. A 50% deposit is required; refund 1 week prior.

LOCATION: 3 hours west of Chicago, 3 hours east of Des Moines.

CONTACT: Marysue Salmon, Cuisine Cooking School, 1100 - 23rd Ave., Moline, IL 61265; (309) 797-8613, Fax (309) 797-8641.

FOOD FEST
January, March, August, October, November

Publicist Gail Guggenheim conducts cooking school weekends that feature cooking demonstrations, seminars, and tastings. Established in 1984. Maximum class/group size: varies. Facilities: a complete kitchen with overhead mirrors set up on a stage; closed-circuit monitors. Also featured: hotel amenities.

EMPHASIS: Entertaining menus, new food trends, ethnic specialties, techniques, gourmet products.

FACULTY: Area chefs and cooking teachers, usually Certified Members of the IACP.

COSTS: $189-$229 per couple for two nights, including continental breakfasts. Refund policy varies with location.

LOCATION: The Kahler Hotel in Rochester, Minn.; Sheraton San Marcos Resort in Chandler/Phoenix; Lakeview Resort in Morgantown, W.Va.; Olympia Park Hotel in Park City, UT; Plaza One Hotel in Rock Island, Ill.

CONTACT: Gail Guggenheim, Food Fests, 125 Country Lane, Highland Park, IL 60035; (847) 831-4265, Fax (847) 831-4266.

FRONTERA GRILL
Chicago

Owner/Chef Rick Bayless conducts demonstrations and an annual 1-week culinary tour of Oaxaca, Mexico. Program started 1992. Maximum class/group size: 25 demo. Facilities: Frontera Grill restaurant kitchen.

EMPHASIS: Mexican cuisine.

FACULTY: Rick Bayless hosted a PBS TV Mexican cooking series, co-authored *Authentic Mexican*, established Chicago's Frontera Grill and Topolobampo restaurants, 3-star rated by Chicago Tribune, 1995 recipient of the James Beard Award as the Chef of the Year.

COSTS: Demonstrations are $45; the 1-week tour is $2,000.

LOCATION: River North section of Chicago; Oaxaca, Mexico.

CONTACT: Pat Schloeman, Frontera Grill, 445 N. Clark, Chicago, IL 60610; (312) 661-1434, Fax (312) 661-1830, E-mail rbayl10475@aol.com.

LA VENTURÉ
Skokie/November-May

This school in a private residence offers 30 six-session participation courses/month. Established in 1980. Maximum class/group size: 12. Facilities: a 600-sq-ft professional-style kitchen. Also featured: private classes, classes for children.

EMPHASIS: French, Italian, and Chinese cuisines; candy making and cake decorating; baking.

FACULTY: Director-owner Sandra Bisceglie attended the French School Dumas Pere and

Harrington Institute of Interior Design and has a certificate of completion from the National Institute for the Foodservice Industry.

COSTS: $289-$359/course. Refund for cancellations with 10 days notice.

LOCATION: Skokie is adjacent to Chicago, 3 miles from O'Hare airport.

CONTACT: Sandra Bisceglie, La Venturé, 5100 West Jarlath, Skokie, IL 60077; (708) 679-8845.

ORIENTAL FOOD MARKET AND COOKING SCHOOL, INC.
Chicago/Year-round   *(See also page 234)*

This food market, cooking school, and catering service offers 1- and 6-session demonstration classes each month and an annual cultural tour to China. Established in 1971. Maximum class/group size: 50 demo/15 tour. Facilities: L-shaped kitchen adjacent to food market.

EMPHASIS: Thai, Indonesian, Japanese, Korean, Vietnamese, Chinese, and Philippine cuisines.

FACULTY: Pansy and Chu-Yen Luke have operated the market and school since its inception.

COSTS: $21/session, $85 for 6 weeks. 50% deposit required, refund upon cancellation.

CONTACT: Pansy Luke, Oriental Food Market and Cooking School, 2801 West Howard St., Chicago, IL 60645; (312) 274-2826.

TRUFFLES, INC.
O'Fallon/September-June

This school in a private home offers 2-session demonstration and participation courses. Established in 1980. Maximum class/group size: 8-20. Facilities: professional home kitchen with grill and double ovens, overlooking a lake. Also featured: Tours of the Hill (Italian) in St. Louis.

EMPHASIS: Regional and international food, bread and pastry, party themes.

FACULTY: Caterer and food consultant Kathy Kneedler, CCP, has taught cooking for 15 years and is a past newsletter editor for the St. Louis Culinary Society.

COSTS: $25-$32. Deposit required; refunds granted 3 days prior.

LOCATION: About 45 minutes from a major airport and 20 minutes from St. Louis.

CONTACT: Kathy A. Kneedler, President and Director, Truffles, Inc., Cooking School, 910 Indian Springs Rd., O'Fallon, IL 62269; (618) 632-9461, Fax (618) 234-3701.

WHAT'S COOKING
Hinsdale

This school offers demonstration and participation courses and Far East tours that feature classes with professional chefs, gourmet dining, sightseeing, and visits to food markets. Established in 1980. Maximum class/group size: 15 hands-on.

EMPHASIS: The cuisines of China, Thailand, Singapore, Malaysia, Indonesia, India, Korea, the Philippines, Japan, and Hawaii.

FACULTY: Ruth Law is author of *The Southeast Asia Cookbook; Indian Light Cooking*, a nominee for the Julia Child Cookbook Award by the IACP, and *Dim Sum-Fast and Festive Chinese Cooking*. She studied in Thailand, Bali, Taipei, and India.

LOCATION: Hinsdale, a Chicago suburb. Tours visit China, Hong Kong, Thailand, Singapore, Malaysia, Indonesia, India.

CONTACT: Ruth Law, What's Cooking, P.O. Box 323, Hinsdale, IL 60522; (708) 986-1595, Fax (708) 655-0912.

WILTON SCHOOL OF CAKE DECORATING
Woodridge/February-November

This private school offers 1-day to 2-week participation courses. Maximum class/group size: 15-20.

CONTACT: School Secretary, Wilton School of Cake Decorating and Confectionery Art, 2240 W. 75th St., Woodridge, IL 60517; (708) 963-7100 #211, Fax (708) 963-7299.

INDIANA

COUNTRY KITCHEN, SWEETART, INC.
Fort Wayne/Year-round

This school offers basic to advanced cake decorating courses 3 times a year and more than 35 demonstration and participation classes on candies, desserts, and other topics. Established in 1964. Maximum class/group size: 35 hands-on/60 demo. Facilities: classroom with tiered work and observation seating. Also featured: Classes for groups, children's parties.

EMPHASIS: Cake decorating, desserts, candies.

FACULTY: More than 10 instructors.

COSTS: Cake decorating courses range from $65-$70 each. Demonstrations range from $10-$40. Full payment in advance; refunds granted a week prior.

LOCATION: Northeast Indiana.

CONTACT: Vi Whittington, Country Kitchen, SweetArt, Inc., 3225 Wells St., Fort Wayne, IN 46808; (219) 482-4835, Fax (219) 483-4091.

KITCHEN AFFAIRS
Evansville/January-November

This cookware store and school offers 15 demonstration and participation classes/month. Established in 1987. Maximum class/group size: 12 hands-on/20 demo. Facilities: a 350-sq-ft kitchen with 4 work stations. Also featured: children's classes, private classes.

EMPHASIS: Basic techniques, ethnic cuisines, menu planning.

FACULTY: Restaurant chefs, professional instructors, cookbook authors, and school owners Shelly and Mike Sackett. Many instructors are IACP members.

COSTS: $15-$60. Full payment in advance, refund 10 days prior.

LOCATION: Across from Evansville's largest shopping mall.

CONTACT: Shelly Sackett, Director, Kitchen Affairs, Woodland Center, 4610 Vogel Rd., Evansville, IN 47715; (800) 782-6762, (812) 474-1131.

IOWA

COOKING WITH LIZ CLARK
Keokuk/Year-round

This school offers about 35 demonstration and participation classes each quarter. Established in 1977. Maximum class/group size: 12 hands-on/16 demo. Facilities: Elizabeth Clark's renovated antebellum home, which also houses her restaurant. Also featured: weekend intensives that offer continuing education units, culinary tours in the U.S. and abroad.

EMPHASIS: Seasonal and holiday menus and guest chef specialties.

FACULTY: Liz Clark studied in Italy & France, received her diploma in the Cours Intensifs from La Varenne, studied at the Moulin de Mougins with Roger Vergé and at The Oriental in Bangkok. Other instructors have included Janeen Sarlin, William Rice, and Nick Malgieri.

COSTS: $39-$60/class. Bed & breakfast is located nearby. Payment 1 week prior. Credit or refund is granted cancellations 3 days prior.

LOCATION: 50 miles south of Burlington airport.

CONTACT: Sandy Seabold, Director Continuing Education, Southeastern Community College, Box 6007, Keokuk, IA 52632; (319) 752-2731, Fax (319) 524-3221, E-mail southec@interl.net.

KANSAS

THE BARON'S SCHOOL OF PITMASTERS
Kansas City/Year-round

This private school offers 12-20 demonstration/participation 10- to 12-hour one-day intensives. A commercial barbecue school is planned. Founded in 1991. Maximum class/group size: 15, divided into 2-person teams. Facilities: outdoor cooking, indoor sauce and barbecue seasoning development and meat trimming. Also featured: out-of-town courses.

EMPHASIS: Basics of traditional barbecue, backyard barbecue, competition barbecue.

FACULTY: 1 full-, 6 part-time instructors. Full-time instructor Paul Kirk, CWC, is 7-time World Barbecue Champion and winner of over 400 barbecue and cooking awards.

COSTS: Basic course is $250. Lodging is available at local hotels and motels. $100 deposit required, balance due 3 weeks prior. Full refund 3 weeks prior or if space can be filled.

CONTACT: Paul Kirk, CWC, Kansas City Baron of Barbecue, The Baron's School of Pitmasters, 3625 W. 50th Terr., Shawnee Mission, KS 66205-1534; (913) 262-6029, (816) 756-5891, Fax (816) 756-5860.

COOKING AT BONNIE'S PLACE
Wichita/September-May

Cooking instructor Bonnie Aeschliman offers 4-6 demonstrations/month. Established in 1990. Maximum class/group size: 25. Facilities: demonstration kitchen.

EMPHASIS: A variety of topics.

FACULTY: Bonnie Aeschliman, CCP, has a master's degree in food and nutrition; Dr. Phil Aeschliman is a member of the IACP.

COSTS: $20-$30/class.

LOCATION: One mile from Wichita.

CONTACT: Bonnie Aeschliman, Cooking at Bonnie's Place, 5900 E. 47th St., North, Wichita, KS 67220; (316) 744-1981.

ELDERWOOD
Lawrence/Year-round

This private school offers monthly evening and weekend demonstration and participation classes. Established in 1996. Maximum class/group size: 6 hands-on/12 demo. Facilities: home kitchen in a newly built residence in the Alvamar community in West Lawrence. Also featured: group classes, private instruction, culinary tours.

EMPHASIS: international and regional cuisines, guest chef specialties, home entertaining and wine pairing menus.

FACULTY: Founder Debbie J. Elder has been associated with the culinary arts since 1980, planning meal functions, catered events, and group travel. Guest chefs from around the country also teach.

COSTS: Ranges from $45-$95/class. Lodging can be arranged at the historic Eldridge Hotel in downtown Lawrence. Payment with registration. Refund 1 week prior.

LOCATION: Lawrence, home of the University of Kansas, is 45 minutes from Kansas City.

CONTACT: Ms. Debbie J. Elder, Founder, Elderwood, 1972 Carmel Dr., Lawrence, KS 66047; (913) 842-5580, Fax (913) 842-8917.

KENTUCKY

THE COOKBOOK COTTAGE
Louisville/Year-round

This cookbook store and school offers more than 150 demonstration and participation classes per year. Established in 1986. Maximum class/group size: 10 hands-on/20 demo. Facilities: 1,200-sq-ft classroom, which seats 30 and has overhead mirrors.

EMPHASIS: Herb and spice cookery, breads, international and regional cuisines, holiday and seasonal menus, guest chef specialties.

FACULTY: Proprietor/instructor Stephen J. Lee earned a degree in Culinary Arts from the University of Kentucky, is food columnist for the *Louisville Entertainer* and a member of the IACP. Other faculty includes local cooking teachers and guest chefs.

COSTS: $15-$30 for most classes, $48 for guest chefs. Advance registration and payment is required. Credit cards accepted.

LOCATION: Louisville.

CONTACT: Stephen J. Lee, Proprietor, The Cookbook Cottage, 1279 Bardstown Rd., Louisville, KY 40204; (502) 458-5227, Fax (502) 473-7108.

KROGER SCHOOL OF COOKING
Lexington/Year-round

This school in a food market offers 140 one- to four-session demonstration and participation courses per year. Established in 1991. Maximum class/group size: 12 hands-on/16 demo. Facilities: a 180-sq-ft self-contained kitchen with overhead mirror in Kroger market. Also featured: private group classes, children's classes, birthday parties.

EMPHASIS: Ethnic and regional cuisines, techniques, pastry, cake decorating, guest chef specialties.

FACULTY: Instructors include IACP and ACF members, registered dietitians, and guest chefs Beatrice Ojakangas, Nathalie Dupree, Joanne Weir, and Jude Theriot.

COSTS: $10-$28. Payment within 3 days of enrollment. Cancellations 2 days prior receive refund.

LOCATION: Three miles from downtown Lexington.

CONTACT: Dianne Holleran, Consumer Affairs Director, Kroger School of Cooking, 344 Romany Rd., Lexington, KY 40502; (606) 269-1034, Fax (606) 269-1034.

LOUISIANA

CHEF JOHN FOLSE CULINARY INSTITUTE
(See also page 44)   **Thibodaux/Year-round**

This university offers an annual 7-day demonstration/participation program. Established 1995. Maximum class/group size: 30. Facilities: the Institute's two new teaching kitchens. Also featured: market visits, dining in fine restaurants, sightseeing, tours of food producers.

EMPHASIS: Cajun and Creole cuisine.

FACULTY: Chef John Folse, CEC, AAC, executive chef and owner of Chef John Folse & Company, specializing in Cajun and Creole cuisine.

COSTS: The cost of $2,299 includes deluxe lodging, most meals, reception and farewell parties. $100 deposit, balance 1 month prior. Refund granted written cancellation 3 weeks prior. Continuing education units and college credit available.

CONTACT: Dr. Jerald Chesser, Director, Nicholls State University, Chef John Folse Culinary Institute, P.O. 2099, Thibidaux, LA 70310; (504) 449-7100, Fax (504) 449-7089, E-mail jfci-jwc@nich-nsunet.nich.edu, URL http://www.server.nich.edu/~jfolse.

COOKIN' CAJUN COOKING SCHOOL
New Orleans/Year-round

Creole Delicacies, a company specializing in Cajun and Creole gourmet items offers demonstration classes Monday through Sunday mornings. Established in 1988. Maximum class/group size: 1-75. Facilities: theatre-style mirrored kitchen overlooking the Mississippi River. Also featured: private classes, parties, fish classes for anglers.

EMPHASIS: Cajun and Creole cuisine.

FACULTY: Susan Murphy and several other instructors.

COSTS: $17.50/class. Advance reservations are required. Mention ShawGuides and obtain a 10% discount.

LOCATION: Riverwalk Marketplace near the New Orleans Convention Center.

CONTACT: Cookin' Cajun Cooking School, #1 Poydras, Store #116, New Orleans, LA 70130; (504) 523-6425, Fax (504) 523-4787. Also: Riverwalk Marketplace.

CREOLE COOKING DEMONSTRATION
New Orleans/October-May
The Hermann-Grima Historic House conducts demonstrations of Creole cooking in New Orleans in the mid-nineteenth century. The program takes place in a restored 1831 kitchen. Established in 1985. Maximum class/group size: 20.
EMPHASIS: New Orleans food, culture, and history.
COSTS: $5, includes tour of the Hermann-Grima Historic House. Group rates available if booked in advance.
LOCATION: The French Quarter.
CONTACT: The Hermann-Grima Historic House, Cooking Program, 820 St. Louis St., New Orleans, LA 70112; (504) 525-5661, Fax (504) 568-9735.

KAY EWING'S EVERYDAY GOURMET
Baton Rouge/Year-round
This school offers 10-12 participation classes/year. Established in 1985. Maximum class/group size: 6. Facilities: The Panhandler, a gourmet kitchen store. Also featured: classes for youngsters held in the summer and during holiday.
EMPHASIS: International and Cajun cuisines, full participation, menu classes.
FACULTY: Kay Ewing is a member of the IACP and author of *Kay Ewing's Cooking School Cookbook.*
COSTS: $30 for adults, $15 for children. Payment within 1 week of booking, refund 48 hours prior.
CONTACT: Kay Ewing, c/o The Panhandler, Village Square Shopping Center, 3072-A College Dr., Baton Rouge, LA 70808; (504) 927-4371.

NEW ORLEANS SCHOOL OF COOKING
New Orleans/Year-round
This school offers morning demonstrations Monday through Saturday. Established in 1980. Facilities: a large mirrored kitchen. Also featured: classes for private groups.
EMPHASIS: Cajun and Creole cuisine.
FACULTY: Kevin Belton is a self-taught cook and television personality.
COSTS: $20/class.
LOCATION: The Jax Brewery adjacent to the Louisiana General Store, overlooking the Mississippi River and the French Quarter.
CONTACT: The New Orleans School of Cooking, 620 Decatur St., New Orleans, LA 70130; (504) 525-2665, (504) 731-6108, Fax (504) 731-6108.

MAINE

THE WHIP AND SPOON
Portland/Spring, Fall
This gourmet foods and cookware store offers approximately 25 to 30 demonstration classes each quarter. Established in 1980. Maximum class/group size: 25. Facilities: a well-equipped teaching kitchen.
EMPHASIS: Ethnic and regional cuisines, healthful foods, guest chef specialties.
FACULTY: Local cooks, chefs, and caterers, including Rosemarie DeAngelis, Barbara Gulino, Cheryl Lewis, and Avis Layman.
COSTS: $15/class. Refund with 48 hours notice. Credit cards accepted.
LOCATION: The Old Port Exchange on Portland's waterfront.
CONTACT: Cheri Musgrave, Class Coordinator, The Whip and Spoon, 161 Commercial St., Portland, ME 04101; (800) 937-9447, (207) 774-4020, Fax (207) 774-6261.

CAKE COTTAGE, INC.
Baltimore/Year-round

This candy shop and school offers participation courses in basic and advanced cake decorating and demonstration and participation classes in candies, cake writing, puff pastry, petit fours, butter cream flowers, air brush decorating, and party foods. Established in 1977. Maximum class/group size: 30 hands-on/50 demo. Also featured: children's courses.

FACULTY: Carole studied at the Wilton School and has taught for over 20 years; Donna studied candymaking with chocolatiers in the U.S. and abroad for over 19 years.

COSTS: Basic decorating course is $35, advanced course is $40, children's course is $25. Single sessions range from $8-$40. Full nonrefundable payment must accompany registration.

LOCATION: Baltimore's northeast section, 20 minutes from BWI airport.

CONTACT: The Cake Cottage, Inc., 8716 Belair Rd., Baltimore, MD 21236; (410) 529-0200, Fax (410) 529-6867.

THE CHINESE COOKERY, INC.
Silver Spring/Year-round

This private school offers 8 levels of participation and demonstration courses in Chinese cuisine. Established in 1975. Maximum class/group size: 5. Facilities: classroom/lab equipped for Chinese cooking, outdoor Chinese brick oven. Also featured: Japanese sushi class, classes for teenagers, private lessons for cooking professionals, market visits, restaurant kitchen tours, and culinary tours to the Far East.

EMPHASIS: Chinese cuisine: Basic, Advanced, Gourmet I, II, III, Szechuan, Hunan, vegetarian.

FACULTY: Joan Shih, a chemist at the National Institute of Health, received a certificate in Chinese cuisine in Taiwan and has taught Chinese and Japanese cooking on television and in schools.

COSTS: Five-session courses are $135 and the sushi class is $35. A nonrefundable $35 deposit is required. Classes are arranged by appointment.

LOCATION: North suburb of Washington, DC.

CONTACT: Joan Shih, The Chinese Cookery, Inc., 14209 Sturtevant Rd., Silver Spring, MD 20905; (301) 236-5311.

L'ACADEMIE DE CUISINE
Bethesda/Year-round

(See also page 49)

This proprietary vocational school offers 35-40 one- to four-session demonstration and participation courses/month. Maximum class/group size: 21-25. Also featured: children's classes and parties, private dinners, guest chef demonstrations, cultural/culinary trips to France.

EMPHASIS: Techniques, international and regional cuisines, nutritional and low-fat foods, pastry, wine and food pairing, entertaining menus.

COSTS: $27-$55/session. Full payment required, refund 3 business days prior.

LOCATION: The Bethesda campus, 3 miles northwest of D.C.

CONTACT: Carol McClure, Assistant Director, L'Academie de Cuisine, 16006 Industrial Dr., Gaithersburg, MD 20877; (301) 670-8670, (800) 664-CHEF, Fax (301) 670-0450, URL http://www.L'Academie.com.

MASSACHUSETTS

BOSTON UNIVERSITY CULINARY ARTS
Boston/September-May

(See also page 50)

This university offers 20-25 one- to three- demonstration and participation courses/year. Maximum class/group size: 24-130. Also featured: children's classes, market visits, food and wine pairing, domestic and foreign tours hosted by a culinary historian familiar with the region's food and wine.

EMPHASIS: Guest chef specialties.

COSTS: Seminars range from $10-$125, full-day classes and 3-session courses range from $150-

$300. Payment with registration. Refund with 24 hours notice.
CONTACT: Rebecca Alssid, Director of Special Programs, Boston University Culinary Arts, 808 Commonwealth Ave., #109, Boston, MA 02215; (617) 353-9852, Fax (617) 353-4130.

KUSHI INSTITUTE COOKING SEMINARS
Becket/Year-round
This nonprofit educational facility, founded by Michio and Aveline Kushi offers 2 different weekend programs that each feature 4 cooking classes, 2 lecture classes, and morning exercise sessions. Established in 1978. Maximum class/group size: 16. Facilities: former Franciscan Friar monastery. Also featured: Shiatsu massage, macrobiotic diet, and lifestyle consultation.
EMPHASIS: The Essentials of Macrobiotic Cooking, Naturally Gourmet, Macrobiotic Cuisine with an International Flair.
FACULTY: The 10 instructors include Wendy Esko, Diane Avoli, Carry Wolf, Mayumi Nishimura, Gail Jack.
COSTS: Weekend seminars $350, which includes meals and lodging; $25 discount with 30-day pre-registration and payment. Airport pick-up is $75 one-way. Double occupancy country manor or dormitory lodging with shared bath; private bath and single lodging are additional. A $100 deposit is required with balance due on arrival.
LOCATION: The Berkshire mountains, a 3-hour drive from Boston and New York City, near Lenox, Mass.
CONTACT: Chris LeFevre, The Kushi Institute, Program and Services Information, P.O. Box 7, Becket, MA 01223; (413) 623-5741 #101, Fax (413) 623-8827, E-mail kushi@macrobiotics.org.

LE PETIT GOURMET COOKING SCHOOL
Wayland/Year-round
This school offers eight 1- to 4-session demonstration/participation courses per month. Established in 1979 and re-opened in 1993. Maximum class/group size: 8. Facilities: 330-sq-ft kitchen with two workspaces. Also featured: private classes.
EMPHASIS: Beginning to advanced French cuisine, low fat cooking, specific subjects. Specialty is chocolate desserts.
FACULTY: Fran Rosenheim studied with local chefs and at Le Cordon Bleu and La Varenne in Paris.
COSTS: $50/session.
LOCATION: 20 minutes from Boston.
CONTACT: Fran Rosenheim, Le Petit Gourmet Cooking School, 19 Charena Rd., Wayland, MA 01778; (508) 358-4219, Fax (508) 358-4291.

MARGE COHEN
Needham Heights/September-May
Marge Cohen offers 5-session demonstration and participation courses. Established in 1980. Maximum class/group size: 8. Facilities: home kitchen. Also featured: private classes, local culinary tours.
EMPHASIS: Basic to advanced Chinese, low fat, low salt.
FACULTY: Marge Cohen has certificates from the Le Cordon Bleu and Weichuan Cooking School in Taiwan and has hosted a cable TV program.
COSTS: Each 5-session course is $105; culinary tours are $35.
LOCATION: Twenty minutes west of Boston.
CONTACT: Marge Cohen, P.O. Box 53, Needham Heights, MA 02194; (617) 449-2688, Fax (617) 449-7878.

TERENCE JANERICCO COOKING CLASSES
Boston/September-June
This school in a private residence offers 17 one- and six-session demonstration and participation courses per month. Established in 1966. Maximum class/group size: 6 hands-on/14 demo. Also

featured: private classes.

EMPHASIS: Gourmet cooking, baking, ethnic and regional cuisines, specific subjects.

FACULTY: Terence Janericco has operated a catering firm for more than 25 years & teaches at adult education centers in Boston and at schools in New England and Michigan. He is author of 12 books, including *The Book of Great Soups*, & *The Gourmet Galley*.

COSTS: Six-session courses are $360, single-sessions are $60. A $60 deposit is required with balance due at first class; refund 1 week prior.

CONTACT: Terence Janericco, Owner, Terence Janericco Cooking Classes, 42 Fayette St., Boston, MA 02116; (617) 426-7458, Fax (617) 426-7458.

MICHIGAN

KITCHEN GLAMOR. . .THE COOK'S WORLD
Grand River/Year-round

This gourmet cookware store and cooking school offers 3 to 5 demonstration and participation courses/month and 15 to 20 pre-registration classes and guest chef classes each season. Established in 1950. Maximum class/group size: 12-16 pre-reg. classes/25 hands-on/125 demo. Facilities: the kitchen auditorium has a 12-foot counter, 2 four-range burners, and overhead mirror. Also featured: national cookware catalog.

FACULTY: Includes award-winning cake decorator Mary Ann Hollen, food authority Toula Patsalis, and local chefs. Guest chefs have included Anne Willan, Charlie Trotter, and Marcel DeSaulnier.

COSTS: Demonstrations are $3 each, $30 for 12; pre-registration classes are $40 for local chefs, $25-$35 for others; guest chef demonstrations range up to $80 per session. No refunds.

LOCATION: Redford Township location, The West Bloomfield School is in the Orchard Mall; the Rochester school is in the Great Oaks Mall, Walton at Livernols; the Novi location is at the Novi Town Center. The closest major city is Detroit.

CONTACT: Toula Patsalis, Program Director, Kitchen Glamor, 39049 Webb Ct., Westland, MI 48185-7606; (313) 641-1244, Fax (313) 641-1240. Also: Redford, (313) 537-1300, Rochester, (810) 652-0402, W. Bloomfield, (810) 855-4466, Novi, (810) 380-8600.

NELL BENEDICT COOKING CLASSES
Birmingham/September-May

This adult community center offers evening demonstration classes. Established in 1970. Maximum class/group size: 45. Facilities: teaching kitchen at The Community House.

EMPHASIS: Ethnic cuisines, breads, restaurant specialties.

FACULTY: Nell Benedict studied at Le Cordon Bleu, La Varenne, and L'Arts Culinara and with James Beard, Jacques Pépin, and Roger Vergé. She has taught on television and is a Charter Member of the IACP.

COSTS: $16/session. Refund for cancellations 48 hours prior.

LOCATION: Approximately 8 miles north of Detroit.

CONTACT: Nell Benedict, International Cuisine, 380 S. Bates St., Birmingham, MI 48009; (313) 664-5832.

MINNESOTA

BYERLY'S SCHOOL OF CULINARY ARTS
St. Louis Park/Year-round

This school in an upscale market offers an average of 20 one-session demonstration and participation classes each month. Established in 1980. Maximum class/group size: 14 hands-on/25 demo. Facilities: a large teaching kitchen with overhead mirror. Also featured: private and couple's classes, children's birthday classes.

EMPHASIS: Italian, Asian, and French cuisine; entertaining, seasonal, healthy cooking basic cooking series. Guest chefs.

FACULTY: Manager Mary Evans studied at La Varenne & Ecole Lenotre. Other instructors include cookbook authors Antonio Cecconi and Paulette Mitchell, CIA grad. Carol Brown, syndicated columnist Mary Carroll, L'Academie de Cuisine grad. Deidre Schipani.

COSTS: Average $27/class. Full refund with 3 days notice.

LOCATION: St. Louis Park, a suburb of Minneapolis, 15 minutes from downtown Minneapolis.

CONTACT: Mary Evans, Manager, Byerly's School of Culinary Arts, 3777 Park Center Blvd., St. Louis Park, MN 55416; (612) 929-2492, Fax (612) 929-7756.

COOKS OF CROCUS HILL
St. Paul/Year-round

This school in a cookware store offers 20 to 25 one-, three-, and five-session demonstration and participation courses per month. Established in 1976. Maximum class/group size: 12 hands-on/25 demo. Also featured: private group classes.

EMPHASIS: Basics, ethnic cuisines, holiday and seasonal menus, single subjects, guest chef specialties.

FACULTY: The 21-member faculty includes owner Martha Kaemmer, BJ Carpenter, Jennifer Holloway, and Yvonne Moody. Guest chefs include Hugh Carpenter, Jim Dodge, and Joanne Weir.

COSTS: The 3-session course is $125, the 5-session is $250. Classes range from $40-$65. Payment required within 5 working days of registration; refund with 48 hours notice. Credit cards accepted.

CONTACT: Jennifer Holloway, Director, Cooks of Crocus Hill, 877 Grand Ave., St. Paul, MN 55105; (612) 228-1333, Fax (612) 228-9084.

FOOD ON FILM
Minneapolis/April or May

The Twin Cities Chapter of Home Economists in Business sponsors a 2-day intensive food styling seminar, held in even-numbered years, that features 16 rotating demonstration workshops. Started in 1982. Maximum class/group size: 50-75. Facilities: conference rooms of the Minneapolis Hyatt Regency. Also featured: keynote and luncheon speakers, cookbook gallery, social activities.

EMPHASIS: Food styling and photography.

FACULTY: Changes each seminar. Includes food stylists and photographers, cooking instructors, chefs, food writers, and other industry professionals.

COSTS: The 1996 program fee was $395 early bird, $425 regular, which includes breakfasts, lunches, and receptions. Lodging available at the Hyatt Regency Hotel. Payment with registration. Full refund approximately 4 weeks prior.

LOCATION: Downtown Minneapolis.

CONTACT: Nancy Iverson, Administrative Asst., Twin Cities Home Economists in Business, 7227 West Fish Lake Rd., Maple Grove, MN 55311-2511; 612-420-4552, Fax 612-420-2469.

MISSISSIPPI

THE EVERYDAY GOURMET
Jackson/January-November

These schools in two Jackson cookware stores each offer 12 demonstration and participation classes/month. Established in 1982. Maximum class/group size: 12-15 hands-on/36 demo. Also featured: guest chefs, lunch sessions, and classes for children.

FACULTY: Includes Martha McIntosh, Gayle Stone, Butchie Nations, Cheryl Welch, and school director Chan Patterson.

COSTS: $20-$50; children's classes are $18. Advance payment is requested; refund with 48 hours notice. Credit cards accepted.

CONTACT: Chan Patterson, Director, The Everyday Gourmet, Inc., 2905 Old Canton Rd., Jackson, MS 39216; (601) 362-0723, (601) 977-9258, Fax (601) 981-3266. Also: 1625 County Line Rd., Jackson, MS 39211.

MISSOURI

CULINARY INSTITUTE OF SMOKE COOKING
Cape Girardeau/Year-round

CISC's Master BBQ-Cook's School offers 8 train-at-home hands-on master lessons. Established in 1992. Facilities: the student's backyard using own BBQ equipment of pit/smoker/grill, meat, and thermometers. Also featured: private lessons, BBQ restaurant consulting, and on-site classroom demonstrations.

EMPHASIS: Southern-style barbecuing and grilling.

FACULTY: Owners Charles and Ruth Knote, authors of *Barbecuing and Sausage Making Secrets* (CISC textbook), are graduates of Memphis-in-May, American Royal, & BBQ Judging Schools and have 44 years of barbecuing experience.

COSTS: Master BBQ Cook's School is $100 cash or $30 plus four $20 payments.

LOCATION: Train-at-home (correspondence school) format.

CONTACT: Charles Knote, President, CISC's Master BBQ Cook's School, 2323 Brookwood Dr., Cape Girardeau, MO 63701; (573) 334-4621, Fax (573) 334-4621.

DIERBERGS SCHOOL OF COOKING
St. Louis/Year-round

This cooking school with four locations offers 80 one-session demonstration and participation courses per month. Established in 1978. Maximum class/group size: 18. Facilities: sound-proof enclosures in Dierbergs Supermarkets. Also featured: classes for couples, children's classes, parent-child sessions.

EMPHASIS: Home cooking.

FACULTY: In addition to the more than 30-member faculty of home economists and cooking instructors, guest teachers include Gerard Germain, executive chef, Tony's Restaurant; industry spokespersons, traveling chefs, and cookbook authors.

COSTS: Adult classes range from $16-$20, guest classes are $20-$40. Payment within 3 days of enrollment; refund with 4 days notice.

LOCATION: St. Louis county.

CONTACT: Jeannie Ruder, Home Economist, Dierbergs West Oak, Cooking School, 11481 Olive St. Rd., Creve Coeur, MO 63141; (314) 432-6561, (314) 432-6505, Fax (314) 432-2548. Also: 290 Mid Rivers Ctr., St. Peters, (314) 928-1117; 12420 Tesson Ferry Rd., St. Louis, (314) 849-3698; 1322 Clarkson/Clayton Ctr., Ellisville (314) 394-9504.

JASPER'S
Kansas City/August-June

This restaurant offers 2 demonstration classes per month and holiday luncheon classes. Established in 1954. Maximum class/group size: 45 demo. Also featured: private classes for groups of 20 or more, children's and couples' classes, wine classes.

EMPHASIS: Northern Italian cuisine.

FACULTY: Executive Chef Jasper J. Mirabile, Jr., son of Jasper's founder, studied at La Varenne, the Gritti Palace, & U. of Nevada. Jasper's has received the Travel/Holiday Award, the Mobil 4-Star award, the AAA 4-Diamond award.

COSTS: $35/class. Refund with 48 hours notice. Credit cards accepted.

LOCATION: South Kansas City.

CONTACT: Jasper J. Mirabile, Jr., Jasper's, 405 W. 75th St., Kansas City, MO 64114; (816) 363-3003, (800) 35-JASPER, Fax (816) 361-2284.

KEMPER CENTER COOKING SCHOOL
St. Louis/Year-round

The Kemper Center of the Missouri Botanical Garden offers more than 20 one- to three-session demonstration and participation courses each season. Maximum class/group size: 16-20. Also featured: gardening, arts & crafts, nature study.

EMPHASIS: A variety of topics.

FACULTY: Includes caterers, nutritionists, cookbook authors, and cooking teachers.

COSTS: $30-$35/session. Members receive a discount. Refund with 4 days notice.

CONTACT: Glenn E. Kopp, Coordinator, Missouri Botanical Garden, Kemper Center Cooking School, P.O. Box 299, St. Louis, MO 63166-0299; (314) 577-9441, Fax (314) 577-9440.

KITCHEN CONSERVATORY
St. Louis/Year-round

This school in a gourmet shop offers 25 to 30 demonstration and participation classes quarterly. Established in 1984. Maximum class/group size: 18. Also featured: day trips to restaurants and shops, classes for children and teens.

EMPHASIS: Ethnic and regional cuisines, seasonal and entertaining menus, guest chef specialties.

FACULTY: Local chefs, restaurateurs, caterers, dietitians, home economists, and IACP members. Guest instructors have included Hugh Carpenter, Merle Ellis, Martin Yan, Paula Wolfert, and Perla Meyers.

COSTS: $28-$75. Credit cards accepted. Refund with 2 weeks notice.

LOCATION: Minutes from downtown.

CONTACT: Kitchen Conservatory, 8021 Clayton Rd., St. Louis, MO 63117; (314) 862-COOK, Fax (314) 862-2110.

MISSOURI CULINARY INSTITUTE
Lexington/January-November   *(See also page 58)*

This private school offers 12 one- to four-session demonstration and participation courses/year. Maximum class/group size: 12.

EMPHASIS: Gourmet food.

CONTACT: Terry Kopp, Missouri Culinary Institute, Rte. 1, Box 224F, Lexington, MO 64067; (816) 259-6464.

SUZANNE CORBETT – CULINARY RESOURCES
St. Louis/September-May

Suzanne Corbett offers 10 participation courses/year. Established in 1976. Maximum class/group size: 16. Facilities: Suzanne Corbett's home kitchen, vocational schools, historic sites. Also featured: wine instruction, Missouri wine country tours, summer workshops for groups.

EMPHASIS: Historic American foods, hearth-style baking, regional dishes, international cuisines.

FACULTY: Suzanne Corbett, CCP, specializes in foods from the past, is a food & wine writer with 20 years experience, contributing editor to Rodale Press & *Victoria Magazine*.

COSTS: $25-$50/class. Refund with 48 hours notice.

CONTACT: Suzanne Corbett, St. Louis Community College, Institute for Continuing Education, 5850 Pebble Oak, St. Louis, MO 63128-1412; (314) 487-5205, Fax (314) 487-5335, E-mail pncor@aol.com.

TAKE PLEASURE IN COOKING!
Kansas City/Year-round

This school in a private residence offers 4 demonstration and 3 to 4 participation classes per month. Established in 1988. Maximum class/group size: 6 hands-on/20 demo. Facilities: a 280-sq-ft home kitchen with overhead mirror. Also featured: private classes and workshops.

EMPHASIS: Culinary arts for the home, herbs, yeast doughs, regional cuisines, creative techniques, ease of preparation.

FACULTY: Gloria Martin, owner, is an IACP member and has taught cooking for 17 years.
COSTS: $30-$40. Refund with 24 hours notice.
LOCATION: The Kansas City suburb of Raytown, 15 miles from downtown.
CONTACT: Gloria Martin, Take Pleasure in Cooking!, 8612 E. 84th St., Kansas City, MO 64138; (816) 353-6022.

NEBRASKA

WILLOW HOLLOW GOURMET
Lincoln/January-May, August-November

This school in a private residence offers personalized demonstration and participation sessions. Established in 1974. Maximum class/group size: 15 hands-on/20 demo. Also featured: private classes at student's home for groups of 8 or more.
FACULTY: Jackie Swanson, IACP member since 1973.
CONTACT: Jackie Swanson, President, Willow Hollow Gourmet, 1265 So. Cotner Blvd., Lincoln, NE 68502; (402) 483-2665, (800) 397-0230.

NEW HAMPSHIRE

A TASTE OF THE MOUNTAINS COOKING SCHOOL
Glen and Ossipee/Year-round except foliage

This school founded at the Bernerhof Inn (Glen) offers weekend courses in May, June and November, day courses every Wednesday and Thursday during summer and winter. Established in 1980. Maximum class/group size: 10 hands-on. Facilities: two restaurant kitchens: Bernerhof Inn & Whittier House. Also featured: custom seminars for groups of 7 or more.
EMPHASIS: Basic techniques including knife handling, sauces, sauteeing, breads.
FACULTY: Chefs Scott Willard and Richard Spencer, CWC, both culinary school graduates and ACF Chef of the Year recipients; Northern New England area guest chefs.
COSTS: Per person rates for the weekend courses, which include double occupancy lodging and meals, range from $399 (standard room) to $499 (suite); day rate is $205 for the weekend; class rate is $45-$55. A 50% deposit is required; balance due on arrival. Refunds for weekend courses granted 30 days prior. Credit cards accepted.
LOCATION: Bernerhof Inn (Glen) and Whittier House (Ossipee), in the White Mountains, are near Conway, 3 hours north of Boston and 90 minutes west of Portland, Me.
CONTACT: A Taste of the Mountains Cooking School, Box 240, Glen, NH 03838; (603) 383-9132, (800) 548-8007, Fax (603) 383-0809.

NEW JERSEY

CLASSIC RECIPES L.L.C.
Westfield/Year-round

This private school offers demonstration and hands-on classes on a variety of topics. Established in 1995. Maximum class/group size: 12-24. Facilities: Viking-equipped kitchen with overhead mirror and video monitoring. Also featured: wine instruction, classes for youngsters, day trips, market visits, winery tours, fine dining, private instruction.
EMPHASIS: Basic techniques, special subjects.
FACULTY: David P. Martone, CCP, Sheila Turteltaub.
COSTS: From $25-$85/session. Payment required with registration. Full refund 10 days prior.
LOCATION: 45 minutes from New York City.
CONTACT: David P. Martone, Classic Recipes L.L.C., 401 W. Broad St., Westfield, NJ 07090; (908) 232-5445, Fax (908) 233-4930.

COOKINGSTUDIO
West Caldwell/Year-round

This school offers 30 to 35 one- to eight-session demonstration and participation courses/month at its four locations. Maximum class/group size: 15. Also featured: celebrity chef demonstrations, classes for couples and singles, classes for children.

EMPHASIS: Basic and advanced Principles of Cooking, Mastery of Baking and other topics.

FACULTY: The more than 15-member resident and guest faculty includes Rick Rodgers, Carole Walter, and Jean Yueh. Guest chefs have included Giuliano Bugialli and Jacques Pépin. The school is a member of the IACP.

COSTS: Principles courses range from $55-$60/session. Individual sessions range from $15-$45. Children's classes are $25-$35. Payment must accompany registration. Credit cards accepted. Full refund with 3 days notice.

LOCATION: Short Hills, Bedminster, Verona, and Hillsdale.

CONTACT: Susan Loden, Cookingstudio, 2 Dedrick Pl., West Caldwell, NJ 07006; (201) 808-4277, Fax (201) 575-3297.

COOKTIQUE
Tenafly/Year-round

This school offers approximately 150 evening demonstration and participation sessions a year. Established in 1976. Maximum class/group size: 14 hands-on/25 demo. Facilities: a 400-sq-ft demonstration kitchen with overhead mirror. Also featured: children's classes, and birthday parties.

EMPHASIS: Techniques, sauces, fish, guest chef specialties, dessert, pizza, pasta, menu classes.

FACULTY: Culinary professionals and master chefs. Guest chefs have included Giuliano Bugialli, Marcella Hazan, Nicholas Malgieri, Lorenza de'Medici, and Jaques Pépin.

COSTS: From $25; guest chef classes $50-$100. Refund with 10 days notice. Credit cards accepted.

LOCATION: 16 miles from New York City.

CONTACT: Cathy McCauley, Director, Cooktique, 9 W. Railroad Ave., Tenafly, NJ 07670; (201) 568-7990, Fax (201) 568-6480.

EDIBLES. . .NATURALLY! COOKING SCHOOL
Princeton Junction/Year-round

This cafe and cooking school offers 8-10 evening demonstration and participation classes/month. Established in 1994. Maximum class/group size: 12 hands-on/24 demo. Also featured: children's, senior citizen's, and private singles' classes, market visits, field trips.

EMPHASIS: American regional, fusion, herbs and spices, vegetarian and low fat, macrobiotic, baking, basics.

FACULTY: Guest chefs and cookbook authors, including Giuliano Hazan, Craig Shelton, Mark Browngold, Jo Kerrigan.

COSTS: $35-$60/class. Payment required with registration; full refund with 7 days notice. Credit cards accepted.

LOCATION: Central New Jersey, an hour from Philadelphia and New York City.

CONTACT: Alice Miller, Director, Edibles. . .Naturally! Cooking School, 14 Washington Rd., Princeton Junction, NJ 08550; (609) 936-8200, Fax (609) 936-8855.

GOURMET LONG LIFE COOKING SCHOOLS
Springfield and Wayne/Year-round

This school with two locations offers 3-session demonstration courses for individuals concerned with weight control, sound nutrition, and/or medical conditions requiring a modified diet. Established in 1984. Maximum class/group size: 9. Facilities: a 300-sq-ft teaching kitchen.

EMPHASIS: Nutritional counseling; gourmet cooking without added salt, sugar, fats, or oils; vegetarian diets, cultural and ethnic foods; analysis of product labels.

FACULTY: Gloria Rose is author of *Cooking for Good Health*, which is included in the program materials. Instructors are gourmet cooks, registered dietitians or nurses affiliated with New Jersey hospitals.

Costs: The $285 cost per course includes textbook and private nutritional counseling. A $150 nonrefundable deposit is required. Classes are booked 3 months in advance.

Location: The Springfield school (central NJ) is 8 miles from Newark; the Wayne school (northern NJ) is 30 minutes from Manhattan.

Contact: Gloria Rose, Gourmet Long Life Cooking Schools, 48 Norwood Road, Springfield, NJ 07081; (201) 376-0942, (201) 296-3911. Also: 7 Pinecrest Terrace, Wayne, NJ, 07470; (201) 296-3911.

THE STUDIO AT SOUFFLÉ
Princeton/Year-round

This private school offers 1- to 5-session demonstration and participation courses on a variety of topics. Established in 1996. Maximum class/group size: 20. Facilities: demonstration kitchen with overhead mirror and seating for 30 students. Also featured: wine instruction and winery visits, classes for youngsters, day trips, market visits, demonstrations by chefs in their restaurants, adventure menu classes.

Emphasis: A variety of topics, including techniques, entertaining and holiday menus, food chemistry, wine appreciation, guest chef specialties.

Faculty: 8 certified chefs: Executive Chef-Proprietor Shawn C. Lawson, Dennis Normile, Colin Marsh, Elisabeth Hawkey, Susan Valentine, Richard Fitzgerald, Dana Osterman, James Needell.

Costs: $40-$60/session. Payment with registration. Refund 48 hours prior.

Location: 45 minutes from Philadelphia, 1 hour from New York City.

Contact: Shawn C. Lawson, Proprietor, The Studio at Soufflé, 14 Farber Rd., #D, Princeton, NJ 08540; (609) 987-2600, Fax (609) 987-0191.

NEW MEXICO

GILDA LATZKY
Albuquerque/Year-round

This school and catering service (formerly of New York City) offers participation courses. Established in 1977. Maximum class/group size: 5. Also featured: seasonal and private classes.

Emphasis: Italian, French, and American cuisine; baking; recipe modification and menu planning.

Faculty: Gilda Latzky has taught French and Italian cooking and baking for more than 27 years in New York City, and also teaches in New Mexico, Colorado, Dallas, and Scottsdale. She studied in France and Italy and at the CIA.

Costs: $35/session.

Location: Colorado, New Mexico, Texas, Arizona.

Contact: Gilda Latzky, The Epicurean Gallery, 9900 Spain NE #V2120, Albuquerque, NM 87111; (505) 296-1439.

JANE BUTEL'S COOKING SCHOOL
Albuquerque/Year-round

This private school offers 10 five-day and weekend participation courses per year as well as demonstration sessions that are scheduled on an on-going basis. Established in 1983. Maximum class/group size: 15 hands-on. Facilities: new 2,000-sq-ft tiled kitchen with 5 work stations, demonstration area, and overhead mirror. Also featured: advanced and private group lessons, sightseeing, ballooning, visits to markets and wineries.

Emphasis: Traditional, innovative, and low-fat, New Mexican and Southwestern cuisine.

Faculty: Jane Butel, author of 14 cookbooks, including *Jane Butel's Southwestern Kitchen, Southwestern Grill*, and *Chili Madness*, and founder of the Pecos Valley Spice Co.; selected guest chefs and speakers.

Costs: The $1,695 ($695) 5-day (weekend) course fee includes most meals and double occupancy lodging. Demonstrations average $40 each. Lodging at Old Town Sheraton Inn or nearby bed & breakfast. Single supplement $210 ($95 for weekend); non-participant rate is $150 ($75). Deposit

of $400 ($250 weekend) is nonrefundable but can be credited to another course.
LOCATION: Old Town Albuquerque.
CONTACT: Jane Butel, Jane Butel's Cooking School, 800 Rio Grande NW, #14, Albuquerque, NM 87104; (800) 472-8229, (505) 243-2622, Fax (505) 243-8297, E-mail cooki@abg.ros.com, URL http://www.worldcon.com/jane_butel.

SANTA FE SCHOOL OF COOKING
Santa Fe/Year-round
This school, food market, and mail order catalog offers demonstration and participation classes several times weekly and smaller hands-on classes that include shopping at the Farmer's Market. Established in 1989. Maximum class/group size: 15 hands-on/44 demo. Facilities: a Santa Fe-style kitchen with overhead mirrors. Also featured: private classes, shopping trips to the Farmer's Market in August and September, culinary tours of northern New Mexico.
EMPHASIS: New Mexican and contemporary Southwestern cuisines, vegetarian, Mexican light cooking, and cuisines of Mexico classes.
FACULTY: Includes owner/director Susan Curtis, author of *Santa Fe School of Cooking Cookbook*; cookbook authors Cheryl Alters Jamison and Kathi Long; guest chefs Mark Miller and Deborah Madison.
COSTS: Classes range from $30-$65; tours are approximately $800, which includes some meals and field trips. 24 hour cancellation notice for daily classes.
LOCATION: The historic downtown district, 50 miles from Albuquerque International Airport.
CONTACT: Susan Curtis, Owner/Director, Santa Fe School of Cooking, 116 W. San Francisco St., Santa Fe, NM 87501; (505) 983-4511, Fax (505) 983-7540, URL http://www.santafe.org/sfcooking.

NEW YORK

A LA BONNE COCOTTE
New York/Year-round
This school offers beginner, intermediate, and advanced 4-session participation courses. Established in 1971. Maximum class/group size: 10. Facilities: large country kitchen. Also featured: cooking vacations in France.
EMPHASIS: French cuisine, from simple regional recipes to haute cuisine.
FACULTY: Lydie Marshall, author of *Cooking with Lydie Marshall*, *A Passion for Potatoes*, and *Chez Nous*.
COSTS: $400. $100 deposit for 4-class series; money-back refund policy for cancellations.
LOCATION: New York City.
CONTACT: Lydie P. Marshall, A La Bonne Cocotte, 23 Eighth Avenue, New York, NY 10014; (212) 675-7736, (33) 475-26-45-31. Also: Chateau Feodal, Lyons, France, 26110; (33) 475-26-45-31 (Apr.-Oct.).

ANNA TERESA CALLEN ITALIAN COOKING SCHOOL
New York/September-June
This school in a private residence offers 8 five-session participation courses/year. Established in 1978. Maximum class/group size: 6. Facilities: an efficient home kitchen. Also featured: culinary tours to Italy.
EMPHASIS: Italian regional cooking.
FACULTY: IACP-member Anna Teresa Callen is author of *The Wonderful World of Pizzas, Quiches and Savory Pies*, and *Anna Teresa Callen's Menus for Pasta*. She teaches at Peter Kump's New York Cooking School and NYU.
COSTS: $620 for course. $120 deposit required. Refund with 2 weeks notice.
LOCATION: Downtown Manhattan.
CONTACT: Anna Teresa Callen, Anna Teresa Callen Italian Cooking School, 59 West 12th St., New York, NY 10011; (212) 929-5640.

CAROL'S CUISINE, INC.
Staten Island/Year-round

This school in a restaurant offers more than 130 one- to six-session demonstration and participation courses/year. Established in 1972. Maximum class/group size: 17 hands-on/25 demo. Facilities: fully-equipped professional teaching kitchen with overhead mirror. Also featured: private lessons, wine classes.

EMPHASIS: Techniques, baking, cake decorating, international and Italian cuisine.

FACULTY: Owner/Director Carol Frazzetta, IACP accredited, advanced certificate from Le Cordon Bleu; studied at CIA, Wilton School of Cake Decorating, Marcella Hazan's School, L'Academie de Cuisine. Leonard Pickell, wine consultant.

COSTS: $37-$45/session. Deposit required. Partial refund for cancellation 10 days prior.

LOCATION: Central Staten Island, 1 hour from Manhattan by ferry or bus.

CONTACT: Carol Frazzetta, Carol's Cuisine, Inc., 1571 Richmond Rd., Staten Island, NY 10304; (718) 979-5600.

CLUB CUISINE
New York/Year-round

This club offers its model recipe-testing kitchen for television and photo sessions, guest chef demonstrations, food and wine promotion events. Established in 1985. Facilities: throughout tristate area. Also featured: culinary trips to southern France, yacht excursions, wine tastings, French conversation courses.

EMPHASIS: Producers of food and/or wine related events.

FACULTY: Founder-president Michele Lyster trained at La Varenne and her family's restaurant; food stylist and consultant; on program committee of James Beard Foundation. Guest chefs have included Martin Yan, Anna Teresa Callen, Steven Schmidt, Jack Ubaldi.

COSTS: Trips to France range from $2,000 to $2,500, which includes meals and lodging.

LOCATION: Various sites in New York City; trips to France.

CONTACT: Nancy Hoffman, Club Cuisine, Inc., 244 Madison Ave., New York, NY 10016-2815; (212) 557-5702, (800) 831-4206, Fax (212) 286-0214, E-mail mcuisine@aol.com.

COOKHAMPTON – SILVIA LEHRER
Water Mill/Summer, Fall, Winter

This school offers 1- to 4-session demonstration and participation courses. Established in 1988. Maximum class/group size: 15 demo/6 hands-on. Facilities: a 400-sq-ft teaching kitchen. Also featured: culinary tours.

EMPHASIS: A variety of topics, including do-ahead seasonal and entertaining menus, regional Italian cuisine, chef specialties.

FACULTY: IACP-certified instructor Silvia Lehrer, former owner of Cooktique in Tenafly, NJ, is author of *Cooking at Cooktique*. She studied with James Beard, Simca Beck, and Giuliano Bugialli. Guest chefs of the Hamptons.

COSTS: $65 per hands-on session, $60 for guest chefs.

LOCATION: The summer resort area of Southampton township.

CONTACT: Silvia Lehrer, Cookhampton, P.O. Box 765, Water Mill, NY 11976; (516) 537-7831.

COOKING BY THE BOOK, INC.
New York/September-July

This school in a Tribeca loft offers 4 evening participation classes each month that focus on a selected cookbook or chef menu. Established in 1989. Maximum class/group size: 20. Facilities: fully-equipped 500-sq-ft kitchen with 7 work stations. Also featured: private parties and cooking instruction, corporate events, children's programs, wine instruction, customized classes.

EMPHASIS: Menus selected from a variety of cookbooks, such as Jacques Pépin's *Cuisine Economique*, Steven Raichlen's *Miami Spice*, and Julia Child's *Cooking with Master Chefs*.

FACULTY: Suzen and Brian O'Rourke; authors occasionally present.

Costs: $55/class. Payment in advance. Refund with 48 hours notice.
Location: Downtown Manhattan, 25 minutes from Newark and La Guardia airports.
Contact: Suzen O'Rourke, President, Cooking by the Book, Inc., 13 Worth St., New York, NY 10013; (212) 966-9799, Fax (212) 925-1074.

CORNELL'S ADULT UNIVERSITY
Ithaca/July-August
This university offers an annual on-campus 4-week summer program consisting of 1-week workshops and courses in subjects that include cooking, history, current events, ecology, music, literature, architecture, and art. Established in 1968. Maximum class/group size: 12-20. Also featured: a supervised youth program offers activities geared to 5 age groups.
Emphasis: The yearly culinary workshop focuses on menu planning and techniques for creating appetizing and nutritionally sound meals.
Faculty: Cornell University faculty and staff.
Costs: Approximately $775/week for adults and $300-$450 for children, which includes tuition, lodging, meals, and planned activities. A $30 materials fee is extra. Fee includes double occupancy dormitory lodging (single supplement available). A $50 nonrefundable deposit is required; balance is due 30 days prior.
Location: The 13,000-acre campus is in New York's Finger Lakes region.
Contact: Cornell's Adult University, 626 Thurston Ave., Ithaca, NY 14850-2490; (607) 255-6260, Fax (607) 254-4482, E-mail cau@sce.cornell.edu, URL http://www.sce.cornell/sce/cau/<.

THE CULINARY INSTITUTE OF AMERICA
Hyde Park/Year-round   *(See also page 65) (See display ad page 66)*
The CIA's Continuing Education Dept. offers a variety of adult education demonstration and participation courses and travel programs for cooking enthusiasts and home gourmets. Also featured: wine instruction, classes for youngsters, dining in fine restaurants.
Faculty: The Institute's chefs and instructors.
Contact: The Culinary Institute of America, Continuing Education Dept., 433 Albany Post Rd., Hyde Park, NY 12538-1499; (800) 888-7850.

CULINARY TREASURES OF THE HAMPTONS
East Hampton/October-December, January-March
This bed and breakfast establishment offers six sessions a year that concentrate on a single topic. Founded in 1996. Maximum class/group size: 8-12. Facilities: commercial kitchen in the Mill House Inn. Also featured: wine instruction, winery tour, dining in fine restaurants and the bed and breakfast.
Emphasis: Baking and wine tasting.
Faculty: Local chefs.
Costs: $65-$75, which includes dinner. The refurbished 200-year-old Inn's 8 guest rooms, all with private baths, range from $150-$200/night double occupancy. A 50% deposit is required. Refund less $25 with 2 weeks notice.
Location: The village of East Hampton, walking distance of restaurants, shops, and the beach.
Contact: Katherine Hartnett, Proprietor, The Mill House Inn, 33 North Main St., East Hampton, NY 11937; (516) 324-9766, Fax (516) 324-9793.

DE GUSTIBUS AT MACY'S
New York
This independent school held in Macy's department store offers about 40 one-session demonstrations and 2-on location classes each season. Established in 1980. Maximum class/group size: 70 demo. Facilities: a professionally-equipped teaching kitchen. Also featured: wine seminars, a recipe-writing course, and a media skills class.
Emphasis: Regional American cuisine, French and Italian cuisines; wine selection; menus for entertaining; guest chef specialties.

FACULTY: Guest chefs and cookbook authors include David Bouley, Daniel Boulud, Bobby Flay, Anne Rosenzweig, and Alain Sailhac.

COSTS: Range from $70 for 1 session to $260 for a series of 4. Credit cards accepted. Cancellations receive class credit only.

LOCATION: Macy's Herald Square store at 34th Street and 7th Avenue.

CONTACT: Arlene Feltman Sailhac, De Gustibus at Macy's, 343 E. 74th Street, Apt. 9G, New York, NY 10021; (212) 439-1714, Fax (212) 439-1716.

KAREN LEE IMAGINATIVE COOKING CLASSES & CATERING
New York/Year-round

Karen Lee teaches participation classes that include two 5-day courses for out-of-towners, three 4-session courses that meet once weekly, and 3-day weekend seminars. 3- and 5-day courses meet in Oct. and May, 4-session courses meet year-round. Established in 1972. Maximum class/group size: 9 hands-on.

EMPHASIS: Fusion and traditional Chinese cuisine, Italian cuisine, basic technique, vegetarian, entertaining menus.

FACULTY: Owner and caterer Karen Lee apprenticed with Madame Grace Zia Chu and is author of *Nouvelle Chinese Cuisine, Chinese Cooking Secrets*, and *The Occasional Vegetarian.*

COSTS: Tuition, which includes a copy of Ms. Lee's latest book, is $655 for the 5-day course, $440 for the 4-session course ($125/single class), and $380 for the weekend course. A $150 nonrefundable deposit is required; cancellations receive credit.

CONTACT: Karen Lee Imaginative Cooking Classes & Catering, 142 West End Ave., #30V, New York, NY 10023; (212) 787-2227, Fax (212) 496-8178. Also: During July and August, P.O. Box 1998, Amagansett, NY 11930, (516) 267-3653, Fax (516) 267-3114.

LA CUISINE SANS PEUR
New York/Year-round

This school in a private residence offers more than twenty 5- and 6-session demonstration courses/year, including the 6-session basic course, 5-session intermediate, advanced, and baking courses. Specialty classes include desserts, fish, and game. Established in 1978. Maximum class/group size: 4. Also featured: 1-week cooking vacations in Provence.

EMPHASIS: The regional cooking of France with emphasis on Alsace and Provence, cooking without recipes, basic to advanced baking, fish, game, vegetable, and dessert courses.

FACULTY: Chef and proprietor Henri-Etienne Lévy trained and worked in restaurant kitchens in France and Germany for 15 years.

COSTS: $450/course. Payment is due 4 weeks prior. No cash refunds.

LOCATION: On Manhattan's Upper West Side, 10 minutes from Lincoln Center.

CONTACT: Henri-Etienne Lévy, chef/proprietor, La Cuisine Sans Peur, 216 W. 89 St., New York, NY 10024; (212) 362-0638, Fax (212) 873-2029.

LAUREN GROVEMAN'S KITCHEN
Larchmont/Year-round

Lauren Groveman offers 5-session participation courses and individual classes on specific subjects. Established in 1990. Maximum class/group size: 6 hands-on.

EMPHASIS: Techniques and preparation of comfort foods, breads, appetizers, edible gifts.

FACULTY: Cookbook author and columnist Lauren Groveman.

COSTS: Tuition is $375 for the 5-session course and $100 for a specialty class. Deposit is $100 for the 5-session course, $30 for a specialty class.

LOCATION: About 30 minutes from New York City.

CONTACT: Lauren Groveman, President, Lauren Groveman's Kitchen, Inc., 55 Prospect Ave., Larchmont, NY 10538; (914) 834-1372, Fax (914) 834-3802.

LOOK WHO'S COOKING, INC.
Oyster Bay/Year-round
This school offers 20 one- to four-session demonstration and participation courses per month. Established in 1994. Maximum class/group size: 20 demo/10 hands-on. Facilities: 800-sq-ft well-equipped kitchen with 10 workspaces.
EMPHASIS: Gourmet cooking for the everyday cook; low fat cooking; baking; fundamentals and techniques; entertaining menus.
FACULTY: Barbara Sheridan, graduate of N.Y. Institute of Technology Culinary Arts Program, attended Peter Kump's New York Cooking School and Le Cordon Bleu.
COSTS: $50/session. No cash refund, 50% deposit on all classes. Refund with 48 hours notice.
LOCATION: Long Island, 20 miles from New York City.
CONTACT: Barbara M. Sheridan, Look Who's Cooking, Inc., 7 West Main St., Oyster Bay, NY 11771; (516) 922-2400.

MARY BETH CLARK
New York/Year-round   *(See also page 266) (See display ad page 267)*
Mary Beth Clark offers 3-hour custom-designed, full-participation private lessons in Italian cuisine. Established in 1977. Maximum class/group size: 1-2.
EMPHASIS: Italian cuisine.
FACULTY: Cookbook author Mary Beth Clark operates the International Cooking School Of Italian Food And Wine.
COSTS: $300/session plus ingredients. $100 deposit, refundable a week prior.
CONTACT: Mary Beth Clark, 201 E. 28th St., #15B, New York, NY 10016-8538; (212) 779-1921, Fax (212) 779-3248, E-mail MaryBethClark@worldnet.att.net.

MIETTE
New York/September-June
Tartine restaurant offers an 8-session hands-on course for youngsters, ages 8-16. Sessions meet Monday afternoons in the restaurant kitchen and conclude with a student-prepared dinner for parents. Established in 1995. Maximum class/group size: 12.
EMPHASIS: French and other cuisines, etiquette, table setting, French language, healthful recipes.
FACULTY: Chef Paul Vandewoude and his assistant, Mariette Bermowitz.
COSTS: $25/class.
CONTACT: Mariette Bermowitz, Miette, 253 W. 11th St., New York, NY 10014; (212) 229-2611, (718) 336-4009.

THE NATURAL GOURMET COOKERY SCHOOL
New York/Year-round   *(See also page 71)*
This private trade school devoted to healthy cooking offers more than 30 demonstration and participation programs/quarter: evening and weekend classes and series, 2-week (60-hour) basic intensives each summer. Maximum class/group size: 8-25. Also featured: classes for youngsters, beginning and advanced cooking theory.
EMPHASIS: Vegetarian cooking, low/no fat, recipe adaptation, medicinal cooking, tofu, tempeh, seitan, food and healing, international cuisines.
COSTS: $595/week for summer intensives, classes and series are $30-$60/session. Lodging at local hotels, hostels, bed & breakfasts. A $50 or 50% deposit is required, 10% discount for seniors.
CONTACT: Director of Admissions, The Natural Gourmet Cookery School, 48 W. 21st St., 2nd Floor, New York, NY 10010; (212) 645-5170.

NEW SCHOOL CULINARY ARTS
New York/Year-round   *(See also page 71)*
The New School for Social Research offers more than a hundred 1- to 8-session demonstration and participation courses and weekend workshops each trimester. Maximum class/group size: 10-

20. Also featured: on-site restaurant chef demonstrations, lectures on culture and cuisine, classes for youngsters, wine courses.

EMPHASIS: Culinary techniques, ethnic and regional cuisines, holiday menus, home entertaining, baking, light-style cooking.

COSTS: $60-$80/session, $40 for youngsters, $10 for lectures, $325 for weekend workshops, $45-$65 for wine classes. Full refund, less $15, for written cancellation prior to class.

CONTACT: Gary A. Goldberg, Executive Director, New School Culinary Arts, 100 Greenwich Ave., New York, NY 10011; (212) 255-4141, (800) 544-1978, #20, Fax (212) 229-5648, E-mail admissions@newschool.edu, URL http://www.newschool.edu.

NEW YORK UNIVERSITY
New York/Fall, Spring, Summer

(See also page 74)

The Dept. of Nutrition and Food Studies, school of Education offers a variety of lecture and demonstration courses for food professionals and career changers.

EMPHASIS: Food business and management, food history and culture, nutrition, food writing, food marketing.

FACULTY: Foodservice and industry professionals, historians, authors.

COSTS: Approximately $50-$200/session.

CONTACT: Carol Guber, Director of Food Programs, New York University, Dept. of Nutrition and Food Studies, 35 W. 4th St., 10th Flr., New York, NY 10012-1172; (212) 998-5588, Fax (212) 995-4194, E-mail guber@is2.nyu.edu, URL http://www.nyu.edu/education/nutrition/.

NORMAN WEINSTEIN'S BROOKLYN COOKING SCHOOL
Brooklyn/September-June

This school offers private classes. Established in 1974. Maximum class/group size: 6. Facilities: Hot Wok Catering's 150-sq-ft kitchen.

EMPHASIS: Asian cuisines, authentic Western barbecue, knife skills workshops, Asian tasting dinners, Chinatown walking tours.

FACULTY: Norman Weinstein, CCP, is author of two cookbooks and has operated Hot Wok Catering for more than 18 years.

COSTS: $40-$50/session. 50% deposit, no refund 10 days prior to class.

LOCATION: Brooklyn's Kensington area, accessible via subway from Manhattan.

CONTACT: Norman Weinstein, Director, Norman Weinstein's Brooklyn Cooking School, 412 E. 2nd Street, Brooklyn, NY 11218; (718) 438-0577.

PETER KUMP'S SCHOOL OF CULINARY ARTS
New York/Year-round

(See also page 75) (See display ad above)

This private school offers more than 900 recreational hands-on courses or workshops a year, including the 5-session, 25-hour Techniques of Fine Cooking series, offered at least monthly as a 5-day intensive. Also featured: Other Techniques series cover spa cuisine, Italian cooking, pastry and baking, and cake decorating. Other courses include ethnic and regional cuisines, business topics, wine tasting, holiday menus, specific subjects.

FACULTY: An evening demonstration series at the 23rd Street facility features noted chefs and cookbook authors.
COSTS: Hands-on classes range from $35 -$475. Housing and restaurant suggestions are provided to out-of-towners. Deposits required, credit cards accepted.
LOCATION: 50 W. 23rd St. and 307 E. 92nd St. in NYC, as well as Pt. Washington and Larchmont, NY; Hohokus, NJ; Pittsburgh, PA; and Washington, DC.
CONTACT: Peter Kump's School of Culinary Arts, 50 W. 23rd St., New York, NY 10128; (800) 522-4610, Fax (212) 348-6360.

SAPORE DI MARE
Wainscott/June-September
This regional Italian restaurant offers participation classes up to three times weekly. Established in 1990. Maximum class/group size: 15. Facilities: the restaurant kitchen.
EMPHASIS: Appetizers, pasta, main courses, pizza, breads, grilling, desserts.
FACULTY: Restaurateur Pino Luongo, author of *A Tuscan in the Kitchen*, owner of Sapore di Mare in the Hamptons and Le Madri and Coco Pazzo in New York. Instructors include the chefs from the restaurants.
COSTS: $150/class. Nonrefundable.
LOCATION: Long Island, 90 miles from New York City.
CONTACT: Kristen Dell'Aguzzo, Director, Sapore di Mare Summer Cooking Classes, Wainscott Stone Rd. & Montauk Hwy., P.O. Box 1357, Wainscott, NY 11975; (516) 324-5045, Fax (516) 537-1828.

THE SEASONAL KITCHEN
Pittsford/Year-round
This school offers approximately 26 weeks of morning and evening demonstrations annually. Established in 1980. Facilities: a well-equipped country kitchen. Also featured: classes for men, couples, and groups.
EMPHASIS: Easy-to-prepare and seasonal recipes.
FACULTY: Ginger and Dick Howell are members of the IACP.
COSTS: $30-$35. Cancellations receive a 50% refund.
LOCATION: A suburb of Rochester.
CONTACT: The Seasonal Kitchen, 610 W. Bloomfield Rd., Pittsford, NY 14534; (716) 624-3242, E-mail dickhcook@aol.com.

TOPS INTERNATIONAL SUPER CENTER COOKING SCHOOL
Amherst and Greece/Year-round
This school in a supermarket offers 20 to 25 one- to eight-session demonstration and participation courses/month. Established in 1991. Maximum class/group size: 30 demo/15 hands-on. Facilities: modern kitchens with overhead mirrors and seminar seating. Also featured: children's classes, private classes for groups.
FACULTY: CIA-educated chefs, caterers, home economists, dietitians. Guest chefs have included Paul Prudhomme, Tommy Tang, CIA Culinary Dean Fritz Sonnenschmid, and Ron Pickarski.
COSTS: Range from free to $20. Pre-registration and pre-payment required.
LOCATION: Amherst and Greece are 15 minutes from the Buffalo and Rochester airports.
CONTACT: Marcia Scheideman, Manager, The Cooking School - Tops International Super Center, 3980 Maple Rd., Amherst, NY 14226; (716) 834-5177, Fax (716) 515-0097.

NORTH CAROLINA

THE CAROLINA CULINARY CENTER
Raleigh, Durham/Year-round
This school (formerly The Jane Thompson Cooking School) offers demonstration and participation classes and celebrity chef demonstrations by noted chefs from around the world. Established

in 1988. Maximum class/group size: 40 demo/16 hands-on. Facilities: throughout the Triangle.
EMPHASIS: French and Italian cuisine, including fish, poultry, stocks, and sauces.
FACULTY: Jane Thompson, food and wine editor of *Raleigh* magazine, former managing editor of *Master Chef* magazine, has studied in Europe and the U.S. with Simone Beck, Jacques Pépin, Madeleine Kamman, and Giuliano Bugialli.
COSTS: $45/class. Reservations required. Full refund with 14 days notice.
CONTACT: The Carolina Culinary Center, 3616 Sleepy Hollow Rd., Wake Forest, NC 27587; (919) 562-1550, Fax (919) 554-2699, E-mail culinary@aol.com.

COOKS & CONNOISSEURS COOKING SCHOOL
New Bern/February-October

This cookware store and school offers demonstration and participation classes. Established in 1983. Facilities: 200-sq-ft teaching kitchen.
EMPHASIS: Chinese, Italian, French, and regional American cuisines, seasonal and local chef specialties, cookbook recipes, wine selection.
FACULTY: Proprietor Candace H. Lynn and staff, including Laurie Hayes, Willard Doxey, and Karen Askew.
COSTS: One-day classes range from $15-$20; 4-week series, $60-$80.
LOCATION: Near Tryon Palace Restoration and 30 miles from beaches.
CONTACT: Cooks & Connoisseurs Cooking School, 2500 Trent Rd., #24, New Bern, NC 28562; (919) 633-2665.

COOK'S CORNER, LTD.
Greensboro/January-November

This cookware store offers 15-18 demonstration classes/month. Established in 1983. Maximum class/group size: 24. Facilities: fully-equipped teaching kitchen with overhead mirror. Also featured: wine tastings, classes for private groups.
FACULTY: Mary James Lawrence, CCP, and Lucy Hamilton, who holds a Cordon Bleu certificate; guest chefs.
COSTS: $9-$50. Payable by credit card; refund with 48 hours notice.
LOCATION: A restored area of Greensboro.
CONTACT: Cook's Corner, Ltd., 401 State St., Greensboro, NC 27405; (910)-272-2665, Fax (919) 379-9022, E-mail mjml@aol.com.

THE GRANDE GOURMET COOKING SCHOOL
Wilmington/Year-round

This school in a private residence offers a half dozen demonstration and participation classes per month. Established in 1989. Maximum class/group size: 25 demo/10 hands-on. Also featured: children's and private classes.
EMPHASIS: Italian, Chinese, and French cuisines, techniques, low-fat cookery, cake decorating, entertaining menus, wine tastings.
FACULTY: Owner Robin Hackney studied with Nick Malgieri, Karen Lee, and others; Occasional guest instructors.
COSTS: $30-$45/session. A deposit is required; refund with 10 days notice.
LOCATION: The southeastern beach resort of Wilmington, 2 hours from Raleigh.
CONTACT: Robin Hackney, Owner, The Grande Gourmet Cooking School, 1108 Princeton Dr., Wilmington, NC 28403; (910) 763-1764, Fax (910) 763-0658.

THE STOCKED POT & CO.
Winston-Salem/Year-round

This school and catering firm offers 30 classes per quarter. Established in 1980. Maximum class/group size: 34. Facilities: well-equipped teaching kitchen with overhead mirror. Also featured: bridal shower cooking classes, Lunch and Learn sessions, children's and family classes.
EMPHASIS: Ethnic and regional cuisines, seasonal dishes, nutritional foods, wine seminars.

Faculty: Owner/chef Donald C. McMillan, CEC, also owns and operates Gisele's Fine Foods Restaurant and Simple Elegance Catering; Lucy Herrman, Tom Peters, Tim Booras, Bob Werth, CEC. Guest teachers include Hugh Carpenter and Giuliano Hazan.

Costs: Range from $18-$30 per class; Lunch and Learn classes are $10-$12; children's classes are $15; celebrity chef classes are $45. Advance payment required; refund with 72 hours notice, 2 weeks notice for guest chefs.

Location: Winston-Salem's Reynolda Village, the former Richard Joshua Reynolds estate, about 20 miles from the Piedmont airport.

Contact: Nancy Barnes, The Stocked Pot & Co., 111-B Reynolda Village, Winston-Salem, NC 27106; (910) 722-3663, Fax (910) 725-5034.

OHIO

BUEHLER'S FOOD MARKETS
Wooster/Year-round

This food market offers demonstration and participation classes at its 5 locations. Established in 1983. Maximum class/group size: 30 demo/12 hands-on. Facilities: teaching areas with theater-type seating and overhead mirrors. Also featured: child, teen, and parent-child classes.

Emphasis: Seasonal menus, nutrition, children's birthday parties.

Faculty: Staff home economists and guest instructors.

Costs: $6-$20/session.

Location: Delaware, Dover, Medina, Wadsworth, and Wooster, Ohio.

Contact: Mary McMillen, Director of Consumer Affairs, Buehler's Food Markets, P.O. Box 196, 1401 Old Mansfield Rd., Wooster, OH 44691; (330) 264-4355 #256, Fax (330) 264-0874.

THE CLEVELAND RESTAURANT COOKING SCHOOL
Cleveland/Year-round   *(See also page 79)*

This private school offers classes for hobbyists and 1-week seminars in May and September.

Contact: The Cleveland Restaurant Cooking School, 2801 Bridge Ave., Cleveland, OH 44113; (216) 771-7130, Fax (216) 771-8130.

COLUMBUS STATE CULINARY ACADEMY
Columbus/Year-round   *(See also page 80)*

This division of Columbus State Community College offers 160 3-hour demonstration and participation classes/year. Established in 1995. Maximum class/group size: 18-30. Also featured: wine instruction, classes for youngsters.

Emphasis: International cuisines, theme classes, guest chefs, vegetarian and healthy cooking.

Costs: $45 for demonstrations, $65 for hands-on classes. Payment in full with reservation. Full refund for cancellations 4 days prior.

Contact: Columbus State Culinary Academy, 550 East Spring St., Columbus, OH 43215; (614) 227-2579, Fax (614) 227-5146.

COOKS'WARES CULINARY CLASSES
Cincinnati/Spring, Fall, Winter

This kitchenware store offers more than 100 demonstration and participation classes per year. Established in 1992. Maximum class/group size: 24 demo/12 hands-on. Facilities: a 300-sq-ft teaching kitchen with overhead mirror. Also featured: wine tasting, private instruction, children's classes.

Emphasis: Basics, ethnic and regional cuisines, specific subjects.

Faculty: Includes Jude Theriot, Marilyn Harris; Chefs Paul Teal, Michael Cohen, Pamela Lewis.

Costs: Range from $20-$40, $15 for youngsters. Payment in advance; refund with 5 days notice. Credit cards accepted.

Location: Approximately 20 miles from central Cincinnati.

CONTACT: Amy Tobin, Director, Cooks'Wares Culinary Classes, 11344 Montgomery Rd., Cincinnati, OH 45249; (513) 489-6400, Fax (513) 489-1211.

DOROTHY LANE MARKET SCHOOL OF COOKING
Dayton/September-May

This supermarket offers 60-80 demonstrations and a few participation classes/year. Established in 1984. Maximum class/group size: 20 demo/10 hands-on. Facilities: 400-sq-ft teaching kitchen with overhead mirror and new appliances. Also featured: children's classes, wine instruction, market visits, private lessons.

EMPHASIS: Includes basic techniques, ethnic and regional cuisines, entertaining menus, guest chef specialties, specific subjects.

FACULTY: Includes professional chefs, caterers, cookbook authors, home economists, and dietitians. Guest chefs have included Giuliano Bugialli, Hugh Carpenter, Sara Leah Chase, Giuliano Hazan, Perla Meyers, Susan Purdy, George Geary.

COSTS: Range from $20 for children's classes to $45 for guest chefs. Most classes are $35. Prepayment is required. Refund with 7 days notice. Credit cards accepted.

CONTACT: Deb Lackey, School of Cooking Director, Dorothy Lane Market School of Cooking, 2710 Far Hills Ave., Dayton, OH 45419; (513) 299-5132, (513) 299-3561, Fax (513) 299-3568, E-mail cooking@dorothylane.com, URL http://www.dorothylane.com.

GOURMET CURIOSITIES, ETC.
Sylvania/Spring, Fall, Summer

The Creative Cooking School of Gourmet Curiosities offers approximately 75 demonstration and participation courses per year. Established in 1974. Maximum class/group size: 34 demo/16 hands-on. Facilities: a 1,000-sq-ft kitchen with overhead mirror. Also featured: children's classes, wine tastings, private classes, market visits, demonstrations at off-site functions.

FACULTY: Owners Geneva and Bruce Williams attended La Varenne, are members of the ACF, have served on consumer panels, and had recipes accepted for publication. Other instructors include area chefs.

COSTS: $20-$30/session. Payment with registration; refund with 3 days notice.

LOCATION: 11 miles from Toledo and 60 miles from Detroit.

CONTACT: Bruce C. Williams, Gourmet Curiosities, Etc., Starlite Plaza, 5700 Monroe St., Sylvania, OH 43560; (419) 882-2323, Fax (800) 465-8843.

HANDKE'S CUISINE COOKING CLASS
Columbus/September-June

This restaurant offers demonstrations and private classes year-round for groups of 20 or more. Established in 1991. Maximum class/group size: 32.

EMPHASIS: American and European cuisine.

FACULTY: Hartmut Handke, CMC.

COSTS: $39 plus tax and gratuity. Credit cards accepted. Refund with 48 hours notice.

CONTACT: Katie Dougherty, Catering Director, Handke's Cuisine Cooking Class, 520 S. Front St., Columbus, OH 43215; (614) 621-2500, Fax (614) 621-2626.

THE LORETTA PAGANINI SCHOOL OF COOKING
(See also page 81)   **Chesterland/Year-round**

This private school affiliated with Lakeland Community College offers more than 400 one- to four-session demonstration and participation courses/year. Established in 1981. Maximum class/group size: 28 demo/12 hands-on. Also featured: couples classes, a young gourmet series, gastronomic tours to Italy, local trips to food-related sites.

EMPHASIS: Professional techniques.

FACULTY: Owner/director Loretta Paganini, born and schooled in Italy, culinary consultant to area restaurants, food writer for the local newspaper and guest chef on local TV. Guest faculty includes

local chefs, teachers, and visiting professionals from many countries.
Costs: $25-$45/session. One week advance registration is required; refund with 7 days notice.
Location: 25 miles east of Cleveland.
Contact: Loretta Paganini, Owner/Director, The Loretta Paganini School of Cooking, 8613 Mayfield Rd., Chesterland, OH 44026; (216) 729-1110, (216) 729-COOK, Fax (216) 729-6459, E-mail lpscinc@msn.com. Also: Toll-free (888) 434-5987.

UNIVERSITY HOSPITALS SYNERGY
Mayfield Heights/Year-round
This private school offers more than 140 demonstration classes/year. Established in 1993. Maximum class/group size: 10-25. Facilities: newly-equipped facility with video monitor system at University Hospitals Health Center at Landerbrook.
Emphasis: Healthful, high flavor, low fat cuisine.
Faculty: Culinary Director is Michelle M. Gavin, CCP. Registered dietitians are present at each class.
Costs: $30/class or 2 for $50. Refund granted 7 days prior.
Location: 20 minutes east of downtown Cleveland.
Contact: Michelle Gavin, Director, University Hospitals Synergy, 5850 Landerbrook Dr., #110, Mayfield Heights, OH 44124; (216) 646-2300, Fax (216) 646-2322.

WHAT'S COOKING?, INC.
Akron/Year-round
This cookware store offers 14 one- to six-session demonstration and participation courses per month. Established in 1984. Maximum class/group size: 25 demo/14 hands-on. Facilities: teaching kitchen with overhead mirror. Also featured: classes for couples and groups, market visits.
Emphasis: Fundamentals, regional American and international cuisine, health-conscious and quick cooking.
Faculty: John and Bev Shaffer studied with James Beard and Julie Dannenbaum. They are winners of over 120 cooking prizes and producers of a cable TV show. Occasional guest instructors.
Costs: Start at $24. Full payment to register.
Location: Suburban area, 30 miles southeast of Cleveland Airport.
Contact: Bev Shaffer, Director, What's Cooking?, Inc., 843 N. Cleveland Massillon Rd., Akron, OH 44333-2174; (330) 666-3663.

ZONA SPRAY COOKING SCHOOL
Hudson/Year-round
This cookware store offers 26 five- to six-session demonstration and participation courses/month and 24-35 professional technique participation courses/year. Established in 1972. Maximum class/group size: 38 demo/10-24 hands-on. Facilities: a 500-sq-ft kitchen with 3 ovens and 3 work stations. Also featured: private and children's classes, market visits, sessions on catering and food writing, gastronomic bicycle tours.
Emphasis: Techniques, basics, pastry, low-fat cuisine, Japanese cuisine, herbs and spices, cake decorating, breads.
Faculty: Proprietor Zona Spray and 15-20 professional chefs, caterers, and cookbook authors. Guest chefs have included Rick Bayless, Shirley Corriher, Joe Ortiz, Barbara Tropp, Todd English.
Costs: Demonstrations are $28, $45 with visiting chef or author; professional programs are $495; gastronomic tours are $850 to $3,000. Local hotel/motel lodging. Advance registration required; refund with 48 hours notice (3 weeks for professional program).
Location: Western Reserve in Ohio, 20 miles south of Cleveland, 15 miles east of Akron.
Contact: Zona Spray, Zona Spray Cooking School, 140 N. Main, Hudson, OH 44236; (216) 650-1665, Fax (216) 650-1665.

OKLAHOMA

COOKING SCHOOL OF TULSA
Tulsa/Year-round

This cookware shop offers more than 130 demonstration and participation classes/year. Established in 1991. Maximum class/group size: 20 demo/8 hands-on. Facilities: fully-equipped teaching kitchen with overhead mirror. Also featured: wine tastings.

EMPHASIS: Simple techniques, menus for entertaining, ethnic cuisines, guest chef specialties.

FACULTY: Proprietor Keith Lindenberg, local chefs, visiting guest chefs, nutritionists.

COSTS: $25-$45/class. Advance registration and payment required. No refunds within 7 days of class.

CONTACT: Cooking School of Tulsa, 8264 S. Lewis, Tulsa, OK 74137; (918) 298-7110.

GOURMET GADGETRE, LTD.
Lawton/October-June

This cookware store conducts cooking demonstrations. Established in 1980. Maximum class/group size: 20.

EMPHASIS: Breads, candies, ethnic cuisines.

FACULTY: Restaurateurs Hazel Wong and Patty Quarles; June Harris.

COSTS: $15/class. Refund with 48 hours notice.

CONTACT: Gourmet Gadgetre, Ltd., 1105 Ferris, Lawton, OK 73507; (405) 248-1837.

OREGON

CARL'S CUISINE
Salem/Year-round

This specialty kitchen store offers demonstration classes. Established in 1978. Maximum class/group size: 12.

EMPHASIS: Ethnic and regional cuisines, seasonal menus, specific subjects.

FACULTY: Proprietor Carl Meisel has traveled and studied in Europe, Thailand, and regions of the U.S. He is a consultant on menu planning, travel, and kitchen design.

COSTS: $20/class. Advance reservations required.

LOCATION: Downtown Salem.

CONTACT: Carl's Cuisine, 333 Chemeketa St. NE, Salem, OR 97301; (503) 363-1612, Fax (503) 363-5014.

PENNSYLVANIA

CHARLOTTE-ANN ALBERTSON'S COOKING SCHOOL
(See also page 241)   **Philadelphia/Year-round**

This school offers more than 75 one- to four-session demonstration and some participation courses each year. Established in 1973. Maximum class/group size: 25 demo/15 hands-on. Facilities: Madsen Design Center and commercial kitchens. Also featured: market tours, children's classes, wine seminars and dinners, European culinary vacations, winter classes in private homes in Florida.

EMPHASIS: Ethnic cuisines, holiday menus, grilling, wine, kitchen design, food science, food marketing.

FACULTY: Charlotte-Ann Albertson, IACP member and certified teacher, studied at La Varenne and Le Cordon Bleu. Others include CIA-trained Philadelphia chefs, caterers and experts such as Shirley Corriher and Barbara Tropp.

COSTS: $25-$45/session. Hotel lodging included in cost of trip. Advance payment required. No cash refunds.

LOCATION: Madsen Design Center, 8 miles from downtown Philadelphia, and suburban commercial kitchens.
CONTACT: Charlotte-Ann Albertson, P.O. Box 27, Wynnewood, PA 19096-0027; (610) 649-9290, (813) 642-6550, Fax (610) 649-9290.

CLASS COOKING
Bryn Mawr/March-May, October-December
This private school offers morning and evening hands-on and demonstration classes. Established in 1986. Maximum class/group size: 12 maximum. Facilities: 14-foot counter, standard cooking appliances, overhead mirror. Also featured: private classes.
EMPHASIS: French, Italian, and American cuisines, understanding what cooking is about.
FACULTY: IACP-member Susan Winokur earned a BS degree from Cornell University, MS in Education from the University of Pennsylvania.
COSTS: $45-$60/class. Full payment with registration.
LOCATION: 20 minutes from Philadelphia.
CONTACT: Susan Winokur, Owner/teacher, Class Cooking, P.O. Box 751, Bryn Mawr, PA 19010; (610) 527-1338, Fax (610) 527-6069.

THE COOK'S CORNER, INC.
Yardley/Year-round
This school in a cookware store offers 1 demonstration class/week. Established in 1987. Maximum class/group size: 35. Facilities: full demonstration kitchen with overhead mirror.
EMPHASIS: Ethnic and regional cuisines, desserts, pastas, breads, salads, guest chef specialties, wine appreciation.
FACULTY: Owner Catherine Rowan and guest cookbook authors, professional instructors, and restaurant chefs.
COSTS: $40-$45. Nonrefundable payment must accompany registration.
LOCATION: Yardley is 30 miles north of Philadelphia and 1 mile from Trenton, N.J.
CONTACT: The Cook's Corner, 90 W. Afton Ave., Yardley, PA 19067; (215) 493-9093.

COOKING WITH CLASS
Shohola/Spring, Summer
This school offers more than 40 hands-on classes and series each season. Established in 1993. Facilities: commercial kitchen studio and cookbook library. Also featured: private instruction available.
EMPHASIS: Basics, ethnic and regional cuisines, special occasion dishes, cake decorating, sugar artistry and design, guest chef specialties, specific subjects.
FACULTY: Founder Sheila Kaye-Stepkin and guest chefs from New York City and surrounding area.
COSTS: $50-$150/session.
LOCATION: On Twin Lakes, 90 minutes from Manhattan and 5 minutes from Milford.
CONTACT: Sheila Kaye-Stepkin, Cooking with Class, 2221 Twin Lakes Rd., Shohola, PA 18458; (800) 226-6540, Fax (717) 296-2627, E-mail jgek68a@prodigy.com.

THE COOKING COTTAGE AT CEDAR SPRING FARM
Sellersville/Year-round
This cooking school offers 65 demonstration classes and specialized series per year. Established in 1992. Maximum class/group size: 12. Facilities: demonstration kitchen with overhead mirror. Also featured: private group classes and market trips, trips to France and Italy.
EMPHASIS: Various types of cooking.
FACULTY: Winnie McClennen and her daughter, Peggi Clauhs; guest chefs.
COSTS: $35-$45, demo or hands-on with full course meal. Payment with reservation.
LOCATION: Rural Upper Bucks County, between Allentown and Philadelphia.
CONTACT: Peggi Clauhs, Co-owner, The Cooking Cottage at Cedar Spring Farm, 1731 B Old Bethlehem Pike, Sellersville, PA 18960; (215) 453-1828, Fax (215) 257-6177.

CRATE
Pittsburgh/Fall, spring

This retail kitchenware store offers 100-120 day and evening demonstration and participation courses per year. Established in 1978. Maximum class/group size: 40 demo/12 hands-on. Facilities: new demonstration kitchen with 8 burners, regular, convection, and microwave ovens, overhead mirror.

EMPHASIS: Italian, Chinese, Mediterranean, and French cuisines; vegetarian, bread, herbs, biscotti, filo, cookies and cake; guest specialties.

FACULTY: Includes chefs and owners of top local restaurants, owners of culinary businesses, and professional caterers. Guests have included Mary Beth Clark, Joanne Weir, Alice Medrich, Perla Meyers, and Marlene Sorosky.

COSTS: Average class cost is $25-$30; guests are higher. Professional series starts January, 1997. Payment required with registration.

LOCATION: In Pittsburgh's South Hills-Scott Township.

CONTACT: Linda Wernikoff, Owner, Crate, Greentree Road Shopping Ctr, Pittsburgh, PA 15220; (412) 341-5700, Fax (412) 341-6321.

JANE CITRON COOKING CLASSES
(See also page 243)   ### Pittsburgh/September-May

This school in a private home offers 20 demonstration classes/year. Established in 1978. Maximum class/group size: 12. Facilities: well-equipped home kitchen. Also featured: private classes, market visits, culinary tours of Napa Valley and Europe.

FACULTY: Jane Citron studied with Marcella Hazan, Madeleine Kamman, Jacques Pépin, and Roger Vergé. She is food editor and writes a column for *Pittsburgh Magazine*.

COSTS: $55/class. Advance payment required. Refund if replacement found.

LOCATION: The Murdoch Farms section of Pittsburgh.

CONTACT: Jane Citron, 1314 Squirrel Hill Ave., Pittsburgh, PA 15217; (412) 621-0311, Fax (412) 765-2511, E-mail janecooks@aol.com.

KATHY D'ADDARIO'S COOKING TECHNIQUES
Ambler/Year-round

This school offers 70 ten-session participation courses/year. Established in 1994. Maximum class/group size: 6-8. Facilities: large home kitchen. Also featured: wine instruction, market visits, private classes, small group lessons.

EMPHASIS: Traditional techniques, low-fat meals, seasonal menus, holiday entertaining.

FACULTY: Kathy D'Addario is a graduate of The Restaurant School and studied at Le Cordon Bleu, Giuliano Bugialli's in Florence, and Peter Kump's New York Cooking School.

COSTS: $35-$50/session. Payment in advance; refund with 1 week notice.

LOCATION: A 30-minute drive from Philadelphia.

CONTACT: Kathy D'Addario's Cooking Techniques, 858 Tennis Ave., Ambler, PA 19002; (215) 643-5883, Fax (215) 257-6681.

THE KITCHEN SHOPPE AND COOKING SCHOOL
Carlisle/September-May

This kitchenware, gift and gourmet store offers over 150-one session demonstration or hands-on classes each year. Established in 1975. Maximum class/group size: 40 demo/15 hands-on. Facilities: well-equipped professional kitchen with 6 work stations, overhead mirrors, audio system. Also featured: classes for youngsters and private groups.

EMPHASIS: Afternoon tea, breads and pastries, grilling and smoking, ethnic and vegetarian cuisines, guest chef specialties.

FACULTY: Proprietor Suzanne Hoffman, IACP, instructors Diana Povis, Jim Lupia, Kevin Fisher. Guest chefs include Hugh Carpenter, Martin Yan, Marion Cunningham.

COSTS: $25-$45/session; children's classes $15. Full payment is required with registration.

LOCATION: 20 minutes west of Harrisburg; 2-1/2 hours west of Philadelphia; 2-1/2 hours northwest of Washington DC and Baltimore.
CONTACT: Suzanne Hoffman, The Kitchen Shoppe and Cooking School, 101 Shady Lane, Carlisle, PA 17013; (800) 391-COOK, (717) 243-0906, Fax (717) 245-0606.

PERSONAL HEALTH DYNAMICS
Pittsburgh/Year-round
This private school offers over 20 evening, weekday, and weekend hands-on classes each trimester. Established in 1993. Maximum class/group size: 10. Facilities: classroom in a private home. Also featured: private instruction, books and videotapes.
EMPHASIS: Vegetarian and macrobiotic cooking with low fat and no dairy or sugar, health and wellness menus, dietary programs for heart disease, cancer, and diabetes.
FACULTY: Janice Polansky studied at the Natural Gourmet Cookery School with Annemarie Colbin, Ron Pickarski, and Fran Costigan, and at the Kushi Institute with Denny Waxman, Bill Tara, and Murray Snyder. She has a BS and 2 masters degrees from Carnegie-Mellon University.
COSTS: Tuition is $45-$55/class, $30-$35/lecture. Advance payment is required. No refund.
LOCATION: A northern suburb of Pittsburgh, within a half hour of most suburbs and 10 minutes from the Pennsylvania turnpike.
CONTACT: Jan Polansky, Personal Health Dynamics, 4256 Old New England Rd., Allison Park, PA 15101-1534; (412) 492-0767, Fax 412-492-0767.

RANIA'S COOKING SCHOOL
Pittsburgh/Spring, Fall
This restaurant offers over 20 demonstrations each season. Established in 1984. Maximum class/group size: 24. Also featured: children's classes, wine instruction, private classes.
EMPHASIS: Ethnic and regional cuisines, holiday foods, appetizers to desserts.
FACULTY: Proprietor Rania Harris and chefs Michael Barbato (Westin Wm. Penn), Joe Nolan (Cafe Allegro), Bill Fuller (Casbah), Gary Terner (Kaya), Stuart Marks (Rania's Catering); Sharryn Campbell, wine tasting.
COSTS: $30/class; children's class is $18. No refunds.
LOCATION: 7 minutes from downtown Pittsburgh.
CONTACT: Rania's Cooking School, 100 Central Sq., Pittsburgh, PA 15228; (412) 531-2222, Fax (412) 531-7242.

THE RESTAURANT SCHOOL
Philadelphia/October-June   *(See also page 91) (See display ad page 93)*
This proprietary institution offers 3-hour demonstration and participation classes. Maximum class/group size: 24-85. Also featured: wine instruction.
CONTACT: The Restaurant School, 4207 Walnut St., Philadelphia, PA 19104; (215) 222-4200 #6, Fax (215) 222-4219.

RHODE ISLAND

SAKONNET MASTER CHEFS SERIES
Little Compton/September-June
Sakonnet Vineyards offers 10 full-day demonstration and participation classes per year. Established in 1980. Maximum class/group size: 12. Facilities: a large main work table and counter, which serves as individual work areas.
EMPHASIS: Guest chef specialties; wine selection and food pairing.
FACULTY: Has included Johanne Killeen and George Germon of Al Forno Restaurant in Providence; Maureen Pothier of Bluepoint Oyster Bar & Restaurant; Jasper White of Jasper's in Boston; Todd English of Olives in Boston.
COSTS: $80-$100. Accommodations can be arranged. Advance reservation required.

LOCATION: 30 minutes from New Bedford and Fall River, Mass., 40 minutes from Providence, 75 minutes from Boston.

CONTACT: Sakonnet Vineyards, P.O. Box 197, Little Compton, RI 02837; (401) 635-8486, Fax (401) 635-2101.

SWINBURNE SCHOOL
Newport/Year-round

The Civic League of Newport, Inc., an adult education center offers 300 classes annually on a variety of topics, including cooking. Established in 1924. Maximum class/group size: 5-15.

EMPHASIS: Ethnic cuisines, vegetarian foods, seasonal and special occasion menus, breads, sauces, wine appreciation, beer making.

FACULTY: Local cooks, chefs, and cookbook authors.

COSTS: $30-$75/session. No refunds within 1 week of class unless space can be filled.

CONTACT: Eloise "Sis" Held, Program Coordinator, Swinburne School, 115 Pelham St., Newport, RI 02840; (401) 846-1496, Fax (401) 847-3750.

SOUTH CAROLINA

BOBBI COOKS II
Hilton Head Island/Year-round

This school in a private residence offers more than 60 demonstration and participation classes/year. Established in 1993. Maximum class/group size: 12 hands-on/20 demo. Facilities: large fully-equipped professional kitchen. Also featured: classes for youngsters, wine and food pairing, couples' classes, private instruction.

EMPHASIS: Smoking and grilling, ethnic, entertaining, heart healthy, techniques.

FACULTY: Bobbi Leavitt studied at Johnson & Wales, RI; Master Chefs Institute, Bermuda; Michael James French Chefs School, CA. Past president NYACT. IACP, AIWF, and James Beard Foundation member. Guest instructors.

COSTS: $28-$40/class. Resort facilities, tennis, golf, ocean are nearby. Deposit required.

LOCATION: 35 miles north of Savannah airport, 10 minutes from Hilton Head airport.

CONTACT: Bobbi Leavitt, Bobbi Cooks II, 9 Baynard Park, Hilton Head Island, SC 29928; (803) 671-5902, Fax (803) 671-5902. Also: Linda Russell, registrar (803) 842-9885.

IN GOOD TASTE
Charleston/Year-round

This gourmet shop offers demonstration and participation classes. Established in 1983. Maximum class/group size: 8-14. Facilities: well-equipped teaching kitchen. Also featured: bed and breakfast tours.

EMPHASIS: Ethnic and regional cuisines, techniques, breads, wine appreciation.

FACULTY: School owner Jacki Boyd, Roland Gilg, and Bonnie Caracciolo; local chefs.

COSTS: $30-$60/session. Payment required to reserve space.

CONTACT: Jacki Boyd, In Good Taste, 1901 Ashley River Rd., Charleston, SC 29407; (803) 763-5597, Fax (803) 763-5597.

TENNESSEE

CHEF DOUGH DOUGH & CO.
Memphis/Year-round

Dolores Katsotis (Chef Dough Dough) offers demonstration and participation classes for adults and youngsters. Established in 1989. Maximum class/group size: 20 demo/12 hands-on.

EMPHASIS: A variety of topics.

FACULTY: Dolores Katsotis, a CIA graduate and author of *Cooking Adventures with Chef Dough Dough*, is the daughter of the late John Grisanti, a Memphis restaurateur and wine expert.

LOCATION: Community centers and museums.
CONTACT: Dolores Katsotis, Chef Dough Dough & Co., 8370 Stavenger Cove, Cordova, TN 38018; (901) 754-0698, Fax (901) 754-0698.

CLASSIC GOURMET COOKING SCHOOL
Nashville/Year-round except August and December
This cookware and gourmet foods store offers more than 125 demonstration and participation classes per year. Established in 1991. Maximum class/group size: 30 demo/12 hands-on. Facilities: teaching kitchen with overhead mirror. Also featured: wine and food classes, private classes.
EMPHASIS: French techniques, Oriental, Italian, dinner parties.
FACULTY: Owner/Chef Hilda Pope, Mary Clarke, Susan Hudgens, and Rachel Blair. Guest chefs include area chefs and cookbook authors.
COSTS: $35-$80. Full payment must accompany reservation. Refund with 48 hours notice.
LOCATION: Near Opryland, The Hermitage, and Belle Meade Mansion.
CONTACT: Hilda Pope, Classic Gourmet Cooking School, Hillsboro Plaza, 3900 Hillsboro Rd., Nashville, TN 37215; (615) 383-8700, Fax (615) 383-8788.

RAJI RESTAURANT
Memphis/February, November
This restaurant offers full-day workshops. Maximum class/group size: 15. Facilities: Raji Restaurant kitchen.
EMPHASIS: Fusion (French Indian) cooking.
FACULTY: Chef Raji Jallepalli.
COSTS: $250.
CONTACT: Raji Jallepalli, Raji Restaurant, 712 W. Brookhaven Circle, Memphis, TN 38117; (901) 685-8723, Fax (901) 767-2266.

UT COMMUNITY PROGRAMS
Knoxville/Year-round
The University of Tennessee's community programs include weekly lectured, demonstration and hands-on classes. Established in 1970. Maximum class/group size: 20. Also featured: wine instruction, market visits.
EMPHASIS: Multi-ethnic cuisines, vegetarian, low-fat cooking.
FACULTY: Culinary and wine professionals.
COSTS: Ranges from $15-$30/session. Full refund less $10 fee granted cancellations 2 working days prior.
CONTACT: Elaine Keener, Program Manager, UT Community Programs, 600 Henley St., Knoxville, TN 37996-4110; (423) 974-0150, Fax (423) 974-0264, E-mail utcommunity@gateway.ce.utk.edu.

TEXAS

CREATING CULINARY OPPORTUNITIES
Houston/February, July, October
Ann Iverson offers 1- and 2-day participation courses in a variety of cuisines. Established in 1993. Maximum class/group size: 12. Facilities: 340-sq-ft private kitchen with 12 work areas.
EMPHASIS: Northern Italian and Mediterranean cuisines.
FACULTY: Guest chefs and authors and Ann Iverson, who studied with Giuliano Bugialli, Mary Beth Clark, Marcella and Victor Hazan, and Lorenza di Medici.
COSTS: Range from $80-$135/session. Full payment required, refund granted with 3 weeks notice.
LOCATION: Galleria area.
CONTACT: Ann Iverson, Owner, Creating Culinary Opportunities, 2902 West Lane, Unit E, Houston, TX 77027; (713) 622-6936, Fax (713) 622-2924, E-mail annci@aol.com.

CUISINE CONCEPTS
Fort Worth/Year-round

Author, food stylist, and food and wine writer Renie Steves offers private wine and cooking instruction designed to the student's requests. Founded in 1979. Maximum class/group size: 1-2. Facilities: kitchen in a private home. Also featured: Group classes for up to 26 persons, hands-on classes for up to 9.

EMPHASIS: A variety of topics, including stocks, sauces, low-fat cooking, menu planning, techniques.

FACULTY: Renie Steves, CCP, chair of the IACP Foundation and owner of The French Apron, studied with Madeleine Kamman, James Beard, Julia Child, Nick Malgieri, and the Hazans.

COSTS: $75/hour for one student, $100 for two, plus a $7/hour assistant fee and minimal marketing expense. Each class is a 4-hour minimum. A 50% deposit is required 7 days in advance.

LOCATION: Ft. Worth's west side, near the Kimbell Museum, 35 minutes west of DFW Airport.

CONTACT: Renie Steves, Cuisine Concepts, 1406 Thomas Pl., Ft. Worth, TX 76107-2432; (817) 732-4758, Fax (817) 732-3247, E-mail RenieSteves@msn.com.

DESIGNER EVENTS COOKING SCHOOL
Bryan/Year-round

This school established by Merrill Bonarrigo offers 1 participation class per month. Food and wine pairing seminars are provided by Messina Hof Wine Cellars. Established in 1992. Maximum class/group size: 15.

EMPHASIS: Menus prepared by Texas chefs.

COSTS: $35-$75/session. Lodging is available at bed & breakfast at Vineyard.

LOCATION: The Messina Hof Winery estate in the Brazos Valley, 100 miles from Houston and 90 miles east of Austin.

CONTACT: Merrill Bonarrigo, Owner, Designer Events Cooking School, 4545 Old Reliance Rd., Bryan, TX 77808; (409) 778-9463, Fax (409) 778-1729, E-mail pmvb7th@cy.com.

DOLORES SNYDER GOURMET COOKERY SCHOOL
Irving/February-May, September-November

This private school offers 16 classes/year. Established in 1976. Maximum class/group size: 10 hands-on/16 demo. Facilities: kitchen with 6 work stations. Also featured: wine classes, private instruction, dining in fine restaurants.

EMPHASIS: Entertaining with English tea, French, Asian.

FACULTY: Dolores Snyder, CCP.

COSTS: $40-$50/class. Refund 1 week prior.

LOCATION: Near Dallas.

CONTACT: Dolores Snyder, Owner, Dolores Snyder Gourmet Cookery School, P.O. Box 140071, Irving, TX 75014-0071; (214) 717-4189, Fax (214) 717-4189, E-mail rhsgedl@worldnet.att.com.

HEART OF TEXAS COOKING SCHOOL
September-May

This traveling cooking school sponsored by cookware and food companies offers 30 to 35 demonstration classes per year through county agents, home economics teachers, churches, clubs, and organizations in Texas. Established in 1980. Maximum class/group size: 50-500.

EMPHASIS: Heart healthy, down home, Southwest regional cuisines.

FACULTY: Lenore Angel has written 9 cookbooks, is a former food editor and stylist, and had a cable TV series. Joan Lyons has a degree in food research, was a food and drug agent, and co-authored 2 cookbooks.

COSTS: Sponsors Pioneer Flour Mills, Fiesta Seasonings, and Chantal Cookware pay for the classes.

LOCATION: Throughout Texas.

CONTACT: Lenore Angel, Heart of Texas, 4080 Menger, San Antonio, TX 78259; (210) 497-3151.

HUDSON'S ON THE BEND COOKING SCHOOL
Austin/Year-round
This restaurant conducts one demonstration/participation class the third Sunday of each month. Established in 1993. Maximum class/group size: 20-25. Facilities: Hudson's on the Bend restaurant kitchen. Also featured: sightseeing.
EMPHASIS: Wild game, seafood, smoking, sauces, chef specialties.
FACULTY: Executive Chef Jay Moore, a CIA graduate, and Owner/Chef Jeff Blank, creators of Hudson's on the Bend Gourmet Sauces.
COSTS: $65 per session.
LOCATION: West of the city in a restored rock ranch house.
CONTACT: Shanny Lott, Hudson's on the Bend, 3509 RR 620, Austin, TX 78734; (512) 266-1369, (800) 996-7655, Fax (512) 266-1399. Also: 4304 Hudson Bend Rd., Austin, TX 78734.

THE KITCHEN SHOP AT THE GREEN BEANERY
Beaumont/Year-round
This cafe and cookware store offers about 75 demonstration and limited participation classes a year. Established in 1992. Maximum class/group size: 30 demo/15 hands-on. Facilities: a 20-seat demonstration kitchen area. Also featured: culinary tours.
EMPHASIS: Basics, ethnic and regional cuisines, pastries, specific subjects.
FACULTY: Glenn Watz, chef/owner of the Green Beanery Cafe for 19 years; local and visiting instructors.
COSTS: $20-$35/class. Credit cards accepted.
LOCATION: Beaumont is 90 miles east of Houston.
CONTACT: Glenn Watz, Owner, The Kitchen Shop at the Green Beanery, 2121 McFaddin Ave., Beaumont, TX 77701; (409) 832-9738, Fax (409) 832-9738.

LE PANIER
Houston/Year-round
This cooking school offers approximately 200 demonstration and participation classes a year. Established in 1980. Maximum class/group size: 45 demo/15 hands-on. Facilities: a well-equipped teaching area that offers theater seating, a large overhead mirror, and several cooking and work spaces. Also featured: classes for youngsters, basic techniques series, catering courses.
EMPHASIS: Ethnic cuisines, breads, entertaining menus, cooking for health, main course dishes, pastries and desserts.
FACULTY: Owner/Director LaVerl Daily teaches basic techniques. Most other classes are taught by guest chefs, teachers, and cookbook authors, including Giuliano Bugialli, Giuliano Hazan, Nicholas Malgieri, Hugh Carpenter, and Shirley Corriher.
COSTS: Range from $35-$60 per session, children's classes are $20. Phone reservations are required; payment is due 3 days prior.
LOCATION: Near intersection of Kirby and Holcombe Streets.
CONTACT: LaVerl Daily, Director, Le Panier, 7275 Brompton Rd., Houston, TX 77025; (713) 664-9848, (713) 666-2038, Fax (713) 666-2037.

THE MANSION ON TURTLE CREEK
Dallas/Year-round
This hotel and restaurant offers a demonstration class, special dinner, or both each month. Maximum class/group size: 200. Facilities: usually the Pavilion Ballroom.
EMPHASIS: Specific cuisines.
FACULTY: Chef Dean Fearing co-hosts the classes. Guest chefs have included Wolfgang Puck, Julia Child, and Jacques Pépin.
COSTS: Classes range from $145-$185, including tax. Special room rates begin at $195 per night.
CONTACT: Tamara Deel, The Mansion on Turtle Creek, Food & Beverage Dept., 2821 Turtle Creek Blvd., Dallas, TX 75219; (214) 559-2100, Fax (214) 520-5896.

NATURAL FOODS COOKING SCHOOL
Houston/September-July

This school offers 8 demonstrations per month. Established in 1989. Maximum class/group size: 30. Facilities: Houston locations. Also featured: classes for youngsters, market tours, private classes.

EMPHASIS: Macrobiotic cuisine.

FACULTY: Nutritional counselor Marian Bell has taught for more than 15 years. Guest instructors include Chef Carl of Moveable Feast.

COSTS: $10-$15/class. Cancellations receive a full refund.

CONTACT: Natural Foods Cooking School, 4418 Woodvalley, Houston, TX 77096; (713) 523-0171.

RICE EPICUREAN MARKETS COOKING SCHOOL
Houston/Year-round

This school offers 30 three-session demonstration and participation courses/month. Established in 1990. Maximum class/group size: 45 demo/16 hands-on. Facilities: 1,100-sq-ft classroom with overhead mirror. Also featured: private classes, children's classes and cooking camp, market tours.

FACULTY: Local and out-of-town chefs, including Mark Miller, Emeril Lagasse, Stephen Pyles, Michael Romano, Michael Chiarello.

COSTS: $20-$60/session, $100 for a 3-session course. Payment is required with registration; refund with 72 hours notice.

LOCATION: On a major road in a fine residential area.

CONTACT: Peg Lee, Director, Rice Epicurean Markets, 6425 San Felipe, Houston, TX 77057; (713) 789-6233, (713) 789-5426, Fax (713) 789-9853.

STAR CANYON COOKING SCHOOL
Dallas/Year-round

This restaurant offers 4 demonstration courses per month. Established in 1994. Maximum class/group size: 50. Facilities: demonstration kitchen, classroom, and closed-circuit TV monitors.

EMPHASIS: New Texas cuisine.

FACULTY: Chef Stephan Pyles, a founder of Southwestern cuisine.

COSTS: Demonstration and tasting is $60-$75.

LOCATION: Minutes from Love Field, 5 minutes from downtown.

CONTACT: Marilyn McAdam, Special Project Manager, Star Canyon, 3102 Oak Lawn Ave., No. 144, Dallas, TX 75219; (214) 520-8111, (214) 520-STAR, Fax (214) 520-2667.

WYNDHAM ANATOLE HOTEL'S YOUNG CULINARIANS
Dallas/July-August

This resort hotel offers 5-day summer cooking school for youngsters, ages 8 to 15. Started in 1987. Maximum class/group size: 15. Facilities: The Verandah Club. Also featured: advanced camp for prior attendees.

FACULTY: Verandah Chef Megan Barnes.

COSTS: $175/course.

CONTACT: Stacy Peteet Barry, Wyndham Anatole Hotel, The Young Culinarians, 2201 Stemmons Fwy., Dallas, TX 75207; (214) 761-7290, Fax (214) 761-7353.

VERMONT

CULINARY MAGIC COOKING SEMINARS
Ludlow/June-August, October

The Mobil 4-Star Governor's Inn offers four 3-day weekend hands-on cooking vacations per year. Started in 1992. Maximum class/group size: 16. Also featured: winery tour and visit to an antique cooperative.

EMPHASIS: The Inn's healthy gourmet specialties, presentation.

FACULTY: Deedy Marble, innkeeper and chef since 1982, studied with Madeleine Kamman,

Lorenza de Medici, and Roger Vergé. She and her husband, Charlie, have received 17 national culinary awards and placed fifth in the World Chef Competition.

COSTS: Cost is $370-$428 double, $540-$600 single occupancy, which includes Inn lodging, all taxes and gratuities, most meals, planned activities. The Inn has 8 guest rooms, one suite. Full payment with registration; refund with 90 days notice.

LOCATION: The Okemo Valley, 132 miles from Hartford Airport, 135 miles from Boston, and 230 miles from New York.

CONTACT: Chef Deedy Marble, Culinary Magic Cooking Seminars, The Governor's Inn, Ludlow, VT 05149; (800) 468-3766, (802) 228-8830.

NEW ENGLAND CULINARY INSTITUTE
Essex/Year-round *(See also page 101) (See display ad page 102)*

This private institution offers four culinary vacation weekends/year. Maximum class/group size: 112.

COSTS: Cost is $400, which includes double occupancy lodging; single supplement $75.

LOCATION: Essex is a Burlington suburb.

CONTACT: New England Culinary Institute, 250 Main St., Dept. S, Montpelier, VT 05602; (802) 223-6324, Fax (802) 223-0634.

VIRGINIA

HELEN WORTH'S CULINARY INSTRUCTION
Charlottesville (Ivy)/Year-round

This school founded in Cleveland 1940, NYC 1947, Virginia 1980 offers one-on-one lessons in her fully-equipped kitchen. Established in 1940. Maximum class/group size: 1.

EMPHASIS: Essential skills, cooking equipment, kitchen efficiency, food purchasing, aesthetics, table refinements, wine appreciation.

FACULTY: Helen Worth, Les Dames d'Escoffier member and author of *Cooking Without Recipes* and *Hostess Without Help*, initiated a food and wine appreciation course at Columbia University and Charlottesville's University of Virginia.

COSTS: $75/hour. A $25 nonrefundable deposit is required.

LOCATION: 68 miles west of Richmond, 118 miles from Washington, D.C.

CONTACT: Helen Worth, 1701 Owensville Rd., Charlottesville, VA 22901-8825; (804) 296-4380.

JUDY HARRIS' COOKING SCHOOL
Alexandria/September-June

This school offers more than 65 participation and demonstration classes/year. Founded in 1978. Maximum class/group size: 12 hands-on/20 demo. Facilities: a large, well-equipped kitchen, culinary herb and vegetable gardens. Also featured: private group classes, culinary tours, restaurant trips.

EMPHASIS: International and American regional cuisines, basic techniques, healthy cooking, baking, holiday and entertaining menus.

FACULTY: Judy Harris studied at La Varenne in Paris. Well known guest chefs, teachers, and cookbook authors also teach, including Hugh Carpenter, Jacques Blanc, and Jacques Haeringer.

COSTS: $32-$60/session. Refund with 7 days notice.

LOCATION: Ten miles from Washington, D.C., five miles from Old Town, Alexandria, and Washington National Airport.

CONTACT: Judy Harris, 2402 Nordok Place, Alexandria, VA 22306; (703) 768-3767.

WILLIAMSBURG INN CLASSIC AFFAIR WEEKENDS
Williamsburg/February, March, August

The Colonial Williamsburg Foundation offers four 2-day weekends in 1997 that include lectures and demonstrations by noted chefs and wine experts. Also featured: reception, wine tastings, guest ticket to the Historic Area, tour of the Williamsburg Winery, fitness center, golf.

EMPHASIS: Guest chef specialties.

FACULTY: Has included André Soltner, retired chef of New York City's Lutece restaurant; Gerard Pangaud of Gerard's Place in Washington, DC, and Jimmy Sneed of The Frog and the Redneck in Richmond, VA.

COSTS: From $375-$425, including double occupancy lodging, continental breakfasts, gourmet dinner, and planned activities. The Mobil 5-star Williamsburg Inn, Providence Hall, Colonial Houses & Taverns, and Williamsburg Lodge. Payment with registration. Full refund 5 days prior.

LOCATION: Colonial Williamsburg.

CONTACT: Trudy Moyles, Concierge, Williamsburg Inn Classic Affair Weekends, P.O. Box 1776, Williamsburg, VA 23187-1776; (804) 220-7979, (800) HISTORY.

WASHINGTON

BON VIVANT SCHOOL OF COOKING
Seattle/Year-round

This school founded by Louise Hasson offers three 9-session certificate courses, two 4-session certificate courses, and over 150 demonstration classes/year. Established in 1977. Maximum class/group size: 20 demo. Facilities: home kitchens. Also featured: assistant program for graduates of certificate courses.

EMPHASIS: Basic techniques, foundations of fine cuisine, breads, pastry, seasonal specialties, regional and international cuisines.

FACULTY: Louise Hasson has a BA in education, 20 years of teaching and catering experience, and is a certified member of the IACP. She studied at the Cordon Bleu, Badia a Coltibuono and Regalaeli. Other instructors include Northwest chefs and teachers.

COSTS: $295 for 12 classes, $275 for an additional 12 classes, $469 for 20 classes. Full payment must be made in advance. Credit cards and two installment payments are accepted. No refunds.

LOCATION: Seattle and suburban areas.

CONTACT: Louise Hasson, Bon Vivant School of Cooking, 4925 NE 86th, Seattle, WA 98115; (206) 525-7537, Fax (206) 525-7537.

COOK'S WORLD COOKING SCHOOL
Seattle/Year-round

This cookware store offers 20 demonstration and participation courses per month. Established in 1990. Maximum class/group size: 20 demo/12 hands-on. Facilities: a 400-sq-ft professionally-designed instruction kitchen with overhead mirrors. Also featured: wine instruction, private classes.

EMPHASIS: French, Italian, Indian, Pacific Northwest, gourmet vegetarian, baking, Thai, basics and intermediate series.

FACULTY: Nancie Brecher, IACP member, who studied at the CIA, Peter Kump's, and La Varenne; local chefs and professional food experts.

COSTS: $20-$32/class. Deposit required; refund with 1 week notice.

CONTACT: Nancie Brecher, Cook's World, 2900 NE Blakeley St., Seattle, WA 98105; (206) 528-8192.

EVERYDAY GOURMET SCHOOL OF COOKING
Seattle/September-June

This school founded by Beverly Gruber offers 10- and 18-session hands-on certificate courses and 1- to 6-session participation and demonstration courses. Established in 1988. Maximum class/group size: 12 hands-on certificate/33 hands-on and demo courses. Facilities: large, multi-station work island in Larry's Markets. Also featured: apprentice/assistant program, custom classes, culinary travel.

EMPHASIS: Basic techniques, pastry, kitchen survival skills, ethnic specialties.

FACULTY: Beverly Gruber is a cum laude graduate of Madeleine Kamman's 2-year professional cooking school, an IACP-Certified Teacher, and has taught professionally for more than 5 years.

COSTS: $30-$35/class. Lodging varies with location. A $35-$50 nonrefundable deposit is required with balance due 15 days prior to class. No refunds thereafter.

LOCATION: Larry's Market in Bellevue, Seattle area.

CONTACT: Beverly Gruber, Director, Everyday Gourmet School of Cooking, Larry's Market, 677 120th Ave. NE, #155, Bellevue, WA 98005; (206) 363-1602, (206) 451-2080, Fax (206) 363-1602, E-mail gormayschl@aol.com.

THE GOURMET'S GALLEY/IN SEASON
Friday Harbor/Year-round

This school in a private residence offers 2 to 4 demonstration and participation classes per month. Established in 1991. Maximum class/group size: 12 demo/8 hands-on. Facilities: large commercial kitchen with professional range and refrigerator.

EMPHASIS: Northwest cuisine, seafood, island-grown vegetables, bistro food.

FACULTY: Greg Atkinson, CCP, is executive chef at Friday Harbor House, writes weekly newspaper columns and authored a cookbook.

COSTS: $35-$65/class. Accommodation list on request. Payable with registration.

LOCATION: San Juan Island, northwest of Seattle, 30 minutes by air from SEATAC.

CONTACT: Patricia DeStaffany, The Gourmet's Galley, P.O. Box 578/9 Spring St. W., Friday Harbor, WA 98250; (206) 378-2251.

THE HERBFARM
Fall City/Year-round

This restaurant and herb nursery offers more than 300 demonstration classes and events each year. Established in 1974. Maximum class/group size: 28. Facilities: the open kitchen of The Herbfarm Restaurant, top-rated in the Northwest by the Zagat Guide. Also featured: classes in horticulture, basketry, herbal crafts, herbal medicine, wines of the Pacific Northwest, a Father's Day weekend microbrewery festival, and the Northwest Wine Festival in August.

EMPHASIS: Pacific Northwest cuisines, herbs.

FACULTY: Jerry Traunfeld, The Herbfarm Restaurant chef and co-author of *Seasonal Favorites* from The Herbfarm, and local guest chefs.

COSTS: $27-$45/class. Refund with 48 hours notice. Credit cards accepted.

LOCATION: Situated on 13 rural acres 30 minutes east of Seattle, The Herbfarm has 17 public gardens, an organic garden , and a gift shop.

CONTACT: Ellen Pardee, Cooking School Director, The Herbfarm, 32804 Issaquah-Fall City Rd., Fall City, WA 98024; (206) 784-2222, Fax (206) 789-2279, E-mail herborder@aol.com, URL http://www.theherbfarm.com.

LE GOURMAND RESTAURANT
Seattle/Year-round

This restaurant offers a demonstration class the last Sunday and Monday of each month. Established in 1986. Maximum class/group size: 20.

EMPHASIS: French and Northwest regional cuisine.

FACULTY: Le Gourmand Chef Bruce Naftaly, a founder of the Northwest cuisine movement.

COSTS: $30. Payment must accompany reservation. Refund with 1 week notice.

LOCATION: Near Seattle's Ballard District, 25 minutes from SEATAC airport.

CONTACT: Bruce Naftaly, Chef/Owner, Le Gourmand Restaurant, 425 N.W. Market St., Seattle, WA 98107; (206) 784-3463.

WEST VIRGINIA

LA VARENNE AT THE GREENBRIER
White Sulphur Springs/February-May

The Greenbrier and La Varenne offer eight 5-day cooking vacations/year that feature daily demonstration classes and optional hands-on instruction. Program started 1977. Maximum class/group size: 60. Facilities: large demonstration kitchen with overhead mirror. Also featured: receptions, dinners, resort amenities.

EMPHASIS: Contemporary American and French cuisine, culinary technique.

FACULTY: Anne Willan, founder and director of Ecole de Cuisine La Varenne, food columnist, TV show food host, and author of more than a dozen cookbooks; Greenbrier chefs; guest food personalities.

COSTS: $1,925 includes lodging and meals. Hands-on class is $100 extra. Cost includes lodging. Resort amenities include golf, tennis, horseback riding, skeet and trap, hiking, spa, swimming, concerts, live music, dancing. Deposit required.

LOCATION: The Mobil 5-Star, AAA 5-Diamond resort is in the Allegheny mountains, 15 minutes from the Greenbrier Valley Airport in Lewisburg. Amtrak service is available.

CONTACT: Riki Senn, Cooking School Coordinator, La Varenne at the Greenbrier, 300 West Main St., White Sulphur Springs, WV 24986; (800) 624-6070, Fax (304) 536-7893, URL http://www.greenbrier.com.

WISCONSIN

CREATIVE CUISINE COOKING SCHOOL
Milwaukee/April-December

This school offers 2 or 3 demonstrations per week. Established in 1977. Maximum class/group size: 20. Also featured: private demonstrations, programs for groups.

EMPHASIS: Ethnic cuisines, food processor, pasta, vegetarian, heart-healthy, entertaining menus.

FACULTY: Food consultant and IACP-Certified Member Karen Maihofer studied with Julia Child, James Beard, and Guiliano Bugialli. She is author of 5 cookbooks, including *Foods For Entertaining*, *Holiday Cuisine*, and *Salads & Muffins*.

COSTS: $25-$30/class. No refunds.

LOCATION: Twenty minutes north of downtown Milwaukee; Naples, on Florida's Gulf Coast.

CONTACT: Karen Maihofer, Creative Cuisine Cooking School, P.O. Box 17664, Milwaukee, WI 53217; (414) 352-0975, (941) 947-9879, FL. Also: 20962 Blacksmith Forge, Estero, FL, 33928; (941) 947-9879 (Nov-April).

ECOLE DE CUISINE
Kohler/Year-round

(See also page 219)

This school of professional cooking for the home chef offers intensive weekend participation courses, 5-day classic cuisine courses, demonstration classes, and an annual Food Tour of Paris escorted by Jill Prescott. Established in 1988. Maximum class/group size: 10 hands-on/48 demo. Facilities: a 1,400-sq-ft professionally equipped facility. Also featured: private tours to food producers, restaurants, and special events with notable culinary professionals, customized events or courses for groups.

EMPHASIS: Classic French cuisine, bistro cooking, Italian cuisine, bread baking, pastry, cooking of Provence and Mediterranean, wine course, sauces, stocks, soups.

FACULTY: Jill L. Prescott, professionally trained in Paris in cuisine, pastry and bread baking at Ecole Lenotre, Ecole de Cuisine La Varenne, and Ecole de Cuisine Gastronomie Ritz-Escoffier. Guest chefs.

COSTS: Participation courses $375-$1,200, single demonstration classes start at $35. Lodging is available at resorts and hotels with restaurants, golfing, fishing, cross country skiing, hiking, biking, health spas and a unique shopping mall. Full payment with registration. No refunds, but substitute may attend.

LOCATION: 55 miles from Mitchell International Airport in Milwaukee, in a Wisconsin resort area. About 100 miles from Chicago's Internationall O'Hare Airport.

CONTACT: Jill L. Prescott, Owner, Ecole de Cuisine, 765 H Woodlake Dr., Kohler, WI 53044; (414) 451-9151, Fax (414) 451-9152.

WISCONSIN SCHOOL OF COOKERY
Cascade/Year-round
This school offers 2 demonstrations/month. Established in 1991. Maximum class/group size: 35. Facilities: vary.
FACULTY: Richard Baumann, member of ICP and FWA, writes for *Lake Home* and *Home Gallery* magazines and is the author of *Wisecrackers*.
COSTS: $20/session.
CONTACT: Wisconsin School of Cookery, W6248 Lake Ellen Dr., Cascade, WI 53011-1322; (414) 528-8015.

WYOMING

WYOMING CATTLEWOMEN BEEF COOKING SCHOOL
Cheyenne or Riverton/April
The Wyoming Cattlewomen sponsor a demonstration cooking program in April of even-numbered years. Established in 1993. Maximum class/group size: 75 maximum.
EMPHASIS: Beef cooking techniques.
FACULTY: Chef R. Allen Smith of Peter Kump's New York Cooking School.
COSTS: $25/session.
LOCATION: Little America in Cheyenne or Holiday Inn in Riverton.
CONTACT: Dianne Kirkbride, Wyoming Cattlewomen, 3206 Road 139, Meriden, WY 82081; (307) 246-3242, Fax (307) 246-3397.

AUSTRALIA

ACCOUTREMENT COOKING SCHOOL
Sydney/April-October
This school offers culinary tours and approximately 100 sessions (30 shifts) a year. Established in 1976.
EMPHASIS: Thai, Japanese, Italian, French, Middle Eastern, and Indian cuisines, seafood, salads, desserts, guest chef specialties.
FACULTY: Proprietor Susan Jenkins, who trained at Ecole Lenotre and worked with many chefs; Australian guest chefs; chefs from abroad.
COSTS: US$60/course.
CONTACT: Susan A. Jenkins, Accoutrement Cooking School, 611 Military Road, Mosman, Sydney, NSW 2088 Australia; (61) 2-969-7929 (phone/fax).

AMANO
Perth/Year-round
This cookware store offers 80 to 90 two- to three-session demonstration and participation courses per year. Established in 1982. Maximum class/group size: 16 hands-on/36 demo. Facilities: teaching kitchen with overhead mirror and individual work areas. Also featured: culinary tours to France.
FACULTY: School director is IACP-member Beverly Sprague. Instruction is given by prominent Australian and international culinary professionals.
COSTS: Range from A$40-A$70 per session; series range from A$70-A$160. Full payment required; no refunds.
LOCATION: The beach-side suburb of Perth, Western Australia's capitol.
CONTACT: Beverly Sprague, Director, Amano, 12 Station St., Cottesloe, Perth, 6011 Western Australia; (61) 9-384-0378, Fax (61) 9-385-0379.

ARTE AL DENTE
Sydney/February-April, July-October

This school in a private home offers approximately 10 three-session demonstration courses/year. Established in 1991. Maximum class/group size: 8. Also featured: culinary courses near Rome in spring and fall.

EMPHASIS: Italian home cooking, specializing in Roman cuisine.

FACULTY: Libby Mangosi, a resident of Italy for 26 years.

COSTS: A$170 per course. Culinary tours are approximately A$2,195, which includes lodging.

LOCATION: Five minutes from city center.

CONTACT: Libby Mangosi, Arte al Dente, P.O. Box 277, Double Bay, 2028 Australia; (61) 2-9365-4684, Fax (61) 2-9365-4684.

ARTIS – ARTIS NOOSA COOKING SCHOOL
Noosa Heads/February-October

This restaurant and private cooking school offers a variety of hands-on 3-day events. Established in 1995. Maximum class/group size: 20 hands-on/40 demo. Facilities: modern demonstration kitchen and licensed restaurant. Also featured: tours to local food producers and growers, wine tastings and lectures, tours of So. Australian wineries.

EMPHASIS: Regional and international cuisines.

FACULTY: The restaurant's executive chef and guest chefs.

COSTS: Begin at A$85/day. A center for tourism, Noosa offers a range of hotels and motels. 50% deposit with booking.

LOCATION: On Queensland's Sunshine Coast, about 100 miles north of Brisbane.

CONTACT: David. Horton, ARTIS, Artis Noosa Cooking School, 8 Noosa Dr., Noosa Heads, QLD 4567 Australia; (61) 74 472 300, Fax (61) 74 472 383.

AUSTRALIAN GAS COOKING SCHOOL
Chatswood, Bondi/February-November

This school offers evening courses. Maximum class/group size: 45. Facilities: well-equipped gas kitchen.

EMPHASIS: Basic techniques, guest chef specialties, specific topics.

FACULTY: Head of School Lyn Sykes, author of magazine and newspaper columns with 25 years of food experience; qualified cooking instructors; guest chefs from Australia and abroad.

COSTS: Range from A$35-A$150. Nonrefundable tuition must accompany application. Credit cards accepted. No refunds.

CONTACT: Lyn Sykes, Head of School, Australian Gas Cooking School, Chatswood School, 544 Pacific Highway, Chatswood, NSW 2067 Australia; (61) 2-9414-6663, Fax 61-2-9412-3786. Also: Bondi School, 31 Newland St., Bondi, NSW, 2026 Australia.

BEVERLEY SUTHERLAND SMITH COOKING SCHOOL
Mt. Waverley/Year-round

This school offers 2 to 3 one- to three-session demonstration courses/month. Established in 1967. Maximum class/group size: 25. Facilities: mirrored teaching kitchen that overlooks an herb garden.

EMPHASIS: Instructor and guest chef specialties, ethnic and regional dishes.

FACULTY: Beverley Sutherland Smith, Vice Conseillere Culinaire Chaine des Rotisseurs, contributed to *Epicurean* and *Gourmet*, authored 15 books and won the Australian Gold Book award, food writer for *The Age* newspaper and *New Idea* magazine.

COSTS: Starts at A$45.

LOCATION: Mt. Waverley, a Melbourne suburb, is about 12 miles from city center.

CONTACT: Beverley Sutherland Smith, Beverley Sutherland Smith Cooking School, 29 Regent St., Mt. Waverley, VIC 3149 Australia; (61) 3-9802-5544, Fax 61-39-802-7683.

CLARE GOURMET WEEKEND
Sydney, Clare Valley/May

Clare Valley Winemakers sponsors a 2-day food and wine festival. Also featured: structured vintage tasting, anniversary dinner, and gourmet food day.

EMPHASIS: Showcasing regional food and wine.

COSTS: A$7 admission. Events are priced individually. A$300 for purchase of a glass, this acts as a passport to all wineries. Lodging at bed & breakfasts, retreats, guesthouses, to be booked by individual.

LOCATION: 90 miles north of Adelaide, in South Australia.

CONTACT: Lisa Turnsull, Natl. Media Coordinator, South Australian Tourism Commission, Level 2, 1 York St., Sydney, NSW 2000 Australia; (61) 2-9258-5007, Fax (61) 2-9258-5056, E-mail turnlisa@tourism.sa.gov.au.

THE COOK, THE ARTIST COOKERY SCHOOL
Brisbane/February-December

This school in a private residence offers 3-session demonstration and participation courses. Founded in 1992. Maximum class/group size: 7 hands-on/12 demo. Facilities: professional kitchen in private home. Also featured: escorted overseas cooking tours.

EMPHASIS: Italian, Thai, Asian cuisines, entertaining in warm climates.

FACULTY: Director Roz MacAllan and home economist Leisel Rogers. The school publishes *Food Art*, a quarterly newsletter.

COSTS: A$55/session, A$155/course, payable in advance. No refunds, classes are transferable.

LOCATION: About 3 miles from city center.

CONTACT: Roz MacAllan, MS, The Cook, The Artist Cookery School, P.O. Box 152, Brisbane Market, QLD 4106 Australia; (61) 7-3870-4101, Fax (61) 7-3870-3760. Also: 30 Aston St., Toowong, QLD, Australia.

COUNCIL OF ADULT EDUCATION
Melbourne/Year-round

This educational organization offers more than 70 two- to six-session cooking and catering courses and full-day classes/year. Also featured: workshops, and travel programs on a wide range of topics, including art, crafts, photography, performing arts, recreation, personal development, history, writing, languages, literature, and nature.

EMPHASIS: International cuisines, microwave, breads, vegetarian cookery, catering, wine appreciation.

FACULTY: Cooking instructors and guest chefs.

COSTS: Nonrefundable tuition ranges from A$20-A$40 per session for multi-session courses and from A$60-A$75 for a full-day class. Discounts for seniors and pensioners. Credit cards accepted.

CONTACT: Dianne Berlin, Asst. Director, Council of Adult Education, 256 Flinders Street, Melbourne, VIC 3000 Australia; (61) 3-9652-0611, Fax (61) 3-9652-0793.

DAVID EGAN COOKING SCHOOL
Applecross/Year-round

This school offers 7-session demonstration courses. Established in 1991. Maximum class/group size: 8. Facilities: 750-square-foot room with overhead mirror and individual work spaces.

EMPHASIS: Vegetarian Chinese, Indian, Italian, French, Mexican, and Australian cuisines; eggless cakes and desserts.

FACULTY: A cook and chef since 1968, David Egan has worked in London, France, Switzerland, and as a chef at the Southern Cross Intercontinental Hotel in Melbourne and the Sheraton Perth Hotel.

COSTS: A$140 per course. A videotape of the 7 lessons is A$45, payable by bank draft.

LOCATION: Near public transportation.

CONTACT: David Egan, David Egan Cooking School, P.O. Box 435, Applecross, 6153 Western Australia; (61) 9-337-9514, Fax (61) 9-330-6808.

DIANA MARSLAND COOKING
Armadale/February-December

This school offers 1- to 5-session demonstration and participation courses and culinary tours. Established in 1991. Facilities: large kitchen with overhead mirror.

FACULTY: Diana Marsland studied at Le Cordon Bleu and Leith's School in London.

COSTS: Range from A$40-A$50 per session.

LOCATION: A residential suburb of Melbourne.

CONTACT: Diana Marsland, Diana Marsland Cooking, 24 Barkly Ave., Armadale, VIC 3143 Australia; (61) 3-9509-3971, Fax (61) 3-9509-3971.

ELISE PASCOE COOKING SCHOOL
Darling Point/Spring, Fall, Winter

This school in a private residence offers 50 one- to three-session demonstration and participation courses and weekend workshops per year. Established in 1975. Maximum class/group size: 6 hands-on/20 demo. Facilities: home kitchen with 3 work stations and overhead mirror. Also featured: private and men only classes, culinary tours of Australia.

EMPHASIS: Technique and theory, Mediterranean cuisine, Italian, Thai, and modern Australian cuisines, pastry.

FACULTY: Elise Pascoe is a free-lance food writer, television presenter, and author of 5 cook books. She trained at Le Cordon Bleu and La Varenne in Paris and with Roger Vergé in France and Angelo Paracucchi in Italy.

COSTS: A$170 per 3-session course, single session A$60, workshop A$125. Full payment required with booking. Credit cards accepted.

LOCATION: Sydney's Eastern suburbs, 10 minutes from central Sydney and 30 minutes from Sydney airport.

CONTACT: Elise Pascoe, Managing Director, Elise Pascoe Cooking School, 1/44 Darling Point Road, Darling Point, NSW 2027 Australia; (61) 2-9363-0406, Fax (61) 2-9363-3122.

ELIZABETH CHONG COOKING SCHOOL AND GOURMET TOURS
Melbourne/Year-round

This school offers participation courses. Founded in 1961. Maximum class/group size: 30. Facilities: kitchen with overhead mirror and individual work areas. Also featured: an annual culinary tour to China, Hong Kong, Taiwan.

EMPHASIS: Chinese cuisine.

FACULTY: Elizabeth Chong, author of 7 books, including *The Heritage of Chinese Cooking*, a food writer for periodicals, and recipient of the Prix La Mazille, 1994.

COSTS: Range from A$120-A$195 (single lesson, A$50). A$30 nonrefundable deposit is required with balance due 2 weeks prior.

CONTACT: Elizabeth Chong, Elizabeth Chong Cooking School and Gourmet Tours, 68 Hawthorn Grove, Hawthorn, Melbourne, VIC 3122 Australia; (61) 3-9819-3666, Fax (61) 3-9818-1870.

THE FOODLOVERS WORKSHOP
Melbourne/Year-round

This private school offers more than 20 hands-on and demonstration classes and weekend workshops/year and gourmet tours of Melbourne. Established in 1993. Maximum class/group size: 8.

EMPHASIS: New Australian cuisine, quick and easy meals, entertaining menus, international dishes.

FACULTY: School Director/Instructor Sherry Clewlow is an executive chef who trained in Canada and Australia.

COSTS: Range from A$35-A$65/session to A$250 for a weekend intensive.

CONTACT: Sherry Clewlow, Executive Chef, The Foodlovers Workshop, 6 Sewell St., Box Hill North, Melbourne, VIC 3129 Australia; (61) 3-9899-9292, Fax (61)3-9899-9292.

FRENCH KITCHEN
Armadale/Year-round

This school offers 1- to 5-session demonstration courses, two levels of 5-day hands-on intensives, and local and international guest chefs. Established in 1969. Maximum class/group size: 15 hands-on/25 demo. Facilities: French country-style kitchen, which has an overhead mirror.

EMPHASIS: Classic French cuisine and its modern derivatives.

FACULTY: Director Diane Holuigue studied at Le Cordon Bleu, Ecole Lenotre, and with Paul Bocuse, Julia Child, and Roger Vergé. She was food editor of *Home Beautiful* and *Epicurean* magazines and is food editor of *The Australian Newspaper.*

COSTS: Range from A$40-A$75 per session; A$640 for the 5-day intensive.

LOCATION: A residential suburb of Melbourne.

CONTACT: Diane Holuigue, French Kitchen, 3 Avondale Road, Armadale, VIC 3143 Australia; (61) 3-9509-3638, Fax (61) 3-9500-9650.

GRETTA ANNA SCHOOL OF COOKING
Sydney/Year-round

This school offers 3-session demonstrations and 4-day live-in courses. Established in 1958. Maximum class/group size: 32. Facilities: lecture room, commercial kitchen, shop, herb garden.

EMPHASIS: French, Continental, and Italian cuisines.

FACULTY: Gretta Anna Teplitzky studied at Le Cordon Bleu, has worked in Michelin 3-star restaurants in France, writes cookbooks and for food magazines, and has appeared on TV and radio.

COSTS: Each 3-hour lesson is A$41.

LOCATION: Demonstrations are held at the school, in a Sydney suburb; live-in courses are held in the country, where meals and lodging are provided at a nominal extra cost.

CONTACT: Gretta Anna Teplitzky, Gretta Anna School of Cooking, 67 Clissold Rd., Wahroonga, Sydney, NSW Australia; (61) 2-9487-2425, Fax (61) 2-9487-3847.

H.T.A. COOKERY SCHOOL WITH BARBARA HARMAN
Brisbane/February-December

The Hospitality Training Association offers 1- to 2-session demonstration and 3- to 4-session participation courses. Established in 1996. Maximum class/group size: 16 hands-on/35 demo. Facilities: auditorium with overhead mirror and professional kitchen. Also featured: recipe advice, local food tours.

EMPHASIS: Australian and Asian cuisines, vegetarian recipes, regional foods, entertaining.

FACULTY: Barbara Harman, cookery school head, has 18 year experience and was previously head of the Boral Gas Cookery Service.

COSTS: A$35-A$60 per session, A$60 for visiting chef classes. Payment is due 1 week prior to course, refund up to 1 week prior to start of class.

LOCATION: Five minutes from Brisbane in Fortitude Valley. Near Chinatown and Bistro district.

CONTACT: Barbara Harman, H.T.A. Cookery School with Barbara Harman, Floor 1. K. Tower, 269 Wickham St., Fortitude Valley, Brisbane, QLD 4006 Australia; (61) 7-3257-0377. Also: P.O. Box 906, Fortitude Valley, Brisbane, QLD 4006 Australia.

HARRY'S CHINESE COOKING CLASSES
Sydney/February-December

This school offers three 7-session demonstration courses on a rotating basis. Established in 1977. Maximum class/group size: 20. Facilities: rented halls and schools with kitchen facilities. Also featured: children's classes, private classes, 4-week courses.

EMPHASIS: Basic Chinese, advanced Chinese, and Thai cuisines.

FACULTY: A third generation chef, Harry Quay has more than 30 years experience.

COSTS: A$20/session, includes full meal, payable at class.

CONTACT: Harry Quay, Harry's Chinese Cooking Classes, 47 Bruce Street, Brighton-le-Sands, NSW 2216 Australia; (61) 2-9567-6353.

HOWQUA-DALE GOURMET RETREAT
Mansfield/March-November

This small country house-hotel resort offers a dozen 4-day and weekend participation courses and 3 to 4 six-day gourmet cycling tours of Australia's wine regions per year. Founded in 1977. Maximum class/group size: 12. Facilities: horse-shoe shaped pavilion with specialized equipment. Also featured: fishing, skiing, swimming, horseback riding, bird-watching.

EMPHASIS: Fresh local foods and modern Australian cuisine; wine appreciation.

FACULTY: Co-owner Marieke Brugman, a noted food writer and cooking demonstrator, conducts the classes. Her partner, Sarah Stegley, acts as hostess and instructs students in wine selection.

COSTS: All-inclusive fee is approximately A$600 for the weekend course, A$1,100 for the 4-day course, and A$2,200 for the tour, excluding transport. Deposit is A$200, nonrefundable unless space is filled.

LOCATION: A 40-acre estate on the Howqua River 18 miles from Mansfield, a country town 128 miles northeast of Melbourne.

CONTACT: Marieke Brugman, Howqua-Dale Gourmet Retreat, P.O. Box 379, Mansfield, VIC 3722 Australia; (61) 5-777-3503, Fax (61) 5-777-3896.

MARCEA WEBER'S COOKING SCHOOL
Faulconbridge/Year-round

This private school offers demonstration and hands-on classes. Founded in 1980. Maximum class/group size: 12-14.

EMPHASIS: Macrobiotic and Chinese-herbal cuisine.

COSTS: A$25/class.

LOCATION: An hour from Sydney.

CONTACT: Marcea Weber, Marcea Weber's Cooking School, 56 St. George's Crescent, Faulconbridge, NSW 2776 Australia; (61) 4-751-1680, Fax (61) 4-751-1680.

MARGARET RIVER WINE & FOOD FESTIVAL
Margaret River/November

This annual festival features a 3-day master class sponsored by Amano Cooking School at a wine estate.

CONTACT: Pauline McLeod, Margaret River Wine & Food Festival, Augusta-Margaret River Tourist Bureau, Bussell Highway, Margaret River, 6285 Western Australia; (61) 97-572911, Fax (61) 97-573287.

MELBOURNE FOOD & WINE FESTIVAL
Melbourne/March-April

This annual four-week festival offers 30 events that include master classes, dinners with chefs and vintners, market and vineyard tours, quality produce, award-winning wines, fine restaurants, bistros, and cafes. Established in 1993. Events range from A$20-A$185 each.

CONTACT: Sylvia Johnson, Melbourne Food & Wine Festival, P.O. Box 128, Belgrave, VIC 3160 Australia; (61) 3-9754-2722, Fax (61) 3-9754-2722.

NATURAL FOODS VEGETARIAN COOKING SCHOOL
Sydney/May and November

This school in a private residence offers 2 five-session demonstration and participation courses per year. Established in 1987. Maximum class/group size: 4 hands-on/36 demo. Facilities: private kitchen with 4 work stations.

EMPHASIS: Nutrition, fruits, legumes, wholegrains.

FACULTY: Certified cooking demonstrator Myrna Fenn.

COSTS: A$125.

CONTACT: Myrna Fenn, Natural Foods Vegetarian Cooking School, 20/21 Rangers Road, Cremorne, Sydney, NSW 2090 Australia; (61) 2-9953-7175.

PARIS INTERNATIONAL COOKING SCHOOL
Sydney/Year-round
This school offers 9-session courses that meet once weekly, shorter courses and workshops. Facilities: high school and community center kitchens throughout Sydney. Also featured: classes for youngsters, classes taught in English or French for interstate and foreign visitors.
EMPHASIS: Australian and international cuisines, low calorie, basics, pastries. Workshops cover holiday menus and single subjects.
FACULTY: French native teacher and coordinator Laurent Villoing has 20 years experience in catering, was cookery teacher in a London catering college, and has a monthly radio segment.
COSTS: Range from A$40 for workshops to A$100 for a 9-week course.
LOCATION: Includes Chatswood, Vaucluse, Maroubra, Matraville, North Sydney.
CONTACT: Laurent Villoing, Paris International Cooking School, 21/1 Mosman St., Mosman, NSW 2088 Australia; (61) 2-9969-4687, Fax (61) 2-9969-4687.

ROSA MATTO COOKING SCHOOL
Adelaide/Year-round
Chef Rosa Matto conducts cooking classes that emphasize European and Italian cuisines. Founded in 1989. Maximum class/group size: 20. Also featured: amateur wine making, olive oil production.
COSTS: A$45/class.
LOCATION: Central Adelaide.
CONTACT: Rosa Matto, Rosa Matto Cooking School, 2A Union St., Goodwood, 5034 Australia; (61) 8-344-7419, (61) 8-373-6106, Fax (61) 8-344-3055.

THE SCHOOL HOUSE PORT DOUGLAS COOKING SCHOOL
Port Douglas/May-September
This private school offers once monthly 1-week vacation programs that include five hands-on half-day classes. Established in 1993. Maximum class/group size: 8. Facilities: air-conditioned restaurant kitchen. Also featured: day trip and picnic in Far North Queensland, private wildlife boat tour, swimming in the Mossman Gorge, market visits, sightseeing, tours of food producers.
EMPHASIS: Specialties of noted Australian chefs.
FACULTY: Noted Australian restaurant chefs conduct each session.
COSTS: A$2,150, which includes double occupancy lodging, most meals, planned activities. Lodging is at The School House, which has 5 guest bedrooms, 2 with ensuite. 25% deposit required, balance due 2 months prior.
LOCATION: 50 minutes north of Cairns, in Far North Queensland.
CONTACT: Michael Edwards, The School House, P.O. Box 275, Port Douglas, QLD 4871 Australia; (61) 70-995-573, Fax (61) 70-994-250. Also: 61 Lower Fort St., Millers Point, 2000, Australia.

SYDNEY SEAFOOD SCHOOL
Pyrmont, Sydney/Year-round
This school established by the Fish Marketing Authority offers 5 demonstration and participation courses per week. Established in 1989. Maximum class/group size: 40 hands-on/66 demo. Facilities: a practical kitchen and 66-seat demo auditorium with tiered seating and overhead mirror. Also featured: children's classes, trade program for commercial cooks, gourmet tours in Sydney.
EMPHASIS: Seafood cookery, guest chef specialties, advanced techniques, seafood buying and handling, sushi and sashimi.
FACULTY: Qualified home economists who are seafood specialists; guest chefs.
COSTS: Nonrefundable tuition, payable in advance, ranges from A$38-A$120 per course.
LOCATION: The Sydney Fish Market, a complex that incorporates the Fish Marketing Authority, fish auction hall, fish retail outlets, and a sushi bar.
CONTACT: Vicki Wild, Manager, Sydney Seafood School, Sydney Fish Market, Blackwattle Bay, Pyrmont, NSW 2009 Australia; (61) 2-9660-1611, Fax (61) 2-9552-3632. Also: P.O. Box 247, Pyrmont, NSW 2009 Australia.

TAMARA'S KITCHEN
Melbourne/Year-round

This cookware store and school offers forty 3- to 5-session demonstration and participation courses per year. Founded in 1989. Maximum class/group size: 12. Facilities: large shopfront with 12 workspaces. Also featured: market visits, private classes, children's classes.

EMPHASIS: Breadmaking, pasta, risotto, Italian and Jewish menus, desserts, modern vegetarian, specific subjects.

FACULTY: Tamara Milstein, who trained in Europe and the U.S.

COSTS: A$150-A$220/course. A$50 deposit is required.

CONTACT: Tamara Milstein, Tamara's Kitchen, 490 Tooronga Rd., Hawthorn East, VIC 3123 Australia; (61) 3-9882-1450, Fax (61) 3-9882-3436, E-mail tamara@1access.com.au.

THORN PARK COOKING SCHOOL
Clare Valley/January-March, July-September, November

This country inn offers 2- and 3-day weekend and midweek programs. Founded in 1992. Maximum class/group size: 8-10. Facilities: 2 kitchens, small hotel/inn, commercial. Also featured: wine tours and art classes.

EMPHASIS: A variety of topics, including seasonal and entertaining menus, wines, and specific subjects.

COSTS: Approximately A$350-A$400 includes accommodations for 2 nights. 4-1/2 star accommodations. A$75 deposit, no refund.

LOCATION: South Australia.

CONTACT: David Hay, Co-owner, Thorn Park Country House, College Rd., Sevenhill via Clare, 5453 S. Australia; (61) 8-8843-4304, Fax (61) 8-8843-4296. Also: CMB63, Sevenhill via Clare, 5453, S. Australia.

VICTORIA'S KITCHEN OF CREATIVE COOKING
Mt. Hawthorn/February-September

This school offers 12 to 15 one and two-session demonstration courses a year. Established in 1981.

EMPHASIS: International cuisines, entertaining menus, vegetarian cookery, microwave, beef, poultry and seafood preparation, purchasing, storage, economy.

FACULTY: Food consultant Victoria Blackadder was named *Australian Women's Weekly* Best Cook in Australia in 1981 and established a catering business in 1986. She is author of *Victoria's Kitchen*.

COSTS: Range from A$14-A$20 per session, payable in advance.

LOCATION: The Home Base Exhibition Centre Auditorium, 10 minutes from Perth city center.

CONTACT: Victoria Blackadder, Victoria's Kitchen of Creative Cooking, P.O. Box 278, Mt. Hawthorn, 6016 Western Australia; (61) 9-443-2266.

WILLIAM ANGLISS INSTITUTE
(See also page 111)
Melbourne/Year-round

This career institute offers a variety of participation courses and wine programs.

CONTACT: Chris Coates, Associate Director, William Angliss Institute, 555 La Trobe St., P.O. Box 4052, Melbourne, VIC 3000 Australia; (61) 3-96062111, Fax (61) 3-96701330, URL http://www.angliss.vic.edu.au.

YALUMBA WINERY COOKING SCHOOL
Barossa Valley/April, July, November

This winery offers classes and 1-day weekend workshops. Founded in 1985. Maximum class/group size: 60. Facilities: kitchen, cooking school, dining room, tasting rooms, cellars, petanque pitch. Also featured: winery tours, specialized tastings.

EMPHASIS: Wine and food combinations.

COSTS: Local bed & breakfast details available.

LOCATION: About 40 miles from Adelaide.

CONTACT: Jane Ferrari, Yalumba Winery Cooking School, P.O. Box 10, Angaston, SA 5353 Australia; (61) 8-561-3200, Fax (61) 8-561-3393.

BRAZIL

ACADEMY OF COOKING AND OTHER PLEASURES
Ouro Preto and Paraty/January-April, July-September

Brazilian cuisine expert Yara Castro Roberts conducts 10 one-week vacation programs/year that feature hands-on classes in Brazilian cuisine, including the regional dishes of Amazon, Bahia, and Minas Gerais. Established in 1996. Maximum class/group size: 10-16. Facilities: hands-on classes are held in professional kitchens of 5-star hotels; lectures and videos are presented in conference rooms. Also featured: day trips to islands, sugar cane distillery tour, coffee plantation, underground gold mine, fine dining, market visits, cultural activities, dancing, craft workshops, sports.

EMPHASIS: Brazilian culinary arts and its relationship with the various aspects of Brazilian culture.

FACULTY: Academy founder Yara Castro Roberts is Emmy Award nominee host for PBS-WGBH cooking show series and graduate of the Boston U. Culinary Arts Program. Dr. Moacyr Laterza is a Brazilian history professor. Local chefs and food artisans teach their specialties.

COSTS: $2,950, which includes double occupancy lodging, breakfasts, other meals in fine restaurants, planned activities. Lower rate for non-participant guest. Lodging in individually decorated rooms with private baths. $600 deposit is required, $400 refund 50 days prior, balance of payment due 40 days prior, no refunds thereafter but credit is possible.

LOCATION: January-April: Ouro Preto, in the mountains of Minas Gerais. July-September: Paraty, 140 miles from Rio de Janeiro on Brazil's Emerald Coast.

CONTACT: Yara Castro Roberts, Director/Instructor, Academy of Cooking and Other Pleasures, 256 Marlborough St., Boston, MA 02116 USA; (617) 262-8455, Fax (617) 267-0786, E-mail rroberts@tiac.net.

CANADA

ACADEMIE DE CUISINE
Dollard des Ormeaux/May, June, September-January

This school offers 12 seven-session demonstration and participation courses per year. Established in 1974. Maximum class/group size: 8 hands-on/12 demo. Facilities: 500-square-foot kitchen with overhead mirror. Also featured: five lessons in Mexican gourmet cooking, children's classes, wine tasting, private classes, culinary tours in Canada, the U.S., and Italy.

EMPHASIS: Regional Italian and international cuisines; cake decorating.

FACULTY: Mario Novati received his training in Venice and at the Lewis Hotel Training School in Washington, D.C. He has published 3 cookbooks and hosted a weekly television cooking series in Ottawa and Montreal.

COSTS: Range from C$38-C$50 per session, payable in advance. A nonrefundable 50% deposit is required.

LOCATION: 10 miles from Montreal.

CONTACT: Mario Novati, Academie de Cuisine, 60 Paddington Place, Dollard des Ormeaux, QB H9G 2S4 Canada; (514) 696-6110, (514) 683-0006, Fax (514) 685-7055.

ART OF FOOD COOKING SCHOOL
Toronto/Year-round

This school in a private residence offers 3 weekly demonstration classes. Established in 1991. Maximum class/group size: 10. Also featured: spring culinary tours to Provence, private instruction.

EMPHASIS: International cuisines and special occasion menus.

FACULTY: Merla McMenomy, IACP member, who studied at Peter Kump's New York Cooking School and La Varenne; local guest chefs.

COSTS: C$65, payable with registration.

LOCATION: Mid-town Toronto, 15 miles from Toronto International Airport.

CONTACT: Merla McMenomy, Art of Food Cooking School, 98 Walker Ave., Toronto, ON M4V 1G2 Canada; (416) 975-5088, Fax (416) 960-9337.

BENKRIS COOKING SCHOOL
Calgary/September-June

This cookware store offers 20 one- to six-session demonstration and participation courses/month. Founded in 1979. Maximum class/group size: 24 hands-on/40 demo. Facilities: well-equipped, mirrored kitchen. Also featured: kids camp, wine seminars, private classes, tourist programs, Italian market tours.

EMPHASIS: Ethnic and regional cuisines, breads, wine and food harmonies.

FACULTY: Owner Richard Durvin, senior assistant Becky Monroe, J. Webb Wine Merchants, and more than 20 local chefs and caterers. Guest instructors include Hugh Carpenter, Deborah Madison, Caren McSherry-Valagao.

COSTS: Range from C$45-C$85 per class, full payment upon registration. Cancellations 48 hours prior receive credit.

LOCATION: Calgary, in the downtown Eau Claire Market.

CONTACT: Richard Durvin, Co-Owner, Benkris Cooking School, 200 Barclay Parade S.W., Box 102, Calgary, AB T2P 4R5 Canada; (403) 290-1952, Fax (403) 290-0430.

BIRTHE MARIE'S COOKING SCHOOL
Brampton/September-June

This school offers 1 or 2 demonstrations per week. Established in 1977. Maximum class/group size: 12. Facilities: home kitchen.

FACULTY: Toronto Culinary Guild and IACP-member Birthe Macdonald learned to cook in Denmark.

COSTS: Approximately C$50 per session.

LOCATION: Toronto.

CONTACT: Birthe Macdonald, Birthe Marie's Cooking School, 88 Hillside Dr., Brampton, ON L6S 1A6 Canada; (905) 453-6647.

BONNIE STERN SCHOOL OF COOKING
Toronto/Year-round

This school offers 12 to 15 demonstration and participation classes and series/month. Founded in 1973. Maximum class/group size: 30 demo. Facilities: interchangeable demonstration/participation area with overhead mirror. Also featured: private group classes.

EMPHASIS: Basic techniques, ethnic and regional cuisines, low fat cookery, holiday menus.

FACULTY: Bonnie Stern, a George Brown College graduate, studied with Simone Beck and Marcella Hazan and authored 6 cookbooks, including *Simply Heartsmart Cooking* and *Bonnie Stern's Appetizers*; Linda Stephen, a George Brown College graduate; and guest instructors.

COSTS: C$70/session, C$260/6-week course. A C$45 deposit is required. Cancellations with 1 week notice forfeit C$20.

CONTACT: Bonnie Stern, Bonnie Stern School of Cooking, 6 Erskine Avenue, Toronto, ON M4P 1Y2 Canada; (416) 484-4810, Fax (416) 484-4820, E-mail bonstern@inforamp.net, URL http://www.bonniestern.com.

CAREN'S COOKING SCHOOL
Vancouver/September-May

This school offers 60 three- to four-session evening demonstration courses/year. Founded in 1978. Maximum class/group size: 32. Facilities: overhead mirror, butcher block demonstration table, 8 gas burners. Also featured: wine classes, classes for children, culinary tours to Europe.

EMPHASIS: Italian, French, and Continental Asian cuisine.

FACULTY: Owner Caren McSherry-Valagao, CCP, trained at the Cordon Bleu, the CIA, and The Oriental in Bangkok. She studied with Julia Child, Jacques Pépin, and Paul Prudhomme.

Costs: Range from C$40-C$50 per class. Cancellations with 1 week notice receive credit.
Location: Ten minutes from downtown, near Victoria and Hastings St.
Contact: Caren McSherry-Valagao, Caren's Cooking School, 1856 Pandora Street, Vancouver, BC V5L 1M5 Canada; (604) 255-5119, Fax (604) 253-1331.

CHEZ SOLEIL
Stratford/Year-round
This bed & breakfast offers demonstration and hands-on cooking weekends and 4 classes/month. Established in 1996. Maximum class/group size: 6. Facilities: commercial kitchen. Also featured: wine instruction, classes for youngsters, day trips, market visits, private instruction.
Emphasis: The guests' choice. Can include vegetarian, Tuscan, food styling, food economy, appetizers, breads.
Faculty: Liz Mountain, 13 years chef experience, graduate of George Brown College; Janet Sinclair, graduate and valedictorian of Stratford Chefs School class of 1995.
Costs: C$220 for a weekend, which includes 2 nights lodging, breakfasts, and dinner originating from the day's class. 73-year-old English Tudor cottage bed & breakfast with 3 private rooms and baths. 50% deposit required for weekend programs.
Location: Near Stratford Shakespeare Theatre, 3 minutes from downtown, 90 minutes from the Toronto airport.
Contact: Janet Sinclair, Chez Soleil, 120 Brunswick St., Stratford, ON N5A 3M1 Canada; (519) 271-7404.

COOKING LITE
Montreal/September-May
This school in a private home offers demonstration and participation classes. Founded in 1989.
Emphasis: Healthful foods.
Faculty: Marilyn Flaherty earned a bachelor's degree in Home Economics.
Costs: A 3-class series is C$75.
Location: Pointe Claire, a Montreal suburb.
Contact: Marilyn Calder Flaherty, Cooking Lite, Fish, Beans, Grains & Lentils, 29 Cedar Ave., Pointe Claire, QB H9S 4X9 Canada; (514) 695-4117.

COOKING STUDIO
Winnipeg/Year-round except summer
This private school offers 4- and 6-session demonstration and participation courses. Established in 1994. Maximum class/group size: 14. Facilities: 1,000-foot commercial kitchen. Also featured: children's birthday parties, private dinners, Saturday workshops.
Emphasis: Ethnic and regional cuisines, nutrition, guest chef specialties.
Faculty: Owner Marisa Curatolo earned a degree in Foods and Nutrition from the University of Manitoba, completed Chef Training at the Dubrulle French Culinary School, and studied at Peter Kump's New York School, Ecole LeNotre and Le Cordon Bleu.
Costs: The 4-session course is $149.80, 4-session course is $150; Saturday workshops range from $40-$45 each. Full payment prior to class.
Contact: Marisa Curatolo, Cooking Studio, 3200 Roblin Blvd., Winnipeg, MAN R3R OC3 Canada; (204) 896-5174, Fax (204) 888-0628.

COOKING WITH SUSAN LEE
London/Year-round except April, August, December
This school in a private residence offers 3-hour participation classes. Founded in 1988. Maximum class/group size: 12. Facilities: large family kitchen. Also featured: private lessons.
Emphasis: Seasonal foods, ethnic and regional cuisines, entertaining menus.
Faculty: Home economist and food writer Susan Lee and local chefs.
Costs: Classes are C$45 each. Refund with 2 days notice.

CONTACT: Susan Lee, Cooking with Susan Lee, 1011 Wellington St., London, ON N6A 3T5 Canada; (519) 439-1423.

COOKING WORKSHOP
Toronto/Fall, Winter, Spring

This school offers 15 weekend hands-on workshops/year. Established in 1985. Maximum class/group size: 8-12. Facilities: industrial kitchen of Dufflet Pastries, a cafe/bakery equipped with skylights and double ovens; a private home kitchen. Also featured: wine-tastings, private classes, culinary tours to Italy and Toronto.

EMPHASIS: Italian cuisine, breads, pastry, foundations (soups, stocks, sauces, dressings).

FACULTY: Maria Pace, author of *The Little Italy Cookbook*, studied at La Varenne, with Marcella Hazan and has taught cooking since 1981 and on CTV's "What's Cooking". Baker Paula Bambrick trained at George Brown College. Doris Eisen develops bread and pastry recipes.

COSTS: Range from C$65-C$90. Advance nonrefundable payment is required.

LOCATION: Three blocks west of Bathurst Street in Toronto's "Little Italy"; Dufflet Pastries (787 Queen St. West).

CONTACT: Maria Pace, Owner, Cooking Workshop, 33 Clinton St., Toronto, ON M6J 3H9 Canada; (416) 588-1954.

COOKSCHOOL AT THE COOKSHOP
Vancouver/Year-round

This cookware store offers 22 evening and 28 daytime demonstration and participation classes each month. Founded in 1992. Maximum class/group size: 8-20. Facilities: 1,000-square-foot area with overhead mirror. Also featured: private lessons/functions, wine pairing, nutrition counseling, cookbook author signings, guided tours of wineries and other facilities.

EMPHASIS: Fresh and healthy.

FACULTY: School director, restaurateur, and teacher Nathan Hyam; 60 guest chefs from local hotels and restaurants.

COSTS: Range from C$19-C$199 per class. Payment in advance. Good hotels within 5 minute walk. Payment in advance, full refund with 7 days notice.

LOCATION: Downtown Vancouver.

CONTACT: Peter Haseltine, COOKSCHOOL at the COOKSHOP, 3-555 W. 12th Ave., Vancouver, BC V5Z 3X7 Canada; (604) 873-5683, Fax (604) 876-4391.

DUBRULLE FRENCH CULINARY SCHOOL
Vancouver
(See also page 113)

This private school offers hands-on evening and weekend classes and 2-week techniques courses. Also featured: wine instruction, classes for youngsters, custom classes.

EMPHASIS: Basic and advanced techniques, regional Italian cuisine, Thai cooking, Provencal French cuisine.

COSTS: C$55-C$785. Payment with registration.

CONTACT: Robert Sung, Director of Admissions, Dubrulle French Culinary School, 1522 W. 8th Ave., Vancouver, BC V6J 4R8 Canada; (604) 738-3155, (800) 667-7288, Fax (604) 738-3205.

EMPIRE COOKING SCHOOL
Woodstock

This school offers demonstration classes. Established in 1983.

EMPHASIS: Microwave cookery.

FACULTY: Home economist and cookbook author Charlotte Empringham.

COSTS: C$25 per hour for private classes, C$185 for a group, plus food and mileage.

CONTACT: Charlotte Empringham, Empire Cooking School, 124 John Davies Dr., Woodstock, ON N4T 1N2 Canada; (519) 421-2837.

GREAT COOKS
Toronto/September-June
This cooking school in a pastry shop offers more than 60 afternoon and evening demonstration classes annually. Established in 1989. Maximum class/group size: 24. Facilities: a 600-square-foot teaching kitchen with overhead mirrors. Also featured: wine tastings, group classes, culinary trips.
EMPHASIS: International and regional cuisines, menus for entertaining, vegetarian meals, local and out of town guest chef specialties, wine appreciation.
FACULTY: More than 30 Toronto chefs, including Mark McEwan, Arpi Magyar, Jean Pierre Challet, Martin Kouprie and Dufflet Rosenberg, owner of Dufflet Pastries.
COSTS: Range from C$70-C$100 per class. A 5% discount is granted those who register for 3 classes or more. Credit with 48 hours notice.
LOCATION: Downtown Toronto.
CONTACT: Esther Rosenberg, Great Cooks, 787 Queen Street West, Toronto, ON M6J 1G1 Canada; (416) 703-0388, Fax (416) 703-9832, E-mail 76433.1103@compuserve.com, URL http://www.foodserviceworld.com/dufflet/cooks.htm.

HOLLYHOCK FARM
Cortes Island/May-November
Hollyhock Farm offers more than 70 workshops annually in the practical, creative, spiritual, and healing arts, including cooking. Founded in 1983. Also featured: yoga, meditation, birdwalks, body work, star talks, drawing, painting, dancing, ceramics, photography, writing, kayaking.
EMPHASIS: Open-pit style cooking of seafood and fresh produce.
FACULTY: Includes cook, teacher, and author James Barber.
COSTS: C$900, which includes dormitory or semi-private lodging and meals. C$250 deposit required, balance due on arrival. Cancellations 3 weeks prior receive C$200 credit.
LOCATION: About 100 miles north of Vancouver, Canada.
CONTACT: Oriane Lee Johnston, Program Director, Hollyhock Farm, Box 127, Manson's Landing, Cortes Island, BC V0P 1K0 Canada; (800) 933-6339, Fax (604) 935-6424, E-mail hollyhock@oberon.ark.com, URL http://www.go-interface.com/hollyhock.

THE INN AT BAY FORTUNE
Bay Fortune/May-October
This country inn rated three stars by *Where to Eat in Canada* offers half-day to 2-day participation sessions that feature enhancing tasting ability and understanding of ingredients. Founded in 1992. Maximum class/group size: 4. Facilities: fully-equipped professional kitchen, library, herb gardens. Also featured: wild mushroom picking, herb and vegetable gardening, field trips.
EMPHASIS: Contemporary creative cuisine.
FACULTY: New York Chef Michael Smith, a CIA graduate.
COSTS: Tuition is C$50-C$225/person. Double occupancy country inn rooms are C$120 to C$175 with full breakfast. C$100 deposit required.
LOCATION: 45 minutes from the nearest airport in Charlottetown.
CONTACT: Chef Michael Smith, The Inn at Bay Fortune, Bay Fortune, PEI C0A 2B0 Canada; (902) 687-3745, Fax (902) 687-3540, E-mail innbayft@peinet.ca. Winter phone (860) 296-1348.

LANGDON HALL COUNTRY HOUSE HOTEL
Cambridge
This country house hotel offers occasional cooking classes. Founded in 1991.
FACULTY: Ms. Louise Duhamel and guest chefs.
COSTS: Lodging in the 38-room Langdon Hall, situated on 200 acres of gardens and woodlands. Amenities include a tennis court, croquet, heated pool, exercise facilities.
LOCATION: An hour from Toronto.
CONTACT: Robin Graham, Langdon Hall Country House Hotel, R.R. #33, Cambridge, ON N3H 4RB Canada; (800) 268-1898, (519) 740-2100, Fax (519) 740-8161.

MAMMA WANDA COOKING SCHOOL
Kirkland/May-August

This private school offers demonstration and hands-on classes. Maximum class/group size: 8.
EMPHASIS: Northern Italian cuisine.
LOCATION: 10 minutes from Montreal City.
CONTACT: Wanda Calcagni, Mamma Wanda Cooking School, 1 Viger St., Kirkland, QB H9J 2E4 Canada; (514) 695-0864.

MANOR CUISINE'S CREATIVE COOKING
Pointe Claire/September-June

This private school offers ten 6- to 8-session beginner to advanced courses (7 levels) per year. Founded in 1984.
EMPHASIS: Techniques, creative presentation, boning and butterflying, garnishing, napkin folding, cake decorating, contemporary low fat and low cholesterol cuisine, and fruit, vegetable, and ice sculpture.
FACULTY: Ausma Groskaufmanis, B.Sc.
COSTS: C$23 to C$25 per session. No refunds.
LOCATION: Montreal.
CONTACT: Ausma Groskaufmanis, Manor Cuisine's Creative Cooking, 6 Manor Crescent, Pointe Claire, QB H9R 4S9 Canada; (514) 697-7015.

McCALL'S SCHOOL OF CAKE DECORATION, INC.
Etobicoke
(See also page 115)

This school offers all-day hands-on workshops and 1- to 4-session cake decorating, baking, chocolate, and specialty courses.
COSTS: C$50-C$100/session. Lodging available at area hotels.
CONTACT: Nick McCall, President, McCall's School of Cake Decoration, Inc., 3810 Bloor St. West, Etobicoke, ON M9B 6C2 Canada; (416) 231-8040, Fax (416) 231-9956, E-mail decorate@mccalls-cakes, URL http://www.mccalls-cakes.com.

NATURAL FOODS COOKING SCHOOL
Montreal/Year-round

This school offers The Basics of Healthy and Inter-natural Cooking program, which consists of 6-session participation classes and Saturday workshops. Founded in 1988. Maximum class/group size: 8. Facilities: private kitchen with large gas stove and oven, working island. Also featured: individual instruction and group classes on specific themes.
EMPHASIS: Healthy and low-fat foods, food history, ethnic cuisine, cutting techniques.
FACULTY: Founder Bonnie Tees has 10 years' experience in natural cooking. She was head cook at the Macrobiotic Institute of Switzerland and studied at The Natural Gourmet Cooking School in New York.
COSTS: C$175 for 6 sessions. C$150 is refundable after first class, C$100 after second, no refunds thereafter.
CONTACT: Bonnie Tees, Natural Foods Cooking School, 4865 Harvard, #6, Montreal, QB H3X 3P1 Canada; (514) 482-1508.

NEELAM KUMAR'S NORTH INDIAN CUISINE
Kirkland/January, April, September

This school in a private home offers 4 six-session participation courses/year. Established in 1984. Maximum class/group size: 7. Facilities: a 140-square-foot kitchen.
EMPHASIS: Vegetarian and non-vegetarian Indian cuisine.
FACULTY: Neelam Kumar has a university degree in Home Science.
COSTS: C$100. Refund 1 week prior.
LOCATION: Western Montreal.

CONTACT: Neelam Kumar, Neelam Kumar's North Indian Cuisine, 6 Daudelin St., Kirkland, QB H9J 1L8 Canada; (514) 697-4029.

SHERWOOD INN COUNTRY COOKING WEEKENDS
Port Carling/November-January, March, May
This country inn offers hands-on theme weekends. Founded in 1992. Also featured: wine discussion and restaurant kitchen tour.
FACULTY: The chefs of Sherwood Inn.
COSTS: Cost ranges from C$338 to C$427, depending on accommodation, and includes lodging, most meals, health club, mountain biking, and cross country skiing equipment in the winter. Lodging: the CAA/AAA 4-Diamond Sherwood Inn.
LOCATION: 2 hours north of Toronto.
CONTACT: Philip Meyer, Sherwood Inn Country Cooking Weekends, P.O. Box 400, Port Carling, ON P0B 1J0 Canada; (705) 765-3131, Fax (705) 765-6668.

CENTRAL AMERICA

CHAA CREEK SCHOOL OF CARIBBEAN COOKERY
San Ignacio/June-December
The Chaa Creek hotel offers 1-week hands-on cooking vacations. Founded in 1993. Maximum class/group size: 10. Facilities: The Chaa Creek hotel kitchen, which has 4 work stations. Also featured: market visits, a canoe trip, a class in a native kitchen, visits to the Mayan sites of Cahal Pech and Xunantunich, shopping in Guatemala.
EMPHASIS: Belizean, Mexican, and Caribbean cuisines.
FACULTY: Bill Altman, a chef and restaurant owner since 1972, has taught cooking in Washington and Arizona and has more than 20 years of experience with tropical cuisines.
COSTS: Cost is $1,500, which includes meals, ground transport, planned activities, and double occupancy lodging at Chaa Creek Cottages. Single supplement is $205. A $350 deposit is required with balance due 90 days prior to arrival. Full refund less $50 for cancellations 90 days prior.
LOCATION: On the Macal River, 8 miles from San Ignacio, in western Belize.
CONTACT: Bill Altman, Chef, Chaa Creek School of Caribbean Cookery, P.O. Box 53, San Ignacio, Cayo, Belize, Central America; (501) 92-2037, Fax (501) 92-2501, E-mail chaa_creek@btl.net, URL http://www.belizenet.com/chaacreek.html.

CHINA

ORIENTAL FOOD MARKET AND COOKING SCHOOL, INC.
China/July   *(See also page 59)*
This food market conducts an annual 19-day culinary and cultural tour to China in July. Maximum class/group size: 15.
COSTS: $4,500, which includes airfare.
CONTACT: Pansy Luke, Oriental Food Market and Cooking School, 2801 West Howard St., Chicago, IL 60645 USA; (312) 274-2826.

ENGLAND

ACORN ACTIVITIES
Herefordshire/April, June, September, November
This activity holiday provider conducts a 2-day gourmet cooking course. Founded in 1989. Maximum class/group size: 12. Facilities: a well-equipped kitchen with individual work areas and cookers. Also featured: study tours, courses, and programs relating to air sports, water sports, ball sports, horseback riding, hunting, shooting, falconry, fishing, motor sports, arts & crafts, music, and languages.

EMPHASIS: Low-fat gourmet cooking.

FACULTY: A professional chef who has appeared on the BBC2 Food and Drink program.

COSTS: Tuition is £100. Accommodations, including breakfast, range from farmhouses and cottages at £20 per night to luxury hotels at £95 per night. A £20 deposit is required with balance due/refund granted 60 days prior.

LOCATION: Herefordshire, near the Welsh border, 120 miles (a 3-hour train ride) west of London.

CONTACT: Charles Cordle, Managing Director, Acorn Activities, P.O. Box 120, Hereford, HR4 8YB England; (44) 1432-830083, Fax (44) 1432-830110.

AGA WORKSHOP
Buckinghamshire/Year-round except August and December

This school in a private residence offers about 50 one- and two-day Aga demonstration workshops per year. Maximum class/group size: 20. Facilities: Watercroft, Mary Berry's home.

EMPHASIS: Using the Aga cooker for grilling and frying, saving fuel, fresh herbs and vegetables, entertaining and holiday cookery, specialized equipment.

FACULTY: Mary Berry studied at the Paris Cordon Bleu and the Bath College of Home Economics and has a City and Guilds teaching qualification. Author of 20 cookery books, she was cookery editor of *Ideal Home Magazine* and contributes to *Family Circle*.

COSTS: One-day (two-day) workshop is £76 (£146), which includes lunch and VAT. Group bookings of 4 or more for 1 day are £71 per person. A list of nearby bed & breakfasts is provided. Payment with booking; refund with 4 weeks notice.

LOCATION: Watercroft, situated on 3 acres of informal garden, is 30 miles from London and Heathrow airport, accessible by railway from London Marylebone.

CONTACT: Mary Berry, Aga Workshop, Watercroft, Church Rd., Penn, Buckinghamshire, HP10 8NX England; (44) 1494-816535, Fax (44) 1494-816535.

THE BATH SCHOOL OF COOKERY
Bath, Somerset/Year-round

Bassett House, a listed grade II 18th-century country house offers more than thirty 1-day, weekend, 4-day, and 4-week demonstration and participation courses per year. Founded in 1988. Maximum class/group size: 10. Facilities: large kitchen equipped with Aga cookers, microwaves, and modern appliances and a smaller kitchen for vegetable/salad preparation, pastry, and chocolate work. Also featured: tennis, cycling, croquet, walking.

EMPHASIS: Everyday French, basic to advanced food preparation and technique, creative cuisine, seasonal, holiday, and special occasion dishes, ethnic menus.

FACULTY: Sallie Caldwell studied in France and the Far East, operated a catering firm and restaurant in Bath, and was principal teacher of a cookery school.

COSTS: Resident (non-resident) tuition, which includes meals, is £420 (£360) for the 4-day courses, £1,490 (£1,290) for the 4-week Master Course; day demonstrations are £55 each, weekends are £210. Bassett House is situated in the Lixpley Stoke Valley on 6 acres of herb, fruit, and vegetable gardens with direct access to the Kenner and Avon canal and the River Avon. Deposit (£150 for 4-week course, £50 for others) is required with balance due/refund granted 6 weeks prior.

LOCATION: A 70-minute train ride from London.

CONTACT: D.K.S. Caldwell, Director, The Bath School of Cookery, Bassett House, Claverton, Bath, Somerset, BA2 7BL England; (44) 1225-722498, Fax (44) 1225-722980.

BONNE BOUCHE
Devon/Year-round

(See also pages 118, 284)

Bonne Bouche offers week-long hands-on cooking courses and gourmet tours in England. Maximum class/group size: 6. Also featured: dining at private manors and Michelin-star restaurants, other food related activities, customized programs.

EMPHASIS: Classical, regional, and modern cuisines of Europe and Asia.

COSTS: £100-£1,200, which includes lodging and meals. Lodging: private room and bath in Bonne

Bouche's 16th-century Devon longhouse, which offers leisure activities and a fitness center. A 25% deposit is required.

CONTACT: Anne Nicholls, Program Coordinator, Bonne Bouche, Lower Beers House, Brithem Bottom, Cullompton, Devon, EX15 1NB England; (44) 884-32257, Fax (44) 1884-32257.

BUTLERS WHARF CHEF SCHOOL
London/Year-round   *(See also page 118)*

This private vocational school offers a range of demonstration classes and weekend courses.

CONTACT: Mr. John Roberts, Director, Butlers Wharf Chef School, Cardamom Bldg., 31 Shad Thames, London, SE1 2YR England; (44) 171-357-8842, Fax (44) 171-403-2638.

COOKERY AT THE GRANGE
Frome/Year-round   *(See also page 119)*

This private school offers 10 weekend and 5-day hands-on courses in addition to its certificate program. Established in 1981. Maximum class/group size: 14. Also featured: wine instruction.

EMPHASIS: European and international cuisines, herbs, wine tasting.

COSTS: All-inclusive rates range from £275 for the weekend to £480 for the 5-day program.

CONTACT: Jane and William Averill, Cookery at The Grange, Whatley, Frome, Somerset, BA11 3JU England; (44) 1373-836579, Fax (44) 1373-836579, URL http://www.hi-media.co.uk/grange-cookery.

COOKERY HOLIDAYS FOR CHILDREN
Chichester, West Sussex/August

The Young Cooks Club encourages young people to learn more about food through 5-day summer cooking and activity vacations for 11 to 16-year-olds. Established in 1983. Maximum class/group size: 20. Also featured: restaurant tour, competitions, swimming, tennis, riding, organized sports.

EMPHASIS: Breads, casseroles, roasts, stir-fry, fish, sauces, meringue, pastries.

FACULTY: Food writers Sophie Grigson, Janet Laurence, and Rosemary Moon.

COSTS: Cost of £280 includes meals, lodging, planned activities, and lunch for a guest the last day of class. Lodging at a 16th century farmhouse. A £80 deposit is required, refundable only if space can be filled.

LOCATION: 70 miles from London.

CONTACT: Anna Best, Cookery Holidays for Children, Bridge Courtyard, Donnington, Chichester, West Sussex, PO20 7PP England; (44) 1243-779239, Fax (44) 1243-784241.

THE CORDON VERT COOKERY SCHOOL
Altrincham/Year-round   *(See also page 119)*

The Vegetarian Society UK offers 8- to 10- weekend and 30 day courses on a variety of vegetarian topics in addition to its diploma course. Established in 1984.

COSTS: Weekend residential (non-residential) courses range from £180-£190 (£150-£160); day courses are £45, which includes lunch.

CONTACT: Heather Mairs, Cordon Vert Cookery School, The Vegetarian Society, Parkdale, Dunham Road, Altrincham, Cheshire, WA14 4QG England; (44) 61-928-0793, Fax (44) 61-926-9182, E-mail vegsoc@vegsoc.demon.co.uk, URL http://www.veg.org/veg/orgs/vegsocuk/.

CREATIVE COOKERY SCHOOL AT OLD HALL LEISURE
Chester/Year-round except January

This school in a renovated turn-of-the-century farmhouse offers 1-day and once monthly 3-day weekend mainly demonstration courses. Founded in 1990. Maximum class/group size: 10. Facilities: the well-equipped teaching kitchen of Old Hall Leisure. Also featured: clay pigeon shooting, swimming, tennis, golf, classes for youngsters, wine instruction, private classes, market visits.

EMPHASIS: Mediterranean, Thai, and Indian cuisines.

FACULTY: Su Bloomberg graduated from the California Culinary Academy and worked in several restaurants, including her own in St. Annes on Sea. Guest chefs include Italian vegetarian food writer Ursula Ferrigano.

COSTS: Tuition, which includes VAT, is £43 for the 1-day class, £115 for the weekend course, which includes meals, exercise classes, and use of facilities. Nightly lodging at Old Hall Leisure ranges from £25-£50, including VAT. All rooms have ensuite shower or bath. Amenities include indoor and outdoor pools, tennis courts, gymnasium, therapy center, beauty spa, and Cafe-Bar. Full payment required with booking.

LOCATION: The Cheshire countryside, less than 5 minutes from Chester and 30 minutes from Manchester airport.

CONTACT: Su Bloomberg, Principal, Creative Cookery School at Old Hall Leisure, Old Hall Leisure, Aldford Rd., Huntington, Chester, Cheshire, CH3 6EA England; (44) 1244-350873, Fax (44) 1244-313785.

CUISINE ECLAIREÉ
Marrick, North Yorkshire/Year-round

This culinary travel company offers 1-day to 1-week vacations that include daily hands-on cooking classes. Established in 1994. Maximum class/group size: 8. Facilities: the restaurant's country kitchen.

EMPHASIS: Vegetarian, appetizers, seasonal and holiday specialties.

FACULTY: Elaine Lemm, Chef de Cuisine and owner, studied at the Ritz Escoffier in Paris.

COSTS: Range from £50-£295, which includes shared lodging and meals. National Trust Stately Homes, including Old Vicarage Farm, overlooking the Swale Valley, and Beningbrough Hall, 30 minutes from York. 10% nonrefundable deposit required.

LOCATION: Marrick, North Yorkshire. Programs are also offered in Sweden and Italy.

CONTACT: Elaine M. Lemm, Owner, Cuisine Eclaireé, 5, the Poplars, Newton-on-Ouse, York, Y06 2BL England; (44) 1347-848557, (44) 1904-448963, Fax (44) 1347-848557.

EARNLEY CONCOURSE
Chichester, Sussex/Year-round

This residential center for courses and conferences established by the Earnley Trust, Ltd. educational charity offers 15 weekend demonstration and participation courses annually. Established in 1975. Maximum class/group size: 12. Facilities: fully-equipped kitchen workshop, which has demonstration and dining areas.

EMPHASIS: Indian and Chinese cookery, cooking for health, vegetarian dishes, advanced techniques, special occasion dishes.

FACULTY: Includes Savita Burke, Deh-Ta Hsiung, Steven Page, and Mary Whiting.

COSTS: Each course is priced from £140, which includes lodging, and meals. Nonresident tuition is £97, which includes lunch. The cost of ingredients is additional. Amenities include art & craft studios, computer room, heated pool, squash court, gardens. A deposit is required with balance due 28 days prior; cancellations 28 days prior receive 50% deposit refund.

LOCATION: A rural setting in West Sussex, 6 miles south of Chichester.

CONTACT: Owain Roberts, Earnley Concourse, Earnley, Chichester, West Sussex, PO20 7JL England; (44) 1243-670392, Fax (44) 1243-670832, E-mail earnley@interalpha.co.uk.

FRANCES KITCHIN COOKING COURSES
Somerset/January -December

This school in a private home offers 1-day demonstration courses alternate months and a 3-day Cooking and a Candlelit Dinners course. Founded in 1987. Maximum class/group size: 10. Facilities: large kitchen in a country house. Also featured: flower arranging courses, color and style.

EMPHASIS: English, French, Italian, and Indian cuisine.

FACULTY: Frances Kitchin, a qualified home economist and chef who has lectured at Strode College for 21 years, is a freelance writer and author of 2 cookbooks, and has a weekly cookery spot on radio, (BBC).

COSTS: Cooking and Candlelit Dinners are £210, which includes breakfasts, dinners and lodging. Day courses are £20, including lunch. A nonrefundable £50 deposit is required.

LOCATION: Stoney Mead, a country house, is 12 miles from Taunton, on the railway line from Paddington (London).

CONTACT: Frances Kitchin, Frances Kitchin Cooking Courses, Stoney Mead, Curry Rivel, Langport, Somerset, TA10 0HW England; (44) 1458-251203, Fax (44) 1458-251203.

HARROW HOUSE
East Sussex/Year-round   *(See also page 120)*

This school offers half-day to 1-week demonstration and participation courses. Maximum class/group size: 66. Also featured: winery tours and instruction, classes for youngsters, day trips, visits to food producers, dining in fine restaurants and private homes, sightseeing.

EMPHASIS: International and British cuisine, sugarcraft.

COSTS: Lodging begins at £75/week.

CONTACT: Harrow House, 1 Silverdale Road, Eastbourne, BN20 7AA England; (44) 1323-730851, Fax (44) 1323-416924, E-mail harrowhouse@mailhost.lds.co.uk.

HINTLESHAM HALL
Suffolk/Year-round

This luxury country hotel offers approximately 20 demonstration classes a year. Maximum class/group size: 12.

EMPHASIS: Vegetarian and fish dishes, seasonal menus, herb cookery, sugarcraft, specific topics.

FACULTY: Hintlesham's Chef Alan Ford and guest instructors.

COSTS: Each class is £48. Nightly lodging, which includes continental breakfast and VAT, begins at £85 single, £110 double occupancy. Hintlesham Hall, situated on 175 acres, offers golf, tennis, snooker, trout fishing, clay pigeon shooting, horseback riding, pool, and spa.

LOCATION: About five miles west of Ipswich, Suffolk, an hour drive from Stansted Airport, and an hour train ride from London.

CONTACT: Claire Hills, Hintlesham Hall, Hintlesham, Ipswich, IP8 3NS England; (44) 1473-652268, (44) 1473-652334, Fax (44) 1473-652463.

JILL PROBERT'S COOKERY DEMONSTRATION COURSES
Cheshire/Spring and Fall

This school in a private residence offers 6-session intermediate and advanced courses. Established in 1983. Maximum class/group size: 14. Facilities: farmhouse kitchen dating from 1910.

EMPHASIS: Dinner party/freezer cookery and food processor techniques.

FACULTY: Jill Probert, a magazine and newspaper food editor, is a member of the Guild of Food Writers and the Institute of Home Economics.

COSTS: Each course is £40.

LOCATION: 5 miles from Chester.

CONTACT: Jill Probert, Jill Probert's Cookery Demonstration Courses, Hillfield, Barton Rd., Farndon, Nr. Chester, Cheshire, CH3 6NL England; (44) 1829-271469.

LA CUISINE IMAGINAIRE VEGETARIAN COOKERY SCHOOL
Hertfordshire/Year-round

This private school offers one- and half-day demonstration courses and a 4-day practical certificate course. Founded in 1989. Maximum class/group size: 6 hands-on/12 demo. Facilities: a well-equipped kitchen and lounge in St. Albans. Also featured: private instruction.

EMPHASIS: Vegetarian cuisine, including quick meals, dinner parties, international dishes.

FACULTY: Director and instructor Roselyne Masselin is a food writer, cookbook author, qualified home economist, and runs Catering Imaginaire.

COSTS: One-day London course is £50, half-day St. Albans course is £30, four-day course is £330; all include lunch and notes. Full payment is required for short courses, deposit for four-day courses; cancellations receive course credit where possible.

LOCATION: Shepherds Bush in London; St. Albans, Hertfordshire, 30 minutes from Heathrow airport and central London.
CONTACT: Roselyne Masselin, La Cuisine Imaginaire Diploma & Day Courses, 18 Belmont Ct., Belmont Hill, S. Albans, Hertfordshire, AL1 1RB England; (44) 1727-837643, Fax (44) 1727-847646.

LA PETITE CUISINE
London/Year-round
This private school offers 6-session master classes and fortnightly demonstrations. Established in 1977. Maximum class/group size: 6-28. Facilities: bulthaup's kitchen studio (master classes) and a small theatre in Divertimenti cookware store (demonstrations). Also featured: private hands-on 5-lesson courses in Lyn Hall's home teaching kitchen.
EMPHASIS: Modern gourmet cuisine, French, Italian, Chinese, Thai, guest chef specialties.
FACULTY: Owner Lyn Hall, BA, MFCA holds certificates in wine, bread, cake decorating, and butchery, and is an Olympic Culinary Gold Medalist. Guest chefs include British cookbook writers and TV chefs.
COSTS: Master class series is £495, demonstrations are £28, private courses are £750 for five lessons.
LOCATION: South Kensington in French London, Divertimenti in Chelsea, bulthaup on Wigmore St.
CONTACT: Lyn Hall, La Petite Cuisine, 21 Queen's Gate Terrace, London, SW7 5PR England; (44) 1715-846841, Fax (44) 1712-250169. Also: Divertimenti, 139 Fulham Rd., Chelsea, London SW3 6SD England; (44) 171-581-8065, Fax (44) 171-823-9429.

LE CORDON BLEU
London/Year-round
(See also page 120) (See display ad page 127)
This private school acquired by Le Cordon Bleu-Paris in 1990 offers daily half-day demonstrations, 3- to 5-day gourmet hands-on sessions, evening classes, and 1-month initiation courses. Also featured: children's workshops, wine classes, cheese courses, guest chef demonstrations.
EMPHASIS: Intensive and comprehensive culinary cuisine and pastry courses.
COSTS: From £180-£385. Lodging information available. Payment in full confirms registration.
CONTACT: Le Cordon Bleu, Enrollment Office, 114 Marylebone Lane, London, W1M 6HH England; (44) 171-935-3503, (800) 457-CHEF, Fax (44) 171-935-7621, URL http://www.cordonbleu.edu.

LEITH'S SCHOOL OF FOOD AND WINE
London/September-August
(See also page 121)
This private school offers 1-week and 4-week holiday courses; 1-week fish, dinner party, and Christmas cooking courses; 10-session beginner and advanced evening courses, Saturday demonstrations, 5-session Certificate in Wine course, specialty wine and food classes. Maximum class/group size: 16-40. Also featured: private instruction.
COSTS: Basic Certificate course is £1,370, 10-session courses are £355, demonstrations are £40, Wine Certificate course is £192. Housing list provided.
CONTACT: Judy Van DerSande, Registrar, Leith's School of Food and Wine, 21 St. Alban's Grove, London, W85 BPX England; (44) 171-229-0177, Fax (44) 171-937-0257.

THE MANOR SCHOOL OF FINE CUISINE
Widmerpool/Year-round
(See also page 121)
This private school offers a 5-day Foundation course, 4-day Entertaining course, theme weekends, and day and evening courses. Also featured: water sports, clay pigeon shooting, horseback riding, golf.
EMPHASIS: Healthy eating, holiday cookery, seasonal menus, Aga cookery, specific topics.
COSTS: Inclusive of VAT, tuition is £390 resident (£295 nonresident) for Foundation course, £330 (£285) for Entertaining course, £130 for weekend courses. Lodging at the Manor. £50 nonrefundable deposit required, balance due/refund granted 6 weeks prior.

CONTACT: The Manor School of Fine Cuisine, Old Melton Road, Widmerpool, Nottinghamshire, NG12 5QL England; (44) 1949-81371.

MILLER HOWE COOKERY COURSES
Cumbria/Spring and Fall
This country house and school offers residential 5-day courses. Established in 1971. Maximum class/group size: 15. Facilities: the main restaurant kitchen.
EMPHASIS: Fresh ingredients, starters, main courses, sweets, tea accompaniments, sauces and garnishes.
FACULTY: Miller Howe chef-proprietor John Tovey, a graduate of Le Cordon Bleu, cookbook author, and TV chef.
COSTS: All-inclusive cost is £400 (includes VAT). Miller Howe, an Edwardian country house, has three lounges, a conservatory overlooking the lake, and 13 centrally-heated private bedrooms. Refund for cancellation only if space is filled.
LOCATION: In The Lakes district above Lake Windermere near the Langdale Pikes and accessible to London by train.
CONTACT: John J. Tovey, Miller Howe Cookery Courses, Windermere, The English Lakes, Cumbria, LA23 1EY England; (44) 15394-42536, Fax (44) 15394-45664.

RAYMOND BLANC'S LE PETIT BLANC ECOLE DE CUISINE
Oxford/October-April   *(See display ad page 242)*
This 5-day cooking vacation school offers hands-on stage 1, stage 2, and stage 3 classes. Founded in 1991. Maximum class/group size: 8. Facilities: individual work areas in the restaurant kitchen.
EMPHASIS: Contemporary French cuisine, including appetizers, fish and vegetables, meat and vegetables, pastries.
FACULTY: Chef Raymond Blanc owns and operates Le Manoir. Sessions are taught by head chef Clive Fretwell.
COSTS: Course cost of £1,150 includes all meals, service, VAT, and lodging. Le Manoir aux Quat' Saisons, which has the highest classification of Relais & Chateaux. Lodging is free for non-cooking guests. A £150 deposit is required with balance due four weeks prior. No refunds unless space can be filled.
LOCATION: Seven miles from Oxford and 40 miles from London.
CONTACT: Judy Ebrey, Owner Cuisine International, P.O. Box 25228, Dallas, TX 75225 USA; (214) 373-1161, Fax (214) 373-1162, E-mail CuisineInt@aol.com, URL http://www.-iglobal.net/cuisineint.

SQUIRES KITCHEN SUGARCRAFT SCHOOL
Farnham, Surrey/Year-round   *(See also page 122)*
This private school offers a 1-hour to 3-day demonstration and participation courses. Maximum class/group size: 12 hands-on/35 demo. Also featured: classes for youngsters, private instruction.
CONTACT: Beverley Dutton, Course Coordinator, Squires Kitchen Sugarcraft School of Cake Decoration, 3 Waverly Lane, Farnham, Surrey, GU9 8BB England; (44) 1252-734309, Fax (44) 1252-714714.

TANTE MARIE SCHOOL OF COOKERY
Surrey/Year-round   *(See also page 122)*
This private school offers certificate courses thrice yearly, 3- to 5-day hands-on courses, 1-day theme demonstrations. Maximum class/group size: 48. Also featured: wine instruction, private group demonstrations.
EMPHASIS: Basic and advanced skills, wine appreciation, specific subjects.
COSTS: 10% of course fee.
CONTACT: Margaret A. Stubbington, Registrar, Tante Marie School of Cookery, Woodham House, Carlton Rd., Woking, Surrey, GU21 4HF England; (44) 1483-726957, Fax (44) 1483-724173.

EUROPE

ANNEMARIE VICTORY ORGANIZATION, INC.
St. Tropez, Siena/Year-round

This travel company that conducts and represents deluxe culinary tours and cooking school programs in Europe offers Provence Cooking School at Chateau de la Messardiere in St. Tropez, A Gourmet Experience in Paris, and Relais Borgo in San Felice, Siena. Established in 1978. Maximum class/group size: 15.

EMPHASIS: Deluxe culinary travel programs.

FACULTY: Austrian-born Annemarie Victory studied at the Sorbonne, attended the hotel and interpreter school in Switzerland, and currently hosts the Discovery Channel's TV series, *World Class Cuisine*.

COSTS: $500 deposit required.

LOCATION: Europe, including France, Italy.

CONTACT: Annemarie Victory, Annemarie Victory Organization, Inc., 136 East 64 St., New York, NY 10021 USA; (212) 486-0353, Fax (212) 751-3149.

CAPITAL TOURS LTD.
Italy and France/Spring and Fall

This tour operator offers monthly 1-week vacations that include 5 daily hands-on classes. Founded in 1973. Maximum class/group size: 12-20. Also featured: market visits, excursions to nearby towns.

EMPHASIS: Regional cooking of Tuscany, Umbria, and the Cote d'Azur (Cuisine Du Soleil with Chef Roger Vergé).

FACULTY: Chefs from various restaurants.

COSTS: C$2,000, which includes lodging and meals. Farm estates with modern conveniences. C$500 deposit required 60 days prior, balance due 45 days prior.

LOCATION: In Italy: Florence and Perugia. In France: Mougins, 5 miles north of Cannes.

CONTACT: Carlo Bertasi, Capital Tours Ltd., 427 Preston St., #204, Ottawa, ON K1S 4N3 Canada; (613) 230-1955, Fax (613) 230-8811.

CAROLINE HOLMES CAPITAL TOURS LTD.
England and France/Year-round

Caroline Holmes offers 1-day demonstration courses and 1-week tours that visit local food producers and herb gardens in Northern France and the Loire Valley, weekends in conjunction with Hilton Hotels. Founded in 1983. Maximum class/group size: minimum 10. Also featured: tailored itineraries for groups.

EMPHASIS: Growing, maintaining, and using herbs: East Anglian specialties.

FACULTY: Caroline Holmes holds a Certificate in Gourmet Cookery and City and Guilds Horticulture. She works with the Museum of Garden History, Hintlesham Hall, Hilton Hotels, BBC *Good Food* magazine and is chairman of the Herb Society.

COSTS: One-day courses begin at £40; 1-week courses, U.K.-based, from £150 excluding accommodations; French-based from £330; UK weekends from £150. Simple to 4-Star by agreement. 10% deposit on booking (non-refundable).

LOCATION: London, Ipswich, Portsmouth in England; Paris, France.

CONTACT: Mrs. Susan Standley, Caroline Holmes - Gourmet Gardening, Denham End Farm, Bury St. Edmunds, Suffolk, IP29 5EE England; (44) 1284-810653, Fax (44) 1284-810653.

CHARLOTTE-ANN ALBERTSON'S COOKING SCHOOL
(See also page 207)　　　　　　　　　　　　　　　**Locations in Europe**

Charlotte-Ann Albertson offers European culinary vacations that include demonstrations, market and city tours, and winery visits. Maximum class/group size: 14.

COSTS: $3,000, which includes airfare from New York, hotel lodging, most meals, and planned excursions.
CONTACT: Charlotte-Ann Albertson, P.O. Box 27, Wynnewood, PA 19096-0027 USA; (610) 649-9290, (813) 642-6550, Fax (610) 649-9290.

CUISINE INTERNATIONAL
Year-round　　　　　　　　　　　　　　　*(See display ad above)*
Cuisine International represents cooking schools and culinary tours in Italy, France, Spain, and England. Established in 1988. Maximum class/group size: 20, depending on program. Facilities: hotel and restaurant kitchens, private homes, castles, monasteries. Also featured: excursions to food-related and historical sites; visits to wineries, tastings of local products, shopping for local products.
EMPHASIS: Culinary tours and cooking classes in regional cuisines.
FACULTY: Owner Judy Ebrey, CCP.
LOCATION: Italy: Badia a Coltibuono in Tuscany, Hotel Le Sirenuse in Positano, Luna Convento in Amalfi, Il Melograno in Puglia, The World of Regaleali in Sicily, Venetian Cooking in a Venetian Palace in Venice, Italian Cookery Weeks in Umbria, Villa Michaela in Lucca, Il Casale La Pietra in the Marche. France: Le Mas Oliviers in Provence, Savoir Faire Tours in Paris, Ecole de Cuisine du Domaine d'Esperance in Gascony. Spain: Flavors of the Real Spain in Catalonia and Andalucia. England: Le Manoir aux Quat' Saisons in Great Milton.
CONTACT: Judy Ebrey, Owner, Cuisine International, P.O. Box 25228, Dallas, TX 75225 USA; (214) 373-1161, Fax (214) 373-1162, E-mail CuisineInt@aol.com, URL http://www.iglobal.net/cuisineint.

EDUVACATIONS
Locations in Europe

This special interest travel company offers personalized programs that feature cooking and/or language instruction.

CONTACT: Mary Ann Puglisi, eduVacations, 1431-21st St., NW, #302, Washington, DC 20036 USA; (202) 857-8384, Fax (202) 835-3756.

EUROPEAN CULINARY ADVENTURES
Gascony and Tuscany/Spring, Summer, Fall

Culinary travel provider Kate Ratliffe offers week-long cooks tours to the Southwest of France and Tuscany and Umbria. Established in 1987. Facilities: farmhouse kitchens. Also featured: visits to markets, villas, foie gras farms, Armagnac and wine cellars, and fine restaurants.

EMPHASIS: Regional country cooking of Gascony and Tuscany.

FACULTY: Kate Ratliffe, owner/chef of the luxury canal barge, the Julia Hoyt, has lived and worked in Europe since 1987 and is author of *A Culinary Journey in Gascony*; local chefs, restaurateurs, and food producers.

COSTS: Land cost is $2,250 per person for Gascony, which includes double occupancy lodging in a 3-star hotel, meals, and planned activities.

LOCATION: The Duchy of Gascony, an area of southwestern France between Bordeaux and Toulouse.

CONTACT: Kate Ratliffe, European Culinary Adventures, 5 Ledgewood Way, #6, Peabody, MA 01960 USA; (800) 852-2625, Fax (508) 535-5738, E-mail juliahoyt@aol.com.

THE INTERNATIONAL KITCHEN
Italy and France/Year-round

This travel company offers weekly cooking vacations in Italy and France that include hands-on instruction. Established in 1995. Also featured: visits to markets, wineries, olive groves, historic and cultural sites.

COSTS: First class or deluxe accommodations.

LOCATION: Destinations for 1997 include Tuscany, Umbria, and the Amalfi coast in Italy; Provence and the Cote d'Azur in France.

CONTACT: Karen Herbst, The International Kitchen, Inc., 2685 Crestwood Ln., Riverwoods, IL 60015 USA; (800) 945-8606, (847) 945-0820, Fax (847) 821-0476, E-mail info@intl-kitchen.com, URL http://www.intl-kitchen.com.

JC FOOD & WINE TOURS
Italy and France/Year-round

Special interest tour operator Joyce Capece offers customized itineraries to Italy and France and occasional trips to other countries in Europe and southeast Asia. Founded in 1992. Maximum class/group size: 8-15. Also featured: visits to wineries and private villas, dining at fine restaurants, visits to agritourismos, markets, food producers, truffle hunts, sightseeing, meeting locals.

EMPHASIS: Food and wine travel focusing on specialties of the regions.

FACULTY: Winemakers, producers, chefs, culinary consultants. Joyce Capece, a 30-year travel professional, specializes in food and wine.

COSTS: Rates are based on regions, seasons, and length of program, usually 10-12 days.

CONTACT: Joyce Capece, CTC, DS, JC Food & Wine Tours, 480 Madera Ave., #2, Sunnyvale, CA 94086 USA; (408) 732-0891, Fax (408) 749-9479.

JANE CITRON COOKING CLASSES
Locations in Europe/September

(See also page 209)

Cooking teacher Jane Citron conducts a culinary trip to the Cote Basque and Riviera. Maximum class/group size: 12.

CONTACT: Jane Citron, 1314 Squirrel Hill Ave., Pittsburgh, PA 15217 USA; (412) 621-0311, Fax (412) 765-2511, E-mail janecooks@aol.com.

SARA MONICK CULINARY TOURS
France, Italy, Spain/Spring and Fall

This culinary tour operator offers 5- to 11-day hands-on and demonstration culinary tours in France (Provence and the Loire Valley), Italy (Tuscany and the Amalfi Coast), Spain (Madrid and Southern Spain) and Morocco. Established in 1986. Maximum class/group size: 8-14. Also featured: visits to markets, food producers, wineries, private homes and gardens; dining at fine restaurants; sightseeing; language classes; custom tours for private groups.

EMPHASIS: French, Italian, Spanish, and Moroccan cuisines.

FACULTY: Sara Monick, a cooking instructor since 1977 and Certified Member of the IACP, owns The Cookery in Minneapolis. She studied with Madeleine Kamman, Jacques Pépin, Nicholas Malgieri, and Giuliano Bugialli.

COSTS: Cost, which includes double occupancy lodging, most meals, and planned excursions, ranges from $2,300-$4,000. $500 deposit required; cancellation penalty ranges from $50 (60 days prior) to $500 (less than 45 days prior).

CONTACT: Sara Monick, Sara Monick Culinary Tours, Hilliard & Olander, Ltd., 608 Second Ave. So., Minneapolis, MN 55402 USA; (612) 333-1440, Fax (612) 333-3554.

TRAVEL CONCEPTS
Locations in Europe/Year-round

This specialty travel company offers customized European culinary and wine tours for groups. Established in 1982.

EMPHASIS: Culinary and wine travel programs.

COSTS: Group rates vary. Some programs can accommodate individuals who are not group members.

LOCATION: The Loire Valley, northern France, northern Burgundy, northern Italy, England, Ireland, and Switzerland.

CONTACT: Patricia A. McNally, Travel Concepts, 62 Commonwealth Ave., #3, Boston, MA 02116 USA; (617) 266-8450, Fax (617) 267-2477.

WANDERING SPOON
Greece and Portugal/Spring and Fall

Cookbook author Lucille Haley Schechter offers 1-week hands-on culinary programs for private groups. Established in 1983. Maximum class/group size: 10. Also featured: dining in fine restaurants, visits to markets, vineyards, and cultural centers.

EMPHASIS: Mediterranean and international cooking techniques.

FACULTY: Former *Harper's Bazaar* magazine editor Lucille Haley Schechter is co-author of *The International Menu Diabetic Cookbook* and is a Professional Member of the James Beard Foundation.

COSTS: One-week session, excluding airfare, is $1,990, double occupancy. Students often are housed in deluxe Mediterranean hotels.

LOCATION: Greece and Portugal, including Crete, Corfu, Santorini, and the Algarve.

CONTACT: Lucille H. Schechter, Wandering Spoon, 340 East 57th St., New York, NY 10022 USA; (212) 751-4532, Fax (212) 753-1714.

WINE ENTHUSIAST ULTIMATE WINE COURSES
France and Italy/February-June, September-December

The Wine Enthusiast magazine offers 1-week wine course vacations that feature daily wine instruction, a cooking demonstration by a noted restaurateur, and tours of wineries and chateaux. Maximum class/group size: 14. Also featured: Japanese course offered for large enough groups.

FACULTY: Masters of Wine and noted restaurateurs.

COSTS: About $4,000, which includes double occupancy lodging, meals, and planned activities.

LOCATION: Bordeaux, Champagne and Burgundy.

CONTACT: Mark Golodetz, Dir., Travel Serv., Wine Enthusiast Ultimate Wine Courses, 8 Saw Mill River Rd., Hawthorne, NY 10532 USA; (800) 356-8466, Fax (800) 833-8466.

FRANCE

A LA BONNE COCOTTE
Provence/Summer

(See also page 245)
Cooking and Living with Lydie in Provence is a 5-day program that features cooking classes and sightseeing. Maximum class/group size: 6.

EMPHASIS: French cuisine, from simple regional recipes to haute cuisine.

COSTS: $1,200, which includes lodging. Lydie Marshall's small chateau. $400 deposit required, refundable only if space can be filled.

LOCATION: Nyons, France, about 45 miles northeast of Avignon.

CONTACT: Lydie P. Marshall, A La Bonne Cocotte, 23 Eighth Ave., New York, NY 10014 USA; (212) 675-7736, (33) 475-26-45-31. Also: Chateau Feodal, Nyons, France, 26110; (33) 475-26-45-31 (Apr.-Oct.).

A WEEK IN BORDEAUX
Bordeaux/June-September

Jean-Pierre and Denise Moulle offer four 6-day culinary participation vacations each summer. Established in 1988. Maximum class/group size: 8. Facilities: the professional kitchen of Chateau La Louviere and a small farmhouse kitchen with a grilling fireplace. Also featured: visits to chateaux, wine estates, markets, cheese shops, medieval villages, oyster beds, regional inns, and Michelin-starred restaurants. Also available: sight-seeing and shopping.

EMPHASIS: French classic cuisine, regional cuisine of Gascony, wine appreciation.

FACULTY: Jean-Pierre Moulle graduated from Ecole Hoteliere in Toulouse, served as chef at Chez Panisse, and consults for restaurants. Bordeaux native Denise Moulle opened wine shops in California's Bay Area and markets her family's French chateau wines in the U.S.

COSTS: Cost of $2,800 (single supplement $200) includes lodging, meals, planned excursions, and ground transport. Lodging is at the private Chateau Mouchac. $500 deposit required, balance due 45 days prior; cancellations over 45 days prior forfeit $150.

LOCATION: France's Bordeaux region.

CONTACT: Denise Lurton-Moulle, A Week in Bordeaux, P.O. Box 8191, Berkeley, CA 94707-8191 USA; (510) 848-8741, Fax (510) 845-3100.

A WEEK IN PROVENCE
Gordes/February-June, September-December

Sarah and Michael Brown offer week-long vacation programs, scheduled every other week, that include daily cooking demonstrations with as much hands-on participation as desired. Founded in 1995. Maximum class/group size: 6. Also featured: history, architecture, and art tours of the region, visits to food markets and wineries.

EMPHASIS: Provence cuisine and culture.

FACULTY: Sarah Brown spent her childhood in France, has a Ph.D. in Art History, and studied cooking since she was 7; gallery owner Michael Brown represented agricultural and food interests as a lobbyist in Washington, DC, and exports wines to the U.S.

COSTS: Cost of $1,500 includes lodging in the Brown's converted village farmhouse, breakfasts and dinners, planned excursions. Lodging: 2 double and 4 single bedrooms, 4 bathrooms. Amenities include swimming pool, library, hiking, riding, biking, golfing. $500 deposit required, balance due 30 days prior. Cancellations over 45 days prior forfeit $150.

LOCATION: 45 minutes from Marseilles-Provence airport, 30 minutes from Avignon train station.

CONTACT: Sarah and Michael Brown, A Week in Provence, Vaucluse, Les Martins, Gordes, 84220 France; (33) 490-72-26-56, Fax (33) 490-72-23-83. Also: Sheppard Ferguson, c/o Schoenhof's Foreign Books, 486 Green St., Cambridge, MA 02139; (617) 547-8534, Fax (617) 547-8565.

ANDRE DAGUIN HOTEL DE FRANCE
Gascogne/October-April
This hotel offers 3-day to 2-week courses. Founded in 1985. Maximum class/group size: 6. Facilities: the hotel's restaurant kitchen. Also featured: a tour of the Armagnac region with visits to wine cellars, a foie gras duck farm, and a farmer's market.
EMPHASIS: The cuisine of Gascony; foie gras, confit de canard, and other duck preparations.
FACULTY: Under supervision of Chef Andre Daguin, proprietor.
COSTS: Fee, which includes meals and hotel lodging, is approximately 2,850 FF for 3 days. A 25% deposit is required with balance due 3 weeks prior.
LOCATION: Auch en Gascogne.
CONTACT: Andre Daguin, Andre Daguin Hotel de France, 2, place de la Liberation, Auch en Gascogne, 32003 France; (33) 562-61-71-71, Fax (33) 562-61-71-81, E-mail hotelfrance@relais-chateaux.fr., URL http://www.integra.fr/relaischateaux/hotelfrance.htm.

AT HOME WITH PATRICIA WELLS: COOKING IN PROVENCE
Vaison-La-Romaine/February, May, June, September
American journalist and author Patricia Wells offers 5-day cooking vacations that include 4 hours of daily hands-on instruction. Founded in 1995. Maximum class/group size: 10. Facilities: Ms. Wells' 18th-century farmhouse kitchen, which has a wood-fired bread oven. Also featured: visits to local markets, wine tastings, dinner at a fine restaurant; February truffle workshop.
EMPHASIS: Provencal cuisine.
FACULTY: Patricia Wells has lived in France since 1980, is restaurant critic of *The International Herald Tribune*, and authored 6 books, including *Bistro Cooking* and *Simply French*.
COSTS: $2,750, which includes meals and planned activities. A list of recommended lodging is supplied. $1,000 deposit required, balance due 90 days prior.
LOCATION: Ms. Wells' hilltop home is just outside Vaison-la-Romaine, about 30 miles northeast of Avignon.
CONTACT: Judith Jones, Program Coordinator, Cooking in Provence, 708 Sandown Place, Raleigh, NC 27615 USA; (919) 870-5955, Fax (919) 846-2081, E-mail jj708@nando.net.

CHATEAU COUNTRY COOKING SCHOOL
Montbazon-en-Touraine/Spring and Fall
Denise Olivereau-Capron and her son, Xavier offer 6-day participation courses. Established in 1986. Maximum class/group size: 15. Facilities: the chateau's renovated L'Orangerie restaurant. Also featured: dining at fine restaurants and visits to the Tours flower market, the chateaux of the region, a goat cheese farm, the Chinon markets, and the caves of Vouvray.
EMPHASIS: French regional cuisine.
FACULTY: Chef Edouard Wehrlin.
COSTS: Course fee of 14,000 FF single, 13,500 FF double, includes chateau lodging, meals, wine tastings, and planned excursions.
LOCATION: Le Domaine de la Tortiniere, a 19th century manor-house chateau, is in the Loire Valley.
CONTACT: Denise Olivereau-Capron, Chateau Country Cooking School, Montbazon en Touraine, Veigne, 37250 France; (33) 247-34-35-00, Fax (33) 247-65-95-70, E-mail U.S. Contact: Sara Monick, The Cookery, 4215 Poplar Dr., Minneapolis, MN 55422; (612) 374-2444, Fax (612) 333-3554.

COOKERY LESSONS AND TOURAINE VISIT
Brehemont/Spring and Fall
Maxime and Eliane Rochereau in the 18th-century Le Castel de Bray et Monts offer 1-week hands-on vacation programs scheduled 6 times a year that include daily instruction. Founded in 1983. Maximum class/group size: 15. Facilities: the manor's restaurant kitchen. Also featured: visits to chateaux, wineries, pastry shops, sightseeing, shopping.

EMPHASIS: French cuisine.

FACULTY: Chef Maxime Rochereau, who was chef at the Ritz Hotel in Paris.

COSTS: Cost is 5,800 FF (10% discount for a couple), which includes lodging at the manor, meals, and planned activities. A $150 deposit is required; refund with 30 days notice.

LOCATION: A vineyard village on the Loire River in the chateau region, 16 miles from Tours and a one-hour train ride from Paris.

CONTACT: Maxime Rochereau, Cookery Lessons and Touraine Visit, Le Castel de Bray et Monts, Brehemont, Langeais, 37130 France; (33) 247-96-70-47, (33) 247-96-63-98, Fax (33) 247-96-57-36.

COOKING AT THE ABBEY
Salon-de-Provence/March-April, November-December

The Hostellerie Abbaye de Sainte Croix resort offers 3-, 4-, and 7-day vacation participation courses; afternoon classes (minimum 4 students) on request. Established in 1987. Maximum class/group size: 12. Facilities: the restaurant kitchen, which has 4 ovens and 12 work stations. Also featured: local sightseeing and vineyard visits.

EMPHASIS: Provencal cuisine.

FACULTY: Chef P. Morel of the Abbey's Michelin 1-star restaurant.

COSTS: 3,670 FF (380 FF) for 3 days to 10,180 FF (1,575 FF) for 7 days, includin most meals, double (single supplement) lodging, and planned activities. Afternoon class is 600 FF. Lodging in the 12th-century Abbey's Roman-style rooms. 30% deposit due 60 days prior, balance on arrival.

LOCATION: The Abbey, a member of Relais & Chateaux, is 2 miles from Salon, 20 miles northeast of the nearest airport, 20 miles west of Aix-en-Provence.

CONTACT: Catherine Bossard, General Manager, Cooking at the Abbey, Route Val-de-Cuech, Salon-de-Provence, 13300 France; (33) 490-56-24-55, Fax (33) 490-56-31-12, URL http://www.integra.fr/relaischateaux. Also: Relais & Chateaux, NY (212) 856-0115.

---

cooking with friends in F R A N C E

Come cook with us in Julia Child's Provence kitchen! This week-long cultural immersion includes classes in English given by French chefs, most meals, market/village tours, restaurant visits, and accommodations. Afternoons free to explore the French Riviera

United States: (617) 350.3837   *France:* (33) 493.60.10.56

COOKING WITH FRIENDS IN FRANCE
Chateauneuf de Grasse/Year-round

(See display ad above)

This vacation school on the property once shared by Julia Child and Simone Beck offers 28-30 six-day participation courses per year. Founded in 1993. Maximum class/group size: 8. Also featured: visits to the Forville Market, a butcher shop, cheese ripener, cutlery shop, and Michelin 2-star restaurant kitchens; demonstration by a French chef.

EMPHASIS: French cuisine, including techniques, tricks, menu-planning, lighter dishes.

FACULTY: Proprietor/instructor Kathie Alex apprenticed at Roger Vergé's Le Moulin de Mougins, assisted well-known chefs at the Robert Mondavi Winery, studied catering at Ecole Lenotre, and studied with and assisted Simone Beck at her school.

COSTS: $1,850, which includes double occupancy lodging (some private baths), breakfasts and lunches, wine tastings, and planned excursions (car required). Students stay in either La Pitchoune or La Campanette, private homes originally owned by Julia Child and Simone Beck. Golf and horseback riding are nearby. A $450 deposit is required and $375 is refunded for cancellations 90 days prior.

LOCATION: On the Cote d'Azur, about 9 miles from Cannes, 4 miles from Grasse, and 20 miles from Nice International Airport.

CONTACT: Kathie Alex, Cooking with Friends in France, La Pitchoune, Domaine de Bramafam, Chateauneuf de Grasse, 06740 France; (33) 493-60-10-56, Fax (33) 493-60-05-56.

COOKING WITH THE MASTERS
Bouilland and Jouy-en-Josas/Fall, Winter, Spring

Michel Bouit offers 1- to 2-week hands-on programs per season (1-week at Le Vieux Moulin, 1- to 2-weeks at Tecomah). Founded in 1990. Maximum class/group size: 10-20. Facilities: full service restaurant/hotel kitchens. Also featured: excursions to local artisans, markets, and vineyards; sight-seeing and shopping in Paris.

EMPHASIS: Classical and regional French cuisine, culinary terms and service, industry-related visits, customized tours.

FACULTY: Jean-Pierre Silva, chef-owner of Le Vieux Moulin; Alain LeCourtois, director of Tecomah; 1989 ACF National Chef of the Year Michel Bouit, CEC, AAC, president of MBI Inc., which specializes in culinary tours, competitions, consulting, public relations.

COSTS: 2-week student course at Tecomah $3,500; 1-week gourmet/professional course at Le Vieux Moulin $2,550 ($330 single supp.). Fees include airfare, lodging, ground transport, most meals, excursions. Lodging: Le Vieux Moulin, luxury country Auberge; Tecomah Educational Center, dormitory accommodations. Deposit is 50%, balance is due 60 days prior to departure, $100 penalty for cancellation 30 days prior.

LOCATION: Le Vieux Moulin, Bouilland, 9 miles from Beaune, wine capitol of Burgundy. Tecomah, Jouy-en-josas, a suburb of Paris near Versailles.

CONTACT: Michel Bouit, President, Cooking with the Masters, c/o MBI, Inc., P.O. Box 1801, Chicago, IL 60690 USA; (312) 663-5701, Fax (312) 663-5702.

COOKING IN PROVENCE
Crillon le Brave/March, April, November

Hostellerie de Crillon le Brave offers five 6-day hands-on cooking vacations a year. Founded in 1992. Maximum class/group size: 8. Facilities: the hotel's restaurant kitchen. Also featured: market visits, winery tour, visits to Avignon and other Provence sites, dining at the hotel and fine restaurants, golf, tennis, cycling, hiking.

EMPHASIS: Provencal and Mediterranean cuisine.

FACULTY: Chef de Cuisine Philippe Monti, a native of Provence, trained at Pic, l'Esperance, Auberge de l'Ill, and Taillevent.

COSTS: Cost is $2,500 ($2,800), which includes meals, double (single) occupancy lodging, and planned excursions; supplement for non-cooking partners is $850. Hostellerie de Crillon le Brave, a member of Relais & Chateaux and named Country House Hotel of the Year in 1992 by *Andrew Harper's Hideaway Report*. An $800 deposit is required, refundable 60 days in advance.

LOCATION: 25 miles from Avignon.

CONTACT: Craig Miller, Cooking in Provence, Place de l'Eglise, Crillon le Brave, 84410 France; (33) 490-65-61-61, Fax (33) 490-65-62-86.

COOKING IN PROVENCE
Provence/Spring and Fall

Travel agent Cathy Kinloch offers 12 one-week cooking vacations per year that include 4 hours of daily instruction. Maximum class/group size: 8. Also featured: visits to markets and wineries, swimming pool.

EMPHASIS: Provencal cuisine.

FACULTY: Chef Sylvie L'Allemande.

COSTS: 3,300 FF, which includes meals and lodging. A 25% deposit is required.

LOCATION: One hour from Avignon.

CONTACT: Cathy Kinloch, Cooking in Provence, Teachers' Travel Service, Ltd., 21 St. Clair Ave. E., #1003, Toronto, ON M4T 1L9 Canada; (800) 268-7229, (416) 922-2232, Fax (416) 922-8410.

CUISINIERES DU MONDE
Chavagnac/Year-round

Daniele Delpeuch offers 1 and 2-week participation courses year-round and Foie Gras and Truffles Weekends during the winter. Maximum class/group size: 7. Facilities: Ms. Delpeuch's 16th-century stone farmhouse. Also featured: visits to the market, neighboring farms, a well-known baker, a foie gras farm, the region's prehistoric caves, and a 17th century walnut oil mill.

EMPHASIS: Traditional French cooking; duck and goose preparations.

FACULTY: Daniele Delpeuch contributed to the Time-Life *Great Meals in Minutes* series, served as guest lecturer at La Varenne, conducted workshops in the U.S., and was private chef to French president M. Francois Mitterrand.

COSTS: $2,000/week, which includes meals, farmhouse lodging, planned activities.

LOCATION: The Perigord region, near the town of Sarlat.

CONTACT: Daniele Mazet-Delpeuch, Cuisinieres du Monde, La Borderie, 24120 Chavagnac, France; (33) 153-51-00-24, Fax (33) 153-23-60-25.

ÉCOLE DES ARTS CULINAIRES ET DE L'HÔTELLERIE
(See also page 124)
Lyon/Ecully/Year-round

In addition to career courses, this school offers 1-week introductory courses for amateurs of French gastronomic tradition. Established in 1990. Also featured: A la carte sessions taught in various languages can be organized (minimum 6 students).

EMPHASIS: French cuisine and pastry, menu composition, restaurant-quality desserts and decorative accompaniments, wines.

COSTS: 5,200 FF fee includes 3 meals daily. Residence hall lodging is 1,000 FF/week.

LOCATION: The restored 19th century Château du Vivier, in a 17-acre wooded park in the Lyon-Ecully University-Research Zone, 10 minutes from downtown Lyon.

CONTACT: Eleonore Vial, Anne-Catherine Laure, International Programs, École des Arts Culinaires et de l'Hôtellerie, Office of International Programs, Château du Vivier, B.P. 25, Écully, Cedex, 69131 France; (33) 478-43-36-10, Fax (33) 4-78-43-33-51, URL http://www.mairie-lyon.fr.

ECOLE DE CUISINE
(See also page 219)
September

This school of professional cooking for the home chef offers an annual 8-day Food Tour of Paris that includes a cooking class and chocolate tasting seminar. Also featured: wine and food tastings, visits to markets, meals at a bistro and Michelin-starred restaurant, tours of bread and pastry shops, restaurant kitchens, cookware shops.

CONTACT: Jill L. Prescott, Owner, Ecole de Cuisine, 765 H Woodlake Dr., Kohler, WI 53044 USA; (414) 451-9151, Fax (414) 451-9152.

ECOLE LENOTRE
(See also page 124)
Plaisir Cedex/Year-round

This French gastronomy school offers 2- to 4-day participation courses for amateur cooks.

EMPHASIS: Basics, regional specialties, pastries, wine and food pairing, theme menus.

COSTS: 2,400 FF-4,800 FF (1,500 FF-4,000 FF) for French residents (non-residents).

CONTACT: Marcel Derrien, Ecole Lenotre, 40, rue Pierre Curie-BP 6, Plaisir Cedex, 787373 France; (33) 130-81-46-34, (33) 1-30-81-46-35, Fax (33) 1-30-54-73-70.

ECOLE DES TROIS PONTS
(See display ad page 250)
Roanne/July, August, October

This language school in a chateau offers four 1-week Cooking and French Courses that feature morning language classes, afternoon hands-on cooking classes, and an optional wine course. Founded in 1991. Maximum class/group size: 6-8 cooking, 6 language. Also featured: a cooking-only option (instruction in English), courses in general and intensive French, a stress management course, courses for professional florists, and a Taste of France course.

EMPHASIS: Provincial French cuisine and sauces; French language instruction.

FACULTY: Professional chef, experienced French language teachers.

COSTS: 5,900 FF-6,600 FF for Cooking and French and 4,700 FF-5,400 FF for cooking only option, which includes lodging, most meals and planned excursions. Share twin, single rooms. ensuite or shared facilities. 1,000 FF/week for single room with private bath. Pool and tennis are nearby, bikes available. Non-refundable 10% deposit due with reservation. Balance due 4 weeks prior, nonrefundable after course starts.

LOCATION: The 17th-century Chateau de Matel is set in 32 acres of park and woodland, 5 minutes from the center of Roanne in the Burgundy/Beaujolais region, near Lyons, Vichy, and Auvergne.

CONTACT: Mrs. O'Loan, Director, Ecole de Trois Ponts, Chateau de Matel, Roanne, 42300 France; (33) 433-77-71-53-00, Fax (33) 433-77-70-80-01, E-mail 3ponts@ntmdp.ardep.fr. U.S. Contact: Michael Giammarella, EMI International, Box 640713, Oakland Gardens, NY 11364-0713; (800) 484-1235 #0096, (718) 631-0096; Fax (718) 631-0316.

ETOILE BLEU MARINE
La Rochelle/Spring and Fall
Maybelle Iribe offers 1-week cooking vacations (12 hours of hands-on instruction) six times/year. Established in 1991. Maximum class/group size: 8. Facilities: a 200-square-foot kitchen with garden. Also featured: visits to cognac distilleries, wineries, oyster beds, food producers, market tour, sightseeing.

EMPHASIS: Regional French cooking and seafood.

FACULTY: Emi Taya, a graduate of the University of Tokyo; restaurateurs Fred Nillson and Mirko Bettini, oenologist George Caviste.

COSTS: Cost is $2,000, which includes meals, lodging, and planned activities. 6-twin and double rooms with bath in Maybelle's Bed & Breakfast. $500 deposit with reservation, balance 30 days prior. 50% refundable thereafter.

LOCATION: La Rochelle is 3 hours from Paris by TGV train and one hour by airline TAT direct.

CONTACT: Maybelle Iribe, Charente Maritime, Etoile Bleu Marine, 33, rue Thiers, La Rochelle, 17000 France; (33) 546-41-62-63, Fax (33) 546-41-10-7. U.S. Contact: Ms. M.J. Drinkwater, Town & Country Travel, Sacramento, CA; (916) 483-4621.

FOOD IN FRANCE
Gourgé/May-July
This village house offers four 6-day participation courses/year. Established in 1990. Maximum class/group size: 7. Facilities: 2 well-equipped domestic kitchens with 6 work stations. Also featured: visits to markets, wineries, cheese producers, and restaurants, cycling, water-color sketching.

EMPHASIS: French regional cuisine, wine appreciation.

FACULTY: Pat Cove specialized in French regional cuisines at Morley College in London.

COSTS: £395 per person (20% less for non-participating partners) includes lodging and full board. Lodging is at Les Belles Etoiles, 2 adjoining houses in the center of the village. A 10% nonrefundable deposit is required with balance due 6 weeks prior.

LOCATION: Gourgé, a rural village in the Deux Sevres, is 25 miles west of Poitiers and 185 miles southwest of Paris.

CONTACT: Pat Cove, Food in France, 14 Thorpewood Avenue, London, SE26 4BX England; (44) 181-699-3437, Fax (44) 181-699-3437.

FRANCE AUTHENTIQUE
Domfront, Normandy/Year-round

France on Your Plate offers a 1-week customized vacation program that features cooking classes in restaurant kitchens. Established in 1994. Maximum class/group size: 8-10. Also featured: visits to local food producers, the copper-making center of Villedieu-les-Poeles, and the World War II landing beaches, cycling, fishing, horseback riding, swimming, tennis, and golf.

EMPHASIS: Cuisine of Normandy.

FACULTY: Prominent local chefs.

COSTS: $1,200-$2,000 per week, which includes most meals, planned activities, and lodging at La Maison de la Resistance.

LOCATION: The Normandy region, 3 hours from Paris.

CONTACT: William T. Fleming, Jr., France Authentique, 1413 Sandhurst Pl., W. Vancouver, BC V7S 2P4 Canada; (604) 925-3095, Fax (604) 926-1084, E-mail fleming@helix.net, URL http://www.helix.net/~fleming.

FRENCH LANGUAGE AND COOKING PROGRAM
St. Malo/July

This travel company offers a 2-week program that includes 20 hours of hands-on cooking and 5 hours of French language instruction/week. Maximum class/group size: 12.

EMPHASIS: Sauces, pastries, seasonings, and wine. Language classes focus on conversation.

FACULTY: Local chefs and French language instructors.

COSTS: Include half-board lodging in a private home. Nonrefundable $100 registration fee required.

LOCATION: About three hours from Paris by train.

CONTACT: Director, Lingua Service Worldwide, 216 E. 45th St., 17th Flr., New York, NY 10017 USA; (800) 394-LEARN, (212) 867-1225, Fax (212) 867-7666.

HOLIDAYS IN THE SUN IN THE SOUTH OF FRANCE
Gordes/Spring, Fall, December

Les Mégalithes school in a private country home offers 1-week participation courses with instruction in English, French, and German. Established in 1980. Maximum class/group size: 6. Facilities: indoor and outdoor home kitchen. Also featured: market visits, horseback and bicycle riding, handicraft shopping, visits to museums and historic sites.

EMPHASIS: Cuisine of Provence, including appetizers, main courses, breads, jellies, holiday dishes.

FACULTY: Sylvie Lallemand, president/founder of the Association des amis de la cuisine et des traditions provencales, learned to cook from her mother and grandmother and studied with Roger Vergé.

COSTS: 3,200 FF, which includes private room and bath at Les Mégalithes, pool, and meals. A nonrefundable 200 FF deposit is required.

LOCATION: Gordes, near Avignon, a 3½-hour drive from Nice.

CONTACT: Sylvie Lallemand, Les Mégalithes, Gordes, 84220 France; (33) 490-72-23-41.

LA CUISINE DE MARIE BLANCHE
Paris/Year-round except August

This school (formerly Princess Ere 2001) in a private apartment offers 1- to 4-week participation courses with instruction in French, English, or Spanish. Established in 1975. Maximum class/group size: 6-8. Facilities: 50-sq-meter kitchen. Also featured: food-related visits to museums and champagne caves in Reims.

EMPHASIS: French cuisine for at-home entertaining.
FACULTY: Marie-Blanche de Broglie, founder and director, is author of *The Cuisine of Normandy*.
COSTS: One class is 600 FF, 5 classes are 2,750 FF, 10 classes are 5,250 FF, 20 classes are 10,000 FF. A 10% nonrefundable deposit is required.
LOCATION: Near the Eiffel Tower.
CONTACT: Marie Blanche de Broglie, La Cuisine de Marie Blanche, 18 Ave. de la Motte-Picquet, Paris, 75007 France; (33) 145-51-36-34, Fax (33) 145-51-90-19.

LA VARENNE
Burgundy/May-November   *(See also page 126) (See display ad below)*
In addition to its residential courses, La Varenne offers a Summer Series (5 half-day hands-on classes, 3 demonstrations, wine tasting) in June and July and the Grand Luxe Gastronomic Course (4 hands-on classes, a master chef demonstration, 3 wine tastings) in the fall. Maximum class/group size: 15. Facilities: the school is in the 17th-century Château du Feÿ, a registered historic monument owned by founder Anne Willan. Also featured: Summer Series: visits to Joigny and Chablis, dinner at a fine country restaurant. Grand Luxe Course: visits to a cheese producer, baker, Chablis vineyard, dining at 2 noted restaurants.
EMPHASIS: Classic, contemporary, and regional French cuisine, bistro cooking, pastry, wine appreciation, guest chef specialties.
FACULTY: Summer Series features different chef-instructors each week; Grand Luxe Course is hosted by Anne Willan and her husband, Mark Cherniavsky.
COSTS: $2,850 ($3,565) for the Summer Series (Grand Luxe Course), which includes transport from Paris, full board, shared twin lodging at Château du Feÿ, and planned activities. Single supplement $400. Payment with registration; cancellations over 90 days prior forfeit $100.
CONTACT: La Varenne, P.O. Box 25574, Washington, DC 20007 USA; (800) 537-6486, (202) 337-0073, Fax (703) 823-5438, E-mail 102635.2040@compuserve.com.

L'ACADEMIE DE CUISINE
Gascony/Year-round   *(See also pages 49, 187) (See display ad page 49)*
This proprietary vocational school offers 1-week culinary vacations to France. Also featured: trips to an Armagnac distillery, Bordeaux wineries, and duck farm; dining at Michelin-star restaurants.
COSTS: $2,500, which includes lodging meals, planned excursions, ground transport.
LOCATION: Domaine de Bassibe in Gascony.
CONTACT: Carol McClure, Assistant Director, L'Academie de Cuisine, 16006 Industrial Dr., Gaithersburg, MD 20877 USA; (301) 670-8670, (800) 664-CHEF, Fax (301) 670-0450, URL http://www.L'Academie.com.

LE CORDON BLEU
Paris/Year-round   *(See also page 126) (See display ad page 127)*
This private school offers half-day to one-month courses, including daily half-day demonstrations, 3- to 5-day gourmet sessions, Saturday hands-on workshops, 1-month initiation courses in cuisine

and pastry, market tours and demonstrations. Also featured: workshops for children, floral art, evening wine classes, cheese courses, guest chef demonstrations.

EMPHASIS: The Classic Cycle.

COSTS: Range from 220 FF/$45 (half-day) to 750 FF/$150 (one-day hands-on workshop) to 4,950 FF/$920 (4-day session).

CONTACT: Le Cordon Bleu, 8, rue Léon Delhomme, Paris, 75015 France; (800) 457-CHEF, (33) 1-53-68-22-50, Fax (33) 1-48-56-03-96, URL http://www.cordonbleu.edu.

LE MARMITON – COOKING IN PROVENCE
Avignon/September-June

This hotel-restaurant offers 1- or 4-day participation courses. Established in 1994. Maximum class/group size: 12. Facilities: restored 19th century kitchen with its original wood-fired cast-iron stove and restored counters.

EMPHASIS: Provencal cuisine.

FACULTY: Olga Manguin, a specialist in Provencal cuisine, and Christian Etienne, Robert Brunel, Jean-Claude Aubertin.

COSTS: 1,745 FF daily (6,580 FF 4 days) double, 2,440 FF (9,360 FF) single, 1,145 FF (4,100 FF) non-cook guest, includes breakfast and lunch. Nonresident daily 600 FF (250FF non-cook guest). 25% deposit required, cancellations 3 weeks prior forfeit 350 FF.

LOCATION: La Mirande, a period town house, is about 65 miles from Marseille international airport and 6 miles from Avignon's domestic airport.

CONTACT: Martin Stein, Artist Director, Le Marmiton - Cooking in Provence, 4, place de La Mirande, Avignon, 84000 France; (33) 490-85-93-93, Fax (33) 490-86-26-85.

L'ECOLE DE CUISINE DU DOMAINE D'ESPÉRANCE
La Bastide d'Armagnac/January, April, June, October-December

This 18th-century country house offers six 1-week hands-on vacations per year that include theoretical instruction in the mornings and preparation of the evening meal in the afternoons. Founded in 1993. Maximum class/group size: 9. Facilities: large country kitchen with 8 work areas. Also featured: market trip, visits to nearby wine cellars; weekend courses for groups of 6 or more.

EMPHASIS: Seasonal French cuisine.

FACULTY: Natalia Arizmendi, recipient of the Cordon Bleu Grand Diplome, has taught cooking and pastry for more than 10 years. She is tri-lingual in French, English, and Spanish.

COSTS: 8,500 FF, which includes double occupancy lodging (private bath) and meals at the Domaine. Domaine amenities include outdoor swimming pool and tennis court. A nonrefundable 10% deposit is required with balance due 10 days prior.

LOCATION: Gascony, in southwest France, 90 minutes from Bordeaux.

CONTACT: Claire de Montesquiou, L'Ecole de Cuisine du Domaine d'Espérance, Domaine d'Espérance, Mauvezin d'Armagnac, La Bastide d'Armagnac, 40240 France; (33) 558-44-68-33, Fax (33) 558-44-85-93, E-mail U.S Contact: Judy Ebrey, Cuisine International, P.O. Box 25228, Dallas, TX 75225 USA; (214) 373-1161; Fax (214) 373-1162.

LES CASSEROLES DU MIDI
Avignon/September-June

This school in an 18th-century country home offers one-week courses that cover 20-30 recipes. Established in 1993. Maximum class/group size: 4. Also featured: shopping for ingredients, visits to farms, wineries, and food producers, sightseeing in Provence, swimming and tennis. Relative or friend can travel with you and pay as traveling guest.

EMPHASIS: Provencal, Italian, North African cuisine.

FACULTY: Italian-born Olga Manguin was owner/chef of Le Cafe des Nattes in Avignon for 15 years and speaks English, Italian, and German.

COSTS: Daily rate of 1,000 FF includes meals, single or double lodging, ground transport, and excursions. The Manguin home has 4 bedrooms with ensuite bath. 1,000 FF deposit required with booking.

LOCATION: About 70 miles from Marseille, 140 miles from Nice, 450 miles from Paris.
CONTACT: Olga Manguin, Les Casseroles du Midi, L'Anastasy, Ile de la Barthelasse, Avignon, 84000 France; (33) 490-85-55-94, Fax (33) 490-82-59-40.

LES LIAISONS DÉLICIEUSES
Fall, Winter, Spring
This culinary tour company offers 6-8 one-week vacations/year, each in a different province, that include 15 hours of hands-on cooking instruction. Founded in 1994. Maximum class/group size: 8-10. Facilities: hotel and restaurant kitchens with individual workspaces. Also featured: visits to wineries, food producers, markets, and restaurants, sightseeing, hiking and biking.
EMPHASIS: French regional cuisine.
FACULTY: Founder Patti Ravenscroft is tour director and translator. Classes are taught by Michelin-star restaurant chefs and proprietors.
COSTS: $1,950-$2,490, which includes lodging, meals, and planned activities. Lodging: Hotel Les Pyrenees in the Basque region, Hostellerie du Vieux Moulin in Burgundy, and L'Auberge de la Truffe in the Dordogne. $600-$800 deposit required. Refund less $100 for cancellations over 45 days prior.
LOCATION: Includes Burgundy, Brittany, Normandy, the Dordogne, the Jura, Provence, the Pays-Basque.
CONTACT: Patti R. Ravenscroft, Les Liaisons Délicieuses, 4710 - 30th St. N.W., Washington, DC 20008 USA; (202) 966-4091, Fax (202) 966-4091.

LES SAVEURS DE PROVENCE
Mérindol-les-Oliviers/March-June, September-October
This gastronomic association offers one or two 6-day hands-on programs per month, including 3 grape harvest weeks in autumn. Established in 1995. Maximum class/group size: 6-10. Facilities: custom-built fully-equipped kitchen, library of wine and cook books. Also featured: winery tours and instruction, market visits, dining in private homes and local restaurants, sightseeing, visits to food producers.
EMPHASIS: French Mediterranean cooking, wine and food pairing.
FACULTY: Elizabeth Miller, graduate of City & Guilds of London in Hotel & Restaurant Catering and L'Académie du Vin in Paris; Isabelle Bachelard, former director of L'Académie du Vin.
COSTS: 5,500 FF/person, which includes lodging for 6 nights, all meals and local wines, ground transport, and planned activities. Bed & breakfast lodging in private country houses with bilingual hosts. 20% deposit required with booking, balance due 6 weeks prior, refund thereafter only if space can be filled.
LOCATION: In Provence, 40 miles from Avignon.
CONTACT: Elizabeth Miller, President, L'Association Les Saveurs de Provence, La Lumiere, Quartier Grand Vignes, 26170 Mérindol-les-Oliviers, Drome Provencale, France; (33) 475-28-78-12, Fax (33) 475-28-90-11.

LEVERNOIS CULINARY SCHOOL
Beaune/January-March
This culinary school at the Relais and Chateaux of Hostellerie de Levernois offers 4-day optional hands-on courses with preparation of a complete menu. Maximum class/group size: 10. Facilities: large, well-equipped professional kitchen of the Restaurant Hostellerie de Levernois. Also featured: wine instruction, private classes, afternoon excursions to cultural and historic sites, market visits, winery tours, goat cheese farm tours, fine dining, shopping, golf and tennis.
EMPHASIS: Classical and traditional French cooking, seafood, fois gras, escargot, pastry and desserts, cheese, wine appreciation.
FACULTY: The Crotet family of chefs includes father Jean and sons Christophe and Guillaume. Christophe, who conducts the classes, was at Troisgros, Bocuse, Girardet, and now at Hostellerie de Levernois.

COSTS: $1,600 ($1,220) single (double) occupancy, which includes all meals and excursions. Lodging is at the Michelin 2-star rated Relais and Chateaux of Hostellerie de Levernois. A $250 deposit is required, balance is due 90 days prior.

LOCATION: A 10-acre estate in the village of Levernois, 3 miles from Beaune, 2 hours southeast of Paris by train. Credit cards accepted.

CONTACT: Lynn Parks, Culinary Director, Levernois Culinary School, 13760 NW 19th Ave., #8, Miami, FL 33054 United States; (305) 688-4007, Fax (305) 688-5008, E-mail images@hafdigital.comAlso: Mrs. Gaby Crotet, Hostellerie de Levernois, 21200 Beaune, France; (33) 380-24-73-58, Fax (33) 380-22-78-00, URL http://www-integra.fr/relaischateaux/levernois.

MAS DE CORNUD
St. Remy-de-Provence/Year-round

David and Nitockrees Carpita's cooking school in their 18th-century Provencal country inn offers a one-week Home Cooking in Provence course that features daily market shopping for ingredients and participation classes. Founded in 1993. Maximum class/group size: 6. Facilities: the schools well-equipped kitchen and herb garden. Also featured: visits to farmer's markets, artisanal bakers, cheese and olive oil producers, wine tastings; customized culinary programs for small groups.

EMPHASIS: Provencal and Mediterranean cuisine.

FACULTY: Nitockrees Carpita, CCP is originally from Egypt. She is a member of the IACP and received culinary training in France.

COSTS: Cost of $1,950 includes double occupancy lodging ($1,750 for non-participant guest) at Mas de Cornud, most meals, ground transport, transfers to Avignon or Marseilles, planned activities. Mas de Cornud is a restored Provencal 18th-century stone farmhouse with four guest rooms (all with private bath), swimming pool and boules court. 50% deposit required, balance due 60 days prior.

LOCATION: 20 minutes to Avignon by train, 50 minutes to Marseilles by air.

CONTACT: David Carpita, School Administrator, Mas de Cornud, Route de Mas Blanc, St. Remy-de-Provence, 13210 France; (33) 490-92-39-32, Fax (33) 490-92-55-99, E-mail 74333.237@compuserve.com.

PROVENÇAL GETAWAY VACATIONS
Curnier/May-June, September-October

Cooking instructor Eileen Dwillies offers seven 6-day participation vacations/year in a restored 16th century house. Established in 1994. Maximum class/group size: 4. Facilities: home-style kitchen. Also featured: daily tours of outdoor markets, vintners caves, artists' workshops, and olive mills.

EMPHASIS: Provencal cuisine.

FACULTY: Eileen Dwillies, author of 9 cookbooks, has taught cooking for 20 years and is a former food editor and TV show host.

COSTS: $950, which includes meals, tours, and twin lodging with shared bath. $350 deposit is nonrefundable unless replacement is found.

LOCATION: 75 minutes south of Avignon, 2-3 hours north of Lyon.

CONTACT: Eileen Dwillies, Provencal Getaway Vacations, #222, 525 Wheelhouse Square, Vancouver, BC V5Z 4L8 Canada; (604) 876-8722, Fax (604) 876-1497.

PROVENCE COOKING SCHOOL
St. Tropez/May-October

The Chateau de la Messardiere offers four to six week-long vacations/year that include daily hands-on cooking classes. Also featured: sightseeing in Provence, dining in fine restaurants, visits to food markets, wineries, and museums.

EMPHASIS: Provence cuisine.

COSTS: All-inclusive land cost is $2,800, single supplement $750.

LOCATION: Overlooking St. Tropez and the Mediterranean.

CONTACT: Annemarie Victory, The Annemarie Victory Organization, Inc., 136 E. 64th St., New York, NY 10021 USA; (212) 486-0353, Fax (212) 751-3149.

PROVENCE IN 3 DIMENSIONS
Carpentras/Year-round

This private school offers demonstration and hands-on sessions scheduled weekly. Established in 1996. Maximum class/group size: 6-20. Facilities: professional kitchen in a chateau, plus dining room. Also featured: winery tours and instruction, day trips, visits to markets and food producers, master classes for culinary professionals.

EMPHASIS: Authenticity of products and artisans, Provencal cuisine.

FACULTY: Michel Depardon, trained at Lausanne, owner/chef of Sous les Micocouliers in Eygalieres; Robert Reynolds, French-trained chef and former restaurateur in San Francisco, academic director of Cooking School of the Rockies.

COSTS: $2,250 for a 5-day session, which includes single occupancy lodging, meals, and ground transport. Lodging is at local first class hotels. Tuition is reduced for those making their own lodging arrangements. 50% deposit required 30 days prior. Cancellations 7 days prior forfeit deposit less 25% administrative fee.

LOCATION: Carpentras, which has a population of 40,000 and is 30 minutes from Avignon.

CONTACT: Michel Depardon, President, Provence in 3 Dimensions, Chateau de la Roseraie, Impasse des Tilleuls, Carpentras, 84000 France; (33) 490-67-02-90, Fax (33) 490-67-02-90. Also: Robert Reynolds, 1267 Balsam, Boulder, CO 80304; (303) 440-8928, Fax (303) 440-8923.

Join us for a truly exceptional culinary experience in the South of France

You will stay with us at our beautiful villa on the coast, with a breathtaking view of the Mediterranean. Our esteemed chef, Frédéric Rivière, will share with you his secrets to provençale and classical French cuisine.

Our course is flexible, to give you what you want from a learning vacation. Between classes, those interested can take advantage of cultural excursions, wine tastings, language lessons, decorative painting, hiking or biking in the Esterels — or, you may choose to simply lounge by the pool or spend time in the Jacuzzi. The choice is yours.

For more information, contact the *Rhode School of Cuisine:*
phone ➤ 800.447.1311

Or *Cuisine International:*
phone ➤ 214.373.1161

THE RHODE SCHOOL OF CUISINE
Théoule-sur-Mer/April-October   *(See also page 273) (See display ad above)*

This school offers weekly 7-day hands-on vacation programs. Also featured: cultural excursions, dining at Michelin-star restaurants, market visits, activities for non-cooking guests.

EMPHASIS: French cuisine, sauces, pastry, wine and cheese.

FACULTY: Chef Frederic Riviere, a graduate of Les Sorbets, who has cooked at Michelin-star restaurants.

COSTS: $1,895, which includes double occupancy lodging, ground transport, and food and wine consumed at the school. Premium room supplement is $200, non-cook guest rate is $1,395. Le Mas des Oliviers, a modernized 5-bedroom/5-bath villa, has a 3,500 sq-ft terrace, pool, and jacuzzi. 50% deposit with booking, balance due 6 weeks prior.

LOCATION: On the coast in the Esterels, overlooking the Mediterranean.

CONTACT: The Rhode School of Cuisine, (800) 447-1311, Fax (800) 447-1311. Also: Cuisine International (214) 373-1161 or Rhode School of Cuisine, c/o Carola Strowick, 25 Blvd. Helvetique, Geneva 1207, Switzerland; (41) 22-736-7878, Fax (41) 22-736-7919.

RITZ-ESCOFFIER ECOLE DE GASTRONOMIE FRANCAISE
(See also page 127) (See display ad page 128) **Paris/Year-round**

This culinary school in the Hotel Ritz offers 1-week hands-on theme courses in June-July, September-November, half-day workshops year-round, demonstrations Monday-Thursday afternoons, alternate Tuesday evenings, and the last Saturday morning of the month. Maximum class/group size: 8-10 hands-on/40 demo. Also featured: floral arranging, wine tastings, children's courses, custom-designed programs for groups.

EMPHASIS: Themes include brasserie and bistro cooking, fish, Provencal specialties, sauces, wild game, chocolate, wine.

COSTS: Demonstrations are 275 FF each (6 for the price of 5), themed courses range from 5,750 FF to 10,000/week. Lodging packages are available on a limited basis. Demonstration reservations must be made by noon the day of class.

LOCATION: Central Paris, near 3 main subway entrances and most major department stores.

CONTACT: Marie-Anne Dufeu, Ritz-Escoffier Ecole de Gastronomie Francaise, 15, Place Vendome, Paris Cedex 01, 75041 France; (33) 143-16-30-50, (800) 966-5758, Fax (33) 143-16-31-50.

ROGER VERGÉ COOKING SCHOOL
Mougins/September-July

This school in Restaurant l'Amandier offers 2-hour demonstrations from Tuesday through Saturday. Founded in 1984. Maximum class/group size: 20. Facilities: the restaurant kitchen.

EMPHASIS: Seasonal menus, Provencal cuisine.

FACULTY: Michel Duhamel and other chefs from the Moulin de Mougins restaurant.

COSTS: 300 FF per class, 1,350 FF for 5 classes. Booking is desired 48 hours in advance.

LOCATION: Near Cannes.

CONTACT: Sylvie Auffrey, Proprietor, Roger Vergé Cooking School, Ecole du Moulin, Restaurant l'Amandier, Mougins Village, 06250 France; (33) 493-75-35-70, Fax (33) 493-90-18-55.

SAVOIR FAIRE TOURS – FOOD LOVERS TOUR OF PARIS
(See display ad page 242) **Paris/Spring and Fall**

Savoir Faire owner Deborah Kearns conducts 1-week culinary vacations that combine three cooking lessons and tastings with touring and shopping of interest to food lovers. Established in 1996. Maximum class/group size: 6-12. Also featured: dining at the Michelin-starred restaurant atop the Eiffel Tower, tour of Les Halles food market, visit to the Sevres porcelain factory, tea salons.

EMPHASIS: French cuisine.

FACULTY: Includes Princess Marie-Blanche de Broglie, Commandeur de l'Ordre des Cordons Bleus, and master chefs of the Hotel Plaza Athenee. Savoir Tours owner/guide Deborah Kearns.

COSTS: Range between $2,600 and $3,250, which includes lodging and some meals. Hotel is a restored villa on the left bank, near the Champs Elysees. A $500 deposit is required. Balance is due 60 days prior. Full refund if space can be filled.

CONTACT: Judy Ebrey, Owner, Cuisine International, P.O. Box 25228, Dallas, TX 75225 United States; (214) 373-1161, Fax (214) 373-1162, E-mail CuisineInt@aol.com, URL http://www.iglobal.net/cuisineint.

HONG KONG

CHOPSTICKS COOKING CENTRE
Kowloon/September-December, March-June   *(See also page 129)*
This private trade school offers a 4-day gourmet tour that includes a demonstration lesson, restaurant kitchen visits, seafood and wet market visits, and dining in local restaurants. Maximum class/group size: 24. Also featured: 1- to 4-hour demonstration classes, half-day tourist classes, 1-day courses, 1- and 4-week intensive.

COSTS: Tour cost begins at $1,200, which includes shared lodging, most meals, ground transport. Classes begin at $90 for a 2-hour demonstration, $500 for a 1-day course. Lodging: 4- or 5-star hotels.
CONTACT: Cecilia Au-Yang, Principal, Chopsticks Cooking Centre, 108 Boundary St., G/Fl., Kowloon, Hong Kong; (852) 2336-8433, (852) 2336-8037, Fax (852) 2338-1462.

HONG KONG FOOD FESTIVAL
March
The Hong Kong Tourist Association sponsors an annual two-week event featuring approximately 20 Cooking with Great Chefs demonstration classes that are held in the kitchens of participating hotels and restaurants. Maximum class/group size: 15. Also featured: culinary Awards Photo Exhibition, t'ai chi lessons, theme parties and banquets, and tours of tea companies, wedding cake bakeries, and Sai Kung villages.

EMPHASIS: Thai, Cantonese, Japanese, and European specialties.
CONTACT: Hong Kong Tourist Assn., 11th Flr, Citicorp Centre, 18 Whitfield Rd., North Point, Hong Kong; (852) 2807-6543, (852) 2807-6177, URL http://www.hkta.org. U.S. Contacts: New York NY (212) 869-5008; Los Angeles, CA (310) 208-4582; Oakbrook, IL (630) 575-2828.

INDIA

CULINARY SPLENDORS OF INDIA WITH JULIE SAHNI
October   *(See also page 67)*
Cooking school owner and food writer Julie Sahni conducts a 17-day cultural and culinary tour of India that includes visits to farm kitchens and cooking demonstrations. Also featured: visits to spice and tea plantations, markets and bazaars, private receptions.

EMPHASIS: Indian cuisine.
FACULTY: Julie Sahni is author of *Classic Indian Cooking* and *Indian Vegetarian Cooking*. She is a member of the IACP and Les Dames D'Escoffier and has degrees in Architecture and Classical Dance.
COSTS: $4,975, which includes double occupancy lodging (single supplement $1,175), most meals, ground transport, planned activities. Lodging in deluxe hotels or, in smaller cities, best available. A $500 deposit reserves a space; balance due 60 days prior.
LOCATION: Western, southern, and northern India.
CONTACT: Julie Sahni, Julie Sahni's School of Indian Cooking, 101 Clark St., #13A, Brooklyn Heights, NY 11201 USA; (718) 625-3958, Fax (718) 625-3958.

IRELAND

BALLYMALOE COOKERY SCHOOL
Midleton/September-July   *(See also page 129)*
This proprietary school offers 1- to 5-day hands-on vacation programs that include a 1-day Christmas cooking demonstration and a weekend Entertaining course. Maximum class/group size: 44 hands-on/60 demo. Also featured: fishing and golf.

EMPHASIS: A variety of topics, including entertaining menus, seafood, vegetarian dishes.

COSTS: 1-day courses are IR£95, weekend courses are IR£225, 5-day courses are IR£355. Accommodation in self-catering cottages at school during short courses is IR£12/night shared, IR£14.50/night single. 55% deposit required.

CONTACT: Tim Allen, Ballymaloe Cookery School, Kinoith, Shanagarry, County Cork, Midleton, Ireland; (353) 21-646785, Fax (353) 21-646909.

BALTIMORE INTERNATIONAL CULINARY COLLEGE
(See also page 48)   **Lough Ramor/March-October**

The college's European Educational Centre offers programs that are open to nonprofessionals. Also featured: golf, tennis, fishing, boating.

COSTS: Lodging at The Park Hotel-Deer Park Lodge.

LOCATION: The 100-acre campus is 50 miles from Dublin.

CONTACT: Baltimore International Culinary College, 17 Commerce St., Baltimore, M/d 21202 USA; (800) 624-9926, (410) 752-4710, Fax (410) 752-3730.

COUNTRY HOUSE COOKERY – BERRY LODGE
Miltown Malbay, Co. Clare/Year-round

This school in a recently renovated, Victorian country house offers day, weekend, 3-day midweek and week-long participation courses. Founded in 1994. Maximum class/group size: 10. Facilities: a modern traditional farmhouse kitchen, bed & breakfast accommodations, restaurant. Also featured: day tour of local cultural and historical sites, dinners at local restaurants, golf, fishing, swimming, sightseeing.

EMPHASIS: Traditional and modern Irish country cuisine, French and international cuisine.

FACULTY: Rita Meade learned to cook from her mother and qualified as a Home Economist. She studied in England, France and Italy and has taught cooking for nearly 30 years.

COSTS: One-week/22 hours tuition is IR£200. Dinner is IR£20. Two morning summer program is IR£50, tuition only. Lodging at Berry Lodge, a 19th-century country house, is IR£20 per night. One week tuition and accommodation for April-June, September and October is IR£356. A IR£150 deposit is required; balance is due 4 weeks prior.

LOCATION: Rural western Ireland, 200 yards from the sea in West Clare, 160 miles from Dublin, and 38 miles from Shannon International Airport.

CONTACT: Rita Meade, Country House Cookery-Berry Lodge, Berry Lodge, Annagh, Miltown Malbay, Co. Clare, Ireland; (44) 353-6587022, Fax (44) 353-6587022.

ISRAEL

TNUVA, TRAINING CENTER FOR FOOD CULTURE
(See display ad page 260)   **Tel Aviv/September-July**

Tnuva, the largest food distributing company in Israel offers three demonstration classes daily, Sunday-Thursday, that teach adults and children how to prepare food inexpensively and efficiently. Established in 1973. Maximum class/group size: 15-40. Facilities: amphitheater. Also featured: sessions in English for groups of 25 or more.

EMPHASIS: Russian, Middle Eastern, Moroccan, Italian, and Chinese cuisines; microwave, vegetarian, and nutritional cookery; baking; fruit preparation and marzipan garnishing.

FACULTY: School director Tova Aran and a teaching staff of food writers, home economics instructors, hotel/restaurant chefs, pastry chefs, and caterers.

COSTS: Classes for English-speaking groups are about 65 Shekels/person.

LOCATION: Central Tel-Aviv.

CONTACT: Tova Aran, Tnuva, Training Center for Food Culture, 47 Ben-Gurion Blvd., Tel Aviv, Israel; (972) 3-5243-157, (972) 3-5243-158, Fax (972) 3-5230-055.

ITALY

A TAVOLA CON LO CHEF
Rome/Year-round
This school offers 1-week demonstration courses. Maximum class/group size: 20. Facilities: well-equipped professional kitchen. Also featured: dining in selected restaurants, guided tours of Rome.
EMPHASIS: Traditional and modern Italian and regional cuisine.
FACULTY: Chefs of selected Italian restaurants.
COSTS: $3,000 ($2,200 for non-cooking guest), which includes double occupancy luxury hotel, meals, and planned activities. Single supplement $500. $250 deposit required, of which $50 is non-refundable, balance due 60 days prior. Refund for cancellation 30 days prior.
LOCATION: Rome's historic center, next to St. Peter Cathedral.
CONTACT: Maria Teresa Meloni, A Tavola con lo Chef, Via dei Gracchi 60, Rome, Italy; (39) 6-320-3402, Fax (39) 6-320-3402.

ALASTAIR LITTLE COOKERY WEEKS – LA CACCIATA
Orvieto/May-July, September-October
This school offers 4 seven-day courses/month (17/year). Founded in 1994. Maximum class/group size: 20. Facilities: 12-sq-meter kitchen area with inglenook fireplace, wood-fired oven outside. Also featured: visits to Perugia, Assissi, or Siena, shopping at Orvieto market, dinner with estate owners.
EMPHASIS: Simple, fresh italian food preparation, including risottos, pastas, truffles, focaccia, breads, pizza, gelati.

FACULTY: Alastair Little, British chef/owner of a restaurant in London's Soho and co-author of *Keep It Simple* and a weekly food column. Local Italian chefs.

COSTS: £850 cost includes lodging, meals, planned excursions. Lodging in bedrooms (with bathrooms) in converted farmhouses. The estate, a working farm noted for its extra virgin olive oil, has a swimming pool and riding school. £200 deposit, balance due 8 weeks prior.

LOCATION: Overlooking Orvieto in Umbria, 90 miles north of Rome.

CONTACT: Sarah Robson, Manager, La Cacciata, Alastair Little Cookery, 15 Dawson Pl., London, W2 4TH England; (44) 181-675-9034, Fax (44) 181-675-9034.

AVIGNONESI WINE AND FOOD WORKSHOPS
(See also page 130)   **Florence/April-June, September-November**

This wine-producing estate sponsors more than a dozen 1-week cooking vacations/year that include demonstrations and hands-on classes. Maximum class/group size: 12. Facilities: professional kitchen in an 11th-century castle. Also featured: visits to markets, an olive oil mill, and prosciutto, bread, and chocolate producers. Programs for food professionals.

EMPHASIS: Tuscan cuisine, including pasta, game, cold buffet; food and wine pairing.

FACULTY: Culinary Director Rolando Beramendi, brand manager of Avignonesi, Chef Sara Jenkins, Burton Anderson, Chef Fabio Picchi of Cibreo, Chef Carlo Cioni of Da Delfina, Master of Wine Nick Belfrage.

COSTS: $2,300, which includes double occupancy lodging, meals and wine, ground transport, and planned activities. Lodging in 4-star hotel in Florence, restored rooms in castle with private bath. $500 deposit required, balance due 30 days prior. Full refund 60 days prior.

CONTACT: Pamela Sheldon Johns, Avignonesi Wine and Food Workshops, 1324 State St., #J-157, Santa Barbara, CA 93101 USA; (805) 963-7289, E-mail CulinarArt@aol.comAlso: Palazzo Avignonesi, 53045 Montepulciano, Italy; (39) 578-757874, Fax (39) 578-757847.

BADIA A COLTIBUONO
Siena/May-July, September-October

Cookbook author Lorenza de'Medici offers about a dozen 5-day vacation courses/year that include demonstration and participation cooking classes. Established in 1985. Maximum class/group size: 15. Facilities: large teaching kitchen. Also featured: visits to food producers, wineries, private estates; dining as guests of Lorenza and at private homes, villas and castles; trip to the Palio horse race (July); dinner as guests at a Siena contrada.

EMPHASIS: Regional Italian cooking and wines.

FACULTY: Lorenza de' Medici, author of several cookbooks and cooking manuals and a PBS TV series; Master of Wine Nicolas Belfrage.

COSTS: Land cost is $4,700 single, $4,200 double occupancy. Badia a Coltibuono, an 11th century estate, produces wine, vinegar, honey, olive oil, and other products. Amenities include a cookbook library, swimming pool, and sauna.

LOCATION: 20 miles north of Siena, 40 miles south of Florence.

CONTACT: Lorenza de' Medici, Badia a Coltibuono, Gaiole in Chianti, Siena, 53013 Italy; , Fax (39)

577-749235, E-mail U.S. Contact: Judy Ebrey, P.O. Box 25228, Dallas, TX 75225 USA; (214) 373-1162, E-mail VillaTable@aol.com, URL http://www.iglobal.net/cuisineint.

BED AND BREAKFAST IN TUSCANY
Tuscany/May, October, November
This bed & breakfast offers 3 or 4 one-week and mini-courses/year. Established in 1985. Maximum class/group size: 10. Facilities: Ms. Luhan's family farm/bed & breakfast has a farm kitchen with individual work areas. Also featured: shopping and sightseeing.
EMPHASIS: Tuscan cuisine, including pastas and pizza.
FACULTY: Restaurateur and caterer Lucia Ana Luhan completed master's degree studies in public relations from Boston University and studied in Europe and South America. She owns What's Cooking? in Newport Beach and Luciana's Ristorante in Dana Point, California.
COSTS: $1,800 for one week includes lodging and most meals.
LOCATION: Central Italy's wine country, a 5-minute drive from Montecatini Terme, less than 30 minutes from Florence, 90 minutes from Siena.
CONTACT: Food and Wine Appreciation Program, B & B in Tuscany, P.O. Box 5246, Balboa Island, CA 92662 USA; (714) 488-7694, Fax (714) 488-7694, E-mail In Italy: (39) 572-628817 phone/fax.

CHIANTI IN TUSCANY – ITALIAN COOKERY AND WINE
Gaiole in Chianti/April-October
This school offers continuous 1-week hands-on cooking courses and Italian language lessons. Founded in 1986. Maximum class/group size: 10. Facilities: Podere Le Rose, the instructors' home, which has a well-equipped typical country kitchen. Also featured: wine lesson, winery tour, Chianti tour.
EMPHASIS: Northern and southern Italian cookery, fresh ingredients, easy-to-make recipes; Italian language.
FACULTY: The Bevilacqua de'Mari family assisted by a Tuscan chef.
COSTS: 900,000 Lira for classes only. Lodging upon request. Various packages offered. Lodging at a 13th-century restored Italian farmhouse. 30% deposit, refund less expenses 30 days prior.
LOCATION: A 30-minute drive from Siena and an hour from Florence.
CONTACT: Countess Simonetta de'Mari di Altamura, Chianti in Tuscany, Podere Le Rose, Poggio S. Polo 2, Lecchi, Gaiole (SI), 53013 Italy; (39) 55 294511, Fax (39) 55 2396887.

COOKING WITH MARIA
Assisi/May-July, September-October   *(See display ad page 264)*
This travel company offers two 1-week cooking vacations/month that include 5 hands-on classes. Started in 1992. Maximum class/group size: 8. Also featured: day trips, market visits, winery tours and instruction, dining in fine restaurants, sightseeing, visits to food producers, ceramics shopping.
EMPHASIS: Umbrian home cooking, fresh herbs and vegetables, roasted meats, game, truffles.
FACULTY: Maria Maurillo-Fabrizi.
COSTS: $1,589, which includes meals, double occupancy lodging and private bath, excursions. Lodging at a country estate with private baths and antique furnishings. $300 deposit with booking, balance due and full refund granted 45 days prior, no refund within 45 days.
LOCATION: 2 miles east of Assisi, in Umbria.
CONTACT: Gabriele Dellanave, Owner, Gabriele's Travels to Italy, 3037 14th Ave., NW, Rochester, MN 55901 USA; (507) 287-8733, Fax (507) 287-8733, E-mail gabriele@infonet.isl.net, URL http://www.isl.net/gabriel/gabriel.html.

CUCINA CASALINGA
April-May, October   *(See also page 171)*
This cooking school offers culinary tours of Italy that include Chef Enrico Franzese's Cooking Classes in Amalfi and Venetian Cooking in a Venetian Palace with Fulvia Sesani. Maximum class/group size: 20. Also featured: optional excursions to golf courses, tour of the Lake Country, dining at a Michelin 2-star restaurant, excursions to Ravello, and Pompeii, shopping in Sorrento.

EMPHASIS: Italian regional cuisine.

COSTS: Amalfi tour is $2,700, including double occupancy lodging, most meals, and excursions.

CONTACT: Sally Ann Maraventano, Owner, Cucina Casalinga, 171 Drum Hill Rd., Wilton, CT 06897 USA; (203) 762-0767, Fax (203) 762-0768, E-mail cucina@juno.com.

CUCINA TOSCANA
Florence/Year-round

This culinary travel service offers customized 1-day to 1-month gastronomic excursions in Italy. Founded in 1983. Maximum class/group size: 2-25. Facilities: restaurant kitchens. Also featured: antique hunting, garden visits, walking tours of Florence, insider shopping, excursions to the Tuscan countryside.

EMPHASIS: Regional Italian cuisine.

FACULTY: Proprietor Faith Heller Willinger is author of *Red, White and Greens: The Italian Way with Vegetables* and directs the Hotel Cipriani culinary program. Her assistant, Laura Kramer, has a degree in Medieval studies and leads tours to Tuscany.

COSTS: From $275/day plus expenses for 1-3 persons. Group rates start at $150/day and include meals and transport. Rates are lower for longer trips.

LOCATION: Regions of Tuscany.

CONTACT: Faith Heller Willinger, Cucina Toscana, via della Chiesa, 7, Florence, 50125 Italy; (39) 55-2337014, Fax (39) 55-2337014, E-mail U.S. Contact: Vivian (847) 432-1814, Fax (847) 432-1889.

CUISINE ECLAIREÉ
Tuscany/Spring and Fall

This culinary travel company offers 1-week hands-on courses in Tuscan cooking. Established in 1994. Maximum class/group size: 8. Also featured: market visits in Lucca or Florence, swimming.

EMPHASIS: Tuscan cooking using fresh, local ingredients.

FACULTY: Elaine Lemm, Chef de Cuisine and owner, studied at the Ritz Escoffier in Paris.

COSTS: Range from £650-£850, which includes shared lodging and meals. Villa Catureglio, an 11th-century Tuscan estate with swimming pool. 10% nonrefundable deposit required.

LOCATION: The hills above Lucca.

CONTACT: Elaine M. Lemm, Owner, Cuisine Eclaireé, 5, the Poplars, Newton-on-Ouse, York, Y06 2BL England; (44) 1347-848557, (44) 1904-448963, Fax (44) 1347-848557.

DIANE SEED'S CULINARY EXPERIENCES
Rome, Puglia/April-June, September-November

This private school offers 5 demonstration and hands-on classes/week in Rome and six 6-day hands-on cooking vacations/year in Puglia. First offered in 1996. Maximum class/group size: 12 Rome/15 Puglia. Also featured: Rome: market visits, dining in fine restaurants, private instruction; Puglia: visits to a cheese maker, olive grove, and oil production plant.

EMPHASIS: Italian regional cuisine.

FACULTY: Diane Seed, British cooking teacher and author, who has lived in Rome for 28 years.

COSTS: Puglia: $2,500, which includes meals and lodging. Lodging in Puglia at Il Melograno, a family owned 5-star Relais & Chateaux hotel decorated with antiques collected by the owners. Amenities include a Mediterranean health center, heated indoor pool, solarium, gymnasium, pool, tennis courts. Refund minus administration costs up to 1 month prior.

LOCATION: Central Rome, near the Palazzo Piazza Venezia; Puglia, in the Truilly region on the Adriatic, south of Bari.

CONTACT: Diane Seed, Diane Seed's Roman Kitchen, Via del Plebiscito 112, Rome, 00186 Italy; (39) 6 6797 103, Fax (39) 6 6797 109, E-mail 100525.1613@compuserve.comU.S. Contact: Judy Ebrey, Cuisine International, P.O. Box 25228, Dallas, TX 75225 USA; (214) 373-1161, (214) 373-1162, E-mail CuisineInt@aol.com, URL http://www.iglobal.net/cuisineint.

GABRIELE'S TRAVELS TO ITALY
Amalfi, Assisi/May-July, September-October   *(See display ad below)*

This special interest travel company offers cooking, food, and wine tours that include demonstrations and hands-on instruction. Established in 1992. Maximum class/group size: 8-16. Also featured: market visits, winery tours, sightseeing, visits to food producers, day trips, shopping for ceramics.

EMPHASIS: Italian regional cuisine.

LOCATION: In Amalfi: Mediterranean Cooking in Amalfi. In Assisi: Cooking with Maria.

CONTACT: Gabriele Dellanave, Owner, Gabriele's Travels to Italy, , 3037 14th Ave. NW, Rochester, MN 55901 USA; (507) 287-8733, Fax (507) 287-8733, E-mail gabriele@infonet.isl.net, URL http://www.isl.net/gabriel/gabriel.html.

GIULIANO BUGIALLI'S COOKING IN FLORENCE
Florence/May-July, September-October, December   *(See display ad page 265)*

Cookbook author Giuliano Bugialli offers 1-week hands-on vacation programs. Established in 1973. Maximum class/group size: 18. Facilities: large newly-equipped kitchens in a Chianti villa, wood-burning brick oven and hearth. Also featured: dining in fine restaurants and trattorias, gastronomic and oenologic trips, tastings.

EMPHASIS: Italian authentic cooking of all regions.

FACULTY: Giuliano Bugialli teaches all classes, He is author of *The Fine Art of Italian Cooking*, Tastemaker-award winners *Giuliano Bugialli's Classic Techniques of Italian Cooking* and *Giuliano Bugialli's Foods of Italy*.

COSTS: $3,400-$4,000, which includes most meals, planned excursions, and first class or superior hotel lodging in central Florence. $500 deposit required, $450 refund 90 days prior, balance due 90 days prior.

LOCATION: In Florence with classes in a Chianti country villa.

CONTACT: Giuliano Bugialli's Cooking in Florence, P.O. Box 1650, Canal St. Station, New York, NY 10013 USA; (212) 966-5325, Fax (212) 226-0601.

GRITTI PALACE SCHOOL OF FINE COOKING
Venice/January-March, July, November-December

This luxury resort hotel offers 5-day vacation demonstration courses. Established in 1974. Maximum class/group size: 22-25. Facilities: specially-equipped mirrored room fitted with a stove.

EMPHASIS: Regional Italian cuisine, seasonal ingredients, wine selection, setting of a table, flower arrangements.

FACULTY: Gritti's chef Celestino Giacomello.

LOCATION: The hotel Gritti Palace, palace of Doge Andrea Gritti in the 15th century, overlooking the Grand Canal, is 30 minutes by boat from Venice Airport.

CONTACT: Laura Fanecco, Gritti Palace School of Fine Cooking, Campo Santa Maria del Giglio, Venice 2467, Italy; (800) 325-3589, Fax (512) 834-7598.

HORIZONS – THE NEW ENGLAND CRAFT PROGRAM
Italy

This craft school offers gastronomic trips to Italy that include daily classes and shopping at village markets. Founded in 1983.

CONTACT: Jane Sinauer, Director, Horizons, 108 N. Main St., Sunderland, MA 01375 USA; (413) 665-0300, Fax (413) 665-4141.

HOTEL CIPRIANI COOKING SCHOOL
Venice/April, September-November

This luxury resort hotel offers seven 5-day demonstration programs per year that are taught by noted culinarians and include visits and dining in private palazzos and homes. Founded in 1978. Maximum class/group size: 24. Facilities: demonstration kitchen in a large meeting room overlooking the Venetian lagoon, video, 3 gas burners and oven. Also featured: visit to the Rialto market, a lagoon or mainland excursion, wine presentations, fine dining, concluding banquet.

EMPHASIS: Italian and international cuisines utilizing the foods and wines of Venice.

FACULTY: Well-known instructors, including Julia Child, Marcella Hazan, Renato Piccolotto, Nobu Matsuhisa, and Giuliano Hazan. Program coordinator is Faith Willinger.

COSTS: $3,385, which includes double occupancy deluxe lodging at the Hotel Cipriani, meals, and planned activities. Non-participant guest $2,530; single supplement $290. Hotel amenities include a heated pool, tennis, and sauna. Full payment with booking; full refund 15 days prior to arrival.

LOCATION: Approximately 30 minutes by water-taxi from the airport.

CONTACT: Dr. Natale Rusconi, Managing Director, Hotel Cipriani Cooking School: Meet the Stars of Gastronomy, Guidecca 10, Venice, 30133 Italy; (39) 41-520-7744, Fax (39) 41-520-3930, E-mail U.S. Contact: Orient Express Hotels (800) 237-1236 or (212) 838-7874.

IL BORGHETTO COOKING SCHOOL
Florence/April, May, September, October
This country villa offers 6-day vacation programs. Founded in 1995. Maximum class/group size: 8. Facilities: a newly constructed restaurant kitchen with 4 work areas. Also featured: visits to local markets and castles, guided tours, shopping in Florence and Siena.

EMPHASIS: The theoretical and practical aspects of Tuscan cuisine, including ingredient selection and techniques.

FACULTY: Francesca Cianchi, former chef at Mezzaluna in New York City.

COSTS: The $3,000 fee includes lodging and meals; $1,000 additional for nonparticipant in double room, $5,000 for 2 participants sharing a room. The 15th-century Il Borghetto is on a 30-hectare estate with olive groves, medieval grain silos, swimming pool, and cookbook library. All rooms have baths. 35% deposit to reserve, balance 3 weeks prior; 25% cancellation penalty a month prior.

LOCATION: The central Chianti region, 10 miles south of Florence.

CONTACT: Francesca Cianchi, Il Borghetto Cooking School, San Casciano Val di Pesa, Florence, 50020 Italy; (39) 55-8244442, Fax (39) 55-8244247, E-mail U.S. Contact: Elaine Muoio, Italian Rentals, 3801 Ingomar St., NW, Washington, DC 20015 USA; (202) 244-5345, Fax (202) 362-0520.

IL CASALE LA PIETRA
Montecosaro/Summer *(See display ad page 242)*
This cooking instructor offers 1-week cooking vacations that feature demonstration and participation classes and cultural excursions. Established in 1995. Maximum class/group size: 6. Facilities: La Pietra, the country home of Emilia Corelli. Also featured: visits to the Caldarola castle, the town of Loreto, and mountain caves. Activities include swimming, tennis, golf, and horseback riding.

EMPHASIS: Regional cuisine of central Italy, home-grown produce.

FACULTY: Emilia Cucchi Corelli and her daughter, Beatrice.

COSTS: $1,950 ($2,150) double (single) occupancy. Includes 6 nights lodging, all meals, excursions (except for tickets). Lodging is at the Villa Eugenia Hotel. A $400 deposit is required.

LOCATION: In the Marche on the Adriatic. Transfers are from Rome.

CONTACT: Judy Ebrey, Owner, Cuisine International, P.O. Box 25228, Dallas, TX 75225 United States; (214) 373-1161, Fax (214) 373-1162, E-mail CuisineInt@aol.com, URL http://www.iglobal.net/cuisineint.

INTERNATIONAL COOKING SCHOOL OF ITALIAN FOOD AND WINE
Bologna/Year-round *(See also page 200) (See display ad page 267)*
This school established in 1987 by Mary Beth Clark offers 5 participation courses per year that include the 6-day Basic certificate course and the 7-day Piedmont Truffle Festival. Maximum class/group size: 14. Facilities: modern, professional kitchen with individual work areas. Also featured: visits to food producers and markets, olive oil tastings, private winery tours, a truffle hunt, dining in Michelin-star restaurants with private demonstrations.

EMPHASIS: Traditional and new light Italian cuisines with fresh ingredients and ease of preparation, techniques, antipasti, hand-made pasta, risotto, truffle dishes, seasonal main dishes, desserts.

FACULTY: Mary Beth Clark, owner of International Food And Wine Consultants, Inc., is chef trained, author of *Trattoria* and contributor to *Italy: A Culinary Journey*, magazine feature writer, and has a cooking video. Other instructors include a pasta maker.

COSTS: $3,000-$3,450 ($2,400-$3,100 for non-cooking guest, $275 single supplement), which includes most meals, first class lodging, ground transport, and planned activities. $300 deposit ($150 nonrefundable) required, balance due 60 days prior.

LOCATION: Central Bologna.

CONTACT: Mary Beth Clark, International Cooking School Of Italian Food And Wine, 201 E. 28th St., #15B, New York, NY 10016-8538 USA; (212) 779-1921, Fax (212) 779-3248, E-mail MaryBethClark@worldnet.att.net.

THE INTERNATIONAL COOKING SCHOOL OF ITALIAN FOOD AND WINE
in Bologna, Italy

Join Mary Beth Clark, award-winning cooking teacher and author, for hands-on cooking in the "Gastronomic Capital of Italy". Learn authentic delectable dishes from *l'antipasto* through *il dolce*. Special techniques of traditional and new light cooking. Conducted in English in a modern professional kitchen. Classes conclude with food-and-wine pairing dinners.

Dine in Michelin-starred restaurants. Exclusive estate visits. Truffle hunt!

Recommended as the only school in Italy for "The Best Cooking Class Vacations." Exceptional week-long courses in June, July, September, October. Video available.

BROCHURE: THE INTERNATIONAL COOKING SCHOOL OF ITALIAN FOOD AND WINE
201 East 28 Street, Suite 15B, New York, NY 10016-8538
Tel (212) 779-1921 Fax (212) 779-3248 E-mail: MaryBethClark@worldnet.att.net

ITALIAN COOKERY WEEKS
Orvieto and Ostuni/May-September

This individual offers weekly 6-day hands-on courses in Orvieto and Ostuni. Founded in 1990. Maximum class/group size: 20. Also featured: shopping at the local market, sightseeing in Assisi and Perugia (Orvieto) and Lecce and Alberobello (Ostuni), truffle hunt. Also available: tailor-made group classes, swimming, golf, horseback riding.
EMPHASIS: Italian regional cuisine.
FACULTY: Susanna Gelmetti, who was chef at London's Accademia Italiana delle Arti and author of *Italian Country Cooking*; well-known Italian chefs and guest English chefs.
COSTS: £900 includes meals, lodging at century farm estates with ensuite baths, planned excursions.
LOCATION: A farm estate in Orvieto, and a converted 15th century castle near Ostuni.
CONTACT: Susanna Gelmetti, Italian Cookery Weeks, Box 2482, London, NW10 1HW England; (44) 181-208-0112, Fax (44) 171-401-8763, E-mail U.S. Contact: Judy Ebrey, Box 25228, Dallas, TX USA 75225; (214) 373-1161; Fax (214) 373-1162; E-mail CuisineInt@aol.com; URL http://www.iglobal.net/cuisineint.

ITALIAN COUNTRY COOKING CLASSES WITH DIANA FOLONARI
Positano/May-June, September-October

Diana Folonari offers 1-week participation courses. Established in 1980. Maximum class/group size: 12. Facilities: Ms. Folonari's home.
EMPHASIS: Italian cuisine.
FACULTY: Diana and Vic Folonari.
COSTS: Fee for classes is $1,500; 8 nights at the Villa Franca Hotel (other hotels available) is $690-$840/person. $300 deposit required.

LOCATION: Via del Canovaccio 10 in Positano
CONTACT: Martha Morano, E & M Associates, 211 E. 43rd Street, New York, NY 10017 USA; (800) 223-9832, (212) 599-8280, Fax (212) 599-1755, E-mail emrom@ichange.com, URL http://www.lesromantiques.com.

ITALIAN CUISINE IN FLORENCE
Florence/Year-round

This school in a private apartment offers a dozen 3- to 5-day demonstration and participation courses/year. Special 1- or 2-day demo classes for larger groups with travel agencies (with Japan). Established in 1983. Maximum class/group size: 8 hands-on/18 demo. Facilities: a 300-square-foot kitchen with modern equipment. Also featured: demonstrations for groups, private instruction.
EMPHASIS: Classical, regional, and new Italian cuisine; desserts.
FACULTY: Masha Innocenti, CCP, a member of the IACP, holds a diploma from Scuola di Arte Culinaria Cordon Bleu and is a member of the Associazione Italiana Sommeliers and the Commanderie des Cordons Bleus de France.
COSTS: 1,300,000 Lira for the gourmet cuisine courses, 850,000 Lira for the desserts course. Rates include meals. Private classes are 300,000 Lira per day. One-day demo 95,000 Lira. A nonrefundable 30% deposit is required; balance is due 6 weeks prior. Payment by bank check in Italian currency.
LOCATION: Near the center of Florence.
CONTACT: Masha Innocenti, Italian Cuisine in Florence, Via Trieste 1, Florence, 50139 Italy; (39) 55-480041, (39) 55-499503, Fax (39) 55-480041.

ITALIAN LANGUAGE AND CUISINE
Siena/Year-round

This sponsor of language learning vacations offers 4-week participation courses that include daily cooking and language instruction. Established in 1990. Maximum class/group size: 12. Also featured: cocktail parties, movies, guided museum visits, excursions, conferences.
EMPHASIS: Tuscan cuisine, pasta; Italian language.
FACULTY: Local chefs and native Italian language instructors.
COSTS: $1,600, including half-board lodging in a private home. Nonrefundable deposit of $100.
CONTACT: Director, Italian Language and Cuisine, 216 E. 45th St., 17th Flr., New York, NY 10017 USA; (212) 867-1225, (800) 394-LEARN, Fax (212) 867-7666.

LA BOTTEGA DEL 30 COOKING SCHOOL
Villa a Sesta, Siena/Year-round

This private school offers twenty 5-day hands-on cooking courses/year. Daily classes on a space-available basis. Founded 1995. Maximum group size: 8-10. Facilities: dining room, library, wine cellar, wood-burning oven, modern kitchen with 10 work areas. Also featured: wine instruction, day trips, market visits, winery tours, fine dining , sightseeing, visits to food producers.
EMPHASIS: Tuscan cooking, using fresh ingredients. Includes appetizers, soups and sauces, home-made pasta, main courses, desserts. Olive oil and wine are pressed on the premises.
FACULTY: Helen Stoquelet, owner and chef of La Bottega del 30 restaurant, and her husband, Franco Camelia; Diana Place, translator/tour guide.
COSTS: $2,200, which includes 7 nights double occupancy apartment lodging, 4 dinners, 2 excursions. Lodging: 10 newly refurbished apartments with pool, surrounded by vineyards. $600 deposit required, refund less $50 for cancellation 30 days prior.
LOCATION: 20 minutes outside of Siena, 90 miles south of Florence.
CONTACT: Diana Place, La Bottega del 30 Cooking School, via S. Caterina, 2, Villa a Sesta, Siena, 53019 Italy; (39) 577-359226, Fax (39) 577-359226, E-mail EssofItaly@aolU.S. Contact: Diana Place, Essence of Italy, Box 956, Boca Raton, FL 33429 USA; (561) 361-0301 phone/fax.

LA CHIUSA – COUNTRY COOKING IN ITALY
Northern Umbria/May, September, October

This tour operator offers 5-day cooking vacations that include 4 afternoon classes. Non-smoking.

Maximum class/group size: 6-8. Facilities: outdoor wood-fired oven for bread baking. Also featured: mountain biking, sightseeing.
EMPHASIS: Italian regional cuisine utilizing the farm's organic produce and grapes.
FACULTY: Mr. and Mrs. Claudio Rener.
COSTS: 770,000 Lira (about $500), which includes lodging and breakfasts and dinners. apartment with private bath. 25% deposit required, balance due 3 months prior.
LOCATION: Near the Tuscany border.
CONTACT: Cathy Kinloch, Travel Agent, Teachers' Travel Service, 21 St. Clair Ave. E, #1003, Toronto, ON M4T 1L9 Canada; (416) 922-2232, (800) 268-7229, Fax (416) 922-8410, E-mail 1030541107@compuserve.com.

LA CUCINA AL FOCOLARE
Florence, Italy
Immerse yourself into the breadth of Tuscan cuisine.
Hands-on cooking, Wine Courses
1-800-988-2851   •   Free brochure

(See display ad above)

LA CUCINA AL FOCOLARE
Tuscany/April-June, September-November

The Fattoria Degli Usignoli, a converted 15th-century friary conducts ten 1-week hands-on culinary vacations a year. Established in 1992. Maximum class/group size: 10-15. Facilities: the converted wine cellar has a demonstration kitchen with wood-burning oven, rotisserie, and individual work stations. Also featured: sheep farm for ricotta, Tuscan bread bakery, grape picking, outdoor market tour, sightseeing in Florence, Siena, and San Gimignano.
EMPHASIS: Tuscan specialties, pizza, breads, grill and rotisserie dishes, culinary history, wine appreciation.
FACULTY: Piero Ferrini, chef-professor from Florence's scuola Alberghiera "saffi"; Paolo Blasi, sommelier; Peggy Markel, program founder and director.
COSTS: Cost is $2,875 ($2,550, $2,250), which includes single (double, triple) occupancy apartment with private kitchen, meals, planned activities, and transport from Florence. The Fattoria, situated on 55 acres, produces its own Chianti and extra virgin olive oil. Amenities include tennis, horseback riding, and swimming. $500 deposit required, balance due 45 days prior. Cancellations 45 days prior forfeit $100.
LOCATION: Overlooking the Valdarno Valley, 18 miles southeast of Florence.
CONTACT: Peggy Markel, La Cucina al Focolare, P.O. Box 646, Boulder, CO 80306-0646 USA; (800) 988-2851, Fax (303) 440-8598, E-mail 76534,3422@compuserve.com.

LA CUCINA KASHER IN TOSCANA
Pomino/May-September

This travel company offers one-week hands-on kosher culinary vacations. Founded in 1995. Facilities: the kitchen of Locanda di Praticino, with a full-time mashgiach. Also featured: visits to markets, olive oil producers, and a porcelain museum, shopping, a cultural evening in Florence, an Italian language lesson, synagogue visits.
EMPHASIS: Cuisines of the Jews of Rome, Tuscany, Venice, and other regions.
FACULTY: Edda Servi Machlin, teacher of Italian-Jewish cuisine and historian of Italian-Jewish life.
COSTS: $2,600, includes meals, double occupancy lodging at Locanda di Praticino, planned activities. $400 deposit, balance due 45 days prior. Cancellations 60 days prior forfeit $150.

LOCATION: A 30-minute drive from Florence.
CONTACT: Ralph P. Slone, La Cucina Kasher in Toscana, Inland Services, Inc., 360 Lexington Ave., New York, NY 10017 USA; (212) 687-9898.

LA SETTIMANA DELLA CUCINA
Bologna/Year-round
This travel company offers 7-day programs that include daily hands-on classes. Established in 1996. Maximum group size: 15-18. Facilities: I Notai restaurant, off Bologna's main square. Also featured: winery tours, tour of ceramic factory, visits to markets and producers of cheese, balsamic vinegar, and prosciutto, dinner and demonstration by chef of San Domenico in Imola.
EMPHASIS: Traditional Bolognese and Emilia Romagna regional cuisine.
FACULTY: Cookbook author Monica Cesari Sartoni, who has over 15 years experience and writes for gastronomy publications and the Gambero Rosso restaurant guide.
COSTS: 3,800,000 Lira, which includes double occupancy lodging, meals in fine restaurants and trattorias, and guided tours. Lodging is at a 4-star hotel in city center. 30% deposit with booking, balance due 6 weeks prior.
LOCATION: Central Bologna.
CONTACT: Marcello Tori, Owner, Bluone Tour Operator, Via Parigi, 11, Bologna, 40121 Italy; (39) 51-263546, Fax (39) 51-267774, E-mail Available in 1997.

L'AMORE DI CUCINA ITALIANA
Pomino/April-May, July, October
This travel company offers 1-week hands-on culinary vacations. Established in 1992. Facilities: the kitchen of the Locanda di Praticino. Also featured: shopping expeditions; visits to an outdoor market, winery, cheese and olive oil producers, the museum of a noted porcelain manufacturer; a cultural evening in Florence; dining at fine restaurants.
EMPHASIS: Tuscan and regional Italian cuisines.
FACULTY: Cristina Blasi and Gabriella Mari, owners of a cooking school in Florence and authors of a book about the cooking of ancient Rome; wine and olive oil experts.
COSTS: $2,175 ($1,975 for non-cook guest), which includes meals, double occupancy lodging ($300 single supplement) at the Locanda di Praticino, and planned activities. $400 deposit required, balance 45 days prior. Cancellations 60 days prior forfeit $100, no refund thereafter.
LOCATION: Pomino, about a half-hour drive from Florence.
CONTACT: Ralph P. Slone, L'Amore di Cucina Italiana, Inland Services, Inc., 360 Lexington Ave., New York, NY 10017 USA; (212) 687-9898.

LAURA NICCOLAI COOKING SCHOOL
Naples, Siena/March-December
Laura Niccolai offers 1-week demonstration courses (4 classes) in S'Agata sui Due Golfi, Naples, and Locanda Dell'Amorosa in Sinalunga, Siena. Founded in 1987. Maximum class/group size: 20. Facilities: well-equipped, professional kitchens. Also featured: Naples: dinners in selected restaurants, visits to Limoncello liqueur and mozzarella factories, guided tours to Capri and Positano. Siena: wine and olive oil tastings, cultural and gastronomic tours. 1-day and private classes.
EMPHASIS: Traditional and modern Italian, Tuscan, and Neapolitan cuisine with emphasis on light and healthy recipes.
FACULTY: IACP-member Laura Niccolai studied with Michelin 3-star chef Gualtiero Marchesi and French pastry chef Jain Bellouet.
COSTS: $3,000 ($3,500) for the Naples (Siena) program, which includes double occupancy lodging, meals, and planned activities. Single supplement $500. Naples: luxury hotels in Sorrento. Siena: Locanda dell'Amorosa. $250 deposit required, balance due 60 days prior. Refund less $50 for cancellation 30 days prior.
LOCATION: S. Agata sui Due Golfi is between Sorrento and Positano, 30 miles south of Naples; Locanda dell'Amorosa, a small medieval village, is 50 miles south of Florence.

CONTACT: Laura Niccolai, Laura Niccolai Cooking School, 730 Columbus Ave., #9H, New York, NY 10025 USA; (212) 666-1436, Fax (212) 666-1436, E-mail LNCooking@aol.comIn Italy: Laura Niccolai Cooking School, Via Termine 9, S. Agata sui 2 Due Golfi, 80064, Italy; (39) 81-878-0152 phone/fax.

LESSON IN FLAVORS – DONNA FRANCA TOURS
Tuscany/May-October

This tour operator offers 8-10 eleven-day hands-on culinary tours per year. Founded in 1967. Maximum class/group size: 20. Facilities: kitchens of private villas. Also featured: winery tours, private visits to Venice gardens, visits to prosciutto balsamic vinegar producers, medieval banquet, excursions to Lake Como, Ferrara, Siena, San Gimignano, Florence, Perugia, Spoleto.
EMPHASIS: Traditional, nuova cucina, medieval cuisine.
FACULTY: Donna Franca studied at the Hotel Cipriani and has operated culinary tours since 1972. A member of Les Dames d'Escoffier, she conducts lessons in her private villa in Cetona, Siena.
COSTS: Include double occupancy lodging in castles and villas, most meals, land transport, and planned excursions. Single supplement ranges from $150-$300. Lodging: Abbazia di Spineto, an abbey dating from 1085. $250 deposit required, balance due 45 days prior.
CONTACT: Franca Franzaroli, President, Donna Franca Tours, 470 Commonwealth Ave., Boston, MA 02215-2795 USA; (617) 375-9400, (800) 225-6290, Fax (617) 266-1062, E-mail dtours2156@aol.com, URL http://www.astanet.com/get?dfrancatrs.

LIGURIAN SCHOOL OF POETIC COOKING
Tellaro/Spring and Fall

Peggy Markel of La Cucina al Focolare offers hands-on classes, history, simple ingredients, new techniques, fish, fresh vegetables, and herbs. Founded in 1996. Maximum class/group size: 6-8. Facilities: professional kitchen, copper utensils. Also featured: exploration of wines of the Cinque-Terre.
EMPHASIS: Fish, sauces, Ligurian cuisine.
FACULTY: Chef Angelo Cabani, owner of the Michelin 1-star Locanda Miranda Inn.
COSTS: $2,000, which includes meals, lodging at the Inn, and planned excursions.
LOCATION: Overlooking the Bay of Poets (La Specia).
CONTACT: Peggy Markel, P.O. Box 646, Boulder, CO 80306-0646 USA; (800) 988-2851, Fax (303) 440-8598, E-mail soulcookin@aol.com.

LUNA CONVENTO COOKING CLASSES WITH ENRICO FRANZESE
(See display ad page 242) **Amalfi**

This private school offers 1-week culinary vacations that include 4 morning demonstration and participation classes. Founded in 1991. Maximum class/group size: 15-18. Facilities: Luna Convento Hotel's Saracen Tower, overlooking the sea. Also featured: guided excursions to Sorrento, Ravello, Pompeii, and Amalfi; dinner at Don Alfonso, a Michelin 2-star restaurant owned by Alfonso and Livio Iccharino.
EMPHASIS: Regional Neapolitan cuisine.
FACULTY: Enrico Franzese, who trained at the Cipriani in Venice and the Hassler in Rome, won the 1990 Parma Ham Chef's Competition in Bologna, and appears on Italian television; interpreter Rosemary Anastasio.
COSTS: $2,200 ($2,500), which includes meals, planned excursions, transportation from Naples, and first class double (single) occupancy lodging and private bath. The 4-star Luna Convento Hotel, a restored 13th century convent.
LOCATION: Amalfi, a resort area on Italy's west coast, is about 150 miles south of Rome and 40 miles south of Naples.
CONTACT: Judy Ebrey, Owner, Cuisine International, P.O. Box 25228, Dallas, TX 75225 USA; (214) 373-1161, Fax (214) 373-1162, E-mail cuisineint@aol.com, URL http://www.iglobal.net/cuisineint.

MARGHERITA AND VALERIA SIMILI'S COOKING COURSES
Bologna/Fall, Winter, Spring
This private school offers more than 100 hands-on classes a year. Established in 1986. Also featured: 1-week intensives for groups of 10 or less.
EMPHASIS: Most classes focus on breads. Other topics include pasta, sausage, holiday desserts.
FACULTY: Margherita and Valeria Simili.
COSTS: $80-$100 per class.
CONTACT: Margherita Simili, 116 Via San Felice, Bologna, 40122 Italy; (39) 51-52-37-71, (39) 51-55-44-94, Fax (39) 51-52-37-71.

MARIA BATTAGLIA – LA CUCUINA ITALIA
Verona/October-May
Maria Battaglia offers 4-day cooking programs each season at La Foresteria Serego Alighieri, a 14th century villa in Valpolicella. Founded in 1981. Also featured: a trip to the Verona market, a demonstration at the Ferron Rice Mill, and tours of the Masi winery and Serego Alighieri Estate.
EMPHASIS: Northern, central, and southern Italian cuisine.
FACULTY: Maria Battaglia studied Italian cooking in Bologna, Florence, Messina, Sardinia, and Milan. She was a recipe consultant and spokesperson for Contadina Foods and was awarded the Diploma di Merito by the Federazione Italiana Cuochi in Milan and Verona.
COSTS: $2,160 per person, including breakfast, double occupancy lodging at the La Foresteria villa apartments, which have private kitchens, and all cooking classes and excursions. A $300 deposit is required with balance due 6 weeks prior.
LOCATION: A 25-minute drive north of Verona, 10 minutes from Catullo airport in Villafranca.
CONTACT: Maria Battaglia, Maria Battaglia - La Cucina Italiana, P.O. Box 6528, Evanston, IL 60204 USA; (847) 328-1144, Fax (847) 328-1787.

MEDITERRANEAN COOKING IN AMALFI
Amalfi/May-June, September-October *(See display ad page 264)*
This travel company offers three 1-week culinary vacations/year that include 5 hands-on and demo classes. Started in 1996. Maximum class/group size: 8. Also featured: winery visits and instruction, day trips, market visits, sightseeing, visits to food producers, shopping for ceramics.
EMPHASIS: Southern Italian and Mediterranean cuisines.
FACULTY: Giuseppe Liuccio, food historian, president of Academy of Medieval Cooking in Italy.
COSTS: $1,989, which includes meals, double occupancy lodging, and excursions. Lodging at the 19th-century 50-room Hotel Cappuccini Convento, which has a solarium and private beach. $300 deposit with booking, balance due and full refund granted 45 days prior, no refund within 45 days.
LOCATION: The Campania region, on the Amalfi coast.
CONTACT: Gabriele Dellanave, Owner, Gabriele's Travels to Italy, 3037 14th Ave., NW, Rochester, MN 55901 USA; (507) 287-8733, Fax (507) 287-8733, E-mail gabriele@infonet.isl.net, URL http://www.isl.net/gabriel/gabriel.html.

THE MIRABELLA SCHOOL
Mirabella Eclano
This school offers 1-week cooking vacation programs that include four days of hands-on morning and afternoon classes. Maximum class/group size: 6. Also featured: Wednesday excursion to the Isle of Capri in the Bay of Naples.
EMPHASIS: Heart-healthy, low-fat Mediterranean cuisine, including antipasti, risotto, pasta sauces, meat and vegetable dishes.
FACULTY: Carla Dora, hostess/instructor, who grows the produce, olives, walnuts, and grapes that are used in recipes and her private-label wine and olive oil.
LOCATION: In the Apennines 90 minutes from Naples and 3 hours from Rome.
CONTACT: Carolyn B. Shinkle, The Mirabella School, 1300 Sugar Hill Lane, Xenia, OH 45385 USA; (513) 445-1150, Fax (513) 445-0523.

THE RHODE SCHOOL OF CUISINE
(See also page 256) (See display ad below) **Vorno, Tuscany/May-November**

This school offers weekly 7-day hands-on vacation programs. Also featured: cultural excursions, mushroom hunting in season, market visits.

EMPHASIS: Italian cuisine, sauces, wine and cheese.

FACULTY: Chef Frederic Riviere, a graduate of Les Sorbets, who has cooked at Michelin-star restaurants; local Tuscan chefs.

COSTS: $1,895 ($2,195) which includes double (single) occupancy lodging, ground transport, food and wine consumed at the school. Premium room supplement is $200, non-cook guest rate is $1,395. Villa Michaela, a 19th-century modernized 12-bedroom/12-bath villa on 50 acres with swimming pool and tennis court. 50% deposit with booking, balance due 6 weeks prior.

LOCATION: 30 minutes from Pisa, 50 minutes from Florence.

CONTACT: The Rhode School of Cuisine, (800) 447-1311, Fax (800) 447-1311. Also: Cuisine International (214) 373-1161 or Rhode School of Cuisine, c/o Carola Strowick, 25 Blvd. Helvetique, Geneva 1207, Switzerland; (41) 22-736-7878, Fax (41) 22-736-7919.

RICHARD SAN MARZANO'S HEART OF ITALY COURSES
Spoleto/March-April, June, September-November

This cultural travel enterprise offers 4- to 14-night hands-on classes. Established in 1994. Maximum class/group size: 8-12. Facilities: 3 well-equipped kitchens, indoor and outdoor teaching areas. Also featured: winery visits and instruction, day trips, market visits, olive mill tours, dining in fine restaurants and private homes, sightseeing.

EMPHASIS: Umbrian cuisine, tartufo, truffle cuisine, pasta.

COSTS: Includes lodging, restaurant meals, ground transport. Lodging in a 15th-century palazzo in town center.

LOCATION: Central Italy, north of Rome, south of Florence, near Assisi.

CONTACT: Karen Herbst, The International Kitchen, Inc., 2685 Crestwood Ln., Riverwoods, IL 60015 USA; (800) 945-8606, (847) 945-0820, Fax (847) 821-0476, E-mail info@intl-kitchen.com, URL http://www.intl-kitchen.com. Also: Richard di San Marzano, Loc. Vallocchia, 11-06049 Spoleto, Italy; (39) 743-229972 (phone/fax).

SCHOOL OF TRADITIONAL NEAPOLITAN CUISINE
Positano/March-April, October-November

The Hotel Le Sirenuse offers 5-day demonstration culinary vacations. Founded in 1993. Maximum class/group size: 20. Facilities: include an original wood-burning pizza oven. Also featured: visits to mozzarella, pasta, and limoncino factories, a fish monger, and Oplontis, Amalfi, and Ravello.

EMPHASIS: Regional Neapolitan cuisine; wines.

FACULTY: Hotel Le Sirenuse Chef Alfonso Mazzacano and Alfonso Iaccarino, chef-owner of the Michelin 2-star Don Alfonso restaurant. Hotel manager Antonio Sersale translates.

COSTS: $2,990-$3,675, which includes lodging, meals, and planned excursions. The 60-room

Hotel Le Sireneuse, an 18th century palazzo, and member of the Leading Hotels of the World, overlooks the Gulf of Sorrento and islands of Li Galli.

LOCATION: Positano, a fishing village in southern Italy, is 40 miles from Naples.

CONTACT: Antonio Sersale, P.R. & Marketing, School of Traditional Neapolitan Cuisine, Albergo di Positano, Positano, 84017 Italy; (39) 89-875066, Fax (39) 89-811798, E-mail U.S. Contact: Judy Ebrey, Box 25228, Dallas, TX USA 75225; (214) 373-1161; Fax (214) 373-1162; E-mail CuisineInt@aol.com; URL http://www.iglobal.net/cuisineint.

SCUOLA DI ARTE CULINARIA "CORDON BLEU"
Tuscany/Year-round   *(See also page 130)*

This private school offers 1-, 5-, and 7-day cooking vacations in Val di Chiana, 7-day cooking and art vacations at a farmhouse in Tuscany, and 1- to 9-session courses at the school in central Florence. Maximum class/group size: 12. Facilities: 30-sq-meter professional kitchen in Val di Chiana, 50-sq-meter Tuscan kitchen with fireplace and brick oven, the school's 40-sq-meter teaching kitchen. Also featured: visits to markets, food producers, wineries, artisans' workshops; dining in trattorias and fine restaurants, cultural programs, sightseeing.

EMPHASIS: Basic, advanced, Tuscan, and new Italian cuisine; bread; ice cream; history and nutrition; wines.

COSTS: 7-day Tuscany program is $2,500 all-inclusive; classes in Florence begin at 150,000 Lira/session. Tuscany lodgings are farmhouses with swimming pools and wineries. 30% nonrefundable deposit required.

LOCATION: Val di Chiana, a rural hamlet 15 miles from Siena and Arezzo; Pomino, a rural community 45 minutes northeast of Florence; central Florence, 15 minutes from the Florence airport.

CONTACT: Gabriella Mari, Co-Director, Scuola di Arte Culinaria "Cordon Bleu", Via di Mezzo, 55/R, 50121 Firenze-Florence, Italy; (39) 55-2345468, Fax (39) 55-2345468, URL http://www.ats.it/kiosco/cordonbl.

SMITHS ITALIAN COOKING
Tuscany, Umbria, Piedmont/February-June, September-November

This travel enterprise offers 7-day programs that include hands-on classes. Established in 1990. Maximum class/group size: 12. Facilities: hotel and restaurant kitchens. Also featured: wine instruction, day trips, market visits, dining in fine restaurants and private homes, sightseeing, visits to food producers.

EMPHASIS: Italian cuisine, regional cooking, classic and regional wines.

FACULTY: Wendy Smith lectured in food science and owned a restaurant in Bath, UK; local chefs.

COSTS: $2,500-$3,000, including full board. 35% deposit required with balance due 4 weeks prior.

LOCATION: Northern Italy, including Lucca, Siena, Chianti region, Cortona, Torgiaso-Umbria.

CONTACT: Karen Herbst, The International Kitchen, Inc., 2685 Crestwood Ln., Riverwoods, IL 60015 USA; (800) 945-8606, (847) 945-0820, Fax (847) 821-0476, E-mail info@intl-kitchen.com, URL http://www.intl-kitchen.com.

TASTING ITALY
March-June, September-November

This private school offers more than 20 one-week hands-on cookery courses a year in different regions of Italy. Established in 1992. Maximum class/group size: 12-16. Facilities: well-equipped kitchens with pizza ovens, grills, and open fire cooking. Also featured: visits to markets, vineyards, restaurants, and wine tastings.

EMPHASIS: Italian regional cooking; wine tasting.

FACULTY: Valentina Harris, author and presenter of BBC's Regional Italian Cookery; Carla Tomasi, author and proprietor of Turnaround Cooks; Alvaro Maccioni, owner of London's La Famiglia; journalist and food stylist Maxine Clark.

COSTS: From £900, which includes shared lodging, meals and excursions. 3 and 4-star accommodations provided. £175 deposit required, balance due 8 weeks prior.

LOCATION: Sicily: the Ravida family's 18th-century palazzo on the southern coast. Tuscany: the hotel Fattoria Montelluci near Arezzo. Piedmont: La Camilla near Gavi, the country home of the Scavia family. Veneto: the hunting lodge, La Foresteria, near Verona.

CONTACT: Sara Schwartz, Tasting Italy, 97 Bravington Rd., London, W9 3AA England; (44) 181-964-5839, Fax (44) 181-960-3919.

TENUTA DI CAPEZZANA CULINARY PROGRAM IN TUSCANY
Florence/Spring and Fall

This school in a 15th century Medici villa offers 12 week-long participation sessions/year. Founded in 1993. Maximum class/group size: 12. Facilities: Capezzana's family kitchen. Also featured: visits to markets, specialty shops, sausage and cheese makers, bakeries; wine instruction; comparative tastings, demonstrations and dining at fine restaurants.

EMPHASIS: Italian wines, basics, ingredients, wine, antipasti, home-style Tuscan cooking.

FACULTY: Culinary director is Rolando Beramendi, owner of Italian import company Manicaretti and general manager of Capezzana. Instructors include Contessa Lisa Bonacossi, Fabbio Picchi, Chef Carlo of Da Delfina, and Master of Wine Nicholas Belfrage.

COSTS: Cost is $2,300, which includes double occupancy lodging in the villa, all meals, ground transportation, and planned activities. A $500 deposit is required, balance due 30 days prior. Full refund with 60 days notice. Food and wine professionals receive a discount.

LOCATION: 20-minutes from Florence. The villa is a working olive oil and wine-producing estate.

CONTACT: Pamela Sheldon Johns, Tenuta di Capezzana Culinary Program in Tuscany, Pamela Sheldon Johns, U.S. Representative, 1324-G State St., Santa Barbara, CA 92101 USA; (805) 963-0230, Fax (805) 963-0230.

TWO FOR COOKING – TUSCAN COUNTRY EXPERIENCE
Argenina, Chianti/June, July, September-November

Tuscan native Julia Scartozzoni offers one-week private cooking vacation courses with lodging in a private country home. Established in 1994. Maximum class/group size: 2 (one couple only). Also featured: private tours of the Chianti region, private castles, wineries, food producers; dining in private homes and fine restaurants.

EMPHASIS: Private Tuscan vacation experiences.

FACULTY: Julia Scartozzoni has studied with noted chefs, co-owned a restaurant in Tuscany, and is an artist of interior designs.

COSTS: $8,500/couple includes meals, private lodging and attendants, and planned activities. Non-cook couple rate is $6,900. Lodging and classes are at the Village of Argenina. $2,500 deposit required, balance due 30 days prior, refund 3 months prior.

LOCATION: The Chianti region, 15 miles north of Siena, 30 miles south of Florence.

CONTACT: Julia Scartozzoni, Two for Cooking-Tuscan Country Experience, Argenina, Gaiole in Chianti, Siena, 53013 Italy; (39) 337-79-0032, Fax (39) 577-73-1100.

VENETIAN COOKING IN A VENETIAN PALACE
(See display ad page 242)   ### Venice/January-March, June, September-October

Fulvia Sesani offers cooking classes in her 13th-century Venetian palace. Founded in 1984. Maximum class/group size: 10. Facilities: a modern, fully-equipped kitchen. Also featured: shopping in the Rialto market, visits to the Ducal palace, museums, and private homes, dinner at Harry's Bar, and the Palazzo Morosini. Also available: day classes and private lessons.

EMPHASIS: Traditional Venetian cooking, edible works of art.

FACULTY: Fulvia Sesani.

COSTS: All-inclusive land costs range from $2,950 to $3,250.

LOCATION: The Palazzo Morosini is in the Santa Maria Formosa area of Venice.

CONTACT: Judy Ebrey, Owner, Cuisine International, P.O. Box 25228, Dallas, TX 75225 USA; (214) 373-1161, Fax (214) 373-1162, E-mail CuisineInt@aol.com, URL http://www.-iglobal.net/cuisineint.

VILLA CENNINA/THE ART OF ITALIAN CUISINE
Siena/Year-round

The nonprofit Cultural Society of Siena offers 15 one- to two-week hands-on cooking vacations per year that include 4-8 hours of daily instruction. Founded in 1983. Maximum class/group size: 15. Facilities: the kitchen of the 16th century Villa Cennina. Also featured: visits to wineries, food producers, markets, restaurants, tours to culinary and cultural arts centers.

FACULTY: Gian Luca Pardini, owner/chef of Ristorante Mecenate in Lucca and consultant to a chain of Italian restaurants in Japan.

COSTS: $1,800-$2,800, including lodging, meals, ground transport, and planned activities. Villa amenities include swimming pool, tennis courts, horseback riding, hiking trails, private baths.

LOCATION: 30 miles from Florence.

CONTACT: Pat Kuh, Villa Cennina/The Art of Italian Cuisine, Transitions Abroad, Inc., 197 W. 16th St., Chicago Heights, IL 60411 USA; (708) 756-3655, Fax (708) 756-3420.

VILLA DELIA TUSCANY COOKING SCHOOL
Ripoli di Lari/May-June, September-October

This Tuscan villa offers 10-day vacation packages that include 7 hands-on morning cooking classes. Established in 1995. Maximum class/group size: 12-20. Also featured: wine instruction, day trips, private instruction, market visits, winery tours, dining in fine restaurants, sightseeing.

EMPHASIS: Tuscan cuisine, including breads, pasta, local food.

FACULTY: Owner Umberto Menghi, Ron Lammie, and resident chef Marietta Menghi.

COSTS: $3,150 ($3,550), which includes double (single) occupancy lodging, deluxe lodging with private bath, meals, and excursions. Lodging at modernized 16thy-century Tuscan villa with swimming pool and tennis courts. $500 nonrefundable deposit required, balance due 6 weeks prior. Package is nonrefundable within 30 days.

LOCATION: 20 minutes from Pisa.

CONTACT: Kim Lloyd, Director of Sales, Villa Delia Hotel and Tuscany Cooking School, Umberto Management Ltd., 1380 Hornby Street, Vancouver, BC V6Z 1W5 Canada; (604) 669-3732, Fax (604) 669-9723, E-mail inquire@umberto.com, URL http://www.umberto.com.

WORLD OF REGALEALI
Sicily/April-May, October-November   *(See display ad page 242)*

Marchesa Anna Tasca Lanza offers weekly 2- and 5-day demonstration courses in Regaleali, her ancestral family home. Established in 1989. Maximum group size: 12. Facilities: professional kitchen with wood-burning oven in an 18th century farm house; adjoining estate and winery. Also: visits to archeological sites, markets, and programs on the estate's agricultural enterprises: bread-baking, garden tour, tastings of estate olive oil and wines, cheese-making demonstration.

EMPHASIS: Sicilian cooking utilizing meats, cheeses, vegetables, and wines from the estate.

FACULTY: Anna Tasca Lanza, author of *The Heart of Sicily*; Mario Lo Menzo, the family chef; other local and guest chefs.

COSTS: $1,200 ($2,200), which includes all meals and 2 (5) days lodging at Regaleali. $500 deposit required, remainder due upon arrival.

LOCATION: 2 hours by train from Palermo, in central Sicily.

CONTACT: Judy Ebrey, Owner, Cuisine International, P.O. Box 25228, Dallas, TX 75225 USA; (214) 373-1161, Fax (214) 373-1162, E-mail CuisineInt@aol.com, URL http://www.iglobal.net/cuisineint.

JAPAN

KONISHI JAPANESE COOKING CLASS
Tokyo/Year-round

This private school offers 43 hands-on classes per year. Dates are flexible. Founded in 1969. Maximum class/group size: 10. Facilities: 300-sq-ft kitchen with Japanese utensils. Also featured:

classes for youngsters, market visits, private classes.

EMPHASIS: Healthy Japanese cooking with artistic presentation, including tempura, sukiyaki, soba, sushi and nabemono (one-pot table cooking); homestyle Chinese menus are also included.

FACULTY: Mrs. Kiyoko Konishi has taught foreigners in English for 28 years and is author of *Japanese Cooking for Health and Fitness, Entertaining with a Japanese Flavor*, and 3 cooking videos.

COSTS: 4,000 yen/session, payable on arrival. A list of nearby hotels is available.

LOCATION: Central Tokyo.

CONTACT: Kiyoko Konishi, Konishi Japanese Cooking Class, 3-1-7-1405, Meguro, Meguro-ku, Tokyo, 153 Japan; (81) 3-3714-0085, Fax (81) 3-3714-0085.

LE CORDON BLEU TOKYO
Tokyo/Year-round

(See also page 131) (See display ad page 127)

This private school acquired by Le Cordon Bleu Paris offers half-day to 1-month courses, daily demonstrations, gourmet sessions, cuisine and pastry courses, flower arranging, and Introduction to Cuisine, Pastry, Catering and Bread Baking. Also featured: workshops for children, evening oenology classes, cheese courses, guest chef demonstrations.

EMPHASIS: The Classic Cycle.

COSTS: From 10,000 yen (1 day course) to 550,000 yen (10 weeks). Payment with registration.

CONTACT: Le Cordon Bleu, Roob-1, 28-13 Sarugaku-cho, Daikanyama, Shibuya-ku, Tokyo, 150 Japan; (81) 3 5489 01 41, (800) 457-CHEF, Fax (81) 3 5489 01 45, URL www.cordonbleu.edu.

TASTE OF CULTURE
Tokyo/Year-round

Elizabeth Andoh offers four to six 1- to 4-session slide-illustrated lecture-demonstration and participation courses per year. Founded in 1970. Maximum class/group size: 25 demo/4 hands-on. Facilities: small home-style kitchen, fully equipped for Japanese cooking. Also featured: market field trips, private classes.

EMPHASIS: Japanese cooking: basics, vegetarian temple food, seasonal and ceremonial menus.

FACULTY: Elizabeth Andoh, IACP member and graduate of Yanagihara School of Classical Cuisine.

COSTS: Range from 5,000 yen for a demonstration class to 22,000 yen for a 4-session participation course. A list of nearby hotels is available. Deposit is 5,000 yen for local residents (no refunds) and full fee for overseas students (refund minus 20% for cancellation 3 weeks prior).

CONTACT: Elizabeth Andoh, A Taste of Culture, 3-8-16 Yoga (Hilltop 109 #202), Setagaya-ku, Tokyo, 158 Japan; (81) 33-5716-5751, Fax (81) 33-5716-5751.

MEXICO

FLAVORS OF MEXICO – CULINARY ADVENTURES, INC.
Tabasco, Puebla, Oaxaca/January, February

Marilyn Tausend's Culinary Adventures offers 7- to 10-day hands-on cooking vacations to different regions of Mexico. Established in 1988. Maximum class/group size: 6-18. Facilities: typically indoor and outdoor home and restaurant kitchens. Also featured: visits to food markets and cottage industries, meals and demonstrations in homes of local cooks, tours of historical and archaeological sites and artisans' workshops.

EMPHASIS: Regional Mexican cuisine.

FACULTY: Marilyn Tausend, co-author of *Mexico the Beautiful Cookbook*; Mexican cooking authority Diana Kennedy, author of *The Art of Mexican Cooking*; Mária Dolores Torres Yzábal, author of *The Mexican Gourmet*, Ricardo Muñoz Zurita.

COSTS: Approximately $2,550, which includes meals, double occupancy lodging, planned excursions, and local transport. Lodging in small hotels popular with Mexican families. $300 deposit required, balance due a month prior, 65% of fee refundable 30-60 days prior.

LOCATION: Oaxaca and Tabasco are less than an hour's flight from Mexico City; Puebla is a 2-hour drive.

CONTACT: Marilyn Tausend, Flavors of Mexico, 6023 Reid Dr. N.W., Gig Harbor, WA 98335 USA; (206) 851-7676, Fax (206) 851-9532.

GOURMET ADVENTURES
San Miguel de Allende/Jan-Feb, April, June, Aug, Oct-Nov

This culinary tour/school offers 1-week culinary tours with demonstration and hands-on instruction. Established in 1995. Maximum class/group size: 6-10. Facilities: private villas with professional kitchens. Also featured: day trips, market visits, winery tours, fine dining in restaurants and private homes, sightseeing, spa treatments, shopping, gallery tours, yoga.

EMPHASIS: Regional Mexican and nuevo Latino cuisines.

FACULTY: Victoria Challancin and Kristen Rudolph, professional cooking instructor and restaurant owner with degree in hotel/restaurant administration.

COSTS: $1,700-$2,200, which includes lodging, meals, and planned activities. Lodging is in fully-staffed villas in a colonial Mexican setting. $800 deposit is required. Full refund 60 days prior.

LOCATION: 90 minutes from Leon, 3 ½ hours from Mexico City.

CONTACT: Kristen Rudolph, Gourmet Adventures, 432 Mainsail Ct., Lake Mary, FL 32746 USA; (52) 415-21852 (Mexico), Fax (52) 415-21852, E-mail gourtadv@unisono, ciateq.mx, URL http://unisono.ciateq.mx/gourtadv/. Also: Victoria Challancin, APDO 429, San Miguel de Allende, GTO. 37700, Mexico.

MEXICAN CUISINE SEMINARS WITH LULA BERTRAN
Mexico City/Year-round

Lula Bertran offers Be My Guest for One Day, a program for visitors. Hands-on seminars and personalized programs for individuals and groups by appointment. Founded in 1980. Maximum class/group size: 1-8. Facilities: conference room and fully-equipped kitchen. Also featured: guided market visits, dining at traditional restaurants, short trips to nearby towns.

EMPHASIS: Mexican cuisine, food history, eating customs; Mexico City's food world.

FACULTY: Food writer and teacher Lula Bertran is founding member of three food associations in Mexico and international advisor of the board of the IACP Foundation.

COSTS: $150 for day-long session includes market visit, breakfast, cooking class, lunch, food shops-city tour, and dinner. Mexican-type deluxe hotel lodging is approximately $50/night. 50% deposit a month prior for seminars over 3 days; 50% refundable/balance due 2 weeks prior.

CONTACT: Lula Bertran, Mexican Cuisine Seminar, 9051-C Siempre Viva Rd., #60-158, Mexico City, 11000 Mexico, D.F.; (52) 5-202-7251, Fax (52) 5-540-3633, E-mail abertran@spin.com.mx. Also: D.F. Cordoba, #135 Mexico City, 11000 Mexico.

MEXICAN HOME COOKING
Tlaxcala/Year-round

This private school offers monthly 5- to 10-day and customized hands-on cooking vacations. Established in 1996. Maximum class/group size: 6. Facilities: fully-equipped 500-sq-ft kitchen, on-site garden and farm. Also featured: day trips, market visits, dining in private homes, sightseeing, visits to food producers.

EMPHASIS: Mexican home cooking, pre-Hispanic to modern.

FACULTY: Estela Salas Silva, chef in Mexico City and San Francisco since 1974; Rogelio Salas Silva, chef and restaurant owner in Mexico City since 1989; local cooks.

COSTS: Land cost begins at approximately $960, which includes double occupancy lodging and meals. Single supplement $100. Lodging: private room in the Silva family home with use of house kitchen and grounds. 30% deposit required, balance due 90 days prior. Full refund less $100 for cancellations 90 days prior.

LOCATION: 10 minutes outside the city of Tlaxcala, 90 minutes east of Mexico City.

CONTACT: Estela Salas Silva, Mexican Home Cooking, Apartado 64, Tlaxcala, Tlaxcala, 90000 Mexico.

SEASONS OF MY HEART COOKING SCHOOL
(See also page 131)   **Oaxaca/Year-round**

This private school offers 2 or more week-long classes/year and on-going 4-day weekend courses and day classes, all hands-on. Maximum class/group size: 2-20. Also featured: visits to corn and chocolate mills, mezcal factory, markets, archaeological sites, farms, weavers, pottery makers, private homes; private group tours and lectures.

EMPHASIS: Native and pre-Hispanic foods, chiles, wild plants and herbs, contemporary dishes.

COSTS: Day classes begin at $65; 4-day bed & breakfast $650, 1-week courses $1,295, including meals, lodging, and planned activities. Lodging in Oaxaca hotel (Casa Colonial) or other posada, private casita on ranch for bed & breakfast. $200 deposit for 1-week course, $150 nonrefundable, half balance due 2 months prior.

LOCATION: Ranch surrounded by archeological sites in the mountains outside Oaxaca.

CONTACT: Susana Trilling, Seasons of My Heart Cooking School, Rancho Aurora, P.O. Box AP 42, Admon 3, Oaxaca, 68101 Mexico; (52) 951-65280, (800) 758-1697 (US), Fax (52) 951-65280.

MOROCCO

LA CARAVANE ADVENTURES IN FOOD AND TRAVEL
Spring and Fall

Cookbook author Kitty Morse offers a fully-escorted 2-week tour emphasizing local cuisine and culture, including 2 days of seminars with Kitty Morse and local experts. Established in 1983. Maximum class/group size: 22. Facilities: private homes, deluxe or first class hotel kitchens. Also featured: demonstrations in Morse's home and visits with personal friends; excursions to historic local marketplaces; special events; golf and tennis available.

EMPHASIS: Moroccan cuisine and culture.

FACULTY: Kitty Morse was born in Casablanca and is author of 6 cookbooks including *The Vegetarian Table: North Africa* and the forthcoming *Cooking at the Kasbah!*. She is a member of the IACP, and the So. Cal. Culinary Guild.

COSTS: Approximately $4,000, which includes airfare from New York to Casablanca, land transport, 2 meals daily, planned activities. Double occupancy first class or deluxe hotels.

LOCATION: Coastal cities of Casablanca, El Jadida, Azemmour, Essaouira; Imperial cities of Fez, Marrakech, Meknes, Rabat; Fall only: desert kasbahs of Erfoud, Tinherir, Ouarzazate, Taroudant.

CONTACT: Kitty Morse, La Caravane Adventures in Food and Travel, P.O. Box 433, Vista, CA 92085-0433 USA; (619) 758-8631, Fax (619) 758-8631.

NETHERLANDS

LA CUISINE FRANCAISE
Amsterdam/September-June

This school offers 60 one- or four-session demonstration and participation courses per year. Established in 1980. Maximum class/group size: 25 demo/16 hands-on. Facilities: 90-sq-meter kitchen rebuilt in 1994, private dining room. Also featured: sessions in English for groups, private classes, and market visits.

EMPHASIS: French, Italian, and English/Dutch cuisines.

FACULTY: School owner Patricia I. van den Wall Bake-Thompson was born in Great Britain, studied home economics at Harrow Technical College, and is a consultant to food companies.

COSTS: Each session is $45 (75-105 Dutch Guilder), payable in advance. Lodging by arrangement in nearby hotels. A 10% deposit is required.

LOCATION: In an 18th century canal house, which also houses a private restaurant, in central Amsterdam and 20 minutes from the airport.

CONTACT: Pat van den Wall Bake-Thompson, La Cuisine Francaise, Herengracht 314, Amsterdam CD, 1016 Netherlands; (31) 20-627-8725, Fax (31) 20-620-3491.

NEW ZEALAND

AN EPICUREAN AFFAIR
Blenheim, Marlborough/Year-round
Stone Aerie Estate offers customized half-day programs that include a buffet lunch or dinner, guided tour of the estate, and cooking and/or wine demonstration. Established in 1995. Maximum class/group size: 10-20. Facilities: Designed by Jeremy Jones, Stone Aerie was featured in *New Zealand House and Garden*. The custom-designed kitchen is Gaggenau equipped.
EMPHASIS: Food and wine of the Marlborough region.
FACULTY: Francie Shagin, owner of Stone Aerie, teaches Italian cooking. Jeremy Jones was chef/owner of Sycamore Tree in Wellington and Peppertree Restaurant outside Blenheim. He runs an interior design firm.
COSTS: From A$92 (wine or cooking) to A$150 (wine and cooking).
LOCATION: A 15-minute drive from Marlborough.
CONTACT: Jeremy Jones, An Epicurean Affair, Stone Aerie Estate, Dog Point Road, R.D.2, Blenheim, Marlborough, New Zealand; (64) 3-572-9639, Fax (64) 3-572-9634.

EPICUREAN WORKSHOP
Auckland/Year-round
This cookware store and school offers 80 demonstration and participation classes/year, and 1-hour Gourmet on the Run classes twice weekly. Founded 1989. Maximum class size: 35-40 demo/8 hands-on. Facilities: teaching kitchen, overhead mirrors. Also featured: classes for youngsters, Taste of New Zealand classes for visitors, private classes, and 5-day vacation programs.
EMPHASIS: Seasonal themes, classics, technique and method, ethnic cuisines, local and overseas guest chef specialties.
FACULTY: Director Catherine Bell, CCP is a graduate of Leith's School in London and an IACP member. Local chefs include Ray McVinnie, Greg Heffernan, and Peter Chichester.
COSTS: Demonstrations range from NZ$6-NZ$57; weekend intensive basics is NZ$325; hands-on classes from NZ$100, young chef classes from NZ$43. Full payment required with booking; refund with 14 days notice, credit with 7 days notice.
LOCATION: Newmarket, a major shopping center in Auckland.
CONTACT: Catherine Bell, Epicurean Workshop, 27 Morrow St., P.O. Box 9255, Newmarket, Auckland, New Zealand; (64) 9-524-0906, Fax (64) 9-524-2017.

SMALL KITCHEN SCHOOL
Christchurch/Year-round
This school offers demonstrations, lunch-and-learn classes, and participation sessions. Maximum class/group size: 12-80. Facilities: newly-designed kitchen. Also featured: private lessons for groups, tours, live-in classes at Gov Bay.
EMPHASIS: Various topics and guest chef specialties, workshops.
FACULTY: Owner-instructor Michael Lee-Richards is chef at Michaels of Canterbury, host to the Canterbury Gourmet Society, director Catering, and oversees The Lonsdale, his private catering firm.
COSTS: NZ$43 for 1-day class to NZ$280 for 3-day class. Bed & breakfast and hotels available for out-of-town participants. Full refund granted 5 days prior, 50% 2 days prior.
CONTACT: Michael Lee-Richards, Small Kitchen School, P.O. Box 22-543, Christchurch, New Zealand; (61) 3-365-2837, Fax (61) 3-365-1621.

SINGAPORE

THE RAFFLES CULINARY ACADEMY
Singapore/Year-round

This school in Raffles Hotel offers one or two classes daily, both demonstration and hands-on. Established in 1995. Maximum class/group size: 10-24. Facilities: well-equipped residential-type kitchen with demonstration area. Also featured: wine instruction, classes for youngsters, market visits, dessert and pastry classes, social etiquette classes.

EMPHASIS: Singapore and Asian ethnic cuisines, Raffles Hotel signature dishes.

FACULTY: Raffles Hotel chefs, including Executive Chef Grant MacPherson and Executive Sous Chef Frederic Schmidt.

COSTS: $60-$100/class. Specialty classes range from $35-$75. The 104-suite Raffles Hotel has 14 restaurants and bars, a Victorian-style playhouse, and an arcade of 60 fine shops. Suites range from $480. Full payment with enrollment. Full refund for cancellation 4 weeks prior.

LOCATION: Singapore's civic district.

CONTACT: Antonio Daroyo, Manager, Raffles Culinary Academy, Raffles Hotel, 1 Beach Rd., 189673 Singapore; (65) 331-1747, (65) 337-1886, Fax (65) 339-7013. Also: 328 North Bridge Rd., Raffles Hotel Arcade, #02-17, Singapore 188719.

SOUTH AFRICA

SILWOOD KITCHEN CORDONS BLEUS COOKERY SCHOOL
(See also page 133)   **Rondebosch Cape/Year-round**

This school offers guest chef demonstrations six times a year. Maximum class/group size: 50-60. Also featured: 1-week hands-on classes for children twice yearly.

CONTACT: Mrs. Alicia Wilkinson, Silwood Kitchen, Silwood Rd., Rondebosch Cape, South Africa; (27) 21-686-4894, (27) 21-685-4378, Fax (027) 21-685-4378.

SPAIN

ALAMBIQUE SCHOOL, S.A.
Madrid/October-June

This school in a cookware store established by Clara Maria Amezua offers 1- to 10-session demonstration and participation courses for beginners and professionals. Founded in 1973. Maximum class/group size: 15-20 demo/10-12 hands-on. Facilities: teaching kitchen equipped with microwave, gas, and electric ovens. Also featured: classes for children, tailor-made courses.

EMPHASIS: Classic and regional Spanish, French, Mediterranean, Chinese, Italian, and Japanese.

FACULTY: Includes Victoria Llamas, Gloria Zunzunegui, Isabel Maestre, and Enrique Alvarez de Baste Arechea.

COSTS: Single sessions range from $22-$37, courses from $100-$700.

LOCATION: Alambique has outlets in Vigo.

CONTACT: Clara Maria Gonzalez Amezua, Alambique School, S.A., Calle de la Encarnacion, 2, Madrid, 28013 Spain; (34) 547-88-27, (34) 547-42-20, Fax (34) 559-78-02.

ALTAMIRA TOURS – FOODS OF SPAIN
Javea, Alicante, Cordoba/July, October

This travel company offers 10-day programs. Maximum group size: 15. Also: extension trips.

COSTS: Lodging in paradors.

CONTACT: Jannelle Wilkins, Altamira Tours - Foods of Spain, 860 Detroit St., Denver, CO 80206-3836 USA; (800) 747-2869, (303) 399-3660, Fax (303) 399-3660.

FLAVORS OF THE REAL SPAIN
Andalucia, Catalonia/February-May, October-November   *(See display ad page 242)*

This travel company offers twice monthly 9-day cooking vacations in Andalucia and Catalonia that feature 5 demonstration and participation sessions. Established in 1993. Maximum class/group size: 10-15. Facilities: Andalucia: modern classrooms in an established cooking school. Catalonia: modern kitchen of Michelin 2-star restaurant El Bulli. Also featured: Andalucia programs include excursions to Cordoba, Granada, Seville, horse show and flamenco, product tastings. The Catalonia program features daily excursions, product tastings, and cultural activities.

EMPHASIS: Andalucia: tapas, seafood, regional specialties. Catalonia: historic and modern Catalonian cuisine.

FACULTY: Andalucia: Gary Bedell, former diplomat and Deputy Commissioner General of Canada, chefs in Palma del Rio, Cadiz, Cordoba. Catalonia: El Bulli Chef Fernando Adria.

COSTS: Range from $3,500-$3,650, which includes double occupancy hotel lodging, most meals, ground transport, escorted tours. Lodging is in 4- and 5-star hotels with private baths. A $500 deposit is required with balance due 60 days prior. Full refund if space can be filled.

LOCATION: Andalucia: Seville, the provincial capital, and Jerez de la Frontera, 1.5 hours from Seville. Catalonia: near Figueres, 90 minutes from Barcelona, 15 minutes from Costa Brava.

CONTACT: Judy Ebrey, Owner, Cuisine International, P.O. Box 25228, Dallas, TX 75225 USA; (214) 373-1161, Fax (214) 373-1162, E-mail CuisineInt@aol.com, URL http://www.ig-lobal.net/cuisineint.

SWEDEN

CUISINE ECLAIREÉ
Stockholm

This culinary travel company offers 10-12 hands-on weekend programs each year. Established in 1994. Maximum class/group size: 10. Facilities: restaurant kitchen of the French restaurant Franska Matsalen at the Grand Hotel.

EMPHASIS: Classical French cuisine.

COSTS: 2,750 SEK. 1,000 SEK deposit.

LOCATION: Central Stockholm.

CONTACT: Lena Nilsson Erleman, Cuisine Eclaireé, Fiskarebacken 3, Saltsjo-Duvnas, Stockholm, 131 50 Sweden; (46) 8-716-1584, Fax (46) 8-716-6882.

TAIWAN

TAIPEI CHINESE FOOD FESTIVAL
Taipei/August

The Taipei Tourist Hotel Association and co-sponsor, American Express International offer an annual 3-day event that includes lectures on culinary culture, demonstrations by noted chefs, and professional cooking competitions. Facilities: CETRA Exhibition Hall, Taipei Sungshan Airport. Also featured: Taipei travel agencies organize gourmet tours that include visits to the National Palace Museum, the Fu Hsing Dramatic Arts Academy, the Tsushih Temple at Sanhsia, and the pottery kilns at Yingko.

EMPHASIS: Theme changes each year. In 1996, it was rice foods.

COSTS: Ticket prices $7.70 for adults, $5.80 for children.

LOCATION: Central Taipei.

CONTACT: Alex Hsiao, Deputy Director, Taiwan Visitors Assn., One World Trade Ctr., #7953, New York, NY 10048 USA; (212) 466-0691, Fax (212) 432-6436, URL http://www.tbroc.gov.tw.

THAILAND

SALA SIAM – BOLDER ADVENTURES
Bangkok/Year-round

This tour company offers weekly programs that include daily participation classes. Founded in 1991. Maximum class/group size: 1-5. Facilities: 1,000-square-foot kitchen with 3 work areas. Also featured: tours of Bangkok and environs, Thailand and region.

EMPHASIS: Thai cuisine.

FACULTY: Thai cook Peep Chinsanaboom.

COSTS: Approximately $150 per day. Standard stay is 4 days. Lodging is in a private teak villa.

LOCATION: Bangkok.

CONTACT: Marilyn Staff, Sala Siam - Bolder Adventures - Asia Transpacific Journeys, P.O. Box 1279, Boulder, CO 80306 USA; (800) 642-2742, Fax (303) 443-7078, E-mail bolder@Southeast-Asia.com, URL http://www.SoutheastAsia.com.

THAI COOKING SCHOOL AT THE ORIENTAL, BANGKOK
Bangkok/Year-round

The Oriental, Bangkok offers weekly 4-day demonstration courses (Monday-Thursday). Established in 1986. Maximum class/group size: 15. Facilities: classroom, participation/demonstration room, kitchen, eating area.

EMPHASIS: Contemporary Thai cooking, Northern and Northeastern cooking, Southern cooking, Thai haute cuisine.

COSTS: $1,490 ($2,110), which includes double (single) occupancy lodging, most meals, and planned activities. $950 for non-cook guest, each additional night is $220. Lodging at The Oriental. Amenities include swimming pools, sports center, tennis and squash, Oriental spa and health center. $250 deposit is refundable a month prior, balance due a month prior.

LOCATION: Overlooking the Chao Phraya River, 15 minutes from the main business district.

CONTACT: Duangrudee Siriwan, Personal Assistant to General Manager, Thai Cooking School at the Oriental, The Oriental, Bangkok, 48 Oriental Ave., Bangkok, 10500 Thailand; (662) 2360400, (662) 2360420, Fax (662) 439-7582. U.S. Contact: Mandarin Oriental Hotel Group (800) 526-6566.

WEST INDIES

COOKING IN PARADISE
St. Barthelemy/April

Cookbook author Steven Raichlen offers Cooking in Paradise, a 1-week hands-on culinary vacation in the Caribbean. Established in 1979. Maximum class/group size: 10. Facilities: open-air kitchen. Also featured: visits to top island restaurants, gourmet picnic, sailing cruise; swimming, fishing, scuba diving, shopping in the capital of Gustavia.

EMPHASIS: Healthy Caribbean cuisine.

FACULTY: Cooking teacher, food writer, and syndicated columnist Steven Raichlen contributes to *Eating Well, Prevention,* and the Los Angeles Times Syndicate. His cookbooks, include IACP Julia Child award-winner Miami Spice and *The New Caribbean Pantry.*

COSTS: $2,995 ($2,495 for non-cook guest), which includes meals, activities, and lodging at the Yuana Hotel, overlooking the ocean. $500 deposit required, balance due February 1, no refunds after March 1.

LOCATION: St. Barthelemy's 8 square miles of beaches and hills are 8 miles from St. Maarten.

CONTACT: Steven Raichlen, Cooking in Paradise, P.O. Box 331597, Coconut Grove, FL 33133 USA; (305) 854-9550, Fax (305) 854-2232.

WORLDWIDE

THE ADVENTUROUS APPETITE
Year-round

Bonnie Kassel offers 2-week culinary vacations scheduled six times yearly that include hands-on instruction. Founded in 1994. Maximum class/group size: 10. Also featured: visits to wineries, food producers, and dining at fine restaurants; yacht trips, watersports, exploring historical sites and wildlife reserves.

EMPHASIS: Traditional regional cuisines.

FACULTY: Restaurant chefs, village women.

COSTS: $3,000-$3,500, which includes airfare, lodging, meals, and planned activities. Up-scale lodging. $500 deposit required, refundable 60 days prior.

LOCATION: Destinations include the state of Goa in India, the colonial Caribbean, Bahia in northeastern Brazil (March, 1997), and cruising along the coast of Turkey.

CONTACT: Bonnie Kassel, The Adventurous Appetite, 56 W. 70th St., New York, NY 10023 USA; (212) 873-9067, Fax (212) 496-1846.

THE FLAVORS OF THE WORLD COOKING SCHOOL
January-May

Crystal Cruises and *Bon Appétit* Magazine offer a 103-day, 5-continent cruise that includes cooking classes that complement the destinations visited during each of the five 16- to 25-day segments. Also featured: dinners hosted by guest chefs, wine tastings, lectures on a variety of subjects.

COSTS: $40,830 for the full cruise, segments start at $7,995, which includes first-class air transport from North American gateway cities. Crystal Symphony cruise ship.

LOCATION: Segments are Los Angeles-Sydney, Sydney-Hong Kong, Hong Kong-Bombay, Bombay-Cape Town, Cape Town-Ft. Lauderdale.

CONTACT: Contact your travel agent for information and reservations.

GLOBAL GOURMET
Year-round   *(See also pages 118, 235)*

Global Gourmet (a division of Bonne Bouche) offers 2- to 10-day food, wine, and cooking courses in Europe, Asia and elsewhere.

COSTS: Range from £200-£2,000, which includes lodging, meals, and some transportation. A 25% deposit is required.

CONTACT: Anne Nicholls, Program Coordinator, Bonne Bouche/Global Gourmet, Lower Beers House, Brithem Bottom, Cullompton, Devon, EX15 1NB England; (44) 1884-32257, Fax (44) 1884-32257.

INTERNATIONAL DINING ADVENTURES
Year-round

This travel company conducts 1- to 2-week tours that focus on the cuisine of the country and include 2 or 3 cooking lessons and dining on regional specialties. Established in 1996. Also featured: visits to markets and historical sites.

FACULTY: Local guides who are knowledgeable about the culture and cuisine. Includes Tommy Tang, restaurant owner, PBS host, and cookbook author.

COSTS: Range from $2,490-$4,190. Credit cards accepted.

LOCATION: Destinations include Thailand, Italy, Japan, Spain, India, and the French Alps.

CONTACT: Bruce Burger, Director, International Dining Adventures, 106 Lynn St., Seattle, WA 98109 USA; (800) 447-6080, (206) 281-8880, Fax (206) 281-8977, E-mail info@intldining.com.

3

Wine Courses

*Taught by
Members of the
American Wine Society
(AWS) and
the Society of Wine
Educators (SWE)*

CALIFORNIA

MICHAEL A. AMOROSE
San Francisco/Year-round

First offered 1974. 25 1-session courses per year. Enrollment 20 to 35 per class. Specialties: California and Pacific Northwest wines; 9 wines sampled per session; current vintages; price range $15 to $40 per bottle. Source of wines: instructor's cellar and current purchases. Instructor is author of eight books on wine. Tuition: $25 per session. Class location: meetings and conventions.

CONTACT: Michael A. Amorose, 555 California St., #1700, San Francisco, CA 94104; (415) 951-3377, Fax (415) 951-3296.

MARIAN W. BALDY
Chico/Fall

First offered 1972. One 15-week, 45-session course per year. Enrollment 80 students per class. Specialties: sensory evaluation, label reading, wine & food combining, table & sparkling wine production, viticulture; 4 wines sampled per session; 1995 to 1982 vintages; price range $5 to $85 per bottle. Source of wines: California. Instructor has AB degree in Microbiology and PhD in Genetics, experience as wine maker in commercial cellar, and wrote The University Wine Course and teacher's manual. Tuition: $300. Class location: California State University, Chico.

CONTACT: Marian W. Baldy, PhD, School of Agriculture, California State University, First & Normal Sts., Chico, CA 95929-0310; (916) 898-6250, Fax (916) 898-5845, E-Mail mbaldy@davax.csuchico.edu

ROBERT BECK
Rocklin/Fall, Spring

First offered 1987. 4 4-session courses per year. Enrollment 20 students per class. Specialties: worldwide, some California emphasis, wine & food; 7 to 8 wines sampled per session; various vintages; price range $4 to $60 per bottle. Instructor is member of SWE, grape grower, and wine maker. Tuition: $40 to $50 plus $15 to $20 lab fee.

CONTACT: Robert Beck, Sierra College, Rocklin, CA 96788; (916) 781-0590, Fax (916) 878-7878.

MICHAEL R. BOTWIN
San Luis Obispo/Fall, Winter, Spring

First offered 1983. 3 5-session courses per year. Enrollment approximately 15 students per class. Specialties: California wines with emphasis on central coast; 8 wines sampled per session; current vintages; price range $6 to $20 per bottle. Source of wines: local wine shops. Instructor is member of SWE with 20 years teaching experience. Tuition: $105. Class location: California Polytechnic State University (San Luis Obispo).

CONTACT: Michael R. Botwin, California Polytechnic State University, San Luis Obispo, CA 93407; (805) 543-1200 (home).

JOHN BUECHSENSTEIN
Northern California sites/Year-round

First offered 1978. Year-rond 1- or 2-day workshops and multiple session seminars. Enrollment 25-50 students per class. Specialties: sensory evaluation and winemaking;, wine tasting tours to France. 12-24 wines sampled per session; current vintages to early 1980's; price range $5 to $60 per bottle. Instructor is wine maker with BS from U.C. Davis, and member of AWS, IFT, SWE, and ASEV. Tuition: $150 to $300 per course. Class location: University of California-Davis, Mendocino College. private industry.

CONTACT: John Buechsenstein, Wine Education & Consultation, 309 Hillview Ave., Ukiah, CA 95482; (707) 468-8245, Fax (707)468-8245; E-mail johnb@pacific.net.

JAMES D. CRUM, PH.D.
San Bernardino/Fall, Winter, Spring
First offered 1980. 3 4-session courses per year. Enrollment 15 students per class. Specialties: getting to know wine, sensory evaluation, visits to local wineries; 10 to 12 wines sampled per session; 1994 to 1980 vintages; price range $5 to $20. Source of wines: purchased by instructor. Instructor is professor and Dean Emeritus, CSU-San Bernardino, International Wine Master, consultant, and lecturer. Tuition: $50 per session plus $25 wine fee. Class location: California State University Extension, San Bernardino.

CONTACT: James D. Crum, Ph.D, 5132 Sepulveda, San Bernardino, CA 92404-1134; (909) 886-3186, Fax (909) 886-3186.

ROBERT VERNON HOULEHAN
Berkeley/Year-round
First offered 1973. 3 6-session courses per year. Enrollment 12 students per class. Specialties: European and California wines; 5 wines sampled per session; current vintages to 20 years old; price range $7.50 to $30 per bottle. Instructor is member of SWE; travels to Europe twice a year. Tuition: $150 per course. Class location: private homes of students.

CONTACT: Robert V. Houlehan, 1320 Addison St., #C327, Berkeley, CA 94702; (510) 841-2829,Fax (510) 841-2819.

DENIS KELLY
Oakland/Year-round
First offered 1975. 3 to 5 10-session courses per year. Enrollment 14 to 30 students per class. Specialties: wines of Europe and America; 5 wines sampled per session; price range $7 to $75 per bottle. Instructor writes for *Wines & Spirits, Gourmet,* and other publications; author or co-author of 4 wine books, member of SWE. Tuition: $190 to $215 per course. Class location: University of California Extension-Berkeley, Diablo Valley College, private classes in Oakland and Berkeley.

CONTACT: Denis Kelly, 4482 Montgomery St., Oakland, CA 94611; (510) 658-8615, Fax (510) 428-1456.

FRED McMILLIN
San Francisco/Spring, Summer, Fall
First offered 1965. 5 to 6 3-session courses per year. Enrollment 15 students per class. Specialties: wine history, California wine history, ranking the great varietals; 20 wines sampled per session; current vintages to 1980; price range $5 to $50 per bottle. Source of wines: worldwide. Instructor has 2 degrees in chemical engineering, was offered teaching position in philosophy. Tuition: $60 to $90 plus $20 wine fee. Class location: San Francisco State University-Extended Education, San Francisco City College-Ft. Mason Campus.

CONTACT: Fred McMillin, 2121 Broadway, #6, San Francisco, CA 94115; (415) 563-5712, Fax (415) 567-4468.

G. M. "POOCH" PUCILOWSKI
Sacramento/Year-round
First offered 1973. 10 to 12 1- to 6-session courses per year. Enrollment 15 to 40 students per class. Specialties: California wines; 6 to 9 wines sampled per session; current vintages; price range $5 to $40 per bottle. Instructor and past-president of SWE; offers commercial courses to restaurants, wineries, and wholesalers. Tuition: $50 to $100 per course. Class location: local restaurants.

CONTACT: G.M. "Pooch" Pucilowski, 2701 E St., Sacramento, CA 95815; (916) 448-3664, Fax (916) 448-9115.

MARILYNN VILAS
Davis/October-June

First offered 1940. 10 2- to 3-hour classes per quarter. Enrollment 20 to 30 students per class. Specialties: enology & viticulture; Instructors all have Ph.D's. Tuition: in-state $4,500, out-of-state $14,000 per year. Class location: University of California-Davis.

CONTACT: Marilynn Vilas, University of California, Department of Viticulture & Enology, Davis, CA 95615; (916) 752-2260, Fax (916) 752-0382.

DR. ALAN YOUNG
San Francisco/Year-round

First offered 1974. 20 6-session courses per year. Enrollment 10 students per class. Specialties: Winelovers' Bootcamp 3-day courses and home study programs, study tours to wine areas of the world; 8 wines sampled per session; 1994 to 1980 vintages; price range $3 to $150 per bottle. Source of wines: international. Instructor is Australian wine consultant and author of 12 books. Other faculty members are internationally known winemakers and writers. Tuition: $247 to $347 per course. Class location: Napa and Sonoma Valleys, Long Island, Australia, New Zealand, Europe.

CONTACT: Dr. Alan Young, President, International Wine Academy, 38 Portola Dr., San Francisco, CA 94131-1518; (415) 641-4767, Fax (415) 641-7348, E-mail ayoung@sirius.com, URL http://www.unoweb.com/wine-iwa.

CONNECTICUT

VINCENT J. LESUNAITIS
New Haven/Fall, Spring

First offered 1981. 2 6-8 session courses per year. Enrollment 18 students per class. Specialties: French champagnes, intro to wine, US vs France, identify varietals (blind tastings); 6 wines sampled per session; current vintages; price range under $15-25 per session. Instructor is member of SWE and AWS. Tuition: $160 per course. Class location: Gateway Community & Technical College.

CONTACT: Vincent J. Lesunaitis, Gateway Community & Technical College, 60 Sargent Dr., New Haven, CT 06510; (203) 789-7067.

FLORIDA

LAURENCE J. SAUTER, PH.D.
Ormond Beach

First offered 1978. 2 12-session courses per year. Enrollment 40-50 students per class. 2-3 wines sampled per session; current to 1980's vintages; price range $5 to $25 per bottle. Instructor Ph.D Bus & Public Adm., Prof. Engineering, member SWE. Tuition: $40 per course.

CONTACT: Laurence J. Sauter, Ph.D., 3639 Conifer Ln., Ormond Beach, FL 32174; (904) 677-3488.

GEORGIA

YVES DURAND
Roswell/Winter

First offered 1984. 1session per week on-going for 3 months; 2 European wine trips/yr. Enrollment 15 students per class. Specialties: European varieties, 10-12 wines sampled per session; vintages from 1983 to 1960's; price range $75 to $150 per bottle. Source of wines: own cellar. Instructor Best Sommelier US 1984, 3rd Best Sommelier World 1985, TV show host, president Sommelier Society of America. Tuition: $50-$80/class. Class location: own home.

CONTACT: Yves Durand, 400 Hollyberry Dr., Roswell, GA 30076; (770) 993-4337, Fax (770) 386-4650.

ANITA LOUISE LARAIA
Atlanta/January, March, May, October
First offered 1978. 4 6-session courses per year. Enrollment 60 students per class. Specialties: worldwide varieties, home study course book & audio cassettes; 6 wines sampled per session; current vintages to 1970; price range $6 to $80 per bottle. Instructor has Certificate from the Wine & Spirits Guild of Great Britain, wine writer for *Atlanta Homes* magazine, and is member of SWE. Tuition: $200 per 6-session course. Class location: Wyndham Garden Hotel, Buckhead; private restaurant and corporate classes.

CONTACT: Anita Louise LaRaia, Director, The Wine School, P.O. Box 52723, Atlanta, GA 30355; (404) 901-9433.

ILLINOIS

PAUL ERNST
Darien/Year-round
First offered 1977. 3 8-session and 3 2-session courses/yr. Enrollment 24 to 50 students per class. Specialties: perception, wine & food pairing. 6 to 30 wines sampled per session; current vintages to 1960's; price range $5 to $100 per bottle. Instructor is past president of Midwest SWE, Director of Chicago Wine Lovers Intl. Tuition: $120 per 6-session course, $10 to $95 per single session. Class location: hotels and restaurants.

CONTACT: Paul Ernst, Bacchus Resource Management, 8321-B Portsmouth Dr., Darien, IL 60561-6601; (708) 654-WINE (9463), Fax 708-789-8186; E-mail wineaprsr@aol.com.

PATRICK W. FEGAN
Chicago/Year-round
First offered 1984. 6 semesters of four 5-week levels and five 1-night seminars 5-session courses per year. Enrollment 100 to 150 students per semester. 5 to 10 wines sampled per session; current to older vintages; price range price range $1.99 to $50 per bottle. Source of wines: retail shops. Instructor is wine columnist and writer, wine judge with 20 years teaching experience. Tuition: $140 to $225 per 5-week course, $35-$50 per 1-night seminar.

CONTACT: Patrick W. Fegan, Director, Chicago Wine School, 1633 N. Halsted St., Chicago, IL 60614; (312) 266-9463, Fax (312) 266-9769, E-Mail pwfegan@aol.com

IRENE HUFFMAN
Moline, Rock Island/Spring, Fall
First offered 1985. 2 to 6 4-session courses per year. Enrollment 10 to 15 students per class. 8 to 10 wines sampled per session; price range $6 to $60 per bottle. Source of wines: purchased. Instructor board member SWE, wine columnist, wine judge. Tuition: $95/4-sessions, $25 to $40 for classes. Class location: Plaza One Hotel (Black Hawk College Outreach Program).

CONTACT: Irene Huffman, 1225 W. 5th St., Milan, IL 61264; (309) 787-6941, Fax (309) 787-0962.

LOUISIANA

FORREST K. DOWTY
Lafayette/Fall, Spring
First offered 1978. Enrollment 50 students per class. Specialties: worldwide varieties, occasional wine trips; 8 wines sampled per session; price range $2 to $100 per bottle. Instructor owns Magnolia & Reliable Marketing of Lafayette (wine wholesaler), has SWE Certificate of Proficiency, and 50 year wine experience. Tuition: $100 beginners, $150 advanced.

CONTACT: Forrest K. Dowty, Box 3587, Lafayette, LA 70502; (318) 233-9244, Fax (318) 261-3570.

NOLAN P. LE COMPTE, JR.
Thibodaux/Fall

First offered 1989. 1 6-7 session courses per year. Enrollment 30 students per class. 6-8 wines sampled per session; current vintages; price range $7 to $15 per bottle. Source of wines: local wine shops. Instructor is SWE member. Tuition: $150 (one credit-hour) plus $35 lab fee. Class location: Nicholls State University, Thibodaux.

CONTACT: Nolan LeCompte, Jr., VP Academic Affairs, Nicholls State University, P.O. Box 2002, Thibodaux, LA 70310; (504) 448-4012, Fax (504) 448-4026.

MASSACHUSETTS

MICHAEL APSTEIN, MD
Boston/Year-round except Summer

First offered 1980. Five 6-session courses per year, except summer. Enrollment 30 students per class. Specialties: worldwide varieties; 5 wines sampled per session; current vintages to 1983; price range $5 to $35 per bottle. Instructor is wine writer and educator for 16 years; wine editor of Grand Diplome Cooking Course; free-lance writer, *The Boston Globe*; judge in national and international wine competition, and gastroenterologist specializing in liver disease. Tuition: $142 per course. Class location: Boston Center for Adult Education.

CONTACT: Michael Apstein, MD, Boston Center for Adult Education, 5 Commonwealth Ave., Boston, MA 02116; (617) 267-4430.

JERRY GOLDMAN
N. Andover/Fall, Winter, Spring

First offered 1972. 4 6 to 8-session courses per year. Enrollment 20 students per class. Specialties: wine appreciation, specific regions; 6 wines sampled per session; current vintages to late 1970's; price range $10 to $50 per bottle. Instructor is SWE and AWS member, appears on TV and radio talk shows, and taught at Northern Essex Community College and Merrimac College. Tuition: $65 to $85 per course. Class location: Messina's Liquor Store, N. Andover.

CONTACT: Jerry Goldman, Messina's Liquor Store, 117 Main St., N. Andover, MA 01845; (508) 686-9649, Fax (508) 681-8498.

DIANE L. HENAULT
Scituate/Year-round

First offered 1976. 5 1 to 6-session courses per year. Enrollment 9 to 16 students per class. Specialties: Italian, German, and Spanish wines; 6 to 8 wines sampled per session. Instructor is author of *Wines of New England, 1981,* and member of SWE. Tuition: $40 to $85 per single session. Class location: Cambridge Center for Adult Education, Cambridge.

CONTACT: Diane L. Henault, Cambridge Center for Adult Education, 39 Ladds Way, Scituate, MA 02066; (617) 545-7309, Fax (617) 545-0344.

MARYLAND

LISA AIREY
Baltimore/Year-round

First offered 1992. 8 3-session courses per year. Enrollment 25 to 35 students per class. 6 wines sampled per session; current vintages to 1985; price range $4 to $20 per bottle. Instructor is wine consultant for Kronheim Co. (wine wholesaler) and member of AWS. Tuition: $65 per course. Class location: Notre Dame Prep School, Towson.

CONTACT: Lisa Airey, 99 Ray Rd., Baltimore, MD 21227; (410) 242-8000, Fax (410) 242-3493.

MINNESOTA

GEORGE RENIER
Duluth/Fall, Spring
First offered 1979. 2 8-10-session courses per year. Enrollment 18-35 students per class. Specialties: wine & beer making at home; 3 wines sampled per session. Instructor is AWS judge and winemaker since 1950. Tuition: $15 to $20 per course plus fee. Class location: Duluth Jr. High Schools.

CONTACT: George Renier, 2418 E. 4th St., Duluth, MN 55812; (218) 724-2558.

MONTANA

GREGORY B. CARTER
Missoula/Year-round
First offered 1982. 6 6-session courses per year. Enrollment 25 to 30 students per class. Specialties: California, French, and German wines, local wine education & restaurant tours; 4 to 5 wines sampled per session; current vintages to 15 years old. Instructor is member of SWE. Tuition: $50 per course. Class location: local restaurants.

CONTACT: Gregory B. Carter, P.O. Box 5596, Missoula, MT 59806; (406) 543-6634, Fax (406) 728-4405.

NEW JERSEY

JOSEPH FIOLA, PH.D.
Cream Ridge, Jamesburg/Fall, Spring, Summer
First offered 1989. 2 to 3 single-session-session courses per year. Enrollment 50 to 100 students per class. Specialties: Northeastern U.S. wines; 3 to 8 wines sampled per session. Instructor has Ph.D in Horticulture; won the AWS gold and bronze awards for wines produced. Tuition: $50 per course. Class location: Rutgers University-Cooper Extension, New Brunswick.

CONTACT: Joseph Fiola, Rutgers Fruit R&E Center, 283 Rte. 539, Cream Ridge, NJ 08514; (609) 758-7311, Fax (609) 758-7085; E-mail fiola@aesop.rutgers.edu.

ROBERT LEVINE
Princeton/Fall, Spring
First offered 1970. 2 5-session courses per year. Enrollment 32 students per class. Specialties: classical varietals, label reading, component identification, recognizing spoiled wines; 5 to 8 wines sampled per session; current vintages to 1965; price range $5 to $100 per bottle. Instructor Founder & President Emeritus of SWE, member AWS, conducts many seminars in NY, Paris and elsewhere. Tuition: $110 per course. Class location: Princeton Adult School.

CONTACT: Robert Levine, 29 Linwood Circle, Princeton, NJ 08540; (609) 924-6328.

GARY C. PAVLIS, PH.D.
Mays Landing/Fall, Spring
First offered 1992. 2 14-session courses per year. Enrollment 25 students per class. Specialties: worldwide; 6 wines sampled per session; 1974 to 1994 vintages; price range $3 to $30 per bottle. Source of wines: various. Instructor is member of SWE and AWS Certified Judge. Tuition: $125. Class location: Rutgers University.

CONTACT: Gary C. Pavlis, PhD., 6260 Old Harding Hwy., Mays Landing, NJ 08330; (609) 625-0056, Fax (609) 625-3646.

NEW YORK

GREG GIORGIO
Altamonte/Year-round

First offered 1987. 1 to 2 single-session-session courses per year. Enrollment 20 students per class. Specialties: current vintages; 3 to 4 wines sampled per session; price range $7 to $15 per bottle. Instructor is SWE member. Tuition: $10 to $20 per session. Class location: local restaurants.

CONTACT: Greg Giorgio, P.O. Box 74, Altamonte, NY 12009.

INTERNATIONAL WINE CENTER
New York/Year-round

First offered 1981. 25 to 30 1 to 14-session courses per year. Enrollment 12 to 35 students per class. Specialties: worldwide; 7 to 10 wines sampled per session; various vintages; price range $3 to $40 per bottle. Source of wines: purchased. Instructors with various backgrounds and director Mary Ewing Mulligan. a Master of Wine. Tuition: $40 to $950. Class location: International Wine Center.

CONTACT: Steven Miller, Manager, International Wine Center, 231 W. 29th St., New York, NY 10001; (212) 268-7517, Fax (212) 239-4497.

RONALD A. KAPON
New York/Fall, Spring

First offered 1969. 2 6-session courses per year. Enrollment 20 to 100 students per class. Specialties: worldwide; 6 to 12 wines sampled per session; price range $6 to $80 per bottle. Instructor is graduate of German Wine Academy and a Ph.D. in Economics. Tuition: $100. Class location: Queens College, Gramercy Park Hotel, Wine Workshop.

CONTACT: Ronald Kapon, 230 W. 79th St., #42, New York, NY 10024; (212) 799-6311.

HARRIET LEMBECK
New York City/Fall, Spring

First offered 1975. 2 10-session courses/yr. & 4-session spirits course in Fall at Helmsley Hotel; more than 30 1-4-session courses/yr. through New School, NY. Enrollment 50 students. Specialties: worldwide wines and spirits; 10 wines sampled per session; all current, some old vintages; price range $8 to $150 per bottle. Source of wines: retail stores, importers. Instructor is author of *Grossman's Guide to Wines, Beers, & Spirits, 7th ed.* and Director of New School wine and wine & spirits program. Tuition: $525/10-session course, $700 with spirits ($200 spirits alone), $60 to $225/course at New School. Class location: N.Y. Helmsley Hotel, New School.

CONTACT: Harriet Lembeck, Director, Wine & Spirits Program, 54 Continental Ave., Forest Hills, NY 11375; (718) 263-3134, Fax (718) 263-3750.

HARVARD LYMAN
Stony Brook/Fall

First offered 1974. 1 15-session courses per year. Enrollment 25 to 40 students per course. Specialties: all major regions, wine making, appreciation; 6 wines sampled per session; current to late 1990 vintages; price range $5 to $30 per bottle. Source of wines: local. Instructor is member of AWS and Charter Member SWE. Tuition: $270/3 credits plus $40-$45 lab fee, $90 for 1 credit otion. Class location: SUNY-Stony Brook.

CONTACT: Harvard Lyman, Dept. Biochemistry/Cell Biology, SUNY-Stony Brook, Stony Brook, NY 11794-5215; (516) 632-8534, Fax (516) 632-8575, E-Mail hlyman@cc.allin1.sunysb.edu

DAVID G MALE
Williamsville/Fall, Spring
First offered 1986. 2 10-session courses per year. Enrollment 30 students per class. Specialties: New and Old World wines; 6-8 wines sampled per session; 1970 to current vintages; price range $15-$60 per bottle. Instructor: vice-president of Intervin (intl. wine competition), 30 years teaching experience, member AWS and SWE. Tuition: $235. Class location: Eagle House Restaurant, Williamsville, in affiliation with Amherst Continuing Ed.

CONTACT: David G. Male, President, Vintage Hous, 441 Sprucewood Terr., Williamsville, NY 14221-3910; (716) 634-2456, Fax (716) 634-7061,; E-mail vinehous@aol.com.

PAUL S. MANDALA, M.D.
West Islip/Fall, Winter, Spring
First offered 1980. 5 to 6 5-session courses per year. Enrollment 12 students per class. Specialties: worldwide; 8 wines sampled per session; Instructor is member SWE. Tuition: $200 to $250. Class location: office.

CONTACT: Paul S. Mandala M.D., 1111 Montauk Hwy, W. Islip, NY 11795; (516) 665-8098, Fax (516) 665-8098.

TAO PORCHON-LYNCH
White Plains/Fall, Winter, Spring
First offered 1985. 2 8-session courses per year. Enrollment 24 students. Specialties: Worldwide varieties, wine and food seminars; 8 wines sampled per session; price range $10 to $150 per bottle. Instructor is a member and regional VP of AWS (Life), SWE member, certified wine judge, and wine writer/publisher. Tuition: $280/course, $45-$60/5-course dinner & wine. Class location: Westchester Marriott Inn & Restaurant. Also offers wine tours to France, Italy, Spain/Portugal, Australia, Argentina/Chile.

CONTACT: Tao Porchon-Lynch, Les Amoreux Du Vin, 5 Barker Ave., #501, White Plains, NY 10601; (914) 761-7700 ext.2501, Fax (914) 997-2617.

DR. HERBERT F. SPASSER
New York/Fall
First offered 1976. 2 5-session courses per year. Enrollment 20 students. Specialties: Italy, France, Germany, U.S.; 5 to 6 wines sampled per session; 1978 to 1992 vintages; price range $7 to $40 per bottle. Source of wines: purchased and donated. Instructor is Certificate Member of SWE, Chevalier/Commandeur Chaine de Rotisseurs, and wine advisor to the Restaurant Society of N.Y. Tuition: $225. Class location: Midtown Manhattan.

CONTACT: Dr. Herbert F. Spasser, 116 Central Park So., New York, NY 10019; (212)765-1877.

THE WINE SCHOOL AT WINDOWS ON THE WORLD
New York/Spring, Summer, Fall
First offered 1976. 5 8-session courses per year. Enrollment 125 students per class. Specialties: major wine regions of the world; 10 wines sampled per session; 1970's to present vintages; price range $10 to $150 per bottle. Source of wines: purchased. Instructor is Wine Director of Windows on the World, author of *Windows on the World Complete Wine Course,* Board member SWE, 1993 James Beard Wine & Spirits Professional of the Year. Tuition: $575. Class location: New York.

CONTACT: Kevin Charles Zraly, The Wine School at Windows on the World, 16 Woodstock Ln., New Paltz, NY 12561; (914) 255-1456, Fax (914) 255-2041.

OHIO

MATTHEW CITRIGLIA
Columbus/Year-round

First offered 1988. 2 1-session courses per year. Enrollment minimum 5 students per class. Specialties: basic grape varieties and where grown, Italy. 5 to 6 wines sampled per session; price range $8 to $25 per bottle. Instructor is AWS certified judge, Segrams School of Hospitality graduate, 12 years in business. Tuition: $20 to $25. Class location: Vintage Wine, Columbus.

CONTACT: Matthew Citriglia, The Wine Mentor, 1692 Wyandotte Rd., Clolumbus, OH 443212; (614) 781-2815. Fax (216) 248-9242.

OREGON

ROBERT LINER/MATTHEW ELSEN — WINE MERCHANTS
Portland/Winter, Summer, Fall

First offered 1990. 3 3-session courses per year. Enrollment 20 students per class. Specialties: France and West Coast U.S.; 8 wines sampled per session; 1985 to current vintages; price range $10 to $80 per bottle. Instructors have 17 to 20 years experience. Tuition: $85. Class location: in store.

CONTACT: , Liner & Elsen Wine Merchants, 202 N.W. 21st Ave., Portland, OR 97209; (503) 241-9463, Fax (503) 243-6706, E-mail wineguys@northwest.com.

PENNSYLVANIA

WILLIAM H. CLARK
Langhorne/Fall, Spring

First offered 1976. 2 10-session courses per year. Enrollment 50 students per class. Specialties: U.S., European, South America; 5 wines sampled per session; price range $15 to $50 per bottle. Instructor is member SWE. Tuition: $120. Class location: Neshaminy Adult School.

CONTACT: William H. Clark, 74 Hollybrooke Dr., Langhorne, PA 19047; (215) 752-4895, Fax (215) 752-4895; E-mail bill_clark@prodigy.com, URL http://pages.prodigy.com/pa/bordeaux/bordeaux.html.

LOUIS J. DIGIACOMO
Paoli/Spring, Fall

First offered 1979. 4 8-session courses per year. Enrollment 42 students. Specialties: all regions; 6 wines sampled per session; current vintages; price range $7 to $25 per bottle. Source of wines: local. Instructor is a wine writer/lecturer. Tuition: $60. Class location: Main Line School Night, Radnor.

CONTACT: Louis J. DiGiacomo, 204 Country Rd., Berwyn, PA 19312; (215) 563-7700, Fax (215) 563-3337.

JOHN ELD
Pittsburgh/Spring, Summer, Fall

First offered 1988. 6 4-session courses per year. Enrollment 16 students per class. Specialties: California; 5 to 6 wines sampled per session. Instructor is wine wholesaler and AWS member. Tuition: $42.

CONTACT: John Eld, Community College of Allegheny County, 8701 Perry Hwy., Pittsburgh, PA 15237-9987; (412) 369-3736.

ALTON LONG
Bryn Mawr/Year-round

Instructor is member of AIWF. Tuition: $25 per seminar, $48 per dinner. Class location: Yangming restaurant.

CONTACT: Charlotte Ann Albertson, P.O. Box 27, Wynnewood, PA 19096-0027; (610) 649-9290.

SHIRLEY MARTIN COUNTRY WINES
Pittsburgh/September-October

First offered 1975. 2 3-session courses per year. Enrollment 5 to 20 students per class. Specialties: wine making. 6-8 wines sampled last session only. Source of wines: mostly home made, some commercial. Instructor is AWS member & Certified Wine Judge and a graduate of Penn. State Univ. with major in home economics. Tuition: $18. Class location: Country Wines, Pittsburgh.

CONTACT: Shirley Martin, 3333 Babcock Blvd., Pittsburgh, PA 15237; (412) 366-0151, Fax (412) 366-9809; URL: http://www.ontv.com//pp/ctrywide/index/htm.

PAUL G. MOFFITI
Drexel Hill/Fall, Spring

First offered 1989. 2 8-session courses per year. Enrollment 20 students per class. Specialties: wine evaluation-judging; 6 wines sampled per session; varied vintages; price range $5 to $15 per bottle. Source of wines: local. Instructor is AWS certified judge and teaches AWS certification classes. Tuition: $60. Class location: Main Line school night adult education.

CONTACT: Paul G. Moffiti, 834 Alexander Ave., Drexel Hill, PA 19026; (215) 789-0198.

DICK NAYLOR
Stewartstown/Year-round

First offered 1980. 2 6-session courses per year. Enrollment 20 to 30 students per class. Specialties: dry red wine; 4 to 6 wines sampled per session; current to late 1980's vintages; price range $5 to $15 per bottle. Source of wines: Naylor and private collections. Instructor is winemaker, AWS and SWE member and lecturer. Tuition: $55. Class location: Naylor Wine Cellars.

CONTACT: Dick Naylor, Naylor Wine Cellars, RFD #3, Box 424, Stewartstown, PA 17363; (717) 993-2431, Fax (717) 993-9460.

RICHARD SAUL
Slatington

First offered 1986. Specialties: all regions and subjects; price range varies. Instructor is AWS member and wine judge examiner. Tuition: varies.

CONTACT: Richard Saul, 2391 Rockdale Rd., Slatington, PA 18080; (610) 767-0282.

SYLVIA H. SCHRAFF
Altoona/Spring, Fall

First offered 1987. 2 2-session courses per year. Enrollment 25 students. Specialties: basic wine appreciation; 5-6 wines sampled per session; 1989 to 1994 vintages; price range $6 to $12 per bottle. Instructor is owner/wine maker of Oak Spring Winery and has M.S. degree in Nursing Science. Tuition: $25. Class location: Oak Spring Winery.

CONTACT: Sylvia Schraff, President, Oak Spring Winery, R.D.1, Box 612, Altoona, PA 16601; (814) 946-3799.

EDWARD TURBA
Pittsburgh/Winter, Summer

First offered 1988. 8 courses per year. Enrollment 20 students. Specialties: worldwide; 5 wines sampled per session; 7 year spread in vintages; price range 10 to $40 per bottle. Instructor is SWE member, taught at Intl. Culinary Academy, Le Mont restaurant sommelier for 8 years. Tuition: $200/3-hour session excl. wine. Class location: privately arranged.

CONTACT: Edward Turba, Sommelier, LeMont Restaurant, 3 Soffel St., Pittsburgh, PA 15211; (412) 488-8499/431-3100, Fax (412) 431-1204; E-mail info@le-mont.com, URL www.le-mont.com.

TENNESSEE

SHIELDS T. HOOD
Memphis/Fall, Spring

First offered 1978. 5 3-session courses per year. Enrollment 18 to 30 students per class. Specialties: California and worldwide; 10 wines sampled per session; current vintages; price range $5 to $50 per bottle. Instructor is SWE certified with 23 years wine experience. Tuition: $20 per session. Class location: local restaurants.

CONTACT: Shields T. Hood, 905 James St., Memphis, TN 38106; (901) 774-8888, Fax (901) 946-4751.

JOHN IACOVINO
Oak Ridge/Fall, Spring, Summer

First offered 1989. 3 4- to 6-session courses per year. Enrollment 25 to 30 students per class. Specialties: Burgundy. 6 to 9 wines sampled per session; current to early 1980's vintages; price range $8 to $80 per bottle. Source of wines: local stores, winery direct, personal cellar. Instructor is member AWS, Senechal of Ducal Order of Croix du Burgogne, and judge for Tennessee Intl. Wine Festival. Tuition: $100 to $125. Class location: local restaurants and homes.

CONTACT: John Iacovino, 120 Westlook Circle, Oak Ridge, TN 37830; (423) 483-8330, Fax (423) 482-2495; E-mail 70673.376@compuserve.com.

UT COMMUNITY PROGRAMS
Knoxville/Year-round

First offered 1978. 6 7-session courses per year. Enrollment 18 students per class. Specialties: French, Italian, Australian, Chilean, California and eastern U.S.; 7 to 8 wines sampled per session; 1970 to 1990 vintages; price range $6 to $35 per bottle. Source of wines: retail outlets. Instructor is member AWS and Cross of Burgundy Wine Society with 20 years teaching experience. Tuition: $145. Class location: University of Tennessee.

CONTACT: Elaine Keener, Program Coordinator, University of Tennessee, 600 Henley St., Ste. 105, Knoxville, TN 37996-4110; (423) 974-0150, Fax (423) 974-0264; E-mail utcommunity@gateway.ce.utk.edu.

VIRGINIA

DR. JOSEPH V. FORMICA
Richmond/Fall

First offered 1992. 1 15-session courses per year. Enrollment 20 students. Specialties: sensory evaluation, physical and chemical compatibilities with food; 6 wines sampled per session; late 1980's to current vintages; price range $7 to $50 per bottle. Source of wines: local. Instructor is SWE member, certified by Wine & Spirit Education Trust of England and SWE, and a Ph.D. in microbiology. Tuition: $140 plus $85 lab fee. Class location: J. Sargent Reynolds Community College.

CONTACT: Dr. Joseph V. Formica, Director, The Wine School, 8402 Gaylord Rd., Richmond, VA 23229-4126; (804) 747-8163, fax (804) 828-9946.

STEFAN GRABINSKI
Richmond/Spring, Fall, Winter

First offered 1970. 3 to 6 8-session courses per year. Enrollment 16 students per class. Specialties: wine countries and regions, wine making and evaluations; 6 wines sampled per session; 1970 to current vintages; price range $7 to $20 per bottle. Source of wines: local. Instructor is SWE and AWS member, founding member of Richmond Wine Society, and former vineyard owner. Tuition: $100 plus wine fee. Class location: local college and restaurants.

CONTACT: Stefan Grabinski, 4944 Farrell Ct., Richmond, VA 23228; (804) 270-6255.

JOHN KEATING
Poquoson/Fall, Spring

First offered 1977. 2 8-session courses per year. Enrollment 20 students per class. Specialties: worldwide; 6 wines sampled per session; price range $10 per bottle. Instructor teaches at Johnson & Wales. Tuition: $150. Class location: College of William & Mary.

CONTACT: John E. Keating, 7 Roberts Landing, Poquoson, VA 23662; (804) 868-7543.

CANADA

MICHAEL BOTNER, C.A. — ACCOUNTING FOR TASTE
Ottawa/Fall, Winter, Spring

First offered 1996. 4 4-session courses, 1 8-session courses per year. Enrollment 24 students per class. Specialties: The Wine Course and the Discovery Series. 6 wines sampled per session; 1978 and later vintages; price range averages $8 to $100 per bottle. Instructor is a wine judge and consultant and a wine writer/columnist since 1979. Tuition: $85 for Wine Course, $200 Discovery Series. Class location: Echo Cafe/Wine Bar.

CONTACT: Michael Botner, Accounting for Taste, Apt. #512, 1081 Ambleside Dr., Ottawa, ON K2B 8C8, Canada; (613) 829-9223, Fax (613) 829-9223ß.

JIM CRAWFORD —MANITOBA LIQUOR CONTROL COMMISSION
Winnipeg/Year-round

First offered 1992. 5 to 10 5-session courses per year. Enrollment 20 students per class. Specialties: all major wine regions; 12 wines sampled per session; last 10 years vintages; price range $5 to $100 per bottle. Instructors are graduates of British Wine & Spirit Education Certificate course. Tuition: $50. Class location: in-house.

CONTACT: Jim Crawford, Coordinator Product Education, Manitoba Liquor Control Commission, P.O. Box 1023, Winnipeg, MB R3T 1L9; (204) 474-5553, Fax (474) 475-7686.

HANS W. TEUNISSEN
Willowdale/Irregularly year-round

First offered 1983. 2 to 3 10-session courses per year. Enrollment 15 students per class. Specialties: worldwide; 8 wines sampled per session; varied vintages; price range $5 to $50 per bottle. Instructor is SWE member. Tuition: C$120. Class location: community college.

CONTACT: Hans Teunissen, 31 Wedgewood Dr., Willowdale, ON M2M 2H2; (416) 733-9441.

4

Food & Wine Organizations

AMERICAN CULINARY FEDERATION (ACF)
St. Augustine, Florida

Founded in 1929. Membership 25,000. Oldest nationwide professional cooks' association recognized by other leading food service organizations. Objectives: to further the advancement of the culinary profession and offer training, education, and fellowship. More than 295 local chapters in the U.S. and Caribbean. Membership benefits include: educational seminars at national convention and regional meetings; subscription to monthly magazine, *The National Culinary Review*, competitions for gold, silver, and bronze medals in ACF-approved culinary arts shows sponsored by local chapters. The ACF and the National Restaurant Association jointly sponsor the United States Culinary "Olympic" Team, which represents the American culinary profession in the largest and oldest international cooking competition, the Culinary "Olympics", held every 4 years in Germany. Membership dues vary from chapter to chapter.

The American Culinary Federation Educational Institute (ACFEI), an ACF subsidiary, accredits culinary schools through its Accrediting Commission, certifies chefs on the basis of knowledge and experience, awards loans and scholarships to students, and provides a U.S. Department of Labor recognized 3-year National Apprenticeship Training Program for Cooks. Certification categories include Certified Cook/Pastry Cook (CC, CPC), Certified Sous Chef/Certified Chef de Cuisine and/or Pastry Chef (CSC, CCC, CPC), Certified Culinary Educator (CCE), Certified Executive Chef and/or Executive Pastry Chef (CEC, CEPC), and the highest level, Certified Master Chef/Pastry Chef (CMC, CMPC). Another ACF subsidiary, The American Academy of Chefs, is the honor society of American chefs.

CONTACT: ACF, P.O. Box 3466, St. Augustine, FL 32085; (800) 624-9458 or (904) 824-4468, Fax (904) 825-4758.

AMERICAN DIETETIC ASSOCIATION (ADA)
Chicago, Illinois

Founded in 1917. Membership 69,000, of which 75% are registered dietitians in diverse areas of practice, including clinical dietetics, hospital, school and foodservice administration, community and public health, organizations, extended care facilities. Promotes optimal nutrition, health, and well-being through various activities, publications, educational meetings, media and marketing programs. Establishes and enforces quality standards for more than 600 educational programs and internships in dietetics and nutrition. Maintains a legislative affairs office in Washington, DC, and has a nonprofit foundation established for charitable, educational, and scientific research and scholarship purposes.

CONTACT: American Dietetic Association, 216 W. Jackson Blvd., Chicago, IL 60606-6995; (312) 899-0400, Fax (312) 899-4845; URL http://www.eatright.org.

AMERICAN INSTITUTE OF BAKING (AIB)
Manhattan, Kansas

Founded in 1919. This non-profit educational organization's objective is to promote the cause of education in nutrition and in the science and art of baking and bakery management. The AIB employs about 135 full-time personnel and is supported by the contributions of more than 600 member companies. Programs include the 16-week Baking Science and Technology course, the 10-week Bakery Maintenance Engineering program, and short courses and seminars (page 41). Correspondence courses include Science of Applied Baking, Bakery Maintenance Engineering, and Maintenance Engineering. Scholarships and financial aid are available. The AIB's Certified Baker Program provides companies with training that does not require lengthy stays away from the job; the research department develops new techniques and evaluates new ingredients; the Technical Assistance group provides information on scientific, technical, and regulatory subjects; the Department of Food Product Safety offers training and in-plant inspection; the Department of Safety Education offers training and in-plant audits; and the Library responds to information requests. The Food Labeling Program provides information for FDA-required food labels.

CONTACT: AIB, 1213 Bakers Way, Manhattan, KS 66502; (800) 633-5137 or (913) 537-4750.

AMERICAN INSTITUTE OF WINE & FOOD (AIWF)
San Francisco, California
Founded in 1981 by Julia Child, Robert Mondavi, and Richard Graff. Membership nearly 10,000. This non-profit educational organization's objectives are to advance the appreciation of wine and food and stimulate greater scholarly education in gastronomy. Membership is open to all and benefits include a discounted invitation to the annual Conference on Gastronomy, invitation to national and chapter programs, special prices on national educational conferences and seminars, and savings on wine and food publications. Publications include the annual *Journal of Gastronomy, Wine, Food and The Arts* and *American Wine & Food* newsletter. There are more than 30 AIWF chapters in the U.S. and abroad. Annual membership contributions range from $35 for students to $500 for corporations

CONTACT: AIWF, 1550 Bryant St., Ste. 700, San Francisco, CA 94103; (415) 255-3000, (800) 274-AIWF.

AMERICAN VEGAN SOCIETY(AVS)
Malaga, New Jersey
Founded in 1960. Nonprofit educational organization dedicated to teaching a compassionate way of living and abstinence from animal products. Lectures, discussions, and live-in weekend classes in vegan cooking are available. Member services: books & videos available by mail order including cookbooks on nutrition and health. An educational convention is held annually. Members receive a subscription to the *Ahimsa* quarterly newsletter. Annual dues are $18.

CONTACT: AVS, 56 Dinshah Ln., P.O. Box H, Malaga, NJ 08328-0908; (609) 694-2887.

AMERICAN WINE SOCIETY (AWS)
Rochester, New York
Founded in 1967. 5,000 members. Non-profit consumer organization dedicated to bringing together wine lovers and educating people about wine production and use. The national conference, held in November, features tastings, contests, tours of wineries and vineyards, and well-known speakers. Publications include a quarterly journal, specialized technical manuals, and lists of related books and publications. The organization assists in publicizing regional events and helps organize local chapters (currently 90), which sponsor tastings, tours, wine making and other social and educational events. Members with at least 2 years of chapter comparative tastings or equivalent are eligible for the AWS Wine Judge Certification Program. Membership is open to all and annual dues are $36 per individual or couple. Professional Memberships are $58 per year and Lifetime Memberships, for ages 60 and over, are $280.

CONTACT: AWS, 3006 Latta Rd., Rochester, NY 14612; (716) 225-7613.

THE BREAD BAKERS GUILD OF AMERICA
Pittsburgh, Pennsylvania
Nonprofit educational organization founded in 1993 by bakery owner Tom McMahon. Objectives are to bring together individuals involved in the production of high quality bread products, to raise professional standards, and to encourage the education and training of people interested in careers as bread baking professionals. It also seeks to promote the exchange of information between artisan bakers, their suppliers, and specialists in the science of baking and baking ingredients. The Guild publishes a newsletter and sponsors seminars and workshops in the U.S. and abroad, as well as regional and national baking competitions. Membership is open to anyone but the focus of the Guild is professional bread bakers. Business membership yearly dues are based upon annual company sales, starting at $100; non-business yearly dues: $35 students, $50 educators, $65 all others.

CONTACT: Gina Renée Piccolino, Director of Activities and Membership Services, The Bread Bakers Guild of America, P.O. Box 22254, Pittsburgh, PA 15222; (412) 322-8275, Fax (412) 322-3412.

CONFRERIE DE LA CHAINE DES ROTISSEURS

International gastronomic organization, originally founded in Paris in 1248 as a guild of masters in the art of roasting geese for the royal table, disbanded in 1791, reincorporated in 1950. In the U.S. the Chaine has approximately 140 local chapters with about 7,000 members. Its purpose is to encourage educational functions and promote fellowship among individuals with a serious interest in wine and cuisine. The nonprofit, tax-exempt Chaine Foundation supports educational and charitable programs. Membership benefits at the local level include gastronomic functions, usually 4-6 formal dinners per year supplemented by 2-4 smaller events. On a regional and national level, members can join in Chaine-sponsored excursions, attend the national convention, and share, by invitation, activities of other chapters. Professionals make up approximately 30% of the membership and include authors, critics, and food service professionals. Membership is normally by invitation only. Interested individuals who do not know a member should contact the National Office for information.

CONTACT: Confrerie de la Chaine des Rotisseurs, National Administrative Office: 444 Park Ave. So., New York, NY 10016; (212) 683-3770, Fax (212) 683-3882

COOKING TOGETHER FOUNDATION (CTF)
Williamsburg, Virginia

Founded in 1995. This nonprofit educational organization is dedicated to teaching children to cook and bake. Activities include workshops conducted by culinary professionals for children and their parents or caregivers. Annual dues range from $5 for youths/$25 for individuals to $500 for corporations.

CONTACT: Cooking Together Foundation, P.O. Box 34066, Washington, DC 20043-4066; (800) 464-8835, (202) 342-1944, Fax (202) 842-3867.

COUNCIL ON HOTEL, REST. AND INSTIT. EDUCATION (CHRIE)
Washington, D.C.

Founded in 1946. 2,400 members from 50 countries. This trade and professional organization's mission is to foster the international advancement of teaching and training in the field of hospitality and tourism management and facilitate the professional development of its members, who include administrators, educators, industry professionals, and government executives. Membership benefits include an annual conference and several publications: The *CHRIE Communique* monthly newsletter, the *Hospitality & Tourism Educator* interdisciplinary quarterly, the 4 times yearly *Hospitality Research Journal*, *HOSTEUR* magazine for students at member schools, and the *Annual Directory of CHRIE Members*. CHRIE also publishes *A Guide to College Programs in Hospitality & Tourism*, which describes curricula, admission requirements, scholarships, and internships.

CONTACT: CHRIE, 1200 17th St., N.W., Washington, DC 20036-3097; (202) 331-5990, Fax (202) 785-2511.

EDUCATIONAL FOUNDATION OF THE NRA
Chicago, Illinois

Established in 1987. Nonprofit organization created to advance the professional standards of food-service management through education. The Foundation develops courses, video training, seminars, and other programs that help managers gain proficiency. The Professional Management Program (ProMgmt.), for undergraduate hospitality students, covers five foodservice areas: unit revenue/cost management, risk management, human resources/diversity management, operations, and marketing. Students receive a certificate upon completion of the course and program. The organization also offers ProMgmt. scholarships. More than 150 schoools are partners in the program.

CONTACT: Educational Foundation of the NRA, 250 S. Wacker Dr., Ste. 1400, Chicago, IL 60606; (312) 715-1010.

INTERNATIONAL ASSN. OF CULINARY PROFESSIONALS (IACP)
Louisville, Kentucky

Founded in 1978. More than 3,300 members representing over 32 countries. This not-for-profit professional association's objectives include: providing continuing education and professional development, sponsoring of the annual IACP Julia Child Cookbook Awards, promoting the exchange of culinary information among members of the professional food community, establishing professional and ethical standards, and funding scholarships. Membership benefits include the annual spring and regional conferences, newsletters and research reports, the annual IACP Membership Directory, the Certified Culinary Professional (CCP) certification program. Annual dues are $150 (plus $50 one-time fee) for Professional Members, $250 (plus $50) for Cooking School Members, $300 (plus $50) for Business Members; $750 (plus $100) for Corporate Members, and $50 for Student/Apprentice Members.

CONTACT: IACP, 304 W. Liberty St., Suite 201, Louisville, KY 40202; (502) 581-9786, Fax (502) 589-3602; E-mail iacp@aol.com, URL http://www. iacp-online.org.

IACP FOUNDATION Tuition-Credit Scholarships Cash-Award Scholarships Work-Study

Approximately 70 awards for partial or full tuition credit in a wide range of schools and culinary programs and for work-study (formerly "sojourns"). Respected food professionals review all complete applications and determine recipients. To receive an application, send a $5 check/money order made payable to the IACP Foundation at 304 West Liberty Street, Suite 201, Louisville, Kentucky 40202; Telephone 502-587-7953, Fax 502-589-3602. **Deadline: December 1st.**

IACP FOUNDATION
Louisville, Kentucky

Founded in 1984. Supports the IACP by soliciting, managing, and distributing funds for educational and charitable work related to the culinary profession. Maintains programming in four emphasis areas: library funding, research, scholarship, and world hunger. Provides and administers tuition-credit and tuition-cash awards for professional training at both the primary and continuing education level. Publications: the annual *Perspectives*. Committee members meet during the annual IACP conference.

CONTACT: Debbie Arnold, Director of Administration, IACP Foundation, 304 W. Liberty St., Suite 201, Louisville, KY 40202; (502) 587-7953, Fax (502) 589-3602.

INTL. ASSN. OF WOMEN CHEFS AND RESTAURATEURS (IAWCR)
San Francisco, California

Established in 1993 by eight well-known women chefs and restaurateurs. Mission is to promote the education and advancement of women in the restaurant industry and the betterment of the industry as a whole. The IAWCR publishes the quarterly newsletter *Entrez!*, and conducts an annual convention and regional events to promote networking and discussion of such issues as flexible working arrangements, job sharing, and child care. Provides nationwide job networking, publishes membership and service directory, and awards grants and scholarships. Membership categories/annual dues include Executive (restaurant chef/owners)/$175, Professional (employed in the restaurant industry)/$75, Student/$35, Affiliate (supporting the association's mission)/$125, Small Business/$250, and Corporate/$1,500.

CONTACT: IAWCR, 110 Sutter St., Ste. 305, San Francisco, CA 94104; (415) 362-7336, Fax (415) 362-7335, E-mail iawcr@well.com.

INTERNATIONAL FOOD SERVICE EXECUTIVES ASSOCIATION
Margate, Florida

Founded 1901. Membership 5,000. Nonprofit educational and community service organization. Services include student scholarships, monthly gatherings, savings on rental cars and cruise lines, and *Hotline Magazine*. Also has certification program for executives, chefs, managers, bar managers, and others. Memberships are Active (management, ownership, purchasing), Associate (supplier/vendor), Member-at-Large (reside more than 50 miles from an IFSEA branch) and Corporate. Annual dues are $130 for certification only, $150 for certification and IFSEA membership.

CONTACT: IFSEA, 1100 S. State Road 7, Suite 103, Margate, Florida 33068; (954) 977-0767, Fax (954) 977-0874.

INTERNATIONAL FOODSERVICE EDITORIAL COUNCIL (IFEC)
Hyde Park, New York

Founded in 1956 by a group of foodservice magazine editors and public relations executives. Membership 250. This nonprofit association is dedicated to improving the quality of media communications in the foodservice industry. Membership benefits include an annual directory and conference, newsletter, and networking. Four to six scholarships ranging from $1,000 to $2,500 are awarded annually to students whose career aspirations combine foodservice and communications. Membership is open to individuals employed in editorial functions within the industry.

CONTACT: Carol Metz, Executive Director, IFEC, P.O. Box 491, Hyde Park, NY 12538; (914) 452-4345, Fax (914) 452-0532.

INTERNATIONAL WINE & FOOD SOCIETY
London, England

Founded in 1933. Educational organization devoted to bringing together wine and food lovers and promoting a wider knowledge of the wines of the world. Membership benefits include yearly festivals, monthly wine events, dinners, seminars, day trips, and a journal. Branches in 50 countries operate autonomously with admission at the discretion of each branch. Application to The Wine and Food Society, Inc. of New York, the largest overseas branch, requires a sponsor. Prospective members must attend 2 events and a Membership Committee reception. Initiation fee is $150 per person; annual dues are $225 (single), $400 (couple).

CONTACT: International Wine & Food Society, 9 Fitzmaurice Place, Berkeley Square. London, W1X 6JD, England; (44) 171-495 4191, Fax (44) 171-495 4172.

JAMES BEARD FOUNDATION, INC.
New York, New York

Established in 1986. Nonprofit organization whose mission is to keep alive the ideals and activities that made James Beard the "Father of American Cooking" and to maintain his home as the first historical culinary center in North America. Membership benefits include discounts on the more than 200 events (workshops and dinners featuring well-known American chefs) each year; a subscription to *Beard House* magazine; the Foundation directory, which lists professional members; and the annual James Beard Awards (first weekend in May), which includes cookbook, journalism, chef, and restaurant categories. A scholarship and apprenticeship program and library have been developed. Tax-deductible annual dues begin at $60 for nonprofessionals and $125 ($250 for members within 75 miles of Manhattan) for professionals.

CONTACT: James Beard Foundation, Inc., 167 W. 12th St., New York, NY 10011; (212) 675-4984, (800)-36-BEARD, Fax (212) 645-1438.

NAPA VALLEY WINE LIBRARY ASSOCIATION (NVWLA)
St. Helena, California

Established in 1963. Dedicated to preserving and sharing information regarding viticulture, enology, and wine lore, particularly as it pertains to the Napa Valley. Acquires books and other publications for the Napa Valley Wine Library, a more than 4,000-title collection including oral history transcripts and historic photographs, which is housed at the St. Helena Public Library. Membership benefits include the seasonal *Wine Library Report,* first notice of wine appreciation weekends and one-day seminars, and admission to the annual winetasting, an August event that presents the wines of more than 100 Napa Valley wineries. Membership is open to anyone and dues are $20 per year.

CONTACT: Napa Valley Wine Library Association, P.O. Box 328, St. Helena, CA 94574; (707) 963-5145.

NATIONAL RESTAURANT ASSOCIATION (NRA)
Washington, D.C.
Established in 1919. Membership over 30,000. This national trade association for the foodservice industry provides educational, research, communications, convention, and government services; interacts with legislators and political leaders; offers a media relations program and speech bank; has a toll-free information hotline. The nonprofit Educational Foundation subsidiary advances industry professional standards. Publications: the monthly *Restaurants USA* magazine, Washington Weekly political report, operations manuals. Sponsors Restaurant, Hotel-Motel Show in Chicago each May. Membership is open to any entity that operates facilities and/or supplies meal service to others on a regular basis. Dues are revenue-based and begin at $140 for annual sales under $250,000.

CONTACT: National Restaurant Association, 1200-17th St., NW, Washington, DC 20036-3097; (202) 331-5900, Fax (202) 331-2429; E-mail isal@restaurant.org, URL http://www.restaurant.org.

NATIONAL ASSN. FOR THE SPECIALTY FOOD TRADE, INC.
New York, New York
Established in 1952. Membership 2,000 companies in the U.S. and overseas. Nonprofit business trade association that fosters trade, commerce, and interest in the specialty food industry. Sponsors the semi-annual International Fancy Food and Confection Show every winter (West Coast) and summer (East Coast), attracting 25,000-35,000 attendees. Other services include the Annual Product Awards held every summer, the Scholarship and Research Fund, and the bimonthly *NASFT Showcase Magazine.* Membership requires that a company be in business for a minimum of one year. The Admissions Committee reviews applications and makes recommendations to the Board of Directors for a final decision. Annual dues are $200 (for annual sales under $1 million), $400 ($1-$5 million), and $600 (over $5 million).

CONTACT: NASFT, 120 Wall St., 27th Floor, New York, NY 10005-4001; (212) 482-6440, Fax (212) 482-6455.

NORTH AMERICAN VEGETARIAN SOCIETY (NAVS)
Dolgeville, New York
Established in 1974. Nonprofit educational organization dedicated to promoting the vegetarian way of life. Affiliated with the International Vegetarian Union. Sponsors an annual Vegetarian Summerfest conference and World Vegetarian Day (Oct. 1). Provides information to members, the public, and the media. Members receive the quarterly magazine, *Vegetarian Voice.* Membership begins as $20 annually.

CONTACT: NAVS, PO Box 72, Dolgeville, NY 13329; (518) 568-7970.

OLDWAYS PRESERVATION AND EXCHANGE TRUST
Boston, Massachusetts
Established 1990. This nonprofit educational institution is dedicated to preserving healthy food traditions and fostering cultural exchange in the fields of food, cooking, and agriculture. It seeks to bring together experts to evaluate cultural traditions and to define sustainable food choices. The Chefs Collaborative: 2000, an educational initiative launched in 1993, works to expand links

between chefs and growers who are committed to farming in an ecologically responsible way. It jointly founded and is a cosponsor of Chefs Helping to Enhance Food Safety (C.H.E.F.S). Conferences, retreats, workshops, and a fund-raising campaign are planned. Membership in Oldways and the Collaborative is open to all through signing of the Chefs Collaborative Charter and subscribing to a newsletter.

CONTACT: Oldways Preservation and Exchange Trust., 25 First St., Cambridge, MA 02141; (617) 621-3000, Fax (617) 621-1230.

SOCIETY OF WINE EDUCATORS (SWE)
East Longmeadow, Massachusetts

Formed in 1977. Membership 1,500. Nonprofit organization dedicated to improving information about the various aspects of wine making, including wine service, wine and food pairing, wine and health. Membership services include the annual conference (held near a different wine-producing area each summer), educational programs, and trips to wine regions worldwide. The Society provides an annual test of proficiency and awards a Certificate of Proficiency. Publications include the quarterly *SWE Chronicle,* and the *SWE Resource Manual* of teaching materials. Annual dues are $55 (single), $82.50 (couple), plus a $15 application fee the first year. Industry membership is $200 annually in addition to a $15 application fee.

CONTACT: SWE, 132 Shaker Rd., Ste. 14, East Longmeadow, MA 01028; (413) 567-8272, Fax (413) 567-2051.

TASTERS GUILD INTERNATIONAL
Ft. Lauderdale, Florida

Established in 1985 by wine consultant Joseph J. Schagrin. Objective is to promote the appreciation and moderate use of wine and food through education, tastings, consumer benefits, and travel opportunities. Conducts an Annual International Wine Judging each spring, publishes *Tasters Guild Journal,* and sponsors an annual Food and Wine Cruise and other excursions. Local Guilds sponsor wine and food events and discounts are offered to members by affiliated wine and gourmet establishments. Annual membership dues are $35 per family.

CONTACT: Joseph J. Schagrin, President, Tasters Guild, International, 1451 W. Cypress Creek Rd., Ste. 300-26, Ft. Lauderdale, FL 33309; (954) 928-2823, Fax (954) 928-2824

UNITED STATES PERSONAL CHEF ASSOCIATION (USPCA)
Corrales, New Mexico

Established in 1991 by David E. MacKay and Susan P. Titcomb, proprietors of Personally Yours Personal Chef Service. More than 1,000 members. For-profit association that trains personal chefs. Member services: continuing education, business support, regional training, referral system. Publications: quarterly newsletter. Meals are customized to the client's taste and prepared in the client's home.

CONTACT: David E. Mac Kay, Executive Director, USPCA, 4769 Corrales Rd., Corrales, New Mexico 87048; (800) 995-2138, Fax (505) 898-6866; E-mail uspcainc@interramp.com, URL http://www.uspca.com.

WINE INSTITUTE
San Francisco, California

Formed in 1934. Membership 440 California winemakers. Trade association dedicated to initiating and advocating public policy to enhance the environment for the responsible consumption and enjoyment of wine. Individuals and companies providing goods and services to the industry can become associate members. Based in San Francisco, with offices in Sacramento, Washington, DC, 6 regions of the United States, and 8 foreign countries.

CONTACT: Wine Institute, Communications Dept., 425 Market St., Ste. 1000, San Francisco, CA 94105; (415) 512-0151, Fax (415) 442-0742.

5

Appendix

AMERICAN CULINARY FEDERATION EDUCATIONAL INSTITUTE (ACFEI) ACCREDITING COMMISSION

Annapolis, Maryland

Accreditation by the American Culinary Federation Educational Institute Accrediting Commission, the educational arm of the American Culinary Federation and is a review process that evaluates the quality of an educationally-accredited post-secondary institution's program in culinary arts and foodservice management. The program's objectives, staff, facilities, policies, curriculum, instructional methods, and procedures are examined to determine if they meet ACFEI standards, which were developed to meet the requirements for entry-level culinarians. To be eligible, a program must contain a majority of required competencies; must be offered by a school that is accredited by an agency recognized by the U.S. Dept. of Education; must be full-time, include at least 1,000 contact hours, and result in a certificate, diploma, or degree; must have a full-time coordinator who has qualifications equivalent to a Certified Culinary Educator, Executive Chef, or Executive Pastry Chef, or has earned a master's degree in an appropriate discipline; and must have been in continuous existence for at least two years and have graduated a sufficient number of students in order to be evaluated. Application for accreditation must be authorized by the department Dean and 50% of the full-time faculty in the technical phase of the program must have credentials equivalent to an ACFEI Certified Culinary Educator, Sous Chef, or Pastry Chef.

CONTACT: For a current list of accredited programs: The Educational Institute, American Culinary Federation, P.O. Box 3466, St. Augustine, FL 32085; (904) 824-4468. For accreditation application: The American Culinary Federation Educational Institute Accrediting Commission, 959 Melvin Rd., Annapolis, MD 21403; (410) 268-5659, Fax (410) 263-3110.

ACFEI-Accredited schools as of July, 1996:

ALABAMA

JEFFERSON STATE COMMUNITY COLLEGE
Pinson Valley Pkwy. at 2601 Carson Rd., Birmingham, AL 35215 **CONTACT:** Joe Morris (205) 853-1200

ARIZONA

SCOTTSDALE CULINARY INSTITUTE
8100 Camelback Road, Scottsdale, AZ 85251 **CONTACT:** Elizabeth Leite (602) 990-3773

CALIFORNIA

CALIFORNIA CULINARY ACADEMY
625 Polk Street, San Francisco, CA 94102 **CONTACT:** Admissions office (800) 229-2433

CITY COLLEGE OF SAN FRANCISCO
50 Phelan Ave., San Francisco, CA 94112 **CONTACT:** Frank Ambrozic (415) 239-3154

DIABLO VALLEY COLLEGE
321 Golf Club Road, Pleasant Hill, CA 94523 **CONTACT:** Jack Hendrickson (510) 685-1230, ext. 556

LOS ANGELES TRADE-TECH. COLLEGE
400 W. Washington Blvd., Los Angeles, CA 90015 **CONTACT:** Steven Kasmar (213) 744-9480

ORANGE COAST COLLEGE
2710 Fairview Blvd., Costa Mesa, CA 92625 **CONTACT:** Daniel Beard (714) 432-5835

SANTA BARBARA CITY COLLEGE
721 Cliff Drive, Santa Barbara, CA 93100 **CONTACT:** John Dunn (805) 965-0581

CONNECTICUT

MANCHESTER COMMUNITY COLLEGE
P.O. Box 1046, 60 Bidwell St., Manchester, CT 06040 **CONTACT:** Sandra Jenkins (203) 647-6121

FLORIDA

ART INSTITUTE OF FT. LAUDERDALE
1799 S.E. 17th St., Ft. Lauderdale, FL 33316 **CONTACT:** Klaus Friedenreich (305) 463-3000, ext. 208

ATLANTIC VOCATIONAL TECHNICAL CENTER
4700 Coconut Creek Parkway, Coconut Creek, FL 33066 **CONTACT:** Moses Ball (305) 977-2066

FLORIDA COMMUNITY COLLEGE AT JAX
4501 Capper Road, Jacksonville, FL 32218 **CONTACT:** Al Fricke (904) 766-6652

THE FLORIDA CULINARY INSTITUTE
a Division of New England Tech. 1126 53rd Court, West Palm Beach, FL 33407
CONTACT: David Pantone (407) 842-8324

GULF COAST COMMUNITY COLLEGE
5230 W. U.S. Highway 98, Panama City, FL 32401 **CONTACT:** Travis Herr (904) 769-1551, ext. 3850

PINELLAS TECHNICAL EDUCATION CENTER CLEARWATER CAMPUS
6100 154th Avenue, North Clearwater, FL 33516 **CONTACT:** Vincent Calandra (813) 531-3531

SOUTHEAST INST. OF CULINARY ARTS
Collins at Del Monte Ave., St. Augustine, FL 32084 **CONTACT:** David Bearl (904) 824-4401

GEORGIA

ART INSTITUTE OF ATLANTA/SCHOOL OF CULINARY ARTS
3391 Peachtree Rd., NE, Atlanta, GA 30326 **CONTACT:** Jim Morris (404) 266-1341, ext. 227

SAVANNAH TECHNICAL INSTITUTE
5717 White Bluff Rd., Savannah, GA 31499 **CONTACT:** Marvis Hinson (912) 351-6362, ext. 360

HAWAII

KAPIOLANI COMMUNITY COLLEGE
University of Hawaii, 4303 Diamond Head Rd., Honolulu, HI 96816 **CONTACT:** Frank Leake (808) 734-9483

LEEWARD COMMUNITY COLLEGE
96-045 Ala Ike, Pearl City, HI 96782 **CONTACT:** Fern Tomisato (808) 455-0375

MAUI COMMUNITY COLLEGE
Food Service Dept., 310 Kaahumanu Ave., Kahului, HI 96732 **CONTACT:** Karen Tanaka (808) 242-1225

IDAHO

BOISE STATE UNIVERSITY
1910 University Drive, Boise, ID 83725 **CONTACT:** Manly Ed Slough (208) 385-1532

ILLINOIS

COLLEGE OF DUPAGE
22nd St. and Lambert Rd., Glen Ellyn, IL 60137 CONTACT: George Macht (708) 858-2800, ext. 2315

COOKING & HOSPITALITY INSTITUTE OF CHICAGO, INC.
361 W. Chestnut, Chicago, IL 60610 CONTACT: Linda Calafiiore (312) 944-0882

ELGIN COMMUNITY COLLEGE
1700 Spartan Dr., Elgin, IL 60120 CONTACT: Mike Zema (708) 697-1000, ext. 7461

JOLIET JUNIOR COLLEGE
1216 Houbolt Ave., Joliet, IL 60436 CONTACT: Patrick Hagerty (815) 729-9020, ext. 2448

KENDALL COLLEGE
2408 Orrington Ave., Evanston, IL 60201 CONTACT: Michael Carmel (708) 866-1300

INDIANA

IVY TECH STATE COLLEGE
3800 N. Anthony Blvd., Ft. Wayne, IN 46805 CONTACT: Allen Eiler (219) 480-4240

IVY TECH STATE COLLEGE
One West 26th St., Indianapolis, IN 46208 CONTACT: Vincent Kinkade (317) 921-4619

IOWA

DES MOINES AREA COMMUNITY COLLEGE
2006 South Ankeny Blvd., Ankeny, IA 50021 CONTACT: Robert Anderson (515) 964-6532

KIRKWOOD COMMUNITY COLLEGE
6301 Kirkwood Blvd., P.O. Box 2068 Cedar Rapids, IA 52406 CONTACT: Carol Wohlleben (319) 398-5468

KANSAS

JOHNSON COUNTY COMMUNITY COLLEGE
12345 College at Quivira, Overland Park, KS 66210 CONTACT: Jerry Vincent (913) 469-8500

KENTUCKY

JEFFERSON COMMUNITY COLLEGE
109 East Broadway, Louisville, KY 40202 CONTACT: Patricia Heyman (502) 584-0181, ext. 317

NATIONAL CENTER FOR HOSPITALITY STUDIES AT SULLIVAN COLLEGE
3101 Bardstown Rd., Louisville, KY 40232 CONTACT: Thomas Hickey (502) 456-6504, ext. 329

LOUISIANA

BOSSIER PARISH COMMUNITY COLLEGE
2719 Airline Dr., N., Bossier City, LA 71111 CONTACT: Tommy Sibley (318) 746-6120

DELGADO COMMUNITY COLLEGE
615 City Park Ave., New Orleans, LA 70119 CONTACT: Iva Bergeron (504) 483-4208

LOUISIANA TECHNICAL COLLEGE-LAFAYETTE CAMPUS
1101 Bertrand Dr., Lafayette, LA 70502 CONTACT: Jerry Sonnier (318) 262-5962, ext. 232

LOUISIANA TECHNICAL COLLEGE-NEW ORLEANS CAMPUS
9800 Navarre Ave., New Orleans, LA 70124 **CONTACT:** Tim Gourley (504) 483-4626

MICHIGAN

GRAND RAPIDS COMMUNITY COLLEGE
151 Fountain, N.E., Grand Rapids, MI 49503 **CONTACT:** Robert Garlough (616) 771-3690

HENRY FORD COMMUNITY COLLEGE
5101 Evergreen Road, Dearborn, MI 48128 **CONTACT:** Dennis Konarski (313) 845-6360

MACOMB COMMUNITY COLLEGE
44575 Garfield Rd., Clinton Twp., MI 48038-1139 **CONTACT:** David Schneider (810) 286-2088

MONROE COUNTY COMMUNITY COLLEGE
1555 S. Raisinville Rd., Monroe, MI 48161 **CONTACT:** Kevin Thomas (313) 242-7300

NORTHWESTERN MICHIGAN COLLEGE
1701 East Front St., Traverse City, MI 49684 **CONTACT:** Fred Laughlin (616) 922-1197

OAKLAND COMMUNITY COLLEGE
27055 Orchard Lake Rd., Farmington Hills, MI 48018 **CONTACT:** Susan Baier (313) 471-7779

MINNESOTA

HENNEPIN TECHNICAL COLLEGE
Brooklyn Park Campus, 9000 Brooklyn Blvd., Brooklyn Park, MN 55445
Eden Prairie Campus, 9200 Flying Cloud Dr., Eden Prairie, MN 55445
CONTACT: Mike Jung (612) 425-3800, ext. 2553

ST. PAUL TECHNICAL COLLEGE
235 Marshall Ave., St. Paul, MN 55102 **CONTACT:** Eberhard Werthmann (612) 221-1300

MONTANA

UNIVERSITY OF MONTANA COLLEGE OF TECHNOLOGY IN MISSOULA
909 S. Avenue West, Missoula, MT 59801 **CONTACT:** Dennis Lerum (406) 542-6811

NEBRASKA

METROPOLITAN COMMUNITY COLLEGE
P.O. Box 3777, Omaha, NE 68103 **CONTACT:** Mr. Dana Goodrich (402) 449-8309

NEVADA

COMMUNITY COLLEGE OF SOUTHERN NEVADA
3200 E. Cheyenne Ave. S2D, N. Las Vegas, NV 89030-4296 **CONTACT:** Joe DelRosario (702) 651-4193

NEW HAMPSHIRE

NEW HAMPSHIRE COLLEGE – THE CULINARY INSTITUTE
2500 North River Rd., Manchester, NH 03104 **CONTACT:** (603) 644-3128

NEW MEXICO

ALBUQUERQUE TECHNICAL VOCATIONAL INSTITUTE
525 Buena Vista SE, Albuquerque, NM 87106 CONTACT: Kayleigh Carabajal (505) 224-3765

NEW YORK

PAUL SMITH'S COLLEGE
Paul Smiths, New York 12970 CONTACT: Paul Sorgule (518) 327-6218

SCHENECTADY COUNTY COMMUNITY COLLEGE
78 Washington Ave., Schenectady, NY 12035 CONTACT: Anthony Strianese (518) 346-6211

SULLIVAN COUNTY COMMUNITY COLLEGE — HOSPITALITY DEPT.
Box 4002, Le Roy Rd. Loch Sheldrake, NY 12759 CONTACT: Ed Nadeau (914) 434-5750

SUNY/COBLESKILL AG. & TECH. COLLEGE
P.O. Box 4002, Cobleskill, NY 12043 CONTACT: Alan Roer (518) 234-5425

OHIO

CINCINNATI TECHNICAL COLLEGE
3520 Central Parkway, Cincinnati, OH 45223 CONTACT: Richard Hendrix (513) 569-1662

COLUMBUS STATE COMMUNITY COLLEGE
550 East Spring St., Columbus, OH 43215 CONTACT: Carol Kizer (614) 227-2579

HOCKING TECHNICAL COLLEGE
3301 Hocking Parkway, Nelsonville, OH 45764 CONTACT: Doug Weber (614) 753-3591

OREGON

WESTERN CULINARY INSTITUTE
316 SW 13th Ave., Portland, OR 97201 CONTACT: Mary Harris, Dir. of Admissions (503) 223-2245

PENNSYLVANIA

IUP ACADEMY OF CULINARY ARTS – INDIANA UNIVERSITY OF PA
125 S. Gilpin St., Punxsutawney, PA 15767 CONTACT: Al Wutsch (800) 438-6424

INTERNATIONAL CULINARY ACADEMY
107 Sixth St., Fulton Bldg., Pittsburgh, PA 15222 CONTACT: Larry Brudy (412) 471-9330

PENNSYLVANIA INSTITUTE OF CULINARY ARTS
700 Clark Bldg., 717 Liberty Ave. Pittsburgh, PA 15222 CONTACT: Dieter Kiessling (412) 566-2444

PENNSYLVANIA COLLEGE OF TECHNOLOGY
One College Ave., Williamsport, PA 17701 CONTACT: Bill Butler (713) 326-3761, ext. 3761

WESTMORELAND COUNTY COMMUNITY COLLEGE
Armbrust Rd., College Station Youngwood, PA 15697 CONTACT: Dr. Paul Lonigro (412) 925-4016

SOUTH CAROLINA

GREENVILLE TECHNICAL COLLEGE
P.O. Box 5616, Station B, Greenville, SC 19606 CONTACT: Dr. Margaret Condrasky (803) 250-8000, ext. 8404

HORRY-GEORGETOWN TECHNICAL COLLEGE
P.O. Box 1966, Hwy. 501 East, Conway, SC 29526 **CONTACT:** Mr. Carmen Catino (803) 347-3186

TRIDENT TECHNICAL COLLEGE
P.O. Box 118067, Charleston, SC 29423-8067 **CONTACT:** Scott Roark (803) 722-5571

TENNESSEE

OPRYLAND HOTEL CULINARY INSTITUTE
2800 Opreyland Drive, Nashville, TN 37214 **CONTACT:** Dina Starks (615) 871-7765

TEXAS

ART INSTITUTE OF HOUSTON
1900 Yorktown, Houston, TX 77056 **CONTACT:** Michael Nenes (713) 623-2040

ST. PHILIP'S COLLEGE
2111 Nevada St., San Antonio, TX 78203 **CONTACT:** Mary Kunz (512) 531-3315

UTAH

SALT LAKE COMMUNITY COLLEGE
4600 S. Redwood Rd., Salt Lake City UT 84130 **CONTACT:** LeslieSeiferle/Ricco Renzetti (801) 957-4066

WASHINGTON

BELLINGHAM TECHNICAL COLLEGE
3028 Lindbergh Ave., Bellingham, WA 98225 **CONTACT:** Patricia McKeown (206) 676-7761

RENTON TECHNICAL COLLEGE
3000 Northeast Fourth St., Renton, WA 98056 **CONTACT:** Kristi Frambach (206) 235-2372

SEATTLE CENTRAL COMMUNITY COLLEGE
1701 Broadway, Seattle, WA 98122 **CONTACT:** Dr. Melissa Dallas (206) 344-4331

SKAGIT VALLEY COLLEGE
2405 E. College Way, Mount Vernon, WA 98273 **CONTACT:** Lyle Hildahl (360) 428-1109

SOUTH SEATTLE COMMUNITY COLLEGE
6000 16th Avenue, SW, Seattle, WA 98106 **CONTACT:** Dan Cassidy (206) 764-5344

SPOKANE COMMUNITY COLLEGE
North 1810 Greene St., Spokane, WA 99207 **CONTACT:** Doug Fisher (509) 533-7284

WISCONSIN

BLACKHAWK TECHNICAL COLLEGE
6004 Prairie Rd., P.O. Box 5009, Janesville, WI 53547 **CONTACT:** Joe Wollinger (608) 757-7690

MADISON AREA TECHNICAL COLLEGE
3550 Anderson St., Madison, WI 53704 **CONTACT:** Mary Hill (608) 246-6368

MILWAUKEE AREA TECHNICAL COLLEGE
1015 N. Sixth St., Milwaukee, WI 53203 **CONTACT:** Gus Kelly (414) 278-6507

WAUKESHA COUNTY TECHNICAL COLLEGE
800 Main Street, Pewaukee, WI 53072 **CONTACT:** William Griesemer (414) 691-5254

RECOMMENDED READING

In addition to the following newsletters, magazines, and books, many culinary food and wine organizations offer publications as a membership benefit.

THE ART OF EATING

Quarterly newsletter. Established 1986. Address: Box 242, Peacham, VT 05862-0242; Fax (802) 592-3400. Writer: Edward Behr. Annual subscription: $30 worldwide.
Monographs about food, and occasionally wine, emphasizing tradition and the relationship of food to place.

ART CULINAIRE

Quarterly magazine. Established 1986. Publisher: Culinaire, Inc., 40 Mills St., Morristown, NJ 07960; (201) 993-5500, Fax (201) 993-8779, E-mail getartc@aol.com. Editor: Jennifer N. Lindner. Per issue (annual subscription) price: $18 ($59) U.S., $22 ($75) other countries. Subscriptions: P.O. Box 9268, Morristown, NJ 07963.
Hardcover magazine with 80 pages of color photographs, industry-related articles, recipes.

THE ASIAN FOODBOOKERY

Quarterly magazine. Established 1996. Publisher: R.W. Lucky, P.O. Box 15947, Seattle, WA 98115-0947; (206) 523-3575. Annual subscription price: $14 U.S., Canada, Mexico; $18 other countries.
Features the food and cooking of Asia through book reviews, essays, and travel accounts.

AUSTRALIAN GOURMET TRAVELLER

Monthly magazine. Established 1989. Publisher: Australian Consolidated Press, 54 Park St., Sydney NSW, 2000, Australia; (61) 2-282-8000, Fax (61) 2-267-8037. Editor Carolyn Lockhart. Per issue (annual subscription) price A$5.95 (A$59 in Australia, A$128.65 overseas air). Subscriptions: Reply paid 764, ACP Subscriptions Services, GPO Box 5252, Sydney, NSW 2001, Australia; (61) 2-267-4363, Fax (61) 2-260-0022.
A color glossy devoted to food, wine and travel, with the latest news in restaurants, recipes, and travel.

BBC GOOD FOOD

Monthly magazine. Established 1989. Publisher: BBC Worldwide Publishing, Woodlands, 80 Wood Lane, London W12 OTT, England; (44)181-576-2000, Fax (44) 181-576-3824. Editor: Mitzie Wilson. Annual subscription £49.35. Subscriptions: P.O. Box 425, Woking GU21 1GP; (44) 1483-733724 (order line), (44) 1483-733754 (inquiry line), Fax (44) 1483-756792.
Monthly magazine covering recipes, celebrity chefs, food issues, wines and shopping news.

BBC VEGETARIAN GOOD FOOD

Monthly magazine. Established 1992. Publisher: BBC Worldwide Publishing, Woodlands, 80 Wood Lane, London W12 OTT, England; (44) 181-576-3767, Fax (44) 181-576-3825. Annual subscription £45.60. Subscriptions: P.O. Box 425, Woking GU21 1GP; (44) 1483-733712 (order line), (44) 1483-733742 (inquiry line).
Promotes vegetarian food. Includes recipes, food news, nutrition, health, and environment updates.

BECOMING A CHEF

320-page paperback. Published in 1995 by Van Nostrand Reinhold, 115 Fifth Ave., New York, NY 10003; (212) 254-3232. Authors: Andrew Dornenburg and Karen Page. ISBN 0-442-01513-5. Price

$29.95. Orders: International Thomson Publishing, Inc. (800) 842-3636 or (606) 525-6600, Fax (606) 525-7778.
Interviews with over 60 noted U.S. chefs about their early influences, training, personal and career experiences, restaurants; includes recipes.

BON APPÉTIT
Monthly magazine. Established 1955. Publisher: Conde Nast Publications, 6300 Wilshire Blvd., Los Angeles, CA 90048; (213) 965-3600, Fax (213) 937-1206. Editor: William J. Garry. Per issue (annual subscription) price: $2.95 ($18) in U.S.; ($30) in Canada & abroad. Subscriptions: P.O. Box 59191, Boulder, CO 80322; (800) 765-9419; URL http://www.epicurious.com/b_ba/b00_home/ba.html.
Features kitchen & tableware design, chefs, travel & restaurants, recipes for home cooks, wine & spirits tasting panel, wine reviews, articles about vineyards.

CAREER OPPORTUNITIES IN THE FOOD & BEVERAGE INDUSTRY
240-page paperback. Published in 1994 by Facts on File, Inc., 460 Park Ave. South, New York, NY 10016; (212) 683-2244. Author: Barbara Sims-Bell. ISBN 0-8160-2913-X. Price $14.95. Orders: (800) 322-8755 or (212) 683-2244, Fax (212) 213-4578.
Provides career profiles of 70 jobs, including duties, salary range, employment and advancement prospects, prerequisites, best locations.

CHEF
Monthly magazine. Established 1952. Publisher: Talcott Communications Corp., 20 North Wacker Dr., Ste. 3230, Chicago, IL 60606; (312) 849-2220, Fax (312) 849-2174, E-mail chefmag@aol.com. Editor: Paul Clarke. Per issue (annual subscription) price: $2.95 ($24) U.S., ($35) Canada, ($60) other; (800) 229-1967 #60.
Information on current news and trends, interviews with chefs, columns on marketing, management, career mobility, menu and restaurant design.

CHILE PEPPER
Bimonthly magazine. Established 1987. Publisher: Magnolia Media Group. Address: 1227 W. Magnolia, Ft. Worth, TX 76104; (888) SPICYHOT, Fax (817) 921-9313, E-mail jgregory@flash.net., URL http://www.chilepeppermag.com. Editor: Joel C. Gregory. Per issue (annual subscription) price: $3.95 ($15.95). Subscriptions: P.O. Box 769, Mt. Morris, IL 61054-8234; (800) 959-5468.
Cooking and travel magazine devoted to spicy foods from around the world.

CHOCOLATIER
Bimonthly magazine. Established 1984. Publisher: Haymarket Group Ltd., 45 W. 34th St., Room 600, New York, NY 10001; (212) 239-0855, Fax (212) 967-4184. Editor: Michael Schneider. Per issue (annual subscription) price: $4.95 ($23.95).
Focuses on chocolate and elegant desserts, their preparation and presentation, with photographs and recipes.

COFFEE JOURNAL
Quarterly magazine. Established 1995. Publisher: Tiger Oak Publications, 123 N. 3rd St., Ste. 508, Minneapolis, MN 55401; (612) 338-4125, Fax (612) 338-0532, E-mail coffeejrnl@aol.com. Editor: Susan Bonne. Per issue (annual subscription) price: $3.95 ($12.97)U.S., $4.95 Canada. Subscriptions: P.O. Box 3000, Denville, NJ 07834-9479; (800) 783-4903. Online through the electric newstand at http://www.enews.com.
Lifestyle magazine featuring gourmet coffees and teas, new blends, brewing techniques, exotic travel, recipes, fiction, recommendations.

COOK'S ILLUSTRATED

Bimonthly magazine. Established 1992. Publisher: Boston Common Press, 17 Station St., Box 569, Brookline, MA 02147-0569; (617) 232-1000, Fax (617) 232-1572, E-mail cooksill@aol.com. Publisher & Editor: Christopher Kimball. Per issue (annual subscription) price: $4 ($19.95) U.S., $4.95 Canada. Subscriptions: Box 7444, Red Oak, IA 51591-0444; (800) 526-8442.

Magazine for home cooks emphasizing cooking technique; narrowly focused articles cover topics in depth and include comparisons of kitchen-tested methods and products.

COOKING LIGHT

Ten issues per year. Established 1987. Publisher: Southern Progress Corp., 2100 Lakeshore Drive, Birmingham, AL 35209; (205) 877-6000, Fax (205) 877-6469, E-mail cooking-light@pathfinder.com. URL http://pathfinder.com/cl; digital cookbook on CD-ROM. Editor: Doug Crichton. Per issue (annual subscription) price: $2.95 ($18) U.S., $3.50 ($24) Canada, ($24) other countries. Subscriptions: Box 830656, Birmingham, AL 35282-9086; (800) 999-1750, Fax (205) 877-6504.

Healthy lifestyle magazine; 65% devoted to food & preparation, 35% to personal care and fitness.

CULINARY REVIEW

Monthly magazine. Established 1975. Publisher: Gourmet on the Go, Inc. Address: 25W441 Plamondon Rd., Wheaton, IL 60187-7364; (708) 653-4413, Fax (708) 653-4445. Editor: Edward Robert Brooks, Sr.

Publishes material of interest to chefs, culinarians, food & beverage directors, catering directors, club managers, restaurateurs, hoteliers, members of gastronomic societies.

CULINARY TRENDS

Quarterly magazine. Established 1990. Publisher: Fred Mensinga, 6285 East Spring St., Ste. 107, Long Beach, CA 90808-9927; (714) 826-9188, Fax (714) 826-0333. Editor: Tim Linden. Subscription price: $21.60/yr U.S., $40/yr foreign.

Features stories and recipes of interest to the career culinarian, as well as home chefs.

EATING WELL

Bimonthly magazine. Established 1990. Publisher: EW Communications, LP, Ferry Road, Charlotte, VT 05445; (802) 425-3961, Fax (802) 425-3675, E-mail EwellEdit@aol.com. Editor: Marcelle Langan Di Falco. Per issue (annual subscription) price: $2.95 ($18) U.S., $3.95 ($24) Canada, Subscriptions: P.O. Box 52919, Boulder, CO 80322; (800) 678-0541. Online EWellEdit@aol.com.

Healthy eating magazine; reports and comments on the dietary movement in America; nutrition reports, food and cooking articles and recipes.

FINE COOKING

Bimonthly magazine. Established 1994. Publisher: The Taunton Press, 63 South Main St., Newtown, CT 06470; (203) 426-8171, Fax (203) 426-3434; E-mail finecooking@aol.com, Compuserve: 74602,2651, URL finecook@taunton.com. Editor: Martha Holmberg. Per issue (annual subscription) price: $4.95 ($26) U.S., $5.95 ($32) other. Subscriptions: P.O. Box 5507, Newtown, CT 06470-9879; (800) 888-8286.

Emphasis on the hows and whys of cooking technique, complementd by detailed information on food, food preparation, and principles of good cooking. Recipes relate to cooking methods covered in each article.

FOOD & WINE

Monthly magazine. Established 1978. Publisher: American Express Publishing Corp., 1120 6th Ave., New York, NY 10036; (212) 382-5618, Fax (212) 764-2177, E-mail food&wine-

@amexpub.com, URL http://www.pathfinder.com/foodwine/. For CD-Rom: (800) 850-7272. Editor: Dana B. Cowin. Per issue (annual subscription) price: $3.50 ($29). Subscriptions: P.O. Box 3003, Harlan, IA, 51593-0022, (800) 333-6569.
Lifestyle magazine that focuses on food stories, recipes, tabletop design stories, travel.

FOOD ARTS
Ten issues per year. Established 1988. Publisher: M. Shanken Communications, 387 Park Ave. South, New York, NY 10016; (212) 684-4224, Fax (212) 684-5424. Editor: Michael & Ariane Batterberry. Per issue (annual subscription) price: $4 ($30) U.S., $5 Canada, $7 other. Subscriptions: P.O. Box 7808, Riverton, NJ 08077; Fax (212) 481-0722.
Magazine designed for chefs, restaurateurs, food & beverage directors, caterers; provides editorial on various aspects of the food business.

FOOD MANAGEMENT
Monthly magazine. Established 1972. Publisher: Gerald J. White, 1100 Superior Ave., Cleveland, OH 44114; (216) 696-7000, Fax (216) 696-0836, E-mail fmeditor@aol.com. Editor: John Lawn. Per issue (annual subscription) price: $4.95 ($55) U.S., ($75) Canada, ($125) international. Subscriptions: Penton Publishing, Subscription Lockbox, P.O. Box 96732, Chicago, IL 60693.
Serves the professional, managerial, and operational interests of foodservice directors & dietitians in non-commercial operations. Contains articles on health, nutrition, business, labor & service .

THE FOOD PAPER
On-line only. Editor: Alain Gayot, 5900 Wilshire Blvd., #650, Los Angeles, CA 90036; (213) 965-3593, Fax (213) 936-2883, E-mail gayots@aol.com, URL http://www.thefoodpaper.com.

THE FOODSERVICE DISTRIBUTOR
Bimonthly magazine. Established 1987. Publisher: Jim Maddox, 1100 Superior Ave., Cleveland, OH 44114; (216) 696-7000, Fax (216) 696-0836. Editor: Michael Buzalka. Annual subscription price: $35 U.S., $50 Canada, $80 international. Subscription: Penton Publishing, Subscription Lockbox, P.O. Box 96732, Chicago, IL 60693.
Written for foodservice distributors, management & sales personnel. Articles on managing staff operations, analyzing competition, future growth planning, new product presentation, and improving sales.

GOURMET
Monthly magazine. Established 1941. Publisher: Conde Nast Publications, 560 Lexington Ave., New York, NY 10022; (212) 880-8800, Fax (212) 753-2596, URL http://www.epicurious.com. Editor: Gail Zweigenthal. Per issue (annual subscription) price: $2.95 ($20) U.S., $3.50 ($34) Canada. Subscriptions: (800) 365-2454.
Lifestyle magazine; balanced coverage of travel, food, culture, and entertainment.

ICR – THE INTERNATIONAL COOKBOOK REVUE
Bimonthly magazine. Established 1996. Publisher: S.P.A., Lagasca, 27-1-E, Madrid, 28001 Spain; (34) 1-575 93 50, Fax (34) 1-575 99 62. Editor: David Brubaker. Per issue (annual subscription) price: $5 ($39) U.S., ($55) Canada. Subscriptions: S.P.A., 645 Fifth Ave., Ste. 703, New York, NY 10022; (212) 753-6849, Fax (212) 753-6948.
Features cookbooks, publishing, and culinary news.

THE JOURNAL OF ITALIAN FOOD, WINE, & TRAVEL
Bimonthly magazine. Established 1991. Address: 609 W. 114th St., #77, New York, NY 10025; (212) 316-3026, Fax (212) 316-3476, E-mail bibendi@aol.com Editor: Robert DiLallo. Per issue (annual

subscription) price: $2.95 ($17) U.S., $5 Canada. Subscriptions: (800)-438-2385.

Covers food, wine & travel in Italy, North America, and other countries; recipes, book reviews, restaurant and chef profiles, regional Italian articles, wine reviews, commentary.

THE MAGAZINE OF LA CUCINA ITALIANA

Bimonthly magazine. Established 1991. Publisher: The Mediterranean Gourmet & Travel Co., Inc. Address: 6230 Fifth Ave., Ste. 1111, New York, NY 10001; (212) 725-8764, Fax (212) 889-3907, E-mail piacere@earthlink.net, URL http://www.piacere.com. Editor: Paolo Villoresi de Loche. Per issue (annual subscription) price: $4.95 ($24) U.S., $5.95 ($32) Canada, ($40) other.
Emphasis on Italian cooking and culture.

NATION'S RESTAURANT NEWS

Weekly. Established 1956. Publisher: Lebhar-Friedman, Inc., 425 Park Ave., New York, NY 10022; (212) 756-5000, Fax (212) 756-5215, URL http://www.nrn.com. Editor: Rick Van Warner. Per issue (annual subscription) price: $5 ($34.50) U.S., $44.50 Canada, $295 other. Subscriptions: P.O. Box 31182, Tampa, Fl 33631; (813) 664-6700, (800) 447-7133; Fax (813) 664-6884. CD-ROM: Buyer's Advantage; an electronic database of non-food products, services, and vendors.
News publication covering the foodservice industry; editorially directed to foodservice decision-makers.

NORTH CAROLINA'S TASTE FULL

Bimonthly magazine. Established 1990. Publisher: Taste Full Magazine, 1202 S. Sixteenth St., P.O. Box 1712, Wilmington, NC 28402; (910) 763-1601, Fax (910) 763-0321, E-mail nctf@aol.com. Editor: Elizabeth K. Norfleet. Annual subscription: $19.95 U.S., $27.50 Canada, $32 other.
Focuses on food, travel, and entertaining in N.C. with emphasis on the state's current culture and talent; explores national food trends from a Tarheel perspective.

NW PALATE

Bimonthly magazine. Established 1987. Publisher: NW Palate Magazine, P.O. Box 10860, Portland, OR 97296-0860 (503) 224-6039, Fax (503) 222-5312, E-mail nwpalate@teleport.com. Editor: Cameron Nagel. Per issue (annual subscription) price: $3.95 ($21) U.S., $5.95 ($33) Canada.
Features food, wine, and travel of the Pacific Northwest; includes recipes, wine & food personalities, getaways, wine reviews, news and events.

PASTRY ART & DESIGN

Quarterly magazine. Established 1995. Publisher: Haymarket Group Ltd., 45 W. 34th St., Room 600, New York, NY 10001; (212) 239-0855, Fax (212) 967-4184. Editor: Michael Schneider. Per issue (annual subscription) price: $5.95 ($30).
Features articles on pastry kitchen/bakery profitability, kitchen equipment, dessert beverages, tabletop presentations, pastry school curricula; includes interviews, techniques, trends, competition updates, an employment hotline.

RESTAURANTS USA

Eleven issues per year. Established 1981. Publisher: National Restaurant Assn., 1200 17th St. NW, Washington, DC 20036-3097; (202) 331-5900, Fax (202) 296-2529. Editor: Jennifer Batty. Per issue (annual subscription) price: $15 ($125) U.S.
Carries how-to articles and reports on recent research relevant to operating a foodservice establishment.

RESTAURANT HOSPITALITY

Monthly magazine. Established 1919. Publisher: Rob Dorfmeyer. 1100 Superior Ave., Cleveland, OH 44114; (216) 696-7000, Fax (216) 696-0836, E-mail rheditors@aol.com. Editor: Michael

DeLuca. Per issue (annual subscription) price: $5.95 ($60) U.S. Subscriptions: Penton Publishing, Subscription: Penton Publishing, Subscription Lockbox, P.O. Box 96732, Chicago, IL 60693.
Edited for commercial food service professionals. Intent is to keep readers informed of industry trends and happenings, and to assist them in running profitable operations.

SAVEUR
Eight issues per year. Established 1994. Publisher: Meigher Communications, 100 Ave. of the Americas, New York, NY 10013; (212) 334-1212, Fax (212) 334-1260, E-mail saveur@here.com. Editor: Dorothy Kalins. Per issue (annual subscription) price: $5 ($24) U.S. ($38) other. Subscriptions: (800) 462-0209.
Examines the gourmet world of food with emphasis on its origins, regional & cultural diversities, and the people who create it.

SIMPLE COOKING
Bimonthly newsletter. Established 1980. Address: P.O. Box 8, Steuben, ME 04680; E-mail outlaw-cook@earthlink.net, URL http://home.earthlink.net/~outlawcook/ Editors: John & Matt Lewis Thorne. Per issue (annual subscription) price: $4 ($24) U.S., $4.25 Canada, $5 other.
Features essays on food, cooking and the culinary life; includes recipes, food book reviews, product notes for the home cook.

SIMPLY SEAFOOD
Quarterly magazine. Established 1991. Publisher: Waterfront Press, 5305 Shilshole Ave. NW, Ste. 200, Seattle, WA 98107; (206) 789-6506, Fax (206) 789-9193. Editor: Peter Redmayne. Per issue (annual subscription) price: $2.95 ($8.95) U.S., $3.55 ($11) Canada.
Informational writing, practical instruction, recipes related to handling and preparation of seafood.

VEGETARIAN JOURNAL
Bimonthly magazine. Established 1990. Publisher: The Vegetarian Resource Group, P.O. Box 1463, Baltimore, MD 21203; (410) 366-8343, E-mail TheVRG@aol.com. Editor: Debra Wasserman. Per issue (annual subscription) price: $4 ($20) U.S., ($30) Canada. Internet: www:http://envirolink.-org/arrs/VRG/home.html.
Covers vegetarian meal planning, nutrition, recipes, and natural food product reviews. Nutrition articles reviewed by registered dietitian or medical doctor. Advertising not accepted.

VEGETARIAN JOURNAL'S FOODSERVICE UPDATE
Quarterly magazine. Established 1993. Publisher: The Vegetarian Resource Group, P.O. Box 1463, Baltimore, MD 21203; (410) 366-8343, E-mail TheVRG@aol.com. Editor: Charles Stahler & Debra Wasserman. Annual subscription: $20 U.S., $30 Canada. For free sample issue send SASE. Internet: www:http://envirolink.org/arrs/VRG/home.html.
For foodservice personnel in schools, restaurants, hospitals, and other institutions; offers advice and recipes, spotlights industry leaders.

VEGETARIAN TIMES
Monthly magazine. Established 1974. Publisher: Cowles Enthusiast Media, Inc. Address: 1140 Lake St., Ste. 500, Oak Park, IL 60301; (708) 848-8100, Fax (708) 848-8175, E-mail 74651.215@compuserve.com. Editor: Toni Apgar. Per issue (annual subscription) price: $3.50 ($29.95) U.S., ($41.95) Canada, ($54.91) other. Subscriptions: Vegetarian Times, P.O. Box 420235, Palm Coast, FL 32142-0235; (800) 829-3340.
Features vegetarian recipes, nutritional breakdowns, photography; articles on health, nutrition, fitness; profiles, product news and reviews.

VEGGIE LIFE

Bimonthly magazine. Established 1993. Publisher: EGW Publishing Co., 1041 Shary Circle, Concord, CA 94518; (800) 777-1164, Fax (510) 671-0692, URL http://www.egw.com. Editor: Sharon Barela. Per issue price: $3.50 U.S., $4.50 Canada.
Growing green cooking lean, feeling good.

VOGUE AUSTRALIA ENTERTAINING GUIDE

Bimonthly magazine. Publisher: Conde Nast Publications Pty Ltd, Locked Bag 2550, Crows Nest, NSW 2065, Australia; (61) 2-964-3888, Fax (61) 2-964-3882. Editor: Sharyn Storrier Lyneham. Annual subscription: A$33 in Australia.
Lifestyle magazine featuring food, entertaining, travel.

WEIGHT WATCHERS MAGAZINE

Monthly magazine. Established 1968. Publisher: Weight Watchers Publishing Group, 360 Lexington Ave., New York, NY 10017; (212) 370-0644, Fax (212) 687-4398. Editor: Nancy Gagliardi. Per issue price: $1.95 U.S., $2.50 Canada. Subscriptions: (800) 876-8441.
Information and news on women's health, wellness, nutrition, and fitness; low-fat cooking techniques and recipes.

THE WINE ADVOCATE

Bimonthly newsletter. Established 1978. Address: P.O. Box 311, Monkton, MD 21111; (410) 329-6477, Fax (410) 357-4504. Editor: Robert M. Parker, Jr. Annual subscription: $40 U.S., $50 Canada, $70 other. On-line Prodigy.
Consumer guide to fine wine; accepts no advertising.

THE WINE ENTHUSIAST

Fourteen issues per year. Established 1988. Address: 8 Saw Mill River Rd., Hawthorne, NY 10532; (800) 356-8466, Fax (914) 345-3028, E-mail wineenth@aol.com. Editor: W.R. Tish. Annual subscription: $24.95 U.S., $49.95 other. Subscriptions: (800) 356-8466. All tasting notes can be found on America Online at the Food & Drink Network.
Focuses on wine for both new and experienced wine drinkers.

WINE SPECTATOR

Nineteen issues per year. Established 1976. Publisher: M. Shanken Communications Inc., 387 Park Ave. South, New York, NY 10016; (212) 684-4224, Fax (212) 684-5424. Editor: Jim Gordon. Per issue price: $2.95 ($40) U.S., $3.95 ($53.50) Canada, 39FF, £2.50 ($125) other countries. Subscriptions: P.O. Box 50463, Boulder, CO 80323-0463, (800) 752-7799.
Wine features, ratings and tasting notes, fine restaurants, cooking and entertaining, world travel and the arts, unusual shopping and collectibles.

WINE & SPIRITS

Eight issues per year. Established 1981. Address: P.O. Box 1548, Princeton, NJ 10016; (609) 921-2196, E-Mail winespir@aol.com. Editor: Joshua Green. Per issue price (special issues) $2.95 ($4.95) U.S., $3.50 ($5.95) Canada. Subscriptions: P.O. Box 50463, Boulder, CO 80323-0463, (800) 395-3364.
The practical guide to wine, for consumers and buyers.

CAREER SCHOOL TUITION RANKINGS

Use this index for guidance only. Programs are indexed by total tuition for those that are less than nine months and by annual tuition for those that are nine months or more. Additional costs, such as housing, meals, fees, books, and supplies are not included. Schools whose in-state (in-county, in-district) and out-of-state (out-of-country) tuition costs fall in different categories are indicated by IS (IC, ID) or OS (OC) following the state or country. Consult individual listings and schools for more specific information.

TOTAL TUITION FOR PROGRAMS OF LESS THAN NINE MONTHS

LESS THAN $2,500
Epicurean Ckg. School (CA)
Le Trou (CA)
Let's Get Cookin' (CA)
Loretta Paganini School of Cooking (OH)
New School Culinary Arts (NY)
Northampton Comm. College (PA) IS
San Juaquin Delta (CA)
School of Natural Cookery (CO)
Sclafani's Cooking School

$2,500 TO $4,999
Cleveland Restaurant School (OH)
Cookery Centre of Ireland (Ireland)
Ecole Superieure de Cuisine (France)
Le Chef College (TX)
Missouri Culinary Inst. (MO)
New Zealand School of Food & Wine (NZ)
Orleans Technical Institute (PA)

$5,000 TO $9,999
Ballymaloe Cookery School (Ireland)
Boston University (MA)
Ckg. & Hosp. Inst. of Chicago (IL)
Connecticut Culinary Institute (CT)
Dubrulle French Cul. Schl. (Canada)
Lederwolff (CA)
Natural Gourmet Cookery School (NY)
New York Restaurant School (NY)
Northampton Comm. College (PA) OS
Pacific Inst. of Culinary Arts (Canada)
Peter Kump's NY Cooking School (NY)
Southeastern Academy (FL)

$10,000 OR OVER
California Cul. Academy (CA)
Cooking School of the Rockies (CO)
Ecole des Arts Culinaires (France)
French Culinary Institute (NY)
Le Cordon Bleu-London (England)
New York Restaurant School (NY)
Ritz-Escoffier (France)
Tante Marie's (CA)

ANNUAL TUITION FOR PROGRAMS OF NINE MONTHS OR LONGER

LESS THAN $1,000
Asheville Buncombe (NC) IS
Atlanta Area Tech. School (GA)
Atlantic Voc-Tech Ctr. (FL)
Augu₃ta Technical Institute (GA)
Burlington County College (NJ) IS
Cabrillo College (CA) IS
Central Piedmont Comm. College (NC) IS
City College of SF (CA) IS
Clark County Comm. College (NV) IS
College of DuPage (IL)
Colorado Mntn. Cul. Inst. (CO)
Columbia College (CA) IS
Contra Costa College (CA)
Crows Nest College of TAFE (Australia)
Cuyahoga Community College (OH)
Cypress College (CA) IS
Daytona Beach Comm. College (FL)
Diablo Valley College (CA)
El Centro College (TX) IS
Elizabethtn. State Voc-Tech (KY) IS
Galveston College (TX)
Glendale Comm. College (CA) IS
Great Plains Voc-Tech (OK)
Grossmont College (CA) IS
Guilford Tech (NC) IS
Gulf Coast Comm. College (FL) IS
Humber College (Canada) IS
Inst. of So. for Hosp. (FL) IS
Jefferson Community College (KY) IS
Joliet Junior College (IL) IS
Kansas City Ks. Voc-Tech (KS)
Kapiolani Community College (HI) IS
Kentucky Tech-Daviess (KY)
Laney College (CA) IS
Lawson State (AL)
Leeward Community College (HI)
Los Angeles Trade-Tech (CA)
Louisiana Tech. College (LA)
Manchester Community College (CT) IS
Massasoit Community College (MA) IS
Maui Community College (HI) IS
McFatter Sch. of Culinary Arts (FL)
Metropolitan Comm. College (NE) IS
NE Ks Area Voc-Tech (KS) IS

No. Tech. Education Ctr. (FL)
Odessa College (TX)
Okaloosa-Walton (FL) IS
Oklahoma State University (OK)
Olympic College (WA)
Orange Coast College (CA) IS
Oxnard College (CA) IS
Pima Comm. College (AZ) IS
Pinellas Tech-Clearwater (FL)
Pinellas Tech-St. Pete (FL)
Pioneer Area Voc-Tech (OK)
San Joaquin Delta (CA) IS
Santa Barbara City College (CA) IS
Santa Fe Community College (NM) IS
Santa Rosa Jr. College (CA) IS
Savannah Technical Institute (GA)
SE Inst. of Culinary Art (FL) IS
Shasta College (CA) IS
Sinclair Comm. College (OH) IS
So. Oklahoma Area Voc-Tech (OK)
So. Puget Sound Comm. College (WA) IS
Southeast Community College (NE)
St. Philip's College (TX)
Truckee Meadows (NV) IS
Tucson Culinary Alliance (AZ)
Utah Valley Comm. College (UT) IS
West Ky State Voc-Tech (KY)

$1,000 TO $1,999
Adirondack Community College (NY)
Algonquin College (Canada) IS
Bellingham Tech. College (WA)
Black Hawk College (IL) IS
Boise State University (ID)
Bucks County Community College (PA)
Bunker Hill Community College (MA) IS
Burlington County College (NJ) OS
Canadore College (Canada) IS
Central Community College (NE)
Chippewa Valley Tech (WI) IS
Clark College (WA)
College of Lake County (IL)
Columbus State Community College (OH) IS
Del Mar College (TX)
Des Moines Comm. College (IA) IS
Edmonds Community College (WA) IS
Elgin Community College (IL)
Elizabethtn. State Voc-Tech (KY) OS
Erie Community College (NY) IS
Essex Ag-Tech Inst. (MA) IS
Food Arts Studio (IL)
Gateway Comm-Tech College (CT) IS
Georgian College (Canada) IS
Greenville Tech. College (SC)
Hocking Technical College (OH) IS
Horry-Georgetown (SC) IS
Hudson County Comm. College (NJ) IS
Indian Meridian Voc-Tech (OK)
Iowa Western Comm. College (IA) IS

Ivy Tech-Ft. Wayne (IN) IS
Ivy Tech-Gary (IN) IS
Ivy Tech-Indianapolis (IN)
Jefferson Community College (NY) IS
Johnson Cty. Comm. College (KS) IS
Kirkwood Community College (IA) IS
Lane Community College (OR) IS
Linn-Benton Community College (OR) IS
Macomb Community College (MI) IS
Madison Area Tech. College (WI)
Massasoit Community College (MA) OS
Metropolitan Comm. College (NE) OS
Missoula Voc-Tech Center (MT) IS
Mitchell Technical Institute (SD)
Mohawk Valley Comm. College (NY) IS
Monroe Cty. Comm. College (MI) IS
Moraine Park Technical College (WI)
Niagara College (Canada) IS
Niagara County Comm. College (NY)
North Dakota State College (ND) IS
North Seattle Comm. College (WA) IS
Northwest Technical College (MN) IS
Northwestern Mich. College (MI)
Oakland Community College (MI)
Onondaga Community College (NY) IS
Renton Technical College (WA)
Richardson Researches (CA)
St. Clair College (Canada) IS
St. Louis Comm. College (MO)
St. Paul Technical College (MN) IS
Salt Lake Comm. College (UT) IS
Santa Fe Community College (NM) OS
Schenectady Cty. Comm. College (NY) IS
Schoolcraft College (MI)
Scott Community College (IA)
Scottsdale Comm. College (AZ) IS
SE Inst. of Culinary Art (FL) OS
Seattle Central Comm. College (WA) IS
Sinclair Comm. College (OH) OS
Skagit Valley College (WA) IS
So. Seattle Comm. College (WA) IS
South Central Tech. College (MN) IS
Spokane Community College (WA) IS
Trident Technical College (SC) IS
Triton College (IL)
Univ. College of Cariboo (Canada) IS
University of Alaska (AK) IS
Vincennes University (IN) IS
W, Va. Northern Comm. College (WV) IS
Wallace State (AL)
Warren Occup-Tech Ctr. (CO) IS
Washtenaw Community College (MI) IS
Waukesha County Tech. College (WI) IS
Westmoreland Cty. Comm. College (PA)
Wichita Area Voc-Tech (KS)
William Rainey Harper (IL) IS
$2,000 TO $2,999
Berkshire Community College (MA) IS

Bristol Community College (MA) IS
Clark County Comm. College (NV) OS
College of Technology (MT) IS
Columbia College (CA) OS
Comm. College-Allegheny Cty. (PA) IC
Cypress College (CA) OS
El Centro College (TX) OS
Fox Valley Tech. Institute (WI) IS
George Brown College (Canada) IS
Glendale Comm. College (CA) OS
Grossmont College (CA) OS
Hennepin Tech (MN) IS
Holyoke Community College (MA) IS
Horry-Georgetown (SC) OS
Hudson County Comm. College (NJ) OS
Indian Hills Comm. College (IA) IS
Instituto del Arte Moderno (PR)
Iowa Lakes Comm. College (IA) IS
Iowa Western Comm. College (IA) OS
Jefferson Comm. College (KY) OS
Jefferson Community College (NY) OS
Kapiolani Community College (HI) OS
Kirkwood Community College (IA) OS
Laney College (CA)
Manchester Community College (CT) OS
Maui Community College (HI) OS
Middlesex County College (NJ) IS
Milwaukee Area Tech. College (WI) IS
Missoula Voc-Tech Center (MT) OS
Monroe Community College (NY)
Monroe Cty. Comm. College (MI) OS
New Hampshire Tech (NH) IS
North Dakota State College (ND) OS
Northern Mich. University (MI) IS
Northwest Technical College (MN) OS
Okaloosa-Walton (FL) OS
Onondaga Community College (NY) OS
Orange Coast College (CA) OS
Oxnard College (CA) OS
Penn Valley Comm. College (MO) OS
Salem County Voc-Tech (NJ)
San Joaquin Delta (CA) OS
Santa Rosa Jr. College (CA) OS
Shasta College (CA) OS
South Central Tech. College (CA) OS
Southern Maine Tech (ME) IS
St. Paul Technical College (MN) OS
Stratford Chefs School (Canada) IS
Sullivan County Comm. College (NY) IS
SUNY-Cobleskill (NY) IS
Trident Technical College (SC) OS
Truckee Meadows (NV) OS
University of Akron (OH) IS
University of Toledo (OH) IS
Utah Valley Comm. College (UT) OS
Wake Tech. Comm. College (NC)
Washtenaw Community College (MI) OS
Waukesha County Tech. College (WI) OS

Westchester Community College (NY)

$3,000 TO $4,999
American Institute of Baking (KS)
Bossier Parish Comm. College (LA)
Bunker Hill Community College (MA) OS
Cabrillo College (CA) OS
Central Piedmont Comm. College (NC) OS
Cincinnati Technical College (OH) IS
City College of SF (CA) OS
Columbus State Community College (OH) OS
Community Coll. of Alleghenny Cty. (PA) OS/IS
Cooking Academy of Chicago (IL)
Culinary Inst. of Canada (Canada)
Culinary Inst. of Colorado Springs (CO)
Des Moines Comm. College (IA) OS
Ecole Superieure de Cuisine ()
Edmonds Community College (WA) OS
Erie Community College (NY) OS
Essex Ag-Tech Inst. (MA) OS
Gateway Comm-Tech College () OS
Grand Rapids Comm. College (MI) IS
Guilford Tech (NC) OS
Gulf Coast Comm. College (FL) OS
Harrisburg Area Comm. College (PA)
Hennepin Tech-Brooklyn Pk. () OS
Hennepin Tech-Eden Prairie (MN) OS
Hocking Technical College (OH) OS
Indian Hills Comm. College (IA) OS
Inst. of So. for Hosp. (FL) OS
Iowa Lakes Comm. College (IA) OS
Ivy Tech-Ft. Wayne (IN) OS
Ivy Tech-Gary (IN) OS
Joliet Junior College (IL) OS
Lane Community College (OR) OS
Le Cordon Bleu Paris (Canada)
Macomb Community College (MI) OS
Memphis Culinary Academy (TN)
Middlesex County College (NJ) OS
Mohawk Valley Comm. College (NY) OS
New York City Technical College (NY) IS
Northern Mich. University (MI) OS
Northwest Technical College (MN) OS
Pima Comm. Colege (AZ) OS
Salt Lake Comm. College (UT) OS
Santa Barbara City College (CA) OS
Schenectady Cty. Comm. College (NY) OS
Seattle Central Comm. College (WA) OS
Silwood Kitchen (South Africa)
So. Alberta Inst. (Canada)
So. Puget Sound Comm. College (WA) OS
Southern Maine Tech (ME) OS
Spokane Community College (WA) OS
Sullivan County Comm. College (NY) OS
SUNY-Cobleskill (NY) OS
University of Toledo (OH) OS
Vincennes University (IN) OS
W, Va. Northern Comm. College (WV) OS
Warren Occup-Tech Ctr. (CO) OS

Washburne Trade School (IL)

$5,000 TO $7,499

Academy of Culinary Arts (NJ)
Asheville Buncombe (NC) OS
Berkshire Community College (MA) OS
Black Hawk College (IL) OS
Bristol Community College (MA) OS
Century Business College (CA)
Cincinnati Technical College (OH) OS
College of Technology (MT) OS
Community College of Alleghenny Cty. (PA) OS
Ckg. & Hosp. Inst. of Chicago (IL) IS
Dandenong College (Australia)
Grand Rapids Comm. College (MI) OS
Holyoke Community College (MA) OS
Humber College (Canada) OS
Indiana University of Pa. (PA)
Int. Culinary Academy (PA)
Johnson Cty. Comm. College (KS) OS
Leeward Community College (HI) OS
Lexington Institute (IL)
Linn-Benton Community College (OR) OS
Mercyhurst College (PA)
Minuteman Tech (MA)
NE KS Area Voc-Tech (KS) OS
New Hampshire Tech (NH) OS
New York City Technical College (NY) OS
New York Food & Hotel Mgmt. Schl. (NY)
North Seattle Comm. College (WA) OS
Pa. College of Technology (PA)
Scottsdale Comm. College (AZ) OS
Skagit Valley College (WA) OS
So. Seattle Comm. College (WA) OS
Stratford Chefs School (Canada) OS
Thames Valley University (England)
UCLA Extension (CA)
University of Akron (OH) OS
University of Alaska (AK) OS
William Rainey Harper (IL) OS

$7,500 TO $9,999

Algonquin College (Canada) OS
Art Inst. of Ft. Lauderdale (FL) ATI
Art Inst. of Phoenix (AZ)
Art Inst. of Seattle (WA)
ATI Career Institute (VA)
Baltimore Int. Cul. College (MD)
Cambridge School (MA)
Canadore College (Canada) OS
Chippewa Valley Tech (WI) OS
Colorado Inst. of Art (CO)
Fla. Culinary Institute (FL)
Georgian College (Canada) OS
Milwaukee Area Tech. College (WI) OS
Napa Valley Cooking School (CA)
New Hamp. College Cul. Inst. (NH)
Newbury College (MA)
Niagara College (Canada) OS
Pa. Institute of Cul. Arts (PA)

Paul Smith's College (NY)
Peter Kump's NY Cooking Schl. (NY)
St. Clair College (Canada) OS
Southeastern Academy (FL)
Sullivan College (KY)

$10,000 OR OVER

Art Institute of Atlanta (GA)
Art Institute of Houston (TX)
Cul. Arts Inst. of La. (LA)
Cul. Schl. of Kendall College (IL)
Culinary Institute of America (NY)
Fox Valley Tech. Institute (WI) OS
George Brown College (Canada) OS
Johnson & Wales Univ. (CO)
Johnson & Wales Univ. (RI)
L'Academie de Cuisine (MD)
Le Chef Culinary Arts (TX) OS
New England Cul. Institute (VT)
New York Institute Restaurant School (NY)
Restaurant School (PA)
Scottsdale Culinary Inst. (AZ)
Southern California School Culinary Arts (CA)
Tante Marie School of Cookery (England)
Western Culinry Institute (OR)

SCHOOLS & ORGANIZATIONS THAT OFFER SCHOLARSHIPS

See individual listings for specific information about number and dollar amount awarded last year.

Albuquerque Technical Vocational Institute, 64
American Culinary Federation, 301
American Dietetic Assn., 301
American Institute of Baking, 301
Art Institute of Atlanta, 27
Art Institute of Ft. Lauderdale, 21
Art Institute of Houston, 97
Art Institute of Phoenix, 1
Art Institute of Seattle, 103
Atlantic Community College, 62
Atlantic Vocational Technical Center, 22
Bellingham Technical College, 103
Black Hawk College-Quad Cities Campus, 31
Bucks County Community College, 86
Butlers Wharf Chef School, 118
Cabrillo College, 5
Central Community College, 60
Chef John Folse Culinary Institute at Nicholls State University, 44
Cincinnati State Technical & Community College, 79
City College of San Francisco, 6
Clark College Culinary Arts Program, 104
College of DuPage, 31

**SCHOOLS THAT OFFER
CLASSES FOR CHILDREN
AND TEENS**

ACCREDITING AGENCIES

ACCSCT Accrediting Commission of Career Schools/Colleges of Technology

ACFEI American Culinary Federation Educational Institute

MSA Middle States Association of Colleges and Schools

NASC Northwest Association of Schools and Colleges

NCA North Central Association of Colleges and Schools

NEASC New England Association of Schools and Colleges

SACS Southern Association of Colleges and Schools

State State Department of Education

WASC Western Association of Schools and Colleges

CURRENCY CONVERSION TABLE
(as of September 12, 1996)

Country	Currency per U.S. $1	Country	Currency per U.S. $1
Australia (A$)	1.25	Israel (Shekel)	3.17
Canada (C$)	1.37	Italy (Lira)	1521.00
France (FF)	5.16	New Zealand (NZ$)	1.44
Great Britain (£)	.64	South Africa (R)	4.50
Ireland (IR£)	.62	Spain (Pts)	127.78

INTERNET ADDRESSES

Andre Daguin Hotel de France: http://www.integra.fr/relaischateaux/hotelfrance
Art Institutes: http:/www.aii.edu
Art of Thai Cooking: http:/users.lanminds.com/~kasma
Atlantic Community College: http://www.atlantic.edu
Bonnie Stern School of Cooking: http://www.bonniestern.com
Border Grill: http://www.bordergrill.com
California Culinary Academy: http://www.baychef.com
Celebration of Hawaii Regional Cuisine; A: http://maui.net/~events
Chaa Creek School of Caribbean Cookery: http://www.belizenet.com/chaacreek.html
Chef John Folse Culinary Institute at Nicholls State University: http://server.nich.edu/~jfolse
Colorado Mountain Culinary Institute: http://www.coloradomtn.edu
Cookery at The Grange: http://www.hi-media.co.uk/grange-cookery
Cooking and Hospitality Institute of Chicago: http://www.chicnet.org
Cooking at the Abbey: http://www.integra.fr/relaischateaux
Cooking with Maria: http://www.isl.net/gabriel/gabriel.html
Cordon Vert Cookery School: http://www.veg.org/veg/orgs/vegsocuk/
Cornell's Adult University: http://www.sce.cornell/sce/cau/<
Cuisine International: vwww.iglobal.net/cuisineint
Culinary Arts Center at Ocean Reef Club: http://www.reefnet.com
Culinary Arts Institute of Louisiana: http://www.explore-br.com-caila
Culinary Institute of America; The: http://www.ciachef.edu
Cuyahoga Community College: http://www.tri-c.cc.oh.us
Dorothy Lane Market School of Cooking: http://www.dorothylane.com
Ecole des Arts Culinaires et de l'Hotellerie: http://www.mairie-lyon.fr
Flavors of the Real Spain: http://www.iglobal.net/cuisineint
Fox Valley Technical Institute: http://www.foxvalley.tec.wi.us
France Authentique: http://www.helix.net/~fleming
Gabriele's Travels to Italy: http://www.isl.net/gabriel/gabriel.html
George Brown College of Applied Arts & Technology: http://www.gbrownc.on.ca
Georgian College of Applied Arts and Technology: http://www.georcoll.on.ca
Gourmet Adventures: http://unisono.ciateq.mx/gourtadv/
Grand Chefs On Tour: http://www.kealani.com/
Great Chefs at the Robert Mondavi Winery: http://www.mondavi.com
Great Cooks: http://www.foodserviceworld.com/dufflet/cooks.htm
The Herbfarm: http://www.theherbfarm.com
Hollyhock Farm: http://www.go-interface.com/hollyhock
Homechef Cooking School: http://www.homechef.com
Hong Kong Food Festival:http:// www.hkta.org
Il Casale la Pietra: http://www.iglobal.net/cuisineint
Indiana University of Penn. Acad of Culinary Arts: http://www.iup.edu/cularts/index.html
International Culinary Academy: http://www.intlculinary.com
International Kitchen: http://www.intl-kitchen.com
International School of Baking: http://www.empnet.com/domocorp/
Italian Country Cooking Classes with Diana Folonari:http:// www.lesromantiques.com
Jane Butel's Cooking School: http://www.wrldcon.com/jane_butel
Johnson & Wales University: http://www.jwu.edu
L'Academie de Cuisine: http://www.L'Academie.com
La Varenne at the Greenbrier: http://greenbrier.com
Le Chef College of Hospitality Careers: http://www.onr.com/chef/lechef.html
Le Cordon Bleu: http://www.cordonbleu.edu
Le Cordon Bleu Paris Cooking School: http://www.lebottawa.com
Lesson in Flavors - Donna Franca Tours: http://www.astanet.com/get?dfrancatrs
Lily Loh's Chinese Cooking Classes: http://www.sandiego-online.com/forums/chinese/

Luna Convento Cooking Classes with Enrico Franzese:v www.iglobal.net/cuisineint
McCall's School of Cake Decoration: http://www.mccalls-cakes.com
Mediterranean Cooking in Amalfi: http://www.isl.net/gabriel/gabriel.html
Moraine Park Technical College: http://www.job.careernet.org
New School Culinary Arts: http://www.newschool.edu
New York University: http://www.nyu.edu/education/nutrition/
Newbury College: http://www.newbury.edu
Nutritiously Gourmet: http://www.aimnet.com/~gourmet
Paul Smith's College: http://www.paulsmiths.edu
Pennsylvania College of Technology: http://www.pct.edu
Pennsylvania Culinary: http://www.pacul.com
Raymond Blanc's Le Petit Blanc Ecole de Cuisine: http://www.iglobal.net/cuisineint
Richard San Marzano's Heart of Italy Cooking Courses: http://www.intl-kitchen.com
Sala Siam - Bolder Adventures: http://www.SoutheastAsia.com
Santa Fe School of Cooking: http://www.santafe.org/sfcooking
Sarasota Food and Wine Academy: http://www.bestfood.com
Savoir Faire Tours - Food Lovers Tour of Paris: http://www.iglobal.net/cuisineint
Sclafani's Cooking School, Inc.: http://www.neworleans.com/sclafani-cooking-school
Scottsdale Culinary Institute: http://www.chefs.com/culinary/
Scuola di Arte Culinaria "Cordon Bleu": http://www.ats.it/kiosco/cordonbl
Seattle Central Community College: http://www.edison.sccd.ctc.edu/instruct/
Smiths Italian Cooking: http://www.intl-kitchen.com
St. Paul Technical College: http://www.sptc.tec.mn.us
Taipei Chinese Food Festival: http://www.tbroc.gov.tw
Venetian Cooking in a Venetian Palace: http://www.iglobal.net/cuisineint
Villa Delia Tuscany Cooking School: http://www.umberto.com
William Angliss Institute: http://www.angliss.vic.edu.au
World of Regaleali: http://www.iglobal.net/cuisineint

INDEX OF ADVERTISERS

Master Index

M

N

Tops International Super Center, 202
Travel Concepts, 244
Trident Technical College, 96
Triton College, 35
Truckee Meadows Community College, 61
Truffles, Inc., 182
Tucson Culinary Alliance, 3
Two for Cooking-Tuscan Country Experience, 275

U

UCLA Extension, 16, 167
UT Community Programs, 212
United States Personal Chef Assn., 307
University College of the Cariboo, 117
University Hospitals Synergy, 206
University of Akron, 82
University of Alaska-Fairbanks, 1
University of Montana, 59
University of Toledo, 82
Ursula's Cooking School, Inc., 177
Utah Valley State College, 100

V

Vandermarliere, Linda, 157
Venetian Cooking in a Venetian Palace, 275
Verge, Roger, 257
Victoria's Kitchen of Creative Cooking, 227
Victory, Annemarie, 241
Villa Cennina/The Art of Italian Cuisine, 276
Villa Delia Tuscany Cooking School, 276
Vincennes University, 38

W

Wake Technical Community College, 78
Wallace State Community College, 1
Wandering Spoon, 244
Warren Occupational Technical Center, 20
Washburne Trade School, 36
Washtenaw Community College, 56

Waukesha County Technical College, 110
Weber, Marcia, 225
Week in Bordeaux, 245
Week in Provence, 245
Weinstein, Norman, 201
Weir Cooking, 167
Wells, Patricia, 246
West Kentucky State Voc-Tech, 44
West Virginia Northern Comm. College, 108
Westchester Community College, 77
Western Culinary Institute, 84
Westlake Culinary Institute, 11, 162
Westmoreland County Community College, 93
What's Cooking, 182
What's Cooking?, Inc., 20
What's Cooking at the Kitchen Sink, 172
Whip and Spoon, 186
Wichita Area Technical College, 42
Wilkinson, Diane, 176
William Angliss Institute, 111, 227
William Rainey Harper College, 36
Williamsburg Inn, 216
Willow Hollow Gourmet, 193
Wilton School of Cake Decorating, 36, 182
Wine Enthusiast Ultimate Wine Courses, 244
Wine Institute, 307
Wisconsin School of Cookery, 220
World of Regaleali, 276
Worth, Helen, 216
Wyndham Anatole Hotel's Young Culinarians, 215
Wyoming Cattlewomen Beef Cooking Sch., 220

Y

Yalumba Winery Cooking School, 227
Yankee Hill Winery-What's Cooking at the Winery, 167
Yosemite Chefs' & Vintners' Holidays, 168

Z

Zona Spray Cooking School, 206